ORIENTALIA CHRISTIANA ANALECTA
N. 213

THE FOUR AUTHENTIC LETTERS
OF IGNATIUS, THE MARTYR

ORIENTALIA CHRISTIANA ANALECTA
213

SERIES ''XPICTIANICMOC '' - N° 2

J. Rius-Camps

THE FOUR AUTHENTIC LETTERS OF IGNATIUS, THE MARTYR

PONTIFICIUM INSTITUTUM ORIENTALIUM STUDIORUM
Piazza S. Maria Maggiore, 7
00185 ROMA
1980

De Licentia Superiorum

TYPIS PONTIFICIAE UNIVERSITATIS GREGORIANAE — ROMAE

PREFACE

Two years after the publication of my two long articles on the Ignatian Problem in the Revista Catalana de Teologia (2, 1977, 31-149 and 285-371) I am able to fulfil the promise then made to offer it in English dress. This, however, is not a mere translation but an elaboration with the addition of a completely new third section. The translation has been made by Kathleen England, to whom I wish here to express my deep gratitude, not only for her fidelity to the original text but also for her painstaking care in revising it with me. Although the original was written in Castilian I think the present English translation corresponds faithfully to my purpose. English-language readers will pardon any deficiencies.

I wish also to take the opportunity to express my gratitude to my friend and colleague, P. Juan Mateos, at the Oriental and Biblical Institutes (Rome), who has discussed with me each and every finding I have tried to express in these pages; to the other members of the team who read the original text and offered valuable criticisms. Finally, I wish to record the helpful contribution of the students in the seminar held during the first semester of 1976 in the Pontifical Oriental Institute (Rome), where this new view of the problem was born and developed.

The present work includes the two above-mentioned articles (first and second sections) and a third in which I make a comparative study of the authentic recension of the four Ignatian letters and the text introduced into them by the interpolator. In the first two sections some alterations are due to suggestions made by colleagues to whom I had sent offprints. Other remarks led to my publishing a critical appendix of the authentic recension of the four letters. There follow a bibliography, together with reference, quotation and subject indices. In the bibliography I have limited myself to works quoted in the present volume, omitting innumerable others consulted, since, given the novel character of the present view of the problem, I could not have mentioned them without reservations. The quotation index is exhaustive.

To help the reader I have italicized some of the more interesting passages. The subject index contains entries both in English and Greek. I do not claim to be exhaustive either in the selection of terms or indication of passages. The omission of the index of authors is due to the orientation given to the bibliography and the desire to avoid interminable references to commentators.

The methodology used in the present work, according to indications made further on in the state of the question, consists of a systematic and exhaustive analysis of the greater and lesser anomalies to be found in what is commonly known as the Ignatian textus receptus or Middle recension. Although many of these have been detected and treated by the commentators, they have not been sufficiently inter-related; on the contrary, separate solutions have been attempted for each one on its own. From the moment they were linked up with each other they automatically became so many milestones along the new road that opened up. None of them taken in isolation constituted an apodictic argument that could validate one more of the innumerable hypotheses already formulated during almost half a millennium of uninterrupted discussions on the Ignatian letters. Hence the scarce attention many of them have deserved. The novelty and strength of the present way of looking at the problem resides, I think, in the inter-connexions that have appeared and the coherence gradually acquired by the Ignatian text once it was freed from the gangue introduced by one of the most astute interpolators ever known. In presenting these findings to the reader I have respected the order in which I found them, so that he may make the same journey that brought me to such unexpected conclusions. The ensuing repetitions as well as certain obscurities are simply due to the method chosen.

I have deliberately omitted those arguments external to the Ignatian letters, so as to avoid setting the discussion on lines that have paralyzed it for centuries (see for example the most recent review of my articles by R. Joly, Le Dossier d'Ignace d'Antioche, Université Livre de Bruxelles 1979, pp. 120-127). Opening of ecumenical dialogue between the churches and growing renewal through the gifts of the Holy Spirit have contributed largely to the possibility of formulating our hypotheses and made it possible to syntonize with the genuine Ignatian text.

MAIN ABBREVIATIONS

A	Armenian version
AA.FF.	Apostolic Fathers, The
AA.VV.	Apostolischen Väter, Die
A.C.	Apostolic Constitutions
A.Ch.W.	Ancient Christian Writers
A.H.	Adversus Haereses
Am	Armenian version of Rom. inserted in the Martyrium Colbertinum
Ant.	Antiochenes, Ps.-Ignatius' letter to the
B	Arab version
Bm	Arab version of Rom. inserted in the Martyrium
C	Coptic version
Did.	Didascalia Apostolorum
E.H.	Ecclesiastical History
Eph.	Ephesians, Ignatius' letter to the
Eph*	Ephesians, Primitive letter to the
G	Greek text of the Middle rec. / Codex Parisiensis (Colbertinus) of Rom.
g	Greek text of the Long rec.
G.Ch.S.	Griechische Christliche Schriftsteller
H	Codex Hierosolymitanus of Rom.
Her.	Hero, Ps.-Ignatius' letter to the deacon
I.d'A.	Ignace d'Antioche
Ign.Mar.	Ignatius' letter to Mary
inscr.	inscription
I. of A.	Ignatius of Antioch
I.v.A.	Ignatius von Antiochien
K	Codex Synaiticus of Rom.
L	Latin version
l	Latin version of the Long rec.
Lm	Latin version of Rom. inserted in the Martyrium
M	Recasting of Rom. made by Simon Metaphrastes
Mar.Ign.	Mary's letter to Ignatius
Mg.	Magnesians, Ignatius' letter to the
Mg*	Magnesians, Primitive letter to the

P	Papyrus
Phil.	Philippians, Ps.-Ignatius' letter to the
Phld.	Philadelphians, Ignatius' letter to the
Pol.	Polycarp, Ignatius' letter to
Pol.Phil.	Polycarp's letter to the Philippians
PP.AA.	Patres Apostolici / Pères Apostoliques
Ps.	Pseudo
rec.	recension
Rom.	Romans, Ignatius' letter to the
Rom*m*	Rom. inserted in the Martyrium Colbertinum
Σ	Syriac version of the Short rec.
S	Syriac version
S.Ch.	Sources Chrétiennes
Sf Sfg.	Syriac fragments
Sm	Syriac version of Rom. inserted in the Martyrium
Sm.	Smyrnaeans, Ignatius' letter to the
T	Codex Taurinensis of Rom.
Tar.	Tarsians, Ps.-Ignatius' letter to the
Tr.	Trallians, Ignatius' letter to the
T.U.	Texte und Untersuchungen
W.z.N.T.	Wörterbuch zum Neuen Testament
x	Greek compilation on the basis of the ASBC versions
z	= GHKT

INDEX

PART ONE

THE AUTHENTIC LETTERS OF IGNATIUS, THE BISHOP OF SYRIA

I. INTRODUCTION

The text of Ignatius has come down to us in three very different recensions: Long, Middle and Short. The *Long* recension consists of thirteen letters, of which seven are also found in the Middle recension, but with a notably more concise text. The *Middle* recension contains only seven letters. Finally, the *Short* recension has only three, with a much shorter text than the Middle one.

As to their transmission, while the Long and Short recensions have been transmitted in independent compilations, the Middle one has been preserved in a mixed compilation, made up of the seven letters of the Middle recension and the six remaining ones of the Long recension that do not appear in the Middle one.

In order to facilitate the reading of the present work we give a list of the various letters with their corresponding symbols:

Middle rec.	Magnesians	= Mg.		
	Trallians	= Tr.		
	Philadelphians	= Phld.		
	Smyrnaeans	= Sm.		
	Polycarp	= Pol.		
	Ephesians	= Eph.	Short rec.	Long rec.
	Romans	= Rom.		
	Mary to Ignatius	= Mar. Ign.		
	Ignatius to Mary	= Ign. Mar.		
	Tarsians	= Tar.		
	Philippians	= Phil.		
	Antiochenes	= Ant.		
	Hero, the deacon	= Her.		

Every time a new recension or version of the letters of Ignatius of Antioch has been published, it has provoked an endless series of reactions in favour of, or against, their authenticity. As a result, after a period of more than four centuries of extended polemics we have come to recognize as textus receptus that which is known as the Middle or Eusebian recension,[1] consisting of seven letters with a middle text between the Longer (interpolated and forged) and the Shorter (epitomized) form.

Medieval recension. — The first printed Corpus Ignatianum appeared in Paris, in the year 1495, annexed to the life of Thomas à Becket. It consists of four very short letters (three supposedly Ignatian — two to Saint John the Evangelist and one to Saint Mary the Virgin — besides one of Saint Mary the Virgin to Ignatius), written directly in Latin, with a totally fictitious text that has no relation to the three above-mentioned recensions.[2] Their composition dates from the XII century.

Long recension. — Jacobus Faber Stapulensis published a *Latin* version in Paris in 1498, which came to be known later as the *Long* recension (symbol l, in small letters: Long rec. in Latin version). It contains twelve letters attributed to Ignatius. Six of them (Tr., Mg., Phld., Sm., Pol. and Eph.) present a text which is notably amplified if compared with today's textus receptus. On the contrary, the text of Romans (Rom.) is rather close to that of the Middle recension, with slight additions and omissions. The remaining five (Ign. Mar., Tar., Phil., Ant. and Her.) do not appear in the Eusebian collection. The letters are not arranged according to objective (chronological or topological) criteria. It seems as if the author of the collection wanted to mix the *inter-*

---

[1] The collection known by EUSEBIUS' *Ecclesiastical History* (= *E. H.*) III. 36 dates at least from the beginning of the IV century.

[2] After their publication, some take them for genuine (Peter Canisius). Baronius, Posevin and, above all, St. Robert Bellarmine consider them fictitious and wholly spurious. The difficulties that critical-minded authors had to face, can still be appreciated in J. USSHER's *Dissertationes* ... ch. XIX (re-edited by J. B. COTELIER, *SS. Patrum, qui temporibus Apostolicis floruerunt* ..., vol. II, Amsterdam 1724, App. pp. 247ff.). According to Th. ZAHN, *Ignatius von Antiochien*, Gotha 1873, pp. 80-82, Bernard of Clairvaux and Denis the Carthusian knew of only the Long recension.

polated (in italics) letters with the apocryphal ones,[3] as follows: (1) Ign. Mar., (2) *Tr.*, (3) *Mg.*, (4) Tar., (5) Phil., (6) *Phld.*, (7) *Sm.*, (8) *Pol.*,[4] (9) Ant., (10) Her., (11) *Eph.*, (12) *Rom.* This translation was probably made in the VII-VIII centuries.[5] The original Greek (symbol **g**, in small letters: Greek text of the Long rec.) was published in Dilligen in 1557 by Valentinus Hartung, called Frid or Paceus. This recension also consisted of twelve letters. Much later Ussher and Voss respectively published the Latin (l) and Greek (g) text of Mary of Cassabola's letter to Ignatius (Mar. Ign.),[6] placing it before Ignatius' answer (Ign. Mar.).

Up to the appearance of Ussher's critical study, the Long recension was taken to be authentic and exercised considerable influence in dogmatic controversies and ecclesiastical legislation.[7] Basing himself exclusively on Eusebius' remarks, Abraham Scultetus (1598) and later, relying on him, Nicholaus Vedelius (1623) already attempted to distinguish the authentic from the spurious letters.[8]

Middle recension. — As a result of his collation of the Long recension with quotations from Ignatius in earlier authors,[9] James Ussher, archbishop of Armagh guessed that in some English library there must exist a shorter recension, agreeing with the quotations of Eusebius and Theodoretus.

His discovery was published in Oxford in 1644,[10] together

---

[3] ZAHN, *I. v. A.* 85: "Die Vertheilung lässt es so erscheinen, als ob es dem Ordner darum zu thun gewesen wäre, Altes und Junges möglichst bunt zu mischen."

[4] All the Latin MSS interrupt the letter to Pol. at ch. 3 (ZAHN, *I. v. A.* 84f.; J. B. LIGHTFOOT, *The Apostolic Fathers*, London 1885, II: I 124).

[5] LIGHTFOOT, *AA. FF.* II: I 117f.

[6] ZAHN, *I. v. A.* 83f.

[7] USSHER, *Dissertationes* 231, complains: "Contendunt ex *Eusebio* Pontificii (he alludes to Bellarmine, Baronius, Mestraeus) id in primis *Ignatio* fuisse propositum, ut in epistolis suis Apostolicas Traditiones Ecclesiis testatas relinquerit; inter quas ex Epistola ad *Philippenses* et istas recensent: Festivitates esse celebrandas, et Quadragessimae ieiunium observandum." See on this subject the testimony of Mericus Casaubonus, adduced by Ussher (p. 246).

[8] ZAHN, *I. v. A.* 86.

[9] Robert Grosstesse (ca. 1250), John Tyssington (ca. 1381) and William Wodeford (ca. 1396).

[10] Complete title of the work of J. USSHER, *Polycarpi et Ignatii Epistolae ...* in

with a perceptive criticism of the recensions known up to then.
What he has discovered was a very literal Latin version of a *mixed*
collection (symbol **L**, in capitals: Latin version of mixed col.),
probably done by Robert Grosseteste, bishop of Lincoln, in the
XIII century. It contains fifteen Ignatian letters, namely: (a) six
belonging to what is known as the *Middle* recension, with a shorter and more archaic text than the Long form (lg) known up to
then; (b) five belonging to the *Long* recension; (c) Rom. inserted
in the *Martyrium* (**L~m~**: m specifies this insertion in the Colbertian
Martyrium); and (d) three letters belonging to the *Medieval* fiction.

Ussher, like Vedelius, accepts only the letters mentioned by
Eusebius as authentic, with exception however of the letter to
Polycarp which he considers spurious on the strength of both inter-
nal critical arguments and external evidence.[11]

The order in which the various components of this mixed
collection (also called Ussherian) appear, still shows how four
different layers were superimposed: (a) *Primitive* collection, that
is, the group of six letters of the *Middle* recension; they appear
in the following order: (1) Sm. and (2) Pol.; (3) Eph., (4) Mg.,
(5) Phld. and (6) Tr. The first two are precisely the letters Ignatius sent to Polycarp, as we learn from Polycarp's letter to the
Philippians 13,2 (τὰς πεμφθείσας ἡμῖν ὑπ' αὐτοῦ); the four remaining ones are those which Polycarp himself gathered from the
nearby communities (καὶ ἄλλας, ὅσας εἴχομεν παρ' ἡμῖν). Rom.
was not available to him. For this reason we call this primitive
compilation, in which Rom. is lacking, *Polycarpiana*. (b) *Amplified*
collection: of the eleven letters that make up the *Long* recension
the compiler picks out only those not figuring in the *Middle* recension, keeping to the order in that collection:[12] (7) Mar. Ign.,

---

W. Cureton, *Corpus Ignatianum*, London 1849, Introd. p. IX. Index in Zahn,
I v. A. 93, n. 1. Account of the findings in Lightfoot, *AA. FF.* II: I 76f.

[11] Ussher manages to support his intuition with Jerome's authority (*De Viris
illustribus* 16) in opposition to Eusebius' more primitive account (*E. H.* III. 36) in
spite of the fact that Baronius had already unmasked Jerome's error in translating
Eusebius. It is easy to perceive the difference between the style of Pol. and the
other six letters. But the first argument had no validity whatever. Today it is
demonstrated that Jerome had no personal acquaintance with the writings of Ignatius. He knew him only through Eusebius.

[12] The compiler inadvertently missed out the letter to the Phil. which came
after Tar., because he probably confused it with the inscr. of Phld. that followed

(8) Ign. Mar., (9) Tar., (10) Ant., (11) Her. (c) The letter to the *Romans* embedded in the " Acts of Ignatius " (L_m). (d) *Medieval* collection.

Two years later, in 1646, Isaac Voss published in Amsterdam the original *Greek* text of this mixed collection (**G**, in capitals: original Greek of mixed col.), but incomplete, due to the accidental fact that the Medicean codex had been cut short in Tar. 7. — In 1689, in Paris, Th. Ruinart completed the publication of the original Greek of the Middle recension by publishing the Colbertine Martyrium with the letter to the Romans embedded in it (**Rom_m**: Rom. inserted in the Martyrium). Later, three other codices of this Martyrium including Rom. were found (**H**: Hierosolymitanus, X cent.; **K**: Sinaiticus, X cent.; **T**: Taurinensis, XIII cent.). The Colbertine codex (**G**: Parisiensis, X-XI cent.) and the other three codices derive from one family (symbol **z** = GHKT).

The first layer (a) of this mixed collection points to a very ancient compilation, which dates from before Eusebius *(E. H.* III. 36), since it does not yet comprise Rom. nor does it follow the topological order of the Eusebian recension (I. Letters from *Smyrna*: (1) Eph., (2) Mg., (3) Tr., (4) Rom. — II. Letters from *Troas*: (5) Phld., (6) Sm., (7) Pol.). However, this shows both in the number of letters as well as in their arrangement that it is the compilation made by Polycarp. On the other hand, the third layer (c), that is, the Martyrium with Rom. embodied in it, clearly shows that the joining of the three first layers (obviously the medieval collection was added later) is independent of the other mixed compilation on which, as we shall see later, the Armenian, Syriac, Arab and Coptic versions were based.

Short recension. — Between the publication of the original text of the Middle recension and the edition of the Short recension (in Syriac) by Cureton, London 1845, the controversy between

---

immediately after. But it could well be that this letter (Phil.) was not in the *primitive* amplified collection (note that in the Armenian version it is placed last). The reason for this addition could have been that of satisfying the Philippians, to avoid Ignatius' seeming inferior to Polycarp (remember that Polycarp wrote them one letter). The strong invective addressed to the devil, in the second person sing., of Phil. 3,3-12 would rather support this hypothesis; several parallels on the other hand, above all with Ps.-Phld., -Sm. and -Pol. suggest strongly the retaining of Ps.-Ignatius as author of the whole compilation including Phil.

2

Episcopalians and Presbyterians, Anglicans, Catholics and Protes-
tants continued, some appealing to Ignatius and others rejecting
his letters, depending on their theological position.[13]

With the edition, in Syriac, of the *Short* recension (symbol Σ)
of three Ignatian letters (Pol., Eph. and Rom.)[14] the controversies
received yet another impulse. According to Cureton, the Short
recension in its original Greek (now lost) from which the Syriac
version derived is the only authentic one. On it, in his opinion,
depend both the Middle and Long recensions. Of the same opinion were Bunsen, Ritschl, Weiss, Lipsius, Pressensé, Ewald, Mil-
man, Böhringer, among others. Against it were Wordsworth, von
Baur, Hefele, Petermann, Denzinger, Uhlhorn, Hilgenfeld, Jacobson, Merx, Zahn, Lightfoot, Harnack, von der Goltz, Rackl, etc.

The publication of the *Armenian* version (A) in 1849, made
from an ancient Syriac one by J. B. Petermann,[15] the careful criticism undergone by Cureton's hypothesis, Zahn's[16] and Funk's[17]
critical editions and commentaries, and Lightfoot's monumen-
tal work[18] vouched for by the authority of Harnack him-

---

[13] A short history of the controversy in W. CURETON, *Corpus Ignatianum*, London 1849, Intr. pp. XVIff.

[14] W. CURETON, *The ancient Syriac version of the Epistles of St. Ignatius to
St. Polycarp, the Ephesians, and the Romans ...*, London 1845; *Vindiciae Ignatianae
or the genuine writings of St. Ignatius as exhibited in the ancient Syriac version vindicated of the charge of heresy*, London 1846; *Corpus Ignatianum: a complete collection of the Ignatian Epistles ... in Syriac, Greek and Latin ...*, London 1849.

[15] *S. Ignatii Patris Apostolici quae feruntur Epistolae una cum eiusdem Martyrio*,
Leipzig 1849. It was published earlier by Minas, an Armenian bishop in Constan-
tinople, 1783. This *editio princeps*, reproduced by Petermann, " is wholly un-
critical ", hence " the value of this version for textual purposes is very seriously
impaired " (LIGHTFOOT, *AA. FF.* II: I 85). Pl. S. SOMAL, *Quadro delle opere di
vari autori anticamente tradotto in Armeno*, Venice 1885, attributes it to the V cent.
(CURETON, *Corpus Ignatianum*, Intr. XVI). LIGHTFOOT, *AA. FF.* II: I 85f. holds
that the arguments of this critic in favour of this date are inconclusive.

[16] Th. ZAHN, *Ignatius von Antiochien*, Gotha 1873; *Patrum Apostolicorum opera
II: Ignatii et Polycarpi Epistulae, Martyria, Fragmenta*, Leipzig 1876.

[17] F. X. FUNK, *Die Echtheit der Ignatianischen Briefe aufs neue vertheidigt*, Tübingen 1883; *Patres Apostolici*, vol. I, Tübingen 1901; F. X. FUNK – F. DIEKAMP, *Patres
Apostolici*, vol. II, Tübingen 1913.

[18] J. B. LIGHTFOOT, *The Apostolic Fathers, Part II: S. Ignatius. S. Polycarp*,
vols. I, II/1, II/2, London 1885. We quote from the *first* edition. In [ ] we give
vol. and p. of the reprinting (Hildesheim 1973) made on the second edition, *The
Apostolic Fathers, Part II, 1.2.3, Revised Texts with Introductions, Notes, Disser-*

self,[19] all contributed to the calming of the atmosphere, and the final acceptance of the Short recension as an *epitome* made of an elder complete Syriac version (S) of the letters included in the *mixed* collection. From this Syriac version, made from the Greek, we still have a series of fragments (**Sfg**),[20] besides the three epitomized letters.

Oriental versions. — The Syriac version (**S**), as can be inferred from the Armenian one, included (a) the seven letters attested to by Eusebius, that is, the six letters compiled by Polycarp and the letter to the Romans, and (b) the remaining six spurious ones coming from the Long recension. The *Greek* compilation on which that version was based (symbol **x**, thus distinguishing it from the Ussherian also mixed collection), goes back to the end of the IV century. It forces us to date the interpolator of the Ignatian letters and author of the forged ones — that is, the author of the Long recension or Pseudo-Ignatius — between the Apostolic Constitutions, on which he depends literally — or of which he is possibly the author —, and the mixed compilation (x), hence in the second half of the IV century (about 360-380).[21]

---

tution and Translations, London 1889, with different numeration of the vols. (I, II, and III instead of I, II/1, and II/2) and total repagination of the third. Omitted when they coincide.

[19] A. HARNACK, *Bishop Lightfoot's " Ignatius and Polycarp "*, The Expositor 22 (1885) 401-414; 23 (1886) 9-22; 175-192.

[20] There are three collections: S_1 contains ffg. of the following letters (in the order in which they appear): Eph., Mg., Tr.; Pol., Phld. Sm., Mg., Tr., Pol. Date: A. D. 687. S_2: Rom., Eph., Mg., Sm., Her. Date: ca. 932. S_3: Rom. Date: A. D. 675. All these extracts come from one complete Syriac version. Cureton preferred deriving them from the Greek, "which was afterwards translated into Syriac" (*Corpus Ignatianum* 345). LIGHTFOOT, *AA. FF.* II: I 92f. refutes this supposition, which is supported rather by prejudices, and he demonstrates its Syriac source: "The conclusion from the facts adduced is irresistible. We have plainly in these fragments ($S_1 S_2 S_3$) portions of the lost Syriac version from which the Armenian text was translated" (p. 97) [104]. And about the close likeness between $S_1 S_2 S_3$ and the Epitome (Σ) of the complete Syriac version (S): "It is strange that Cureton should not have been struck by the close resemblance between the Syriac fragments ($S_1 S_2 S_3$), and the Syriac version of the three epistles in the Short recension (Σ), in those passages which are common to both" (ib.).

[21] Scholars waver between identifying the author of the Const. as Ps.-Ign. (Lagarde, Harnack, Funk) or verifying the strict dependence of the latter on the Const. (Zahn, Lightfoot, Perler). The hypothesis that the author of the Const. was an

The Armenian version (**A**) comes from the ancient Syriac one (S).[22] It contains two compilations. The first one is a *pre-Eusebian* collection. This collection is distinguished from that made by Polycarp, but although depending on it, because it already contains *Rom.*; it is also independent from Eusebius' collection, since the order of the letters is different, viz.: (1) Sm. and (2) Pol.; (3) Eph., (4) Mg., (5) Tr. and (6) Phld.; (7) *Rom.* The second compilation comes from the *Long* recension *amplified* by addition of *Phil.*, namly: (8) Ant., (9) Mar. Ign., (10) Ign. Mar., (11) Tar., (12) Her., (13) *Phil.*

If we compare this mixed collection with the so-called Ussherian one, we see that in both the first (a) and second (b) layer the mixed collection (x) that served as a model for the Oriental versions increased the number of the letters by adding, respectively, Rom., that is the letter written to Italy by Ignatius himself, and Phil., probably composed from Reggio to complete the cycle before Ignatius' sailing for Rome.

On examining the order of the letters, we observe that in the first layer (a) the archtype of the Armenian version (x) retains the primitive order of the Polycarpian collection, with addition of Rom. at the end, whereas the Ussherian collection changes the order of the last two letters. The order of the first layer (a) of the archtype x is perfectly attested in the series of quotations from Ignatius contained in the writings of Severus of Antioch and John Damascene.[23] As for the second layer (b), the Ussherian collec-

---

Apollinarist (Funk, Bardenhewer, Bardy, Diekamp) has been shelved to give place to a semi-Arian writer (Zahn, Harnack, Duchesne, Turner, Schwartz, Perler, Wagner). Zahn (*J. v. A.* 141f.) proposed Acatius of Cesarea; Turner (*J. Th. S.* 31, 1930, p. 130) agreed; O. PERLER, *Pseudo-Ignatius und Eusebius von Emessa, Hist. Jb.* 77 (1958) 73-82, suggests Silvanus of Tarsus (p. 82, n. 46) as author of Ps.-Ign.; G. WAGNER, *Zur Herkunft der Apostolischen Konstitutionen, Mélanges Liturgiques* offered to B. Botte, Louvain 1972, pp. 525-537, proposes Eunomius as author of the Const. and interpolator of Ign. Recently D. HAGEDORN, *Der Hiobkommentar des Arianers Julian*, Berlin 1973, pp. XXXVII-LVII, shows that Julian of Halikarnass, the Arian, is the author of both compilations, the Apostolical Constitutions and the Ps.-Ign.

[22] LIGHTFOOT, *AA. FF.* II: I 86f.

[23] Severus (VI cent.) knows Rom. and testifies to the sequence Pol. – Eph. – Mg. – Tr. in one of his quotations. Of the *Sacra Parallela Rupefucaldina*, compiled a century earlier than John Damascene, we can infer the sequences Eph. – (Mg.) –

tion reflects the original order given by pseudo-Ignatius according to the place of writing, while x changes the order and adds the letter to the Philippians at the end.

The *Arab* version (**B**), recently published by B. Basile,[24] has not yet been incorporated in the critical editions. This version was made also from the Syriac one: hence A B Σ Sfg = S. There also exists an Arab version of Rom. inserted in the Martyrium (Rom.-B$_m$).[25] This version does not come from the corresponding Syriac one (S$_m$) and is notably different from the original Greek (G$_m$).

The *Coptic* version (**C**) [26] derives directly from a Greek manuscript that probably belongs to the same archtype x as the Armenian, Arab and Syriac versions, for the letters of the Middle recension are found in the same order, and contains Her. which comes from the Long text. A fragment of Pol. 7,2 has been published in Coptic by C. Wesely.[27]

Finally, we possess a Greek *Papyrus* (**P**) of Sm. 3,3-12,1, published by C. Schmidt.[28]

Letter to the Romans: independent manuscript transmission. — As we already suggested, the letter to the Romans could not be part of the compilation made by Polycarp. Because of geogra-

---

Tr. – Phld. and Sm. – Pol. – Eph. – Mg. – Tr. – Phld. Rom. does not appear in these *Parallela* nor in the *Vaticana*. See below n. 161.

[24] *Un ancien témoin arabe des Lettres d'Ignace d'Antioche, Melto* 4 (1968) 107-191. The order of the letters is the same as in A (S) and in C: Sm. – Pol. – Eph. – Mg. – Tr. – Phld. – Rom.

[25] *Une autre version arabe de la Lettre aux Romains de St. Ignace d'Antioche, Melto* 5 (1969) 269-287.

[26] Both the Papyrus Borgia (C$_1$) edited by l. P. Paulinus Martinus and the Papyrus of Vienna (C$_2$) edited by C. WESELY, *Neue Materialien zur Textkritik der Ignatius-Briefe*, Vienna 1913, come from the same MS (p. 7). Wesely re-edits the Borgian fragment (pp. 57-66), as also the fg. of Rom. 6,2-9,1 (C$_3$), edited by W. E. Crum (pp. 53-54). This last fg. does not belong to the same MS (p. 8). The collection represented by C$_1$C$_2$ begins with the letter to Hero (pp. 1-6 of the MS) followed by Sm. (pp. 6-8 of the same MS), Pol., Eph., Mg. (the middle pp. are missing), Tr. Phld. and Rom. (pp. 31-42 of the MS). Rom. is incomplete. However on p. 47 of the MS a text of another author follows (p. 8).

[27] *Griechische und Koptische Texte theologisches Inhalts*, Studien zur Paleographie und Papyruskunde XVIII, Leipzig 1917, pp. 94-96.

[28] C. SCHMIDT – W. SCHUBART, *Berliner Klassikertexten, VI. Altchristliche Texte*, Berlin 1910, pp. 3-12: see A. von HARNACK, *Th. L.* 31 (1906) 596f.

phical distance, Polycarp had no access to this letter (he had not even had time to find out what happened to Ignatius and his followers, cf. Pol. Phil. 13,2). This letter has come down to us through the following channels:

I. *Apart* from the Martyrium it has been transmitted in the following documents, in which it always occupies the last position: (a) In the Greek and Latin manuscripts of the Long recension (gl), after the interpolated and spurious letters; (b) In A and B and, hence, also in S, after the letters belonging to the Middle recension (even in the epitome Σ it is placed at the end); (c) In C, in which the translation was made directly from the Greek.

II. As *inserted* in the Martyrium it appears: (a) In the Colbertine Martyrium (codices GHKT = z); (b) In Ussher's mixed Latin collection (L), after the Middle and Long recensions; (c) In S_m[29] A_m[30] and B_m[31]; (d) In the recasting made by Simon Metaphrastes (**M**) in the X century, with additions common to z and gl.[32]

The particular manuscript transmission of Rom.,[33] the fact of its unavailability to Polycarp because of geographical and chronological reasons,[34] its inconsiderable interpolation by Pseudo-Igna-

---

[29] The Syriac version of the Mart. + Rom. preserved by three MSS has been made directly from the Greek. It is very free and paraphrastic: LIGHTFOOT, *AA. FF.* II: I 99-101 [106-108].

[30] According to Aucher, Petermann and Lightfoot the translation has been made directly from the Greek, although keeping in mind A, while Zahn derives it from the Syriac (*I. v. A.* 21). See LIGHTFOOT, *AA. FF.* II: I 89 [90].

[31] The Arab version of the Mart. + Rom. contained in two MSS (Sin. ar. 443 and 482) has recently been published by B. Basile (see above n. 25).

[32] Unlike LSABCSmAmBm, the letter to the Rom. contained in M (Metaphrastes), gl (Long rec.) and z (Colbertine Mart. + Rom.: codices GHKT) includes a series of amplifications (most often based on Biblical quotations) that reveal a common archtype (Mart^corr) posterior to Mart*(m) and to the Middle rec. of Rom. (LSABC): see the critical apparatus of F. X. FUNK - K. BIHLMEYER, *Die Apostolischen Väter*, Tübingen ²1956, on Rom. 2,1.2; 3,2; 4,3; 5,3; 6,1.2; 7,3.

[33] FUNK-BIHLMEYER, *Die Apostolischen Väter*, p. XXXV: "Auch der R ö m e r - b r i e f lässt sich trotz seiner an sich auffallenden Sonderüberlieferung von der übrigen Ignatianen nicht trennen, denn er stimmt in Stil und Grundcharakter ganz mit ihnen überein." We have 16 authorities for it: L*x* (= CSfgΣAB) *m* (= SmAmBm) *z* (= GHKT) Mgl.

[34] Note for the moment (later we shall display irrefutable arguments arising from internal evidence) that in the Ussherian collection (Middle rec.: Sm. and Pol.; Eph., Mg., Phld. and Tr.; completed with the Long rec.: Ign.Mar., Tar.,

tius [35] and the existence of two slightly differing recensions of Rom. incorporated in the Martyrium [36] give this particular letter a privileged position among the others that, taken as a whole, suffered together the same vicissitudes.

II. STATE OF THE QUESTION

The consensus of scholars taking as textus receptus the middle recension of seven letters was arrived at gradually and for want of any better solution after more than four centuries of polemics. The main contribution is due above all to arguments put forward by Zahn, Lightfoot, Funk and Harnack.

However, discordant voices were not lacking. When Harrison wrote his history of the theories formulated since Lightfoot's voluminous monograph, he listed Hilgenfeld, Völter, Killen, Steck, Cotterill, Van der Bergh, Lipsius, Jenkins, Owen, Delafosse, who did not admit Lightfoot's thesis; some reject the Ignatian letters wholly or in part, others favour the theory of a massive inter-

---

Ant., Her.: crowned with the Colbertine Martyrium: Rom.) the letter to the Rom. *does not yet appear* between the letters of the Polycarpian coll., and that in the mixed coll. (x = CS[SfgΣAB]) it is *still placed last* after the letters of the Middle rec.

[35] According to LIGHTFOOT, *AA. FF.* II: I 263-266 [275-279], against Zahn's thesis (*I. v. A.* 115, 128, 161f.; *PP. AA.* II, p. VIIf.): " The *Epistle to the Romans* from the beginning formed part of the collection of thirteen letters contained in the Long Recension " (p. 263 [275]).

[36] See n. 32. The letter to the Rom. was quickly incorporated into the *Polycarpian* coll.: Eusebius (*E. H.* III. 36) is the first who gives direct witness to this amplified compilation (we have indirect information from Origen's quotation of Rom. and Eph., that these two letters were already in circulation together). Much later on it was again incorporated by the author of the *Acta Antiochena* in the centre of his account of Ignatius' martyrdom. From notable discrepancies between the data contained in the Polycarpian and Eusebian compilations on the one hand, and the *Acta Antiochena* on the other (see LIGHTFOOT, *AA. FF.* II: II/1, 383f.), it can been inferred that these last are posterior, though they had remote knowledge of the existence of the former. The author of the *Long* rec., in his turn, probably incorporated Rom. with the Martyrium, in a slightly *lengthened* version. Thus we can explain that both the Greek codices of the Mart. + Rom. (z = GHKT) as well as the Greek and Latin codices of the Long rec. (gl) and the paraphrase of Metaphrastes (M) have *common* readings. Such readings are not to be found either in the versions arising from a common Greek archtype (x = CS[SfgΣAB]) nor in the Oriental versions of the Mart. + Rom. (SmAmBm).

polation.[37]   Recently, however, there have been authors who even contest the authenticity of the Ignatian letters themselves: Simon, Grégoire, Moreau, J. Schwartz, etc.[38]

But the greatest uproar was produced by R. WEIJENBORG's monograph.[39]   After weighing the pros and cons, lining up positive and negative proofs, he concludes that the Middle recension depends literally on the Long form.   His conclusions have been received on the whole rather sceptically.[40]   Indeed, it shows that not everything is clear and resolved once and for all, and that there are still internal and external problems of textual criticism that await fully satisfactory solutions.   Weijenborg's line of argument gives the impression that he is continually begging the question (his hypothesis that the Longer rec. is the older), building up on a series of fallacies:

(1)   Firstly, after a *sui generis* criticism of internal and external arguments put forward by scholars who favour the authenticity of the Ignatian letters, he concludes that " he has found no convincing argument either external or internal to prove that the seven letters of the current mixed recension present the original text of the seven letters, that some authors, relying on the authority of Eusebius of Caesarea, supposed were written by a bishop Ignatius at the beginning of the II century " (p. 32).

(2)   He then denies the validity of the comparison of the mixed recension text of the seven Ignatian letters with the six forged ones of the Long recension.   Any comparison should be made with the two recensions taken as a whole (p. 33).   On the

---

[37] P. N. HARRISON, *Polycarp's two Epistles to the Philippians*, Cambridge 1936, pp. 66-72.   Harrison, however, affirms that the genuiness of the Eusebian compilation (Middle rec.) is " accepted, by almost universal consent, as one of the most thoroughly assured results of modern scientific research, for which the chief credit is due — as all agree — to Lightfoot ..." (p. 122).

[38] B. ALTANER – A. STUIBER (D. IRENEO), *Patrologia*, Turin 1968, p. 52.

[39] *Les Lettres d'Ignace d'Antioche. Étude de critique littéraire et de théologie*, Leiden 1969.

[40] Reviews of Weijenborg's work: *Bibl.* 51 (1970) 560-564 (Camelot); *R. H. E.* 65 (1970) 1095f. (Gribomont); *R. Et. Gr.* 88 (1970) 582f. (Jaubert); *B. L. E.* 71 (1970) 141f. (Hamman); *J. B. L.* 89 (1970) 517f. (Brown); *J. Th. St.* 22 (1971) 227-229 (de Mendieta); *R. Bén.* 81 (1971) 154f. (Bogaert); *R. S. L. R.* 7 (1971) 152-161 (Pizzolato); *T. R.* 67 (1971) 531f. (Barbel); *R. Et. Byz.* 29 (1971) 313-316 (Wenger); *Greg.* 53 (1972) 169f. (Orbe); *R. H. Ph. Rel.* 52 (1972) 220f. (Prigent); *R. H. R.* 182 (1972) 98 (Nautin); *Z. K. G.* 84 (1973) 101-103 (Staats), etc.

one hand, with a stroke of the pen, this discredits M. P. BROWN's study [41] based on linguistic criteria through comparison of the seven authentic letters and the six spurious ones; on the other, it sets up a principle that makes any textual confrontation between the two (Middle and Long) recensions impossible, on the plea that we possess no other manuscript tradition independent of the seven letters. The fact that only the Middle recension has come down to us within the mixed collection does not forbid collating the shorter letters with the longer ones and with the remaining spurious letters of the Long recension.

(3)   Once demonstrated (!) that the Long recension is more primitive than the Middle recension and not anterior to 360, he affirms without proof that " it is extremely difficult to admit that authentic Ignatian letters — type L (= Long rec.) or M (= Middle rec.) — existed before 360 " (p. 394f.).

(4)   Finally, to avoid the grave difficulty of Eusebius' information on the seven Ignatian letters, he went on to suppose that the *Ecclesiastical History* was already written after 360 (sic!) (p. 394).

For my part, the most objective method of coming to a sure judgement on the relationship between the Long and Middle recension (not to be mistaken for M!) seems to be the elaboration of a complete index of the Long recension (the thirteen letters),[42] so as to confront them with H. KRAFT's index on the Middle recension.[43]   After verifying the presence or absence in both recensions of typically Ignatian expressions and idioms, studying parallels and checking doctrinal evolution of such matters as heresy, ecclesiastical organization, theological and trinitarian formulas, etc.,[44] I came to the conclusion that there is not the slightest

---

[41] *The authentic Writings of Ignatius. A Study of linguistic Criteria*, Durham, N. C. 1963.

[42] Indices drawn up through photomechanic process according to the technique I acquired in the elaboration of the complete Greek and Latin indices of the *Clementine Homelies and Recognitions* (see *Las Pseudoclementinas. Bases filológicas para una nueva interpretación*, R. Cat. Teol. 1, 1976, pp. 79-158). They include all the terms and particles of the 13 letters of the Long rec. with their corresponding context.

[43] *Clavis Patrum Apostolicorum. Konkordanz zu den Schriften der Apostolischen Väter*, München 1963.

[44] I limit myself to a few examples: (a) Rectification of archaizing formulas in

probability that the Middle recension can derive from the Long one, whereas everything points to the opposite hypothesis. In spite of negative results, comparison between the two recensions and the different treatment accorded by Ps.-Ignatius to certain problems raised by the Middle recension, led me to concentrate on them and to open up a new type of procedure.

Our point of departure was the textus receptus of the seven Ignatian letters making up the Middle recension. Starting from the problems and anomalies found in the text, some of them already noted by commentators, I searched for ways to resolve the complex problem that has harassed critics for centuries, but which, through defective posing, has not led to the hoped-for solution.

---

the Long. rec. of *Eph.* (letter studied by Weijenborg); Eph. inscr. Ἰῦ Χῦ τοῦ θεοῦ ἡμῶν G: τοῦ σωτῆρος ἡμῶν g | 1,1 ἐν αἵματι θεοῦ G: ἐν αἵματι Χριστοῦ g | 1,2 ὑπὲρ τοῦ κοινοῦ ὀνόματος καὶ ἐλπίδος G: ὑπὲρ Χριστοῦ τῆς κοινῆς ἐλπίδος g | 18,2 ὁ γὰρ θεὸς ἡμῶν Ἰς ὁ Χὸς G: ὁ γὰρ τοῦ θεοῦ υἱός ... g | 19,2 πῶς οὖν ἐφανερώθη τοῖς αἰῶσιν; G: ἡμῖν δὲ ἐφανερώθη g. (b) Elimination of problematic clauses: The Middle rec. of *Eph.* 20,1 speaks of a " second tract " or letter, in which Ignatius promises to continue the exposition on the subject (the economy of the Incarnation) here interrupted. There is no trace of this second letter. The Long rec. eliminates this clause. Weijenborg's argument borders on the absurd: " Par *dans un deuxième livret* il désigne la lettre *aux Ephésiens* déjà écrite par L (...) Il ne s'agit pas d'une vraie *lettre* mais d'un *livret* forgé dans le bureau d'un faussaire. Comme il parle d'un *deuxième livret*, tout semble impliquer qu'aussi bien L que *M* [le premier livret] sont des faux " (p. 304). " Par conséquent M nous présente L comme un livret qui n'a pas été écrit par Ignace, mais qui faussement porte son nom. Ainsi il nous trompe une seconde fois, semble-t-il, parce qu'il se donne lui-meme pour Ignace. En réalité M n'est qu'une séconde édition de ce L qu'il cherche à discréditer " (p. 308). (c) Correction of difficult clauses: With regard to the expression σύνδουλός μου of the Middle rec., the Long text corrects its meaning by slight retouches. Thus in *Eph.* 2,1 it changes μου for ἡμῶν; in *Mg.* 2 συνδούλου for συμβιωτοῦ. These are the only two cases in which the Middle rec. uses this expression applied to a deacon in the singular. In *Sm.* 12,2 it attempts to give an explanation of said clause: τοὺς χριστοφόρους διακόνους κτλ. In *Ant.* 11,3 Ign. presents himself οὐχ ὡς ἀπόστολος ... ἀλλ᾽ ὡς σύνδουλος ὑμῶν. — We could multiply examples. It suffices to compare some hard or difficult expression of the Middle rec. with its corresponding one in the Long text to find a more smooth and intelligible reading.

III. Problems posed by the Ignatian textus receptus

Before starting out on the *central section* of this first part, we must trace the broad lines of our work. To facilitate reading we have adopted *titles* and *subtitles*, thus distinguishing the main sections and the internal divisions. Then, to emphasize the progressive stages of the exposition and simplify internal quotations, we have adopted an on-going numeration (independent of titles and subtitles) to mark successive paragraphs that, to us, appeared to introduce a new element of proof. We start with certain *topographical* data hard to reconcile (nrs. 1-7). Then follows the problem of Ignatius' real *identity* (nrs. 8f.). After this, as required by the exposition itself, we (simultaneously) treat of two types of problems: anomalies in the *structure* of certain letters (nrs. 10f. and 18-23) and *thematic* similarities in the two groups of letters, Eph.–Tr.–Sm. and Mg.–Phld. (nrs. 12-17 and 24-28). The results obtained oblige us to study the *inscriptions* of certain letters (nr. 29) and the *conclusions* of the four letters examined up to then (nrs. 30-35). All this leads us to go into the *relationship between Ignatius and Polycarp*, based on evidence of the same period. Among external witnesses we have Irenaeus, who as a young man listened to Polycarp when he lived in Smyrna. Then we shall examine firstly, *Irenaeus' account on Polycarp* (nr. 36) and on the *Letter to the Philippians* (nr. 37). Once we have discussed the problem arising from *two contradictory statements on Ignatius* contained in the above-mentioned letter (nrs. 38f.), we shall then deal with the somewhat singular reference in *Philippians* 13 (nrs. 40f.). Secondly, we shall analyse the *brief mentions of Polycarp* to be found in the Ignatian letters (nrs. 42f.). All this will finally lead us to examine *Ignatius' Letter to Polycarp* (nrs. 44-51). The accumulation of new materials and possession of new elements on which to base our judgement demand a detailed analysis of the *genuine ending of Ephesians* (nrs. 52f.) and a global study of the *genuine final greetings of this letter* (nrs. 54f.). With this we shall have reached the end of the first section, exclusively devoted to examining the primitive *structure* of Ignatius' letters. In the *conclusions*, besides summing up results, we shall try to draw new inferences in so far as the newly-discovered structure will allow.

a) *Two places of writing*: *Smyrna and Troas*

1. We start by noting a detail that has escaped commentators because at first sight it seems of slight importance. Critical editions usually set out the Ignatian letters in the order of the Eusebian recension, instead of following the well-attested order in the series of quotations given by Theodoret and John Damascene, in Ussher's mixed compilation and in the Oriental versions (ASB and C), that is, the primitive Polycarpian order (see p. 16).

But EUSEBIUS, *E. H.* III. 36, follows the order of the data they contain. In the first four letters it is specified that they were written from *Smyrna*: (1) Eph. 21,1; (2) Mg. 15; (3) Tr. 12,1; (4) Rom. 10,1. The three remaining are said to have been written from *Troas*: (5) Phld. 11,2; (6) Sm. 12,1; (7) Pol. 8,1 (understood).

Besides, Ignatius had intended to write to all the Asia Minor communities (πάσαις ταῖς ἐκκλησίαις), but he was unable to do so because of his sudden sailing from Troas in the direction of Neapolis (Macedon), the port of Philippi. To make up for his omission, he asked Polycarp to write to the communities "in front" (ἔμπροσθεν), [45] that is, Sardes, Laodicea, Colossae and

---

[45] Pol. 8,1. The phrase ταῖς ἔμπροσθεν ἐκκλησίαις, because of its lack of concreteness, has given rise to numerous interpretations. ZAHN, *I. v. A.* 284, after excluding the solutions proposed by Lipsius, Uhlhorn and Hilgenfeld, takes Pearson's, that is, "die gewöhnliche örtliche Bedeutung": "Auf diesem Wege (from Smyrna to Antioch of Syria) liegen von Smyrna aus weiter vorwärts z. B. Ephesus, Tralles und Magnesia." The same in his commentary, *PP. AA.* II 105. A similar interpretation in LIGHTFOOT, *AA. FF.* II: II/1, 358: "'*the churches lying in front*', i. e. nearer to Syria than Smyrna itself", without further specification. BAUER, *W. z. N. T.*, s. v. translates: "Die Kirchen weiter vorwärts", fully accepting in his commentary (*AA. VV.* II 280f.) Zahn's solution, but not limiting its meaning to the three cities. LELONG, *PP. AA.* III 106, makes it a little more precise: "Presque tous les commentateurs entendent par là *les églises qu'aura devant lui* le délégué en se rendant de Smyrne à Antioche, par conséquent *les églises situées entre Smyrne et Antioche.*" KLEIST, *I. of A.* 146,23, questions the current translations: "The current translations of ἔμπροσθεν are too artificial to be correct: 'in front of', 'on the hither side', that is, in the context, 'this side and *nearer to Syria* than to Churches beyond Antioch'! The adverb, when not further qualified, is used in the sense of 'preferred'; hence 'principal, chief'." FISCHER, *AA. VV.* 223, opposes Kleist's translation and returns to the traditional interpretation of Zahn, Bauer, Lelong: "D. h. in Richtung auf Antiochien, am Weg, den Ignatius zurückgelegt hat". — Given the geographical situation of Smyrna, the adverb ἔμ-

perhaps even Antioch of Pisidia, situated on the κοινὴ ὁδός taken
by Ignatius to reach Philadelphia. The invitation Ignatius made
to the various communities, directly or through Polycarp, to send
messengers or letters to Antioch of Syria, he repeated to the Philippians as he passed through that city, as we learn from Polycarp's letter to them (Pol. Phil. 13,1).

2. Not only was the writing done in two places, but in each
group of letters the requests were different. Whereas in the letters
written from *Smyrna*, Ignatius limits himself to asking *prayers for
the church established in the province of Syria* (Eph. 21,2; Mg. 14;
Tr. 13,1; Rom. 9,1), in those written from *Troas* he asks all the
communities to send *messengers*, or at least *letters to the church
established in Antioch of Syria* (Phld. 10; Sm. 11; Pol. 7-8). The
obvious explanation of this sudden change is due to the good
news from the community of Antioch in Syria brought by Philo
and Gaius: see Phld. 10,1 and Pol. 7,1 (someone announced it)
collating with Phld. 11,1 and Sm. 10,1 (Philo and Gaius have
followed in his footsteps from Cilicia and Syria respectively).
This news reached him when he was already in Troas; which
explains why there is no mention of messengers or messages in
the first letters. The messengers followed the same road as Ignatius (Sm. 10,1), bringing him news of the welcome which had
been given in Philadelphia (with divided opinions: Phld. 11,1) and
in Smyrna (most cordial: Sm. 10,1). The communities of Asia
Minor (Philadelphia and Smyrna directly, and through Polycarp,
the other communities that Ignatius greets on his way) are requested, like the Philippians, to send letters or messengers to Ignatius'
community. Nothing is specified of the communities he wrote to
from Smyrna (Ephesus, Magnesia and Tralles). The Ephesians
like the Magnesians and the Trallians sent a delegation to Smyrna.
Only the deacon Burrhus, of Ephesus, accompanied him to Troas,
sent by the Ephesians and Smyrnaeans (Phld. 11,2 and Sm. 12,1).
Was he the one charged with bringing them the new invitation?

προσθεν refers, naturally, to the Asian communities of the hinterland with whom
Ignatius has been in contact but to whom he has not yet been able to write. Up
to now he has written from Smyrna to those communities who had sent delegates
there (Eph., Mg. and Tr.) and from Troas, to two of the communities who received him as he passed by (Phld. and Sm.). Polycarp is charged to carry out his
purpose.

The procession of ambassadors to Antioch had already started in Syria (" Even as the churches nearer [to Antioch] have sent bishops, others [further away] presbyters and deacons ", Phld. 10,2). Ignatius invites the Philadelphians to send a deacon (10,1); the Smyrnaeans, of Polycarp's see, to send an ambassador (Sm. 11,2); and Polycarp himself, to send messenger/s (Pol. 7,2/8,1; Polycarp will interpret this either as a personal invitation or a request to send an ambassador: Pol. Phil. 13,1). Ignatius also asks the other churches to send messengers on foot or letters (Pol. 8,1). All this contrasts with the simplicity of Rom. 9,1: " Remember in your prayer the church (established) in Syria; it has God for its Shepherd now in place of myself: Jesus the Messiah alone will supervise (ἐπισκοπήσει) it, with your communion also." However, this passage and similar invitations in Eph., Mg. and Tr., even letters written from Smyrna, contain a new problem which we shall now look at.

b)   *Syria or Antioch of Syria?*

3.   Together with the twofold place of writing — Smyrna and Troas — we observe an anomalous change in the designation of Ignatius' own community. In the letters written from *Smyrna* he calls his community simply " the church that (is) in (the province of) *Syria* " (Eph. 21,2; Mg. 14; Tr. 13,1; Rom. 9,1). On the contrary, in the letters from *Troas*, his community is limited to " the church that (is) in *Antioch of Syria* " (Phld. 10,1; Sm. 11,1; Pol. 7,1).

ZAHN tries to sidestep this anomaly by explaining the first by the second. He holds that it is not a question of Ignatius having jurisdiction over the whole Syrian province, as Pearson thinks, but only over the Antiochian communities, near which are other communities with their own bishops.[46] LIGHTFOOT is of the same

---

[46] *I. v. A.* 244: " Denn der in allen vier von Smyrna aus geschriebenen Briefen wiederkehrende Ausdruck τῆς ἐν Συρίᾳ ἐκκλησίας (Rom. 9. Eph. 21. Mgn. 14. Tr. 13) kann nichts Anderes bedeuten, als der an den entsprechenden Stellen der drei späteren Briefe (Phil. 10. Sm. 11. Pol. 7) ebenso constante Ausdruck τὴν ἐκκλησίαν τὴν ἐν Ἀντιοχείᾳ τῆς Συρίας." P. 307: " Man hat aus mehreren Stellen herauslesen wollen, dass Ignatius selbst ganz Syrien zum Sprengel gehabt habe. Er nennt allerdings in den vier von Smyrna aus geschriebenen Briefen fünf Mal seine Gemeinde ‘ die Gemeinde in Syrien ’, aber es wurde schon oben S. 244 daran

opinion, in his interpretation of Rom. 2,2. Basing himself on
Zahn, he concludes that to admit a " bishop of Syria " would be
an anachronism " as great in the third or fourth century, as in
the second ".[47] BAUER grants still more: Ignatius had jurisdiction
not only over the city of Antioch but also over part of the province of Syria; but not over the province of Cilicia, which also
at that time belonged to the Roman province of Syria.[48]

To avoid begging the question, materials derived from letters
written from Smyrna should not be confused with those from
Troas. The letter to the *Romans*, written precisely from *Smyrna*,
contains information that decisively supports the simple denomination " Syria ". In *Rom.* 2,2 — the only time Ignatius reveals
his identity — he presents himself as " the bishop (or " supervisor ") of Syria " (τὸν ἐπίσκοπον Συρίας). The text clearly affirms
that Ignatius exercises supervision over all the *Roman province of
Syria*. This item fits in perfectly with repeated invitations to the
communities of Ephesus, Magnesia and Tralles (letters also written
from Smyrna) to remember in their prayers the church that is in
the province of *Syria*. Besides, *Rom.* 9,1 confirms the function of
Ignatius and its extension, thus excluding any concordist interpretation: " Remember in your prayer the church (established) in
(the province of) Syria; it has God for its Shepherd now, in place
of myself: Jesus the Messiah alone will supervise it, with your

erinnert, dass dieselbe in den drei späteren Briefen ' die Gemeinde im syrischen
Antiochien ' heisst und deutlich als Ortsgemeinde vorgestellt wird, in deren Nähe
andere Gemeinden mit eigenen Bischöfen sich befinden (Phil. 10).''

[47] *AA. FF.* II: II/1, 201: " ' *The bishop belonging to Syria* ', i. e. ' from the
distant east '; the genitive denoting, not the extent of his jurisdiction, but the
place of his abode. On the supposition that episcopal jurisdiction is implied,
objection has been taken to Συρίας (...) as an anachronism in the time of Ignatius
(...) But the anachronism would be as great in the third or fourth century, as in
the second; see Zahn *I. v. A.* p. 308.''

[48] *AA. VV.* II 242: " Die Kirche Antiochiens zwar auch syrische Kirche ist,
diese jedoch nicht ausmacht, da noch anderes syrisches Gebiet, dem Ign. gleichfalls
als Bischof vorsteht (Rom. 2,2) hinzugehört.'' P. 262: " Die Nachbarkirchen sind
gewiss in der Nähe von Antiochien zu suchen, nicht in der von Philadelphia. Sonst
wäre der Gegensatz von Nachbarkirchen, die Bischöfe abordnen, und andere Kirchen, die Presbyter und Diakonen schicken, unverständlich (s. oben S. 203). Das
Vorhandensein s y r i s c h e r Bischofskirchen neben Antiochien (s. zu Rom. inscr.)
wird dadurch nicht bewiesen. Die unmittelbar folgende Erwähnung des Diakonen
Philo aus Cilicien (...) legt den Gedanken z. B. an jene Provinz nahe.''

communion also " (ἥτις ἀντὶ ἐμοῦ ποιμένι τῷ θεῷ χρῆται· μόνος αὐτὴν Ἰησοῦς Χριστὸς ἐπισκοπήσει καὶ ἡ ὑμῶν ἀγάπη).

God, with the article, seems to allude to God the Father. The following phrase, however, suggests it should be applied to Jesus the Messiah. Given the Ignatian use of ὁ θεὸς ἡμῶν,[49] as predicated of Jesus, it probably has to be understood of him, in his condition of unique Shepherd and Overseer/Supervisor of the orphaned community. Μόνος suggests that Ignatius was not thinking of a human substitute, but that his community would remain in the hands of Jesus, after his condemnation and deportation; "your communion" also fits into the supervision: it is a supervision on the spiritual level, that can be exercised at a distance through prayer in common, in the same way as that of Jesus through his spiritual presence in the midst of the community gathered together into one.

4. On the other hand, the notice contained in *Phld.* 10,2 accords perfectly with the denomination *Antioch of Syria* which is common to the letters written from *Troas*: "Even as the churches nearer (to Antioch) have sent bishops, others (further away) presbyters and deacons" (ὡς καὶ αἱ ἔγγιστα ἐκκλησίαι ἔπεμψαν ἐπισκόπους, αἱ δὲ πρεσβυτέρους καὶ διακόνους). Here it is taken for granted that Ignatius comes from *Antioch* and that the near-by cities have their own bishops. So as not to leave their communities without a head, the more distant communities only send presbyters and deacons (see n. 48). This organization is similar to that also found in the letters concerning the bishops of Ephesus, Magnesia and Tralles. In the *province* of Asia there are monarchical bishops in the main cities, including Smyrna, whose bishop is Polycarp. Thus in the Roman *province* of Syria, it would seem, the same organization prevails.

5. We find ourselves, then, faced with *two irreconcilable positions* as to the function of "supervision" entrusted to the bishop: according to one, such supervision includes the whole area of a Roman province (*Syria*: Ignatius-Rom.); for the other, it is limited to those communities grouped round a city (*Antioch of Syria*: according Phld., Sm. and Pol.; *Smyrna*: Polycarp-Ign.

---

[49] Eph. inscr.; 15,3; 18,2; 19,3 (θεοῦ ἀνθρωπίνως φανερουμένου); Tr. 7,1 (θεοῦ Ἰῦ Χῦ); Rom. inscr. (2x); 3,3; 6,3 (μου); Phld. 6,3 (μου); Sm. 1,1 (Ἰν Χν τὸν θεὸν); 10,1 (Χῦ θεοῦ); Pol. 8,3.

Pol.; *Ephesus*: Onesimus-Eph.; *Magnesia*: Damas-Mg.; *Tralles*: Polybius-Tr., etc.). Which of the two conceptions is the oldest? The information about " the bishop of Syria " is found in Rom. the better attested letter as much by external evidence as by the manuscript transmission. Rom., thanks to the remoteness of the addressees, was unknown in proconsular Asia and thus remained free from any later adaptation. Besides, in Rom. the simple name *Syria* appears no less than four times (2,2; 5,1; 9,1 and 10,2), applied as much to Ignatius' supervising *function* (2,2) as to the *area* in which it was exercised (9,1). Consequently, given the incompatibility of the two conceptions and the certainty of the first, the information contained in the three letters composed in Troas seems to be an anachronism as regards the ecclesiastical organization of Ignatius' time. It supposes a far more evolved episcopate already confined to the more important cities.

6. Furthermore, there exists evidence about Polycarp, who was almost contemporary with Ignatius, that confirms our solution. IRENAEUS, in his work *Adversus Haereses* (*A. H.* III. 3,4), referring to Polycarp says that " he was established by some of the Apostles as supervisor, for the (province of) Asia from the community (residing) in Smyrna " (ὑπὸ ἀποστόλων κατασταθεὶς εἰς τὴν Ἀσίαν ἐν τῇ ἐν Σμύρνῃ ἐκκλησίᾳ ἐπίσκοπος). As witnesses to the apostolic preaching, Irenaeus mentions *Polycarp* and all the churches spread over the *province of Asia* as well as *those who succeeded Polycarp* in the supervision of this province up to the moment of writing.[50] This statement from the pen of a man who knew Polycarp personally in his youth, corresponds perfectly with the self-presentation Ignatius makes in Rom. 2,2 as " the bishop of (the province of) Syria " and with the formulas contained in the letters sent from Smyrna.

7. Once established that the denomination " Antioch of Syria " is a much later one, the presence of the simple denomination *Syria* will guarantee the authenticity of those passages in which it appears. In fact there is another series of extracts where reference is made to *Syria*. In Eph. 1,2 and Rom. 5,1 Ignatius says he is on the way to Rome in chains *from Syria*, to be de-

---

[50] Μαρτυροῦσιν τούτοις αἱ κατὰ τὴν Ἀσίαν ἐκκλησίαι πᾶσαι καὶ οἱ μέχρι νῦν διαδεδεγμένοι τὸν Πολύκαρπον.

voured by wild beasts. On the way *from Syria* to Rome he has
been left to the mercy of a detachment of ten soldiers who, like
ferocious leopards, harass him day and night, on land and on sea.
Some members of his community had gone on ahead *from Syria*
to Rome to meet the Roman community beforehand (Rom. 10,2).
Philo and Gaius followed him (Sm. 10,1), one from Cilicia, the
other *from Syria* (Phld. 11,1), with the news of the restoration
of peace *in the community of Syria* (Sm. 11,2). Ignatius invites
the community of Smyrna to choose an ambassador whom they
would send *to Syria* to congratulate that community (Sm. 11,2;
Pol. 7,2), and he greets cordially the one chosen for this embassy
to Syria (Pol. 8,2). There is not the slightest doubt that it is a
question of an important personage. The Romans understood it
thus when they chained, guarded and deported *the bishop of Syria*.

These passages in the Ignatian letters where the denomination
Syria is found repeatedly, fully haimonize with Rom. 2,2 where
the bishop of Syria is spoken of, and consequently, they betray
the existence of later retouching in the letters from Troas.

We have seen that some topographical data in the letters are
contradictory. But there is another graver contradiction concerning Ignatius' identity.

c) *Bishop or deacon?*

8. In the present text the role played by Ignatius in the
community is not treated uniformly. Only in Rom. 2,2 he presents himself as τὸν ἐπίσκοπον Συρίας, *the bishop* (with article) of
the Roman province of Syria. In the other letters, however,
integrating the so-called *Polycarpian compilation*, he *never* associates
himself with the category of bishop, in spite of his insistence on
the three hierarchical grades (bishop, presbyters and deacons).[51]
He does not even use the second person plural in places where
it would be much more logical to count himself among them
(thus in Eph. 3,2 he writes εἰσίν instead of ἐσμέν). On the contrary, he identifies himself much more with the community as distinguished from the bishop: σπουδάσωμεν οὖν μὴ ἀντιτάσσεσθαι τῷ

---

[51] In the Long rec. (g) Ignatius also introduces himself as bishop in Ps.-Mg.
14,1: ἧς οὐκ ἄξιός εἰμι καλεῖσθαι ἐπίσκοπος.

ἐπισκόπῳ, ἵνα ὦμεν θεῷ ὑποτασσόμενοι (Eph. 5,3); οὕτως δεῖ ἡμᾶς αὐτὸν (τὸν ἐπίσκοπον) δέχεσθαι, ὡς αὐτὸν τὸν πέμψαντα (6,1).

Still more, in places where he mentions the three hierarchical grades, instead of making common cause with the bishop, he solidarizes with the *deacons*, calling them his fellow-servants: ἀσπάζομαι τὸν ἀξιόθεον ἐπίσκοπον ... καὶ τοὺς συνδούλους μου διακόνους (Sm. 12,2); ὡς εἷς ἐπίσκοπος ἅμα τῷ πρεσβυτερίῳ καὶ διακόνοις, τοῖς συνδούλοις μου (Phld. 4). And what is more, as if he wanted to avoid any concordist interpretation, he applies the same adjective in the singular to specific deacons mentioned by name: περὶ δὲ τοῦ συνδούλου μου Βούρρου, τοῦ κατὰ θεὸν διακόνου ὑμῶν (Eph. 2,1); καὶ τοῦ συνδούλου μου διακόνου Ζωτίωνος, οὗ ἐγὼ ὀναίμην κτλ. (Mg. 2). Similarly, speaking only of the deacons he uses the expression τῶν ἐμοὶ γλυκυτάτων (Mg. 6,1). In identifying the martyr of Antioch with the deacons he himself contradicts information contained in Rom. 2,2: τὸν ἐπίσκοπον Συρίας.

Scholars have already been aware of this anomaly. Some use it as a pretext to reject the authenticity of Ignatius or of some of his letters;[52] others try to avoid the difficulty by referring to similar Pauline expressions and/or theological speculations.[53]

---

[52] Thus E. Bruston, *Ignace d'Antioche, ses épîtres, sa vie, sa théologie*, Paris 1897, pp. 30-35 (Ign. was no more than a deacon; the letter to the Rom. in which he presents himself as bishop would be a forgery). Recently R. Weijenborg, *Les Lettres d'Ignace d'Antioche*, p. 66.

[53] W. Bauer, *AA. VV.* II 199, replies to Bruston: "Doch Ton und Haltung der Schreiben sind (auch abgesehen davon, dass ihr Verfasser kein anderer ist als der von Rom., der sich den Bischof von Syrien nennt 2,2; 9,1; s. auch zu Eph. 21,2) dieser Annahme (i. e. Bruston's thesis) ungünstig. Und das Nebeneinander von 'Mitsklave' und 'Diakon' lässt sich vielleicht auch ohne sie aus dem Vorbild des Paulus (Col 1,7; 4,7) befriedigend erklären." Lightfoot, *AA. FF.* II: II/1, 33f., attempts to give a theological explanation to this singular expression: "This expression is with great propriety confined in Ignatius to *deacons*, since the function which the bishop had in common with them was *ministration* (...) The limitation observed by Ignatius is not regarded in other early writers (...) where presbyters and others are so addressed by a bishop." Zahn, *I. v. A.* 443, holds the same limitation to be characteristic of Ignatius. Camelot, *I. d'A.* (S. Ch. 10A) 59,4, offers another explanation: "L'évêque, captif et, comme Paul, 'esclave du Christ Jésus', se rapproche volontiers des diacres, les 'serviteurs'." J. Moffat, *An Approach to Ignatius, H. Th. R.* 29 (1936) 1-38, complicates matters: "These hyperbolical terms about the diaconate in Trallians and elsewhere do not imply that in calling deacons his 'fellow-servants' Ignatius meant 'co-deacons' literally. It was not that he intended to define his own position in the Church as a διάκο-

The explanations given, however, are not convincing. The Pauline use in Col. 1,7 and 4,7 is very different from the restrictive sense given by Ignatius. *Paul* is not a bishop; Epaphras and Tychicus are not, technically speaking, " deacons ", the third degree of the ecclesiastical hierarchy. Referring to Epaphras, Paul does not use the expression in an exclusive sense, but preaches it to the whole community (" *our* dear fellow-servant "); finally, speaking of Tychicus, he explains that it is in the " service of the Lord ".[54] *Ignatius*, on the contrary, limits very precisely the scope of this expression to the deacons as distinct from the bishop and presbyters. If Ignatius had wanted to build a bridge between the ministry of the bishop and that of the deacons, he would have extended this expression to include the bishop. Finally, the explanation based on the fact that Ignatius, " captive ", identifies himself with the deacons, " servants of the community ", confuses two levels, the real and the metaphorical, due to the ambiguity of the term δοῦλος. Where Ignatius and Paul-Col. meet is in δεδεμένος. But neither of them relate this to σύνδουλος.

The different usage of the term σύνδουλος in the New Testament always contains a double connotation: (1) a relationship of dependence (expressed by the term δοῦλος) towards another who is " lord " in the strictly literal or the analogical sense of the word, and (2) a relationship of belonging to a social group or state (prepos. συν-). If the relationship of dependence between κύριος (βασιλεύς) and δοῦλος is understood in a strict sense (" lord "/" slave "), σύνδουλοι designates the fellow-slaves (Mtt. 24,49) or fellow-servants (18,28.29.31.33). But if it is understood analogically of God or Jesus the Messiah (" Lord ") and those

---

νος, nor to express his great humility, nor simply because Paul had called Epaphras ἀγαπητὸς σύνδουλος and Tychicus ἀγαπητὸς ἀδελφὸς καὶ πιστὸς διάκονος καὶ σύνδουλος ἐν κυρίῳ (Coloss. 1,7 and 4,7). What all this language suggests is the intimate associations between an ἐπίσκοπος and his henchmen the διάκονοι, particularly when there was any risk or trace of local disaffection on the part of presbyters " (p. 12f.).

[54] J. A. KLEIST, *I. of A.* 120,8, besides reproducing Lightfoot's explanation, adds: " Note, however, that St. Paul, in calling Epaphras and Tychicus ' fellow servants ' or ' fellow slaves ' in Col. 1.7 and 4.7, seems to put these co-workers on a level with himself, both being ' slaves ' of Christ like himself (Phil. 1.1)." See also C. SPICQ, *Le vocabulaire de l'esclavage dans le Nouveau Testament*, R. Bi. 85 (1978), p. 208f.

who are in their service ("servants"), σύνδουλοι are plainly the fellow-servants in a wide sense. According to the service they render to the cause of God or the Messiah will be the qualification of the "fellowship". Thus, in Col. 1,7 and 4,7 Epaphras and Tychicus are διάκονοι of the Messiah and, therefore, fellow-servants of Paul and the other community members in the preaching of the Gospel. Re. 6,11 mentions those who have borne witness to God's message with their death ("martyrs") and the fellow-martyrs who will do the same. Finally, in Re. 19,10 and 22,9 the angel/messenger of the prophecy refuses to be worshipped by John since he considers himself his fellow-servant and that of the other prophets.

In the Apostolic Fathers this term occurs only in the Shepherd of Hermas, in a sense very close to Matthew's parable (Sim. 55, 9.10), and in the present passages ascribed to Ignatius.

In the last case the term is applied to Ignatius as "fellow-servant" of the deacons, and it is understood in a stereotyped sense, that is, as an ecclesiastical state below the bishop and presbytery. The relationship of dependence exists between the deacon/s and the bishop (with his presbytery). The prepos. συν- shows him to be a member of this state. When Ignatius introduces himself as σύνδουλος of the deacons, he includes himself in the same ministry.

9. How then are we to explain this contradiction? Instead of an occasional solution (to escape from the deadlock), we have to look for a global one, since this expression recurs, except for Romans, in all the letters. The peculiar transmission of the letter to the Romans kept Ignatius' identity hidden from readers of the so-called Polycarpian compilation, where it was included much later. The compiler himself, attempting to assign to the distinguished martyr, Ignatius, a hierarchical grade, carried away by the cluster of phrases where Ignatius considers himself "trash", "the least", "the most unworthy of all", etc., without further ado places him in the list of deacons. Furthermore, conditioned by the mentality of his times, when the deacons were already closely bound to the *local* bishop, he limited Ignatius' diaconal service to the city of *Antioch* in Syria, as appears in the letters from *Troas*.

To sum up what has been said up to this point, we see that the twofold place of redaction corresponds with the double localization of the function assigned to Ignatius: Smyrna, to the church of the province of Syria; Troas, to the community of Antioch in Syria. If we add to that, that in Romans he appears clearly as the bishop of Syria, while in the rest of the letters he is still more clearly deacon from Antioch in Syria, we have logically to conclude that *Smyrna*, as place of writing, together with *Syria*, as area of the bishop Ignatius, reflect a much more primitive text than that of Troas, Antioch of Syria and the assignation of the diaconate to Ignatius.

d)   *The end of Ephesians*: *promise of a second letter*

10.   Coming now to analyse in detail the actual letters, we shall see that the end of the letter to the Ephesians contains the promise of a second letter that was never written:

"If Jesus Christ should count me worthy through your prayer, and it should be allowed, in the second tract, which I intend to write to you, I will further set before you the account I have begun of (God's) plan [55] for the new man Jesus Christ, with faith in him and love for him, thanks to his passion and resurrection [56]" (Eph. 20,1).

God's plan mentioned by Ignatius was exposed from chapter 18, up to the end of the letter, and consisted of an anti-Docetic exposition on the reality of Jesus Christ's humanity: the cross is a scandal for those who disbelieve (18,1) in the salvation of the flesh. It is surprising that two chapters later, without any apparent motive, he abruptly interrupts the exposition, promising to continue in a second tract or letter.[57] However, to carry out this

---

[55] BAUER, *W. z. N. T.*, s. v. οἰκονομία; LIGHTFOOT, *AA. FF.* II: II/1,85; FISCHER, *AA. VV.* 159; ZAHN, *I. v. A.* 457, n. 1 and 467f.; in *PP. AA.* II 26 he retracts this interpretation and understands it of the "doctoris expositio, qui bona domus divinae, quae administranda accepit et thesauros scientiae distribuit".

[56] ZAHN, *PP. AA.* II 26, interprets all the genitives as subj. gen. (the faith and love of J. Ch., etc.): "De virtutibus omnino Domini rebusque ab illo gestis disserendum erat Ignatio"; LIGHTFOOT, *AA. FF.* II: II/1, 86, however, understands it as obj. gen. distinguishing very well between the first clause (faith and love), subjective element, and the second (passion and resurrection), objective element of the dispensation.

[57] LIGHTFOOT, *AA. FF.* II: II/1, 18: "Towards the close he enters upon what

promise he lays down two conditions. The first refers to himself: that " Jesus Christ should count me worthy " and that " it should be allowed ". The second refers to the community and is unusual: " Especially, if the Lord should reveal to me that you are all united down to the last man, personally ..." (Eph. 20,2).

Thus, Ignatius awaits a revelation from the Lord before writing the second tract. The content of this revelation is clearly explained: an orderly assembly of the community obedient to the bishop and presbytery in the Eucharistic celebration (ib.). Therefore, before going on with his anti-Docetic exposition, Ignatius wants to be certain that the community is truly united in the Eucharist (see Ch. 13). The Docetists, in fact, as he says in Sm. 7,1, withdraw from the Eucharistic meetings, because they will not accept that the Eucharist is the Body of the Lord.

This promise was not fulfilled. It does not appear that Ignatius ever wrote this second tract. To explain why, scholars have referred to Pol. 8,1, where it is said that the forced and sudden departure from Troas for Neapolis prevented him from writing to the other communities.[58]

11. What are we to think of this solution? The bare fact supplied by the letter to Pol., last of the letters from Troas, is only indirectly connected with Eph. The interruption of the development is too abrupt. In Eph. 20, no reason is given to justify this interruption (lack of time, excessive length of the letter, unreadiness of the Ephesians to follow the argument ...). Ignatius seems here to have forgotten what he had written in Rom. 5,1 (Ἀπὸ Συρίας μέχρι Ῥώμης θηριομαχῶ, διὰ γῆς καὶ θαλάσσης, νυκτὸς καὶ ἡμέρας, ἐνδεδεμένος δέκα λεοπάρδοις κτλ.). If it had been the soldiers who prevented his writing he would not have omitted to mention it. The fact that he is able to make plans for the immediate future supposes that he enjoys a certain liberty of movement (" if it should be allowed ").

---

looks like a systematic discussion of the doctrine of the Incarnation (§ 19). But he breaks off abruptly, promising, if it be God's will, to send them a second tract (βιβλίδιον) wherein he will continue the subject upon which he has entered ..."

[58] ZAHN, PP. AA. II 25: " Quid Ignatium impediverit, quominus disputationem inchoatam ad finem perduceret, ignoramus; sed licet suspicari, simile quid Smyrnae accidisse, quam quod postea a scribendis pluribus epistulis eum prohibuit (ad Pol. VIII,1)." The correlation ἐὰν ... θέλημα ᾖ (Eph. 20,1) — ὡς τὸ θέλημα προστάσσει (Pol. 8,1) is deliberate. See below n. 182.

Even the way the interrupting clause is introduced leaves much to be desired. Instead of a motivation ('Επειδὴ κτλ.), he imposes a double condition ('Εὰν ... μάλιστα ἐὰν ...)

To clarify the question, we have to examine the theme of the above-mentioned tract on God's plan from the elements contained in chapters 18-19 and in the clause of chapter 20 that causes the difficulty. First, however, there is a wider problem that concerns the various tendencies Ignatius has to fight.

e) *Gnostics (Eph., Tr. and Sm.) and Judaizers (Mg. and Phld.):*
   two tendencies fought by Ignatius.

12. At least at first sight Ignatius seems to be fighting two tendencies: one, mainly anti-Docetic; the other, overwhelmingly anti-Judaizing.

(1) He warns the communities of Eph., Tr. and Sm. against the propaganda of certain false teachers from Syria (Eph. 9,1). They do not confess the Lord took human flesh (σαρκοφόρον, Sm. 5,2); if he suffered and died it was only apparently (τὸ δοκεῖν πεπονθέναι αὐτόν, Tr. 10; cf. Sm. 2; 4,2). On the one hand, they ignore the needs of their neighbour (Sm. 6,2); on the other, they keep away from the Eucharistic meetings and community prayer, so as not to have to confess that the Eucharist is the Flesh (τὴν εὐχαριστίαν σάρκα εἶναι) of our Saviour Jesus Christ (7,1).

Here, evidently, we have to do with the *Docetic-Gnostics* who despised matter as a contaminating element. For this reason they held that the Saviour, either simply passed through Mary, or descended on Jesus at baptism, and in any case, withdrew his strength before the passion, suffering only apparently (Tr. 10; Sm. 2; 4,2; 5,2; 7,1; Eph. 18,1).

(2) Ignatius warns the communities of Mg. and Phld. against the seduction of certain Christians. Although they confess in words that Jesus is the Messiah, in fact they remain attached to Judaism (Mg. 10,3): they invoke ancient Jewish myths (8,1), urge the Sabbath observance (9,1) and other Jewish practices that they consider reasonable on the private level (7,1). Ignatius exhorts them not to listen to those who propound Judaism (Phld. 6,1); he alludes even to his own personal discussion with certain Judaizing exegetes who subordinate the Gospel to the ancient — canonical — docu-

ments preserved in the Archives of the Jews, the Old Testament Scriptures (8,2).

Here it is clearly a question of *Judaizing* tendencies similar to those that sprang up in the Pauline communities, but with a noteworthy difference: these propagandists do not insist on circumcision, even going to the point of presenting themselves as uncircumcised (Phld. 6,1).

13. We have seen that there are two tendencies. The question is: can these be reduced to only one or are they incompatible? Scholars do not agree. They differ on the basic question: in spite of the emphasis in various letters, was Ignatius really fighting only *one heresy*, accusing its followers sometimes of Docetism and at others of Judaism, or did he rather clearly *distinguish* Docetic-Gnostics from the Judaizing groups? [59] The partisans of Judeo-Gnostic syncretism fence with the arguments supplied by the exhaustive studies of Zahn and Lightfoot, supporting them with recent discoveries of Gnostic documents of Nag Hammadi (evidence of late Jewish speculations in Gnostic treatises) and with Qumrân documents (presence of Hellenistic ideas in Palestinian Judaism). [60] MOLLAND calls this current of ideas *communis opinio*, and holds that Zahn and Lightfoot have definitely refuted BARTSCH's most more recent effort to distinguish two different

---

[59] Huther, Uhlhorn, Lipsius, Pfleiderer, Zahn, Funk, Lightfoot, Von der Goltz, Lelong, Rackl, Bauer, Barnard, Molland, Prigent, among others, reduce the two tendencies to *a single type of Judaizing-Gnosticism*. Copious bibliography of the ancient authors in M. RACKL, *Die Christologie des heiligen Ignatius von Antiochien*, Freiburg i. Br. 1914, p. 118, n. 2. Rackl gives a whole chapter, *Der häretische Gegensatz*, pp. 89-127, to the above-mentioned tendencies. Ample and critical study of the question in Th. ZAHN, *I. v. A.* 356-399: 5. *Die häretische Bewegung*. Concise, dense and very influential on later writers is the chapter on the subject by J. B. LIGHTFOOT, *AA. FF.* II: I 359-375 [373-388], *Theological Polemics*, especially pp. 359-363 [373-377]. — On the contrary, Harnack, Völter, Hilgenfeld, Richardson, Bartsch, Corwin, Grant, Kraft, among others, distinguish adequately *two irreducible tendencies*, one *Docetic-Gnostic*, and the other *Judaizing*. See M. RACKL, *Christologie* 118, n. 3; V. CORWIN, *St. Ignatius and Christianity in Antioch*, New Haven 1960, pp. 52-61; P. PRIGENT, *L'hérésie asiate et l'église confessante de l'Apocalypse à Ignace*, *V. Ch.* 31 (1977) 1-22. — After my two articles on Ignatius had been published (*R. Cat. Teol.* 2, 1977, pp. 31-149 and 285-371) P. J. DONAHUE, *Jewish Cristianity in the Letters of Ignatius of Antioch*, *V. Ch.* 32 (1978) 81-93, reached the same conclusions following a parallel method.

[60] L. W. BARNARD, *Studies in the Apostolic Fathers and their Background*, Oxford 1966, p. 24f.

groups of adversaries.[61] According to LIGHTFOOT, " a nearer examination shows the two (tendencies) to be so close interwoven that they can only be regarded as different sides of one and the same heresy ".[62] His argument is based on the fact that the terminology used by Ignatius to describe the one and the other tendency is generally more or less the same, and that those very false teachers who inculcated Judaism also propagate Docetism, according to what can be inferred from passages contained in the letters with markedly Judaizing tendencies, Mg. 8-11 and Phld. 2-9.[63]

14.   Does this generally accepted opinion rest on an irrefutable basis? We can admit without difficulty the existence of a Jewish gnosis and the presence of definite speculations of late Judaism at the heart of Christian Gnosticism. This, however, does not prove the possibility of a *Judaizing Gnosticism* in the technical sense of the word *Judaizing*, that is, which inculcates Jewish observances and practices and subordinates the Gospel to the Old Testament Canon. The terminology used by scholars to designate this hybrid of Gnostic presuppositions (Docetism) and Judaizing practices validated by Jewish hermeneutic principles (Judaizing tendencies), is notably lacking in precision.[64] On the other hand, besides Ignatius, there is no documentary proof of such syncretism.[65] Does it necessarily follow from his letters?

---

[61] E. MOLLAND, *The Heretics Combatted by Ignatius of Antioch*, in *Opuscula Patristica*, Oslo 1970 (= *J. E. H.* 5, 1954, pp. 1-6), p. 17f. – H. W. BARTSCH, *Gnostisches Gut und Gemeindetradition bei Ignatius von Antiochien*, Gütersloh 1940.

[62] *AA. FF.* II: I 361 [374f.].

[63] I 361-363 [375-377].

[64] Lightfoot speaks of " a type of *Gnostic Judaism* " (I 359 [373]); " In other words their *Judaism* was *Docetic* or *Gnostic* " (I 363 [377]); agreeing with the thesis " sufficiently confirmed from other quarters, that *the earliest forms of Christian Gnosticism were Judaic* " (I 364 [378]). BARNARD, *Background* 24, speaks of " a form of Judaeo-Docetism or Judaeo-Gnosticism ". To avoid confusion, they should speak of a form of Judaizing Gnosticism, that is, a Gnosticism that inculcates into its followers the legal practices and the hermeneutics of the Judaizers. DONAHUE, *Jewish Christianity* 87, agrees with our conclusions: " Finally, but importantly, we know of no such mélange as Jewish Christian Gnosticism; a Gnosticism of a much later period, influenced by Jewish literature, but not Jewish in any other sense, does not provide such a model."

[65] ZAHN, *I. v. A.* 356-399: *Die häretische Bewegung*, endeavours to identify the heretical, Judaeo-Gnostic movement, that appears in the Ignatian letters with some

15. We shall answer the arguments proposed by scholars. (1) The first is that Ignatius uses *identical terms* to label each class of adversary and to warn the Asian communities of their propagandists. This proves at most that Ignatius considers both equally dangerous because they come camouflaged under the name of " Christians ". Later on, when we deal with the common " origin " of both heresies, " the Chief of this world ", we shall come back to this point (see nr. 17).

(2) Neither do the proofs drawn from certain passages seem conclusive. *Mg.* 8,1 speak of " antiquated fables, which are profitless " (μυθεύμασιν τοῖς παλαιοῖς ἀνωφελέσιν οὖσιν). LIGHTFOOT, turning to the Pastoral letters (1Tim. 1,4; 4,7; 2Tim. 4,4; Tit. 1,14 and 3,9), sees here a hint of the emanations of the Gnostic systems.[66] However, ZAHN, who is also partisan of a single heretical current, denies that the Pastoral letters, and still less Ignatius' letters, refer to such Gnostic lucubrations.[67] In fact, the imme-

---

well-known names. Zahn is convinced that Irenaeus, *A. H.* III. 16,1; 18,5-6, etc., when referring to the Docetists who despised even the martyrs, is directly inspired by Ign. Sm. 4-5 and Tr. 10 (pp. 393-395). By exclusion, he concludes, the only Docetic heretic Ignatius could fight was his compatriot Saturninus (p. 395). Now it is sufficient to read Irenaeus' notice on Saturninus, *A. H.* I. 24,1, taken probably from Justin's lost *Syntagma*, to realize that Saturninus ill-treated the God of the Jews, however much he makes use of their angelology, anthropology, etc. LIGHTFOOT, *AA. FF.* II: I 367 [380], perceived this incongruence: " For they (Simon Magus, Saturninus, Marcion) do not satisfy the condition of being Judaic. Saturninus and Marcion are distinguished by their direct opposition to Judaism, while Simonianism lies altogether in another sphere." Then, he tries to identify our Docetists with those of 1 John 4,3 (Cerinthian Docetism), according to the very ancient Western variant that reads ὃ λύει for μὴ ὁμολογεῖ, to end by saying: " From the foregoing discussion it will have appeared that *the strongly marked type of Docetism assailed in these letters, so far from being a difficulty, is rather an indication of an early date* ..." (I 368 [382]).

[66] *AA. FF.* II: II/1, 124: " The ' antiquated fables ' are probably myths relating to cosmogony and angelology "; I 362 [375]: " Thus a closely allied form of Gnostic Judaism is suggested, which taught by myths or fables — the main subject of these myths being (as in the later systems of Valentinus and others) the genealogy of angelic beings or emanations, which were intended to bridge over the chasm between God and the World."

[67] *I. v. A.* 372: " Aber noch viel weniger als an diesen paulinischen Stellen kann hier an gnostische Aeonenlehren und an Travestieen alttestamentlicher Stoffe oder gar heidnischer Mythologeme gedacht werden ..." DONAHUE, *Jewish Christianity* 83f., concludes after a similar argumentation: " While there may indeed be a connection between the heretics attacked in the Pastorals and Ignatius' opponents

diate Ignatian context contrasts " living in conformity with Juda-ism " or " living according to the Jewish law " [68] to " living in conformity with the Messiah, Jesus " (Mg. 8,1-2). It is simply a case of Judaic fallacies.

(3) In *Mg.* 9,1 there is a sentence, they say,[69] markedly anti-Docetic. The context is as follows:

" If then those (the Prophets) who lived surrounded by antiquated practices came to a new hope, no longer observing the Sabbath but living according to the Lord's Day — a Day on which our life also began to shine thanks to him and his death (which mystery some deny, though owing to it we have received the faith and for this reason we persevere, that we may be found disciples of Jesus the Messiah, our only Teacher) —, how can we live without him, of whom even the Prophets were disciples through the Spirit and to whom they looked forward as their Teacher? And for this reason he, for whom they rightly waited, when he came, raised them from the dead " (Mg. 9, 1-2).

The parenthetical sentence " which mystery some deny ", refers obviously [70] to what is affirmed in the previous digression,

---

in Magnesia and Philadelphia, such a link would suggest that the former were Jewish Christians rather than that the latter were Gnostics."

[68] The fact that GgAB (hence S!) read νόμον, against L, suggest to retain this variant. I read νόμον ἰουδαϊκὸν with gAB.

[69] LIGHTFOOT, *AA. FF.* II: I 362 [376]: " Incidentally he mentions that Christ's death was denied by certain persons, obviously meaning these Docetic teachers, as his language elsewhere clearly shows." See also the following note. BARNARD, *Background* 23: " In IX. 1 he refers by implication to those who keep the sab-bath — now superseded by the Lord's Day — as denying the death of Christ." MOLLAND, *Heretics* 17: " In IX, 1 docetism is attacked (ὅ τινες ἀρνοῦνται)."

[70] ὅ τινες (quod quidam L) ἀρνοῦνται is a parenthetical sentence, referring to the whole preceding phrase. Lightfoot suggests correcting οἵτινες G with ὅν τινες and refers it to τὸν θάνατον αὐτοῦ: " The allusion is to Docetism, which denied the reality of our Lord's passion." In case of retaining the reading ὅ he specifies: " In this case ὅ may be referred either (1) to the whole sentence ἡ ζωὴ ἡμῶν ἀνέ-τειλεν δι' αὐτοῦ κ.τ.λ., the denial of this truth being involved in the denial of the reality of the passion and resurrection; or (2) to the words τοῦ θανάτου αὐτοῦ alone" (*AA. FF.* II: II/1, 130). What we are discussing however is not whether the negation of the principal sentence of the digression, " Our life also began to shine on the Lord's Day " (ἐν ᾗ καὶ ἡ ζωὴ ἡμῶν ἀνέτειλεν), is involved in the denial of the reality of the passion and resurrection, but whether the negation of the principal sentence should be interpreted as the denial of the Lord's reality. — Of course the text is uncertain at this point. The Oriental versions A and B are

that is, that " our life also began to shine on the Lord's Day ", namely, on the Day of the resurrection of Jesus the Messiah. We can only speak of " life ", according to Ignatius, from the moment of the resurrection of the Messiah. Even the Prophets who, thanks to the gift of the Spirit, lived " in conformity with the Messiah, Jesus " (8,2), had to wait for his coming to be raised from the dead (9,2). Those who deny this mystery are precisely the Judaizers who reject the radical newness of Christianity.

There is no trace then of anti-Docetic polemics. Ignatius insistently attacks " the Jewish way of living ", their trust in their own works and religious practices which are diametrically opposed to the divine gratuitousness (χάρις, 8,1) and goodness (χρηστότης, 10,1), to the point of saying that if Jesus the Messiah (" the Christ ") were to imitate our insensitivity towards his goodness, showing himself to be insensitive to us, we would cease " to be " (" Christians ") [71]. " To be ", for Ignatius, means the identification of the disciple with his Teacher, until death if necessary.[72]

(4) *Mg.* 11 is also usually interpreted in an anti-Docetic sense. We came now to Ignatius' explanation of the meaning of his exhortation. He does not write as though he had learned that Judaizing tendencies are found among the Magnesians, but to warn them beforehand against the propagandists of Judaism For this reason he begs them to be

---

of no help in deciding this textual problem. Only if we read ὅν and restrict the antecedent to " his death " " would a reference to Ignatius' Gnostic opponents be at all probable " (DONAHUE, *Jewish Cristianity* 84f.). I prefer to retain the well-attested reading of L and make ὅ agree with μυστήριον.

[71] Μὴ οὖν ἀναισθητῶμεν τῆς χρηστότητος αὐτοῦ · ἐὰν γὰρ ἡμᾶς μιμήσεται καθὰ πράσσομεν, οὐκέτι ἐσμέν. διὰ τοῦτο, μαθηταὶ αὐτοῦ γενόμενοι, μάθωμεν κατὰ Χριστιανισμὸν ζῆν (Mg. 10,1). Our insensitivity towards Jesus the Messiah's goodness (Χριστός/χρηστότης) would cause him to be insensitive towards our Christian identity (Χριστιανοί/Χριστιανισμός). To be insensitive to his " goodness/favour " (Mg. 8,1; 10,1: cf. Sm. 6,2) is equivalent to " not to be " (οὐκέτι ἐσμέν). See Mg. 4, a; Eph. 14,2; Rom. 3,2. The possible play upon the words Χριστός/χρηστότης/Χριστιανισμός is to be found in JUSTIN, *Apol.* I 4,1.5; THEOPHILUS OF ANT., *Ad Autol.* 1,1.

[72] Μαθητής-μαθητεύεσθαι sometimes means the beginning of the process of imitation (Eph. 3,1; Rom. 5,3), sometimes the process itself (Eph. 10,1; Mg. 10,1), at other times its culmination (Eph. 1,2; Mg. 9,1; Tr. 5,2; Rom. 4,2; Pol. 7,1), or else the whole process (Mg. 9,2).

" fully convinced of the birth and the passion and resurrection that happened at the time of Pontius Pilate's government; which facts were truly and irrefutably (ἀληθῶς καὶ βεβαίως) done by Jesus the Messiah, our hope. May none of you even be turned from that hope " (Mg. 11).

The supporters of only one group of adversaries, take this passage as proof that the Judaizers, alluded to above, denied just as the Docetists the reality of the Lord's humanity, his incarnation, passion and resurrection.[73] The terminology here used by Ignatius is very close to that in the anti-Docetic letters (Tr. 9 and Sm. 1-3). But the stress was not the same.

Firstly, in the present passage the accent is on the *resurrection* (note the chronological date, τῇ ἀναστάσει τῇ γενομένῃ ἐν καιρῷ τῆς ἡγεμονίας Ποντίου Πιλάτου), while in the above-mentioned and other analogous passages (Eph. 16-18; Tr. 10-11; Sm. 5-6,1) the insistence is preferably on the reality of the passion and death on the cross. The explanation is simple. The Docetists dislike to think the Saviour could die; but the Judaizers refused to accept that our life began on the Day of the resurrection of Jesus, since this amounted to denying the salvific value of the Jewish institutions.

Secondly, in the present passage Ignatius uses two adverbs (the *only time* we find together ἀληθῶς καὶ βεβαίως), to point out against the Judaizers the *reality* of the salvific facts — birth, passion and resurrection of the Messiah Jesus — and its *demonstrability*, whereas in the anti-Docetic letters he underlines the reality and importance of Jesus' historical life (*repeated* use of the adverb ἀληθῶς) [74].

16. It remains for us to examine the passage of *Phld.* 8,2. Ignatius speaks of having, on a certain occasion, exchanged words with his adversaries. Those who favour a single heresy take this

---

[73] LIGHTFOOT, *AA. FF.* II: II/1, 135; BARNARD, *Background* 23.

[74] Tr. 9: ὃς ἀληθῶς ἐγεννήθη..., ἀ. ἐδιώχθη..., ἀ. ἐσταυρώθη καὶ ἀπέθανεν..., ὃς καὶ ἀ. ἡγέρθη ἀπὸ νεκρῶν; Sm. 1-2: ἀ. ὄντα ἐκ γένους Δαυὶδ κατὰ σάρκα..., γεγεννημένον ἀ. ἐκ παρθένου..., ἀ. ἐπὶ Ποντίου Πιλάτου καὶ Ἡρώδου τετράρχου καθηλωμένον ὑπὲρ ἡμῶν ἐν σαρκί... καὶ ἀ. ἔπαθεν, ὡς καὶ ἀ. ἀνέστησεν ἑαυτόν. In Mg. 11, on the contrary, " there is no particular stress on the reality of the incarnation or of the passion. The stress is rather on what has really been accomplished in Christ, on the radical newness of Christianity " (DONAHUE, *Jewish Christianity* 85).

as proof of an anti-Docetic polemic that arose in Philadelphia between Ignatius and the Judaizers.[75] The passage is difficult, as much from the point of view of textual criticism as for interpretation. In the translation critical variants and philological annotations are indicated; in the commentary, the main interpretations:

" I entreat you to do nothing in a sectarian spirit but rather after the teaching of the Messiah. For I heard certain persons saying, ' If I find it not in the Archives, I do not believe the Gospel ' [76]. And when I told them, ' It is Scripture ',[77] they answered me, ' That

---

[75] E. F. VON DER GOLTZ, *Ignatius von Antiochien als Christ und Theologe. Eine dogmengeschichtliche Untersuchung*, Leipzig 1894, T. U. XII,3, p. 81, n. 1: " Das Alles erklärt sich besser bei der oben gegebenen Auslegung, nach welcher es sich in dem Streit um das γέγραπται um Weissagungen für die von den Doketen bestrittenen Thatsachen des Leidens und der Auferstehung handelt." And a little further on: " Da nach Phld. 6 die Gegner heidnischer Abstammung waren, so ist diese Kombination judaistischer Forderungen und eines spiritualisirenden Doketismus besonders leicht denkbar, wie wir denn eine Spur dieser Verbindung auch in der Polemik der Past. Briefe, vielleicht des Eph. Briefs und des Joh. Ev.'s finden. Das A. T. war zur buchstäblichen Autorität geworden in der Sabbathfrage und einigen dem griech. Geist naheliegenden asketischen Vorschriften (...) Danach hätten wir also in Philadelphia jedenfalls eine Kombination beider Irrlehren bei denselben Gegnern, *obgleich an und für sich Beides aus verschiedener Quelle stammte*." I have emphasized the last sentence, to bring out the perplexity of defenders of a single syncretist tendency.

[76] I read ἀρχείοις with g and almost all commentators, against GL that read ἀρχαίοις (scripturis antiquis A; B seems to read ἀρχαίοις). See the convincing arguments of LIGHTFOOT, *AA. FF.* II: II/1, 271; BAUER, *AA. VV.* II 260. I hold against Zahn, Funk, Battiffol, Lelong, Lebreton, etc., the punctuation of Hilgenfeld, Krüger, Lightfoot, Von der Goltz, Bauer, Bihlmeyer, Kleist, Camelot, etc.: Ignatius' adversaries oppose τὰ ἀρχεῖα to τὸ εὐαγγέλιον.

[77] γέγραπται, in the perf., is used by Ignatius, not only to quote the O. T. (Eph. 5,3 and Mg. 12) but to designate the sepulchral inscriptions (Phld. 6,1). In the N. T. it is employed to quote O. T. passages (BAUER, *W. z. N. T.* s. v.). Ignatius here extends it to N. T. books. See Barnabas 4,14 compared with 4,3ff.; 5,2, etc.; Polycarp, Phil. 12,1, and our n. 85 as well.

Against his adversaries who take as canonical only the Archives or O. T. writings (see LIGHTFOOT, *AA. FF.* II: II/1, 270ff. and the majority of modern commentators) Ignatius considers the Gospel also as a canonical writing: in Phld. 5,1 he compares it with the flesh of Jesus (ὡς σαρκὶ Ἰησοῦ); in 5,2 and 9,2, as well as in Sm. 5,1 and 7,2 he places the Gospel above the writings of the Prophets or the Law of Moses; in the present passage of Phld. 8,2 he compares it with the Archives (preceded like them with ἐν with dat., as in 5,2f and Sm. 7,2); in Sm. 7,2 he uses the perfects δεδήλωται and τετελείωται speaking of the passion and resurrection respectively, thus stating that we have in the Gospel the demonstration

is the question ' [78]. Well, to me the Archives are Jesus the Messiah: the inviolable Archives are his cross, and death, and resurrection, and the faith that comes to us through him; — in these, and through your prayer, I desire to be justified " (Phld. 8,2).

According to ZAHN, Ignatius' adversaries demanded written proofs taken from the documents of the evangelical preaching themselves, in contrast with the oral tradition of Christian faith evoked by Ignatius.[79] But LIGHTFOOT held that his opponents refuse to defer to any modern writings, whether Gospels or Epistles, unless they harmonized with the Jewish Archives or the canon of the Old Testament.[80] VON DER GOLTZ gives still more detail: the adversaries demand proofs from the Old Testament, not on liberty from Old Testament Law, but on the passion, death and resurrection of the Messiah.[81] BAUER, on the contrary, holds that they asked written proofs from the Old Testament on the question of a Gospel free from the Law.[82] On the other hand,

---

of the passion and the verification of the resurrection; finally, in Phld. 9,2 he says that ἐξαίρετον δέ τι ἔχει τὸ εὐαγγέλιον (comp. Sm. 7,2), namely the coming of the Saviour, his passion and resurrection, unlike the Prophets who only contain the announcement of his coming, but not the realization: for this reason, he goes on saying that τὸ δὲ εὐαγγέλιον ἀπάρτισμά ἐστιν ἀφθαρσίας, since it contains the demonstration and verification of the promise.

ZAHN, I. v. A. 430-434, admits the *technical* meaning of the Gospel as writing, only in Sm. 7,2; Phld. 5,1 and 8,2 (p. 433). Arguing with Zahn, VON DER GOLTZ, *Ignatius* 78-80, does not admit the meaning of *written* Gospel (Schriftliche fixierung), interpreting all the passages in the sense of its content (Inhalt der Heilsbotschaft).

[78] γέγραπται and πρόκειται are opposites. For the meaning of this last term, see LIGHTFOOT, *AA. FF.* II: II/1, 272f.: " ' *This is the question before us, this remains to be proved* ' ", against Pearson, Bull, Credner, etc. His interpretation is upheld by the majority of modern commentators. What do Ignatius' adversaries not admit as proved? The O. T. proofs adduced by him, or that the Gospel is Scripture? Ign. has given no proof whatever; he has simply stated: " It is also written " (just as their O. T. Archives!). The Judaizers counter-attack with: " This has to be proved ".

[79] *I. v. A.* 374-379.

[80] *AA. FF.* II: II/1, 270f.

[81] *Ignatius* 81 (and n. 1): " Es kann sich aber nur um Tod und Auferstehung des Messias gehandelt haben, da auf die F r e i h e i t vom alttestamentlichen Gesetze Ign. sich doch nicht mit einem ' γέγραπται ' berufen konnte."

[82] *AA. VV.* II 261: " Wir dürfen annehmen, dass Ign. bei jener Diskussion, auf die er im Brief nur einen flüchtigen Rückblick wirft, den Schriftbeweis für sein gesetzesfreies Evangelium geführt hat."

KLEVINGHAUS thinks the matter concerns Christian Jewish-Gnostic heretics, who refused to accept as " gospel " anything not to be found in their secret books.[83] Finally, CAMELOT understands it in a global sense: the Judaizing heretics denied *a priori* that the new Economy could find its justification in the Prophets.[84]

The problem remains complex due to want of agreement on the meaning of certain terms and the different possible combinations. Attempting to resolve them we shall take the data in order:

(1) In Phld. as in Mg. the context is clearly anti-Judaizing. This being so, the *Archives* can be none other than the canonical writings of the Old Testament, and the opponents' position consists in subordinating the Gospel to its inspired and fully recognized writings. At that time, the canon of the New Testament was still in process of formation.

(2) As for Ignatius, he alleges that the Gospel is also a type of canonical Scripture, and the Judaizers reply that it is precisely this that has to be proved. As far as I know, no commentator has proposed this interpretation, though Lightfoot already admitted the possibility of Ignatius' alluding here to some Evangelical or Apostolical writings.[85]

(3) In his discussion with the Judaizers, it is impossible that Ignatius held all the newness of the Gospel " is written " in the Old Testament. This would be as much as to accept its hermeneutic postulate without question. Indeed, if Ignatius' plain answer, γέγραπται, means that he includes proofs from the Old Testament on liberty from the Law (Bauer), or death and resurrection (Von der Goltz), it would seem to indicate that he has accepted the condition laid down by the Judaizers. So what are the Judaizers denying?

(4) According to Mg. 9,1, as we have seen, they deny that " also our life began to shine on the Lord's Day ". They will

---

[83] *Die theologische Stellung der Apostolischen Väter zur alttestamentlichen Offenbarung*, Gütersloh 1948, pp. 98-102.

[84] *I. d'A.* (S. Ch. 10A) 128 (note): " ... refusant *a priori* de trouver dans les Prophètes une justification de l'économie nouvelle."

[85] *AA. FF.* II: II/1, 272: " Though it is not impossible that Ignatius might have applied γέγραπται to some Evangelical or Apostolical writings (as e. g. Barnab. 4; comp. Polyc. *Phil.* 12)."

4

not admit then the newness of the resurrection of Jesus and the new life of his disciples. Could Ignatius demonstrate that this was contained in their Archives? The most he could concede was that the Gospel and their Archives were equally Scriptural.

(5) Since they would not learn from the Messiah (κατὰ χρι-στομαθίαν), and continued to argue in a sectarian spirit (κατ᾽ ἐρίθειαν), he gives up the discussion and simply stresses his position: " Well, to me the Archives are Jesus the Messiah ".

What counts for Ignatius are not words stored up in archives but the person of the Messiah and his adhesion to him. The Prophets too, already gave their adhesion to the Messiah, no longer observing the Sabbath but living according to the Lord's Day. For this reason, as disciples instructed by the Spirit they awaited him as Teacher and announced his coming. When he came, he raised them from the dead (Mg. 8-9). Hence, for Ignatius the Gospel is the canonical book par excellence; it contains the coming of the Saviour, his passion and the resurrection, foretold by the Prophets: it is the completion of incorruptibility (Phld. 9,2: cf. Sm. 7,2 and Phld. 5,2).[86]

17. As we have just seen, the arguments adduced by scholars in favour of a Gnostic-Judaizing syncretism lack solid proof. For in neither of the two letters (Mg.-Phld.) where Ignatius deals with Judaizing polemics is there evidence of the anti-Docetic struggle. However, there exist new elements, not adverted to up to now.

(1) Even the use of certain terms to brand the Gnostics and Judaizers is justified. Both heretical tendencies have a common origin, " the Chief of this world " (Eph. 17,1; 19,1; Mg. 1,2; Tr. 4,2; Rom. 7,1; Phld. 6,2). To defend the communities from their common enemy, Ignatius is not afraid to use the same denigrating terms to expose them.

(2) Nevertheless, in the question of clarifying the greater or lesser separation of one or other tendency before the community, he keeps to the term αἵρεσις for the anti-Docetic letters (Eph. 6,2 and Tr. 6,1), to indicate individuals who have deliberately " separated " themselves from the Eucharistic community meeting (Sm.

---

[86] DONAHUE, *Jewish Christianity* 86: " For Ignatius, the central mysteries of Christian faith must illumine interpretation of the Old Testament (...) Ignatius could not win his exegetical argument with his opponents, so he changes the rules; he appeals to a higher, more decisive standard."

7,1); while in the anti-Judaizing letters he uses slightly gentler words: μερίσαι (Mg. 6,2), μερισμός (Phld. 2,1; 3,1; 7,2 and 8,1),[87] σχίζων (Phld. 3,3); he names thus the " divisions " that had arisen in the heart of the community through conservative members who had upset unity.

(3) Both parties are in need of a deep conversion (μετανοῆ-σαι): the Docetic-Gnostics, should recognize the *salvific value of the passion* (μέχρις οὗ μετανοήσωσιν εἰς τὸ πάθος, Sm. 5,3), which is very difficult (4,1); the Judaizers, should enter into the *unity of the church* (ὅσοι ἂν μετανοήσαντες ἔλθωσιν ἐπὶ τὴν ἑνότητα τῆς ἐκκλησίας, Phld. 3,2), which is the unity of God (ἐὰν μετανοήσωσιν εἰς ἑνότητα θεοῦ, 8,1).

(4) The main danger of the *Docetic* heretics is brought out in the qualifying adjectives ἄθεοι = ἄπιστοι Ignatius repeatedly applies them (Tr. 10; Sm. 2; 5,3; οἱ ἀπιστοῦντες, Eph. 18,1), re-commending insistently not to receive them and if possible not even to meet them (Sm. 4,1); to avoid speaking of them either privately or in public (7,2); neither naming them in writing nor remembering them (5,3).

f) *The beginning of Smyrnaeans and the end of Ephesians*

18. The analysis of the themes of the Ignatian letters has confirmed the existence of a double line of defence that, without confusing the issues, gives some letters an anti-Docetic and others an anti-Judaizing nuance. Besides this it has made it possible to classify them into two groups, each with its own specific themes.

But this analysis itself reveals another anomaly. If we omit the inscription of Sm., we see that the *opening* of the letter differs notably from the way others begin, especially those written from Smyrna. Indeed, the letter to the Smyrnaeans starts *ex abrupto* making no allusion to the receiving community, naming no bishop, presbyters or deacons, when we should have logically expected to find an extensive mention of Polycarp and other noteworthy mem-bers of the community of Smyrna, where the first four letters came from.

---

[87] The sentence of Sm. 7,2f is probably inspired by Phld. 7,2g as we shall see later.

It could be objected that the circumstances were different, for the letter was sent to a community that Ignatius had known personally and not through some delegates as was the case with Eph., Mg. and Tr. But then, how do we explain that at the end of the letter the greetings to the bishop, presbytery and deacons are not given by name (Sm. 12,2; see 8-9,1)? In the whole letter, which contains a number of proper names, there is no mention of Polycarp. On the other hand, anonymous greetings appear in one of the passages where Ignatius identifies himself with the category of deacons.

19. Closer examination of the opening of Smyrnaeans shows, however, a series of *coincidences with the end of Ephesians*. In fact, if we compare Eph. 20 with Sm. 1 we discover (1) a similar vocabulary organized in binary structures and (2) corresponding contents between the second condition posed in Eph. 20,2 (μάλιστα ἐὰν ὁ κύριός μοι ἀποκαλύψῃ κτλ.) and the motives of the solemn praise with which Sm. 1,1 begins.

(1) In both passages a similar *vocabulary* is organized into *binary structures* of which the first member expresses the human and the second the divine dimension. We shall examine this in detail.

(a) The theme of the second tract (2Eph.), according to Eph. 20,1c, should deal with " the new man, Jesus Christ " (εἰς τὸν καινὸν ἄνθρωπον Ἰησοῦν Χριστόν) continuing the exposition of " God's plan [88] I have (just) begun " (ἧς ἠρξάμην οἰκονομίας), but has been abruptly interrupted. On the other hand, Sm. 1,1a starts off: " I glorify Jesus Christ, the God who has instructed you in such a way " (Δοξάζω Ἰησοῦν Χριστὸν τὸν θεὸν τὸν οὕτως ὑμᾶς σοφίσαντα).

(b) Ignatius goes on to enumerate the perfect dispositions he had observed in the community: faith and love, firm convictions. The *first* binomial of Eph 20,1d, ἐν τῇ αὐτοῦ πίστει καὶ ἐν τῇ αὐτοῦ ἀγάπῃ,[89] sums up the two basic dispositions, which can be verified in Sm. 1,1b.d: ἐνόησα γὰρ ὑμᾶς κατηρτισμένους ἐν ἀκινήτῳ πίστει ... καὶ ἡδρασμένους ἐν ἀγάπῃ ... The *second* binomial of Eph. 20,1e, ἐν πάθει αὐτοῦ καὶ ἀναστάσει, appears more fully developed in Sm. 1,2b: ἀπὸ τοῦ θεομακαρίτου αὐτοῦ πάθους ... διὰ τῆς ἀναστά-

---

[88] See n. 55.
[89] See n. 56 and nr. 10.

σεως ... The *third* binomial, which in Eph. 20,2 is bound up in
the second condition laid down for continuing the tract, ἐν Ἰησοῦ
Χριστῷ, τῷ κατὰ σάρκα ἐκ γένους Δαυίδ, τῷ υἱῷ ἀνθρώπου καὶ υἱῷ
θεοῦ, figures in Sm. 1,1e-g, after the first binomial, being part of
a *sequence* of four perfects: πεπληροφορημένους εἰς τὸν κύριον
ἡμῶν, ἀληθῶς ὄντα ἐκ γένους Δαυίδ κατὰ σάρκα, υἱὸν θεοῦ κατὰ
θέλημα καὶ δύναμιν θεοῦ. This far we have looked at verbal and
structural similarities.

(2) If we now turn to the content of the unusual condition
formulated in Eph. 20,2: " Especially, if the Lord should reveal
to me ...", we shall see that there is exact correspondence between
Eph. 20,2b, συνέρχεσθε ἐν μιᾷ πίστει, and Sm. 1,1b, ἐνόησα γὰρ
ὑμᾶς κατηρτισμένους ἐν ἀκινήτῳ πίστει; while to the second phrase
of Eph. 20,2b, καὶ ἐν Ἰησοῦ Χριστῷ, τῷ κατὰ σάρκα ἐκ γένους
Δαυίδ κτλ., Sm. 1,1e responds with πεπληροφορημένους εἰς τὸν
κύριον ἡμῶν, ἀληθῶς ὄντα ἐκ γένους Δαυίδ κατὰ σάρκα κτλ. That
is, what is expected to be known by way of *revelation* in Eph.
20,2 is known in Sm. 1,1 by way of *verification*. The exposition
of God's plan about Jesus Christ was interrupted in Eph. 20,
waiting for a revelation to be sure that the community had some
specific dispositions; in Sm. 1 Ignatius seems to verify their existence (οὕτως), and the tract continues.

20. What is the basis of these suspicious *coincidences* and
correspondences? The interrupting clause of Eph. 20 appears like
a deliberated *summing up* of Sm. 1. To explain this phenomenon
two hypotheses are possible: either (1) the letter to the Smyrnaeans
was originally the second letter to the Ephesians, and the addres-
see's name was changed by some later writer; or (2) the letters
to the Ephesians and Smyrnaeans originally formed only one letter
and some later writer had cut it in two, justifying the interruption
by the Eph. 20 clause.

Redactional as well as thematic indications go to support the
second hypothesis, which is, that Eph. and Sm. are really one
single letter. (1) Indeed, if these two letters were composed independently, there would be no explanation on the *redactional anomalies* we find in *Eph.* 20 (sudden interruption of the exposition,
promise of a second tract, conditions for a future continuation
and obvious imitation of Sm. 1) and in *Sm.* 1 (abrupt beginning,
anonymous nature of greetings to the hierarchy). Even more

inexplicable would be the *change of addressees* in the second letter (first 2Eph. and now Sm.).

(2) On the other hand, if we omit the interrupting clause (Eph. 20), we shall see that the themes of Eph. 18-19 and Sm. 1-3 fit perfectly together. So that the reader may grasp this more clearly, we shall recompose the text in translation bringing out and italicizing the *four articles of Ignatius' creed* and the *four of that of the Ephesian community*:

(A) Eph. 18,1 " My spirit is a humble servant (περίψημα)[90] of the cross: *to unbelievers a scandal*; but to us, salvation and eternal life.

(B) 18,1d Where is a wise man, where is a scholar? Where does the pride of the so-called knowledgeable end?[91] 18,2 For our God, Jesus the Messiah,

(a) was *carried by Mary in her womb according to God's plan*, that is, *of the seed of David* but *by the work of the Holy Spirit*;
(b) he was *born*
(c) and *baptized*,
(d) that *by his passion* he might cleanse the water[92].

---

[90] See also Eph. 8,1: περίψημα ὑμῶν καὶ ἁγνίζομαι ὑμῶν. LIGHTFOOT, *AA. FF.* II: II/1, 50f. and 74, gives this term in the Ignatian context the twofold meaning of " abasement and self-sacrifice ": " ' My spirit bows itself at the foot of the Cross,' and ' My spirit devotes itself for the sake of the Cross ' " (p. 74); only much later, towards the middle of the third century, it would acquire the sense of a " common expression of formal compliment ' your humble and devoted servant ' " (p. 51). This is related to the other Ignatian formula ἀντίψυχον (see Eph. 21,1 and Sm. 10,2). BAUER, *W. z. N. T.*, s. v.. inclines to the meaning of " allerunter-tänigster Diener ". The Pauline sense of 1Cor. 4,13, " the scum (περικαθάρματα) of the world, the offscouring (περίψημα) of humanity ", does not make sense in the present context. The sense of " expiatory victim " given by Lightfoot, Lelong, Camelot, among others, is bestowed on it by ἁγνίζομαι in Eph. 8,1 (see Tr. 13,3). In Ignatius as in Barnabas 4,9 and 6,5 the sense of " humble servant " fits well. Ignatius cannot say that his " spirit is an expiatory victim of the cross ".

[91] 1Cor. 1,20(19); cf. Rom. 3,27.

[92] Much disputed clause, because of its theological content. Abundant biblio-graphy in A. ORBE, *La unción del Verbo*, Rome 1961, *E. V.* III, p. 9, n. 25. The parallel of CLEMENT ALEX., *Ecl. Proph.* 7, supposes a separate theological approach. For Clement, " the Saviour was baptized without needing it personally, so as to consecrate the whole water in view of those who would be regenerated " (7,2); the water thus consecrated filtered the unclean spirits that were entangled with the soul (5,3: see ORBE, *E. V.* IV 662f.). For Ignatius, however, the cleansing of the water in view of the future baptism was made through the passion, thus stressing, against the Docetic Gnostics, the salvific value of the cross. Ignatius gives more weight to the virginal birth, with the manifestation of Jesus' Star to the heavenly

(C)   19,1 And *hidden* from the Chief of this world were
    (a)   the *virginity* of Mary
    (b)   and her *child-bearing*,
    (c)   as also the *death* of the Lord:
        three loudly proclaimed mysteries, that God brought
        about silently.[93]

(C′)   19,2 How then were they made *manifest* to the other (heavenly) Chiefs [94]? A Star began to shine in heaven above all the other stars: its light was unutterable and its novelty caused bewilderment. All the rest of the heavenly bodies, the sun and moon as well, gathered round this Star in chorus, but its light far outshone them all; there was also (great) commotion (asking) where this novelty, so unlike themselves, had come from.   19,3 From that time (ὅθεν) all magic arts started to vanish and all bonds of evil to disappear; ignorance to be removed; the ancient kingdom to be overthrown, when God appeared as man (ἀνθρωπίνως) to inaugurate a life without end.   Thus began the plan God had drawn up.   At once (ἔνθεν) the universe began to be moved, for it foresaw the annihilation of death ".

(B′)   Sm. 1,1 " So [95] I glorify Jesus the Messiah, the God who has instructed you in such a way.[96]   For I have observed that you form a compact block with faith immovable, materially and spiritually nailed on the cross of the Lord Jesus, the Messiah, and that you are solidly established in love by the blood of the Messiah, fully persuaded that our Lord,
    (a)   *by fleshly descendence*, is really *of David's stock*, but *Son of God by the divine design and power*;

---

hierarchies, than to the descent of the Spirit in the Jordan.   In the virginal conception the two components, the divine and human in Jesus, are perfectly delimited; to stress them with regard to the baptism could have favoured the adoptianist thesis of his adversaries.

[93] ἅτινα ἐν ἡσυχίᾳ θεοῦ ἐπράχθη. Lit.: " Those (mysteries) which were brought about in God's repose ".   The (theological) passive ἐπράχθη has God as agent: the modal clause ἐν ἡ. θ. denotes the state of repose/silence in which God has carried out those mysteries.   We can turn the clause into the active voice and translate: " God has brought about these mysteries during his repose " or " silently ".

[94] οἱ αἰῶνες, in pl. and personified, only here and in Eph. 8,1 (" the future generations "). Here they are ' the aeons ' who inhabit the heavenly regions (τὰ ἐπουράνια) in opposition to the earthly and subterranean regions, invisible Chiefs distinguished from the visible ones (see above all Tr. 5,2 and Sm. 6,1).

[95] In the original sequence there was probably an οὖν marking the continuation of the sequence.

[96] " τὸν Θεὸν must be closely connected with the words following " (LIGHTFOOT, *AA. FF.* II: II/1, 289).   The sentence τὸν οὕτως ὑμᾶς σοφίσαντα is anaphorical.   It refers to the initiation Jesus conferred on the community.

(b) he has been really *born of a Virgin*;

(c) he has been *baptized* by John, so that ' in him would be accomplished all that had been ordained ' (Mtt. 3,15);

(d) 1,2a under Pontius Pilate and Herod the tetrarch he was really *nailed to the cross*, in mortal flesh, for our sake.

(A') 1,2b Fruit of his divine and blessed passion are we:[97] thus, through the resurrection,[98] ' he raised an ensign ' (Is. 5,26) for all time to gather[99] his consecrated and faithful people, whether among Jews

---

[97] From Lightfoot on, modern commentators consider ἀφ' οὗ καρποῦ ἡμεῖς, ἀπὸ τοῦ θεομακαρίτου (sic: G) αὐτοῦ πάθους, as a parenthetic sentence, " so that ἵνα ἄρη is connected with the preceding sentence " (*AA. FF.* II: II/1, 291f.). But there is enough evidence to affirm that a *new* development begins here (A'): (1) Up to now the weight of the phrase has fallen on ὑμᾶς, i. e. the community as distinct from Ign.: (a) 4 perfects agreeing with ὑμᾶς (κατηρτισμένους, καθηλωμένους, ἡδρασμένους, πεπληροφορημένους) and (b) 4 participles depending on the last participial sentence (ὄντα, γεγεννημένον, βεβαπτισμένον, καθηλωμένον); whereas ἡμεῖς implies Ign. + community; (2) Both Ign.' creed (Eph. 18,2) and that of the community (Sm. 1,1e-2a) culminate in the cross (which was, in fact, denied by the Docetists); here however Ign. introduces a new theme, the *resurrection*; (3) The connection through the conj. ἵνα between crucifixion and resurrection, once excluded the parenthesis, is too forced (" ... you are fully persuaded that our Lord ... was really nailed to the cross ... that he raised an ensign through the resurrection "); but maintaining ἀφ' οὗ as introduction of a new development, with its antecedent explained at once (ἀπὸ... πάθους), Ign. encloses with a golden brooch the sequence solemnly begun in Eph. 18,1 (" the cross ... is *to us* salvation and eternal life "): " of which *we* (are) the fruit " i. e. " of his ... passion " (Sm. 1,2b), for " the passion is *our* resurrection " (Sm. 5,3). καρποῦ should be considered, then, attracted by the relative.   Zahn seems already to insinuate this: " Christiani ipsi pertinere dicuntur ad fructum Christi, quod subinde sic exponitur: *i. e. ad fructum passionis eius* " (*PP. AA.* II 84).   Funk follows him: " Crucem tanquam arborem cogitans Ign. de fructu arboris loquitur " (*PP. AA.* I 276).   It is the image clearly expressed in Tr. 11,2: The cross is the tree of life; we are its branches, that give incorruptible fruit. Lightfoot, on the contrary, prefers to identify the " fruit " with Christ: " But it is more naturally rendered *a quo fructu* " (*AA. FF.* II: II/1, 291). It is Pearson's interpretation against which Zahn, with good reason, protested.   Christians do not come from a fruit but from a tree: for they themselves are the fruit.

[98] ἵνα is a consecutive conj.; διὰ τῆς ἀναστάσεως is the instrument by which " he raised the ensign ". ZAHN, *PP. AA.* II 85, expresses it very well: " resurgens Christus crucis signum erexit ".

[99] Besides Is. (see 11,12; 49,22; 62,10) we have here the underlying Johannine theology of the cross as exaltation and pole of attraction for believers (John 12,32), which in turn connotes the image of the bronze Serpent: see Eph. 9,1 (ἀναφερόμενοι εἰς τὰ ὕψη διὰ τῆς μηχανῆς Ἰησοῦ Χριστοῦ, ὅς ἐστιν σταυρός). σύσσημον contains besides the idea of " signal " or " ensign ", that of " convergence " (συν-σημεῖον): " il a levé son étendard ... pour grouper " (LELONG, *PP. AA.* III 83).   Patristic parallels in LIGHTFOOT, *AA. FF.* II: II/1, 292f.

or among Pagans, ' into one body ', his church (Ephes. 2,16).[100]   2 For he suffered all these things for our sake, that we might be saved. And he suffered really, just as he really raised himself; *not as certain unbelievers say*, that ' he merely suffered in appearance ', being themselves ' mere appearance '; and as they mean so shall it happen to them, since they will be bodiless and ghost-like shapes.   3,1 For myself, I know and believe that he was in the flesh even after the resurrection. 3,2 And when he came to Peter and his companions, he said to them: ' Lay hold, feel me and see that I am not a bodiless ghost ' (*Preaching of Peter*: cf. Lk. 24,39).   And immediately they touched him and, being mixed with his flesh and spirit, believed.   For this reason also they despised death, nay they were found superior to death.   3,3 Again, after the resurrection, he ate and drank with them like a human being, though spiritually he was united with the Father ".

21.   In this long sequence it is easy to distinguish six steps, arranged in the form of *chiasm*:

(A)   The cross, *a scandal for the Docetic heretics*, is for us *liberation and eternal life* (see Sm. 5,3: " The passion is our resurrection "): *our life* starts on the cross (Eph. 18,1a-c).

(B)   *Anti-Docetic Christological creed* of Ignatius' community: it insists on the articles denied or attenuated by the Gnostics, supporters of an apparent body, and subordinates the salvific value of baptism to the passion that purifies the water, thus demythologizing the descent of the Saviour into the Jordan over Jesus and his withdrawal before the passion (Eph. 18,1d-2).

(C)   *Hiding* of the three loudly proclaimed mysteries from the Chief of the present order: all heretical teaching comes from this Chief (cf. 17,1); the Docetists, therefore, ignored the same mysteries as their Chief (Eph. 19,1).

(C')   *Manifestation* of God as man to the other Chiefs of the heavenly regions by means of the Star: agitation and commotion of the universe (Eph. 19,2-3).

---

[100] The paraphrase of *Ephes.* 2,14-16 is not limited to the present development. The whole sequence seems a paraphrase of this Pauline passage (end of the domination of the heavenly chiefs, thanks to the cross, and the raising of a standard to gather together the dispersed into one single body). Ign. had just told the Ephesians they were Παύλου συμμύσται... ὃς ἐν πάσῃ ἐπιστολῇ μνημονεύει ὑμῶν (Eph. 12,2).

(B') *Anti-Docetic Christological creed* of the Ephesian community: immovable in faith, stable in love, strong in conviction (Sm. 1,1-2a).

(A') The *resurrection* gives evidence that he really suffered, *against the Docetic heretics* (Sm. 1,2b-3,3).

The coupling of Eph. 18-19 with Sm. 1-3 takes place between the fourth (C') and fifth (B') steps. Not only the sequence, with its evident anti-Docetic theme, but also its suture, is perfect: the *agitation* and deep *commotion* of the universe, produced by the manifestation of the Star, with the consequent *annihilation* of death (C'), follows the verification by Ignatius of the immovable faith, stable love and firm convictions of the Ephesian community, to end with the *setting up* of a new and definitive order in the Church, as alternative to a society that is in process of crumbling away (B').

Ignatius was aware of the situation in the Ephesian community, not only through his representatives (Eph. 1,3-2,2 and 6,2), but also probably through a few families, whom he greets by name at the end of the letter (Sm. 13). The community of Ephesus was closely knitted both humanly and spiritually, through its firm adhesion to Jesus the Messiah, and well consolidated in mutual love. Thanks to its firm convictions, it was refractory to the perverse teaching of the Docetic missionaries (Eph. 9,1; Sm. 4,1) from Syria (Eph. 9,1).

Once Ignatius had affirmed his own convictions and those of the Ephesians, he went on directly to warn the Ephesian community and to refute the Docetic presuppositions (Sm. 4-5).

To sum up developments to this point, we see that behind the well-known promise of a second tract is hidden the hand of an astute interpolator. So that his abrupt interruption of the text may pass unnoticed he makes use of a literary device. By the promise of a second booklet the reader fails to be interested in the logical continuation of the newly begun exposition and accepts the vague excuse the interpolator himself let fall in Pol. 8,1. Once the reader has been distracted, the interpolator is able, without fear of discovery, to make use of the second half of Ephesians to compose one letter adressed to Polycarp's community in Smyrna.

g) *The inscription and opening of Philadelphians*

Thanks to the anomalies detected in the end section of Eph., it has been possible to unmask the tactics of the interpolator. Once aware of his shrewd stratagem, we intensified our investigation of a similar pattern in the other letters.

22. The letter to the Phld. starts out by two anomalies.

(1) In the *inscription* we miss the ritual formula πλεῖστα χαίρειν, ending of all other Ignatian inscriptions. In its place we find mention of three hierarchical grades, introduced with μάλιστα ἐὰν (as in the interpolated clause in Eph. 20,2).[101]

(2) In no other inscription is there mention of the hierarchy. It seems as if its introduction has displaced the primitive formula of epistolary blessing.

23. On the other hand, (3) the letter *begins* by an *anonymous* allusion to the bishop without naming him, although Ignatius pretends to know him in person: Ὃν ἐπίσκοπον ἔγνων κτλ. It is strange that if Ignatius has passed by Philadelphia, as Phld. 7 suggests, he does not mention the names of the bishop, presbyters and deacons instead of limiting himself to generic enumerations (inscr.; 7,1, etc.), while in Eph. Mg. and Tr., communities that Ignatius — it seems — has not visited, he names its representatives and their respective order in the hierarchy (Eph. 1,3-2,1; Mg. 2; Tr. 1,1).

Commentators pay no heed to these anomalies. LIGHTFOOT sees the difficulty and attempts to justify the use of the third person (ἐν ἑνὶ ὦσιν) in the inscription because it is found in the address of the letter.[102] The ritual blessing formula is missing too, and he notes that it has been substituted by a justification of ecclesiastical offices and particularly by praise of the bishop.[103]

---

[101] The formula μάλιστα ἐὰν is to be found only in these two passages. μάλιστα δὲ appears in Pol. 3,1.

[102] *AA. FF.* II: II/1, 250: " He still uses the third person, because the address of the letter is not yet concluded (...) The difficulty has occasioned the substitution of the first or second person in the versions ..."

[103] *Ibid.* 251: " After the words ἣν καὶ ἀσπάζομαι κ.τ.λ. would naturally have followed καὶ εὔχομαι πλεῖστα χαίρειν (...) This however is forgotten; there is no opening benediction, such as we find in the other six letters; but instead of this Ignatius runs off into a justification of the Church officers thus accidentally mentioned (ἀποδεδειγμένοις κ.τ.λ.), and more especially into a eulogy of the bishop

Is there any explanation of this anomaly? This we shall now see.

h) *Was there only one letter with anti-Judaizing content?*

24. To confront this problem we have as pattern the results of research on the end of Eph. and the beginning of Sm., together with the anti-Docetic theme common to both letters. These inclined to the hypothesis of a single letter, Eph*, unfolded by a later writer into the actual Eph. and Sm. To cover up the artificial interruption of the anti-Docetic argument just begun, he invented the excuse of a second booklet (Eph. 20,1) conditioning its writing to a divine revelation on the degree of obedience of the community to its bishop and presbytery (20,2). The division of the original letter into two halves left the chiastic structure of the sequence Eph. 18-19 + Sm. 1-3 unrecognizable. Are we now facing a similar case?

The *anti-Judaizing* theme is to be found in two letters, Mg. and Phld. On the one hand, the anomalies observed at the opening of Phld., with the omission of the bishop's name and that of the other ecclesiastical grades of the Philadelphian community, where Ignatius claims he has been.[104] On the other hand, the presence in both letters not only of a similar anti-Judaizing theme, but also of the same key-expressions,[105] lead to the suspicion that here also the original letter (Mg*) has been divided into two halves, Mg. and Phld. If the case is parallel with Eph*, the first half of the letter should clearly be found where the names of the messengers from the community of Magnesia are mentioned (Mg. 2); the second half, in the development that comes after the supposed heading of Phld., that is, Phld. 2ff.

Eph* was divided by an interrupting clause (Eph. 20). Was the same artifice used in the present case? We have to examine the ending of Mg., to see if there is a similar clause (nrs. 25-28).

(ὃν ἐπίσκοπον ἔγνων)." See H. J. SIEBEN, *Die Ignatianen als Briefe, V. Ch.* 32 (1978), p. 5.

[104] ZAHN, *I. v. A.* 261-272; LIGHTFOOT, *AA. FF.* II: II/1, 241 and 267.

[105] Μερισμός/μερίζειν/σχίζειν; Ἰουδαϊσμός/Χριστιανισμός; οἱ προφῆται/τὸ εὐαγ-γέλιον; Ἰησοῦν Χριστὸν λαλεῖν καὶ ἰουδαΐζειν (Mg. 10,3)/Ἰουδαϊσμὸν ἑρμηνεύειν — περὶ Ἰησοῦ Χριστοῦ μὴ λαλεῖν (Phld. 6,1), etc.

On the other hand, given that the interpolation has deformed the very *inscription* of Phld., it would be advisable to compare those of Mg. and Phld. to ascertain which is authentic, or else to reconstruct — in case both possess some original material — the genuine inscription of Mg* from the two existing ones (nr. 29).

As for the *conclusion* of the letter, the request for prayers for the church of Syria and the greetings and final recomendations of Mg. 14-15 seem more primitive than Phld. 10-11. However, given that this conclusion is closely connected with Sm. 10-13, and that this last probably contains a large part of the original conclusion of Eph*, we have to examine the problem of the conclusions (nrs. 30-35).

i)　*The interrupting clause of Magnesians: continuity between the theme of Magnesians and that of Philadelphians*

25. To support the hypothesis of a single original letter (Mg*) actually divided in two, Mg. and Phld., we have to demonstrate that between the theme of each of them there is a close connexion and that between the two halves there is a clause that is meant to soften the break. Everyone admits that the *theme* of Mg. and Phld. is, *in recto* at least, *anti-Judaizing* in tone. Are there substantial repetitions that make it impossible to fuse the two letters? Or is it demonstrable, on the contrary, that the exposition has a single unifying thread? Let us look at the *structure* of the main section of the letter to the Magnesians.

(1) The *introduction* develops thus: (a) Ignatius alludes to the orderly communion of the community as being according to God's criteria (Mg. 1,1a); (b) He expresses his decision to address them as a believer in Jesus the Messiah (1,1b); (c) Ignatius justifies his initiative in writing to the various communities that they may work in favour of unity (1,2); (d) He enumerates the messengers through whom he has contacted the community: Damas, Bassus, Apollonius and Zotion (2); (e) He stresses the need to be Christians not only in name but in deed (4), given the imminence of the end of the world (5,1); (f) He begins the exhortation by alluding again to his knowledge of the community acquired through his representatives (6,1).

This opening, unlike Phld. (see nrs. 22f.), seems to be original. Indeed, the three letters from Smyrna to the Asian communities have similar openings (see Eph. 1-2; Tr. 1 and Mg. 2). However, the two written from Troas to the Smyrnaean and Philadelphian communities show anomalies: *Sm.* has no opening section; *Phld.* has attempted to make up for this with an anonymous allusion to the bishop, without mentioning names of community leaders. These two letters do not mention delegates, taking for granted that Ignatius has visited both places. In both letters it is noticeable that there is no mention of proper names: in *Phld.* the writer has not dared to invent leaders' names and in *Sm.*, strangely enough, it does not even refer to Polycarp, as would be natural. We see the notable difference existing between the letters written to the Asian communities from Smyrna and those from Troas. The openings of the letters of the first group contain names of persons, but not those of the second.

26. (2) From the opening Ignatius goes on to *exhort* the community to " strive to do all things in conformity with God " (Mg. 6,1); so that, " because they have received the likeness of God ", they avoid human aims and all that could divide them (6,2), as also any private judgement however pious it may seem (7,1). Consequently, he invites them to gather all together in a single community meeting (7,1-2).

(3) From this point on Ignatius enters fully into the *exposition of the danger* lying in wait for the community, the Judaizing propaganda (Mg. 8-10), reinforcing his argument with the " Christian " behaviour, *ante litteram*, of the Prophets (8,2-9,2).

(4) That his exhortation may not be taken amiss, he makes the same *reserve* formulated in the other two thematic letters (Sm. = Eph* 4,1 and Tr. 8,1):

" (I say) this, my beloved, not because I have learned that any of you behave in this way, but as the least of you I want to warn you beforehand, etc." (Mg. 11).

This is a *stereotyped formula* that regularly (see Sm. = Eph* 4; Tr. 8) follows denunciation of adversaries against whom Ignatius wants to warn: Judaizers (Mg. 8-10) or Docetists (Sm. = Eph* 2-3 and Tr. 6-7).

(5) There follows an *enumeration of main truths of faith* in which the community should firmly stand (Mg. 11), similar to Tr. 9,1-2. In *Eph** (see nrs. 20f.) this enumeration appears twice (Eph. 18,2 and Sm. 1) before the mention of the Docetists (Sm. 2). In Mg. the profession of faith is limited to three truths; birth, passion and resurrection; that the resurrection was the burning theme in the controversy with the Judaizers is emphasized by the chronological date accompanying it (Mg. 11d-f).

(6) Then follows a sensitive opening of Ignatius' heart insisting once more on the praise of the community and his own littleness (Mg. 12).

We are already near the end of the letter and have not yet met the interrupting clause. The last two chapters of the letter (Mg. 14 and 15) clearly belong to the conclusion and are authentic (twice there is mention of the church in Syria, as in Eph. 21; Tr. 13 and Rom. 9, and of Smyrna, as place of writing, as we saw before). It remains to examine chapter 13. Is it authentic or not?

27. An attentive reading of *Mg.* 13 is sufficient to show that it is a *recapitulating* chapter. At present we cannot undertake a terminological and thematic analysis, because we do not yet know the extent of the interpolation in Ignatius' letters. But, confronting Mg. 13 with the interpolated clause of Eph. 20 that interrupts the exposition (see nr. 10), we find a stylistic resemblance (asyndeton) and similar terminology. Apart from these coincidences, other motives are not lacking to make us doubt the authenticity of Mg. 13. Momently let us take only the *double trinitarian enumeration* (ἐν υἱῷ [106] καὶ πατρὶ καὶ ἐν πνεύματι, 13,1; τῷ Χριστῷ καὶ τῷ πατρὶ καὶ τῷ πνεύματι, 13,2). Though Ignatius knows the function of each of the divine persons (see Eph. 9,1), there is no similar formula in the other letters. Nevertheless, for the moment it is impossible to draw a conclusion based on these doubts. This can only be done in the course of the analysis.

28. If we set aside the above-mentioned clause and reserve the conclusive chapters (Mg. 14-15) for the end of the original letter, we find that the exposition we have just ended on Mg. 12

---

[106] The mention of the Son before the Father is very rare: see FUNK, *PP. AA.* I 240.

follows without a break in Phld. 2, that is, exactly after the opening of Phld. that already appeared doubtful (see nrs. 22-23).

A particular detail confirms this to be the correct line. At
first sight Phld. 2,1: " Where the shepherd is, there you must
follow like sheep ", refers to the bishop of Philadelphia, about
whom we have an eulogy in previous paragraphs. By suppressing
the inscription and opening of the letter and joining Phld. 2 to
Mg. 12, the " shepherd " can be no other than Jesus, as in Rom.
9,1. Indeed, the following chapter — with a change of image —
presents him as a " gardener " who cultivates the planting of the
Father (Phld. 3,1).

By joining Phld. with Mg. the text appears in all its primitive
clarity. It is necessary — goes on Ignatius — to avoid divisions
and perverse teachings, following the shepherd as sheep, for there
are many wolves pretending to be worthy of faith trying to lay
evil traps to capture the runners in God's way (Phld. 2); the
community must abstain from the weeds that are not cultivated
by Jesus the Messiah, since these are not the planting of the
Father (3,1); unless they (the Judaizers) repent and enter into the
unity of the community, living in conformity with Jesus the Messiah (κατὰ ᾽Ιησοῦν Χριστὸν ζῶντες, 3,2).

Ignatius closes this first expositive cycle with the same recommendations, both negative and positive, that we met in the beginning of Mg. 6-8 (Phld. 3,3-4).

When we examine the sequence of Mg. 6-12 and Phld. 2-4
we can appreciate a perfect *concentric structure*, which hinges on
nothing else but the preventive explanatory clause of Mg. 11-12.
Ignatius, thus, gives us to understand the precise object of his
letter: *To warn the Magnesians beforehand of the approaching
assault of Judaizing propagandists.* To enable the reader to form
his own judgement on the perfect concordance of Mg. and Phld.,
we have drawn up a table of the outstanding elements of this
concentric structure:

(A) *Aim*: ᾽Επεὶ οὖν... ἐθεώρησα... παραινῶ... σπουδάζετε... (in pres.:
" strive ")

    (a) ἐν ὁμονοίᾳ θεοῦ... πάντα πράσσειν... πάντες οὖν ὁμοήθειαν
θεοῦ λαβόντες... (God, Jesus the Messiah, norm of behaviour) (Mg. 6),

(b) ἐπὶ τὸ αὐτὸ μία προσευχή... ὡς εἰς ἕνα ναὸν συντρέχετε θεοῦ, ὡς ἐπὶ ἓν θυσιαστήριον... (the Eucharist polarizes unity) (Mg. 7).

(B) *Warning*: Μὴ πλανᾶσθε... (a) εἰ ... κατὰ νόμον ἰουδαϊκὸν (see n. 68) ζῶμεν (adhesion to Judaism),

(b) ὁμολογοῦμεν χάριν μὴ εἰληφέναι (negation of Christianity) (Mg. 8-9).

(C) *Exhortation*: Μὴ οὖν (a) ἀναισθητῶμεν τῆς χρηστότητος αὐτοῦ... (to avoid Judaism),

(b) μάθωμεν κατὰ Χριστιανισμὸν ζῆν (to live Christianity) (Mg. 10).

(D) *Explanation*: Ταῦτα δέ...

— οὐκ ἐπεὶ ἔγνων τινὰς ἐξ ὑμῶν οὕτως ἔχοντας (negative constatation),

+ ἀλλ’... θέλω προφυλάσσεσθαι ὑμᾶς... (object of the letter: to warn beforehand against the Judaizers) (Mg. 11-12).

(C′) *Exhortation*: Τέκνα οὖν...

(a′) φεύγετε τὸν μερισμὸν... ἀπέχεσθε τῶν κακῶν βοτανῶν (to avoid Judaism),

(b′) κατὰ ’Ιησοῦν Χριστὸν ζῶντες (to live Christianity) (Phld. 2,1-3,2).

(B′) *Warning*: Μὴ πλανᾶσθε... (a′) εἴ τις σχίζοντι ἀκολουθεῖ (adhesion to Judaism),

(b′) βασιλείαν θεοῦ οὐ κληρονομεῖ (negation of Christianity) (Phld. 3,3).

(A′) *Aim*: Σπουδάσατε οὖν (in aor.: " strive for once ")

(b′) μιᾷ εὐχαριστίᾳ χρῆσθαι... ἓν θυσιαστήριον... (the Eucharist polarizes unity),

(a′) ἵνα, ὃ ἐὰν πράσσητε, κατὰ θεὸν πράσσητε (God, Jesus the Messiah, norm of behaviour) (Phld. 4).

5

This layout cannot be merely casual. The anomalies found in the opening of Phld. also have their reasons. The clause in Mg. 13, too, whose authenticity we did not decide on above (nr. 27), now shows its true function. As for Eph. 20, it serves to cover up the cutting, so that the reader will not notice the interruption.

There is also a very similar case to the one we observed before where Eph* was cut in two to make Eph. and Sm. The interpolator has constructed *four* letters utilizing materials contained in *two* authentic ones. For this: (a) He has divided each letter into two halves (Eph* = Eph. + Sm.; Mg* = Mg. + Phld.); (b) He has drawn up interrupting clauses (Eph. 20 and Mg. 13) to soften the breaks; (c) He has invented new community addressees (Sm. and Phld.); (d) He has composed suitable conclusions that will be examined further on (see nrs. 30-35).

j) *One inscription shared between Magnesians and Philadelphians?*

29. The unity of the two letters being established, we turn back to examine the inscriptions. In Phld. we saw there was a foreign body, mention of the hierarchy, and the consequent disappearance of the ritual blessing formula. This invites us to compare it with the Mg. inscription.

Unlike the other inscriptions, that of *Mg.* is extremely brief. On the other hand, in the first sentence (τῇ εὐλογημένη κτλ.) the word ἐκκλησία is missing, though present in all the others. *Phld.* inscription, however, retains this word and enumerates a series of distinctive qualities of the community. Finally, the ritual blessing formula missing in Phld. reappears in the last sentence of Mg. Given that elements missing in one are present in the other, the two inscriptions must be complementary. Everything leads us to think that the forger distributed the primitive Mg* inscription between Mg. and Phld. In fact, putting together both inscriptions we get a complete one, with no more repetitions that the artificial summaries composed by the forger:

" Ignatius (named) also ' God-bearer ',

— to the ‹community› blessed by the favour of God through Jesus the Messiah, our Saviour, at Magnesia-on-the-Meander (Mg. inscr[a].),

— object of mercy and consolidated in conformity with God, rejoicing indistinctly[107] in the passion of our Lord and his resurrection,
— filled with all kinds of mercy:
— to whom I send my greetings in the blood of Jesus the Messiah, that[108] is joy eternal and abiding (Phld. inscr.ᵃ),
— and heartily beg that they may rejoice in God the Father and in Jesus the Messiah (Mg. inscr.ᵇ)."

The leit-motiv of the original letter to the Magnesians (Mg*) is given by the sentence " in conformity with God " (ἐν ὁμονοίᾳ θεοῦ) that appears in the present *Phld. inscription*. Faced with the *divisions* that the Judaizers were trying to sow in the heart of the community, Ignatius insists on the complete *conformity* of the community *with God*. Hence he repeats this sentence at the *beginning of the exhortation* too (Mg. 6,1; note his equivalent, ὁμοή-θειαν θεοῦ, in 6,2) as at the *end of the letter* (Mg. 15) as well as at the *end of the exhortation* in this paraphrase: " In order that whatever you do, you may do it in conformity with God (κατὰ θεόν) " (Phld. 4).

The *programmatic* content of the inscription shows up also in the selection of the adverb " indistinctly " (ἀδιακρίτως) to stress that the community " rejoices in the passion of our Lord and his resurrection ". Its significance can only be understood correctly by keeping in mind the words of Mg. 9,1, when the Judaizers deny precisely that our life began on the Lord's Day and therefore they went on inculcating sabbatical practices. Here the relief given to the resurrection, through the adverb ἀδιακρίτως, is brought out in Mg. 11 through chronological date joined to the mention of the resurrection (see above nr. 15,4).

k) *The conclusions of Eph* and Mg**

In dealing with the division of Eph* into Eph. and Sm. as they stand today, we did not study their conclusions, as it was

---

[107] Against the majority of commentators I refer ἀδιακρίτως as much to the passion as to the resurrection, placing a comma after the latter. LIGHTFOOT, *AA. FF.* II: II/1, 249, already hints at this possibility: " καὶ ἐν τῇ ἀναστάσει κ.τ.λ. This is perhaps best taken with the preceding words ἀγαλλιωμένη κ.τ.λ., rather than with the following πεπληροφορημένη. "

[108] Lit.: " which is ... " (fem.) referred to " blood " (neut.) for the attraction exercised by " joy " (fem.): see LIGHTFOOT, *AA. FF.* II: II/1, 250, where Zahns' interpretation (*I. v. A.* 350) is also criticized.

not necessary to clarify that question.   However, once established
that Eph. + Sm. made up only one letter (Eph*) and Mg. +
Phld. another (Mg*), we have to face the problem of the four
existing conclusions, to discover the originals.   One line of research
would be the extraordinary analogies existing between the conclusion of Sm. (second part of Eph*) and that of Phld. (second
part of Mg*).

α)   *The present conclusion of Ephesians, summary of the original
one of Eph***

30.   The present *conclusion of Eph.* 21 retains only remains
of the primitive conclusion.   To a great extent, it is a summary
of the genuine conclusion of Eph*, displaced later on to Sm. 10-
11 and 13 (Sm. 12, as we shall see [nr. 32], has been newly coined
for the present letter to the Smyrnaeans).   We shall now analyse
Eph. 21 phrase by phrase:

(1)   Eph. 21,1a is a *summing up of Sm.* 10,2 (verifiable by the
ἀντίψυχον ὑμῶν found in both passages); it retains, however, an
original datum that could not have been transferred into the Smyrnaeans' letter: καὶ ὧν [109] ἐπέμψατε εἰς θεοῦ τιμὴν εἰς Σμύρναν,
that is, the community delegates of Ephesus mentioned at the
beginning of the letter (Eph. 2,1).

(2)   Eph. 21,1b preserves the *original place of writing* of the
letter: ὅθεν καὶ γράφω ὑμῖν. Then came Sm. 10,2 (τὸ πνεῦμά μου
καὶ τὰ δεσμά μου κτλ.), summed up at the beginning (ἐγώ).

(3)   Eph 21,1e and 2a asks the Ephesian community to *pray
for him and for the church of Syria* (see Mg. 14; Tr. 13,1 and Rom.
9,1).   This *fits in with Sm.* 11,1a (according to whether we infer
the presence in both of the same continuation: ὅθεν δεδεμένος
κτλ.), but the formulation is *more archaic* (Syria, instead of An-

---

[109] ὧν g Ussher (" in D. Montacutii codice *et quem misistis*, in Cantabrigiensi
vero ms *et quos misistis* ") Zahn, Lightfoot, Funk, etc.: ὃν GLABl (see the note
of LIGHTFOOT, *AA. FF.* II: II/1, 88). When distributing between Eph. and Sm.
the original datum of Eph*: 'Αντίψυχον ὑμῶν καὶ ὧν ἐπέμψατε εἰς θεοῦ τιμὴν
εἰς Σμύρναν, ὅθεν καὶ γράφω ὑμῖν, τὸ πνεῦμά μου κτλ., the interpolator substitutes
τὸ πνεῦμά μου κτλ. for ἐγώ and intercalates it between the two genitives: 'Αντίψυχον ὑμῶν ἐγὼ καὶ ὧν κτλ., thus making it possible that a subsequent very ancient
scribe confused ὧν with ὄν, interpreting it as the attraction of a nominative (ἐκεῖνος ὄν), due to the presence of ἐγώ.

tioch in Syria, as in Mg., Tr. and Rom.; confronted with Phld., Sm. and Pol.)

(4)   Eph 21,2b keeps the original tenor of the *place from* which Ignatius the prisoner came, *Syria*, and the *destination, Rome*, forming an inclusion with the beginning of the letter (1,2).   This *agrees with Sm.* 11,1b, where the interpolator has fallen into an inconsistency.   Sm. 11,1ab, in fact, says: " Your prayer has already reached the church at Antioch of Syria, *from whence* chained with lordly fetters *I greet everyone*, etc."   Commentators limit themselves to excusing the difficulty in the translation.[110]   How can Ignatius, who to all appearances is in Troas, send greetings from Antioch? The *lapsus* is comprehensible if we compare it with the summary: " Pray for the church of Syria, *from whence I am led* enchained *to Rome*" (Eph. 21,2ab).   This notice did not suit the forger, in that it presupposed that — due to the more or less lengthy stay Ignatius made in Smyrna — the Smyrnaeans ignored neither where he came from nor where he was bound for.   Hence he changed the well-known fact into a general greeting.

(5)   Eph. 21,2cd *sums up Sm.* 11,1c-end. Sm. keeps to the *original* reading.

(6)   Eph. 21,2e, finally, is the *short expression of final greetings* particularized in Sm. 13.

β)   *Sm. 10-11.13, original conclusion of Eph***

31.   The present *conclusion of Smyrnaeans* 10-11.13 is — with the pertinent retouching already mentioned — the *genuine conclusion of Eph**.   The clause of Sm. 12, however, is forged *ex professo* to adapt the former conclusion to the new situation of the Smyrnaeans (see nr. 32).

The transplanting to Smyrna of data originally belonging to Ephesus has only implied slight changes in the letter.   Nevertheless, the new context in which they were inserted has considerably modified the original meaning of the data.   We have reconstructed the contents of the Eph* conclusion and the altered meaning these

---

[110] Lightfoot: " Let your congratulations follow on the same road "; Bauer: " Von dort her (gekommen) ... grüsse ich alle " and comments: " Der knappe Ausdruck ὅθεν δεδεμένος = ' von dort her gebunden a n g e l a n g t (oder: fortgeführt) ' wie Eph. 1,2 " (*AA. VV.* II 272); similarly Fischer, Kleist, Camelot, etc.

same data undergo in the new context. For this reconstruction
we rely on the summing up in Eph. 21 (see nr. 30).

(1) *Eph* original context*: Philo and Gaius and Agathopus [111]
" have come " *from Syria to Smyrna* " following " Ignatius,[112]
passing by Ephesus, in the direction of the ship that transported
Ignatius prisoner. Their mission was to carry " a message from
God " (εἰς λόγον θεοῦ) [113]. When they reached Ephesus, the community " offered them hospitality as servants of God the Messiah " [114] indicating Ignatius' new whereabouts. Immediately they
went on their way till they met with Ignatius in *Smyrna* [115] (**Sm.**
10,1). — *Actual context*: In its new context, the messengers followed
the interior route passing by Philadelphia and descending to *Smyrna*; from there they went on to meet Ignatius in *Troas*.

(2) *Eph**: Ignatius *consecrates his person and his chains* [116]

---

[111] I read Γάϊον with PCgl (see BAUER, *AA. VV.* II 263): against GL (AB).
Add καὶ between Gaius (Raius) and Agathopus LABgl; omit it GP. The same
variants in Phld. 11,1: add καὶ CABgl; omit it GL (G places a full stop between
both names). The authors tend to explain Sm. 10,1 by Phld. 11,1 and this last,
even from Ps.-Ign. Ant. 13 and Phil. 15 (see LIGHTFOOT, *AA. FF.* II: II/1, 280f.),
since in Phld. there are only two sentences corresponding with two persons, in the
singular, and in Ps.-Ign. only two persons are spoken of. Now, Phld. *imitates* Sm.,
as we shall see at once, and nevertheless the " and " is maintained in Phld. We
have, then, to do without Phld. (and, of course, without Ps.-Ign. too!) to interpret
Sm. Philo, named first, would be responsible for the little group. Therefore he
alone greets the Ephesian community in Sm. 13,1c.

[112] οἱ ἐπηκολούθησάν μοι: " follow close behind; go in pursuit of, after " with
dative (BAUER, *W. z. N. T.*: " sie sind mir ... nachgereist "). Since it is a past act
with a mark of continuity, the aor. means the whole journey from Syria to where
Ignatius actually is.

[113] εἰς explains the motive of the travellers in pursuit of Ign.: " to (take) a
message "; θεοῦ qualifies the " message ": " on the part of, in the name of, from
God ". Hence " to (take/carry) a message from God ". (But " in the matter of "
Lightfoot; " in Gottes sache " Bauer; " pour l'amour de Dieu " Lelong, Camelot,
etc.).

[114] ὑποδεξάμενοι ὡς διακόνους Χριστοῦ (GL > PAB) θεοῦ: " you have received/
welcomed/offered hospitality/given entertainment to them as servants of the
Messiah God ". See Rom. 9,3: the community of Ephesus was one of those which
" received " Ignatius " in the name of Jesus the Messiah ". For the archaism,
" Messiah God ", see Tr. 7,1 and our n. 49.

[115] εὐχαριστοῦσιν, in the present: " they are thanking " in Ignatius' presence
" for " what the Ephesians did for them.

[116] The expressions ἀντίψυχον ὑμῶν τὸ πνεῦμά μου καὶ τὰ δεσμά μου (Sm. 10,2:
nevertheless see Eph. 21,1; Pol. 2,3 and 6,1c); περίψημα ὑμῶν καὶ ἁγνίζομαι ὑμῶν

*for the Ephesian community and their delegates to Smyrna from
whence also he is writing to them* (**Eph.** 21,1ab + **Sm.** 10,2). —
Actual context: The forger has been obliged to leave in Eph. the
allusion to the envoys to Smyrna and to the place of redaction,
keeping for Sm. the *development* of the summary in Eph. and
placing further on, in Sm. 12,1, *Troas*, as the place where the new
letter was written.

(3) *Eph**: Ignatius asks that *they remember him, for their
prayer has already reached the church of Syria, from whence he is
being led to Rome enchained ...*[117], because " though he does not
feel worthy to belong to it, being the very last of them " (see
Mg. 14; Tr. 13,1 and Rom. 9,2), " by the grace of God he has
been found worthy " to go to martyrdom, a grace he begs to be
given in full (**Eph.** 21,1e.2a-d + **Sm.** 11,1) — *Actual context*: The
interpolator has need to leave in Eph. the mention of Syria, as
the place of departure for Rome, and has incorrectly replaced
it with a *greeting*; in the same way he has modified Syria to
Antioch of Syria, thus limiting the wide range of Ignatius' action
(the bishop of the province of Syria) to the city of Antioch, considering him merely a *deacon*.[118]

(Eph. 8,1); περίψημα τὸ ἐμὸν πνεῦμα τοῦ σταυροῦ (18,1); ἀγνίζεται ὑμῶν τὸ ἐμὸν
πνεῦμα (Tr. 13,3); ἀσπάζεται ὑμᾶς τὸ ἐμὸν πνεῦμα (Rom. 9,3), on the one hand
avoid *mentioning the first person* and, on the other, stress *the interior attitude* of
Ign. the prisoner — " total consecration ", " humble servant ", " personal sacrifice "
— towards the communities to whom he is writing on the way to martyrdom.
No need to insist, in the direct language Ign. uses, on the purely etymological sense,
even when, given his situation and his idea of martyrdom as sacrifice (θυσία: Rom.
4,2) offered (σπονδισθῆναι: 2,2) on the altar prepared in the arena (θυσιαστήριον:
ibid.), it is not excluded that in certain cases this is what it connotes. See however LIGHTFOOT, *AA. FF.* II : II/1, 50f. (he insists on the etymological sense); BAUER,
AA. VV. II 207 and *W. z. N. T.*, s. v. (" Ausdruck höfflicher Selbsterniedrigung "
for περίψημα; " Lösegeld " for ἀντίψυχον: " sich weihen " for ἀγνίζομαι).

[117] From the more or less stereotyped heading to be found in the conclusions
of the letters from Smyrna (Mg. 14: Μνημονεύετέ μου ἐν ταῖς προσευχαῖς ὑμῶν...
καὶ τῆς ἐν Συρίᾳ ἐκκλησίας, ὅθεν κτλ.; Tr. 13,1 and Rom. 9,1) and of the one
retained by Eph. 21 and Sm. 11,1, it is possible to reconstruct very approximately
the heading of the conclusion of Eph*: Μνημονεύετέ μου · ἡ <γὰρ> προσευχὴ ὑμῶν
ἀπῆλθεν ἐπὶ τὴν ἐκκλησίαν τὴν ἐν Συρίᾳ, ὅθεν δεδεμένος θεοπρεπεστάτοις δεσμοῖς
εἰς Ῥώμην ἀπάγομαι κτλ.

[118] See the earlier developments (a) about the singular transmission of Rom.
(the only letter in which Ign. introduces himself as " the bishop of Syria ") (p. 21ff.);
(b) about the diversity of denominations of Ignatius' own community: Syria (letters

(4) *Eph**: Ignatius has been informed by Philo, Gaius and Agathopus that " thanks to the prayer and deep love of the Ephesians, *the church of Syria is in peace* " (**Phld.** 10,1a). To give tangible sign of this good work,[119] he suggests they " *appoint an ambassador* to go as far as Syria and congratulate them because they are at peace, and have recovered their own strength and their corporate body has been re-established " (**Sm.** 11,2). — *Actual context*: The forger, conditioned by the modifications he introduced in Sm. 11,1,[120] has *omitted* the motivation that caused Ignatius to invite the Ephesians to complete, by sending a messenger, the good work begun (their prayers for the Syrian community). The omitted phrase served to open the Phld. conclusion, as we shall see presently (nr. 33). With no further explanation, *he limits himself to transcribing the invitation.*

(5) *Eph**: As a spur to the Ephesians, he also decides to do what is within his reach, " *sending one of* " the Ephesians who went with him to Smyrna " *with a personal letter from him,* "[121] to show " his pleasure for the God-given calm which had come

---

from Smyrna) or Antioch of Syria (letters from Troas) (nrs. 3-7); (c) about the identification of Ignatius with the deacons (nr. 8) and its logical explanation (nr. 9). In this matter it is curious that Ps.-Ign., in spite of having introduced him as bishop of Antioch of Syria, goes on showing him to be very attached to the deacons to the point of proposing the deacon Heron as his successor in Antioch (see Ant. 12; Her. 7).

[119] ἵνα οὖν τέλειον ὑμῶν γένηται τὸ ἔργον καὶ ἐπὶ γῆς καὶ ἐν οὐρανῷ: " in heaven ", for his prayers; " on the earth ", for the choice and sending of an ambassador to Syria. At the beginning of the letter, referring to the eagerness of their welcome on his arrival in Ephesus from Syria Ign. says: τὸ συγγενικὸν ἔργον τελείως ἀπηρτίσατε (Eph. 1,1). See Eph. 14,2; Rom. 3,3. Further on we shall deal with the parallel in Pol. 7,3: τοῦτο τὸ ἔργον θεοῦ ἐστὶν καὶ ὑμῶν, ὅταν αὐτὸ ἀπαρτίσητε.

[120] The interpolator modified the original conclusion of Eph* (see n. 117), adapting it to the new situation in Sm. as follows: Ἡ προσευχὴ ὑμῶν ἀπῆλθεν ἐπὶ τὴν ἐκκλησίαν τὴν ἐν Ἀ ν τ ι ο χ ε ί ᾳ τ ῆ ς Συρίας, ὅθεν δεδεμένος θεοπρεπεστάτοις δεσμοῖς π ά ν τ α ς ἀ σ π ά ζ ο μ α ι. (We have spaced what is interpolated.)

[121] ἐφάνη μοι οὖν θεοῦ ἄξιον πρᾶγμα, πέμψαι τινὰ τῶν ὑμετέρων μετ' ἐπιστολῆς, ἵνα συνδοξάσῃ κτλ. There is no more news of this letter of Ign. to his " diocese " of Syria. Its contents are immediately hinted at. The Ps.-Ign. has coined a new letter addressed to the Antiochenes, whose heading (borrowed from a letter of Alexander of Jerusalem) reflects this situation (Ant. 1: see LIGHTFOOT, *AA. FF.* II: II/2, 817 [III 233]).

upon them, and because thanks to the prayers of the Ephesians they have already reached a safe haven '' (**Sm.** 11,3a-c). — *Actual context*: The forger has merely influenced the phrase negatively, preventing its normal meaning from being understood. Indeed, by changing the original address of the letter, the conclusion written from Smyrna to the Ephesians has inevitably suffered the influence of the fictitious circumstances in which Ignatius is placed. Thus only Burrhus goes with him to Troas.[122] Consequently, the sentence τινὰ τῶν ὑμετέρων [123] can only refer to *one of the members of the Smyrnaean community*, that is, the one the community had chosen for the embassy to Syria. With a stroke, Sm. 11,3 has been changed into a *simple repetition* of what was said in 11,2; the obvious subject of πέμψαι (Ignatius) has become the *community of Smyrna* (not without straining the syntax)[124]; the letter written by Ignatius to show his pleasure for the calm reached by his church of Syria, has become a *letter drawn up by the community of Smyrna for the community of Antioch in Syria*, as a kind of *credentials* for the embassy that should be carried out by the man chosen to go as far as Syria.

(6) *Eph**: Ignatius supports the invitation to the Ephesians by the *total availability of God to give* any kind of good towards what the community wants to carry out: '' Since [125] you are mature (men), aspire to maturity: because when you wish to do something, God is always ready to grant [126] it '' (**Sm.** 11,3de). — *Actual context*: The incidence of falsification on this sentence seems scarce.

---

[122] See Sm. 12,1 and Phld. 11,2.

[123] While it was addressed to the Ephesian community, it connoted one of the Ephesians sent to Smyrna; when it addresses the Smyrnaeans, it can only point out one of them who is in Smyrna. In the impossibility of Ignatius' sending someone from Troas, the Smyrnaeans had to send an envoy to Syria: the (lost) letter then is no longer from Ign. but from the Smyrnaeans. Thus concludes ZAHN, *I. v. A.* 286: '' Sind es ohne alle Frage nach Allem, was vorangeht und nachfolgt, die Smyrnäer oder ihr bischof, welche den Boten absenden, so muss auch ' ein Brief ', den dieser mitnehmen soll, ein zu dem Ende von den Smyrnäern abzufassender sein.''

[124] All the commentators supply a new subject for πέμψαι, distinct from the one indicated by the preceding phrase, being thus forced simply to negate what is affirmed *in recto*: '' Nicht Ign. will die würdige Aufgabe erfüllen, sondern die Smyrnäer sollen es tun '' (BAUER, *AA. VV.* II 272).

[125] P adds οὖν.

[126] παρέχειν: see critical apparatus, p. 384, l. 1.

(7) *Eph**: Ignatius *personally greets* the families and members of the community whom he met *when he passed through Ephesus* (**Sm.** 13: unrecognizable in Eph. 21,2e). — *Actual context*: Actually the greetings are addressed to the Smyrnaeans.

When we sum up what was been said about the summary of Eph. 21 and the presence in Sm. 10-11.13 of the original conclusion of Eph*, we have evidence of the perfect consistency of the data retained in both conclusions, their complementary nature in some places and their logical connection with the circumstances of the prisoner Ignatius, i.e. those belonging to his condition as prisoner as well as those linked with his position as bishop of Syria and the events that brought about his condemnation.

γ) *The additional clauses*

32. To adapt the original conclusion of Eph* to the new letter to the Smyrnaeans the above-mentioned touching up was insufficient (nrs. 30f.): A *new clause* had to be created to state where the letter came from and its carrier's name. Now, Sm. is one of three letters attributed to the new place of writing, Troas. It will not be strange then to find in the Phld. and Pol. *conclusions* more or less similar analogies with Sm. Still more, in one of them, Phld., there is an inserted clause modelled on the new one composed for Sm. We shall now examine these two newly-created clauses: *Sm. 12* and *Phld. 11,2*.

In both we have the same data: (a) The community of *Troas*, north of Smyrna, from whence Ignatius sailed in direction of Neapolis, the port-town of Philippi (Macedonia); (b) *Burrhus*, one of the delegates sent by the Ephesians to Smyrna (Eph. 2,1), to take the letters written in Troas to Philadelphia and Smyrna (ὅθεν καὶ γράφω ὑμῖν διὰ Βούρρου); (c) *Smyrnaeans and Ephesians*, as senders of Burrhus as well as Ignatius (sic!: ὃν ἀπεστείλατε μετ' ἐμοῦ ἅμα 'Εφεσίοις, Sm.; πεμφθέντος ἅμα ἐμοὶ ἀπὸ 'Εφεσίων καὶ Σμυρναίων, Phld.). The forger once more shows that he is ignorant of the genuine situation described by Ignatius in Rom. 5,1.

When we have sufficient elements to identify the interpolator's style, we shall be able to confirm that both clauses are spurious. Some stylistic characteristics have already emerged. Note, for example, the asyndetic style of Sm. 12,2, compared with Eph. 20, certainly an interpolation; as also the unusual association of terms common to both (τοὺς κατ᾽ ἄνδρα καὶ κοινῇ πάντας ἐν ὀνόματι κτλ., Sm.; οἱ κατ᾽ ἄνδρα κοινῇ πάντες ἐν χάριτι ἐξ ὀνόματος κτλ., Phld.). In Phld. 11,2 appears a trichotomic anthropology (σαρκί, ψυχῇ, πνεύματι), characteristic of the interpolator, as contrasted with the Ignatian dichotomic (σάρξ, πνεῦμα). In the same passage the trilogy faith-love-concord goes beyond Ignatius' binomial faith-love. A tendency to ternary formulas seems to be a constant of the forger (remember the trinitarian synthesis in Mg. 13,1 and 2: see nr. 27).

One more proof that Sm. 12,2 is an interpolation is provided by the anonymous mention of the bishop, presbyters and deacons; the least one could expect was a mention of Polycarp, who lived in Smyrna, and his collaborators. Finally, the mention of the deacons as "fellow-servants" of Ignatius that follows, was precisely one of the anomalies detected from the beginning (see nrs. 8f.).

δ) *Phld.* 10, *copy of Sm.* 11

33. The *conclusion of Phld.* 10 is an imitation of Sm. 11. We leave aside for the moment its resemblance to Pol. 7-8. Except for the beginning (10,1a), that is to a large extent authentic, the rest of the conclusion imitates or paraphrases Sm.:

(1) Phld. 10,1a, as we already hinted (nr. 31,4), retains — with the necessary touching up (note the change of Syria for Antioch of Syria) — the *genuine motivation* of Ignatius' invitation to the Ephesians (actually Sm. 11,2) to send an ambassador of the community to Syria (note that Syria is still mentioned, in a general way, in all the passages where this envoy is named: Sm. 11,2; Pol. 7,2 and 8,2). The construction of the phrase, κατὰ τὰ σπλάγχνα, ἃ ἔχετε ἐν Χριστῷ Ἰησοῦ, is very primitive. The forger never inverts Ἰησοῦς Χριστός into Χριστὸς Ἰησοῦς; for him "Jesus Christ" has become a compound name.

(2) Phld. 10,1b (πρέπον ἐστὶν ὑμῖν ὡς ἐκκλησίᾳ θεοῦ χειροτονῆσαι διάκονον) *imitates* Sm. 11,2b (πρέπει εἰς τιμὴν θεοῦ χειροτονῆσαι τὴν ἐκκλησίαν ὑμῶν θεοπρεσβευτήν).

(3) Phld. 10,1c *paraphrases* the technical term θεο-πρεσβευτὴν in εἰς τὸ πρεσβεῦσαι ἐκεῖ θεοῦ πρεσβείαν.

(4) Phld. 10,1d (εἰς τὸ συγχαρῆναι αὐτοῖς ἐπὶ τὸ αὐτὸ γενομένοις) again *imitates* Sm. 11,2c (εἰς τὸ γενόμενον ἕως Συρίας συγχαρῆναι αὐτοῖς).

(5) On the other hand, the following sentence, Phld. 10,1e
(καὶ δοξάσαι τὸ ὄνομα), *sums up generically* the motivations specified in Sm. 11,2d-f.3b (ὅτι εἰρηνεύουσιν κτλ., ἵνα συνδοξάσῃ κτλ.).

Before going on with the comparison, we should observe how
the forger forces the original data on the embassy to the Syrian
communities, narrowing its area to the community of Antioch,
and changes its contents, speaking of a *deacon* instead of a messenger, paraphrasing the original and reducing the motives of
congratulation to a generic *praise* of God.

(6) Phld. 10,2a-c has a parallel in Sm. 11,3b and in Pol.7,2ef
and 8,2c, as we shall see further on. Indeed, Sm. 11,3a-d contains, in the form of a parenthetic sentence destined to encourage
the Ephesians to do their best, the decision Ignatius took to write
to his communities of Syria by means of a messenger from the
Ephesian community. It seems as if ἵνα συν-δοξάσῃ of Sm. 11,3b
has been paraphrased in Phld. 10,1e-2c: εἰς τὸ... δοξάσαι τὸ ὄνομα...
καὶ ὑμεῖς δοξασθήσεσθε.

(7) Phld. 10,2d (θέλουσιν δὲ ὑμῖν οὐκ ἔστιν ἀδύνατον ὑπὲρ ὀνόματος θεοῦ) tries to imitate Sm. 11,3c (θέλουσιν γὰρ ὑμῖν εὐπράσσειν
θεὸς ἕτοιμος εἰς τὸ παρέχειν).

(8) The last sentence, Phld. 10,2ef, deserves to be specially
noted. Instead of the parenthetic sentence of Sm. 11,3a-d, in which
Ignatius mentioned his letter to Syria, the forger tries to inspire the
Philadelphians with the example of the churches in the Antiochene
region: ὡς καὶ αἱ ἔγγιστα ἐκκλησίαι ἔπεμψαν ἐπισκόπους, αἱ δὲ
πρεσβυτέρους καὶ διακόνους. Again, ignorance of Rom. and the
ecclesiastical situation at the beginning of the II century proved
fatal to the forger. As we have seen, in Rom 2,2 Ignatius introduced himself to the Roman community as " the bishop of Syria ".
Hence, addressing the letters written from Smyrna to the communities of Ephesus, Magnesia and Tralles, belonging to the province
of Asia, and to the community of Rome, he asked them to remember in their prayers " the church that is in Syria ". Convinced that Ignatius belonged to the community of Antioch of
Syria, the interpolator reinterpreted the data, and presented him
as a deacon. Consequently, he organized a procession of bishops,
presbyters and deacons from the churches in the region of Antioch,
to encourage the Philadelphians to send a deacon. It is evident,
therefore, from Rom. 2,2 that in Ignatius' time there was only

one " bishop " or " supervisor " for all the communities in the province of Syria. Furthermore, Ignatius states in Rom. 9,1 that Jesus the Messiah will be the only one who instead of him will supervise his church, together with the communion of the Romans.

ε) *Phld.* 11,1, *a new copy of Sm.* 10,1

34. The interpolator does not limit himself to imitating the conclusion of Sm. For some personal interest, he caused the *messengers* sent from Syria to pass by Philadelphia and he pretends there are two factions among the Philadelphians, one for and the other against the messengers. To express this he imitates, amplifies and paraphrases Sm. 10,1 in Phld. 11,1, thus revealing his tactics and style.

(1) Speaking of *Philo*, he enlarges on the data of Sm.: (a) He introduces him as a *deacon* in the technical sense (in Sm. it is said the messengers were " servants " — in a wide sense [127] — " of God the Messiah "); (b) He has him come from *Cilicia* (in Sm., on the contrary, all the messengers seem to proceed from Syria); (c) He calls him " a man of good repute, who also now assists me in (the ministry of) God's word, together with Gaius and Agathopus, etc.". It is undeniable that the forger is *paraphrasing* Sm. 10,1b, οἱ ἐπηκολούθησάν μοι εἰς λόγον θεοῦ, into ὃς καὶ νῦν ἐν λόγῳ θεοῦ ὑπηρετεῖ μοι, referring to Philo, and ὃς ἀπὸ Συρίας μοι ἀκολουθεῖ ἀποταξάμενος τῷ βίῳ, referring to Agathopus, as we shall see. The resulting expression is far from the original meaning. For it is affirmed that *precisely then* Philo was helping Ignatius in the ministry of the word, letting it be seen that his motive for coming from Cilicia (!) was not to carry a message (εἰς λόγον θεοῦ) but to be at the service of God's word (ἐν λόγῳ θεοῦ).[128]

---

[127] LIGHTFOOT, *AA. FF.* II: II/1, 316, after verifying the affinity of this expression with the Pauline sense of " servants of God or the Christ ", he prefers the technical and more restricted one of " deacon ", " for he (Ign.) never uses it with any other signification ". Even, as we shall see later, this seems to be the only passage where Ign. uses this term. The archaism " Messiah God " should be retained: see above n. 114.

[128] ZAHN, *PP. AA.* II 81, makes the two expressions equivalents. On the contrary, LIGHTFOOT, *AA. FF.* II: II/1, 279, distinguishes them adequately. Also BAUER, *AA. VV.* II 263.

(2)   As for Gaius and Agathopus (sic! see n. 111), the first seems
to be associated with Philo, whereas, speaking of the second he
adds: "An elect man who has followed after me from Syria,
having bidden farewell to this life." Neither here does it appear
that he went to deliver a message from the community of Syria.
Before, in 10,1 he says only "he had received news that the
church at Antioch of Syria is in peace", without stating by what
means. Could the forger have interpreted the clause in Sm. 10,1b
in the sense of another group of prisoners proceeding from Cilicia
and Syria, meant to join Ignatius at Troas, to go together to
Rome? His interpretation of Sm. would be: "Those who have
followed my footsteps/my lot in God's cause."

(3)   The next sentence, Phld. 11,1g-j, is very instructive, as
much for the way the interpolator deals with the original texts as for
the peculiarities of his style. We have here four short sentences
grouped two by two, each one with its own subject and a mark
of reciprocity in each couple. The first couple: οἳ καὶ μαρτυροῦσιν
ὑμῖν, κἀγὼ τῷ θεῷ εὐχαριστῶ ὑπὲρ ὑμῶν is a close paraphrase of
Sm. 10,1d: οἳ καὶ εὐχαριστοῦσιν τῷ κυρίῳ ὑπὲρ ὑμῶν. In the second
couple: ὅτι ἐδέξασθε αὐτούς, ὡς καὶ ὑμᾶς ὁ κύριος, inspired no
doubt by Sm. 10,1c, the reciprocity is detailed by the particle ὡς
with a *conjunctive* function. If we examine carefully we see that,
as the interpolated passages are identified, this tendency to reciprocity becomes clearer (see, for example, Phld. 10,2e[c] and Mg.
13,2).

The poor welcome offered the messengers by a faction among
the Philadelphians (οἱ δὲ ἀτιμάσαντες αὐτοὺς λυτρωθείησαν ἐν τῇ
χάριτι τοῦ [!] Ἰησοῦ Χριστοῦ, Phld. 11,1k) contrasts with the complete availability of the Smyrnaeans (Sm. 10,1ef: in reality, the
Ephesians!). This fact, so surprising in itself, could be an indication of the interpolator's motivation.

ζ)   *The conclusion of Mg**

35.   It remains for us to examine the *conclusion of Mg.* 14-
15. Having set aside the present conclusion of Phld., it was
logical to suppose that the forger had left in its primitive context
the *genuine* conclusion of Mg* (Mg. 14-15). To make up in some
way for the absence of the second part of the letter (actually

Phld. 2-9) and, at the same time, to connect the first part (Mg. 1-12) with the primitive conclusion, he drew up the interrupting clause of Mg. 13.[129] Thus, the genuine letter to the Magnesians included: (1) Inscription (reconstructed from Mg. inscr. + Phld. inscr.); (2) Mg. 1-12 (first part of the letter); (3) Phld. 2-9 (second part); (4) Mg. 14-15 (conclusion). We shall now examine this last in detail, taking into account the parallels with the authentic Ignatian letters:

(1) The first sentence, Mg. 14a: Εἰδώς, ὅτι θεοῦ γέμετε, συντόμως παρεκάλεσα[130] ὑμᾶς, is *characteristic* of the authentic Ignatian letters: Tr. 3,3;[131] Rom. 8,2; Pol. 7,3 (= Eph*, as we shall prove later on). Ignatius did not pretend to "give directives" (οὐ διατάσσομαι ὑμῖν: Eph. 3,1; Tr. 3,3; Rom. 4,3), but on the contrary to "exhort" (Eph. 3,2; Phld. = Mg* 8,2; Tr. 6,1 and 12,2; Rom. 4,1 and 7,2, etc.), so as to "warn beforehand" the Asian communities (Sm. = Eph* 4,1; Mg. 11; Tr. 8,1) against Gnostic and Judaizing propaganda.

(2) So also the second sentence, Mg. 14b-d, where he begs them: "*Remember* in your prayers *both me*, that I may reach God, *and also the church in Syria*", is to be found in all the *authentic* letters (Eph. 21,1e and 2a; Tr. 12,3c and 13,1b; Rom. 8,3a and 9,1a). In the spurious letters, however, there is mention of the effects of the prayer in the community *of Antioch of Syria* (Phld. 10,1; Sm. 11,1; Pol. 7,1).

(3) The following sentence, Mg. 14e: ὅθεν οὐκ ἄξιός εἰμι καλεῖσθαι, expresses briefly the idea of "self-abasement" contained *exclusively* in the authentic letters (Eph. 21,2b-d and Sm. 11,1b-end [complementary]; Tr. 13,1cd; Rom. 9,2).

(4) The last sentence, before the final greetings, Mg. 14fg: "For I *still need the unity* God has conferred on your prayer and your communion, so that thanks to your community the church of Syria may deserve to be refreshed with dew", is similar to Rom.

---

[129] We can now add to what has been said above (nr. 27) that Mg. 13,1 (Σπουδάζετε οὖν βεβαιωθῆναι..., ἵνα πάντα, ὅσα ποιεῖτε, κατευοδωθῆτε κτλ.) probably anticipates the invitation Ign. made later (actually Phld. 4: Σπουδάσατε οὖν μιᾷ εὐχαριστίᾳ χρῆσθαι..., ἵνα, ὃ ἐὰν πράσσητε, κατὰ θεὸν πράσσητε). Note also the mark of reciprocity of Mg. 13,2 (ὡς with conjunctive function).

[130] See critical apparatus, p. 361, l. 20.

[131] συντομώτερον C: see critical apparatus, p. 365, l. 27.

9,1c (" Jesus the Messiah alone will supervise it, with your communion also ") and further on with Tr. 12,3de (" For I have need of your love, by the mercy of God, that I am held worthy to receive the heritage ...").

(5)   In the *final greetings*, Mg. 15, he mentions firstly the Ephesians sent to Smyrna (see Eph. 21,1a); then the Magnesians present there, and the other communities (at least Trallians and Smyrnaeans).   This detail is also *characteristic* of the letters written from Smyrna: see Tr. 12,1 and Rom. 9,3.

Summing up the data we have gathered from examining the four actual conclusions, it appears that only *two* of them are *genuine*: *Sm. and Mg.*   The conclusion of *Eph. sums up* the original one, retaining those data which were only meaningful in the context of the Ephesian community; the conclusion of *Phld.* is a simple *copy* of Sm.

There is a certain logic in the method of the interpolator. For the conclusion of the new letter addressed from Troas to the Smyrnaeans, *detailed* data was needed to give the impression that Ignatius had got to know the community of Smyrna thoroughly during his stay there.   Ignatius certainly stayed in Smyrna.   It is precisely from there that he writes the authentic letters to the Eph*, Mg* and Tr*, communities which have sent delegates to Smyrna, as well as the letter to the Romans, taken to Rome by some members of the Ephesian community (Rom. 10,1).

So far we have established that Ignatius passed through Ephesus on his arrival by sea coming from Syria, but he did not remain there.   When his guards heard that a ship was sailing from Smyrna to Rome, before the " September fast " (Acts 27,9), they forced him to go on foot to Smyrna.   In fact, the letter to the Romans is dated 24 August (Rom. 10,3).   Before leaving, while the ship was being rigged, Ignatius wrote a long letter of thanks to the Ephesians for the many services and kindnesses they had shown him: the warm welcome, the sending of delegates to Smyrna, the messengers who took his letter to Rome, thoughtfulness for the messengers from Syria and readiness to send an envoy there.   The detailed greetings contained in the actual conclusion of Sm. (= Eph*), show that Ignatius, on his way through Ephesus, had met various members of the community.

But he did not write to the Smyrnaeans. Firstly, there was no need, since his stay in Smyrna made it possible to communicate orally. Secondly, he had no chance: from Smyrna he probably sailed to Rome. The interpolator had to modify Ignatius' journey considerably, making him pass through Troas, so that he would have occasion to write to the Smyrnaeans. Thirdly, there was nothing to thank them for since, inexplicably, it was not they who were the messengers to Rome or Syria. Probably the Smyrnaean community of that time was relatively small. Ephesus, on the contrary, was very important.

The conclusion of Mg*, unlike that of Eph*, does not lend itself to evoking Ignatius' passage through Philadelphia. Mg* contains no specific greetings, since Ignatius had not been in Magnesia. For this reason, the interpolator preferred leaving the conclusion of Mg* as it was and drawing up a new one for Phld., on the model he had contrived for Sm.

l) *Relations between Ignatius and Polycarp: external evidence*

The fact that the letter to the Smyrnaeans, Polycarp's community, is not genuine and that two of the letters written from Troas (Sm. and Phld.) have proved spurious, sheds doubts on the authenticity of the third letter (Pol.), presumed to have been written by Ignatius to Polycarp from Troas, a short time before leaving for Neapolis and Philippi. All this obviously puts in question the generally accepted thesis that Ignatius and Polycarp knew each other personally.

Aside from the letter to Pol., we have only two brief references to Polycarp, bishop of Smyrna, in the rest of Ignatius' letters: Eph. 21,1d and Mg. 15d. Sm. only alludes in general terms to the bishop, presbyters and deacons. Two mentions of Ignatius contained in Polycarp's letter to the Philippians (Pol. Phil. 9 and 13), far from settling the question, only raise new ones. Since this is a very complex problem, we shall examine the *external* evidence in the present section (l) and in two further sections (m-n) the *internal* evidence from the Ignatian letters.

Among external witnesses, we have a writer, *Irenaeus*, who knew Polycarp in his youth. We shall consider, then, in the first place his remarks about Polycarp (nr. 36) and the letter he sent

6

to the Philippians (nr. 37). After which, since *Polycarp's letter to the Philippians* contains two contradictory mentions of Ignatius' we shall analyze each of them in the context of the letter (nrs 38f.), before giving an opinion on the so-called Polycarpian compilation (nrs. 40f.).

α) *The testimony of Irenaeus on Polycarp*

36. Irenaeus knew Polycarp, in Smyrna probably, but when he was a child, according to the account in his *Letter to Florinus*. Irenaeus had already written a letter to Florinus, entitled "Treatise on the Monarchy of God or that God is not the author of evil". When Florinus joined the Gnostic sect of the Valentinians because he had not found a satisfactory solution to the problem of the origin of evil, Irenaeus wrote him a second letter entitled "Treatise on the Ogdoada".[132] Eusebius has handed down to us an extract of this second letter. He says to Florinus:

"Such opinions, Florinus (...), not even heretics outside the church would ever dare to express; such opinions were not transmitted to you by the *presbyters who went before us* and were disciples of the Apostles. Indeed, I saw you when I was still a child, on the shores of (the province of) Asia (ἐν τῇ κάτω 'Ασίᾳ) with Polycarp; you held a brillant place in the imperial court and you tried to influence him." [133]

Irenaeus goes on with a detailed description of the place where Polycarp sat and habitually talked to the community (τὸν τόπον ἐν ᾧ καθεζόμενος διελέγετο), on his comings and goings (καὶ τὰς προόδους αὐτοῦ καὶ τὰς εἰσόδους) in his continual visits to the communities he was charged with, on his way of life, his physical aspect, his contacts with John (the Apostle) and others who had seen the Lord, etc.[134]

This information on the *presbyter* Polycarp fits in with the mention he makes of him in his work "*Adversus Haereses*", which passage has also been preserved in the original Greek by Eusebius:

---

[132] Eus., *E. H.* V. 20,1. See Harvey's note in his edition of Irenaeus' work *Adversus Haereses*, vol. II, p. 470, n. 1.

[133] According to Eus., *E. H.* V. 20,5. See G. Bardy's note to his translation of Eusebius' *Histoire Ecclésiastique* (S. Ch. 41), p. 62, n. 4, on the "Basse Asie": it is not an administrative division, but the lower, coastal section of that province.

[134] Eus., *Ibid.* 6.

" Polycarp, too, who was not only taught by some of the Apostles and spoke to many ocular witnesses of the Messiah, but also was established by some of the Apostles as supervisor for (the province of) Asia from the community in Smyrna, and who we also saw in our early youth — he then lived for a long time and to a very advanced age, after having given glorious and brillant witness, he left this life —, he always taught all he had learned from the Apostles, the same that the church transmits, the only truth." [135]

The sentence: ὑπὸ ἀποστόλων κατασταθεὶς εἰς τὴν Ἀσίαν ἐν τῇ ἐν Σμύρνῃ ἐκκλησίᾳ ἐπίσκοπος deserves detailed analysis. Making use of four prepositions with very different meanings, Irenaeus distinguishes: (a) *Apostles* (without the article), indicating that both the instruction and the establishment as bishop-supervisor-inspector had as *agent* (ὑπό) some of the Apostles, reserving the article to designate the Twelve as a group.[136] (b) The *Roman province of Asia*, whose Eastern frontiers (Westwards it was bounded by the Ægean Sea) were Bithynia and Pontus, to the N-E., Galatia, to E., and Lycia, to the S-E. The function of " in-spector " (ἐπίσκοπος) entrusted to Polycarp extended to (εἰς) the whole province of Asia. (c) The *community* in which he had been established and from which (ἐν for ἐν-ἐκ) [137] he exercises his function of supervisor over the other communities. (d) *Smyrna*, the city where (ἐν) the community lives and meets, and to which Polycarp belongs.

Of the four prepositions, the three that define the scope of the function are included between the verb (κατασταθεὶς) and the predicate (ἐπίσκοπος), describing also three concentric circles that become smaller each time, according as to how they are more or

---

[135] *A. H.* III. 3,4 (= Eus., *E. H.* IV. 14,3-4).

[136] Irenaeus uses the term ἀπόστολος 31 times: 28x with article and 3x without it. In the present passage, twice running it is used without the article, to specify that Polycarp " has been instructed " and " established " by some of the Apostles, not by the group. The other case in which it is used without the article, *A. H.* I. 3,2, refers explicitly to the Twelve.

[137] κατασταθεὶς... ἐπίσκοπος indicates the beginning (punctiliar aorist) of a permanent activity, the " supervision " over all the Asian communities, exercised from the community of Smyrna, where he resides; ἐν has here a double value: the place in which he resides and the place from which he exercises his function. This phenomenon is studied for the N. T. by A. URBÁN, *El doble aspecto estático-dinámico de la preposición ἐν en el NT*, in *Estudios de Nuevo Testamento, II. Cuestiones de gramática y léxico*, Madrid 1977, pp. 17-60.

less *related to the function* (εἰς > ἐν/ἐκ > ἐν) placed for emphasis
at the end of the phrase, or vice versa, according to the greater
or lesser *definition of the place* (εἰς → ἐν → ἐν) in which the punctiliar action of the verb (aorist) is verified.

According to Irenaeus, in the time of Polycarp, there was a
single bishop for the whole province of Asia. This information is
confirmed by Irenaeus himself, a little further on, in his well-
known list of witnesses to the true tradition, when he enumerates
all the communities scattered over the province of Asia together
with the *successors of Polycarp* in charge of the supervision of
these communities up to the present (αἱ κατὰ τὴν 'Ασίαν ἐκκλησίαι
πᾶσαι καὶ οἱ μέχρι νῦν διαδεδεγμένοι τὸν Πολύκαρπον).[138] There
is no doubt, then, that for Irenaeus, ἐπίσκοπος, unlike πρεσβύτε-
ρος, still means a function of " in-spection " or " super-vision "
of the communities spread over a vast territory (in our case, the
province of Asia), exercised by a *presbyter or elder* of a determined
community.[139]

Irenaeus' account agrees, besides, with what we found in
Rom. 2,2, where Ignatius introduces himself as " the bishop/
supervisor of the province of Syria " (τὸν ἐπίσκοπον Συρίας).
Thus, not only in Asia (first half of II cent.) but in Syria too,
at the beginning of the II century we meet with a still archaic
exercise of the " bishop's " function with the duty of visiting, over-
seeing and confirming the old or new communities.

β) *Irenaeus' account on Polycarp's letter to the Philippians*

37. Irenaeus gives us precise details on the letter Polycarp
wrote to the Philippians. This account forms part of a much
larger context, in which Irenaeus enumerates the *witnesses to the*

---

[138] *A. H.* III. 3,4 (= Eus., *E. H.* IV. 14,5).

[139] Referring to the church of Rome, Irenaeus sometimes points out the *function*
of " supervision " (ἡ τῆς ἐπισκοπῆς λειτουργία or ἡ ἐπισκοπή: *A. H.* III. 3,3 =
Eus., *E. H.* V. 6) sometimes he describes the *state* of those who exercise it (οἱ πρὸ
Σωτῆρος/πρὸ σοῦ πρεσβύτεροι: *Letter to Vict.*, in Eus., *E. H.* V. 24,14-15; see also
οἱ πρὸ ἡμῶν πρεσβύτεροι: *Letter to Florin.* 2, in Eus., *E. H.* V. 20,4.7). — Irenaeus
himself was sent to the Gauls to exercise the function of " supervision " over the
several " parishes " or Christian communities spread over that province (καὶ τῶν
κατὰ Γαλλίαν δὲ παροικιῶν, ἃς Εἰρηναῖος ἐπεσκόπει: Eus., *E. H.* V. 23,3; ἐκ
προσώπου ὧν ἡγεῖτο κατὰ τὴν Γαλλίαν ἀδελφῶν ἐπιστείλας: 24,11).

true apostolic tradition as contrasted with a secret, oral or written tradition held by the Gnostics: (1) The uninterrupted succession of the presbyters of the church of Rome who exercise the role of "supervision" in the Capital of the Empire; (2) Polycarp, "supervisor" of the communities settled in the Roman province of Asia; (3) All the communities spread over this province and the successors of Polycarp in this function up to the present; (4) The coming of Polycarp to Rome at the time of Anicetus, when he (Pol.) converted many Gnostic heretics; (5) Polycarp's account of a possible meeting of John, disciple of the Lord, with the heresiarch Cerinthus in Ephesus; (6) The well-known reply of Polycarp against Marcion; (7) The letter addressed by *Polycarp to the Philippians*; (8) The testimony of the church of Ephesus, founded by Paul, where John lived up to the time of Trajan.[140]

Notwithstanding the fact that Irenaeus knew various letters of Polycarp — whether to neighbouring communities (ἤτοι ταῖς γειτνιώσαις ἐκκλησίαις) or individual Christians (ἢ τῶν ἀδελφῶν τισί) —,[141] he mentions *only one* letter written by Polycarp to the Philippians.[142]

Furthermore, Irenaeus had no knowledge while he lived in Smyrna (where he has born and spent his youth) of a collection of Ignatius' letters compiled, it seems, by Polycarp (Letters to various Asian churches and others addressed to Polycarp and his Smyrnaean community). Otherwise, Ignatius' testimony as bishop of Syria, his travelling through Smyrna and his contacts with Polycarp, his openly anti-Gnostic tones, etc., would have been mentioned by Irenaeus to confirm his argument on the true apostolic tradition.

But it does not even appear that he had direct knowledge of Ignatius' letter to the Romans. In fact, the quotation he gives from it is in anonymous form:

"As one of ours, who was condemned to the beasts for having witnessed to God, said: 'I am God's wheat, and I am going to be ground by the teeth of wild beasts, that I may be found to be pure bread of God' (Ign. Rom. 4,1)."[143]

---

[140] *A. H.* III. 3,3-4 (= Eus., IV. 14 and III. 23,4); II. 22,5 (= III. 23,3).

[141] *Letter to Florin.*, in Eus., *E. H.* V. 20,8.

[142] *A. H.* III. 3,4 (= Eus., *E. H.* IV. 14,8). See G. Bardy's note, *Histoire Ecclésiastique* (S. Ch. 31), p. 180, n. 6.

[143] *A. H.* V. 28,3 (Original Greek in Eus., *E. H.* III. 36,12, and above all in

Against Lightfoot's opinion,[144] it seems that Irenaeus knows this saying of Ignatius only by hearsay. He mentions neither his name, function nor origin: but only that he is ' one of our ' martyrs. He is unaware of the context of Rom. For that reason he presents Ignatius' saying as though it had been pronounced by a martyr giving public witness of his Christianity, who for this had been condemned to the beasts. In the *context of Rom.* the present ἀλήθομαι leads to a *proximate* future that could however not come about, if the Roman Christians did not learn how to keep silence, and started searching for influential friends; in none of the letters is there question of persecution or public witness given by Ignatius; the cause of his condemnation to the wild beasts is not clear. In the *context of Irenaeus*, on the contrary, the same present points to an *immediate* future. *Jerome*, too, who " was unacquainted with the epistles themselves and in this account of Ignatius depends solely on the passage of Eusebius in which Irenaeus is quoted ",[145] goes much further still and interprets it as the moment when

---

C. Diobouniotis – A. Harnack, *Der Scholien-Kommentar des Origenes zur Apokalypse Johannis. Nebst einem Stück aus Irenaeus, Lib. V, Graece*, Leipzig 1911, T. U. 38,3, Scholion 38, p. 43).

[144] *AA. FF.* II: I 326 [339]: " The language of Irenaeus himself places the saying of Ignatius at the same point of time as it is placed in the Epistle to the Romans ..."; διὰ τὴν πρὸς θεὸν μαρτυρίαν κατακριθεὶς πρὸς θηρία alludes obviously to the public *witness* given by Ignatius before his judges. But it is above all in Lightfoot's second argument that we perceive a false re-translation: " The preceding context of the passage in Irenaeus (extant only in the Latin) indicates a knowledge of the Ignatian letter to the Romans, as the comparison shows ". He then collates the preceding context of *A. H.* V. 28,3 with Ign. Rom. 5,3 and goes on: " Here the three words ' contriti, attenuati, consparsi ', correspond to the three σκορπισμοί, συγκοπαί, ἀλεσμοί, the order however being reversed ...". Lightfoot was unaware of the existence of the Greek fragment of the *Scholia in Apocalypsin* (see the preceding n.), where the original Greek of the Latin translation is conserved: instead of the triadic sequence, the original Greek contained only two participles λεπτυθέντες καὶ συμφυραθέντες which joined to πυρωθέντες (igniti) describe the three proceedings needed before wheat becomes " bread ", i. e. to be ground, kneaded and baked. It has then nothing to do with Ign. Rom. 5,3. Irenaeus quotes Ign., because he associated the idea of " tribulation " with the Ignatian " I am going to be ground by the teeth of wild beasts ": καὶ διὰ τοῦτο καὶ ἡ θλῖψις ἀναγκαία τοῖς σωζομένοις, ἵνα τρόπον τινὰ λεπτυθέντες καὶ συμφυραθέντες διὰ τῆς ὑπομονῆς τῷ λόγῳ τοῦ θεοῦ καὶ πυρωθέντες ἐπιτήδειοι ἔσονται εἰς τὴν τοῦ βασιλέως εὐωχίαν, ὡς εἶπέ τις τῶν ἡμετέρων κτλ.

[145] Lightfoot, *AA. FF.* II: II/1, 376f. [II 337ff.].

Ignatius already glimpses the lions.[146] Something of the sort is also to be found in the *Acta Romana* 10.

γ)   *Two contradictory references to Ignatius in Polycarp's letter
      to the Philippians*

Irenaeus' silence on Ignatius contrasts with the two references to him — especially the second — contained in Polycarp's letter to the Philippians, which was known to Irenaeus. These passages must be examined thoroughly.

38. In the *inscription* of the letter Polycarp and his fellow-presbyters (καὶ οἱ σὺν αὐτῷ πρεσβύτεροι) address the pilgrim community in Philippi. The *motive* of the letter is explained in Phil. 3,1:

" I am writing this, brothers, concerning fidelity (to the message: περὶ τῆς δικαιοσύνης), not on my own initiative, but because you have appealed to me ",

and he *develops* the idea concretely in Phil. 11:

" Nimis contristatus sum pro Valente, qui presbyter factus est aliquando apud vos, quod sic ignoret is locum, qui datus est ei." (Phil. 11,1)

And further on:

" Valde ergo, fratres, contristor pro illo et pro coniuge eius." (11,4)

Valens and his wife had let themselves be carried away by avarice, attacking the chief postulate of the evangelical message, renunciation of riches.[147] Two paragraphs earlier, Polycarp had invited the Philadelphians to follow the *example of the martyrs and apostles*:

" I exhort you all, then, to obey the message of (evangelical) fidelity (τῷ λόγῳ τῆς δικαιοσύνης) and to practise all endurance, the same endurance also you have had under your eyes in the blessed Ignatius,

---

[146] *De Viris illustribus* 16: " Quumque iam damnatus esset ad bestias, ardore patiendi, cum rugientes audiret leones, ait: *Frumentum* ...". See ZAHN, *I. v. A.* 32.

[147] Polycarp chooses the first and last Beatitudes " guided by the fact that to these two alone the promise of the kingdom of heaven is attached " (LIGHTFOOT, *AA. FF.* II: II/2, 910 [III 326]): Pol. Phil. 2,3.

Zosimus and Rufus, yea, and in others also of your own townsmen, as well as in Paul himself and the other Apostles " (Phil. 9,1).

The sentence ἣν καὶ εἴδατε κατ' ὀφθαλμοὺς [148] distinguishes three classes of witnesses: (a) recent outstanding martyrs of other communities: Ignatius, Zosimus and Rufus; (b) martyrs of their own Philippian community; (c) Paul and the other Apostles. Not an ocular vision (the third group excludes it), but a few examples well-known to all. Ignatius appears associated with two other martyrs, unknown to us, but in Polycarp's time as familiar as Ignatius. Distinguishing them from their own martyrs (who are probably referred to at the beginning of the letter: 1,1) [149] and from Paul and the other Apostles, remembering besides that they are mentioned firstly and by name, there is no doubt that they are considered *outstanding martyrs of other communities of sub-apostolic times*. It is impossible to deduce from this passage that Ignatius passed by Philippi, as the letters from Troas seem to suggest (Sm., Phld. and above all Pol. 8,1).

39. On the other hand, the information contained in *Phil.* 13 agrees perfectly with the itinerary followed by Ignatius according to the letters written from *Troas* (Troas → Neapolis → Philippi), as well as with Ignatius' proposal to the Phld. and Sm., and also to Polycarp, to send messengers to Antioch of Syria. One serious difficulty remains, however, that is in flagrant contradiction with the earlier statement in *Phil.* 9. Here is the text to start with:

" You wrote to me, both yourselves and Ignatius, asking that if any one should go to Syria he might carry thither a letter from you as well. And this I will do at once as soon as I get a fit opportunity — either myself, or by someone whom I shall send to be ambassador

---

[148] G reads ἴδατε; Eus., Zahn read εἴδετε; Lightf. corrects to εἴδατε, mixed form of the aorist 1 and 2 of εἶδον (BAUER, *W. z. N. T.*, s. v.). The (phonetic) reading of the MS could be kept. In any case, it does not indicate a direct vision (τοῖς ὀφθαλμοῖς) but like Gal. 3,1 something the community has *under* its eyes, as testimony that has remained impressed on its mind.

[149] δεξαμένοις τὰ μιμήματα τῆς ἀληθοῦς ἀγάπης καὶ προπέμψασιν, ὡς ἐπέβαλεν ὑμῖν, τοὺς ἐνειλημένους τοῖς ἁγιοπρεπέσιν δεσμοῖς κτλ. LIGHTFOOT, *AA. FF.* II: II/2, 906 [III 322], interprets it rather of Ign. and his companions. So also ZAHN, *I. v. A.* 290f.; CAMELOT, *I. d'A.* (S. Ch. 10A) 177, n. 2, etc. The identification of the said martyrs with Ign. and his companions has been influenced by Pol. Phil. 13, a chapter that, as we shall see at once, is usually separated in more modern editions from the rest of the letter.

on your behalf also. We sent you Ignatius' letters, as you requested, both those he wrote to us and the others we have in hand. They are appended to this letter. You will be able to gain great profit from them, for they contain his faith and endurance and every kind of edification which pertain to our Lord. Moreover, if you should have any certain news of Ignatius himself and his companions, let me know it " (Pol. Phil. 13).

According to this evidence we can infer that Polycarp thought not only that Ignatius had not yet been martyred, but that he had quite recently passed through Philippi. But Polycarp had not so far found a fit opportunity to carry out the embassy Ignatius as well as the Philippians had entrusted to him. Hopefully, he had fulfilled the other charge, which was to write to the near-by communities (since Ignatius had been unable to do so because of his sudden sailing for Neapolis), so that they too sent messengers, or at least letters by Polycarp's envoys (Pol. 8,1).

So evident is the contradiction that most recent commentators have published the note or notice contained in chapter 13 apart, as the first *letter* of Polycarp to the Philippians. Following this, they have edited the already known letter to the Philippians, as the *second* letter.[150]

Commentators have gradually become aware of this contradiction. In 1873, Th. ZAHN, following J. Pearson (1672), still wrote: " That from the *sunt* of the Latin translation it is not possible to deduce, in contrast with Ch. 9, that Ignatius and his companions were still alive (as Schwegler, Baur and naturally also, Bunsen hold, having got it from Daillé) as has been demonstrated by Pearson from the Greek re-translation: καὶ περὶ 'Ιγνατίου καὶ περὶ τῶν μετ' αὐτοῦ." [151] In 1885, J. B. LIGHTFOOT proposes in place of the " qui cum eo sunt " to read " those that *were* with him ": " The Latin translator thus makes Polycarp speak as though Ignatius were still living, but this is inconsistent with § 9. The expression

---

[150] J. A. KLEIST, *I. of A.*, in A. Ch. W. I, London 1948; J. FISCHER, *AA. VV.*, München 1956; Th. CAMELOT, *I. d'A.*, in S. Ch. 10A, Paris 1969.

[151] " Dass aus dem sunt der lateinischen Uebersetzung nicht etwa im Widerspruch mit c. 9 sich ergebe, dass Ignatius und seine Gefährten noch am Leben sind, wie noch Schwegler II, 154, Baur II, 129 und, da Dall. p. 427sq. es bemerkt hatte, selbstverständlich auch Bunsen II, 108ff. behaupten, hatte schon Pearson II, 72 durch seine Rückübersetzung ins Griechische gezeigt: καὶ περὶ 'Ιγνατίου καὶ περὶ τῶν μετ' αὐτοῦ " (*I. v. A.* 290).

in the original was doubtless neutral as regards time, probably τοῖς σὺν αὐτῷ ' his companions ', as in the opening of this epistle where τοῖς σὺν αὐτῷ is translated in the same way ' qui cum eo sunt ', and thus has been wrongly rendered by a present (...). This letter of Polycarp must have been written shortly after the death of Ignatius, and before the particulars of his martyrdom had reached Smyrna ".[152] The explanation based on a re-translation did not, seemingly, eliminate the problem. In 1886, A. HILGEN-FELD, after a new edition of the letter, insists once more on the hypothesis of a massive interpolation.[153] But in 1920, W. BAUER remains fully convinced that there is no contradiction whatever with Chap. 9. One has only to read in 13,2, οἱ σὺν αὐτῷ, to be sure that all Polycarp wants to stress is that he had travelling-companions.[154] But here suddenly an ingenious hypothesis suc-ceeds in setting aside the old re-translations. In 1936, P. N. HAR-RISON develops an idea he had already anticipated in 1929.[155] He had no difficulty in showing that the explanations given up to that time were altogether too simple (pp. 133-140) and proposes to resolve definitely the contradiction existing between Chap. 9 and 13, by simply dividing the letter in two: on the one hand we should have Pol. Phil. 13 (14), in the form of a covering note written beforehand by Polycarp, just at the time Ignatius was travelling through Philippi, to go with his compilation of Ignatian letters; on the other, Pol. Phil. 1-12 would contain Polycarp's answer to the question raised by the Philippians, in the form of a separate letter drawn up much later (ca. 135). Harrison's thesis was very well received. F. C. Burkitt, B. H. Streeter (in a " Pre-fatory Note "), F. L. Cross, J. A. Kleist, P. Meinhold, J. Fischer,

---

[152] *AA. FF.* I: II/2, 933 [III 349].

[153] *Der Brief des Polycarpus an die Philipper*: *Z. W. Th.* 29 (1886) 180-206, esp. 201f.

[154] *AA. VV.* II 298.

[155] *Polycarp's Two Epistles to the Philippians*, Cambridge 1936. Harrison makes a detailed study of the *History of Criticism* concerning both Ign. and Pol. (pp. 27-72). The first part ends with a short Chap. dedicated to *The crux of our Problem* (pp. 73-75). To eliminate the grave still unsolved problem he devotes a second part to prove that Chap. 13 was written before Ignatius' martyrdom (pp. 79-140) and a third to show that Chaps. 1-12 were written after Ignatius' death, when he had passed already into history (pp. 143-206). In the fourth part he studies the chronology of Ign. and Pol.

Th. Camelot, L. W. Barnard, etc. have accepted as established [156] the division of Polycarp's letter into Phil. I (Chap. 13) and Phil. II (Chaps. 1-12 and 14), but not the late dating of the second letter.

For the moment this seems to have calmed things down. The same has happened to the textus receptus (Middle recension) of the Ignatian letters. However this succession of hypotheses — brought up merely to solve emergency situations, is both confusing and discouraging to the reader and ends up by leaving him completely sceptical. Instead of facing the problem squarely, scholars have chosen either radical solutions (massive interpolation of Phil.) or compromise (several attempts at re-translation) or else, finally, when the situation had become practically desperate, adopting extreme solutions (division into two parts: one note and the letter properly so-called).

If recourse to the re-translation was a valid solution, at least for the authors who adopted them, how then do we explain that when Harrison proposed the new one, they rejected the former as insufficient? Who can be sure that this last will not also be held as insufficient when another better one turns up? Eagerness to solve problems of detail, without linking them or waiting until they appeared in their totality has had fatal consequences for Ignatius as well as for Polycarp. For the moment one concession was made: the Ignatian problem has carried with it Polycarp's letter to the Philippians, throwing it into a tangle of hypotheses that can swallow up the most disparate approaches. For example, during the controversy raised by the discovery of the Curetonian recension, in one and the same review, at a few years' distance, two well-known scholars managed to reach diametrically opposite conclusions from the laborious examination of the same materials.[157]

---

[156] BARNARD, *Background* 39: " The thesis that Polycarp's Epistle to the Philippians is in fact two letters written on different occasions may be regarded as established beyond doubt and its wide acceptance by scholars is a mark of the importance of the author's (Harrison's) work."

[157] G. UHLHORN, *Das Verhältnis der kürzeren griechischen Recension der Ignatianischen Briefe zur syrischen Uebersetzung, und die Authentie der Briefe überhaupt,* in *Z. H. Th.* 21 (1851) 3-65; 247-341. He concludes in favour of the Middle rec.: " Die sieben Briefe nach der kürzeren griechischen Recension sind ächte Producte des Ignatius von Antiochien " (p. 341). R. A. LIPSIUS, *Ueber die Echtheit der*

One thing is certain: from this long and hard-fought polemic about Phil. 13, the question of mutual relations between Ignatius and Polycarp, far from being confirmed, has been worsened.

Since *Eusebius*[158], and the *Acta Romana*[159] that depended on him, the most varied means[160] has been made use of to eliminate the grave problem of Phil. 13: *suppresion* of the last sentence of Phil. 13,2 (Eusebius and Acta Romana); *rejection* of Phil. as spurious (Schwegler, Baur, Zeller, Hilgenfeld) or — at least — wholly *interpolated* (Ritschl, Lipsius, Böhringer, Volkmar, Hilgenfeld); *elimination* of Phil. 13 as an interpolation (Daillé, Bunsen, among others); several attempts at *re-translation* of the Latin passage of Phil. 13,2 (Pearson, Zahn, Funk, Lightfoot, Bauer, etc.); *division* of Phil. in two, Phil. I and Phil. II (Harrison, Streeter, Burkitt, Cross, Meinhold, etc., recent editors, Barnard).

Harrison's hypothesis, however, has its weakness. *Irenaeus*, who was born and trained as a Christian in Smyrna with Polycarp, had knowledge of only *one* (the) letter to the Philippians, in spite of knowing of other letters of Polycarp, and he completely ignores the compilation of Ignatian letters that Phil. 13 is trying to vouch for. On the other hand, the way this sentence has been drawn up does not favour its isolated dismemberment of the letter. Indeed, in the *context* of the letter to the Philippians, we can deduce from its reference to Polycarp: " We sent you Ignatius' letters, as you requested ... they are appended to this

---

syrischen Recension der Ignatianischen Briefe, Z. H. Th. 26 (1886) 3-160, on the contrary, is in favour of the short or Curetonian rec.: " Die 3 Briefe der syrischen Recension sind die Grundschrift, die 7 Briefe der griechischen die Ueberarbeitung (p. 96; id. pp. 159f.).

[158] EUS., *E. H.* III. 36,13 and 14-15. – BARNARD, *Background* 32f. has perceived this subtle proceeding: " After recording the deaths of the blessed martyrs Ignatius, Rufus and Zosimus in Ch. IX Eusebius quotes Ch. XIII in full, *but significantly omits the last sentence*, which is now only extant in the Latin quoted above. Why did Eusebius omit this when he had the original Greek before him? The only feasible explanation is that he saw that in the original, Chs. IX and XIII were in dire conflict, the one recording the death of Ignatius and the other presupposing he was still alive. Accordingly, as befitted one who assumed the unity of the Epistle, Eusebius removed the contradiction."

[159] In Ch. XII they quote the testimony of Irenaeus and Polycarp exactly as it is found in Eusebius.

[160] Good summary of the state of the question in HARRISON, *Polycarp* 27-72; BARNARD, *Background* 31-39; CAMELOT, *I. d'A.* (S. Ch. 10A) 164-167.

letter (Τὰς ἐπιστολὰς Ἰγνατίου ... ἐπέμψαμεν ὑμῖν καθὼς ἐνετείλασθε · αἵτινες ὑποτεταγμέναι εἰσὶν τῇ ἐπιστολῇ ταύτῃ, Phil. 13,2),
that the compilation of Ignatian letters constitutes an *annex* to the
letter properly so-called. The aorist stresses the *answer to a request*, while the periphrastic perfect indicates the *state* resulting
from the act of adding the recently compiled letters by Polycarp
to his letter to the Philippians. According to this, the *chief* objective of the author of this note is to send " this letter " (τῇ
ἐπιστολῇ ταύτῃ), that is, Phil.; the *secondary*, the remittance of
the compilation making use of (ὑπο-τεταγμέναι) the departure of
the messenger Crescens to Philippi. — By setting this reference of
Polycarp's (Phil. I) *apart* from its natural context (Phil. II), " this
letter " has become the covering *note* for the compilation. What
meaning then has the previous remark that the Ignatian letters
" are appended to this letter ", when by " this letter " is meant
a brief introductory note? Polycarp's reference (αἵτινες) insists
that not only the letters " are put *in order* " (τεταγμέναι) but they
" are *sub-ordinate* " or " *appended* to this letter " (ὑπο-τεταγμέναι
εἰσὶν τῇ ἐπιστολῇ ταύτῃ).

δ) *Phil. 13 has been thought up to support the Polycarpian
    compilation*

Without intending to, by separating the note from the rest
of the letter, Harrison has brought up clearly the true *motive* of
the interpolator's writing of this chapter: to validate the Ignatian
compilation with Polycarp's authority.

40. Thus, in the short passage from Phil. 13, of which we
have already seen the translation (nr. 39), a *triple motivation*
emerges very clearly: (1) *Immediate objective or pretext*: To make
use of the letter to the Philippians to connect up: (a) Philippians
and Ignatius with Polycarp (Ἐγράψατέ μοι καὶ ὑμεῖς καὶ Ἰγνάτιος); (b) The community of the Philippians with Ignatius' community (Philippian's letter addressed to the church of Syria);
(c) Polycarp's own letter to the Philippians with Ignatius' letter
to Pol. (7,2) and other letters written from Troas (Phld. 10,1 and
Sm. 11,2).

(2) *Main objective, disguised as an appendix*: To make use of
Polycarp's authority, especially of his letter to the Phil. to support

the recent compilation of Ignatian letters, done by the same forger. To attain his objective, the forger avails himself of various literary devices: (a) He brings out the request made by the Philippians (καθὼς ἐνετείλασθε); (b) Presumes a special interest Polycarp has for gathering and setting in order Ignatius' letters and, certainly, in the same order as we still have them today, whether in the mixed Ussherian collection (GL) as in the one that is the basis of the Oriental translations (SAB), that is: *Firstly* the letters sent by Ignatius to Polycarp and his community (Sm. and Pol.); τὰς ἐπιστολὰς Ἰγνατίου τὰς πεμφθείσας ἡμῖν ὑπ' αὐτοῦ (note the repeated plural τὰς ... τὰς ..., which supposes there are *two* letters, and the "us" that supports the order Sm. → Pol.); *Secondly*, the other letters Polycarp had procured: καὶ ἄλλας, ὅσας εἴχομεν παρ' ἡμῖν (note the imperf. of ἔχω constructed with παρά + dat.), that is Eph., Mg., Tr. and Phld., in the order given by SAB as well as C and by the *Sacra Parallela, Vaticana and Rupefucaldina*.[161] Initially, Rom. was not included in this compilation [162] (for which reason it always appears last in modern collections), not because Polycarp did not possess a copy but because the forger was unaware of its existence.

(c) The forger takes advantage of Polycarp's genuine letter to the Philippians to authenticate his compilation (literally: that it might serve as a letter of introduction: αἵτινες ὑποτεταγμέναι

---

[161] The *Parallela Rupefucaldina* seem anterior by a century to the *Parallela Vaticana* probably compiled by John Damascene (see LIGHTFOOT, *AA. FF.* II: I 210 [220]). K. HOLL, *Fragmente vornicänischer Kirchenväter aus den Sacra Parallela herausgegeben*, Leipzig 1899, T. U. 20,2, gives a critical edition of the Ignatian fragments contained in the various Chains. From it we infer that the quotation from Rom. 3,3 is extant only in the Cosl. 276, the only one, in fact, which contains the *First Book of the* ἱερά. In the *Parallela Rupefucaldina* I 76 (II 772 Lequien) appears the sequence: (Sm.)–Eph.–Tr.–Phld.; in V 48 (II 779 Lequien) another more complete one: Sm. – Pol. – Eph. – Mg. – Tr. – Phld.; in the *Parallela Vaticana* V 17 (II 514f. Lequien) only the sequence is hinted at: Sm. – Pol.

[162] ZAHN, *I. v. A.* 110-116 (492). LIGHTFOOT, *AA FF.* II: I 409f. [426ff.], on the contrary, includes also Rom. (Polycarp had made do with a copy of that letter!); CAMELOT, *I. d'A.* (S. Ch. 10A), either includes it (p. 14: "peut-être aussi la lettre aux Romains") or as unhesitantly excludes it (p. 165: "qui ne contenait sans doute pas la lettre aux Romains") or leaves it as a simple conjecture (p. 175, n. 2: "On peut conjecturer que par conséquent ce premier recueil ne contenait pas la lettre aux Romains qui nous a été transmise indépendamment des autres"). See what is said in the *introduction*, p. 21ff.

εἰσὶν τῇ ἐπιστολῇ ταύτῃ); (d) The sending of the letter to the Phil. (Haec vobis scripsi per Crescentem: Phil. 14,1) was apparently used to forward the Polycarpian compilation (ἐπέμψαμεν ὑμῖν); basically the letter to the Philippians was useful as a platform to advertize the new Ignatian compilation; (e) The recommendation of the Ignatian letters, finally, served in its turn to recommend his collection and the fresh contents he has placed in the genuine letters (πᾶσαν οἰκοδομὴν τὴν εἰς τὸν κύριον ἡμῶν ἀνήκουσαν).

(3) The *third motivation* seems to be bound up with the first: "If you should have any certain news of Ignatius himself and his companions, let me know it", since after their/his letter he had had no news. This last clause, unlike Phil. 9, has upset the interpolator's plans.

Each motivation contains an explicit reference to Ignatius, without qualifying him "blessed" as in 9,1, taking him to be still alive. In the first and last motivation he appears associated with others (Philippians/companions); in the second, with his letters (τὰς ἐπιστολὰς Ἰγνατίου). The *main* motivation is the one that refers to the compilation of the letters; the other two serve as *historical* framework, so that the reader of this fragment may catch on the fact that the circumstances here described coincided fully with the ones evoked in the letters from *Troas* (Ignatius' passing by Philippi: see Pol. 8,1; sending of letters/messengers to Syria: see Phld. 10; Sm. 11,2-3; Pol. 7,2 and 8,1-2; fellow-travellers with Ignatius: see Phld. 11,1 and nr. 34).

Contrasting with this proliferation of motivations, is Polycarp's sobriety — in the *letter properly so-called to the Philippians* — in the way he introduces the theme of the letter and the motive of its writing (see nr. 38). Polycarp decided to intervene in Philippi not on his own initiative, but because the Philippians had previously appealed to him. The *nucleus* of the letter is made up of the theme of fidelity to the evangelical message (περὶ τῆς δικαιοσύνης: see 2,2-4,1; 5,1-2; 8,1; 9,1-2). The *motive* that caused him to compose it is not apparent until well into the second half (7,2). Something very grave has happened in Philippi: the presbyter Valens and his wife have been taken up for avarice (11, 1.4). Valens had been entrusted with a post of considerable responsibility ("locum, qui datus est ei", 11,1c), probably the administration of the common good, but he had been deposed from his charge as presbyter by the community ("qui presbyter factus est aliquando apud vos ", 11,1b).[163]

The appeal to Polycarp, the "supervisor" of another province, would seem to indicate that Valens held the highest post of responsibility in that province. To fill in the vacancy created by his defection, it has been necessary to turn to Polycarp. As far as we can see, Polycarp did not so much address the community of Philippi as the whole church of Macedonia whose centre was Philippi: (a) Phil. 1,2 (ἐξ ἀρχαίων καταγγελλομένη χρόνων) alludes to 1Thess. 1,8 (see 2,2); (b) Phil. 3,2 (ἀπὼν ὑμῖν ἔγραψεν ἐπιστολάς) presupposes more than one letter from Paul, probably Phil., 1Thess. and 2Thess.; (c) Phil. 11,3 ("qui estis in principio epistulae eius: 'de vobis' etenim 'gloriatur in' omnibus 'ecclesiis', quae Deum solae tunc cognoverant") alludes explicitly to 2Thess. 1,4.[164]

In fact, Polycarp went *personally* to Philippi and recommended Crescens to them, probably as Valens' substitute. Then he recommends him again *by letter*. Crescens had behaved perfectly in Smyrna; Polycarp hopes he will behave in the same way in Philippi. He is not, then, a simple messenger-carrier of the letter to the Philippians but a man trusted by Polycarp to settle there. For this reason he recommends his sister to them.[165] From which we infer that there is a double purpose in the letter to the Phil.: (a) *Development* of themes relative to fidelity to the evangelical message that had suffered from the desertion of Valens and his wife; (b) *Recommendation* of Crescens, the new man who has to put it into practice, with his sister.

41. The presumed covering note of Phil. I (Chap. 13) agrees also with the strange proceedings of Ignatius' interpolator:

---

[163] A. HARNACK, *Miscellen zu den Apostolischen Vätern ... III. Zu Polycarp ad Philipp.* 11, Leipzig 1900, T. U. 20,3: "Man ersieht aber aus dem 'aliquando', dass die Strafe den Missethäter bereits ereilt hat, und er abgesetzt worden ist" (p. 90).

[164] Op. cit., pp. 87-89.

[165] "Haec vobis scripsi per Crescentem, quem in praesenti commendavi vobis et nunc commendo: conversatus est enim nobiscum inculpabiliter; credo quia et vobiscum similiter. Sororem autem eius habebitis commendatam, cum venerit ad vos" (Phil. 14).

(1) *Superfluous multiplication of letters and envoys*: (a) Phil. 13,1a supposes two letters, both addressed to Polycarp, one from the Philippians and the other from Ignatius (Ign. Pol. II), distinct from the letters sent by Ignatius to Polycarp (Ign. Pol. I) and his community (Ign. Sm.), unless we like to give a benevolent sense to the phrase καὶ Ἰγνάτιος not by way of postscript to the letter to the Phil. but as referring to Ignatius' letter to Polycarp (see Pol. 7,2);[166] (b) Phil. 13,1c mentions one more letter to the *Antiochenes* written by the Philippians in the style of Pol. 8,1; (c) Phil. 13,1d makes reference to the future delegate who has to leave for Syria, specifying that he could be Polycarp himself (sic!) as much as his envoy sent to bear his and the Philippians embassy to Syria (ὃν πέμπω πρεσβεύσαντα καὶ περὶ ὑμῶν). It is exactly the same technical term we found in Phld. 10,1 (paraphrase of Sm. 11,2) which underlies the circumlocution θεοδρόμος of Pol. 7,2. Besides, there is an unnecessary succession of letters (Ign. Sm., Ign. Pol. I, Ign. Pol. II; Phil. to Pol., Phil. to Ant.; Pol. to the churches of Asia; the churches of Asia to Ant.; the churches of Syria to Ant.) and an endless procession of delegates, the greater number with hierarchical grades (a deacon from Phld.; bishops, presbyters and deacons of the neighbouring churches of Antioch; Polycarp or his envoy from Sm.; messengers on foot from the other Asian churches), all converging on Antioch of Syria. The only and repeated motive is " to congratulate them because they are at peace " (Sm. 11,2). No one is charged with providing for the vacant see of Antioch. We have already said that the forger — not knowing Rom. — was unaware that Ignatius was " the bishop of Syria " and introduced him as a simple deacon of Antioch.

(2) *Division of the letters into two groups*: Letters sent to Polycarp and his community (Sm. and Pol.) and letters written to the near-by churches and compiled by Polycarp (Eph., Mg.,

---

[166] ZAHN, *I. v. A.* 288; BAUER, *AA. VV.* II 297f.: " Zn, Ign. v. Ant. 288 schliesst daraus, Ign. hätte von Philippi aus eine zweite Zuschrift an Pol. gesandt, worin er ihm den nach Antiochien gerichteten Brief der Philipper zur Weiterbeförderung empfahl. Aber, da Ign., Pol. 8,1 den Smyrnäern aufgegeben wird, sich um die Besorgung der Briefe fremder Kirchen zu kümmern, besteht die Möglichkeit, dass Pol. doch den erhaltenen Ign. brief meint, dessen Aufforderung er mit der von den Philippern an ihn ergangenen zusammenwirft (so Lgft, Krg)."

7

Tr. and Phld.). Sm. and Phld. are the second part, precisely, of Eph* and Mg* respectively. We shall speak of Polycarp's letter later. The intentions of the editor of Phil. 13 are evident.

(3) *Tendency to reciprocity*: This tendency is expressed here by the repeated use of καί in the sense of "also" and the correlatives καὶ ... καὶ ... (et ... et ...), εἴτε... εἴτε...

There have always been those who maintain that the letters of Ignatius and Polycarp have been interpolated. However, all the hypotheses that have more or less upheld a massive interpolation of one letter or other, have been disqualified because of an aprioristic posing of the question and for not having troubled to investigate the motives of the interpolation. Emerging from our analysis, the forger (better than interpolator, since he not merely put in his own sentences, but created fresh letters) has elaborated a compilation of letters in the name of Ignatius of Antioch, mixing authentic materials with his more recent problematic (as we shall see later) and supporting the compilation with Polycarp's authority. Going solely by internal evidence, we have come to the conclusion that the *main motivation* of the forger in this big enterprise was to *set up a framework* that would authenticate the fresh material he wanted to insert into it. We are now speaking of the framework; in the second part, we shall deal with the interpolated material.

m) *Two direct allusions to Polycarp in Eph.* 21,1d *and Mg.* 15d

Apart from Ignatius' letter to Polycarp, there are only two brief allusions to Polycarp, bishop of Smyrna, in the other letters. It interests us to know if these allusions are genuine. Being two very short sentences, the degree of certitude we could arrive at from analysing them is only relative.

42. The mention of Polycarp in Eph. 21,1, *summary* of the primitive conclusion of Ephesians, follows immediately after mention of Smyrna, the place where the letter was written.

" ... to Smyrna, from whence also I am writing to you, *thanking the Lord, being grateful to Polycarp as well as yourselves* " (Eph. 21,1).

As can be seen from the synopsis of Eph. 21,1 and Sm. 10,2 that follows, the two participles relating to Polycarp, εὐχαριστῶν and ἀγαπῶν, that depend on the verb in personal tense, γράφω, are in apposition to the personal *masculine* pronoun ἐγώ. In the reconstruction of the original sequence both the extant conclusions of Eph. and Sm. (the interpolation in brackets { } and in a smaller print) and the data acquired in the foregoing analysis (references in the adjoining column between ( )) have been taken into account:

Eph. 21,1-2

Ἀντίψυχον ὑμῶν {ἐγὼ} [167] καὶ ὧν ἐπέμψατε εἰς θεοῦ τιμὴν εἰς Σμύρναν, ὅθεν καὶ γράφω ὑμῖν, (see 31,2)

{εὐχαριστῶν τῷ κυρίῳ, ἀγαπῶν Πολύκαρπον ὡς καὶ ὑμᾶς.} Μνημονεύετέ μου {, ὡς καὶ ὑμῶν Ἰησοῦς Χριστός.} · Προσεύχ{εσθε ὑπὲρ} (see nr. 31,3) τῆ{ς} ἐκκλησία{ς} τῆ{ς} ἐν Συρίᾳ, ὅθεν δεδεμένος (see nr. 30) εἰς Ῥώμην ἀπάγομαι, (see parallel passages in nr. 30) ἔσχατος ὢν {τῶν ἐκεῖ πιστῶν, ὥσπερ} ἠξιώθην εἰς τιμὴν θεοῦ εὑρεθῆναι.

Sm. 10,2-11,1

Ἀντίψυχον ὑμῶν (see nr. 30 and n. 109)

τὸ πνεῦμά μου καὶ τὰ δεσμά μου, ἃ οὐχ ὑπερηφανήσατε οὐδὲ ἐπησχύνθητε · οὐδὲ ὑμᾶς ἐπαισχυνθήσεται ἡ τελεία ἐλπίς, Ἰησοῦς Χριστός.

(see nr. 35 and n. 116)

ἡ <γὰρ> προσευχὴ ὑμῶν ἀπῆλθεν ἐπὶ τὴν ἐκκλησίαν τὴν ἐν {Ἀντιοχείᾳ τῆς} Συρία{ς}, ὅθεν δεδεμένος θεοπρεπεστάτοις δεσμοῖς {πάντας ἀσπάζομαι}, οὐκ ὢν ἄξιος ἐκεῖθεν εἶναι, ἔσχατος αὐτῶν ὤν, κατὰ θέλημα δὲ κατηξιώθην οὐκ ἐκ συνειδότος κτλ.

By restoring to the predicate ἀντίψυχον ὑμῶν its genuine subject, τὸ πνεῦμά μου καὶ τὰ δεσμά μου κτλ. (Sm.), this cannot obviously be intercalated between ὑμῶν and καὶ ὧν and it must necessarily be placed — given its extension — after the phrase "from

---

[167] See too Pol. 2,3 (κατὰ πάντα σου ἀντίψυχον ἐγὼ καὶ τὰ δεσμά μου) and 6,1 (ἀντίψυχον ἐγὼ τῶν ὑποτασσομένων τῷ ἐπισκόπῳ).

whence also I am writing to you ''. The genuine subject not only dislodges the two participles of the sentence concerning Polycarp from their actual position, but these participles without the pronoun are deprived of textual support. It might be objected that we are arguing from a reconstruction. Apart from the way Eph. and Sm. fit together perfectly, it should be observed that expressions equivalent to ἀντίψυχον ὑμῶν are *never* constructed with the personal pronoun, but either with τὸ ἐμὸν πνεῦμα or simply with the verbal medio-passive form (ἁγνίζομαι, ἀσπάζομαι) (see n. 116). For the rest, the expression ἀντίψυχον ἐγὼ still appears in two passages of the letter to Polycarp (see n. 167), a letter that in its turn will be criticized later. The Pseudo-Ignatius will also make profuse use of the former term to authenticate his forgery.[168]

Finally, we must note that, both in the Polycarpian sentence and the one that follows, the particle ὡς is to be found with a *conjunctive* function, a characteristic that is becoming frequent in the interpolated passages.

43.　The other occasion when Polycarp is mentioned is Mg. 15d:

'' Some Ephesians from Smyrna send you greetings, from whence also I am writing. Like yourselves (see Mg. 2) they are here for the glory of God, and they have relieved me in every way, *together with Polycarp, bishop of the Smyrnaeans* '' (Mg. 15a-d).

Ignatius mentions Smyrna to let the Magnesians know the place from which he was writing and that he is with some Ephesians and the delegates from Magnesia. He makes no reference to the Smyrnaeans, as in the corresponding passage in Rom.:

'' I am writing these things to you from Smyrna by the hand of the Ephesians, who are worthy of all praise. And Crocus also, a name very dear to me, is with me too, with many others '' (Rom. 10,1).

Ignatius' silence with regard to the Smyrnaeans makes itself felt still more by his mention of Crocus, one of the Ephesian delegates who procured all kinds of comforts for him (Eph. 2,1). Rom., having been transmitted independently, could not be tampered with, which shows that Ignatius, in spite of being in Smyrna,

---

[168] Mar. 3,3; Tar. 8,2; Phil. 14,1; Ant. 7,2; 12,1; Her. 1,3; 9,3. See BROWN, *Authentic* 54f.

gave more importance to the Ephesians than to the Smyrnaeans. The only place he mentions them is in Tr. 13,1, together with the Ephesians.

The interpolator tried to make up for this omission by inserting the name of Polycarp, bishop of the Smyrnaeans, in the phrase where Ignatius praises the solicitude of the Ephesians. The way he introduces the sentence (ἅμα with dative, as well as in Phld. 11,1.2 and Sm. 12,1) is very artificial. He wants, at all costs, to avoid arousing in the reader the suspicion that Polycarp ignored his friend when he passed through Smyrna. Note that the title " *bishop of the Smyrnaeans* " does not fit in with the function Irenaeus assigns to Polycarp (see nr. 36).

n) *Ignatius' letter to Polycarp*

Having set aside the two brief mentions of Polycarp, at least as insufficient to prove Ignatius had personal contact with him, we have only a direct witness to this friendly relationship: Ignatius' letter to Polycarp. The testimony of Pol. Phil. 13, in fact, proved to be an interpolation of the same forger. With this clause he claimed the authority of Polycarp to validate his compilation of Ignatian letters. His distinction between " *the letters he wrote to us* " (Sm. and Pol.) and " *others we have in hand* " (Eph., Mg., Tr. and Phld.) still shows up in the present compilations. Besides, one of the two letters sent to Polycarp's community, namely Sm., has been proved to be nothing but the second part of Eph* (concealed by the forger under the euphemism of " second tract " in Eph. 20,1). What can be said of the letter to Polycarp? Is it what gave the forger the chance to venture on an enterprise of such vast proportions or, on the contrary, have we to conclude that even the letter to Polycarp is an invention? Only the document itself can answer the dilemma.

α) *The inscription of Pol.*

44. The inscription is shorter that in the other letters. Ignatius, also known as ' God-bearer ', addresses " *Polycarp, bishop of the church of the Smyrnaeans* " personally (Πολυκάρπῳ ἐπισκόπῳ ἐκκλησίας Σμυρναίων). In the short allusion to Polycarp that we have just examined (nr. 43) he bears a similar title: " *Bishop of*

the Smyrnaeans " (Mg. 15d). Irenaeus, however, who spent his youth in Smyrna, when speaking of Polycarp — whom he knew personally — says he " was established by some of the Apostles as bishop for the province of Asia from the community residing in Smyrna " (see nr. 36).

The confining of Polycarp's activities to Smyrna is similar to limiting the activities of the deacon Ignatius to Antioch of Syria. In both cases we have neighbouring bishops to these sees, that is, it is taken for granted that each important *city* has its bishop (Ephesus, Magnesia, Tralles, Philadelphia, Smyrna; Antioch of Syria, closely linked churches, etc.). But the testimony of Ignatius (Rom. 2,2) and even Irenaeus points to a much more archaic type of " bishop ": a presbyter charged with supervising the communities placed in a definite Roman *province* (Syria, Asia, Gaul).

In the second sentence of the inscription,

" *or rather, who has for bishop God the Father and the Lord Jesus-Christ* ",

there is a play of words on the title " bishop " applied in the first sentence to Polycarp.

Scholars usually quote Mg. 3,2, where there is question of a visible and an invisible Bishop. This is not exactly the same, since the invisible Bishop is God, whom the bishop replaces on earth (Mg. 6,1), for he is his earthly representative (Tr. 3,1); while here Jesus Christ himself is associated in his " supervising " activity (if indeed, it retains this meaning) or " presiding " (see Mg. 6,1) over Polycarp and through him over the whole community. In the second part we shall develop the intricate problems of topology and typology of the three hierarchical grades in the Ignatian letters and their connection with the problem we are now treating.

Ignatius' mentality is very different. As we learn from Rom. 9,1 (collated with 2,2), the vacancy he has left can only be filled by Jesus the Messiah and the communion of the Romans. Jesus, God, is the Shepherd who will henceforth " supervise-shepherd " the Syrian communities. " Bishop " is even a function that can be exercised from afar (through the communion of the Romans) and directly, without human intermediary (through Jesus). At no time in his letters, not even in the actual text, does Ignatius express any preoccupation about his successor. As the interpolator considered him a deacon he was not concerned with this question. The Pseudo-Ignatius, however, who already knew his true identity thanks to the addition of Rom. to the "Polycarpian" compilation, already promises his successor to the Antiochenes (Ant. 12,1) and appoints the deacon Heron (Her. 7).

β)   *A personal or collective letter?*

45.   As other scholars have observed,[169] Polycarp's letter contains a glaring *anomaly*: the *first* section (Chaps. 1-5) is addressed to Polycarp, in the singular (only very indirectly to the community); but the *second* section (Chaps. 6-8) is addressed to the community of Smyrna, in the plural (only indirectly to Polycarp, its bishop).[170]   This anomaly would have less importance if there did not exist a letter expressly addressed to the Smyrnaeans. ZAHN tried to explain this by saying that Ignatius wrote to Polycarp at the last moment, when Burrhus had already left with the two letters to the Sm. and Phld.[171]   Once these two letters

---

[169] ZAHN, *I. v. A.* 282: "Ignatius scheint sogar Mittheilung an die Gemeinde vorauszusetzen, denn unvermerkt geht er von Anweisungen für den Bischof (c. 1-5 init.) zu Regeln für das Gemeindeleben (c. 5 fin.) und dann geradezu in ermahnende Anrede der Gemeinde über (c. 6).   Daher markirt er die Rückkehr zur Anrede des Adressaten durch Nennung des Namens (c. 7); aber auch nachher noch wechseln Anrede des Bischofs und der Gemeinde in einer Weise, welche nur dann natürlich erscheint, wenn der Brief der Gemeindeversammlung mitgetheilt werden sollte." LIGHTFOOT, *AA. FF.* II: II/1, 351; LELONG, *PP. AA.* III 102; CAMELOT, *I. d'A.* (S. Ch. 10A) 151, n. 6. – A. HARNACK, *Miscellen zu den Apostolischen Vätern ... II. Zu Ignatius ad Polycarp.* 6, Leipzig 1900, T. U. 20,3, pp. 80f., observes: "Während Ignatius in seinem Briefe an Polycarp c. 1-5 diesen ausschliesslich anredet, ändert er plötzlich c. 6,1 die Adresse (...) Diese Beobachtung ist höchst paradox und hat anlass gegeben, die Integrität des Briefes zu bemängeln.   Wie kommt Ignatius dazu, ganz unvermittelt und ohne jede Andeutung eines Motivs sich plötzlich an die ganze Gemeinde von Smyrna zu wenden, *der er doch gleichzeitig einen besonderen Brief geschrieben hat?*" Harnack immediately proposes a far more picturesque solution: the plural "you" of Chap. 6 does not refer to the community but to the clergy of Smyrna!

[170] Statistics: *I. part*: (1) *Personal pronouns*: 1. pers. sg. (= Ign.) 2x; 2. sg. (= Pol.) 16x; 1. pl. 5x; (2) *Verbs*: (a) *Imperatives*: 2. pers. sg. (= Pol.) 27x; 3. sg. 3x; 3. pl. (= community?) 6x; (b) *Other pers. forms*: in 2. sg. (= Pol.) 12x; 3. sg. 4x; 3. pl. (= community?) 2x. *II. part*: (1) *Pers. pronouns*: 1. pers. sg. (= Ign.) 8x; 2 sg. (= Pol.) 1x; 1. pl. 1x; 2. pl. (= community) 15x; (2) *Verbs*: (a) *Imperatives*: 3. pers. sg. 1x; 2. pl. (= community) 9x; (b) *Other pers. forms*: in 1. sg. (= Ign.) 11x; 2. sg. (= Pol.) 1x; 3. sg. 12x; 2. pl. (= community) 9x.

[171] ZAHN, *I. v. A.* 282; LIGHTFOOT, *AA. FF.* II: I 355f. [366].

are discarded as fictitious, the difficulty would seem to have dis-
appeared. However, the *prescriptive* tone of the *first* section, by
juxtaposing asyndetic and paratactic imperatives, differs notably
from the exhortative tone that is deliberately not prescriptive
(Eph. 3,1; Tr. 3,3; Rom. 4,3) of the authentic letters.[172]

For the rest, in the *second* section that is *directly addressed to
the community*, we find the same anomalies we observed in the
forged letters: (a) *Anonymous* mention of the bishop, presbyters
and deacons (Pol. 6,1; see Phld. inscr. and Sm. 12,2); (b) Deli-
mitation of Ignatius' activity to the church of *Antioch* (Pol. 7,1;
see Phld. 10,1 and Sm. 11,1); (c) Assignment of the letter to the
second place it was written in, *Troas* (Pol. 8,1; see Phld. 11,2 and
Sm. 12,1); (d) Allusion to the supposed intention of Ignatius to
include all the churches of Asia in his invitation to send *messengers or letters* to Antioch of Syria (Pol. 8,1; see Phld. 10,2 and
Pol. Phil. 13,1).

Now, while in the first section addressed to Polycarp in an
imperative tone there are only traces of the characteristic terminology and style proper to Ignatius, in the section addressed to
the community there are clear signs of the situation described in
Rom. and numerous internal parallels with the actual conclusion
of Sm. This phenomenon can be explained, as we shall see next,
by the fact that the forger has used materials taken from the
genuine conclusion of Ephesians to draw up that of Pol. and thus
make it more plausible. It was written in the plural so as to refer

---

[172] See M. P. BROWN, *The Authentic Writings of Ignatius. A Study of linguistic
Criteria*, Durham 1963, pp. 8, 79f., 81: " This would certainly appear to indicate
in Pol. a distinctly different structural style from the usual in Ign. On closer scrutiny, this proves to be so: Pol. has, on the whole, much shorter and more loosely
connected sentences than do the other letters. Parataxis and asyndeton are much
more in evidence here than elsewhere in Ign." (p. 80). LIGHTFOOT, *AA. FF.* II :
I 233 [244], on the contrary, thinks that " The objections from the internal character of the epistle, which Ussher quotes from Vedelius (*App. Ign.* l. c.) have no
force; and indeed the Epistle to Polycarp, being substantially the same in all the
three recensions, is the best standard and the safest test of the style of S. Ignatius."
The contrast is too obvious to pass unnoticed. The linguistic analysis done by
Brown, even though it has not been especially directed to the letter to Pol., opens
up sufficient perspectives to shed doubts on the categorical affirmation of the English scholar.

to the community of Ephesus; which led the forger to pass unawares
from the singular to the plural. This we shall now see in detail.

γ) *The collective section of Pol. is derived from the conclusion
      of Eph*

The conclusion of Pol. starts just where the section in the
singular addressed to Polycarp ends. At the beginning of this
conclusion we have a passage containing implicit references to the
situation of the prisoner Ignatius as described in Rom. This
allusion to Rom. confirms the fact that there are original materials
in the conclusion of Pol. Once this passage examined, we shall
analyse the rest of the conclusion step by step. The synopsis
pp. 122ff. will serve as guideline to this detailed description.

46. The *allusion to the situation as described in Rom.* 5,1 is
to be found at the beginning of the section addressed to the
community (Pol. 6). In the description in Pol. 6 of the true
soldiers of Christ, Ignatius was inspired by the model he had
continually before his eyes, " by land and sea, by day and night,
a company of soldiers like ten leopards " to whom he is chained,
" who grow the more insolent the more deference is shown to
them " (Rom. 5,1).[173]   The image of these ten soldiers, who share
the same pains and fatigues, who fight for the same aim, who
go to bed and rise at the same hours, at the service of the Roman state; their enrollment for a wage in the army; their remarks
about deserters, about honorariums (" accepta ") and deposit on
credit (" deposita ") in the cohort's supplies;[174] finally, their arms
and the various parts of them, suggest to Ignatius to an application to the Christian community, with its common life, its pains
and fatigues, its common objectives, its enrollment in the army of
God, its spiritual arms, its reward for good services rendered.

---

[173] Ἀπὸ Συρίας μέχρι Ῥώμης θηριομαχῶ, διὰ γῆς καὶ θαλάσσης, νυκτὸς καὶ
ἡμέρας, ἐνδεδεμένος δέκα λεοπάρδοις, ὅ ἐστιν στρατιωτικὸν τάγμα · οἳ καὶ εὐεργετούμενοι χείρους γίνονται. E. Bruston, *Ignace* 115f., while holding Rom. to
be spurious, is forced by the image in Pol. 6 to acknowledge that, " Trés proba-
blement il avait été soldat. Un passage de l'épître à Polycarpe trahit de sa part
une connaissance des usages de l'armée, qui ne peut, à notre sens, s'expliquer
autrement ".

[174] Zahn, *I. v. A.* 530f.; *PP. AA.* II 103f.; Lightfoot, *AA. FF.* II: II/1, 353f.;
Bauer, *W. z. N. T.*, s. vv. ἄκκεπτα and δεπόσιτα.

The unity and perfect concord of the Ephesian community, its firm convictions and its continual demonstration of affection to Ignatius, have made it possible for the prisoner to sublimate entirely the negative, mean and brutish image he had before his eyes.

47. Besides this clear allusion to the letter to the Romans, there are in the conclusion of Pol. numerous parallels to the *conclusion of Sm.* = *Eph** and to the *authentic letter to the Ephesians* that can be reconstructed from Eph. and Sm.

The actual conclusion of Pol. (6,1) begins with an *invitation* to follow the bishop and submit to him, the presbytery and the deacons, without naming them. By way of spurring them on it is said that Ignatius risks his life (ἀντίψυχον ἐγώ) for those who submit. This expression, like that of Pol. 2,3, has been taken from Sm. 10,2. Above (see the n. 109) we have been able to appreciate the change introduced by the interpolator as he adapts the primitive conclusion of Ephesians to Eph. 21,1a and Sm. 10,2. Thus we can already state without hesitation that except for ἀντί-ψυχον ὑμῶν ... τὸ πνεῦμά μου κτλ. that was in the original conclusion of Ephesians (see nr. 31,2), the other three passages in which this singular expression is to be found were deliberately composed by the interpolator to cover up his forgery. It should be noted that in the three cases (Eph. 21,1; Pol. 2,3 and 6,1) he has substituted the archaism τὸ πνεῦμά μου (internal principle of human operation as distinct from σάρξ) with a simple ἐγώ, because his anthropology was not dichotomic (πνεῦμα — σάρξ) but trichotomic (σάρξ — ψυχή — πνεῦμα: see Phld. 11,2 and 1,2, both interpolated). The Pseudo-Ignatius confirms this tendency, including this expression at least once in each of he five letters and supplying in five of the seven instances the optative, which was only understood in the usage of Ignatius.[175]

Every forger tries to cover up his manipulations of original texts by emphasizing the most striking expression they contain in order to affect the style of his model. There is an analogous case in Pol. 1,1, where the forger has used the idiomatic optative of desire, ὀναίμην, to authenticate his letter to Pol. (to collate with Mg. 2). In the same way the Pseudo-Ignatius hides behind this expression that he uses no less than eight times.[176]

---

[175] Brown, *Authentic* 54f.

[176] Brown, *Authentic* 18f (use of this verb form in the Middle rec.); 55 (in the Long rec.).

In the case we are dealing with, most important is the presence of ἀντίψυχον in Pol. 6,1. This gives us a valuable leading to place the exhortation Ignatius addresses to the Ephesians in its primitive context making use of military terminology suggested by his precarious situation as prisoner.

48.   Between the ἀντίψυχον and the exhortation properly so-called is a sentence — applied in the present context to the above-mentioned three hierarchical grades — that are very close to similar expressions used by Ignatius:

"And I desire that I may be able to obtain with them my place [177] in the presence of God" (καὶ μετ᾽ αὐτῶν μοι τὸ μέρος γένοιτο σχεῖν ἐν [178] θεῷ, Pol. 6,1d).

The optative γένοιτο occurs another five times, two of which are followed by the infinitive present, thus indicating the desire to continue in a determined state (Eph. 11,2; Sm. 5,3); and four followed by an infinitive aorist, expressing the desire to enter/get away from a determined state either future/or present (Eph. 11,2; 12,2; Pol. 6,1/Mg. 11). In each case these are genuine Ignatian texts. It should also be observed that five of the six passages concern Eph* (in all of them there is the expression γένοιτό μοι). Although the term μέρος occurs only in this passage, Ignatius frequently uses the equivalent κλῆρος in expressions that have practically the same meaning (Eph. 11,2; Tr. 12,3; Rom. 1,2; Phld. 5,1). Once detached from the interpolator's context, αὐτῶν ceases to refer to the three hierarchical grades, to designate again the Syrian community. Then what was its *original context*?

49.   Most certainly, its *immediate posterior context* is Pol. 6,1e-2, that is, the exhortation to realize positively the "model" of Ignatius' escort. Now if we keep in mind that the following context (Pol. 7,1), collated with Phld. 10,1, fits in perfectly with Sm. 11,2 — as we shall see at once — and that immediately before our sentence there is still a mark, the ἀντίψυχον, of the place it original-ly occupied, the search for its *original* context is notably re-stricted. The mark of Pol. 6,1c comes from *Sm.* 10,2 (see the

---

[177] BAUER, *W. z. N. T.*, s. v. μέρος, proposes as second meaning "*der Anteil*" (participation) and "*der Platz*" (place), and translates: "*mit ihnen möchte ich meinen Platz haben in* (oder *bei*) *Gott*".

[178] See critical apparatus, p. 382, l. 9.

remark in n. 109 about its completion by Eph. 21,1). Sm. 10,2 actually follows Sm. 11,1 (see our explanation in nr. 31,3, and its corresponding n. 117 about its completion by Eph. 21,1e-2). If we are right, Pol. 6,1d-2 should precede Eph. 21,1e + Sm. 11,1, where the petition for a remembrance of himself begins the conclusion of the letter. Indeed, the imperatives that make up the exhortation to the community (συγκοπιᾶτε ἀλλήλοις κτλ.) still belong to the *paraenesis* of the letter. The last sentence, ὀναίμην ὑμῶν διὰ παντός, indicates that we have come to the end. So, what is its *immediately anterior* context? On the one hand it must belong to the paraenesis. On the other, it should contain an explicit allusion to the church of Syria (distinct from that of Sm. 11,1) with which our sentence (καὶ μετ' αὐτῶν) can be linked. Pol. 7,1 + Phld. 10,1a fulfills both conditions. While this passage belongs to the paraenesis, because he refers to the news brought by the envoys from Syria (Sm. 10,1 ~ Phld. 11,1), the desire expressed near the end (εἰς τὸ εὑρεθῆναί με κτλ.) is completed precisely by our initial sentence (καὶ μετ' αὐτῶν μοι τὸ μέρος γένοιτο σχεῖν ἐν θεῷ: see the parallel passage of Eph. 11,2). The interpolator had once more inverted the order of the primitive sequence: Phld. 10,1a (Pol. 7,1a) → Pol. 7,1b-d → 6,1d, etc.

50. After the paraenesis came the petition for prayers for himself (Eph. 21,1e), the verification that the prayers of the Ephesians had reached Syria (Sm. 11,1: see nr. 31,3), and the *invitation to send a delegate from the community to Syria*. Given that *Pol. 7 is partly authentic and partly a copy of the original*, the whole period needs detailed analysis.

(1) In *Pol.* 7,1 (to collate with Phld. 10,1a, a more archaic formulation than Pol. 7,1a) a new period opens with the verification of news from Syria on the pacification reached in the heart of the communities after the condemnation of its pastor and bishop, Ignatius. The interpolator had slightly modified the first sentence (7,1a), so as not to have to repeat the same in the two letters to Phld. and Pol., making clear in both that peace had reached the church of *Antioch of Syria* (he could not imagine it otherwise!). The three following sentences (1b.c.d), however, are *authentic*:

"I myself also have gathered fresh courage since God has banished my care,[179] if so be I may through martyrdom attain to God, so that

---

[179] Γίνομαι joined to an adjective takes the place of a passive (BAUER, *W. z.*

thanks to your prayers[180] I may be found a disciple " (κἀγὼ εὐθυμότερος ἐγενόμην ἐν ἀμεριμνίᾳ θεοῦ, ἐάνπερ διὰ τοῦ παθεῖν θεοῦ ἐπιτύχω,
εἰς τὸ εὑρεθῆναί με ἐν τῇ αἰτήσει ὑμῶν μαθητήν, Pol. 7,1b-d).

There are many parallels with Rom. 1,2 and Eph. 11,2. The
use of ἐάνπερ (conj. + particle), which is characteristic and exclusive to Ignatius,[181] being something belonging to the deepest sub-
conscience of the writer, confirms the fact that the parallels noted
are not brought about by imitation.

(2) In *Pol.* 7,2 comes the invitation to choose a man who
would carry an embassy to Syria. The original text is found in

---

N. T., s. v. I 4b: " zur Umschreibung eines passivs "): " I myself also have been
made more cheerful (through the news received) ". The sentence ἐν ἀμεριμνίᾳ
θεοῦ should be taken in a *dynamic* sense: " for the absence of preoccupations
worked by God " (BAUER, *AA. VV.* II 223, with respect to Mg. 6,1 says: " Der-
artige Wendungen sind bei Ign. (...) aufzulösen mit: ' von Gott gewirkt ...' "), God
being the *principal* (remote) cause of the disappearance of anxiety that worried
Ignatius from his departure from Syria, while the news from there was the *means*
(proximate cause) by which he has become aware of the " pacification " worked
by God. Among the translations there are the literal, that hardly make sense:
" in insollicitudine Dei " L, " in göttlicher Unbesorgtheit " Bauer, Fischer; the
paraphrastic, but exact ones: " et (maintenant que) Dieu m'a rendu la tranquillité,
(je n'ai plus qu'un souci), celui ..." Lelong; faithful versions: " since God has
banished my care " Lightfoot; free versions: " in sorglosem Vertrauen auf Gott "
Fischer, " carefree and confident in God " Kleist, " dans l'abandon à Dieu "
Camelot.

[180] αἰτήσει gA Lightfoot, Bauer: ἀναστάσει GL Zahn, Funk, Hilgenfeld, Fischer,
etc. LIGHTFOOT, *AA. FF.* II: II/1, 355, notes that in case of reading ἀναστάσει,
ὑμῶν μαθητήν " must be taken together "; the same also BAUER, *AA. VV.* II 280:
" Dann muss ὑμῶν zu μαθητήν gehören. Aber der Wunsch, Jünger der Smyrnäer
zu werden (...) scheint mir weder durch Rom. 3,1 noch durch Eph. 3,1 noch durch
irgend eine der beliebten Wendungen der Selbsterniedrigung glaubhaft gemacht zu
sein." In spite of this, the larger number of translators interpret it thus: Lelong
(" parmi vos disciples "), Fischer (" als Euer Jünger "), Kleist (" your disciple "),
Camelot (" votre disciple "). Bauer is right in saying that the expression " your
disciple " makes no sense within Ignatius' thought about discipleship. But what
prevents us from joining ὑμῶν to ἀναστάσει? This reading would make very good
sense: compare Eph. 11,2 (ἵνα ἐν κλήρῳ Ἐφεσίων εὑρεθῶ τῶν Χριστιανῶν contem-
poraries of the Apostles); 12,2 (οὗ γένοιτό μοι ὑπὸ τὰ ἴχνη εὑρεθῆναι, of Paul);
Mg. 9,1, etc. I prefer, however, to read ἐν τῇ αἰτήσει ὑμῶν (cf. Tr. 13,3), because
for Ign. " our resurrection " has begun already since the passion of Jesus (... εἰς
τὸ πάθος, ὅ ἐστιν ἡμῶν ἀνάστασις, Sm. 5,3).

[181] Eph. 2,2; Mg. 12; Rom. 1,1.2 (2x); 4,1: all these passages being authentic.
See BROWN, *Authentic* 78f.

Sm. 11,2. Both Phld. 10,1b-end and Pol. 7,2 are rough imitations (verify in the synopsis, nr. 53F, the way both paraphrase the different elements of Sm.: πρέπει, χειροτονῆσαι, ἐκκλησίαν ὑμῶν, θεοπρεσβευτήν, etc.).

(3) The argument interrupted in Sm. 11,3e (imitated by the forger in Phld. 10,2) is taken up in *Pol.* 7,3a-f:

" A Christian has not power over himself, but devotes himself to God. This work will be God's and yours too, when you shall complete it. For I have every confidence in the grace (that God grants), that you are ready for this good work that concerns God " (Pol. 7,3).

Note the clear correspondence between Sm. 11,2a (ἵνα οὖν τέλειον ὑμῶν γένηται τὸ ἔργον καὶ ἐπὶ γῆς καὶ ἐν οὐρανῷ) and Pol. 7,3cd (τοῦτο τὸ ἔργον θεοῦ ἐστιν καὶ ὑμῶν, ὅταν αὐτὸ ἀπαρτίσητε). Also between Sm. 11,3e (θέλουσιν γὰρ ὑμῖν εὐπράσσειν θεὸς ἕτοιμος εἰς τὸ παρέχειν) and Pol. 7,3f (ὅτι ἕτοιμοί ἐστε εἰς εὐποιΐαν θεῷ ἀνήκουσαν). The original letter to the Ephesians is scattered with allusions to the *work/s* undertaken immediately by this community when they heard of Ignatius' visit: sending of delegates (Eph. 1,1: τὸ συγγενικὸν ἔργον τελείως ἀπηρτίσατε; see 1,3-2,1), care for Ignatius (Mg. 15; Tr. 12,1; Sm. = Eph* 9,2), attention to the messengers from Syria (Sm. = Eph* 10,1), sending of messengers to Rome (Rom. 10,1), messengers for Syria from the community (Sm. = Eph* 11,2), and from Ignatius (11,3).

(4) *Pol.* 7,3gh give us the characteristic *trait* we shall find up to the end of the letter (εἰδὼς ... δι᾽ ὀλίγων ὑμᾶς γραμμάτων παρεκάλεσα). In a first stage it belonged to the letter to the Ephesians; the interpolator used it to give a more authentic touch to his forgery of Pol. Similar traits are to be found in the authentic letters to the Romans (Rom. 8,2) and Magnesians (Mg. 14a). In the brief letter to the Trallians it was placed at the beginning (Tr. 3,3), to justify the epitomatic character of this letter as compared with its homologue (also anti-Docetic), Eph*.

51. Finally, in *Pol.* 8 we have (a) a *clause destined to put an end to Ignatius' letter-writing*, due to his sudden sailing from Troas for Neapolis (8,1); (b) the *final greeting* of the letter (8,2-3). We shall speak of the greetings further on (nr. 54). For the moment, we wish to examine the *concluding clause* of Ignatius' literary activities.

*" Since, then, I could not write to all the churches, because of my
sudden sailing from Troas for Neapolis, as the order* [182] *enjoins, you shall
write to the churches lying in front, as one possessing the mind of God,* [183]
*that they also may do the same thing — those who are able sending foot-
messengers, and others letters through those whom you send — so that
you may be glorified by an enduring work, as you deserve* [184] *"* (Pol.
8,1).

The change to the *singular* (Pol. 6-7 is written in the plural,
including interpolations and copies) and a *series of coincidences*
with other passages certainly interpolated show that this clause is
a recent creation. In fact it has a threefold purpose: (a) To
sanction the new itinerary of Ignatius the prisoner (Troas → Neapolis); (b) *To form a connecting link with the interpolated Chap.* 13
of Polycarp's letter to the Philippians (Neapolis is the port of
Philippi and gives access to the Via Egnatia); (c) *To justify the*

---

[182] I have translated "order" instead of "will" taking into account the
situation of the prisoner Ignatius and his strict dependence on the "orders" given
by "some officer", as KLEIST, *I. of A.* 146, 22, suggests. See also LELONG, *PP.
AA.* III 106. On the contrary, ZAHN, *PP. AA.* II 105; BAUER, *AA. VV.* II 280.

[183] ὡς θεοῦ γνώμην κεκτημένος: the interpolator imitates the Ignatian use of
the perf. of κτάομαι (Eph. 1,1; 14,2; 15,2; Mg. 15) above all in the letter to Pol.
(1,3; 8,1: see also Phld. 1,1), as well as the Ignatian theologumenon, ἡ γνώμη τοῦ
θεοῦ/πατρός, that for Ign. is Jesus the Messiah (see Eph. 3,2cd): to the Mind/Plan
of God or God's way of thinking Ign. opposes the mind/plan of the Chief of this
world (Rom. 8,3; Phld. 3,3; 6,2; Sm. 6,2); while for the interpolator it is the
bishop (Pol. 4,1; 5,2; 8,1 and above all in Eph. 3,2e-4,1c, which we shall deal
with in the second part) who represents and possesses the mind of God.

[184] ὡς ἄξιος ὤν: this sentence, in parallel with the one of the preceding n., is,
however, rather badly placed. LIGHTFOOT, *AA. FF.* II: II/1, 358, considers the
sentence included between "as one possessing ... the same thing" and "as you
deserve" as parenthetical, so that the last will be connected with the first, thus
avoiding unnecessary difficulties of previous translators and commentators of this
singular ἄξιος ὤν. ZAHN, *PP. AA.* II 106, confesses: "Dura sane lectio, quae
explicanda fortasse est ex ancipiti huius epistulae, modo ecclesiam, modo episcopum
alloquentis, ratione." LELONG, *PP. AA.* III 107, observes: "Ignace passe ici sans
transition du pluriel au singulier; *vous* désigne les Smyrniotes (?), et *tu* Polycarpe."
The interrogation mark is mine: the text refers both to Polycarp *with* the nearby
churches that would carry out the request (δοξασθῆτε) and to Polycarp *alone* (ὡς
ἄξιος ὤν). The difficulty is obvious, although the English translation does not
distinguish between "you (2. pl.) may be glorified" and "you (2. sing.) deserve".
It is a similar difficulty to that arising from the twofold origin of the materials,
that is, the interpolator's own materials written in the second pers. sing. and those
coming from the older conclusion of Eph* drawn up in the second pers. pl.

unfulfilled promise made in Eph. 20,1 (to write a "second tract" to the Ephesians) because of the sudden sailing from Troas for Neapolis [185] (note that in the compilation Pol. was placed first, so that the reader of Eph. automatically connected up the two passages). Comparison between Eph. 20,1 (ἐὰν ... θέλημα ᾖ) and Pol. 8,1 (ὡς τὸ θέλημα προστάσσει) shows that this is no accident but an intentional relationship.

With this clause the forger has managed to make his compilation hold together. Indeed, by charging Polycarp to complete his resolution "*by writing to all the churches*", so that they send messengers or letters to his church in Antioch of Syria, the three letters from *Troas* are given unity. At the same time they are distinguished from the writings from *Smyrna*, and he links them up with his interpolation of Polycarp's letter to the *Philippians*. There is a danger, however, that once the apparently well-connected parts of this construction fail, the very means used to give consistency to the whole would change into evidence of interpolation.

Although for the moment we have limited ourselves to the indications the forger had unconsciously left in the text, we can conclude that the letter to Polycarp is the least authentic of the Ignatian letters. The whole of the *first part* (Pol. 1-5), drawn up in the singular, and the clause of *Pol.* 8,1, also in the singular, are spurious. In his redaction he has paid attention to the most outstanding elements of the Ignatian vocabulary and some typical Ignatian turns of phrase. The *second part*, addressed in the plural to the Smyrnaean community, is for the most part made up of the original conclusion of Ephesians. The original amounts to about a quarter of the whole letter.

Once eliminated the letter to Polycarp, Ignatius' supposed relations to the bishop of Smyrna are groundless. The forger has woven this plot to authenticate his compilation. There is hardly a trace of the community of Smyrna in Ignatius' authentic letters, although he spent a few days there. The overwhelming importance of Ephesus at that time, is faithfully reflected in all his letters.

---

[185] See ZAHN, *PP. AA.* II 25 (quoted above in our n. 58); LIGHTFOOT, *AA. FF.* II: II/1, 18; LELONG, *PP. AA.* III 25: "Pourquoi Ignace n'a-t-il pas mis son project à exécution? Peut-être parce qu'on l'a fait partir précipitamment de Troas (cf. *Ép. à Polyc.*, VIII, 1)."

o) *Fresh material for the reconstruction of the ending of Eph**

We have attempted a first reconstruction of the ending of Eph* from those of Eph. and Sm. (see nr. 31). With fresh material coming from the conclusion of Pol., a more exact reconstruction should be undertaken. The importance of this ending is obvious, if we take into account that the forger has made use of it as a model for the three new letters from Troas (Phld., Sm. and Pol.).

α) *The original ending of Eph*, shared between the letters to Eph., Sm., Pol. (and Phld.)*

52.   For the original letter to the Magnesians, the interpolator chose to leave the conclusion of Mg* in *Mg.* (see nr. 35), as a colophon to the first half of the letter. Between this and the conclusion he places the interrupting clause of Mg. 13 (see nrs. 25-28), to substitute in some way for the second half that he thought of reserving for Phld.

In the case of Ephesians he could not do the same. The ending of Eph* was not suitable — except in a few particulars — to terminate *Eph.*, since this community had been reduced to performing a secondary function. On the other hand, the numerous personal details and the itemized greetings to be found in the ending of Eph* were liable to be reinterpreted as demonstrating friendly relationships, created by the interpolator, between Ignatius and Polycarp/the community of Smyrna.

The letter to the *Trallians* could not be divided because it was too short. Ignatius anticipates in Tr. the theme amply developed in Eph*. The interpolator limits himself to inserting his problematic into Tr*, as we shall see in the second part.

As for the three new letters supposedly written from Troas, the forger counted on a single ending (Eph*). The interdependence community/bishop suggested he should divide the ending of Eph* between *Sm.*, Polycarp's community, and *Pol.*, although because of this the last would be profoundly affected by the presence of a terminology clearly communitarian in its second part.

There remains the letter to the *Phld.* The forger had special reasons for demonstrating that Ignatius had passed through Phil-

adelphia.   Nevertheless, to avoid suspicions, he always tried not
to invent proper names for bishop, presbyters and deacons.   The
surest way was to imitate the original ending of Eph*, before
dividing it between Sm. and Pol.   To disguise it better, he inverted the order of the original sequence.   He placed first the invitation to send an envoy to Antioch in Syria (see nr. 33).   Then,
without a connecting link to what went before, he alluded to the
passage of Philo, Gaius and Agathopus by Philadelphia and the
different welcome they received from the community (see nr. 34).
Once these three persons were separated from their original mission, that is, to take good news about the reestablishment of
peace in the community of Syria (see nr. 31,4), only a few slight
retouches were needed in order to present them as a second group
of prisoners going from Cilicia to Syria, as can also be seen in
the interpolated chapter of Philippians (Pol. Phil. 13,2).   If he had
known Rom. he would not have let slip such an incongruity.

      53.   The *reconstruction of the original ending of Ephesians* that
follows, has been made possible thanks to the traces the interpolator has left behind him, the copies he was obliged to make,
sometimes twice over, the summaries, the reminiscences of original
materials, etc.; as also by the internal logic of the original sequence.
Except in the case of Phld., in which he has inverted the logical
order of the narrative (Phld. 10 before 11,1-2), and in that of Pol.
6,1c-2 (placed before its logical context), in all the other sequences
he has scrupulously respected the original order.   To visualize the
original sequence of the ending of Eph*, we shall give in standard
type the text of the ancient conclusion of Ephesians, and in smaller
print the summaries, copies and adaptations made by the interpolator.   All that is not included in brackets { } belongs in some
way to Ignatius.   In the table preceding the text the vicissitudes
suffered by the ending of Eph* are indicated, as also the original
elements (without brackets), the copies (round brackets) and the
fresh interpolations (square brackets).

Vicissitudes of the primitive ending of Eph*:

Ending
of Eph*

Eph.: Summary + details
exclusively Ephesian . . . . . .
- 21,1ab.e and 2b
- (21,1a.cd)
- [21,1cd.f]

Unfolding and adapta-
tion of Eph* for con-
clusions of letters writ-
ten from T r o a s . .

Sm. . .
- 10,1-2; 11,1b-3
- (11,1a)
- [12,1-2]

Pol.. . .
- 6,1d-2; 7,1b-d.3
- (7,1a.2)
- [6,1a-c; 8,1]

Phld. . .
- 10,1a
- (10,1b-11,1)
- [11,2]

Synopsis of the original sequence of the ending of Eph*:

Synopsis of the original sequence

Eph. 21,1-2

A.

Sm. 10,1-11,3

A. [186]

10,1a Φίλωνα καὶ Γάϊον [187] καὶ [188]
         Ἀγαθόπουν,
    b οἳ ἐπηκολούθησάν μοι εἰς λό-
         γον θεοῦ,
    c καλῶς ἐποιήσατε ὑποδεξάμε-
         νοι ὡς διακόνους Χριστοῦ [190]
         θεοῦ ·

    d οἳ καὶ εὐχαριστοῦσιν τῷ κυρίῳ
         ὑπὲρ ὑμῶν,

    e ὅτι αὐτοὺς ἀνεπαύσατε κατὰ
         πάντα τρόπον ·
    f οὐδὲν ὑμῖν οὐ μὴ ἀπολεῖται.

B. [191]

21,1a Ἀντίψυχον ὑμῶν {ἐγὼ} καὶ
         ὧν [192] ἐπέμψατε εἰς θεοῦ τιμὴν
         εἰς Σμύρναν,
    b ὅθεν καὶ γράφω ὑμῖν,
    c {εὐχαριστῶν τῷ κυρίῳ,
    d ἀγαπῶν Πολύκαρπον [195] ὡς καὶ
         ὑμᾶς.}

B. [193]

10,2a Ἀντίψυχον ὑμῶν

         τὸ πνεῦμά μου καὶ τὰ δεσμά
    b μου, ἃ οὐχ ὑπερηφανήσατε
         οὐδὲ ἐπῃσχύνθητε ·
    c οὐδὲ ὑμᾶς ἐπαισχυνθήσεται ἡ
         τελεία ἐλπίς, Ἰησοῦς Χριστός.

---

[186] See nr. 31,1.
[187] See n. 111.
[188] See also n. 111.
[189] See nr. 34.
[190] See n. 114.

of the ending of Eph*:

Pol. 6,1c-7,3
A.

Phld. 11,1; 10,1-2
A. [189]

11,1a {Περὶ δὲ} Φίλων{ος τοῦ} διακόνου
{ἀπὸ Κιλικίας,

   b ἀνδρὸς μεμαρτυρημένου,

   c ὃς καὶ νῦν ἐν} λόγῳ θεοῦ {ὑπη-
ρετεῖ μοι

   d ἅμα} Γαΐῳ [187] καὶ [188] Ἀγαθόπο{δι,

   e ἀνδρὶ ἐκλεκτῷ,

   f ὃς ἀπὸ Συρίας μοι} ἀκολουθ{εῖ
ἀποταξάμενος τῷ βίῳ ·}

   g οἳ καὶ {μαρτυρ}οῦσιν .{ὑμῖν,

   h κἀγὼ} τῷ {θε}ῷ εὐχαριστῶ
ὑπὲρ ὑμῶν,

   i ὅτι {ἐ}δέξα{σθε} αὐτούς,

   j ὡς {καὶ ὑμᾶς ὁ} κύρι{ος.}

   k {οἱ δὲ ἀτιμάσαντες} αὐτοὺς {λυ-
τρωθείησαν ἐν τῇ χάριτι τοῦ Ἰησοῦ Χριστοῦ.}

B. [194]

B.

6,1c Ἀντίψυχον {ἐγὼ τῶν ὑποτασσομένων τῷ ἐπισκόπῳ, πρεσβυτέροις, διακόνοις ·}

---

[191] See nrs. 30 and 31,2 with the n. 116.
[192] See n. 109.
[193] See nr. 31,2 and n. 116.
[194] See nr. 47.
[195] See nr. 42.

Eph.   Sm.

C.   **C.**

D.   **D.**

---

[196] See nr. 50,1.   [198] See nr. 31,4.   [200] See n. 179.
[197] See nr. 33.   [199] See nr. 50,1.   [201] See n. 180.

Pol.

C. [196]

7,1a Ἐπειδὴ ἡ ἐκκλησία ἡ ἐν {Ἀν-
τιοχείᾳ τῆς} Συρία{ς} εἰρηνεύει,
{ὡς ἐδηλώθη} μοι, {διὰ} τὴν
προσευχὴν ὑμῶν,

b κἀγὼ [199] εὐθυμότερος ἐγενόμην ἐν ἀμεριμνίᾳ θεοῦ, [200]

c ἐάνπερ διὰ τοῦ παθεῖν ἐπιτύχω,

d εἰς τὸ εὑρεθῆναί με ἐν τῇ αἰτήσει [201] ὑμῶν μαθητήν,

6,1d καὶ [202] μετ' αὐτῶν μοι τὸ μέρος γένοιτο σχεῖν ἐν [203] θεῷ.

D. [204]

6,1e Συγκοπιᾶτε ἀλλήλοις, f συναθλεῖτε, g συντρέχετε, h συμπάσχετε, i συγκοιμᾶσθε, j συνεγείρεσθε ὡς θεοῦ οἰκονόμοι καὶ
πάρεδροι καὶ ὑπηρέται.

2a ἀρέσκετε ᾧ στρατεύεσθε,

b ἀφ' οὗ καὶ τὰ ὀψώνια κομί-
ζεσθε·

c μή τις ὑμῶν δεσέρτωρ εὑρεθῇ·

d τὸ βάπτισμα ὑμῶν μενέτω ὡς
ὅπλα, ἡ πίστις ὡς περικεφαλαία, ἡ ἀγάπη ὡς δόρυ, ἡ
ὑπομονὴ ὡς πανοπλία·

e τὰ δεπόσιτα ὑμῶν τὰ ἔργα
ὑμῶν,

f ἵνα τὰ ἄκκεπτα ὑμῶν ἄξια
κομίσησθε.

g μακροθυμήσατε οὖν μετ' ἀλλήλων ἐν πραότητι,

h ὡς ὁ θεὸς ὑμῶν [205].

i ὀναίμην ὑμῶν διὰ παντός.

Phld.

C. [197]

10,1 Ἐπειδὴ κατὰ τὴν προσευχὴν
ὑμῶν καὶ κατὰ τὰ σπλάγχνα,
ἃ ἔχετε ἐν Χριστῷ Ἰησοῦ
ἀπηγγέλη μοι, [198] εἰρηνεύειν
τὴν ἐκκλησίαν τὴν ἐν {Ἀντι-
οχείᾳ τῆς} Συρία{ς},

D.

---

[202] See nrs. 48f.

[203] See n. 178.

[204] See nrs. 46-49.

[205] See critical apparatus, p. 382, l. 16.

Eph.

Sm.

E. [206]

E. [207]

21,1e Μνημονεύετέ μου{,
  f ὡς καὶ ὑμῶν Ἰησοῦς Χριστός}
2a προσεύχ{εσθε ὑπὲρ}
       τῆ{ς} ἐκκλησία{ς}
  τῆ{ς} ἐν
  Συρίᾳ,
  b ὅθεν δεδεμένος
       εἰς Ῥώμην ἀπάγομαι,

  c ἔσχατος   ὢν {τῶν ἐκεῖ πιστῶν,
  d ὥσπερ}   ἠξιώθην
       εἰς τιμὴν θεοῦ εὑρεθῆναι,

11,1a ἡ <γὰρ>[208] προσευχὴ ὑμῶν
       ἀπῆλθεν ἐπὶ τὴν ἐκκλησίαν
       τὴν ἐν   {Ἀντιοχείᾳ τῆς}
       Συρία{ς},
  b ὅθεν δεδεμένος θεοπρεστάτοις
       δεσμοῖς {πάντας ἀσπάζομαι}[209],
  c οὐκ ὢν ἄξιος ἐκεῖθεν εἶναι,
  d ἔσχατος αὐτῶν ὤν,
  e κατὰ θέλημα δὲ κατηξιώθην,
               οὐκ ἐκ συν-
       ειδότος, ἀλλ' ἐκ χάριτος θεοῦ,
  f ἣν εὔχομαι τελείαν μοι δοθῆ-
       ναι,
  g ἵνα ἐν τῇ προσευχῇ ὑμῶν θεοῦ
       ἐπιτύχω.

F.

F. [210]

11,2a Ἵνα οὖν τέλειον ὑμῶν γένηται
       τὸ ἔργον καὶ ἐπὶ γῆς καὶ ἐν
       οὐρανῷ,
  b πρέπει εἰς τιμὴν θεοῦ χειροτο-
       νῆσαι τὴν ἐκκλησίαν ὑμῶν
       θεοπρεσβευτήν,

  c εἰς τὸ γενόμενον ἕως Συρίας
       συγχαρῆναι αὐτοῖς,
  d ὅτι εἰρηνεύουσιν
  e καὶ ἀπέλαβον τὸ ἴδιον μέγεθος
  f καὶ ἀπεκατεστάθη αὐτοῖς τὸ
       ἴδιον σωματεῖον.

---

[206] See nrs. 30 and 31,3 with the n. 117.

[207] See nr. 31,3 and nn. 117, 120.

[208] Probably suppressed by the interpolator by separating it from its primitive context.

Pol.   Phld.

E.   E.

F. [211]   F. [212]

7,2a πρέπει {, Πολύκαρπε θεομακαριστότατε, συμβούλιον ἀγαγεῖν θεοπρεπέστατον
   b καὶ} χειροτονῆσαί {τινα,
   c ὃν ἀγαπητὸν λίαν ἔχετε καὶ ἄοκνον,
   d ὃς δυνήσεται} θεο{δρόμος καλεῖσθαι ·
   e τοῦτον καταξιῶσαι,
   f ἵνα πορευθεὶς εἰς} Συρίαν

10,1b πρέπ{ον ἐστὶν ὑμῖν ὡς} ἐκκλησίᾳ {θεοῦ,} χειροτονῆσαι {διά-
κονον

   c εἰς τὸ} πρεσβεῦ{σαι ἐκεῖ} θεοῦ
πρεσβε{ίαν.}

   d εἰς τὸ
συγχαρῆναι αὐτοῖς {ἐπὶ τὸ αὐτὸ
γενομένοις

---

[209] See nrs. 30,4 and 31,3.
[210] See nr. 31,4 and n. 119, and nr. 50 as well.
[211] See nr. 50,2.
[212] See nr. 33.

<table>
<tr><td align="center">Eph.</td><td align="center">Sm.</td></tr>
</table>

G.

G. [213]

11,3a Ἐφάνη μοι οὖν θεοῦ ἄξιον
       πράγμα, πέμψαι τινὰ τῶν ὑμε-
       τέρων μετ' ἐπιστολῆς, [214]

   b ἵνα συνδοξάσῃ τὴν κατὰ θεὸν
     αὐτοῖς γενομένην εὐδίαν,

   c καὶ ὅτι λιμένος ἤδη ἔτυχον ἐν
     τῇ προσευχῇ ὑμῶν.

H.

H. [215]

11,3d Τέλειοι οὖν [216] ὄντες τέλεια
       καὶ φρονεῖτε·

   e θέλουσιν γὰρ ὑμῖν εὐπράσσειν
     θεὸς ἕτοιμος εἰς τὸ παρέ-
     χειν· [219]

I.   **I.**

---

[213] See nr. 31,5.
[214] The sender of the letter = Ign.: see n. 121.
[215] See nr. 31,6.
[216] See n. 125.
[217] See nr. 33,7-8.
[218] See nr. 50,3.

Pol.

G.

Phld.

G.

7,2f δοξάσῃ {ὑμῶν τὴν ἄοκνον ἀγάπην εἰς δόξαν θεοῦ.}

10,1e καὶ} δοξάσαι {τὸ ὄνομα.
2a μακάριος ἐν Ἰησοῦ Χριστῷ,
  b ὃς καταξιωθήσεται τῆς τοιαύτης διακονίας,
  c καὶ ὑμεῖς} δοξοσ{θήσεσθε}.

H. [218]

H. [217]

10,2d θέλουσιν {δὲ} ὑμῖν {οὐκ ἔστιν ἀδύνατον ὑπὲρ ὀνόματος} θεο{ῦ,
  e ὡς καὶ αἱ ἔγγιστα ἐκκλησίαι ἔ-} πεμψα{ν ἐπισκόπους,
  f αἱ δὲ πρεσβυτέρους καὶ διακό-νους.}

7,3a Χριστιανὸς <γὰρ> [219 bis] ἑαυ-τοῦ ἐξουσίαν οὐκ ἔχει,
  b ἀλλὰ θεῷ σχολάζει.
  c τοῦτο [220] τὸ ἔργον θεοῦ ἐστιν καὶ ὑμῶν,
  d ὅταν αὐτὸ ἀπαρτίσητε ·
  e πιστεύω γὰρ τῇ χάριτι,
  f ὅτι ἕτοιμοί ἐστε εἰς εὐποιΐαν θεῷ ἀνήκουσαν.

I. [221]

I.

7,3g Εἰδὼς [222] ὑμῶν τὸ σύντονον τῆς ἀληθείας,
  h δι᾽ ὀλίγων ὑμᾶς γραμμάτων παρεκάλεσα.

---

[219] See critical apparatus, p. 384, l. 1.
[219bis] Probably suppressed by the interpolator by separating it from its primitive context.
[220] See n. 119.
[221] See nr. 35,1.
[222] See critical apparatus, p. 384, l. 8.

β) *Personalized final greetings of Eph*, transferred to Sm. and Pol.*

54.   It remains for us to examine the *farewell greetings* of the four letters, among which the original ending of Ephesians has been distributed.   The surest way of discerning between the archaic elements and those superimposed is through the *proper names.* The interpolator's fear that his forgery was discovered let him to retain, carefully, the names of persons appearing in the Ignatian letters and not to invent proper names, not even for the bishop, presbyters and deacons of the communities of Philadelphia and Smyrna, the only churches that — according to him — Ignatius knew personally (see nrs. 23, 32 and 45).   Analysis of the final greetings of the four letters leads us to infer:

(1) *Eph.,* unlike the other letters, completely lacks farewell greetings.   The *ritual salutation* of Eph.   21,2e (ἔρρωσθε ἐν θεῷ πατρὶ καὶ ἐν Ἰησοῦ Χριστῷ, τῇ κοινῇ ἐλπίδι ἡμῶν) was drawn up — as we shall see at once — by the interpolator from the second farewell formula of Eph* (ἔρρωσθε ἐν χάριτι θεοῦ Ἰησοῦ Χριστοῦ, τῆς κοινῆς ἐλπίδος ἡμῶν: Sm. 13,2d + Eph. 21,2e).

(2) *Phld.* contains no *personalized greetings,* although — according to the interpolator — Ignatius had stayed in Philadelphia. Just as in the authentic letters Ignatius addressed to communities he did not know personally (Mg. 15a; Tr. 13,1a; Rom. 9,3a), the forger limits himself to sending *greetings from the brothers living in Troas* (Phld. 11,2a).   This clause, like the similar one in Sm. 12, was forged, as we have already said (nr. 32), to correspond with the new situation created by the letters attributed to *Troas.*   The *farewell formula* must be authentic.   Note the archaism ἔρρωσθε ἐν Χριστῷ Ἰησοῦ, τῇ κοινῇ ἐλπίδι ἡμῶν, as compared with Eph. 21,2e. It belongs probably to Tr., as we shall see in the second part.

(3) *Sm.* presents *five very diversified types of greetings*: (a) Greetings *sent by the brothers residing in Troas* (Sm. 12,1a), which are spurious as those we found in Phld. 11,2a; (b) *Anonymous greetings from Ignatius* to the bishop (Polycarp!), the presbytery and his fellow-servants, the deacons (typical denomination of the interpolator!), as well as to all and everyone in particular (Sm. 11,2; note the resemblance with Eph. 20,2, also spurious); (c) *Generic greetings sent to the families* of the Christians of Smyrna with their

wives and children, and to the virgins, called " widows " [223] (Sm.
13,1a), modelled on the authentic greetings sent by Ignatius to
the widow [224] of Epitropus, with her family and children, in Pol.
8,2a; (d) The *personal greetings sent by Philo* to the Smyrnaeans
(Sm. 13,1c: read Ephesians!): clearly this alludes to Philo, one of
the three messengers from Syria; he alone is named as being responsible for the mission (note also in Sm. 10,1a, he is named first).
The delegates of Tr. and Mg. having now returned with their respective letters, Ignatius tell the Ephesians that Philo (and probably
the other two messengers) is still with him (σὺν ἐμοὶ ὤν). There
can be no doubt that the sentence of Sm. 13,1c is *authentic*; (e) The
detailed greetings sent by Ignatius to Tavia, the widow and her
family (Sm. 13,2a); to his dear Alce (see also Pol. 8,3c) [225], to

---

[223] The expression: " I greet ... and the virgins, the so-called ' widows ' " implies
that the order of so-called " widows " contained among its ranks persons who
were unmarried virgins. To obviate the consequences derived from this interpretation a number of explanations have been proposed: see ZAHN, *I. v. A.* 334ff.,
580ff.; *PP. AA.* II 95 (where he confesses that he is not satisfied by the previous
explanation — arguing that different churches had different practices — and proposes new solutions); LIGHTFOOT, *AA. FF.* II: II/1, 322ff. (abundant bibliography,
with a new solution; widows called " virgins " by Ignatius " for such they are in
God's sight by their purity and devotion ", p. 324); BAUER, *AA. VV.* II 273f.,
rejects with reason this explanation and comments: " Wir verstehen die Wendung
des Ign. wohl am besten von der Voraussetzung aus, dass in den Orden der kirch-
lichen Witwen aus Mangel an geeigneten Witwen auch Jungfrauen eingestellt werden
mussten." According to LELONG, *PP. AA.* III 95: " Il s'agit sans doute de vierges,
d'un âge avancé, qui avaient été admises dans l'ordre des veuves." Once identified
the author of such generic and anonymous greetings, we should start from the
concrete situation of the interpolator to interpret this sentence. In his time there
already existed *virgins integrated into the order of the widows*, which TERTULLIAN,
De Virg. Vel. 9 denounces vehemently. Here already, " widows " had a technical
ecclesiastical sense (CAMELOT, *I. d'A.*, S. Ch. 10A, p. 143). The many solutions
proposed aimed at obviating this anachronism, which was supported by the adversaries of the authenticity of the Ignatian letters.
[224] In Sm. 13,2ab as in Pol. 8,2a, instead of naming the head of the family,
Ign. names a woman, doubtless the widow. These were two distinct families, as
we shall see in the reconstruction proposed later on. Ign. refers to them in the
first place, precisely because they have been widows. See LIGHTFOOT, *AA. FF.* II:
II/1, 358f. and BAUER, *AA. VV.* II 281.
[225] The repetition of the sentence concerning Alce in Sm. and Pol. will help
to sanction the priority of the one preserved in Sm. See a similar formula, predicated of Crocus (also named in Eph. 2,1), in Rom. 10,1.

Daphnus, Eutecnus and all by name (Sm. 13,2c). These sentences are also *authentic*.

(4) As for the *farewell formula*, Sm. contains a double mention. Are both or only one authentic? Note that there is a double formula of farewell in Pol. 8,3 also. Then, there are indications that the original letter to the Ephesians had *two* farewell formulas. To decide which is original, we have to make a comparative study of the farewell formula of Pol. 8,3, since it seems the interpolator has divided the numerous personalized greetings of Eph* between Sm. and Pol. On the one hand, the first, Sm. 13,1b, must be forged, since it follows immediately after the *generic* greetings of 13,1a, in imitation of Pol. 8,2a. Note the uncommon addition of μοὶ to ἔρρωσθε. The second, on the other hand, is coupled with the greetings to *concrete* persons in the community mentioned by name (13,2d). An apparently insignificant detail inclines us to accept it as *authentic*: unlike Tr. (13,2a: ἔρρωσθε ἐν ᾽Ιησοῦ Χριστῷ), in the other authentic letters Ignatius seems to concentrate his deepest feelings towards each community in this last sentence: ἔρρωσθε ἐν χάριτι θεοῦ (Sm. = Eph* 13,2d); ἔ. ἐν ὁμονοίᾳ θεοῦ (Mg. 15f: see nr. 29); ἔ. ... ἐν ὑπομονῇ ᾽Ιησοῦ Χριστοῦ (Rom. 10,3b). Finally, keeping in mind that this sentence in the authentic conclusions is always directed towards Jesus (Tr. 13,2a; Mg. 15f; Rom. 10,3b) and that in the summary of Eph. 21,2e he qualifies him as " our common hope ", it is very likely that the last farewell formula in Eph* was: ἔρρωσθε ἐν χάριτι θεοῦ ᾽Ιησοῦ Χριστοῦ, τῆς κοινῆς ἐλπίδος ἡμῶν.

(4) *Pol.*, finally, contains, with some repetitions, the rest of the *personal* greetings of the original ending of Ephesians. (a) The first sentence (Pol. 8,2a) probably followed the *collective* greetings in Sm. 13,2a to Tavia's family, once eliminated the transition created by the interpolator (ἀσπάζομαι πάντας ἐξ ὀνόματος). Note, in fact, that Sm. 13,2c-end contains a similar expression which is more in accord with Ignatius' style [226] and better placed that in Pol. [227] (b) In the following sentence (8,2b), the *particular* greet-

---

[226] Insofar as in other two instances the interpolator still uses the construction ἐξ ὀνόματος (Eph. 20,2 and Pol. 4,2).

[227] In Pol. it is placed at the beginning of the greetings; in Sm., at the end. It is logical that a long enumeration of personal greetings should conclude with a global one; " and (I greet) all by name ".

ings to individuals start: " I greet Attalus my beloved. " (c) He then goes on to greet the fortunate man chosen for the mission to Syria, to whom he wishes the favour of God all the way (8,2cd). The extension of this favour to Polycarp is manifestly an interpolation. Note the ingenuous way he inserts the forced mention of Polycarp (in brackets): ἔσται ἡ χάρις μετ' αὐτοῦ διὰ παντὸς [καὶ τοῦ πέμποντος αὐτὸν Πολυκάρπου] (see n. 230). (d) After the first farewell formula, nevertheless, there comes the greeting to *Alce* (8,3c), whom we already know (Sm. 13,2c), followed by the second farewell formula. This greeting is a doublet, deliberately repeated by the interpolator to make believe there is a connection between the letters to the Sm. and to Pol.

As for the *double farewell formula*, in Pol. contrary to Sm., the *first is authentic*: note the second person plural of the pronoun, applied to the *community* (ἐρρῶσθαι ὑμᾶς); the *inclusion* of διὰ παντὸς with 8,2d and the *archaism* ἐν θεῷ ἡμῶν Ἰησοῦ Χριστῷ (see n. 49). But the *second* is a *copy* of Sm. 13,2d.

55. Once weighed up the authenticity or falsehood of the greetings and farewell formulas in the four letters, it is now possible to attempt, very approximately, the *reconstruction of the greetings and farewell formulas of the original letter to the Ephesians*.

Note, to begin with, that, unlike the other three authentic letters, in *Eph** there are no greetings from the communities present in Smyrna, but only one from Philo. Thus, in *Mg.* 15a.e he says: " Some Ephesians from Smyrna send you greetings... and the other communities, too, greet you "; in *Tr.* 12,1 he details: " I greet you from Smyrna, together with the communities of God that are present with me... ", and again in 13,1a: " The Smyrnaeans and the Ephesians send you loving greetings "; lastly, in *Rom.* 9,3 he says: " I send you my personal greetings, and the communities who have welcomed me in the name of the Messiah Jesus also send their loving greetings... ".

What is this omission due to? From the moment he landed in Ephesus up to the time he sailed for Rome, the Ephesians remained with him helping him in every way. In gratitude Ignatius wrote them a long letter, once the delegates from Magnesia and Tralles had returned with their respective letters, as we gather from the fact that it is only in Eph* that we have the good news from his Syrian community and the bare mention of Philo's

greeting. Thus can be explained the brevity of Tr., a simple
sketch of the themes he hoped to develop more fully in Eph*,
Rom. being the first letter he wrote, because of the urgency of its
message and the remoteness of the addressees.

According to the data gathered from the previous analysis,
the *probable sequence* of greetings and farewell formulas in Eph*
are as follows:

   (1) *Greetings from Philo*:

" Philo, who is here with me, greets you " (Sm. 13,1c).

   (2) *Greetings to the families*:

" I greet Tavia's family — I pray she may be steadfast [228] in faith and
love, both human and divine " (Sm. 13,2ab) — " as also the widow [229]
of Epitropus, with her family and children " (Pol. 8,2a).

   (3) *Greetings to individuals* (first series):

" I greet Attalus my beloved (Pol. 8,2b). I greet the man who shall
be held worthy to go to Syria: the favour (of God) shall be with him
all the way " (8,2cd).[230]

   (4) *First farewell formula*:

" I wish that you be always strengthened by our God, Jesus the Messiah, so that you abide in the unity of God and under his oversight "
(Pol. 8,3ab).

---

[228] LIGHTFOOT, *AA. FF.* II: II/1, 325, observes that the form ἑδρᾶσθαι, for
ἡδρᾶσθαι, is possible. In this case it should be translated: " she may remain steadfast ". Similar Ignatian expressions in Eph. 10,2 and Sm. = Eph* 1,1.

[229] See n. 224. The suture between Sm. and Pol. is perfect once eliminated
the transition (in brackets) coined by the interpolator in Pol.: Ἀσπάζομαι τὸν
οἶκον Ταουὶας... (Sm.) [ἀσπάζομαι πάντας ἐξ ὀνόματος] καὶ τὴν τοῦ Ἐπιτρόπου
σὺν ὅλῳ τῷ οἴκῳ αὐτῆς καὶ τῶν τέκνων (Pol.).

[230] The interpolator adds: " *and with the one who sends him, Polycarp* ". Ign.
had written to the Ephesians that the community (τὴν ἐκκλησίαν) should appoint
an ambassador to go as far as Syria (Sm. = Eph* 11,2b). In Phld. the forger has
simply paraphrased this request (Phld. 10,1bc). In Pol. 7,2ab, however, he has
changed it slightly, so that Polycarp was charged to convoke " *a most venerable
plenary meeting* " (συμβούλιον ἀγαγεῖν θεοπρεπέστατον). Now it results that it is
not the community but Polycarp who sends him (τοῦ πέμποντος), thus anticipating
what he will interpolate in Pol. Phil. 13,1: " *And this I will do at once as soon as
I get a fit opportunity — either myself, or by someone whom I shall send* (ὃν πέμπω)
to be ambassador on your behalf also."

(5) *Greetings to the individuals* (second series):

" I greet Alce, a person very dear to me (Pol. 8,3c: see n. 225), and Daphnus, the incomparable, and Eutecnus, and all by name " (Sm. 13,2c).

(6) *Second farewell formula*:

" May you be strengthened by the favour of God " (Sm. 13,2d) " Jesus the Messiah, our common hope " (Eph. 21,2e).[230bis]

Once the personalized greetings that were distributed between Sm. and Pol. have converged in Eph* it becomes evident that this letter to the Ephesians is the only one containing greetings to definite persons. Naturally, since Ephesus is the only city — with the exception of Smyrna, from whence the letters were written — in which Ignatius made a brief stay on his way from Syria.

Thus we have come to the end of this first part. For the moment we have limited ourselves to analyzing those passages that, in some way, could affect the s t r u c t u r e of the authentic Ignatian letters. In the second part we shall determine the extent of the interpolation, its motivation and themes.

We have now to draw up a balance sheet of results. In presenting the conclusions, we shall give a general idea of the fresh image we have of I g n a t i u s through his authentic letters, compared with the deformation the f o r g e r gives us through the interpolated ones.

IV. CONCLUSIONS

(1) *Ignatius' identity*: *the bishop of the province of Syria.* — I g n a t i u s was not properly speaking the bishop of Antioch, in the technical sense of monarchical bishop, resident in an important city, with jurisdiction over the urban and sub-urban communities. Ignatius introduces himself in Rom. 2,2 as " the bishop

---

[230bis] The interpolator has cut up the original phrase, ἔρρωσθε ἐν χάριτι θεοῦ Ἰησοῦ Χριστοῦ..., leaving in Sm. ἔρρωσθε ἐν χάριτι θεοῦ and referring θεοῦ to God the Father in Eph., by separating him from Jesus Christ: ἔρρωσθε ἐν θεῷ πατρὶ καὶ ἐν Ἰησοῦ Χριστῷ...

of Syria " (τὸν ἐπίσκοπον Συρίας), as the administrator, coordinator and supervisor of the communities scattered throughout the Roman province of Syria, possibly residing in Antioch (nrs. 3-7). The denomination " Syria ", standing alone, occurred twelve times in the authentic letters of Ignatius [231]; " bishop ", only in Rom. 2,2.

Neither was *Polycarp* properly speaking bishop of Smyrna. But, as we learn from the ocular testimony of Irenaeus, he was established by some of the Apostles as overseer or inspector for the whole province of Asia from the community residing in Smyrna (κατασταθεὶς εἰς τὴν 'Ασίαν ἐν τῇ ἐν Σμύρνῃ ἐκκλησίᾳ ἐπίσκοπος) (nr. 36). In the same way, according to Eusebius, *Irenaeus* was called to Gaul to exercise the function of overseer of the communities scattered over the Roman province of Gaul (see n. 139).

The f o r g e r supposes a much more evolved ecclesiology, since he places bishops in all the major cities of the provinces of Syria and Asia (nrs. 4f., 43f.). Because, however, he was unaware of the Ignatian letter to the Rom., he ignores that Ignatius was " the bishop of Syria " (Rom. 2,2). For this reason he does not identify him with the bishop (Eph. 3,2), but rather with the community (5,3), and places him with the deacons both in collective enumerations (Phld. 4c; Sm. 12,2; Mg. 6,1) and when he refers to a deacon in the singular (Eph. 2,1; Mg. 2a) (see nrs. 8f.). Carried away by repeated signs of humility in the conclusions of the authentic letters (Eph. 21,2; Sm. = Eph* 11,1; Mg. 14e; Tr. 13,1; Rom. 9,2), he assigns to the martyr Ignatius the lowest grade of deacon and locates him in Antioch in Syria, thus correcting the phrase " the church that is in Syria " of the authentic letters (see n. 231) with " the church that is in *Antioch of* Syria ", only to be found in the spurious letters [232]. In fact, in the letters there is no mention of Ignatius' succession, unlike Ps.-Ignatius (end of IV century) who names Heron as future bishop of Antioch of

---

[231] Namely: 4x in *Rom.* (2,2; 5,1; 9,1; 10,2); 5x in *Eph** (Eph. 1,2; 21,2 [Sm. 11,1]; original of Phld. 10,1a [Pol. 7,1]; Sm. 11,2 [Pol. 7,2]; Pol. 8,2); 2x in *Mg** (Mg. 14d.g) and 1x in *Tr.* (13,1). Another important datum is that " Syria " qualifies 4x the " church " in the *conclusion of each of the authentic letters*: Rom. 9,1; Eph. 21,2; Mg. 14d and Tr. 13,1. " The church of Syria " includes all the communities that are under the " supervision " of the bishop of Syria.

[232] Namely: Phld. 10,1; Sm. 11,1 and Pol. 7,1, the three letters attributed to Troas.

Syria (nr. 44). The forger's tendency to attribute any sort of service to the deacon's office is to be seen in the election of Burrhus, a deacon according to Eph. 2,1, chosen to carry the letters to the Phld. and Sm./Pol. (Phld. 11,2 and Sm. 12,1), and in the assignment of " deacon of Cilicia "[233] to Philo (Phld. 11,1), one of the messengers who, according to Sm. 10,1, came from Syria.

The fact that the forger was unaware of Ignatius' true identity proves that, when Ignatius passed through Asia, ecclesiastical titles were not appreciated so much as fidelity to the Gospel sealed with martyrdom. It also proves that the interpolator did not come from Syria and that he had not been in Rome. His knowledge of the three Ignatian letters sent to three Asian communities (Eph*, Mg* and Tr*), makes it probable that he came from that province.

(2) *Ignatius' route* : *Syria → Ephesus → Smyrna → Rome.* — I g n a t i u s was denounced to the Romans and had been condemned to die devoured by the wild beasts in the Roman amphitheatre for being a " Christian ". Loaded down with chains he was transported from Syria to Rome, escorted by a detachment of ten soldiers, who like leopards harassed him day and night, on land and at sea, and became enraged like beasts at the slightest sign of deference shown them by the prisoner (Rom. 5,1: nr. 46). Probably in Seleucia, after a short (if he travels by way of Antioch) or long journey (if he comes from the interior of the province) he boards a ship sailing to Ephesus. The special security precautions that surrounded him, and Ignatius' total silence about other companions of his fate, emphasize the importance the Romans gave to his person. In Ephesus Ignatius took contact with various members of the community. Since there was no ship there leaving for Italy, he was obliged to go overland to Smyrna where there were some. To relieve his sufferings as far as possible, the Ephesians decided to send five representatives to Smyrna (Onesimus, Burrhus, Crocus, Euplus and Fronto). His stay in Ephesus

---

[233] Compare Eph. 2,1: Περὶ δὲ τοῦ συνδούλου μου Βούρρου, τοῦ κατὰ θεὸν διακόνου ὑμῶν with Phld. 11,1: Περὶ δὲ Φίλωνος τοῦ διακόνου ἀπὸ Κιλικίας... ὃς καὶ νῦν ἐν λόγῳ θεοῦ ὑπηρετεῖ μοι. Note the equivalence between " my fellow servant " and " (he) who also now assists me in the ministry of God's word " (see Tr. 2,3).

must have been very short, since he had not even time to write
to the Romans.   On the way, the nearest Christian communities
went out to meet him, and the more distant ones (Magnesians and
Trallians), hearing from the Ephesians, also decided to send delegates (Damas, Bassus, Apollonius and Zotion from Magnesia;
Polybius from Tralles) who went before him to Smyrna (αἱ μὴ
προσήκουσαί μοι τῇ ὁδῷ, τῇ κατὰ σάρκα, κατὰ πόλιν με προήγαγον,
Rom. 9,3). [234]

From Smyrna he wrote letters to each of the communities
who showed their affection by sending delegates and overwhelming
him with attentions (Mg*, Tr* and Eph*, probably in this order).
Before this he had sent a letter to the members of the Roman community, making use of the Ephesians who had come with him to
Smyrna as couriers (Rom. 10,1).   He dated his letter the day it
was written: 24 August (10,3), so that the Romans might have
some idea of the day of his arrival.   Ignatius begs them warmly
not to put obstacles in his way out of love for his person (1,2),
nor to show inopportune signs of good will towards him (4,1);
they should not hinder him from " living " and belonging to God,
by making him return to the world and the seductions of material
things and wishing him " death " (6,2).   In a word, he asks them
to keep silence: their silence would mean that he could become
" word of God "; their signs of affection shown in their efforts
to save him from martyrdom, would turn him again into a mere
" voice ", devoid of the efficacy that involves witness (2,1) [235].

---

[234] Commentators, influenced by the tour the forger makes Ign. take through
Philadelphia to Smyrna, usually interpret this passage of Rom. taking κατὰ πόλιν
distributively: the communities that did not go out to meet him on the way, because they were too far away, went before him *from city to city* (ZAHN, *I. v. A.*
254ff.; *PP. AA.* II 69; LIGHTFOOT, *AA. FF.* II: II/1, 232; BAUER, *W. z. N. T.*, s. v.
κατά; *AA. VV.* II 253, etc.).   It can be understood, however, also in a *spatial* sense
(motion *to* a place): went before him *to the city*. See Lk. 10,32f.; Acts 8,26; 16,
7; 27,7. Likewise all accept the reading προῆγον of GMΣ, while gL and, as it
seems, AAmSm (see LIGHTFOOT, *AA. FF.* II: II/1, 231) read προήγαγον.   In the
original road taken by Ign. from Ephesus to Smyrna the distributive interpretation does not hold.   But the spatial one seems very likely: the communities of
Magnesia and Tralles which could not go out to meet him by the way, went before
him to the city of Smyrna.   This interpretation fits in with the news of delegates
coming from these cities.   The change from aorist to imperfect seems due to the
distributive interpretation.

[235] See the note of LELONG, *PP. AA.* III 57.

Where does this insistent invitation to the Roman community to keep silence, come from? Did they know Ignatius (*Egnatius*! Lat.; Ἰγνάτιος Gr.; *Nurono* Syr.: his name is of Latin origin) [236] was a Roman citizen? [237] Had Ignatius hidden his condition so that they would not commute his punishment, and does he now fear the Roman Christians would reveal it? From the tone of the letter they could prevent his being condemned to the beasts.

From Smyrna onwards, we lose track of him. The delegates of the Asian communities had returned to their respective churches, each one with a letter from Ignatius. Of the envoys from the Ephesians, some had gone to Rome with the letter to the Romans and others had returned to Ephesus with Eph*. This was the last one written by Ignatius. In fact, only Philo (perhaps also the other messengers from Syria) was with him at the time he wrote his greetings (nr. 53,3d).

The f o r g e r makes considerable changes in Ignatius' route. According to him, the journey of the prisoner Ignatius (remember he is unaware of his precarious situation, described in Rom. 5,1) is more than anything a triumphal way. His starting point was Antioch of Syria. In Seleucia he sailed for a port in Pamphilia (better than Cilicia) [238], Perge or Attalia. From there he would have gone on to Antioch in Pisidia following the κοινὴ ὁδός as far as Laodicea. At the crossroads, instead of taking the usual road through Tralles, Magnesia and Ephesus, he would have gone by way of Hierapolis, Philadelphia and Sardes. In Sardes once again he would have left the main road and stopped at Smyrna. From there he would have travelled to Troas. At Troas he would sail for Neapolis, the port of Philippi, proceeding by the *Via Egnatia* across Macedonia to the Adriatic Sea (Dyrrhachium). [239]

According to the present (Middle) recension, then, Ignatius did not pass through Ephesus (to obtain this effect the original conclusion of Eph* was divided between Sm. and Pol.: see nrs. 52-

---

[236] See LIGHTFOOT, *AA. FF.* II: I 22-25 (ZAHN, *I. v. A.* 73f.). Would Θεοφόρος be his second, Christian, name?

[237] LELONG, *PP. AA.* III, p. I, rejects this hypothesis, because Ign. was condemned to the wild beasts (*En questio!*). S. L. DAVIES, *The Predicament of Ignatius of Antioch*: *V. Ch.* 30 (1976) 175-180, also rejects it.

[238] ZAHN, *I. v. A.* 253.

[239] ZAHN, *I. v. A.* 260ff.

55), but through Philadelphia instead (Phld. 7 and 11,1); he did not embark in Smyrna, but went on by Troas towards Neapolis and Philippi. The reason of this change is obvious: to validate the fresh compilation with the authority of Polycarp's letter to the Philippians, it was necessary to have Ignatius pass through Philippi. The mysterious motive of his visit to Philadelphia will become clear later on.

(3) *Authentic letters: Rom., Mg*, Tr* and Eph**. — I g n a t i u s wrote several letters on his way to martyrdom. His motives for doing so were varied and corresponded with the concerns that arose from his particular situation: (a) To *warn* the Asian communities, with which he had been in contact in Ephesus and Smyrna, about the dangerous teachings of the Gnostics or Judaizers who had caused such grave divisions in the church of Syria (Sm. = Eph* 4,1; Mg. 11; Tr. 8,1); (b) To *prevent* the Romans from using their influence to stand in the way of his condemnation being executed (Rom. passim); (c) To *congratulate* the Syrian community for having reached a safe port after the storm (Sm. = Eph* 11,2-3); d) To *write* to all the churches and to insist all men that he *gives his life willingly for God* (Rom. 4,1).

The letter addressed to the church of *Syria* (Sm. = Eph* 11,3) has not been preserved (nr. 31,5, and n. 121). *Rom.* has come down to us by a double channel: (a) Inserted in the Antiochene Acts of the Martyrdom, independently of the other letters, or in the last position in the mixed compilation of Ussher (after the six letters of the Middle recension and the five letters of the Long one); (b) In the last position also in the mixed compilation that was the basis of the oriental translations (x = SAB and probably C), after the letters of the Middle recension. Its independent transmission or its coming last in the lists show that this letter, destined for Rome, did not form part of the primitive compilation of Asian letters. [240] Therefore it could not have been tampered with.

---

[240] See what is said in the introduction, pp. 21ff. K. LAKE, *Apostolic Fathers* I, London 1975, p. 280f., sums up the question very well: " It is interesting to notice that the one epistle which neither Polycarp nor the Philippians could easily obtain would be that to the Romans, and that it is this letter which in the Ignatian MSS. seems to have had a different textual history from that of the other six."

Of the Ignatian letters written to the *Asian* communities, only three are authentic: *Mg**, actually divided between Mg. (first part + conclusion) and Phld. (second part) (nrs. 22-29); *Tr**, basis of the present Tr., very short but complete, a kind of thematic sketch for Eph*; *Eph**, which can be reconstructed from Eph. (first part) and Sm. (second part + conlusion, completed in turn with the conclusion of Pol.) (nrs. 10, 18-21).

We do not know if Ignatius wrote any other letters. All those of the Long recension that have no corresponding ones in the Middle recension are spurious.

The four authentic letters were written in *Smyrna*. The delegates of each community to Smyrna had undertaken to see they reached their respective communities. The Ephesians undertook, besides, to take Rom. to Rome (Rom. 10,1) and the mislaid congratulatory letter to Syria (Sm. = Eph* 11,3a).

The f o r g e r gathered together the three letters circulating in the Asian province and with them composed another three. *Tr.* has only suffered interpolations and some alterations in the order of the sentences. Mg* served to create a new letter, *Phld.*, and, obviously, *Mg.* To replace the second part of the letter (destined for Phld.) he created the interrupting clause of Mg. 13 (nrs. 25-28). To give a heading to the two letters he divided the inscription of Mg* between Mg. and Phld. (nr. 29). The conclusion of Mg* had to be left in Mg. 14-15 (nr. 35). In the same way, Eph* was distributed between *Eph.* and *Sm.*; creating for it another interrupting clause (Eph. 20). So abrupt was the interruption that the forger was obliged to soften it by promising a continuation in a second letter (nrs. 10f.: see 18-21). The conclusion of Eph* served as a conclusion for both Sm., Polycarp's community, and Pol. in its second part; a short summary remained in Eph.; for Phld. he composed a copy (nrs. 30-34, 45-51 and 52f.).

Once the compilation was ready, he tried to authenticate it by inserting the famous chapter 13 into Polycarp's letter to the Philippians. Thus he sanctioned not only Ignatius' meeting with Polycarp, but also the order of the letters and the compilation itself, distinguishing between letters Ignatius sent to Polycarp (Sm. and Pol.) and the other letters the latter had collected (Eph., Mg., Tr. and Phld.). This order is still reflected in the present compilations (see nr. 41 and the introduction). Much later on, Ps.-

Ignatius will do the same, interpolating over again letters of the Middle recension (Rom. was already part of the so-called Eusebian compilation) and enlarging the collection with spurious letters thus making up the Long recension.

Our forger respected Smyrna as the place where the three letters preserving the original title were written (Mg., Tr. and Eph.) and invented a second place of writing, *Troas*, for the letters with spurious titles (Phld., Sm. and Pol.). Inadvertently he changed the original address of Ignatius' community, Syria, characteristic of the letters from Smyrna (including Rom.), to *Antioch of* Syria, kept exclusively for the letters from Troas. Ps.-Ignatius will do the same reserving Smyrna and Troas for the letters he considers authentic and creating new places of writing for the spurious ones.

(4) *Twofold subject of the Asian letters: anti-Gnostic (Tr* and Eph*) and anti-Judaizing (Mg*).* — The subject of the letters sent to the Asian communities is twofold: anti-Gnostic in Tr. and Eph. + Sm. and anti-Judaizing in Mg. + Phld. I g n a t i u s distinguishes adequately the Docetic-Gnostics from the Judaizers, but he fights them with the same weapons: (a) Warning the Asian communities beforehand against their propaganda; (b) Urging the communities to a shared experience of the reality of the Lord's body in the Eucharistic celebration; (c) Stigmatizing both heretics and schismatics with the same invectives, as offspring of the Chief of this world (nr. 17).

The f o r g e r has not gone directly into the problematic of the letters. Unlike Ps.-Ignatius, who incorporates the new heresies of his time, he limits himself to transcribing Ignatius' past polemics against the Gnostics and Judaizers. His are other preoccupations. What worries our interpolator is the problem of order and the organization of the community, as we shall see in the second part. This theme is reflected in the first half of the letter to Pol., which is addressed in the singular to the bishop of Smyrna. The second half, on the other hand, belongs in great part to the original conclusion of Ephesians.

(5) *Ignatius knew the Ephesian community.* — I g n a t i u s passed through Ephesus and came into contact with the large Christian community there. The personal and detailed news of the

primitive conclusion of Ephesians (reconstructed from Eph., Sm. and Pol., and subject to control thanks to the copy of Phld.: nrs. 30-34 and 52-55) shows that Ignatius took occasion to greet several members of the community. It is not unlikely that he already knew them previously. Ephesus was probably the port of arrival for the ship coming from Syria. The journey overland from Ephesus to Smyrna is due to the fact that the ship did not go on to Rome; but in Smyrna it was another that was about to set sail for Italy. It does not appear that Ignatius spent much time in Ephesus. In fact all his letters are written from Smyrna.

The original letter to the Ephesians contains several allusions to Ignatius' visit there: (a) Once the Ephesians were informed by the messengers who went before Ignatius from Syria to Rome (Rom. 10,2), they hastened to see him and overwhelm him with attentions (Eph. 1,1-2); (b) When Ignatius left for Smyrna, they chose five delegates to go with him (1,3-2,1; 21,1), the latter brought him up-to-date on the community situation (6,2: Onesimus) and its resistance to heretical propagandists (9,1: see Sm. = Eph* 1,1; 4,1); (c) Ephesus was traditionally "the gateway (πάροδος) of those who go through martyrdom to God" (Eph. 12,2); (d) The Ephesians always showed their affection towards Ignatius, "whether present or absent", with all kinds of attentions (Sm. = Eph* 9,2), just as they did for the messengers coming from Syria (10,1); (e) In fact, the prayers Ignatius asked on his way through Ephesus for his church in Syria, had the effect of pacifying the Syrian community (Phld. = Eph* 10,1a ~ Pol. 7,1a). For this reason he begged them to complete the work they had begun with him (Eph. 1,1) by sending an embassy to Syria (Sm. = Eph* 11,2 and Pol. = Eph* 7,3). This is confirmed by the personal greetings in the actual conclusion of Sm. and Pol.

The f o r g e r, however, has no particular interest in the fact that Ignatius passed through Ephesus and needed the personal news of the original conclusion to make Ignatius' meeting with Polycarp and the Smyrnaean community more realistic. For this reason he divided the conclusion of Eph* between Sm. and Pol. (nrs. 52f.). In the same way, to give the impression that Ignatius passed through Philadelphia, he composed the conclusion of Phld. by copying those of Sm. and Pol. (nrs. 32-34). In Eph. he left a brief summary (nrs. 30f.).

The supposed disputes with schismatic elements in Philadelphia are a pure invention of the forger. The autobiographical
notes in Phld. = Mg* 6,3 and 8,2 do not necessarily imply that
Ignatius stayed in Magnesia. The first (Phld. 6,3) refers to the
contents of the letter (see Tr. 12,3). The second (Phld. 8,2) to
a discussion started by Ignatius with the Judaizers, without precise
indication of place. Most probably it alludes to the critical situation created in Syria that ended in his condemnation.

For the rest, Ignatius' journey through Magnesia would have
left some trace in the conclusion. But, like Tr., this contains only
general greetings to the community.

By distributing Mg* between Mg. and Phld., he took special
care to make an exception in Mg. 11 ('' Not because I have learned that any of you behave in this way ... '') that we also found
in Eph* (Sm. 4,1) and Tr. (8,1). Thus he freed himself to work
up a public discussion between Ignatius and his opponents (note
the imitation of the above-mentioned clause in Phld. 7,2). To
make this divergence of opinions more evident, it is taken for granted
that there was also difference of view on the welcome given to the
envoys from Cilicia and Syria (Phld. 11,1: copy of Sm. = Eph*
10,1).

The forgery of the letter to the Philadelphians, the interest
the forger has in making Ignatius pass through Philadelphia and
the twofold mention of schismatic elements disturbing unity, would
suggest that the interpolator of the Ignatian letters came precisely
from Philadelphia, and that he had difficulties with some members
of the community. We shall be able to clarify this further in the
second part of this study.

(6) *Ignatius did not know Polycarp.* — The progressive un-
covering of the forger's methods has led to a quite unexpected
discovery, that is, that the relationship between Ignatius and Polycarp are a pure fabrication of the forger and that there is a reason
for them: to have the compilation placed under Polycarp's authority and, thus, to vouch for the division of the authentic letters
and the interpolation itself.

Nevertheless, from the authentic letters it can be deduced
that I g n a t i u s passed through Asia at a time when Smyrna
hardly counted as a community (see nr. 43). Smyrna, as we learn

from Polycarp himself (Pol. Phil. 11,3), is not a Pauline founda-
tion.   Ephesus, on the contrary, has a flourishing community of
Pauline origin (Eph. 11,2 and 12,2).   But according to Irenaeus,
Polycarp, the bishop of Asia, resided in Smyrna (nr. 36).   Between
Ignatius and Polycarp there had also been a notable spread of
Christianity towards the North and, concretely, of the commu-
nity of Smyrna.

Ephesus, however, at the time Ignatius passed that way, was
full of vitality, and this is perfectly reflected in his letters: (a) Sending of delegates to Smyrna; (b) Readiness to be sent as messengers
to Rome and Syria as much in the name of the community as in
Ignatius' name; (c) Care for Ignatius, whether present or absent,
and for the messengers come after him from Syria; (d) Firmness
in the true doctrine, overlooking and turning a deaf ear to the
propagandists from Syria; etc. (see nr. 50,3).

Among persons mentioned in the authentic Ignatian letters,
outstanding are Crocus, probably known to the Romans (Rom.
10,1: see also Eph. 2,1), and Onesimus, first on the list of delegates
(Eph. 1,3) and spokesman for the group (6,2), both of them Ephesians.

The f o r g e r has built up the whole scheme of his forged
letters and interpolation of the authentic text on presumed friendly
relationship between Ignatius and Polycarp: (a) By composing a
new letter addressed to the Smyrnaeans, Polycarp's community
(nrs. 18-21); (b) By creating a brand new letter addressed to Polycarp (nrs. 44-51); (c) By inserting two brief references to Polycarp
in Eph. and Mg. (nrs. 42f.); (d) By distributing the conclusion of
Eph* between Sm. and Pol. to pretend that Ignatius was very familiar with Polycarp and his Smyrnaean community (nrs. 30f. and
46-53); (e) By interpolating Polycarp's letter to the Philippians,
after having altered Ignatius' itinerary to pass by way of Troas and
Philippi (nrs. 39-41).

(7) *Occasion of Ignatius' condemnation*: *persecution or internal
strife*?. — It is fairly unanimously held by scholars that Ignatius
died during the persecution of Trajan.   In fact, the dating of the
letters has always been based on this hypothesis.   However, there
have been some discordant views.   W. BAUER, on Ignatius' repeated invitations to the Asian leaders, the Philippians and Poly-

carp, brings out the internal struggles that arose in Antioch between orthodoxy and heterodoxy. [241]   But P. N. HARRISON in particular outlined the problem on the Ignatian text, especially the
meaning of εἰρηνεύειν, up to then understood from the viewpoint
of persecution, as if this were the only possible interpretation.
These are his conclusions: (a) εἰρηνεύω, in the setting of primitive
Christian literature (N.T., AA.FF.), usually means "to be at
peace with one another" and is never used in this period to express the cessation of a persecution. [242]   (b) For instance, the
passage of Sm. 11,2, from whence we have motives of "pacification", can scarcely refer to the restoration of the community
as a body decimated by persecution, but rather to the "recovery
of its own strength and the re-establishment of its corporate body"
(ὅτι ... ἀπέλαβον τὸ ἴδιον μέγεθος καὶ ἀπεκατεστάθη αὐτοῖς τὸ ἴδιον
σωματεῖον). [243]   (c) Lastly, Sm. 11,3 speaks of the calm that returned after the storm and the fact of having already reached
a sure port. [244]   J. A. FISCHER rejects this interpretation and emphasizes the repeated expressions in which Ignatius introduces
himself as "the last of the church of Syria" and the insistence
with which the martyr has all the communities of Asia and Syria
make contact with the church of Antioch. [245]   Seeing the results
obtained and the conclusions we have just synthesized, I g n a -
t i u s ' text takes on new light and postulates the re-opening of
nearly all the problems relative to his person and his work.   In
the concrete case that concerns us, the textual evidence supports
the hypothesis whereby Ignatius was not a victim of a persecution

---

[241] W. BAUER, *Rechtgläubigkeit und Ketzerei im ältesten Christentum*, Tübingen
[2]1964, p. 68f.

[242] HARRISON, *Polycarp* 83f.

[243] HARRISON, *Polycarp* 86f.: "Now, to Ignatius' way of thinking, a body of
which some members were temporarily cut off from the rest by banishment or
imprisonment would not really have *lost* them, nor they it (...) On the other hand
any severance due to alienation of spirit must involve *real* loss. And that loss
would be mutual. And a reunion which meant a return to loyalty *would* "restore"
such members to the whole body, and it to them. Such a victory for the peace-
makers, and defeat of the mischief-makers, would indeed seem to Ignatius an
answer to his prayers and to the prayers of all who had shared his grief over those
unhappy divisions." See H. PAULSEN, *Studien* 143 ff.

[244] HARRISON, *Polycarp* 87f.

[245] FISCHER, *AA. VV.* 203.

unchained in Antioch, but of the internal quarrels brought about
by the Gnostic and Judaizing factions at the heart of the communities of the Syrian province. Let us see the more important
arguments:

(a) The allusion to the envoys from Syria (Philo, Gaius and
Agathopus) makes its appearance for the first and only time in
Eph* (actually in Sm. 10,1: imitated by Phld. 11,1). In the rest
of the letters written earlier, Ignatius limits himself to asking for
prayers for his church of Syria (Mg. 14; Tr. 13,1; Rom. 9,1).
The arrival of the envoys has altered the situation. Their mission, in fact, was to bring news of the pacification brought about
in the Syrian community, which had arisen from their repentance
after the bishop's condemnation (Phld. = Eph* 10,1a [correct-
ed] ~ Pol. 7,1a). In the original conclusion of Eph*, mention of
the messengers (Φίλωνα κτλ.) preceded the notification of his message (Ἐπειδὴ κτλ.) (nrs. 31,1.4, 33f., 50,1; reconstruction on nr. 53AC).

(b) Ignatius being relieved by this news (Pol. = Eph* 7,1b),
asked the Ephesians as a body to choose someone who would
take a message of congratulations to Syria (Sm. = Eph* 11,2:
imitated in Pol. 7,2 and Phld. 10,1b-2). He, too, did so by sending one of the Ephesians to Syria with his personal letter of congratulations (Sm. = Eph* 11,3 + Pol. = Eph* 7,3) (nrs. 31,4-5, 50,3).

(c) All the motivations of this petition to the Ephesians and
of Ignatius' letter to the church of Syria allude: (α) To the precarious situation in which it was left after Ignatius' condemnation; (β) To the restoration of peace, strength and the communitarian body, damaged through internal divisions (nrs. 50 and
31,4).

(d) All indications scattered through Ignatius' authentic letters support this hypothesis: (α) Ignatius' concern for the church
of Syria (nrs. 3, 30, 31,2-3); (β) His trust in Jesus the Messiah,
the only shepherd and supervisor (Rom. 9,1: see nr. 44); (γ) His
feeling of lowliness and littleness (nr. 31,2, and n. 116; nr. 35);
(δ) His constant exhortations to the Asian communities to warn
them against false missionaries (Mg. 11; Tr. 8,1; Sm. = Eph*
4,1) coming from Syria (Eph. 9,1), like wolves trying to pass as
believers (Phld. 2,2) and biting furtively like rabid dogs (Eph.
7,1; Sm. 4,1), weeds of the devil (Eph. 10,3; Tr. 6,1; Phld. 3,1),
vile offshoots that engender a deadly fruit (Tr. 11,1), a deadly

drug mixed with honeyed wine (Tr. 6,2); (ε) His insistent urging that they seek unity in the community meeting, in the praise and thanksgiving, in the experience of the Body and Blood of Jesus the Messiah, thus making up a single body, a single temple and a single altar (Eph. 4,2; 5,2-3; 13,1; Sm. = Eph* 7,1; Mg. 7,1c-2; Phld. = Mg* 4ab; Tr. 6,1; 7,2ab; Rom. 7,3 and Tr. 8,1).

(e) Except for the Old Testament Prophets (Mg. 8,2) or for Jesus (Tr. 9,1), he speaks of no one as having been persecuted. There is no mention of other martyrs who were with him or who followed in his footsteps (Phld. 11,1f is a recasting of the original text of Sm. 10,1b). The description in Rom. 5,1 is surprising: ten soldiers to watch over one prisoner. So this is someone important for the Romans. The nature of Rom. supposes that there is not open persecution and that he could be freed through influential intermediaries.

(f) The reason of his condemnation is that he " is a Christian " (Eph. 1,2; 3,1; Tr. 1,1; Rom. 1,1). But what brought about his imprisonment? Denunciation by dissidents, or more likely, a public disturbance due to internal discord, that led to upsetting order in the province of Syria? Were the Romans forced to intervene, demanding the head of the one mainly responsible? In Rom. 4,1 Ignatius says textually: " I am writing to all the churches and insisting to all men that I give my life willingly (ἑκών) for God ". But it is more explicit in Sm. = Eph* 4,2: " And why then have I delivered myself over to death (τί δὲ καὶ ἐαυτὸν ἔκδοτον δέδωκα τῷ θανάτῳ), to (perish) by fire or sword or wild beasts? ". The only plausible explanation is that Ignatius has delivered himself over to the authorities spontaneously as wholly responsible for the uproar. Of the three kinds of death he might have had, the Romans condemned him to be devoured by the wild beasts in Rome.

The f o r g e r interpreted it as a persecution, but without heightening the colours more than necessary. For this, he made use of various subterfuges:

(a) When he composed the conclusions of the three spurious letters from the original conclusion of Eph*, he separated the mention of the three messengers from the allusion to news received. Thus, in *Phld.* 11,1 (copy of Sm. 10,1) he delayed this news after the announcement of the pacification of the church of Antioch in Syria (Phld. 10,1a); in *Sm.* he left the news where it was (Sm. 10,1), but he suppressed the announcement of newfound peace by saying that " his prayer has already reached the church at Antioch of Syria " (11,1a); in *Pol.* he passed over the mention of the messengers, limiting himself to transcribing the news he had received without saying by whom (Pol. 7,1a).

(b) In Phld. 11,1f (copy of Sm. 10,1b) he has hinted that Agathopus has been imprisoned: " An elect man who has followed after me from Syria, having bidden farewell to this life ". He makes Philo come from Cilicia, probably to give the impression that there is a general persecution (nr. 34).

(c) In the interpolated sentence in Polycarp's letter to the Philippians (Pol. Phil. 13,2), he makes Polycarp say: " Et de ipso Ignatio et de his, qui cum eo sunt, quod certius agnoveritis, significate " (" Moreover, if you should have any certain news of Ignatius himself and his companions, let me know it "). He alludes to the prisoners who had joined him in Troas.

(d) For this he has made up an absurd procession of envoys with letters, bishops, presbyters, deacons, messengers on foot, to Antioch, coming from all the churches, from Syria (nr. 36) as well as Asia (nrs. 31,5, 33), on the part of the Philippians (nr. 40) or Polycarp himself (nrs. 41, 51).

(8) *Date: Did Ignatius write at the end of the first century?.* — Traditionally, from Eusebius' *Chronicon*, Ignatius' death and, consequently, the dating of his letters, has been connected with the persecution of Trajan. Eusebius places Ignatius' martyrdom in the tenth year of Trajan (a. D. 107), Lightfoot, after a thorough study, inclines to the years 100-118. [246] The Colbertine Martyrdom places it in the year 107; Jerome, in 109: and both depend on Eusebius.

Every attempt at fixing a date for the letters have up to now been based on two suppositions: (a) that Ignatius was victim of a persecution [247] and (b) that this persecution took place under

---

[246] *AA. FF.* II: II/1, 470 [472]. See also A. HARNACK, *Geschichte der altchristlichen Literatur bis Eusebius, II Chronologie*, vol. I, Leipzig 1897 (reprinting 1958), p. 406; FISCHER, *AA. VV.* 114f.; H. KOESTER, *Synoptische Ueberlieferung bei den apostolischen Vätern*, Berlin 1957, T. U. 65, p. 24.

[247] ORIGEN, *Hom. VI. in Lucam* (G. Ch. S. IX 34f.[37]): ἐν τῷ διωγμῷ.

Trajan. If the hypothesis of a persecution is rejected for lack of documentary evidence in flat contrast with the tone and wording of the letters, the date once more becomes uncertain.

Ignatius does not speak of *John* to the Ephesians, but he does of *Paul* (Eph. 12,2), [248] even when he seems to breathe the same milieu as John's and faces a very similar problematic (Gnosticism). [249] Much later on *Irenaeus* will consider Paul to be the founder of the Ephesian community, but he will add that John stayed in Ephesus up to the time of Trajan (μέχρι τῶν Τραϊανοῦ χρόνων), [250] basing this statement probably on Polycarp's trustworthy testimony who reported he had lived with John (τὴν μετὰ Ἰωάννου συναναστροφήν, ὡς ἀπήγγελλε). [251] Ignatius' silence implies that John was not yet in Ephesus when he passed through. In the same way, his silence about *Polycarp*, whom Irenaeus knew in his youth as a man of advanced age and who, according to the Letter of the Smyrnaeans on the Martyrdom of Polycarp (Mart. Pol. 9,3), was 86 years old when he testified, as well as the little importance Ignatius gives to Smyrna in his authentic letters, suggests a much more primitive situation with regard to the one created later on when John was in Ephesus and Polycarp had been appointed bishop of Asia with residence in Smyrna.

In fact, as Ignatius often points out, in the communities of the province of Asia (Ephesus, Magnesia, Tralles) there had *not yet* appeared the heretical (Gnostic-Docetic) or schismatic (Judaizing) deviations that had caused such a grave uproar in the province of Syria (Eph. 7,1; 8,1; 9,1; Sm. = Eph* 4,1; Mg. 11; Tr. 8,1). Speaking to his favourite community, the Ephesians, he says explicitly that they had not allowed themselves to be deceived (ὥσπερ

---

[248] LIGHTFOOT, *AA. FF.* II: II/1, 64; HARNACK, *Chronologie* I 406, n. 2: " Das negative Verhältniss zu den johanneischen Schriften bei Ignatius darf immerhin auch dafür geltend gemacht werden, mit den Briefen nicht zu weit abwärts zu gehen." Concerning the relations between Ignatius and the Pauline letters, see H. RATHKE, *Ignatius von Antiochien und die Paulusbriefe*, Berlin 1967, T. U. 99.

[249] W. VON LOEWENICH, *Das Johannes-Verständnis in zweiten Jahrhundert*, Giessen 1932, pp. 25-38; HARRISON, *Polycarp* 255-263. See also P. DIETZE, *Die Briefe des Ignatius von Antiochien und das Johannes-Evangelium*, in *Th. Studien und Kritiken*, Gotha, 4 (1905) 563-603; Ch. MAURER, *Ignatius von Antiochien und das Johannesevangelium*, Zürich 1949; FISCHER, *AA. VV.* 122.

[250] *A. H.* III. 3,4 = Eus., *E. H.* III. 23. See n. 140.

[251] *Letter to Florin.* = Eus., *E. H.* V. 20,6.

οὐδὲ ἐξαπατᾶσθε) by certain troublemakers (Eph. 8,1); and had turned a deaf ear to some agitators from Syria passing through Ephesus (παροδεύσαντάς τινας ἐκεῖθεν), who wanted to sow their evil doctrine there (9,1). Of the community of Magnesia he says that it is in perfect and orderly communion in concord with God (Mg. 1,1), while Tralles' community persevered in " an unblameable and steadfast mind " (Tr. 1,1). Thus EUSEBIUS states in his *Ecclesiastical History*: " First of all he exhorted them to take precautions against heresies, that from then on began to multiply. " [252] Bearing in mind that John, in Ephesus, was already face to face with aberrant charismatic elements (" false prophets ") who denied the human reality of Jesus the Messiah (1John 4,1-3), we are led to suppose that the historical moment in which Ignatius lived and suffered his passion was much earlier than that of John's time, since it reflects the transition period between the troubled situation in Syria and the peace of Asia.

On the other hand, Ignatius does not know the Apostles personally. Hence he prays to be found at the moment of the resurrection in the place reserved for the martyrs of Ephesus who moreover were ever of one mind with the Apostles, strengthened by Jesus the Messiah (ἵνα ἐν κλήρῳ Ἐφεσίων εὑρεθῶ τῶν Χριστιανῶν, οἱ καὶ τοῖς ἀποστόλοις πάντοτε συνήνεσαν ἐν δυνάμει Ἰησοῦ Χριστοῦ, Eph. 11,2). Ignatius considers that the Ephesians are initiated in the Christian mystery (Παύλου συμμύσται), like Paul, who was already consecrated, approved as martyr and blessed (12,2). Although obviously this refers to the Ephesian community, as is shown by the sentence in which he tells that Paul " remembers them in every letter " (*ib.*), it is not to be excluded that among the Ephesians there were some who knew Paul. For this reason he repeats three times over (Eph. 3,1; Tr. 3,3; Rom. 4,3) that he is not giving them directives like the Apostles Peter and Paul, though he still considers himself " slave " and a mere " condemned man ", but not yet a " freedman ": " But if I shall suffer martyrdom, then am I a freedman of Jesus the Messiah, and I shall rise free in his companionship " (Rom. 4,3).

Another datum to keep in mind is the imminence of the parousia, stressed twice: Eph. 11,1 (Ἔσχατοι καιροί) and Mg. 5,1 (Ἐπεὶ

---

[252] Eus., *E. H.* III. 36,4: ἐν πρώτοις μάλιστα προφυλάττεσθαι τὰς αἱρέσεις ἄρτι τότε πρῶτον ἐπιπολαζούσας παρῄνει.

οὖν τέλος τὰ πράγματα ἔχει κτλ.). It deals with the beginning of the definitive end (see Eph. 19,3).

It is difficult to date Ignatius' letters with such isolated elements. However, once cleansed from the dross introduced by the f o r g e r, the text and problematic appear very similar to the Johannine writings and the Pauline letters. It could well be that the Ignatian letters were written before the end of the first century, between the years 80 and 100.

PART TWO.

THE INTERPOLATION IN THE LETTERS OF IGNATIUS: CONTENTS, EXTENT, SYMBOLISM, AND ITS RELATIONS WITH THE DIDASCALIA APOSTOLORUM

In the first part we have subjected the letters that make up what is held today to be the textus receptus of Ignatius (Middle recension) to a detailed and rigorous analysis. Led on by an endless number of anomalies detected in the actual letters and thus alerted to the existence of newly created ex professo clauses, we have reached the conclusion that I g n a t i u s wrote only *four letters*: (1) One addressed to the *Romans* (actual Rom.), unknown to the author of the so-called Polycarpian compilation (Pol. Phil. 13), composed in Asia Minor, because of the addressees' geographical distance; (2) Three written to the Asian communities of *Magnesia* (Mg. 1-12 + Phld. 2-9 + the conclusion of Mg. 14-15), *Tralles* (present Tr., without the interpolations) and *Ephesus* (Eph. 1-19 + Sm. 1-11.13 + Pol. 6,1d-7,1.3; 8,2-3 [to complete with Eph. 21 and Phld. 10,1a]). The one addressed to the Syrian community (Sm. = Eph* 11,3) has been hopelessly mislaid.

The clauses newly created by the f o r g e r are: (1) Eph. 20: to interrupt the anti-Docetic exposition (Eph. + Sm.) of the original letter to the Ephesians; (2) Mg. 13: to interrupt the anti-Judaizing exposition (Mg. + Phld.) of the original letter to the Magnesians; (3) Phld. inscr[b].-1: to provide a heading for the freshly created letter to the Philadelphians; (4) Phld. 10-11; Sm. 12 and Pol. 7,2 and 8,1: to finish the three new letters composed by the interpolator.

Thanks to the new structuring of the authentic Ignatian letters it has been possible to reconstruct a fairly approximate picture of what happened. Let us briefly sum up the results obtained to the present.

Ignatius was the only bishop supervising the whole Roman province of Syria (Rom. 2,2) as coordinator of the various communities that made up the church of Syria (see Eph. 21,2; Mg. 14d and Tr. 13,1). The vacuum created by his condemnation would be filled by the divine pastor, Jesus the Messiah, and the communion of the Roman community (Rom. 9,1). In fact, because of a grave public uproar brought about in the church of Syria by antagonistic Gnostic and Judaizing factions, the Roman authorities decided to strike at the roots of any attempt at subversion and demanded the heads of those responsible (hint at Eph. 7,1; 9,1; Sm. 6-7 and, above all, 11,2-3; Mg. 6,2a-e; 7,1c, etc.; Phld. 6 and 8; Tr. 6). To avoid worse trouble, Ignatius has delivered himself over to the authorities spontaneously (Sm. 4,2; Rom. 4,1), and was condemned to die devoured by the wild beasts in the Roman amphitheatre (Eph. 1,2; Tr. 10; Rom. 4-5). Escorted day and night, on land and at sea, by a detachment of ten soldiers, furious like leopards against their only prisoner (Rom. 5,1), on his way through Asia, he took advantage of the delay occasioned by a probable change of ships and the forced transfer from Ephesus to Smyrna (9,3) to write to the community of Rome from this last city, making use of some of the Ephesians who had come with him to Smyrna (10,1). Ignatius earnestly begs the Christians in Rome not to interfere by seeking help from influential people (Rom. passim). In the same way he writes to the Asian communities that showed him signs of affection by sending delegates to Smyrna, to warn them against the propagandists from Syria (Eph. 9,1) trying to sow cockle in those solidly united communities which were so deeply bound together in love (Sm. = Eph* 1,1; 4,1; Mg. 11; Tr. 8,1). In the letter addressed to the Ephesians, probably the last he ever wrote, he asks them to send an embassy to Syria with a personal letter from him (Sm. = Eph* 11,2 and 3), congratulating them for the pacification reached after his condemnation, according to the news brought by the messengers of the church of Syria (10,1).

Ignatius did not know Polycarp. The forger of the so-called Polycarpian compilation made use of Polycarp's authority to authenticate his fresh compilation. By this means he pretended that Ignatius had passed by Philippi, to make a link with the clause he had inserted into Polycarp's letter to the Philippians (Pol. Phil.

13: considered today as Phil.-I because it does not fit with Phil.-II); from Troas, a new place of writing, he makes him send three letters, one to the Philadelphians and two to Polycarp and his community of Smyrna, making use of the materials obtained by dividing respectively Mg* and Eph*. The appointment of Polycarp as bishop of Smyrna on the part of the forger (Mg. 15; Pol. inscr.) contradicts the statement of Irenaeus, Polycarp's contemporary, who says he was established by the Apostles as bishop-supervisor for the whole province of Asia with residence in the community of Smyrna (*A.H.* III. 3,4). At the time of Ignatius, however, there was no such bishop in Asia. Note that Irenaeus, with Polycarp, heads the list of supervising bishops about the communities spread over the province of Asia up to the time he writes (*ibid.*).

Although there was a Christian community in Smyrna (Tr. 13,1), the authentic letters place in the foreground the care of the *Ephesian community* not only at the time of Ignatius' passing through Ephesus (Eph. 1,1-2; Sm. = Eph* 9,2; personal greetings of gratitude in Sm. = Eph* 13 and Pol. = Eph* 8,2-3) but also during his stay in Smyrna (Mg. 15; Tr. 13,1; Rom. 10,1; Sm. = Eph* 10,1 [care for the messengers coming from Syria]; 11,2-3 [sending of an embassy to Syria]; Pol. = Eph* 8,2 [greetings to the ambassador]). From whence we can infer that the most important community at that time was in the capital of Proconsular Asia.

Ignatius' silence over John in his letter to the Ephesians, where he makes explicit mention of Paul and his letters (Eph. 12,2), and the laudatory description he gives of the Asian communities in his authentic letters (Eph. 1,1; 8,1; 9; 11,2; Sm. = Eph* 1; 4,1, etc.; Mg. 1,1; 11a; 12, etc.; Tr. 1; 8,1, etc.) contrasting with the troubled situation of those same communities at the time of John, Polycarp and young Irenaeus, suggest that Ignatius' journey through Asia should be dated earlier that John's stay in Ephesus. If to this we add that the motive of his condemnation is not connected with Trajan's persecution we can shift the date of his letters and his martyrdom back to the end of the first century.

Once reconstructed the primitive s t r u c t u r e of the Ignatian letters from the textus receptus or Middle recension, we shall now treat of the c o n t e n t s (I.), e x t e n t (II.) and s y m - b o l i s m (III.) of the interpolation.

I. CONTENTS OF THE INTERPOLATION

Unlike the first part where we had to start from zero, we have now a series of passages that for internal and external critical reasons are obviously interpolated (henceforth all the interpolated passages are in italics). To state exactly the extent of the interpolation requires a preliminary systematic study of the content and constants of style and terminology of the already identified passages. We shall first analyse the interrupting clauses (Eph. 20 and Mg. 13), the beginning and ending of the spurious letters that were mere imitations (Phld. inscr[b].-1 and Sm. inscr.; Phld. 10-11 and Sm. 12), and also all that concerns the pretended relations between Ignatius and Polycarp (Pol. inscr.-6,1c; 7,2; 8,1 and Pol. Phil. 13) (§ a: nrs. 56-73). Secondly, we shall attempt to define the exact limits of those sections that contain anomalous data (§ b) because the forger did not know the true condition of Ignatius (nrs. 74-78) or because he extrapolated the ecclesiastical organization of the time of Ignatius with a much more evolved ecclesiology (nrs. 79-91).

a) *Systematic analysis of the passages already incriminated*

56. *Eph.* 20. — In the first part we have considered this passage from the point of view of its function, that is, to distract the reader from noticing that the recently started exposition (Eph. 18-19) has been interrupted so as to keep the second part of Eph* for the letter addressed to the Smyrnaeans. To discover the basic concern of the forger when he drew up this clause, we should pay attention to the strange condition to which he has subjected the sending of the " *second tract* ":

" *Especially, if the Lord should reveal to me that* [253] *you are all united down to the last man, personally and gratefully assembled in the same faith and united in Jesus Christ — who by fleshly descendance was of David's stock, son of man and Son of God, so that we may obey the bishop and presbytery with undivided minds in the breaking of one bread, which is medicine of immortality, antidote that we should not die but live in Jesus Christ forever* " (Eph. 20,2).

---

[253] ὅτι GL: See critical apparatus, p. 377, l. 25.

The text is intricate.   Commentators have realized the serious difficulties of interpreting the first phrase.   To lighten it they modify the punctuation and take ὅτι to be a textual corruption to be changed into ἔτι or simply τι. [254]   According to LIGHTFOOT, the redaction of the text " gives a sense altogether unworthy of the writer (Ignatius) and entirely opposed to his mode of speaking elsewhere (e.g. §§ 3, 6, 9, 11, 12) ". [255]   When we know his manner of proceeding it does not surprise us that the interpolator has recourse to a " revelation " to validate his demands (see for ex. Phld. 7, which we shall deal with later on).   We shall gather new elements for judging by a detailed analysis.

The sentence " *all united down to the last man* " has a single parallel in Sm. 12,2, which is also an interpolation. [256]   " *Personally* " (ἐξ ὀνόματος) is a pleonasm: it occurs only here and in the (spurious) letter to Pol. [257]   We have already treated of the theological themes hinted at here in the first part of this study: they are mere summaries of Sm. 1, the primitive continuation of the interrupted development in Eph. 19 (see nrs. 18-21).   The phrase is constructed on two graduated conditions (Ἐὰν ... μάλιστα ἐὰν ...) which converge in the modal clause εἰς τὸ ὑπακούειν ὑμᾶς τῷ ἐπισκόπῳ κτλ.   Ignatius — according to the interpolator — conditions the redaction and sending of the second letter not only to verify something concerning his person (favour of Jesus Christ, orders given by some officer), but above all to the confirmation, by revelation, of the unity of the community as a result of its submission to the bishop and the presbytery.

" *Breaking of bread* " is an archaism (see Acts 2,46): no doubt it means the Eucharistic celebration. [258]   Ignatius does not

---

[254] ZAHN, *I. v. A.* 568f., sees the difficulty ("Ignatius nimmt eine sehr andere Stellung zu diesern lesern an (Eph. 3. 12) ") and tries to obviate it by connecting this phrase with the former context and conjecturing τι for ὅτι. LIGHTFOOT, *AA. FF.* II: II/1, 86, follows Zahn in punctuation and prefers taking ὅτι as a text corruption. Uhlhorn, Hefele, Funk-Bihlmeyer punctuate as we do. The same construction μάλιστα ἐὰν appears in the interpolated inscr. of Phld.

[255] LIGHTFOOT, *AA. FF.* II: II/1, 86f.

[256] Compare οἱ κατ᾽ ἄνδρα κοινῇ πάντες (Eph.) with τοὺς κατ᾽ ἄνδρα καὶ κοινῇ πάντας (Sm.). The expression οἱ κατ᾽ ἄνδρα has been taken from Eph. 4,2; Tr. 13,2; Sm. 5,1.

[257] Pol. 4,2 and 8,2. Ignatius uses κατ᾽ ὄνομα (Sm. 13,2).

[258] ZAHN, *I. v. A.* 341-353; LIGHTFOOT, *AA. FF.* II: II/1, 87; CAMELOT, *I. d'A.* (S. Ch. 10A) 78f.

use this expression when he writes of the Eucharist. Still less does he use expressions describing the Eucharist as the " *breaking of one bread, which is* [259] *medicine of immortality, antidote that we should not die but live in Jesus Christ forever* " (ὅς ἐστιν φάρμακον ἀθανασίας, ἀντίδοτος τοῦ μὴ ἀποθανεῖν, ἀλλὰ ζῆν ἐν Ἰησοῦ Χριστῷ διὰ παντός).

Where did the interpolator get this last phrase with such a characteristic terminology? Th. SCHERMANN is convinced that Ignatius has taken it from medical terminology, so as to set the Christian agape against the ritual meals of other religions. [260] H. LIETZMANN gives us a precious clue. In a liturgical Papyrus of the time of Justinian, coming from the same tradition of the liturgy contained in the Apostolic Constitutions (see VIII. 15,6-9) and transmiting an archaic text older than the liturgy of Mark, there is an ancient *postcommunion* in which are enumerated the " fruits of communion ". [261]   The last " fruit " in the list coincides almost literally with the supposed Ignatian text:

" For a *medicine of immortality*, vital *antidote that we should not die* absolutely *but live in* you *through* your beloved servant " (εἰς φάρμακον ἀθανασίας, ἀντίδοτον ζωῆς ὑπὲρ τοῦ μὴ ἅπαντα ἀποθανεῖν, ἀλλὰ ζῆν ἐν σοὶ διὰ τοῦ ἠγαπημένου σου παιδός).

In the Papyrus text we have italicized what the interpolator took from it. Like all archaic texts, the prayer was addressed primitively to the Father through the Son, " his beloved servant ", this later expression also having a very primitive savour. [262]   The

---

[259] ὅς Gl, distinct from [the Ignatian use ὅ [ἐστιν], refers obviously to ἄρτος. G. F. SNYDER, *The Text and Syntax of Ignatius* ΠΡΟΣ ᾽ΕΦΕΣΙΟΥΣ 20:2c, in *V. Ch.* 22 (1968) 8-13, concludes: " φάρμακον ἀθανασίας in *Eph.* 20,2 is not an element of the eucharist but an action of the Christian community which produces and designates ecclesiastical unity " (p. 13). For this he has had to correct, as Lightfoot does, ὅς Gl (*qui*) in ὅ gL (*quod*). CAMELOT, *I. d'A.* (S. Ch. 10A) 79, specifies: " Il reste cependant que 'la fraction du pain' ne peut signifier autre chose que la liturgie eucharistique ".

[260] *Zur Erklärung der Stelle epist. ad Ephes.* 20,2 *des Ignatius von Antiocheia*: φάρμακον ἀθανασίας κ.τ.λ., in *Th. Q.* 92 (1910) 6-19: " Um einen scharfen Gegensatz zu ausserchristlichen Mahlen zu machen " (p. 13). More bibliography in SNYDER, n. ant., and FISCHER, *AA. VV.* 161, n. 98.

[261] *Ein liturgischer Papyrus des Berliner Museums*, Festgabe für A. Jülicher, Tübingen 1927, pp. 213-228.

[262] See *Didache* 9,2.3; 10,2.3; 1*Clement* 59,2.3.4; *Didascalia* inscr.; *Apostolic*

interpolator had to introduce slight modifications to adapt it to a theological context, [263] and has suppressed what according to him was not strictly necessary, thus the better to conceal his adaptation. [264] The parallel is so evident that only the conviction that Eph. 20,2c belongs to Ignatius has prevented H. LIETZMANN [265] from drawing the last conclusions; the interpolator was inspired by this Eucharistic prayer, doubtless because it belonged to a liturgy attributed to some Apostle.

With this the interpolator has not only brought quite alien terminology into Ignatius' writing, but has also tried to persuade his readers that the redaction of the second letter was subordinated to a divine revelation, by which he was told that the community was united to break one bread in obedience to the bishop and the presbytery. Assistance at Eucharistic community meetings to de-

---

Tradition (assigned to Hippolytus) Can. 69 (Hauler 105; Botte 8 and 10); 70 (Hauler 107; Botte 16); 72 (Hauler 109; Botte 22); 76 (Hauler 115; Botte 76); *Apostolic Constitutions* VII. 25,2 (= Didache 9,2); 26,2 (= Didache 10,2); 27,2; 28,3; VIII. 5,5.7 (= Acts 4,30); 13,10 (= Acts 4,30); 15,2.9; 39,4; 40,2; 41,8; 48,3. LIETZMANN, *Papyrus* 228: "In allen späteren Liturgien wird die Bezeichnung παῖς (θεοῦ) für Jesus vermieden." For primitive liturgical prayers directed to the Father, see J. A. JUNGMANN, *Die Stellung Christi im liturgischen Gebet*, Münster i. W. 1925. In the Syriac tradition, the expression " medicine of life " (*sam ḥayyê*) is a favourite term for the Eucharist (R. MURRAY, *Symbols of Church and Kingdom. A Study in Early Syriac Tradition*, Cambridge 1975, p. 120). It should not to be confused, however, with " medicine of immortality ", which savours distinctly of Greek thought.

[263] Thus ἐν σοὶ (addressed to God the Father) has come to be ἐν 'Ιησοῦ Χριστῷ; διὰ τοῦ ἠγαπημένου σου παιδός has been neutralized by διὰ παντός. Strangely enough g, without knowing it, restores the text to its primitive tenor: ἐν θεῷ διὰ 'Ιησοῦ Χριστοῦ.

[264] In the Papyrus, ἀντίδοτον ζωῆς ὑπὲρ τοῦ μὴ ἄπαντα ἀποθανεῖν stresses the *vital force* contained in the " antidote " and its medical *indications* (ὑπὲρ τοῦ), that is, to avoid *every kind* (ἄπαντα) of death and live in *God*. The revisor has omitted these details.

[265] *Messe und Herrenmahl. Eine Studie zur Geschichte der Liturgie*, Bonn 1926, p. 257: " In der Formel (he quotes Eph. 20,2c) (...) haben wir schwerlich ein Theologumenon des Ignatius, sondern ein Zitat aus der antiochenischen Liturgie zu sehen ", and in the n. 2, on the Berlin Papyrus: " Man wird das für ein Ignatiuszitat halten wollen: aber seit wann zitieren die Liturgien Kirchenväter? Sollte nicht eine liturgische Tradition beide Texte verbinden? " In the edition of the Papyrus (see n. 261), struck by the parallel between 1 *Clement* 59,4 and the intercessions of Mark's liturgy, alters his opinion: " Wir haben demnach in dem fraglichen Satz nicht einen Rest direkter liturgischer Ueberlieferung, sondern ein Ignatiuszitat zu erblicken " (p. 226).

fend themselves from heretics was part of Ignatius' strategy. The real experience of " body " and " unity ", through the palpable presence of the Lord at the heart of the community, was the best defence against those who propagated Judaizing practices or who escaped from human realities under pretext of a disincarnate spirituality. The interpolator has not been impressed by the communitarian experience of the Lord to be found in Ignatius' text. To avoid schisms and divisions it is necessary to *assure unity by submission* to the bishop and presbytery. The community situation has radically changed.

57. *Mg.* 13. — The exhortation here contained fulfills the same function as the interrupting clause of Eph. 20, that is, to supply somehow for the vacuum created by the division of Mg* into two halves. In the case of Eph., the abrupt interruption of the theme obliges the forger to promise a further explanation and to sum up the rest of the theme which will be kept for Sm. In the present case the interruption is less abrupt, since the letter already tends towards the concluding exhortation. The transition is surely inspired by the original exhortation of the letter (actually in Phld. 4), while making use of Psalm 1,2-3:

" *Do you strive therefore to be confirmed ' in the precepts of the Lord ' and of the Apostles, that you may ' prosper in all things you do ' (Ps. 1,2-3), humanly and spiritually, by faith and love, in the Son and the Father and in the Spirit, from beginning to end, with your most revered bishop and the worthily-woven spiritual crown of your presbytery, and with the deacons in agreement with God. Submit to the bishop and to one another, as Jesus Christ did humanly to the Father, and as the Apostles did to Christ and the Father and the Spirit, so that there may be both material and spiritual union* " (Mg. 13).

Together with a string of binary forms typical of Ignatius (σαρκὶ καὶ πνεύματι, πίστει καὶ ἀγάπῃ, σαρκικῇ τε καὶ πνευματικῇ), there appear in the text some very suspicious-looking ternary ones (Father-Jesus Christ-Apostles; Son-Father-Spirit; bishop-presbyters-deacons).

To introduce the third element of the first set of three, the Apostles, he has been obliged to amplify the scope of the Psalm: ' in the precepts of the Lord ' *and of the Apostles.* In the Ignatian textus receptus the Apostles are nearly always found associated with the presbyters, the bishop with God and the deacons with

Jesus Christ, as we shall see later. Hence, the first and third ternary phrases correspond with each other, at least in the mind of the writer of the clause. The second ternary phrase only appears here and is repeated in a very unusual order: Son (Christ)-Father-Spirit. We observe also a tendency to reciprocity, expressed by the particle ὡς with conjunctive function, a constant already remarked in other interpolated passages (see for ex. Phld. 10-11). This particle frequently serves to connect the first and third ternary phrase (ὑποτάγητε τῷ ἐπισκόπῳ καὶ ἀλλήλοις, ὡς Ἰησοῦς Χριστὸς τῷ πατρὶ ... καὶ οἱ ἀπόστολοι τῷ Χριστῷ κτλ.). Δόγμα and κατευοδόω occur only here and depend on the implicit quotation of the Psalm suggested probably by the original sequence of the letter. Compare, in fact, Phld. 4 (σπουδάσατε οὖν μιᾷ εὐχαριστίᾳ χρῆσθαι ..., ἵνα, ὃ ἐὰν πράσσητε, κατὰ θεὸν πράσσητε) with the newly coined exhortation as from the Psalm 1,2-3 (σπουδάζετε οὖν βεβαιωθῆναι ..., ἵνα πάντα, ὅσα ποιεῖτε, κατευοδωθῆτε ...). While Ignatius invited the community to the experience of unity based on a " single act of thanksgiving ", so that the Magnesians could stand up to the Judaizers, the sowers of noxious weeds (Phld. 2-3: see also Eph. 9-10, on the Gnostics), in the style of Eph. 13,1, the interpolator feels the need of having recourse to a confirmation (βεβαιωθῆναι: see also Mg. 4c and Sm. 8,1) based on the precepts of the Lord and the Apostles, specified by submission to the bishop.

Once more we have here the three hierarchical grades, bishop, presbytery and deacons. The only way to reach " *material and spiritual union* " is through " *submission* ". Submission to the bishop is based on the submission of Jesus Christ to the Father; mutual submission, on that of the Apostles to Christ, the Father and the Spirit. Generally, the Apostles are connected with the presbyters (Mg. 6,1c; 7,1ab; Tr. 2,2b; 3,1c; 12,2d; Sm. 8,1b). Here, however, the submission of one to the other is symbolized by the Apostles in so far as in their turn they are submitted to the three persons of the Trinity. The use of this paradigm, to induce to mutual submission, is pushed too far. In Tr. 2,2b it is used correctly: " *Moreover submit to the presbytery as to the Apostles* ". The interpolator tries to soften the categoric affirmation of submission to the bishop with submission to the presbytery and other members of the community. There is no doubt that the centre of the community and fulcrum of unity is the bishop.

The presbytery, described as ,, *the worthily-woven spiritual crown* ",
surrounds the bishop in presiding.

58.   *Phld. inscr*[b].-1. — In the two interrupting clauses of the
theme, respectively, of Eph* and Mg* we have found an extended
mention of the hierarchical trilogy.   If we now pause to consider
the beginning of the two new letters resulting from the division,
Sm. and Phld., we observe that, while Sm. starts without transition
nor heading with the development that follows Eph. 19, Phld.
contains a very peculiar heading.

In the case of *Sm.*, the forger limited himself to composing
an inscription after the Ignatian model.   On the other hand, he
did not see the need for drawing up a heading similar to those in
Eph*, Mg* and Tr*, however much it was a question of Polycarp's community.   Still less did he feel the need to write a transition, since the materials kept for Sm. — which was the continuation of the development just begun in Eph. 18-19 — have their
own specific unity.

On the contrary, in the case of *Phld.*, being a new community,
an introduction was necessary.   Whereas the interruption of the
theme, whose explanation began in Mg. 8-12, required a transition that would somehow substitute it.

The *inscription of Phld.* was obtained by dividing that of Mg*
(see nr. 29).   By inserting an exhortation to unity with the bishop,
presbyters and deacons in the same inscription, the forger reveals
his greatest preoccupation.   Note the disconcerting condition to
which he subjects the ritual greeting to the Philadelphian community:

" *Especially, if they are united with the bishop and with the presbyters
and deacons who are with him, appointed by Jesus Christ's disposition,
whom he has established and confirmed according to his own design by
his Holy Spirit* " (Phld. inscr[b].).

The hierarchical trilogy is to be found, no more no less, where
the ritual Ignatian greeting πλεῖστα χαίρειν was originally placed.
As in Eph. 20,2, he has inserted this sentence with the enigmatic
μάλιστα ἐάν ... (see nr. 22).   Ἀποδείκνυμι, στηρίζω and βεβαιωσύνη are
to be found only here. [266]   The sequence made up of these three

---

[266] Eph. 12,1 uses the passive ἐστηριγμένοι in the sense of " secure ", in contrast with ὑπὸ κίνδυνον, " in danger ". — The adverb βεβαίως is used in Mg. 4d;

terms, ' *appointment, establishment and confirmation* ', refers to the three grades of the hierarchy.   The forger wants to make it appear settled that this trilogy has been appointed by Jesus Christ's disposition, established in conformity with his design or plan and confirmed by the Holy Spirit.

In Eph. 20 he had promised the Ephesians a second letter (the continuation of his incomplete one!) *on condition they were obedient* to the bishop; here he greets (sic!) the community *on condition it was united* with the bishop, presbyters and deacons.   Neither construction is a very fortunate one. Gradually we come to realize that the forger was not so cunning as it seems at first sight. His connections and transitions are awkward.   The style of his phrases are reiterative, with a stressed tendency to comparison. His theology tends to be a kind of scholasticism, based on standardized trilogies (body-soul-spirit; faith-love-concord [Phld. 11,2]; bishop-presbyters-deacons; God-Jesus Christ-Apostles, etc.).

59.   The allusion to the bishop, presbyters and deacons in an inscription is unique of its kind.   The forger has brought it in deliberately, to be able to refer to it in the *opening* of the letter:

" *Bishop, whose ministry for the common weal I have found was not holden by his own initiative* (ἀφ᾽ ἑαυτοῦ) *nor by any human agency* (διά) *nor yet for vanity, but by* (ἐν) *the love of God the Father and the Lord Jesus Christ* " (Phld. 1,1a).

It is obviously a reflexion on Gal. 1,1 ("Paul, apostle, not from human initiative (ἀπό) or by human agency (διά), but through Jesus Christ and God the Father").   The forger wants to escape certain accusations which had arisen against the bishop of Philadelphia, whom he claims to know, but whose name he ignores. The addition κενοδοξία seems to refer to the accusation Ignatius made against the Judaizers in Mg. 11c:

" *I was amazed by his moderation; his silence is more eloquent than other people's vain chatter, for he is attuned in harmony with the commandments, as a zither with its strings* " (Phld. 1,1b-2a).

60.   The description of insistent quarrels among members of the Philadelphian community (remember the different welcome

---

the adjective βέβαιος in Sm. 8,1; βεβαιόω only appears in the interpolated passage of Mg. 13,1, as we have just seen.

meted out to the messengers: see nr. 34), make it likely that his critical situation itself led the forger of the Ignatian letters to send Ignatius a long way round on his journey to Smyrna. [267] The theme of the " *silence of the bishop* " and the analogy of the " *zither with its strings* " will lead further on to the incrimination of other passages (Eph. 6,1 and 4,1a-c).

For the " *silence of the bishop* ", the forger gets inspiration from a specifically Ignatian theme: (a) The three great mysteries of the Incarnation, " that God brought about silently ", were hidden from the Chief of this world and his followers, the Docetic-Gnostics (Eph. 19,1: see nrs. 20f., and n. 93); (b) " God manifested himself through his Son Jesus the Messiah, who is his Word that proceeded from silence " (Mg. 8,2), when he revealed to us his own mystery through his word incarnate; [268] (c) Consequently " it is better to keep silence and be, than to talk and not to be; it is a good thing to teach, provided the speaker practices (what he preaches) " (Eph. 15,1), said of the false Gnostic masters who call themselves " Christians ", but did not act like them, while Ignatius reduced to silence behaves like a true Christian; (d) " For there is one Teacher, who ' spoke ' and ' it was done ' (Ps. 32,9; 148,5; Gen. 1,3); and what he has done in silence is worthy of the Father " (Eph. 15,1), thus distinguishing between creation (works) and revelation (ineffable mysteries); (e) It follows that " he who truly possesses the word of Jesus is able to perceive his secret too, so as to be a mature man who acts through his speech and is known through his silence " (15,2), in contrast with the heretical Docetists who say and do not do; (f) Finally, in Rom. 2,1 he plays on the " silence " of the Romans and his becoming " word of God ", to which he opposes the " speech " of the Romans and his remaining as a mere " voice ". — The forger holds on to this theme, applying it to the bishop who remains silent before those who talk nonsense thus leading them to reverential fear. It seems that the bishop of Philadelphia was contested by some as having arrogated to himself " *the ministry for the common weal* " of the community. As only reply he chose " *moderation* " and " *silence* ". Did the forger project his own problems on Ignatius' letters, trying to uphold the authority of the martyr against his detractors?

---

[267] See above, pp. 133f., 137f. Further on we shall speak of Phld. 7.
[268] See LIGHTFOOT, *AA. FF.* II: II/1, 126-128.

The *analogy of the zither and its strings* reappears in Eph. 4,1a-c: The presbytery is perfectly harmonized (συνήρμοσται) with the bishop, as (ὡς) the strings with the zither. As in the former passage, the bishop is the zither; the strings there (Eph.) represent the presbytery, and here (Phld.), the commandments. Note, in both, the particle ὡς with conjunctive function, one more evidence that they come from the same hand. The metaphor in Phld. is not so clear as in Eph.; in any case, even if the application is not good, it is not necessary to introduce corrections in the text, as Lightfoot does. [269] It is enough to assign them to the forger. To state this analogy he has been inspired by " musical " terminology used by Ignatius in Eph. 4,1d-2, when he describes the community as singing with one voice to the Father through Jesus the Messiah in concord and in an unison communion; image also used in Rom. 2,2.

61.   The interpolated introduction thus concludes:

" *Wherefore my soul praises his attitude to God, for I have acknowledged that it is virtuous and perfect — even his steadfast and passionless temper with all moderation that comes from the living God* " (Phld. 1,2b).

In answer to the sharp criticism of some members of the community — our forger makes Ignatius say! — the bishop of Philadelphia answers in measured tones, with silence, dispassionately but firmly. Note that ψυχή (if we except the gloss of Rom. 6,1, coming from the Long recension) is found only here and in 11,2, also interpolated. Ignatius had used πνεῦμα, which corresponds with his dichotomic anthropology.

As a consequence of this interpolation, the term ποιμήν, that follows immediately (Phld. 2,1), once its primitive term of reference removed to a distance (Jesus the Messiah = Shepherd: Mg. 12 agrees with Phld. 2), comes to mean the bishop as shepherd. In the same way, μερισμός and κακοδιδασκαλίαι, that at first alluded to the Judaizers of Mg. 8-11, are confined to the internal situation of the community and hint — rather worse than better — at the dissidents who gave themselves up to " *vain chatter* ".

---

[269] *AA. FF.* II: II/1, 252f.: " Here however the metaphor is not so clear (...) the application of the metaphor is not good. Perhaps we should read χορδαὶ κιθάρᾳ, as some authorities suggest " (gA against GL!).

62. *Sm. inscr.* — The Smyrnaean inscription was composed
on the model of the authentic ones. Unlike the Phld. inscr., in
this case the interpolator has not used materials from any other
inscription (Eph. inscr. is preserved entirely), but he imitates the
Ignatian structure, which is easy enough. In the first part we did
not treat of this inscription, as it does not contain anomalies worth
mentioning. The forger has left some slight traces of his work:

For example: (a) The emphatic placing of ἐκκλησία, as also
in Phld. inscr., in contrast with its continually delayed position
in the four authentic inscriptions; (b) The determination " *church
of God the Father and the beloved Jesus Christ* ", very similar to
Phld. inscr. (Ignatius never applies the qualification ἠγαπημένος
to Jesus the Messiah); (c) The tautology " *mercifully endowed with
every charism* ", " *lacking in no charism* ": the forger uses χάρισμα
three times (see also Pol. 2,2) for once in Ignatius (τὸ χάρισμα = the
Holy Spirit: Eph. 17,2); the second phrase is a repetitive and very
singular one (ἀνυστερήτῳ [here only] οὔσῃ: construction not found
in the authentic inscriptions); (d) ἐν ἀμώμῳ πνεύματι καὶ λόγῳ θεοῦ
πλεῖστα χαίρειν probably imitates the model of Eph. inscr.: πλεῖστα
ἐν ᾿Ιησοῦ Χριστῷ καὶ ἐν ἀμώμῳ χαρᾷ χαίρειν (see also Rom. inscr.;
Mg. 7,1).

If we compare the headings of Phld. and Sm., we shall see
notable changes in the forger's method: (a) For the inscription
of Phld. he avails himself of materials coming from Mg* inscr.:
for Sm. he does not divide the inscription of Eph*, but limits
himself to plagiarizing it; (b) He has thought necessary to introduce the hierarchical trilogy in the Phld. inscription, but not in
Sm.; (c) For Phld. he has been obliged to make up a heading (Phld.
1), in which he alludes to personal acquaintance with the bishop
of Philadelphia (without mentioning his name!), in the style of
the Eph. Mg. and Tr. headings: in the case of Sm. he begins
abruptly, continuing the interrupted exposition of Eph. 18-19, with
no mention whatever of Polycarp nor presbyters or deacons of
Smyrna. The fact that one is the community of Polycarp (Sm.)
and the other requires introduction (Phld.) is insufficient to explain
this change of method.

63. *Phld.* 10-11. — From the headings of Phld. and Sm. we
pass on to examine the spurious endings of the two letters made
up by dividing Eph* and Mg*. As we have seen, practically the

whole ending of Phld. is a copy of the original of Eph*. [270] We shall therefore pay attention exclusively to the functions attributed to persons whose names and mission are known to us from other passages.

(1) The *delegate from Philadelphia* to Antioch in Syria — remember that the whole development of Phld. 10-11,1 is a copy of Sm. 10-11 — should be a *deacon* (Phld. 10,1); his mission, a *diaconia* (office of a deacon: 10,2). Deacon and diaconia are to be taken here in the strict sense according to the analogy that follows:

" *Even as the nearer churches* (*to Antioch*) *have sent bishops, others* (*further away*) *presbyters and deacons* " (Phld. 10,2).

The only envoy of the Ephesian community to Syria, as appears in the original (Sm. = Eph* 11,2), has become a procession of envoys with hierarchical grade.

(2) Philo, Gaius and Agathopus (see nr. 31,1, and n. 111) in the original (now Sm. 10,1) are " servants of God the Messiah " (διακόνους Χριστοῦ θεοῦ: the only time Ignatius uses διάκονος, in the current sense of " servant, messenger "). They came from Syria following close upon Ignatius to bring him good news about the pacification of his church in Syria. After a brief stay in Ephesus (according to the present text, in Smyrna: Sm. 10,1) they overtook him finally in Smyrna (according to the present text, in Troas: see Sm. 12,1). But the revisor of the text distinguishes their point of departure: *Philo* comes from Cilicia together with Gaius (if for the revisor this personage is distinct from Agathopus); *Agathopus* comes from Syria. Philo is made into a *deacon*.

(3) The original stated that " they followed me to bring me a message from God (εἰς λόγον θεοῦ) " (Sm. 10,1). But according to the revisor:

(a) *Philo* is *the deacon from Cilicia* (note a similar construction in Eph. 2,1, also interpolated), who has already borne witness with his confession. Together with Gaius and Agathopus they " *also now assist him in the ministry of God's word* (ἐν λόγῳ θεοῦ)".

---

[270] Only Phld. 10,1a is mainly original. See nr. 33. The primitive ending of Ephesians has been reconstructed in pp. 116ff.

(b) *Agathopus* is "*an elect man*". He comes from Syria in the footsteps of Ignatius "*having bidden farewell to this life*" (Phld. 11,1).

As can be seen, the revisor not only assigned different points of departure but also very different tasks. According to Ignatius they were bearers of good news about the pacification reached by the Syrian communities (Sm. = Eph* 10,1b). According to the revisor, however, they were a fresh group of prisoners on their way from Syria and Cilicia. Note his tendency to hierarchize the personages: Philo has become a deacon from Cilicia, just as Ignatius turns out to be a deacon of Antioch in Syria.

64. The tendency to set up correspondences that can be observed in the construction of the sentences relating to Philo and Agathopus, are a part of the mental framework of the forger, together with the tendency to reciprocity, that we shall soon verify. Thus, while the original text goes on:

"You did well to give them hospitality as servants of God the Messiah; who also thank God for you, because you refreshed them in every way" (Sm. 10,1cd):

the revisor distinguishes two kinds of welcome:

"*The same also give a good report of you, and I too* (κἀγὼ) *thank God for you that you welcomed them, as also* (ὡς καὶ) *the Lord* (*will welcome*) *you*" (Phld. 11,1g-j),

about the *loyal* faction;

"*But those who treated them with dishonour may be redeemed by the grace of Jesus Christ*" (Phld. 11,1k),

about the *contesting* faction.

According to this, in Philadelphia there were schismatic elements that brought shame upon the community. The forger is logical with the affirmation he made at the beginning of the letter, about the bishop, and in Chap. 7 (that we shall consider further on), about Ignatius. In Philadelphia there are elements tending to trouble unity, either by criticizing the bishop, or setting themselves against Ignatius or dishonouring the guests. To bring about this effect he had to leave in the first part the exceptive clause of Mg. 11, which is also present in the other two authentic letters,

Eph* (Sm. = Eph* 4,1) and Tr* (Tr. 8,1).   We have already noted that the forger consciously projected his own problem in the so-called letter to the Philadelphians.   Probably he himself was the bishop of Philadelphia.   Because of the contestation of which he was the object, he tried to disallow his detractors, throwing in their face similar conduct of members of the same community in Ignatius' time.

65.   *Phld.* 11,2 and *Sm.* 12. — In Phld. 11,2 and Sm. 12 reappears Burrhus, introduced by the interpolator in Eph. 2,1 as " *fellow-servant* " of the deacon Ignatius.   Both clauses were drawn up by the forger to adapt materials coming from Eph* and Mg* to the new letters, Sm. and Phld., and to the new place of redaction, Troas.   We already noted in the first part (see nr. 32) the tendency to ternary enumerations (σαρκί, ψυχῇ, πνεύματι / πίστει, ἀγάπῃ, ὁμονοίᾳ), certain incorrect expressions (πεμφθέντος ἅμα ἐμοὶ κτλ. / ὃν ἀπεστείλατε μετ' ἐμοῦ κτλ.), some stylistic constants (tendency to reciprocity) and the anonymous mention of the bishop and the other hierarchical grades in Sm. 12,2 (Polycarp's community!).

That the forger of the Ignatian letters was preoccupied by the *hierarchical organization* of the church becomes evident in the clauses he drew up to interrupt the sequence of the primitive letters (Eph. 20 and Mg. 13) or to head or end the new ones (Phld. inscr[b].-1; 10-11 and Sm. 12).

66.   *The letter to Polycarp.* — The same obsession for the vertical organization of the community appears in the letter the forger addressed to Polycarp, bishop of Smyrna.   As we saw in the first part (see nr. 36), relying on trustworthy — insofar as contemporary — and detailed evidence of Irenaeus, Polycarp was the bishop of the whole province of Asia, as overseer of all the existing communities there, residing in the Smyrnaean community which was the centre of his comings and goings.   Ignatius, as we learn from his letter to the Romans (Rom. 2,2), was the only bishop of the province of Syria.   In the forger's times, circumstances had changed considerably.   In Asia every important city had its own bishop. For this reason, when he tries to support his compilation with Polycarp's authority, he presented him as bishop of Smyrna (Mg. 15d and Pol. inscr.).   In the letter to the Smyrnaeans he does not name him, limiting himself to an anonymous allusion

to the bishop, presbyters and deacons, doubtless because not knowing the names of the supposed presbyters and deacons he did not
want to be found out.   To avoid anachronisms, the forger decided
not to invent any names and maintains this principle at any cost.
At the beginning of the second part of the letter to Polycarp (Pol.
6,1a-c) he follows the same tactics.

Although he considers Ignatius a deacon, he avails himself
of the authority of his martyrdom to place in his mouth a string
of counsels to Polycarp, in the imperative.

All the *first part* (Pol. 1-5) is built up on coordinated sentences
with hardly a trace of any link (paratactical and asyndetic style),
by short phrases, most of the time in the imperative, where some
terms and expressions, taken from the authentic letters, are mixed
with the favourite themes of the forger.   We shall limit ourselves
to those expressions that directly concern the episcopal order.

67.   " *Approving your disposition so according to God, firmly built
as if on immovable rock* (Mtt. 7,25), *I praise* (God) *exceedingly* ..."
(Pol. 1,1).

Like the original headings of Eph. 1,1 and Tr. 1,2, he asserts
Polycarp's firm disposition which is so much in accord with God.
The conformity of the bishop's plan (ἡ γνώμη) with that of God
is one of his favourite themes (Eph. 3,2e-4,1a; Phld. inscr[b].-1,2;
Pol. 4,1; 5,2; 8,1).   This, as we shall see, is inspired by an original
Ignatian theme: Jesus identifies himself with the Plan of the Father
(Eph. 3,2d).

" *Vindicate your office with all human and spiritual solicitude*: *Take
care of union* (*of the community*), *for there is nothing better* " (1,2).

The theme of the community *union* is also peculiar to Ignatius.
The schisms and divisions provoked by Judaizers and Gnostics
in the heart of the church of Syria were in all probability the motive for his condemnation.   The departure of these troublemakers
from Syria and his passage through Asia, probably on the way
to Rome, caused Ignatius to take advantage of his delay in Smyrna
to warn the Asian communities of the dangers that could come to
them and to urge them to hold together in the Eucharistic meeting.
Ignatius was fully convinced that the best defence against them
was the shared experience of the Lord's presence, truly dead and

truly raised from death, in the community's centre. For him, this was a real experience of a spiritual nature, an effect of the gratuitous manifestation of the Spirit. For the forger, however, the centre of the community is no longer Jesus the Messiah but the bishop. Hence he exhorts Polycarp to maintain unity at all costs, rising in defence of his episcopal dignity. Even Irenaeus, who lived later than Ignatius, never appealed to obedience to the bishop to defend his communities against the Gnostics.

68. " *Let nothing be done without your consent* (ἄνευ γνώμης σου), *neither do you anything without God's consent, as indeed you do not* " (Pol. 4,1).

Once more we have the theme *opinion/consent* of the bishop. God-bishop-community: perfect verticality. A very similar theme in Mg. 7,1ab and Tr. 2,2a (based on the preposition ἄνευ); Mg. 4b; Tr. 7,2c and Sm. 8,1-2 (based on the preposition χωρὶς); Sm. 9,1e (ὁ λάθρα τοῦ ἐπισκόπου τι πράσσων), with which we shall deal further on.

69. " *If any one is able to abide in chastity to honour the human-ity of the Lord, let him not to boast of it; if he boast, he is lost; and if he comes to think himself better than the (married) bishop* [271], *he is totally corrupted. On the other hand, it is fitting that men and women who marry contract their union with the bishop's consent* (μετὰ γνώμης τοῦ ἐπισκόπου), *that the marriage may be after the Lord and not after the passion* " (Pol. 5,2).

The anachronism of a ' canonical marriage ' contracted with the " *bishop's consent* ", at the beginning of the second century, was more than evident. Ignatius' ' authority ', however, caused this anachronism — like many other problems arising from the Ignatian textus receptus thanks to the stratagems of our forger — to pass unnoticed or be considered as something rather strange that, is not explained, neither was any one ready to start to dispute it after so many centuries of polemics.

---

[271] πλέον GL Anton., Zahn, Lightfoot, Bihlmeyer, Kleist, Fischer: πλὴν gSAB (Lightfoot) Camelot. In the second case, it should be translated: " if it (' his purpose or vow of chastity ') be known beyond the bishop ..." (LIGHTFOOT, *AA. FF.* II: II/1, 349; CAMELOT, *I. d'A.*, S. Ch. 10A, p. 151, n. 4). Here however it seems taken for granted that the bishop is married and that the celibate could not only boast of his chastity, but could even think himself better than the bishop. Thus ZAHN, *I. v. A.* 337.

The counsels the forger gives to Polycarp through Ignatius tend to support to the utmost the outstanding, centralizing and overbearing role of the bishop — a kind of " patriarchal regime " — in his respective community, not so much in order to avoid schisms and heresies, as to face up to relaxed discipline, as Zahn very well grasped. [272] It is interesting to note that, unlike Ps.-Ignatius, the forger does not think himself obliged to bring Ignatius' letters up-to-date in the matter of heresy. Insistence on total obedience to the bishop, repeated advice to do nothing without his consent or delegation: all leads us to suppose that in reality his eagerness was an intracommunitarian problem — contestation of his authority —, due perhaps to the novelty of a centralizing regime.

70. In the *second part* of the letter (Pol. 6-8), drawn up for the most part in the plural, for it comes from the primitive conclusion of Eph* (see nrs. 46-51), the interpolated sentences continue in the same key:

" *Heed the bishop, that God may also heed you. I give my life for those who submit to the bishop, presbyters, deacons* " (Pol. 6,1a-c).

In the first sentence we observe the characteristic tendency to reciprocity, almost exclusive to the forger. The second is headed with the formula ἀντίψυχον ἐγώ, exclusive to the forger (Eph. 21,1; Pol. 2,3 and 6,1), based on the genuine Ignatian formula ἀντίψυχον τὸ πνεῦμά μου κτλ. (Sm. 10,2: see nr. 47, as soon as nn. 109 and 116). Note the anonymous mention of the bishop, precisely in the letter addressed to Polycarp (!). Inclusion of materials belonging to the primitive conclusion of Ephesians has obliged him to change the tone of his repeated counsels from singular to plural.

---

[272] ZAHN, *I. v. A.* 319: " Wenn trotzdem so oft ermahnt wird, nichts ohne den Bischof oder ohne die Träger des dreifachen Amtes zu thun, wenn auch da, wo eine versuchung zum Schisma nicht unmittelbar vorliegt, vor aller Vornahme kirchlicher Handlungen ohne den Bischof oder einen von ihm beauftragten Vertreter, ohne seine Ausdrückliche Billigung oder gar mit absichtlicher Umgehung desselben gewarnt wird (Sm. 8. 9), so muss in dieser Hinsicht dort eine laxere Praxis herrschen, als Ignatius der Zeitlage angemessen findet. Er findet es unter anderem auch schicklich, dass die Eheschliessung unter Zustimmung des Bischofs geschehe, damit die Ehe eine christliche sei; dann wird das nicht als kirchliche Ordnung festgestanden haben. Wir gewinnen aus ad Pol., c. 1-6 die allgemeine Vorstellung einer patriarchalischen R e g i e r u n g der Gemeinde durch den Bischof, deren hauptsächliche Form die persönliche Seelsorge ist."

The aim of the forger remains faithfully reflected in Ignatius' mouth with the expression " *I give my life* ", that is, ' I avail myself of the martyr Ignatius' authority ', "*for those who submit etc.* ", that is, ' to inculcate obedience to the bishop and the other hierarchical grades '.

71.   " *It is fitting, most God-blessed Polycarp, to convoke ...*" (Pol. 7,2).

In this clear imitation of Sm. 11,2 he is constrained to name Polycarp (the same will happen in Pol. 8,2d) due to the plural structure of this section. The superlative θεομακαριστότατε, inspired probably by Sm. 1,2, is not very suitable to a person who has not yet died as a martyr, but serves to attenuate the change of addressees of all this second part directed to the community. With the excuse of convoking " *a most venerable plenary meeting* " (συμβούλιον ἀγαγεῖν θεοπρεπέστατον), he returns to the second person plural. Again a superlative to designate " the community meeting " (τὴν ἐκκλησίαν ὑμῶν), as is to be found in the original (Sm. = Eph* 11,2b).

72.   Immediately below, forgetting the communitarian plural of the original conclusion, he addresses Polycarp once again in the singular. The next phrase is, perhaps, the most carefully composed of all the interpolation:

" *Since, then, I could not write to all the churches because of my sudden sailing from Troas for Neapolis, as the (officer's) order enjoins, you shall write to the churches laying in front, as one posssesing the mind of God, that they also may do the same thing — those who are able sending foot-messengers, and others letters through those whom you send —, so that you may be glorified by an enduring work, as you deserve* " (Pol. 8,1: see nr. 51, and corresponding nn.).

Indeed, this apparently simple passage aimed at nothing less than: (a) To allay any suspicion about the amplification of the Ignatian letters (those written from Troas), letting it be supposed that Ignatius' purpose was to " *write to all the churches* " in Asia, so that they all " *send messengers* " to Antioch of Syria: Polycarp should now be commissioned to do so; (b) To sanction the new direction of Ignatius' journey (Troas-Neapolis); (c) To link the compilation with Chap. 13 of Polycarp's letter to the Philippians, also interpolated (Neapolis-Philippi, from whence Ignatius wrote

to Polycarp again, as well as the Philippians); (d) To justify the
unfulfillment of the promise made in Eph. 20,1 (to write " *a second
letter* ") because of his sudden sailing from Troas for Neapolis
(note the deliberate correspondence between Eph. 20.1: ἐὰν ...
θέλημα ᾖ and Pol. 8,1: ὡς τὸ θέλημα προστάσσει); (c) To increase the
number of envoys to Antioch, thus connecting up with a theme
that in the present text is exclusive to the letters from Troas (Phld.
10,1b-2d and 2ef; Sm. 11,2-3; Pol. 7,2 and 8,1; see Pol. Phil. 13,1).
It is a rather ample development of the theme that originally consisted in the genuine letter to the Ephesians (actually Sm. 11,2-3),
the last of Ignatius' writings from Smyrna before sailing for Rome.
While the original speaks of an embassy sent to the whole church
of the province of Syria (εἰς τὸ γενόμενον ἕως Συρίας συγχαρῆναι
αὐτοῖς, Sm. 11,2), in the interpolated letters it is restricted to the
capital of the province, Antioch of Syria (Phld. 10,1a; Pol. 7,1a).
The expression in Pol. 7,2f, πορευθεὶς εἰς Συρίαν, which imitates
the original one of 8,2c, merely indicates the departure for Syria,
as in Pol. Phil. 13,1: ἐάν τις ἀπέρχηται εἰς Συρίαν; the concrete goal
of the journey and the embassy is clearly expressed in Pol. 7,1.

73.   *The covering note of Pol. Phil.* 13. — As we have already
proved, the interpolated clause in Polycarp's letter to the Philippians has a very peculiar aim.   Once the new compilation of Ignatian letters composed (with a new letter addressed to Polycarp
and one to his community in Smyrna) it only remained to finish
off with Polycarp's signature; the themes enunciated in this presumed covering note (Pol. Phil. I according to most recent editions) are the same that the forger has introduced in the Ignatian
letters (see nrs. 40f.).   Given their place in Polycarp's letter to the
Philippians and their specific task, the forger left no trace there
of his organizing preoccupations, unless by emphasizing the privileged position occupied by Polycarp, making him, instead of the
community (see Sm. = Eph* 11,2), send the ambassador to Syria
(ὃν πέμπω πρεσβεύσοντα), just as he did in Pol. 8,1g (διὰ τῶν ὑπό σου
πεμπομένων) and in 8,2d (τοῦ πέμποντος αὐτὸν Πολυκάρπου).

* * *

In all the passages we have just examined we observe the interpolator's same main preoccupation: to settle definitely the vertical

organization of the church — bishop, presbyters, deacons — by
tampering with the letters of Ignatius the martyr.   For this he has
had: (a) To cut up Eph* and Mg* so as to obtain new materials;
(b) To make up three new letters: two to prove there was intimate
relationship between Ignatius and Polycarp (Pol. and Sm.: respectively for the bishop of Smyrna and his community) and one to
make it evident that Ignatius knew the critical situation in Philadelphia (Phld.: for the anonymous bishop and his community);
(c) To twist the contents of the authentic letters so as to bring into
the foreground the figure of the bishop, surrounded by his " spiritual crown ", the presbytery, and seconded by the deacons in every
kind of service.   Consequently, the community that was first
polarized by the figure of Jesus, has now become centred on the
bishop.   Hence his continual exhortations to submission and obedience to the bishop and clergy.

b) *Passages with anomalies due to the forger's ignorance of Ignatius'
   identity*

Of all the passages presenting serious anomalies, we have
up to now only examined those — chosen especially for their linking up of successive discoveries — that bear directly on the *structure* of the text, which are taken by almost all editors and commentators as unquestionably Ignatian.   Having seen that all the
more recent clauses insisted on presenting a perfectly structured
church, and on the Eucharistic celebration in obedience to the bishop
and clergy, we have now to turn again to a series of passages that,
though incidentally suspect because of their anomalies, have not
been treated expressly since they do not bear directly on the structural framework.   Among these passages we distinguish:

(α) Those in which Ignatius is taken to be merely a *deacon*,
"*fellow-servant*" of the deacons in general (Phld. 4c; Sm. 12,2;
Mg. 6,1d) or of Burrhus (Eph. 2,1a) and Zotion (Mg. 2a) in particular, contrasting with Ignatius' introduction of himself to the
Romans:

" God has vouchsafed that the bishop of Syria (τὸν ἐπίσκοπον Συρίας)
shall be found in the West (at the setting of the sun) sent for from
the East (from sun's rising): it is good to set from the world towards
God, that I may rise to him " (Rom. 2,2).

(β) The passages in which it is presumed that in Ignatius' times some communities of the province of Asia already possessed a *monarchical bishop*, of the same type as the Syrians (Phld. 10,2ef), that is: Ephesus with Onesimus (Eph. 1,3c), Magnesia with Damas (Mg. 2a), Tralles with Polybius (Tr. 1,1c), Philadelphia with the bishop supposedly known by Ignatius (Phld. 1,1a), Smyrna with Polycarp (Pol. inscr.; Mg. 15d), the other bishops of neighbouring communities of Smyrna, those Ignatius could not write to and asked Polycarp to do so (Pol. 8,1). All this being contradictory to:

(1) Irenaeus' account of Polycarp, according to whom he " was established by some of the Apostles as bishop for (the province of) Asia (ὑπὸ ἀποστόλων κατασταθεὶς εἰς τὴν Ἀσίαν ... ἐπίσκοπος) in/from the community (residing) in Smyrna " (A.H. III. 3,4: see nr. 36).

(2) Irenaeus' statement as witness of true tradition — with regard to the Gnostics:

" all the communities scattered over (the province of) Asia together with the successors of Polycarp up to the present " (αἱ κατὰ τὴν Ἀσίαν ἐκκλησίαι πᾶσαι καὶ οἱ μέχρι νῦν διαδεδεγμένοι τὸν Πολύκαρπον: A. H. III. 3,4, see nr. 36).

(3) What is stated also in the first part about the forged relationship between Ignatius and Polycarp (see nrs. 36-51).

(4) The ecclesiastical organization in the province of Syria, as it is inferred from Rom. 2,2, and even in Gaul, according to Eusebius (see nrs. 3-9, and n. 139).

As can be seen, contestation of the present structure of seven Ignatian letters carries with it the denunciation of the hierarchical contents inserted by the forger. Nevertheless, we still ignore the exact extent of each of the interpolated passages and the possible existence of very brief sentences, similar to those relative to Polycarp we have already met with. To identify this and delimit it precisely we should set up very definite criteria. For this we shall undertake a methodical analysis of the anomalous passages, before excluding other possible interpolations.

We shall treat, then, in two sections each of these passages. As to the first group (§ α), bearing in mind that three of them are in the same context as those of the second group and that Sm. 12.2 is already known to us, we shall deal only with what is pecu-

liar to each one (nrs. 74-78).   As regards the second group (§ β),
given that the anomaly we have remarked conditions the whole
heading of the letter and that the headings of the spurious letters
(Phld. and Pol.; Sm. has no heading) have been sufficiently studied,
we shall confine ourselves to the headings of the three interpolated
authentic letters (Rom. has remained intact) (nrs. 79-91).

α) *Passages in which Ignatius is taken to be merely a deacon*

As has been seen in the first part, the forger ignored Ignatius'
true identity since he was not acquainted with Rom.   For his
purpose, it was advisable to give Ignatius a deacon's grade, making
sure in this way (deacon is by definition subject to the bishop and
presbytery) of the new orientation he wanted to give to Ignatius'
ecclesiology.   We should now examine all the passages in which
it is presupposed that Ignatius is a deacon, so as to weigh the magni-
tude of the interpolation.

74. *Eph.* 2,1. — Immediately after the praise of Onesimus,
bishop of Ephesus, with which we shall deal in the following paragraph (§ β), comes this sentence:

" *As for my fellow-servant Burrhus, your deacon in agreement with God,
blessed in all things, I pray he may stay at my side both for your and
the bishop's honour* " (Eph. 2,1a-d).

In the spurious conclusions of Philadelphians and Smyrnaeans Burrhus is presented to us as a link between Troas and the
addressees of the letters supposedly written there (Phld. 11,2 and
Sm. 12,1).   In both it is explained that Burrhus has been sent
by the Ephesians and Smyrnaeans to Troas for this mission.   The
supposed petition made by Ignatius has been seconded.   The
interpolator is logical in taking Ignatius to be a deacon: among
the many envoys to Smyrna from the Ephesians, Magnesians and
Trallians, he asks to be accompanied to Troas precisely by a deacon.

In the next paragraph Burrhus and Onesimus appear coupled
with three other names, Crocus, Euplus and Fronto.   Crocus'
name appears also in Rom. 10,1, free from all suspicion of being
interpolated; the expression, " worthy of God and of you ", also
belonging to Crocus, is said in Rom. 10,2 of those who went before
him from Syria to Rome.   But the following sentence: " *whom I
received as an example* (ἐξεμπλάριον) *of your affection* ", was ap-

plied to Burrhus in the spurious conclusion of Smyrnaeans (Sm. 12,1) and will be stated of bishop Polybius in Tr. 3,2. Onesimus appears again in Eph. 6,2, without hierarchical qualification, as spokesman of the Ephesian community.

75. *Mg.* 2. — After enumerating the bishop Damas and the presbyters Bassus and Apollonius, he names the deacon Zotion his " *fellow-servant* ". The assignation to Ignatius of the dea-conry, by excluding the other two hierarchical grades, is very clear here, still more — if possible — than in Eph. 2,1a. The connec-tion between this qualification and the next sentence is deliberate: Ignatius, deacon, rejoices that his " *fellow-servant* " obeys the bishop and the presbytery. The optative ὀναίμην with *singular* comple-ment (οὗ) reappears in Pol. 1,1, also interpolated. In the genuine letters Ignatius uses it four times always with a plural complement (Eph. 2,2a; Mg. 12a; Rom. 5,2a and Pol. = Eph* 6,2i). Ps.-Ignatius also make use of this expression to authenticate his Long recension (Mar. Ign. 2,3; Tar. 8,1 and 10,1; Phil. 15,1; Ant. 12,3 and 14,2; Her. 6,2 and 8,2).

76. *Mg.* 6,1d. — Here too, when he comes to the deacons, after enumerating the bishop and the presbyters without epithet, he adds a qualification, " *my beloved* " (τῶν ἐμοὶ γλυκυτάτων), a stylistic variant of " *fellow-servants* ". The bishop presides in the place of God, the presbyters represent the college of the Apostles, to the deacons has been entrusted the ministry of Jesus Christ. This triple analogy occurs also in the heading of Trallians (Tr. 2,2-3,1) and in many other passages. Undeniable coincidences in analogies and terminology of these passages with the Didascalia have been explained up to now by having them depend on Ignatius. Since it is a very complex problem we shall deal with it in a special section.

77. *Phld.* 4c. — Ignatius thinks it indispensable, as defence against heretics or schismatics, to stir up the experience of unity in the Eucharistic meetings of the community. [273] Firstly, because the heretics keep themselves aloof from the Eucharist and com-mon prayer, " because they allow not that the Eucharist is the Flesh of our Saviour, Jesus the Messiah " (Sm. 7,1); secondly, because " in your unity (with Jesus, Shepherd) they will find no occasion

---

[273] See Eph. 5,2a-c.3a-e; Mg. 7,1c-2; Tr. 7,1a-c.2ab.

(to lead you captives) " (Phld. 2,2). For this reason Ignatius, after labelling the Judaizers as wolves disguised as believers, [274] exhorts the Magnesians (early addressees of the letter) to partake exclusively of Christian food, the Eucharist. [275] As in almost all the passages where the Eucharistic meeting is mentioned, the interpolator inserts his own ecclesiology (in italics), in this case introducing it with the conjunctive particle ὡς:

" So, strive for once to partake of one Eucharist: for, one is the Flesh of our Lord Jesus the Messiah, and one the cup to unite his Blood, and one the altar, *just as one is the bishop with the presbytery and the deacons my fellow-servants*; in order that whatever you do, you may do it in conformity with God " (Phld. 4).

As we have shown on another occasion, the former passage of Mg. 6 and the present one of Phld. 4 originally made up the first and last link of a perfectly concentric structure (see nr. 28). God, Jesus the Messiah, is the only norm of behaviour for the Christian community. This agreement of the community with the mind of God becomes visible in the unanimous concurrence of all the members in one Eucharistic celebration. The Eucharist polarizes the unity in that there is only one Body of the Lord and one cup that unites his Blood, as there is only one altar: Jesus the Messiah. The experience of the Lord, his life, death and oblation are sufficient by themselves to give the community cohesion. This was what Ignatius meant. But not so the interpolator. For him, another unifying pattern was necessary, the bishop with the presbyters and deacons. Not that in Ignatius' time the communities were not organized. Ignatius was the bishop of Syria supervising the communities scattered through the province; Polycarp, in Irenaeus' time, supervised those in the province of Asia; Irenaeus himself was bishop of the parishes distributed throughout Gaul. All the communities possessed a senate of presbyters, or elders, gifted with spiritual discernment and approved by the community. But what gave unity to the whole was not the structure itself but the experience of the Lord communicated by his Spirit.

The only passage that has not been tampered with is Eph. 13,1:

---

[274] Phld. 2,2: compare with Eph. 7,1 (wild beasts — rabid dogs that bite furtively) and Tr. 6,2 (deadly drug mixed with honeyed wine).

[275] Phld. 4a equals Tr. 6,1d.

" So, strive to meet together more frequently for thanksgiving to God and for his praise (εἰς εὐχαριστίαν θεοῦ καὶ εἰς δόξαν). For, when you meet together frequently, the powers of Satan are overthrown and his mischief is brought to nothing by the concord of your faith."

Did the interpolator think this was merely a question of a prayer and praise meeting and not of the Eucharistic celebration properly so-called? Ignatius passes without a break from the literal sense, " thanksgiving ", to the technical sense, " Eucharist ". Hence in Sm. = Eph* 7,1 he says that the Docetic Gnostics

" keep away from (the meeting of) thanksgiving and prayer (εὐχαριστίας καὶ προσευχῆς), because they allow not that this Thanksgiving (τὴν εὐχαριστίαν) is the Flesh of our Saviour, Jesus the Messiah, which Flesh suffered for our sins, the same the Father raised up by his goodness."

For Ignatius the Thanksgiving of the community has a double effect: (a) To actualize the real presence of the Lord as centre of the community (positive); (b) To dissipate any Satanic attempt to neutralize its commitment if necessary till death, by denying the salvific value of Jesus' death (negative).

The forger knows nothing of such language. He understands the Eucharist in a cultic sense. For this he interpolates only those passages in which the Eucharistic Body and Blood are explicitly mentioned and he leaves out this passage which he interprets as a simple prayer meeting.

78. *Sm.* 12,2. — This clause contains a whole series of anomalous data and hints of interpolation (see nrs. 32 and 65): (a) Troas; (b) Burrhus, deacon; (c) Burrhus being sent together with Ignatius by the Smyrnaeans and Ephesians; (d) The Latinism " *exemplarium* "; (e) The anonymous greetings to the bishop, presbyters and deacons; (f) Ignatius' identification with his " *fellow-servants* ", the deacons, etc. To make it credible he has imitated a series of typically Ignatian expressions: " from whence also I am writing to you ", " he has relieved me in every way ", the binary forms: body/blood, passion/resurrection, material/spiritual. It can very well be considered a model of imitation.

*   *   *

The tone of the passages just examined is always the same. Both the clauses written to support the structure of the new Ignatian compilation and the sentences inserted in the exhortations to concord or unity tend to use Ignatius the martyr's authority to back up the ecclesiastical organization in fashion at the interpolator's time. The always anonymous mention of the three hierarchical grades; the stereotyped use of some analogies (bishop/God, presbyters/Apostles, deacons/Jesus Christ), the stylistic mannerisms (repeated use of the particle ὡς with conjunctive function, very singular conditions, several sentences inserted through the conjunction ὡς) imply a speculative, synthetic and scholastic mentality, as compared with the direct, pragmatic and vehement style of the genuine Ignatian letters.

β) *Headings nominally addressed to the bishop of specific communities of the province of Asia*

Once ascertained that ecclesiastical organization, founded on the existence of local bishops (of each chief city) instead of provincial supervisors (of a whole Roman province) does not belong to the epoch of Ignatius, not even to that of Polycarp and Irenaeus, any passage in which a local bishop appears is manifestly a manipulation of the interpolator. Besides this main criterion we shall discover others which confirm the presence of interpolations. In the third part we shall give a list of the means he made use of to introduce his themes.

Up to now — except for Eph. 2,1; Mg. 2; Phld. 11,1 and what concerns Polycarp — allusions to bishop, presbyters and deacons have all been anonymous. In the headings, however, of what have turned out to be the genuine Ignatian letters, that is, those addressed to the Asian communities who sent delegates to Smyrna, bishops of the respective communities with some presbyters and deacons are called by name. On the other hand, a study of the headings and conclusions of the spurious letters written from Troas leads us to discern a characteristic feature of the forger's proceedings: his aversion to making up proper names, for fear of being detected. Thus, in the heading of Phld. he speaks of knowing the bishop, but does not name him; greetings to bishop, presbytery and deacons are always anonymous; the proper names comprised in the conclusions of the three spurious letters come from the original conclusion of Eph* (see nrs. 22, 54f., as well as the passages we have just examined).

How then are we to explain that at the beginning of the three genuine Asian letters he had risked giving the names of the bishop and other collaborators? The explanation is simple. At the beginning of each of these letters are the names of the delegates of the respective communities, through whom Ignatius keeps them in mind. The forger limited himself to assign the rank of bishop to the first and allotted to the rest the remaining hierarchical grades. But his manipulation of the original does not end here. As we already saw apropos of Phld., he used the heading of the letter to introduce his favourite theme. We should, then, examine each of these headings to determine exactly the extent of the interpolation.

79. *Eph.* 1-6. — The heading of Ephesians is clearly delimited by the twofold allusion to Onesimus in 1,3 and 6,2, who informs Ignatius of the total absence of heresy in the community and that it is consecrated exclusively to Jesus the Messiah, " who goes on really speaking (to them) " (6,2). We can distinguish three parts: (I.) The allusion to the solidarity shown by the Ephesians in their eagerness in greeting him when he came from Syria on his way to Rome (Eph. 1,1-2). (II.) The mention of the five delegates through whom he keeps in mind the whole community, with the consequent invitation that the community keep close to the person of Jesus the Messiah (1,3-2,2). (III.) The beginning of the exhortation (3,1-6,2). The forger respected the first part, but has interpolated copiously the second and third ones. Here we shall examine these last two.

The mention of the delegates has given occasion to the interpolation of a number of sentences all tending to centre the attention of the reader on the person of the bishop. These are easy to detect. The one regarding Onesimus (Eph. 1,3c-e), for the mention of the " bishop " at beginning and end. The specification ἐν σαρκὶ ἐπισκόπῳ presupposes the distinction between the visible bishop/invisible Bishop of Mg. 3,2b-d. The first sentence concerning Burrhus (Eph. 2,1ab) is identifiable by the presence of the mark " *my fellow-servant* "; the second (2,1d) for the construction of the sentence with εὔχομαι, on the same pattern as the one on Onesimus. The first sentence belonging Crocus (2,1f), for the

Latinism " *exemplarium* "; the second (2,1h), by the mark of reciprocity (ὡς καὶ) and above all the parallel of Tr. 12,2d.

Reconstruction of the second part of the original sequence could well read as follows: Ἐπεὶ οὖν τὴν πολυπληθίαν ὑμῶν ἐν ὀνόματι θεοῦ ἀπείληφα ἐν Ὀνησίμῳ, τῷ ἐν ἀγάπῃ ἀδιηγήτῳ (Eph. 1,3ab), <καὶ> Βούρρ<ῳ> (2,1a), <τῷ> ἐν πᾶσιν εὐλογημέν<ῳ> (1c), καὶ Κρόκ<ῳ> δέ, <τῷ> θεοῦ ἀξί<ῳ> καὶ ὑμῶν (1e), ὅ<ς> κατὰ πάντα με ἀνέπαυσεν (1g) ἅμα Ὀνησίμῳ καὶ Βούρρῳ καὶ Εὔπλῳ καὶ Φρόντωνι, δι᾽ ὧν πάντας ὑμᾶς κατὰ ἀγάπην εἶδον (1hi) — ὀναίμην ὑμῶν διὰ παντός, ἐάνπερ ἄξιος ὦ —, πρέπον ἐστίν, κατὰ πάντα τρόπον δοξάζειν Ἰησοῦν Χριστὸν τὸν δοξάσαντα ὑμᾶς, ἵνα ἐν μιᾷ ὑποταγῇ κατηρτισμένοι (2,2a-d), κατὰ πάντα ἦτε ἡγιασμένοι (2f).

(1) The *first sentence* (1,3a) has equivalents in Mg. 2a; 6,1a and Tr. 1,1a, as in Eph. 2,1i. The Ephesians had sent five delegates to Smyrna. Through this numerous representation Ignatius kept in mind the whole Ephesian community. Ignatius had known it personally, when he passed through Ephesus, as can be ascertained from the original conclusion of Eph*. Much later, when the envoys from the Syrian community passed by, they were given a warm welcome (Sm. = Eph* 10,1). Some of the delegates — excluding Crocus who stayed behind with him — offered to take the letter addressed to the Romans (Rom. 10,1).

(2) The *parenthetic clause*: " May I rejoice with you always, if I be but worthy (of martyrdom!) " (2,2ab), has a parallel in Mg. 12ab and partly in Pol. 6,2i. The conditional particle ἐάνπερ is used exclusively by Ignatius (7x), whether to express a condition, on whose fulfillment depends the wish expressed in the principal clause (Eph. 2,2b; Mg. 12b and Rom. 1,1d), or to indicate that what is affirmed in the principal clause would largely be without effect if this condition is not fulfilled (Rom. 1,2 [2x]; 4,1c; Pol. = Eph* 7,1c). For the sense of ἄξιος in this clause, can also be seen Tr. 4,2b and Rom. 1,1d.

(3) For each one of the *delegates* we have kept the corresponding appositive sentence which does not contain hierarchical contamination. The one corresponding to Crocus (Eph. 2,1e), " worthy of God and of you ", appears again in Rom. 10,2c. The reconstructed original phrase (2,1g.h): " who has relieved me in every way together with... " is typically Ignatian (Mg. 15d; Tr. 12,1b; Rom. 10,2d; Sm. 9,2c and 10,1e). The forger imitates this in Sm. 12,1d.

12

(4) The corresponding apodosis to Ἐπεὶ οὖν of Eph. 1,3ab is πρέπον ἐστίν of 2,2c (without the intercalated particle οὖν).

80. To facilitate the identification of the interpolated clauses for the reader, we offer a translation of the whole second part showing their position in italics; once the interpolations omitted (in brackets), the Ignatian text flows easily:

" [1,3] *a*Seeing then that I received in God's name your great community in the person of Onesimus, *b*a man of indescribable affection, { *c*humanly your bishop, *d*whom I pray to all to love in agreement with Jesus Christ and that you take him for model. *e*Blessed, then, is he who granted you such a bishop, whom you did indeed deserve. [2,1] *a*As for my fellow-servant} Burrhus, {*b*your deacon in agreement with God} *c*blessed in all things, { *d*I pray he may stay at my side both for your and the bishop's honour;} *e*but Crocus too, worthy of God and of you, {*f*whom I received as an example of your affection,} *g*has relieved me in every way { *h*—that the Father of Jesus Christ may refresh him in turn —} together with Onesimus and Burrhus and Euplus and Fronto, *i*through whom I saw you all with the eyes of love — [2,2] *a* may I rejoice with you always, *b*if I be but worthy (of martyrdom)! —{ *c*Therefore} it is fitting in every way to glorify Jesus the Messiah, who has glorified you, *d*so that being perfectly joined together in one submission { *e*— submitted to the bishop and the presbytery —} *f*you may be consecrated in every respect " (Eph. 1,3-2,2).

In the present text the names of the first two delegates appear invested, the first with rank of bishop, and the second, of deacon. The rest have not been " ordained ". By detaching the initial protasis (Ἐπεὶ οὖν κτλ.) from the corresponding apodosis (πρέπον ἐστίν κτλ.), the former has been left hanging. A similar anacoluthon occurs in the heading to Magnesians. [276]

Once the bishop and his deacon have been introduced, he mentions the presbytery by inserting a sentence (2,2e) in the primitive apodosis that distorts the meaning of the Ignatian one, " being perfectly joined together [277] in one submission (ἐν μιᾷ ὑποταγῇ) "

---

[276] See BROWN, *Authentic* 83f.

[277] In this same sense and with a similar construction, he uses καταρτίζω in Sm. 1,1 (" you form a compact block "). In Eph. 1,1 and Pol. = Eph* 7,3 he uses ἀπαρτίζω, referring to the work the community of Ephesus was bringing to a conclusion. Referring to himself, he employs ἀναπάρτιστος (Phld. = Mg* 5,1), οὔπω ἀπήρτισμαι (Eph. 3,1), εἰς θεόν με ἀπαρτίσει (Phld. = Mg* 5,1) and εἰς ἕνωσιν κατηρτισμένος (8,1). ἀπαρτίζω still appears in Eph. 19,3 and ἀπάρτισμα predicated of the Gospel in Phld. = Mg* 9,2. — The interpolator does not use this

(2,2d), making this "submission" to Jesus the Messiah attained by the community because of her continual attitude of praise and for the glory with which she has corresponded, becomes subjection (ὑποτασσόμενοι) of the community to the bishop and the presbytery. A simple parenthetic clause has sufficed. [278]

81.   The beginning of the exhortation likewise is ful of interpolations. (1) In Eph. 3,2e-4,1c he has changed the meaning of the Ignatian sentence: " For this reason I take the initiative of exhorting you to run in agreement with the Plan of God (ὅπως συντρέχητε τῇ γνώμῃ τοῦ θεοῦ), for Jesus the Messiah also, our unwavering life, is the Plan of the Father (τοῦ πατρὸς ἡ γνώμη) " (3,2b-d). For this he has introduced the bishops in the plan of Jesus: " *Just as* (ὡς καὶ) *the bishops... are included in the plan of Jesus Christ* (ἐν Ἰησοῦ Χριστοῦ γνώμῃ εἰσίν). *Hence it is fitting to you to run in agreement with the plan of the bishop* (συντρέχειν τῇ τοῦ ἐπισκόπου γνώμῃ) " (3,2e-4,1a).   The link is rudimentary, an inclusive addition.   In this way the forger has attained his purpose: to concentrate the attention of the reader on the person of the bishop, while in the original sequence Jesus the Messiah was the centre of the community.

(2)   In the two following sentences the interpolator tampers with the exhortation to unity and to unanimous praise with twin ascending progressions constructed with εἰ γὰρ ... πόσῳ μᾶλλον (Eph. 5,1. 2de).   Both tend to underline the link of the church with the bishop.   The two progressions proceed from minor to major: the first based on the twofold correlation church/Jesus Christ, Jesus Christ/Father, as pattern for the relationship community/bishop; the second based on the progression: private prayer of two → prayer of the whole church with the bishop.

(3)   The last interpolated sentence is based on the Ignatian quotation of Prov. 3,34 (" God resists the proud ": Eph. 5,3e), paraphrasing it as follows: " *Let us strive, therefore, not to ' resist '*

---

terminology. — G, as in many other instances (see for example Eph. 1,2), has let himself be contaminated by g, amplifying the text with a quotation from 1*Cor.* 1,10.

[278] ὑποταγή is found only here. Ign. insists that it is a *unique* act of submission (ἐν μιᾷ ὑποταγῇ), namely, the all-embracing praise given by the community to Jesus the Messiah, the unique *Eucharist*. The interpolator re-interprets it as submission (ὑποτασσόμενοι) to the hierarchy.

the bishop ... " (5,3f). Immediately after by means of another ascending progression (Καὶ ὅσον ... πλειόνως ...) he develops the theme of the silence of the bishop and the reverential fear that should be had for the representative of God sent to us (6,1). We have come across a similar development earlier in Phld. 1.

82. So that the reader may form his own opinion on the awkward way the interpolated clauses are worked in with the Ignatian text in this third part we determine the limits (in brackets) of all the interpolations (in italics):

" 5,1 *a* I give you no directives as though I were someone: *b*for although I am in chains for the (Christian) name's sake, *c*I am not yet completed in Jesus the Messiah. *d*As I am now but at the beginning of my discipleship, *e*I address you as my fellow-disciples. *f*For I ought rather to have been anointed for the contest with your faith, advice, endurance, magnanimity. 3,2 *a*But, since love does not permit me to be silent concerning you, *b*for this reason I take the initiative of exhorting you *c*to run in agreement with the Plan of God, *d*for Jesus the Messiah also, our unwavering life, is the Plan of the Father, {, *ejust as the bishops, established in the most distant regions,*[279] *are included in the plan of Jesus Christ. 4,1 aHence it is fitting to you to run in agreement with the plan of the bishop, bwhich you already do. cIndeed, your justly famous presbytery, worthy of God, is attuned with the bishop as completely as the strings with a zither*}. *d*For this reason your concord and love in unison are a song to Jesus the Messiah. 4,2 *a*And all of you also without exception form a chorus, *b*so that, joining the symphony by your concord *c*and taking the key note of God by your unity, *d*you may sing praises to the Father with one voice through Jesus the Messiah, *e*so that he may both listen to you and by your good works recognize you *f*to be members of his Son. *g*It is therefore profitable for you to maintain yourselves in a blameless unity, *h*in order that you may always be partakers of God. {5,1 *aFor if I in so short a time have reached such confidence with your bishop, certainly not human but spiritual, bhow much more should I praise you who are as united to him as the church is to Jesus Christ and Jesus Christ is to the Father, cso that all things may be in symphony with the unity!*} 5,2 *a*Let no one deceive himself. *b*If any one be not within the precinct of the

---

[279] οἱ κατὰ τὰ πέρατα ὁρισθέντες is a real anachronism in Ignatius' times. ZAHN, *I. v. A.* 299, labels the phrase hyperbolic. It would claim to refer only to the models known to Ign. in Syria and Asia. However, the obvious sense goes much further: " Ignatius would be contemplating regions as distant as Gaul on the one hand and Mesopotamia on the other " (LIGHTFOOT, *AA. FF.* II: II/1, 40); " Die Bischöfen, (selbst) in den fernsten Ländern eingesetzt " (BAUER, *AA. VV.* II 204; *W. z. N. T.* s. v. πέρας).

altar, *c*he lacks the Bread of God. { *dFor, if the prayer of one with another has so much strength* (cf. Mtt. 18,19.20), *ehow much more that of the bishop together with the whole church!*} [5,3] *aSo* then whoever does not come to the common assembly, *bby* that very fact shows pride *cand* has excluded himself. *dFor* it is written: *e« God resists the proud»* (Prov. 3,34). { *fLet us strive, therefore, not to « resist » the bishop, gthat we may be submitted to God.* [6,1] *aAnd the more any one sees that the bishop is silent, bthe more he should respect him. cFor every one whom the owner sends to take charge of his household, dwe ought so to receive as him who has sent him* (cf. Mtt. 10,40). *ePlainly then, we ought to regard the bishop as the Lord himself.*} [6,2] *a*Indeed Onesimus himself praises above measure your orderly conduct according to God, *b*that is, that you all live according to truth, *c*and no sectarianism has a home among you; *d*nay, you do not even listen to any one else *e*but to Jesus the Messiah who goes on really speaking (to you) " (Eph. 3,1-6,2).

As can be seen, in the actual text of Ignatius we are faced with two distinct ecclesiologies. Ignatius' own, based on the trilogy: God as Father, Jesus the Messiah as only Mediator, the community as a gathering of the members of his Body; and the interpolator's one reducible to a binary scheme: bishop/church. Both are fighting the same adversaries who are trying to split the community. But while Ignatius has recourse to " one submission " to Jesus the Messiah, that is, the unanimous gathering of the community members to celebrate the Eucharist, the interpolator directs this submission to the person of the bishop (and the presbytery). Ignatius made use of musical terminology to express the unison triad of a community closely joined by concord and love; the interpolator uses the analogy of the strings with a zither, as we saw in Phld. 1,2, to express the perfect harmony of the presbytery (and therefore of the community) with the bishop. The explanation of this phenomenon can be perceived from the actual text of the Ignatian letters. When Ignatius travels through Asia, the communities are small but well disciplined; the experience of the Lord " speaking to them really " through prophecy, and the sharing of goods among members of the community gives it the best possible defence against heresy. When the interpolator re-interprets the letters, " *the bishops are already established in the most distant regions* ", that is, the Christian communities have spread everywhere, but have lost their internal cohesion. The only humanly viable way of defence against heresy is submission to the bishop.

83. *Mg.* 1-7. — The heading of Magnesians follows the same pattern as Ephesians: (I.) Justification of the letter (less personal, inasmuch as Ignatius did not pass through Magnesia) (Mg. 1); (II.) Mention of the four delegates sent to Smyrna with an invitation to be true Christians in view of the imminence of the end (2-5); (III.) Exhortation to do all in conformity with God through unanimous gathering in the celebration of the Eucharist (6-7). Here too the interpolator has respected the first part. We proceed, now, to deal with the plentiful interpolations of the second and third ones.

In the short space between chapters 2-7 we have three paragraphs starting with 'Επεὶ οὖν (2; 5,1 and 6,1), besides four clauses joined by οὖν (3,2; 4; 6,2 and 7,1). Of the three paragraphs, only the third (6,1) has a corresponding apodosis. The other two, belonging to the second part, are anacolutha due to the introduction of new themes.

The mention of the delegates in the second part (Mg. 2-5) has been of use for the interpolator to assign a hierarchical rank to each one of them. When he introduces the sentence belonging to the deacon Zotion (2bc), *"fellow-servant"* of Ignatius, he forgets the primitive apodosis. Repetition of the verb πρέπω in impersonal form (3,1a.2a; 4a), existence of proper names (2a) and of some typically Ignatian expressions (3,2a; 4a) lead us to suspect that hidden in this sequence lies the original Ignatian period. This would be headed by the first 'Επεὶ οὖν (2a) and would have its corresponding apodosis, which in turn gives rise to a digression. In fact, at the beginning of the third part, Ignatius has been forced to reassume the initial period (2a) with a new 'Επεὶ οὖν (6,1).

The reconstruction we propose of this second part is based on the following considerations: (a) Parallelism between Mg. 2a and Eph. 1,3a and other passages there quoted; (b) Presence of four proper names, belonging to the delegates from Magnesia; (c) Parallel of Mg. 3,2a with Sm. = Eph* 11,2b (πρέπει εἰς τιμὴν θεοῦ); (d) Presence in Rom. inscr. as well as Mg. 3,2a of the same singular locution, τοῦ θελήσαντος, [280] to name God; (e) Inclusion between two πρέπον ἐστὶν (3,2a and 4a) of an interpolated phrase

---

[280] τοῦ θελήσαντος ἡμᾶς. For the construction of θέλω with the accusative, see BAUER, *AA. VV.* II 222. ἡμᾶς GL Dam.: ὑμᾶς AB(g) Lightfoot.

and the consequent logical nexus between the previous phrase
(3,2a) and the one following (4a) the interpolation; (f) Finally,
statement in Mg. 4a of the same distinction as in Rom. 3,2.

Once combined all these elements we have the following heading to Magnesians: Ἐπεὶ οὖν ἠξιώθην ἰδεῖν ὑμᾶς διὰ Δαμᾶ καὶ
Βάσσου καὶ Ἀπολλωνίου καὶ Ζωτίωνος (2a), εἰς τιμὴν ἐκείνου τοῦ θελήσαντος ἡμᾶς πρέπον ἐστὶν (3,2a) μὴ μόνον καλεῖσθαι Χριστιανοὺς ἀλλὰ
καὶ εἶναι (4a), ἐπεὶ τέλος τὰ πράγματα ἔχει κτλ. (5,1).

As can be seen, the presumed second period of 5,1, that starts
with Ἐπεὶ οὖν, but without its corresponding apodosis, once the
οὖν is suppressed, recovers its original function: to motivate the
invitation to be true Christians on the imminent end of all.

84. The interpolator avails himself of this short and simple
heading to develop the theme of the bishop's youth. We shall
now examine the interpolation phrase by phrase:

(1) In the *first* phrase (Mg. 2) he has very logically distributed
the three hierarchical grades between the four delegates from
Magnesia: one bishop, two presbyters (collegial sense!) and a
deacon, Ignatius' "*fellow-servant*". Only in mentioning this last
he stresses with the optative ὀναίμην (typical of Ignatius) [281] that
he submits to the bishop and the presbytery. In this way, the
figure of the deacon, Ignatius/Zotion, appears as guarantor of
perfect submission. ὑποτάσσω, which we have already found in
Eph. 2,2e, is used exclusively by the forger (9 times). The expression ὡς χάριτι θεοῦ is equivalent to ὁ χαρισάμενος ὑμῖν κτλ. of Eph.
1,3; ὡς νόμῳ Ἰησοῦ Χριστοῦ, to ὡς θεοῦ ἐντολήν of Sm. 8,1. [282]

(2) The *second* phrase (Mg. 3,1), entirely spurious, brings
out one of the problems that most worries the forger. However,
it lends itself to a variety of interpretations because of (a) the poly-
valence of the terms integrating the sentence οὐ προσειληφότας τὴν
φαινομένην νεωτερικὴν τάξιν, (b) the task assigned to the phrase introduced by καθὼς (mere comparison or *a fortiori* argument), (c) the

---

[281] Ign. always uses it with a plural complement and as a colophon to a sentence. The interpolator always with a singular complement and in a relative clause
(οὗ ὀναίμην). See nrs. 47, 75.

[282] Perhaps also Tr. 13,2: ὑποτασσόμενοι τῷ ἐπισκόπῳ ὡς τῇ ἐντολῇ, ὁμοίως
καὶ τῷ πρεσβυτερίῳ. In all these cases χάρις, ἐντολή should be translated in the
active sense of "the grace, order that God, Jesus Christ gives" (LIGHTFOOT, *AA.
FF.* II: II/1, 181, "'the voice ordering', not 'the thing ordered'").

correction required by the adversative clause that follows and (d) the historical value in which it claims to be inserted. [283]

Understanding νεωτερικός, predicated of things, in the sense of " recent " [284] and giving to τάξις the obvious meaning of " rank/ office ", theoretically the phrase might be understood as " the newly-created office ". [285] If the presbyters, able to vaunt their age, did not lay claim to this office, giving the presidence to a young man, how much less (a fortiori argument) should the community take advantage of the youthfulness of the bishop. Placing ourselves in the historical context made up by the forger, we find in the Magnesian community a newly-created bishop's office; instead of one of the " elders " a young man has been elected bishop because of his obvious leadership qualities.

ZAHN (following partly Cotelier's interpretation: " recentem illius ordinationem ") grants to τάξις the meaning of " ordination " and proposes to translate: " The presbyters have not taken advantage of the exceptional circumstance that a young man has been ordained bishop ". [286] This interpretation is handicapped

---

[283] A good summing up in LIGHTFOOT, AA. FF. II: II/1, 112-114. The most incisive commentary is still that of PEARSON, vol. I, Ad lectorem (in J. B. COTELIER, SS. Patrum, qui temporibus Apostolicis floruerunt ..., vol. II, Amsterdam 1724, pp. 257ff.).

[284] ZAHN, I. v. A. 304, n. 3, claims to interpret EPIPHANIUS, Panarion haer. 67,3, not in the sense of " new, fresh, modern " but " youthful Psalms ", adducing PLUTARCH, Dion. 7,4, and EUS., E. H. VII. 30,10. However, in Epiphanius it can only have the sense of " recent ": ψαλμούς τε πολλούς νεωτερικούς ἐπλάσσατο, to distinguish them from the " canonical " ones. Other testimony in JULIUS AFRICANUS, Letter 1 to Origen: νεωτερικὸν δὲ (σύγγραμμα) καὶ πεπλανημένον δείκνυταί τε καὶ κατὰ πολλοὺς ἀπελέγχεται τρόπους. Hence, the emphatic statements of ZAHN (" heisst weder neu noch neuerlich ") and LIGHTFOOT, AA. FF. II: II/1, 114 (" never, so far as I am aware, ' recent " ') remain ineffective.

[285] SALMASIUS, Appar. ad Libr. de Prim. Pap. 57, Lyon 1645, meant it of the recent institution of the episcopate as such (" sicut cognovi presbyteros, non ut accipientes eam, quae nova apparet, institutionem, sed tamquam prudentes in Deo, cedentes ipsi "). PETAU, Theol. Dogm. III, De Eccl. Hier. lib. V, Chap. VIII 5, Antwerp 1700, p. 162, retains the forced interpretation of οὐ προσειληφότας (" non assumentes " L: " not recognizing, repudiating "), but translates νεωτερικὴ τάξις by " novitia et recens ordinatio et institutio ", according to which some claimed mature age as aptitudes for government acknowledged by the free election of the community, as was practised from Apostolic times.

[286] I. v. A. 305: " Die Presbyter haben den ' äusserlichen Umstand ', dass ein jüngerer Mann zum Bischof bestellt worden ist, sich nicht zu Nutze gemacht ...".

by the fact that the first sentence and the comparison or *a fortiori* argument deal with different matters (age — ordination), an observation that holds also for the first interpretation (age — office). Neither of these two interpretations explain the use of the perfect tense, for they presuppose punctiliar actions.

The third interpretation, proposed by LIGHTFOOT and followed by BAUER tries to clear away this difficulty. [287] τάξις νεωτερική would be a locution equivalent to ἡλικία. The nexus between the two phrases would be set up by the equivalences: " *age* " (in the context: " youthfulness ")/" *youthful condition* " (in the context: " youthfulness ").

If instead of meaning φαινομένην in the sense of " outwardly ", we understand it as " apparently ", we have a fresh variant: " *of his apparently youthful condition* ". [288] The presbyters or " elders " have never taken advantage (οὐ προσειληφότας: the negative perfect denies not only a punctiliar act but all ulterior ones) of the — more apparent that real — youthful condition of the bishop, rather they respect him, in that they submit not to him but to the Father of Jesus Christ, the universal Bishop.

The theme of youthfulness already appears in 1Tim. 4,12. The nearest parallel shows up in the Didascalia II.1,1-3, where an exception to the norm of fifty years is allowed, when a small community has only a young man having the required capacities for the bishopric. Note how the general norm requiring the bishop to be a man advanced in age is justified: τρόπῳ τινὶ τὰς νεωτερικὰς ἀτάξεις ... ἐκπεφευγώς, inspired in turn by 1Tim. 2,22.

The reason for this respect for a young bishop on the part of the presbyters lies in the prudence they have received from God, [289] enabling them to distinguish between the earthly bishop and the paradigmatic Bishop, God. This is a theme dear to the forger. In Eph. 1,3c he speaks of Onesimus as " *humanly* (ἐν

---

[287] LIGHTFOOT, *AA. FF.* II: II/1, 112f.; he translates: " have not taken advantage of his outwardly youthful estate "; BAUER, *AA. VV.* II 221f., translates: " seine offen for Augen liegende jugendliche Beschaffenheit nicht missbrauchen ". STEPHANOS, *Thesaurus Graecae Linguae* VII, Paris 1848-1854, col. 1820C, also admits this meaning; " Sunt vero qui in nonnullis huiusmodi locis existiment reddi etiam posse Conditio, et Gradus."

[288] As LELONG, *PP. AA.* III 30f., translates.

[289] φρονίμους GLB: φρονίμῳ A(g) Lightfoot. The Arab version (B) has reinforced the GL reading.

σαρκὶ) *your bishop* " ; in Mg. 6,1c he says that " *he takes the place of God* " (εἰς τόπον θεοῦ) and in Tr. 3,1b that he is "*a type of the Father* " (τύπον τοῦ πατρός). But Ignatius, speaking of his church of Syria in Rom. 9,1 says that it now has God for its Shepherd in his own place, that is, Jesus the Messiah, the only one who will *supervise* (ἐπισκοπήσει) it, as in Pol. 8,3 (ἐπισκοπῇ) corresponding to the original conclusion of Ephesians.

(3) In the *third* phrase (Mg. 3,2) the forger insists again on the distinction between visible and invisible bishop. Accounts must be rendered, not to a man but to God.

(4) The *fourth* phrase (Mg. 4b-d) amplifies the original sentence. The rather awkward paraphrase of the original [290] has given rise to conjectures of an assimilation — by some amanuensis — between an hypothetic λαλοῦσιν and the preceding καλεῖσθαι. [291] His tendency to imitate the original (ὥσπερ καὶ) leads him to change the meaning of the phrase, so as to impose his new concept. The interpolator will insist to the point of satiety that nobody " should do anything without the bishop ". [292] The precept here expressed, " *according to the commandment* ", [293] will be elucidated in Sm. 8, as we shall see. Ignatius insisted on assiduous community meetings to ward off heresy and schisms. [294] The interpolator, on the contrary, concentrates on " *validity* ", [295] which in turn depends on the person presiding. [296] It seems, again according to the inter-

---

[290] LIGHTFOOT, *AA. FF.* II: II/1. 116: " But καλοῦσιν is an awkward expression."

[291] ZAHN, *I. v. A.* 302, n. 1, suggests reading λαλοῦσιν. The presumed confirmation in 10,3 belongs to Ign. — The transition from καλεῖσθαι (Ign.) to καλοῦσιν (interp.) is based on the fundamental meaning of " give the title of ".

[292] See Mg. 7,1b; Tr. 2,2ab; Phld. 7,2d; Sm. 8,1-2; 9,1e; Pol. 4,1c-e; 5,2d. An equivalent expression is extant in *Did.* II. 27,1-2 and in den *Apost. Const.* II. 30,2; 31,1; VIII. 47,39.

[293] κατ' ἐντολὴν is found only here. In the *Did.* II. 25,2 it describes the way the bishop should administer (Syr. version), or how the community should contribute (the Greek text of the *Ap. Const.*); in 46,2 it refers to the bishop's manner of living; in III. 10,8 to how widows should behave (see III. 8,1.4). The way the Eucharist should be celebrated is described perfectly in II. 57,2-59,3.

[294] Eph. 4,2; 5,2.3; 6,2; 13,1; Mg. 7; Phld. = Mg* 4; 6,2; Sm. = Eph* 7,1.

[295] Note his predilection for βέβαιος and derivants: Mg. 4d; Sm. 8,1.2; Mg. 13,1; Phld. inscr[b].

[296] Eph. 20,2; Mg. 6,1c.2f; 13,1; etc.

polator, some Christians of Magnesia gather together²⁹⁷ without the bishop's consent; according Ignatius, on the contrary, there
has been no schism in Magnesia, but he warns them beforehand
against the dangers of the Judaizers (Mg. 11).

(5) The *last* phrase (Mg. 5,1), finally, which actually starts
with Ἐπεὶ οὖν, has not been interpolated, but simply modified.
By adding the particle οὖν, the period has become independent (a
fresh anacoluthon!). At first it was a digression: to motivate the
former invitation to be true Christians because of the imminence
of the parousia.

85. As we did in preceding analyses, we offer the translation of the whole second part with the interpolations in italics and
brackets:

" ² ᵃForasmuch then as I have been deemed worthy to see you in the
person of Damas {, *your very worthy bishop,*} and {*the worthy presbyters*} Bassus and Apollonius and {*my fellow-servant the deacon*} Zotion,
{ᵇ*with whom I would rejoice* ᶜ*because he is submitted to the bishop as
to a gift of God and to the presbytery as to an order of Jesus Christ,*
— ³,¹ ᵃ*But for you, too, it is fitting not to seek to profit by the bishop's
youth,* ᵇ*but rather according to the capacity (you have received) of God
the Father you show him all respect,* ᶜ*following the example (καθὼς) of
the venerable presbyters, who — as I heard — have never taken advantage
of his apparently youthful condition,* ᵈ*but rather with their godly prudence
respect him:* ᵉ*yet not him, but the Father of Jesus Christ, the Bishop of
all men.* ³,² ᵃ*Therefore,*} for the honour of him who has shown us his
love, it is fitting {*to obey without dissimulation.* ᵇ*For a man does not
deceive this bishop who is visible,* ᶜ*but defraud rather the invisible one.*
ᵈ*In such a case he must reckon not with man but with God who knows
what is hidden.* ⁴ ᵃ*It is therefore fitting*} not only to be called Christians
by name, but also to be such in fact, {ᵇ*and not like some persons who
call him bishop, but in everything act apart from him.* ᶜ*Such men do
not seem to me to keep a good conscience,* ᵈ*forasmuch as they do not
gather together in a valid way, as is prescribed.* ⁵,¹ ᵃ*Thus,*} since the
concrete realities are coming to an end ᵇand these two issues — death
and life — are set before us at the same time, ᶜand each man shall
go to his own place. ⁵,² ᵃFor just as there are two coinages — the one
of God, the other of the world —, ᵇand each of them has its proper
stamp impressed upon it — ᶜthe unbelievers the stamp of this world;
ᵈthe believers, by love, the stamp of God the Father through Jesus

---

²⁹⁷ συναθροίζω appears only here. This term (see Acts 12,12) is frequent in
the *Did.* II. 57,2; 59,2; 62,1; V. 19,1; 20,12; VI. 22,2 and in the *Apost. Const.* VI.
5,7; VIII. 34,10; 35,2. The *Apost. Const.* likewise use the substantive ἄθροισμα:
II. 61,2; III. 18,1; VIII. 1,20.

the Messiah —, ʿunless through this stamp (δι' οὗ) ²⁹⁸ we are ready to bear willingly his death which links us to his passion, ʲhis life is not in us '' (Mg. 2-5).

This whole interpolation hinges on the problem of the bishop's youth, and there are two attempts to find an issue: (1) The example of the *elders* of the community, gifted with spiritual *discernment*; (2) The close relationship between the visible and invisible bishop. It is to be noted that since all these developments are intentional, at the end of our analysis it will be possible to reconstruct with the many traces scattered through the letters, a close portrait of the personality of the interpolator and a list of the problems that worried him.

86.   The *exhortation* to do all in conformity with God in the third part (Mg. 6-7), also obliged the forger to introduce the necessary corrections.   The original exhortation started with a new allusion to the community situation, made known through the Magnesian delegates, ²⁹⁹ due to the digression in chapter 5 (6,1a). Here follows the exhortation to do all things in concord with God, stated in a lapidary phrase: παραινῶ, ἐν ὁμονοίᾳ θεοῦ σπουδάζετε πάντα πράσσειν (6,1b).   This is the dominant theme of the genuine letter to the Magnesians (Mg. + Phld.), written precisely to face the discords aroused by the Judaizers.   Consequently, the whole letter is pervaded by the theme of '' concord '' (ἐν ὁμονοίᾳ θεοῦ: Phld. = Mg* inscr.; Mg. 6,1b; 15f = subscr*; ὁμοήθειαν θεοῦ, Mg. 6,2a; κατὰ θεόν, Phld. 4d) and '' unity '' (ἕνωσις: Mg. 1,2; Phld. 4b; 8,1a; ἑνότης: Phld. 2,2b; 3,2c; 5,2d; 8,1d; ἐπὶ τὸ αὐτό: Mg. 7,1d; Phld. 6,2d; εἷς, μία, ἕν: Mg. 7,1d-2; Phld. 4ab).   As we have already shown (see nr. 28), the exhortation just beginning goes on through the whole letter to the Magnesians (Mg. 6-12) and part of Philadelphians (Phld. 2-4), Mg. 11-12 being the hinge on which a perfectly concentric structure turns.

---

²⁹⁸ δι' οὗ (sc. χαρακτῆρος) ἐὰν μὴ κτλ. takes the place of the apodosis of the explanatory sentence headed by ὥσπερ γὰρ κτλ., slightly displaced by the parenthetical phrase οἱ ἄπιστοι... Ἰησοῦ Χριστοῦ. The coin symbolizes death (note how Ign., speaking of death in symbolic sense uses τὸ ἀποθανεῖν instead of ὁ θάνατος: Mg. 5,2; Tr. 2,1; 6,2) by which believers are made one with the passion and death of Jesus.

²⁹⁹ Compare Ἐπεὶ οὖν ἠξιώθην ἰδεῖν ὑμᾶς διὰ Δαμᾶ κτλ. of Mg. 2 with Ἐπεὶ οὖν ἐν τοῖς προγεγραμμένοις προσώποις τὸ πᾶν πλῆθος ἐθεώρησα κτλ. of 6,1.

For his part, the forger is also quite sensitive to the "concord" and "unity" theme, but for different motives. Ignatius' insistent invitation to the communities to meet in a single thanksgiving focussed on Jesus the Messiah was already insufficient. It was necessary that this be exteriorized by union with the bishop. For this he always joins the unity attained by the Eucharistic meeting to the unity personified in the bishop together with the presbyters and deacons, as we have seen above with regard precisely to Phld. 4c (see nr. 77). In the present context he has inserted two sentences. We should identify them to make an exact reconstruction of the genuine exhortation.

(1) The *first* interpolated phrase (Mg. 6,1cd) tries to correct the purpose of the Ignatian one, " Strive to do all things in conformity with God, Jesus the Messiah, who was with the Father before time began and was made manifest at the end of time ". Thus the interpolator has divided the first Ignatian sentence, so that ἐν ὁμονοίᾳ θεοῦ becomes a reference to God, the Father, and could introduce, in this manner, through a simple genitive absolute (προκαθημένου), a very important touch, that is, that we cannot reach this " conformity with God " unless someone occupies the " *presidence* " of the community. The " presidence " belongs to the bishop and the presbytery, but not to the deacons. But because he had to connect this with the second part of the interrupted sentence, Ἰησοῦ Χριστοῦ κτλ., he had to introduce the deacons representative of *Jesus Christ* as well, thus forcing the construction of the phrase itself (προκαθημένου ... πεπιστευμένων ...).[300] Reconstructed it runs ἐν ὁμονοίᾳ θεοῦ Ἰησοῦ Χριστοῦ, ὃς πρὸ αἰώνων παρὰ πατρὶ ἦν καὶ ἐν τέλει ἐφάνη, σπουδάζετε πάντα πράσσειν and echoes in Rom. 3,3: ὁ γὰρ θεὸς ἡμῶν Ἰησοῦς Χριστὸς ἐν πατρὶ ὢν μᾶλλον φαίνεται.

---

[300] See LIGHTFOOT, *AA. FF.* II : II/1, 119 : " The same word προκαθημένων may well be understood with the following τῶν πρεσβυτέρων, as it is used of the presbyters just below ; but with τῶν διακόνων it is necessary to supply some other word, such as συμπαρόντων, according to the sense. The clause πεπιστευμένων κ.τ.λ. is added by way of explanation, ' seeing that they have been entrusted etc.' "; LAKE, *AA. FF.* I 203 : " The sentences seem to be unfinished : the Apostolic Constitutions ii.26 say ' Let the Deacon be honoured as a type of Holy Spirit '." (However in the Apost. Const. it is not the deacon who is type of the Holy Spirit but the deaconess: the deacon is a type of Jesus Christ!)

(2) The *second* phrase (Mg. 6,2f-7,1b) takes its rise from the immediately preceding phrase, making it into a positive construction. Ignatius said: " let there be nothing among you that could divide (μερίσαι) you " (6,2e); the interpolator adds: " *on the contrary, be united* (ἐνώθητε) *with the bishop and those who preside as models and a lesson of integrity* " (6,2f). He goes on to explain this " model " with the paradigm Lord (Apostles)/Father, to justify the community/bishop (presbyters) dependence (7,1ab). The paradigm we already know (Eph. 5,1; Mg. 13,2) constitutes one of the interpolator's characteristic turns of phrase (see also Phld. 7,2 and Sm. 8,1).

87. If we eliminate the interpolations, we shall see that after the reassuming sentence and the lapidary exhortation mentioned above its development follows in a chiastic form: a totality, expressed in both negative and positive (= individual relations) form; with a new antithesis containing two negative sentences and one positive, recapitulated for another totality (= communitarian relations). [301] The interpolator has broken the rythm of the phrase by introducing a fresh antithesis and a correlation. [302] Let us look at the position of the interpolated sentences (in brackets and italics) in the translation of the text:

" [6,1] ªSince, then, I have looked on the whole community with eyes of faith and affection [303] through the aforementioned persons,[304] ᵇI exhort you to strive to do all things in conformity with God, { *ᶜpresided over by the bishop in the place of God and the presbyters representing the senate of the Apostles, ᵈto the deacons, my beloved, having been entrusted with the diaconia of*} Jesus the Messiah, who was with the Father before time began and was made manifest at the end of time. [6,2] ªAll of you, then, having been given a resemblance with God, ᵇrespect each other ᶜand let no one regard his neighbour with human intent, ᵈbut love one another at all times like Jesus the Messiah; ᵉlet there be nothing among you that could divide you, { *ᶠon the contrary, be united with the bishop and those who preside as models and a lesson of integrity. [7,1] ªJust as the Lord, then, did nothing without the Father, (being*

---

[301] πάντες οὖν... καὶ μηδείς... ἀλλ'... || μηδέν... μηδὲ... ἀλλ'... πάντες...

[302] πάντες οὖν... || καὶ μηδείς... ἀλλ'... || μηδέν... ἀλλ'... || ὥσπερ... οὕτως... || μηδὲ... ἀλλ... || πάντες...

[303] ἀγάπη: see critical apparatus, p. 356, l. 20.

[304] SAB add: " that is, through the bishop and the presbyters and deacons ". Probably it is a gloss of the Syriac translator.

united with him,)[305] *neither for himself nor for the Apostles*: *[b]so neither should you do anything without the bishop or the presbyters,}* *[c]nor at-*tempt to have any particular revelations, *[d]but rather (let there be) in* common one prayer, one supplication, one mind, one hope, with love, *[e]with this flawless joy, that is Jesus the Messiah, [f]than whom there is* nothing better: *[7,2 a]run together, all of you, as to one sanctuary of* God, as to one altar, to one Jesus the Messiah, *[b]who came forth from* One Father *[c]and has returned and is with the One* " (Mg. 6-7).

According to Ignatius' text, the first member of the chiasm (Mg. 6,2a-d) bases the respect and love we owe our neighbour on the fact that we have received a likeness with God; the second (6,2e + 7,1c-2), warns the community against divisions and pious particularisms by polarizing it wholly in the person of Jesus.

Between God and the community the interpolator places the hierarchical trilogy by adducing as reason the triple analogy: bishop/God, presbyters/Apostles, deacons/Jesus Christ. Then, with another comparison, he warns that nothing should be done without the bishop or the presbyters, just as Jesus Christ did nothing for himself nor for the Apostles without the Father (see Mg. 13,2).

Later we shall examine thoroughly the first trilogy. For the moment it should be noted that by trying to join this to the comparison: Jesus Christ/Father, the forger was obliged to change the logical correlation that would be: community is to the bishop /presbyters what Jesus Christ is to God/Apostles, by modifying the second member: what Jesus Christ/Apostles is to God the Father. Observe, likewise, that in the third member of the trilogy he has let slip an incongruity: deacons (plural)/Jesus Christ (singular), and that the vertical nature of the proposed symbolism is coherent only between the representatives, bishop-presbyters-deacons, and not between those represented, God-Apostles-Jesus Christ. In analyzing the origin of this symbolism, it will be possible to explain these incongruities.

88. *Tr.* 1,1-3,2. — The heading of Trallians follows the same pattern we have found in Ephesians and Magnesians: (I.) Situation of the community making mention of the only delegate sent to Smyrna, Polybius (Tr. 1,1); (II.) Invitation to remain united to God (1,2-3,2); (III.) Beginning of the exhortation (3,3). However, unlike the headings of Eph. and Mg., and in keeping with

---

[305] See critical apparatus, p. 357, l. 2.

the compendious character of the letter, the heading of Tr. was very short. There was a certain relation between the size of the community, number of delegates and length of the letter. Thus, the community of *Ephesus*, placed in the provincial capital of Asia, sent five delegates: the original letter to the Ephesians consisted of actual Eph. and Sm. with a long conclusion that can be reconstructed with Eph.-Sm. (-Phld.)-Pol. conclusions. The community of *Magnesia* sent four delegates: the original letter to the Magnesians included actual Mg. and Phld. *Tralles* sent only one delegate: the original letter to the Trallians is the actual one without interpolations, a kind of anticipation of Eph*.

The interpolator has not taken this detail into account. By means of amplifications he has given the Tr. heading the same length as that of the other two letters. As far as the interpolations are concerned, after mentioning Polybius he has intercalated " *your bishop* " as was to be expected. Then he has cut off the last sentence, to leave one section in the heading (1,2) and make use of the other (2,1bc and 2,2bc) to support his particular ideas. The reconstruction was not easy, because he has inverted the order of the sentences. We shall see this in detail.

89. The existence of authentic Ignatian sentences has been evident thanks to the verification of similarities of style and terminology with other original passages and to slight incongruities in the correlations set up by the interpolator.

(1) A first incongruity appears in the correlation bishop/ Jesus Christ. Jesus Christ is the model of submission to the Father for the community that should be submissive to its bishop (Eph. 5,1; Mg. 7,1ab; 13,2; Phld. 7,2; Sm. 8,1). It fits in logically with his symbolism bishop/God. Why did he change the analogy here? Simply because he is paraphrasing the original text. Indeed, the sentence,

" not living like the people [306] but like Jesus the Messiah, who died for us, so that once linked to his death you might escape dying " (Tr. 2,1bc),

is genuinely Ignatian:

The phrase τὸν δι' ἡμᾶς ἀποθανόντα occurs in Rom. 6,1c (τὸν ὑπὲρ ἡμῶν ἀποθανόντα) and Sm. 2a (ἔπαθεν δι' ἡμᾶς). The construc-

---

[306] κατὰ ἀνθρώπους: see critical apparatus, p. 365, l. 13.

tion πιστεύειν εἰς + acc. is exclusively Ignatian (see Mg. 10,3b.c and Sm. 6,1b), as are other uses of πιστεύω in the sense of " believe in ", " adhere to " (the interpolator uses it only in Mg. 6,1d with the meaning of "to be entrusted with "), θάνατος and ἀποθνήσκω (except for Eph. 20,2, inspired by a liturgical text). See for the rest Sm. 6,1 and Mg. 5,2 (more remotely Rom. 6,1; Mg. 9,2; Sm. 4,2; Tr. 9,2).

(2) Equally Ignatian is the sentence:

" Jesus the Messiah, our hope, in whose company if we persevere we shall be found ..." (Tr. 2,2bc).

The identification of this very short and extremely subtle sentence has been possible thanks to two slight incongruities that the interpolator let slip into his paraphrase: (a) The specification " as to the Apostles *of Jesus Christ* ", unique of its kind (see Mg. 6,1c; 7,1a; 13,1.2; Tr. 3,1c; 7,1d; 12,2d; Sm. 8,1). Even Ignatius mentions it in absolute form (Eph. 11,2f; Phld. = Mg* 5,1h and 9,1e), but still together with adjectival use (Rom. 4,3b; Tr. 3,3d); (b) The passage of the first person plural, " our ", " we shall be found ", to the second plural, " *even as you do* ", " *submit (you)* ".

(3) On the other hand, the formula " Jesus the Messiah, our hope " is typical of Ignatius (Mg. 11e; Tr. inscr.; Sm. = Eph* 10,2c), as well as the ritual greeting, " May you be strengthened by the favour of God, Jesus the Messiah, our common hope ", belonging to the second farewell formula in Eph*, reconstructed from Sm. 13,2d + Eph. 21,2e and Phld. 11,2f (see nr. 54,4), and the archaic farewell formula of Phld. 11,2f, " May you be strengthened by the Messiah Jesus, our common hope " (see for the present nr. 54,2).

(4) But there has been the passive of εὑρίσκω — used no less than 21 times by Ignatius, for once by the interpolator (Pol. 4,3) — and the first person plural (εὑρεθησόμεθα), as well as the absence of its corresponding nominal predicate (ἐν ᾧ goes with διάγοντες) what has put us on the right path. In one case we had μιμητὰς ὄντας θεοῦ, referred in the present text to God, unlike its use by Ignatius who refers always to Jesus the Messiah. [307] In the other,

---

[307] μιμηταὶ θεοῦ, τοῦ κυρίου, etc. always refers, according to Ign., to Jesus the Messiah: see Eph. 1,1; 10,3; Rom. 6,3 (μ. εἶναι τοῦ πάθους τοῦ θεοῦ μου).

the genitive construction of the sentence in question. Joining this
with the former we obtain the desired sense of the original Ignatian phrase: μιμητὰς ὄντας θεοῦ Ἰησοῦ Χριστοῦ. That we are on
Ignatius' track is confirmed by the fact that by the juncture with
the sentence that just before has turned out to be Ignatian, we
obtain a perfect sequence: Ἀποδεξάμενος οὖν τὴν κατὰ θεὸν εὔνοιαν
δι᾿ αὐτοῦ, ἐδόξασα εὑρὼν ὑμᾶς — ὡς ἔγνων — μιμητὰς ὄντας θεοῦ (Tr.
1,2) Ἰησοῦ Χριστοῦ, τῆς ἐλπίδος ἡμῶν, ἐν ᾧ διάγοντες εὑρεθησόμεθα
(2,2bc) οὐ κατὰ ἀνθρώπους ζῶντες, ἀλλὰ κατὰ Ἰησοῦν Χριστὸν τὸν
δι᾿ ἡμᾶς ἀποθανόντα, ἵνα πιστεύσαντες εἰς τὸν θάνατον αὐτοῦ τὸ ἀποθανεῖν ἐκφύγ<ωμεν> (2,1b-d).

At last the nominal predicate of " we shall be found " has
shown up, namely, " not living ... but ... " (see equivalent formulas in Eph. 11,1.2; 12,2; Mg. 9,1; Pol. = Eph* 7,1). We only
had to give ἐκφύγητε the form it had before being adapted to an
exhortation to the community. It is possible that the touching
up also replaced ἡμᾶς for ὑμᾶς, as appears still in LC. Common
sense has brought it back to its primitive form.

(5) The interpolator has not only modified the original sentence referring " imitators " to God (the Father), but with the
introduced changes he makes Ignatius say that only " *when you
are submitted to the bishop as to Jesus Christ you show me that
(you are) living ... like Jesus Christ* ", which is equal to saying that
the only visible model is the bishop. In this way he places him
as mediator between God and the community. Note the use of
the conjunction ὡς to introduce the unusual equivalence bishop/
Jesus Christ.

90. The rest of Tr. 2,1-3,2 has been drawn up by the interpolator. Besides the terminology typical of the forger, there are
a whole series of constants that converge:

(1) Tr. 2,1ab: " *For when you are submitted to the bishop as
to Jesus Christ you appear to me ...* " contains the verb ὑποτάσσω
exclusively used by the interpolator and the mark of reciprocity
with the conjunctive particle ὡς; (2) For the parenthetic sentence
of 2,2a, " *even as you do* ", see Eph. 4,1b; Pol. 1,2f; 4,1e; for
the sentence: " *It is necessary ... that you realize nothing without
the bishop* " see Mg. 7,1a.b; Tr. 2,2a; Pol. 4,1c.d (always with the
preposition ἄνευ, typical of the interpolator; Ignatius only uses
it in Tr. 11,2e), as well as Mg. 4b; Tr. 3,1d; 7,2c; Phld. 7,2d;

Sm. 8,1d.2c (all with the preposition χωρίς; the interpolator always applies it to the hierarchical grades, while Ignatius places it only before Jesus the Messiah: Eph. 11,2a; Mg. 9,2a; Tr. 9,1b.2d); (3) In 2,2b the verb ὑποτάσσω reappears and the conjunctive particle ὡς, both referring this time to the presbyters; (4) In 2,3 the deacons are told they " *must shun blame as* (*they must shun*) *fire* ", where we find the conjunctive particle ὡς once more. (5) This usage is repeated no less than four times in 3,1 to introduce the correspondences: deacons/Jesus Christ, bishop/Father, presbyters/God's senate and college of Apostles, [308] which culminate in the statement : " *Without these we cannot speak of a church* "; (6) In 3,2b we have again the Latinism " *exemplarium* ", predicated this time of the bishop; (7) The last sentence of 3,2e: " *to whom* [*the bishop*] *even the heathen* (τοὺς ἀθέους: lit. " godless "), *I am sure, respect* " contradicts the pejorative meaning given by Ignatius to this epithet in the same letter: " as some atheists (ἄθεοι), that is, disbelievers, say, that he suffered only apparently " (Tr. 10), applied obviously to the Gnostic teachers.

91.   The original sequence follows once more in Tr. 3,3. In the translation we offer of the complete heading of Trallians and the beginning of the exhortation, we have rendered the sequence its original order (2,2 before 2,1) and marked the interpolations (in brackets) with italics, so that the reader may easily follow the thread of the Ignatian argument:

" [1,1] *a*I heard you possess an unblamable and not discriminating disposition in endurance, not an acquired habit, but by nature, *b*according as Polybius { *c your bishop*} informed me, *d*who came to Smyrna by the will of God and of Jesus the Messiah, *e*and so shared my joy at being enchained for the Messiah, Jesus, *f*that in his person I beheld [309] your whole community. [1,2] *a*Having therefore received this show of goodwill so much in agreement with God through him, *b*I praised (God) for having found you — as I heard — to be imitators of God {[2,2] *a It is necessary, then, even as you do, that you realize nothing without the bishop. bMoreover submit to the presbytery as to the Apostles of*} Jesus the Messiah, our hope, *c*in whose company if we persevere, we shall

---

[308] For the meaning of σύνδεσμον see W. F. ARNDT – F. W. GINGRICH, *A Greek English Lexicon of the New Testament and Other Early Christian Literature*, Chicago 1957/1971 (an adaptation of W. BAUER, *W. z. N. T.*), s. v.: " bundle, band, college "; LELONG, *PP. AA.* III 45, has already translated it by " le collège des Apôtres ".

[309] θεωρεῖσθαι: see critical apparatus, p. 364, l. 12.

be found {^{2,1} ^{a}*For when you are submitted to the bishop as to Jesus Christ, ^{b}you appear to me*} not living like the people but like Jesus the Messiah, ^{c}who died for us, ^{d}so that once linked to his death we (lit. *you*) might escape dying.

{^{2,3} ^{a}*It is further needful that those who are deacons of the mysteries of Jesus Christ please all men in every way. ^{b}For they are not deacons of meats and drinks but ministers of the church of God. ^{c}Consequently, they must shun blame as fire.* ^{3,1} ^{a}*As for what concerns all, let them respect the deacons as Jesus Christ, ^{b}even as the bishop as a type of the Father ^{c}and the presbyters as the senate of God and the college of Apostles. ^{d}Without these we cannot speak of a church.* ^{3,2} ^{a}*As for them I am convinced that such is your attitude. ^{b}For I received, and I have with me, the example of your affection in the person of your bishop, ^{c}whose very demeanour is a great lesson ^{d}and his meekness a spun ^{e}— a man whom even the heathen, I am sure, respect.*}

^{3,3} ^{a}Although I love you, I am sparing, ^{b}since I might write you more briefly [310] on this subject. ^{c}It is not my intention to give you directives like an apostle, since I am a condemned man " (Tr. 1-3).

* * *

The interpolations we have found in the heading of the letter to the Trallians confirm that the basic synthesis of the interpolator's ecclesiology circles round the triple analogy: God/bishop, Apostles/presbyters, Jesus Christ/deacons. In Mg. 6,1cd we have already found this expression. Equivalent ones — at least in part — appear in Eph. 6,1; Mg. 3,1-2; 7,1; 13,2 and Sm. 8,1. Not always, however, is the forger consistent in the application of these correspondences. Thus, in Eph. 3,2e-4,1a and Tr. 2,1a he has had to modify — because of the underlying Ignatian text — the analogy God/bishop into Jesus Christ/bishop, in disagreement with the symbolism noted. Further on, once we know the exact extent of the interpolation, we shall deal expressly with this symbolism, as well as with any noteworthy coincidences — already observed by commentators — that exist between the analogies and terminology used by the interpolator and that employed by the Didascalist.

---

[310] For the meaning of this formula, see nr. 35,1. ὑπὲρ τούτου referred originally to the anti-Docetic theme of the real and salvific death of Jesus the Messiah (theme of this letter in synthesis) announced in 2,1bc. The long interpolation of 2,2-3,2 has inevitably separated both sentences.

At the end of this first section — whose object was to deduce the specific content of the interpolation from those passages that either were an integral part of the new imposed structure by the forger to the Ignatian letters, or else contained a series of serious anomalies with regard to other certainly genuine passages — we have acquired important knowledge relative to the characteristic terminology of the interpolator, analogies he uses, certain pronounced stylistic constants, proceedings he makes use of to turn the original meaning of the phrase and, above all, his ecclesiological presuppositions. As we have gone forward grasping the motives of the interpolation, as it takes shape like a script overlying Ignatius' writing, the number of internal parallels have increased.

Nevertheless, it was to be presumed that the forger would not have limited himself to falsifying interrupting clauses, inscriptions and conclusions, and interpolating the genuine headings. There remained the possibility that he had inserted sentences or entire clauses into the body of the genuine Ignatian letters and that, because they presented no structural incongruities or internal contradictions, had escaped a first scrutiny. We shall deal with this matter in the next section.

II. EXACT EXTENT OF THE INTERPOLATION

After verifying the above-mentioned criteria in a second scrutiny of the textus receptus of the Ignatian letters we obtain the following results:

(a) *Eph.* contains no more interpolations that those already outlined (1,3c-2,1b.d.f.h, except the proper names; 2,2e; 3,2e-4,1c; 5,1. 2de. 3f-6,1; 20; and the sentences of 21,1cd.e);

(b) Neither does *Mg.* contain more interpolated passages than those already mentioned (2a partim. bc; 3-4, except 3,2a and 4a; 6,1c-d. 2f-7,1b; 13; and what concerns Polycarp in 15d);

(c) *Tr.* stil includes some interpolated sentences, besides those already identified (1,1c; 2,1a. 2ab. 3-3,2), that is, 7,1d. 2cd (nrs. 92f.); 12,2d and 13,2b (nrs. 94f.);

(d) *Rom.* contains no interpolation;

(e) *Phld.* conceals a considerable interpolation (Chap. 7: nrs. 97-107) and some very short sentences, one concerning the bishop in 3,2b (nr. 96), another the bishop's senate in 8,1e (nr. 108), besides those already identified (inscr[b].-1; 4c and 10-11);

(f) *Sm.* also conceals a notable interpolation (Chap. 8, which really starts in 7,2f: nr. 109) and the sentences relative to the bishop in 9,1c-e (nr. 110); up to now only interpolations in the concluding section have been mentioned (Chap. 12 and 13,1ab);

(g) Finally, the whole first part of *Pol.*, drawn up in the singular, is spurious (inscr.-5: nr. 111); in the second part, addressed in the plural to the community (6-8), there are several interpolated sentences and phrases, all of them already identified (6,1a-c; 7,1a. 2; 8,1. 2d [only that relating to Polycarp]).

As we have done up to now, we shall take each of these interpolations, justify them and set forth their exact extent.

92. *Tr.* 7,1d and 2cd. — Ignatius invites the community of Tralles to take precautions against Docetic-Gnostic propaganda (that is, against heresy: 6,1). After the invitation (7,1a) come two practical pieces of advice: (a) Not to be puffed up (7,1b), and (b) To be inseparable from God Jesus the Messiah (7,1c). The interpolator is not satisfied and adds two more: (c) To be inseparable from the bishop, (d) And from the Prescriptions (τῶν διαταγμάτων) of the Apostles (7,1d).

The inclusion of the bishop (c) is parallel with a passage already studied in 2,1a (*when you are submitted to the bishop as to Jesus Christ*) and in Eph. 3,2e (*the bishops... are included in the plan of Jesus Christ*). The one relative to the Apostles (d) raises an interesting datum. This last piece of advice has not suggested to the commentators of the Ignatian textus receptus any connection with the Apostolic Constitutions, whereas they compared with these the paraphrase of Tr. 7,1 drawn up by the Ps.-Ignatius. [311] Nevertheless, in spite of the fact that the latter depends very often on the

---

[311] In Ign. Tr. 7,1 in general there is no comment. BAUER, *AA. VV.* II 236, translates it for " Vorschriften der Apostel "; in *W. z. N. T.*, s. v., for " die apostolischen Anordnungen "; LELONG and CAMELOT, in loc., translate " préceptes des Apôtres "; LIGHTFOOT, *AA. FF.* II: II/1, 169, comments: " The reference is doubtless to the institution of episcopacy ". — As for Ps.-Ign. Tr. 7,1 however ZAHN, *I. v. A.* 152f., and *PP. AA.* II 187, note: " Constitutiones apostolorum libro conscriptas respicere videtur " (*A. C.* II 34,2.5); LIGHTFOOT, *AA. FF.* II: II/2, 739 [II,3, 155]: " The reference is to the spurious *Apostolical Constitutions*: see esp. ii. 20 "; I 251 [II,1, 263] says that " the Ignatian writer accidentally betrays the source of his obligations ".

Constitutions,[312] and notwithstanding the similarity of the text
with the title of this work (Constitutions = ΔΙΑΤΑΓΑΙ)[313] or its
contents[314], in the present case the Ps.-Ignatius has done no more
than paraphrase the text of Tr. 7,1, as it could be proved by comparing both recensions. In the left-hand column we give the genuine
Ignatian text and the interpolated one (in brackets and smaller
type) and in the right-hand we transcribe line by line the equivalents in Ps.-Ignatius:

Ign. Tr. 7,1   *Ps.-Ign. Tr.* 7,1

Ign. Tr. 7,1	Ps.-Ign. Tr. 7,1
Φυλάττεσθε οὖν τοὺς τοιούτους·	Ἀσφαλίζεσθε οὖν τοὺς τοιούτους ...
τοῦτο δὲ ἔσται ὑμῖν	ἐὰν οὖν καὶ ὑμεῖς
μὴ φυσιουμένοις	ἀποθῆσθε φυσίωσιν ...
καὶ οὖσιν ἀχωρίστοις θεοῦ	δυνατὸν ὑμῖν ἐστιν εἶναι ἀχωρί-
Ἰησοῦ Χριστοῦ	στους θεοῦ ...
{καὶ τοῦ ἐπισκόπου	αἰδεῖσθε δὲ καὶ τὸν ἐπίσκοπον
	ὑμῶν ὡς Χριστόν,
καὶ τῶν διαταγμάτων τῶν	καθὰ ὑμῖν οἱ μακάριοι διετάξαντο
ἀποστόλων}.	ἀπόστολοι.

The Ps.-Ignatius paraphrases the Middle recension, which in
turn has been interpolated. As far as our sentence is concerned,
he scarcely adds anything to be noted, but he shows his fixed aver-

---

[312] See F. X. FUNK, *Die Apostolischen Konstitutionen, Eine literar-historische
Untersuchung* (= *AA. KK.*), Rottenburg 1891, pp. 281-355; *Didascalia et Constitutiones Apostolorum* (= *Did. et CC. AA.*), Paderborn 1905, pp. XV, XIX-XX. In p. XV
he falls into the same error as the above-mentioned authors: " Non solum senten-
tias plurimas cum Constitutionibus communes habet, sed Trallianos 7,3 (sic) adhor-
tans, ut episcopum venerentur tamquam Christum, sicut apostoli constituerint, satis
clare ad eas provocat." Who would have dared say the same of Ign. Tr. 7,1?
See also LIGHTFOOT, *AA. FF.* II : I 250-254 [II, 1, 262-265].

[313] FUNK, *AA. KK.* 342: " Aber das Wort διετάξαντο, mit dem die Verordnung
der Apostel bezeichnet wird, lässt eher an die Konstitutionen, die Διατάξεις oder
Διαταγαί, denken." See however H. CONNOLLY, *Didascalia Apostolorum. The Syriac
Version Translated and Accompanied by the Verona Latin Fragments* (*Did. Ap.*),
Oxford 1929, p. LXXXIV: " Epiphanius is the earliest writer who makes mention
of the *Didascalia*, which he cites as the Διατάξεις of the Apostles. It was formerly
thought that his references were to the *Apostolic Constitutions*, but some of them
could not be identified as from that source, and their true origin was revealed by
the publication of the *Didascalia*."

[314] Compare *A. C.* II. 34,2: οὕτως καὶ ἡμεῖς ὑμῖν περὶ τῶν ἐπισκόπων δια-
τασσόμεθα.

sion to calling Jesus the Messiah, " God " (see n. 44). Have the scholars been mistaken in associating this passage with the Apostolic Constitutions? Yes and no. In place of Ps.-Ignatius they should have related Ign. Tr. 7,1; in place of the Constitutions, the Didascalia. This last claims to be, in fact, a compilation of the *Prescriptions drawn up by the Apostles* at the Council of Jerusalem to fight against heresies. [315]   Was our interpolator convinced that it was apostolic? Was he inspired by it to carry out his thorough recasting? We shall treat of this problem further on.

The other interpolated sentence, Tr. 7,2cd, is very easy to identify, as it is introduced with a simple " *that is* ". Ignatius tries to explain what it means to be " separated from Jesus " with the image of the precinct of the altar, symbol of the community united for the celebration of the Eucharist. [316]   The interpolator has not missed his chance. He cannot conceive of the Eucharist without bishop, presbyters and deacons; " *without them* " — he says in 3,1d — " *we cannot speak of a church* ".

93.   Here is the translation of this passage (interpolations in brackets and italics):

" [7,1] *a*Beware therefore of such men.   *b*And this will be possible for you, if you are not puffed up *c*and cling inseparably to God, Jesus the Messiah {, *dand to the bishop and the Prescriptions of the Apostles*}. [7,2] *a*He that is within the precinct of the altar is clean; *b*but he that is without the altar is not clean{, *cthat is: he that does anything apart from bishop, presbytery and deacon, dthis man is not clean in his conscience*} [317] " (Tr. 7).

" To be clean " for Ignatius implied to remain within the precinct of the community that confesses the human reality of Jesus Messiah-God (see Eph 5,2bc); " to be puffed up " meant " to keep away from the Eucharistic meeting " (see Eph. 5,3a-e). The

---

[315] See above all *Did.* VI. 12,1; 13,1; 23,1.5-6.

[316] Ign. has a certain predilection for the image of the θυσιαστήριον in the metaphorical sense of " the place of sacrifice ", " the court of the altar " (LIGHTFOOT, *AA. FF.* II: II/1, 169), " der Altarraum " (BAUER, *W. z. N. T.*, s. v.) to symbolize the community meeting for the Eucharistic celebration (Eph. 5,2; Tr. 7,2) and for the very oblation of Jesus the Messiah = Altar (Mg. 7,2; Phld. = Mg* 4). In Rom. 2,2 he speaks of the altar or arena in which he is to be sacrificed.

[317] The variant διακόνου of GL (διακόνων gC) is very strange. — τῇ συνειδήσει, form used by the interpolator; ἐκ συνειδότος, form employed by Ign. in Sm. 11,1, according to P (Voss) G (-τως), against gL(A) that read συνειδήσεως.

Gnostics abstain from the thanksgiving and prayer meetings, because they do not allow that the Eucharist is the true Flesh of the Saviour, Jesus the Messiah (Sm. 7,1). Their refusal of the humanity of the Lord and, therefore, of his human commitment besides the security derived from their individual experience of salvation, could not fit in with the real and communitarian experience of the humanity of Jesus the Messiah and of his commitment until death. The interpolator has other problems. He is not worried about the heresy that attacks the person and message of Jesus. He is troubled by the attitude of certain Christians who do not comply with the bishop's orders. The danger is from within. For this reason, in paraphrasing Ignatius' saying, he identifies the " altar " with the three ministries charged with cult (χωρὶς corresponds with ἐκτὸς) and goes on to add the restriction " *in his conscience* " to " clean ". Anyone who acts outside those constituted in the hierarchy cannot have a quiet conscience (see Mg. 4bc).

94. *The conclusion of Trallians* (Tr. 12-13). — In the first part we have examined all the conclusions, except that of Trallians, for the simple reason that this letter, because of its brevity, was not involved in the profound remoulding made in the two long letters to the Ephesians (Eph*) and Magnesians (Mg*). There are, however, two clear interpolations in its conclusion. Furthermore, in examining its structure, we see that the farewell formula (ἔρρωσθε ἐν Ἰησοῦ Χριστῷ: 13,2a) has been removed from its usual position (at the end of the letter). But it seems as if the interpolation of 12,2d (πρέπει γὰρ ὑμῖν τοῖς καθ' ἕνα κτλ.) has in turn displaced the Ignatian sentences that appear at present after the concluding formula in 13,2c-3 (καὶ οἱ κατ' ἄνδρα ἀλλήλους ἀγαπᾶτε κτλ). In fact, this sentence fits in perfectly with 12,2c (διαμένετε ἐν τῇ ὁμονοίᾳ ὑμῶν καὶ τῇ μετ' ἀλλήλων προσευχῇ). The other interpolated sentence (13,2b) emphasizes in the farewell formula itself the above-mentioned submission to the bishop and presbytery, and illustrates it with the analogy of those who submit to oiders given (note once more the use of the conjunctive particle ὡς). [318]

95. We restore the original order of the sequence so that the reader can judge its primitive, simple and orderly structure, once the interpolations removed (in brackets and italics):

[318] ὡς τῇ ἐντολῇ G: + θεοῦ LA (cf. Sm. 8,1). See the statement in n. 282.

" [12,1] *a*I greet you from Smyrna together with the communities of God here present; *b*they have relieved me in everything, both corporal and spiritual. [12,2] *a*My chains exhort you, *b*which for Jesus the Messiah's sake I bear about, begging to attain to God. *c*Abide in mutual concord and in common prayer, { *d*for it is fitting that you severally, and more specially the presbyters, give the bishop refreshment in honour of the Father of Jesus Christ [319] and the Apostles.} [13,2] *c*and all of you without exception love one another with undivided heart. [13,3] *a*My person offers itself for you, not only now, but also when I shall attain to God. *b*For I am still in danger, *c*but the Father is faithful to fulfil both your and my prayer through Jesus the Messiah. *d*May you through him be found blameless! [12,3] *a*I pray that you take heed to me in love, *b*so that I do not, by writing to you, become a witness against you. *c*But also pray for me, *d*for I have need of your love by the mercy of God, *e*that I am held worthy to receive the heritage, *f*that is alloted to me [320] and shall not be disqualified. [13,1] *b*Remember in your prayers the church in Syria, *c*whereof I am not worthy to be called a member, *d*being the least of them. [13,1] *a*The Smyrnaeans and Ephesians greet you affectionatelly. [13,2] *a*May you be strengthened by Jesus the Messiah, < our common hope > { *b*submitted to the bishop as to the commandment (that comes from God), and likewise to the presbytery} " (Tr. 12-13).

---

[319] For textual criticism see ZAHN, *PP. AA.* II 53; LIGHTFOOT, *AA. FF.* II: II/1, 179.

[320] A difficult passage to translate, frequently avoided by conjecturing (see LIGHTFOOT, *AA. FF.* II: II/1, 180; J. MOFFAT, *An Approach to Ignatius, H. Th. R.* 29 [1936] 31, n. 72). BAUER, *W. z. N. T.*, s. v. περίκειμαι 3., observes: " In τοῦ κλήρου, οὗ περίκειμαι ἐπιτυχεῖν ITr 12,3 ist der Text schwerlich in Ordnung und nur mit Vorbehalt die Uebersetzung zu wagen *des Loses, das zu erlangen mir anliegt.*" Note that, on the one hand, the punctuation can be modified, making οὗ περίκειμαι into a parenthetical sentence, in which case ἐπιτυχεῖν would then depend on καταξιωθῆναι and govern τοῦ κλήρου. On the other hand, LIDDELL–SCOTT–JONES, *A Greek-English Lexicon,* 9Oxford 1973, s. v. περίκειμαι, points out that this verb is used as passive voice of παρατίθημι. By changing it into the active voice we get ὃν (κλῆρον) ὁ θεὸς περιτέθηκέν μοι (lot God has assigned me); οὗ would be an attraction of the relative in place of ὅν. In 1Cor. 9,17; Gal. 2,7, etc. we have examples of indirect passives, in that the subject of the passive becomes indirect complement to the active: οἰκονομίαν πεπίστευμαι = ὁ θεὸς πεπίστευκέ μοι οἰκονομίαν. For the rest, see the parallel of *Phld.* 5,1 with a noticeable attraction of the antecedent: ἵνα ἐν ᾧ κλήρῳ ἠλεήθην ἐπιτύχω = ἵνα τοῦ κλήρου ἐπιτύχω ἐν ᾧ ἠλεήθην, and with a passive also, equivalent to ἐν ᾧ ὁ θεὸς ἠλέησέν με (with which lot God has had pity on me). See also Eph. 11,2; Rom. 1,2: κλῆρος is the lot he inherits after death (in Ignatius' case, thanks to martyrdom), without identifying with martyrdom (against BAUER, *AA. VV.* II 257: " Im Märtyrerlos hat Ignatius Erbarmung erfahren "), equivalent to μέρος (see Pol. 6,1d: nr. 49).

The correspondences bishop/Father of Jesus Christ and presbyters/Apostles are familiar to us. Here, though, they are not applied consistently. Something like this occurred in Mg. 13,2 and 7,1ab. The invitation to " *give refreshment* " to the bishop (see Eph. 2,1h) is especially addressed to the presbyters. To distinguish these from the community members, the forger uses a special expression (οἱ καθ᾽ ἕνα), inspired by the Ignatian one (οἱ κατ᾽ ἄνδρα), which has been displaced from its primitive position, as we have already noted. The first of the interpolated sentences has been introduced with a " *for* ", to give the impression that " common prayer " takes place before the bishop. [321] The second has been inserted with a participle in apposition, in the style of Eph. 2,2e; 21,1c.d and Mg. 6,1c. Most probably the interpolator has altered also the order of the final greetings (13,1a) and the farewell formula (13,2a), that we have replaced at the end of the letter. On the other hand, it is very likely that the extant farewell formula was solely an abridgement of the one which is to be found in Phld. 11,2f (ἔρρωσθε ἐν Χριστῷ Ἰησοῦ, τῇ κοινῇ ἐλπίδι ἡμῶν). Probably it has been shortened after being removed from its usual position, so as to make room for the interpolation ὑποτασσόμενοι κτλ. The archaism Χριστῷ Ἰησοῦ of the farewell formula of Phld. shows evidence of authenticity, while the apposition, τῇ κοινῇ ἐλπίδι ἡμῶν, is typical Ignatian (see Eph. 21,2e: nr. 54,1.4; in a shorter form it appears also in Tr. inscr. and 2,2b: τῆς ἐλπίδος ἡμῶν).

96. *Phld.* 3,2b. — The persistence of certain themes dear to the interpolator, which are now familiar, the fact of its being a letter with a false address, and finally, the reference in the heading of the letter to a local bishop, whose name furthermore is not mentioned (because the writer does not know it!), all this shows clearly that the passage in question conceals an interpolation:

" For as many as (ὅσοι) are of God and of Jesus the Messiah, these (οὗτοι) are *with the bishop* " (Phld. 3,2ab).

But the reconstruction of the original drift of the passage is not so easy. The second member, also built up with the correlation ὅσοι ... οὗτοι ... (3,2cd), testifies that in the original there

[321] Thus BAUER, *AA. VV.* II 240f., has understood it: " Die Begründung πρέπει γάρ [XII] 2 zeigt, dass sich Ign. Betätigung wirklicher Eintracht und wirkungsvolles gemeinsames Gebet nur denken kann bei Beteiligung des Bischofs."

was a double correlation. Bearing in mind that the interpolator did not usually modify the literal form of Ignatius' writing, it is most probable that he was satisfied with changing the order of the words, so as to add the clause belonging to the bishop. The most likely reconstruction of the first correlation, taking into account that God (replaced by the bishop) forms the second member of the second correlation and, consequently, also of the first, would be:

ὅσοι γὰρ Ἰησοῦ Χριστοῦ εἰσίν, οὗτοι καὶ θεοῦ εἰσίν (the numbers refer to the order of the textus receptus). Note how the second correlation plainly distinguishes the reintegration in the church and to be of God, " so that they may live according to Jesus the Messiah ". Ignatius' reasoning was *a minore ad maius* (see Paul, Rom. 8,14): As many as belong to Jesus the Messiah/church, these belong to God. The interpolator applies his well-known correlation God/bishop to conclude *a maiore ad minus*: As many as belong to God and Jesus Christ, these belong to the bishop.

97. *Phld.* 7. — As we shall see, the whole sequence of Phld. 7 is interpolated. It supposes there was a public discussion in Philadelphia between Ignatius and schismatic disturbers of the community. When he passed that way, Ignatius would have grasped the situation and taken the part of the bishop who had invited him. The interpolator wants at all costs to make out that Ignatius made a short stay in Philadelphia. The reason is obvious. Ignatius, a " *deacon* " (submitted to the bishop and the presbytery: see Mg. 2) and " in chains for Jesus Christ's sake " (martyrdom as greatest authority), should *also* have had problems with the schismatics, but he cut them short by bidding them submit to the bishop. To bring about this effect, the interpolator has made use of a whole series of means: (1) He split up the primitive letter to the Magnesians (actually Mg. and Phld.: see nrs. 24-28); (2) He tried to leave in Mg. the clause where Ignatius assured that in that community he had not heard of any Judaizing deviations (Mg. 11: see p. 138); (3) He inserted a personal praise of the bishop, but without mentioning his name, in the heading of the new letter, in imitation of the genuine ones (Phld. 1: see nrs. 22, 58-61); (4) He placed the polemic paragraph of Phld. 7 between two passages that — benevolently — could be interpreted in favour of a short stay of Ignatius in Philadelphia (6,3 and 8: see nr. 16); (5) He imitated the primitive conclusion of Ephesians, but reversing the

order of the paragraphs (Phld. 10,1-11,1), so that the envoys coming after him remain released from their first mission and thus
they could be interpreted as a second group of prisoners due to
the persecution (see nrs. 34, 63, and pp. 139-143); (6) Finally,
he gave the impression that they *too*, were received with divided
attitudes (Phld. 11,1i-k: see nrs. 34, 64; in contrast with the original statement, nr. 31). This forced passing of Ignatius through
Philadelphia could reveal the true motive of the forger. We shall
examine the contents of the quarrel.

98. In the present passage of Phld. 7 there appears a new
factor that was not expressed up to now, in spite of the fact that
in the interrupting clause of Eph. 20 the redaction of a second
letter was conditioned by a divine revelation. Ignatius shields
himself — according to the interpolator — behind a prophetic revelation of the Spirit of God:

" [7,1] *[a]For, even though some tried to deceive me humanly, [b]yet the Spirit
does not deceive, since he proceeds from God. [c]Indeed, ' he knows where
he comes from and where he is going ' (John 3,8) [d]and lays bare what
is hidden (1Cor. 14,24.25) [e]I cried out, when I was among you, [f]I began
to speak [322] with a ringing voice, with God's own voice, [g]— 'Give heed
to the bishop, the presbytery and the deacons! ' [7,2] [a]And whoever suspected
me of saying this, because I knew beforehand of the division caused by
certain persons, [b]he for whom I am in chains is my witness, that I had
no knowledge of this from any man, [c]but that the Spirit proclaimed it
saying this: [d]'Without the bishop do nothing. [e]Keep your bodies as temples
of God. [f]Cherish union. [g]Shun divisions. [h]Be imitators of Jesus Christ,
[i]as he himself also was of his Father ' "* (Phld. 7).

There is no doubt that he is feigning a prophecy (cry, ringing voice, God's voice, proclamation of the Spirit). Note, how-

---

[322] ZAHN, *I. v. A.* 268, n. 1, prefers the reading of gl (μεταξὺ ὧν ἐλάλουν) which
is more correct grammatically than the aorist — imperfect succession: "Denn der
Tempuswechsel verbietet eine einfache Coordinirung von ἐκραύγασα und ἐλάλουν.
Aus einem andauernden Reden hebt sich dieser einzelne Ruf heraus." The succession aorist — imperfect, however, is a case well supported by A. T. ROBERTSON,
A Grammar of the Greek New Testament in the Light of Historical Research, London ³1919, pp. 838 and 885, and recently studied by J. MATEOS, *El aspecto verbal
en el Nuevo Testamento*, in *Estudios de Nuevo Testamento*, I., Madrid 1977, nr. 72,
and J. MATEOS – M. ALEPUZ, *El imperfecto sucesivo en el NT*, in *Estudios de
Nuevo Testamento*, II. *Cuestiones de gramática y léxico*, pp. 63-101. The aorist
limits the beginning of the duration expressed by the imperfect (see Mtt. 4,11; 5,2;
Mk. 3,6, etc.).

ever, that he puts in the Spirit's mouth a string of imperatives, in an asyndetic and paratactic style, that is very like the first part of the letter to Polycarp. By appealing to prophetic revelation he claims to settle once and for all the question of the authority of the bishop and his collaborators faced with internal schisms. [323]

The clause is drawn up in such a way that the reader infers from these data that Ignatius had really visited Philadelphia. [324] The interpolator's aim was to create an antagonistic atmosphere in the heart of this community: firstly, between Ignatius and his opponents (Phld. 7); then, between Philo, Gaius and Agathopus who follow in his footsteps and some individuals who treated them with dishonour (11,1k). He is interested in demonstrating that the community is divided in two factions: on the one hand, the bishop, his collaborators, the section of the community that welcomed Ignatius and the other future martyrs; on the other, the dissidents who with their fallacies have tried to win over Ignatius to their cause. [325]

99.   Between the heading of this clause and the interpolation we have detected in the heading of Magnesians (Mg. 3) there are a series of coincidences that cannot be fortuitous. It was the case of a young bishop who could be taken in by feigned obedience, [326] profiting by his youthfulness. Here the community

---

[323] CAMELOT, *I. d'A.* (S. Ch. 10A) 38, n. 2: " Lors de son intervention dans les difficultés de l'Eglise de Philadelphie, c'est l'Esprit qui est en lui qui crie: ' Soumettez-vous à l'évêque ' (*Ad Philad.*, VII, 2). Cf. J. LEBRETON, *Histoire* ..., t. II, p. 328, et n. 1, qui cite une page bien curieuse d'H. MONNIER, *La notion de l'apostolat*, p. 374, montrant comment dans l'Eglise c'est l'autorité qui a hérité de l'Esprit, le préservant ainsi de ces excès mêmes."

[324] ZAHN, *I. v. A.* 261-272; *PP. AA.* II 77: " Ignatium nuper Philadelphiam permeasse "; LIGHTFOOT, *AA. FF.* II: II/1, 267: " It is evident from the whole context that Ignatius had himself visited Philadelphia "; BAUER, *AA. VV.* II 259: " Ign. erinnert an die Worte, die er in Philadelphia gesprochen, und sieht darin einen Beweis dafür, dass er damals schon unter dem Einfluss des Geistes von der Absonderung gewusst hat."

[325] LELONG, *PP. AA.* III 75: " Allusion à une tentative, d'ailleurs inconnue, faite pour tromper Ignace. L'obscurité même de cette allusion est une preuve de l'authenticité de la lettre "; CAMELOT, *I. d'A.* (S. Ch. 10A) 126: " Les détails de cet épisode restent obscurs pour nous. Il semble qu'il s'était formé à Philadelphie un parti opposé à l'évêque, et que les dissidents avaient essayé de circonvenir Ignace pour le compromettre avec eux."

[326] Ign. uses πλανάω only in the middle voice, always applied to the community (μηδεὶς πλανάσθω: Eph. 5,2 and Sm. 6,1; μὴ πλανᾶσθε: Eph. 16,1; Mg. 8,1; Phld.

troublers tried to deceive Ignatius taking advantage of his human condition (κατὰ σάρκα). In the case of the young bishop, the trick could be effective; but since the bishop is representative of God, this would involved God himself, thus deceiving the invisible bishop. [327] For accounts are not given to man (πρὸς σάρκα), but to God (πρὸς θεόν), who knows what is hidden (τὰ κρύφια). In Ignatius' case the tactic has no effect, [328] since his quality of future martyr assures him the assistance of the Spirit who cannot be deceived (οὐ πλανᾶται), for he proceeds from God (ἀπὸ θεοῦ), and searches out what is hidden (τὰ κρυπτὰ). The interpolator insists that Ignatius does not know beforehand, through human means (ἀπὸ σαρκὸς ἀνθρωπίνης), that there are disguised dissidents among the members of the Philadelphian community, only that it was the Spirit himself (τὸ δὲ πνεῦμα) who proclamed it in form of a prophecy.

In all the genuine thematic letters there is a clause by which Ignatius after unmasking his opponents makes it clear that he has no news — through the delegates — that in the communities of Ephesus (Sm. = Eph* 4,1), Magnesia (Mg. 11) and Tralles (Tr. 8,1) there exist schisms or divisions. Here, on the contrary, this situation was made known to him beforehand by the Spirit himself.

To bring out and give greater authority to this " prophecy ", the interpolator has combined John 3,8 (4,14) with 1Cor. 14,24. 25. This is the only literal quotation from John identifiable in the actual text of Ignatius. [329] The indeniable similarity between

---

3,3). — The interpolator uses it in the active voice (Mg. 3,2b; Phld. 7,1a) and in the middle one (Phld. 7,1b) referring to the concrete case of the bishop, of Ign., or the Spirit (in Mg. 3,2c he applies to God, the invisible Bishop, the equivalent παραλογίζεται).

[327] One can deceive (πλανᾷ, present continuous) a young bishop by hypocritical submission, because of his lack of experience; in reality one is deceiving (παραλογίζεται) God.

[328] Note the attempt marked by the (punctiliar) aorist ἠθέλησαν πλανῆσαι.

[329] Ch. MAURER, *Ignatius von Antiochien und das Johannesevangelium*, Zürich 1949, pp. 25ff., adduces three passages of the actual text of Ignatius, in which can be demonstrated with certainty the presence of a Johannine quotation: Phld. 7,1; 9,1 and Rom. 7,3. In reality, only the first probably contains a literal quotation from John. It is not enough to identify Jesus with the Door (Ign. speaks of Jesus as the Door of the Father, through which enter Abraham and Isaac and Jacob and the Prophets, the Apostles and the Church: Phld. 9,1; but John identifies him with the Door through which the sheep go in and out: John 10,7.9) nor will

(the genuine) Ignatius and John, explicable by the fact that they were both faced with the same problems (Gnostics and Judaizers), clashes with Ignatius' silence with regard to John in his authentic letter to the Ephesians (where he quotes Paul), and the peaceful situation of the Asiatic communities described by Ignatius, as they were just about to be attacked by the Docetic and Judaizing missionaries from Syria (see pp. 143-146).

100.   As for the content of the so-called " prophecy ", it can be said that it sums up the burning theological and ecclesiological questions of the interpolator's time.   We shall examine its elements:

(1)   " *Without the bishop do nothing.*
(2)   *Keep your bodies as temples of God.*
(3)   *Cherish union.*
(4)   *Shun divisions.*
(5)   *Be imitators of Jesus Christ,*
        as he himself also was of his Father."

The first (1), third (3), and fourth element (4), respond to a troubled ecclesiastical situation.   It is not yet a question of Gnostic heresy nor of schisms provoked by the Judaizers.   What is contested is the hierarchy on the part of some dissident circles.   The second element (2) seems to indicate a certain slackening of behaviour or else a tendency to moralism.   The last element (5) forms an inclusion with the first (1), in that it subordinates Jesus Christ to God, whose representative is the bishop.

101.   " *Without the bishop do nothing* " (1).   This sentence contains in negative form the same theme as the phrase placed before (Phld. 7,1g) in Ignatius' mouth in prophetic vein.   Both phrases make up the quintessence of the forger's ecclesiology. The first (7,1g) occurs literally in Pol. 6,1a; as equivalents we could quote the repeated invitations to submission (Eph. 2,2e; Mg. 2c; 13,2; Tr. 2,1a.2b; 13,2b), to collaboration (Eph. 4,1a; Mg. 13,1), to obedience (Eph. 20,2; Mg. 3,2), to respect and reverence (Eph. 6,1b; Mg. 3,1; Tr. 3,1; Sm. 9,1cd), etc., which are owed the bishop and the rest of the hierarchy.   The second phrase (Phld. 7,2d) comes up constantly in the interpolated passages (Mg. 4bc; 7,1ab; Tr. 2,2a; 3,1d; 7,2c; Sm. 8,1d. 2c; 9,1e; Pol. 4,1c).

---

recourse to resonances in Ign. Rom. 7,3 (Bread of God, Flesh of Jesus; Drink, Blood of Jesus) and John 6 allow us to infer material dependence from this.

Among the verbs used by the interpolator, to which we have just referred, some never occur in Ignatius' writings, while others are placed in a very different context. Thus ὑποτάσσω is used nine times (Eph. 2,2e; 5,3f; Mg. 2c; 13,2; Tr. 2,1a.2b; 13,2b; Pol. 2,1; 6,1c) by the forger, never by Ignatius. Whereas this latter uses ὑποταγή only once (Eph. 2,2d). Ignatius, on the other hand, employs συντρέχω three times to invite the community to be united in God's Plan (Eph. 3,2cd), in the temple of God which is Jesus the Messiah, the Father's Plan (Mg. 7,2), in the common life (Pol. = Eph* 6,1g); while the interpolator uses it once to direct the community towards the bishop (Eph. 4,1a). ὑπακούω (ἐπ-) is used only by the forger (twice: Eph. 20,2 and Mg. 3,2). ἐντρέπω is understood by Ignatius to mean the mutual respect owed to each other by the members of the community (Mg. 6,2b; 12h); the interpolator channels its meaning towards the bishop, presbytery and deacons (three times: Tr. 3,1.2; Sm. 8,1), as well as ἐντροπή (Mg. 3,1). Ignatius employs τιμή always related to God (Eph. 21,1a.2d; Mg. 3,2a; Sm. 11,2b) or to Jesus the Messiah (Mg. 15e); the interpolator refers it to the bishop/community (Eph. 2,1d; Phld. 11,2: τιμή/τιμάω; and Sm. 9,1d: ὁ τιμῶν ἐπίσκοπον ὑπὸ θεοῦ τετίμηται). προσέχω is applied by the forger always to the bishop and the other hierarchical grades (Phld. 7,1g; Pol. 6,1a); Ignatius refers it to the Prophets (Sm. 7,2c) or the flatterers (Tr. 4,1). προκάθημαι is used exclusively by the interpolator (Mg. 6,1c. 2f).

As for the use of ἐπίσκοπος, the interpolator employs it 53 times in the singular and twice in the plural; of these times in five instances only does he mention the bishops by name, otherwise they are anonymous. 53 times he refers to the bishops allocated in the most important cities (Ephesus, Magnesia, Tralles, Philadelphia and Smyrna in Asia; Antioch of Syria and the neighbouring cities; etc.), and twice to the universal and invisible Bishop, God (Mg. 3,1e.2bc). On the contrary, ἐπισκοπέω is used by him only once (Pol. inscr.: referring to God and Jesus Christ) and never, ἐπισκοπή. — Ignatius uses ἐπίσκοπος only once (Rom. 2,2: referring to the bishop of the whole Roman province of Syria), once ἐπισκοπέω (Rom. 9,1: only Jesus the Messiah and the communion of the Romans will from then on supervise the church in Syria) and another ἐπισκοπή (Pol. = Eph* 8,3: that thanks to Jesus the Messiah our God the Syrian community persevere in

14

unity with God and under his vigilance). From whence we infer that Ignatius still retains the primitive meaning, "function of vigilance", while the interpolator already takes it to be an "office/title".

In referring to the use of the "improper" preposition χωρίς and its equivalent ἄνευ see above nr. 90: the interpolator always employs χωρίς for the hierarchical grades; Ignatius only applies it to Jesus the Messiah. In Sm. 9,1e the interpolator makes use of the particle λάθρα with a prepositional function.

102. "*Keep your bodies* (τὴν σάρκα ὑμῶν) *as temples of God* (ὡς ναὸν θεοῦ)" (2). A similar invitation in Pol. 5,2a-c, directed to the celibates: εἰς τιμὴν τῆς σαρκὸς τοῦ κυρίου,, with reference to the celibate estate of the Lord.

Ignatius knows nothing of this individualistic language. Although he uses ναός three times (in the singular: Eph. 9,1; Mg. 7,2; in the plural: Eph. 15,3) he understands it always in the communitarian sense, like οἰκοδομή (Eph. 9,1), σῶμα (Sm. 1,2) and σωματεῖον (Sm. 11,2).

103. "*Cherish union* (τὴν ἕνωσιν)" (3). Analogous expression in Pol. 1,2d (τῆς ἑνώσεως φρόντιζε). The idea was suggested to him as much by the immediate subsequent context, in which Ignatius states, to relieve his concience, that he has tried to do what lay to hand as a man ready to (create) union (τὸ ἴδιον ἐποίουν ὡς ἄνθρωπος εἰς ἕνωσιν κατηρτισμένος, Phld. 8,1: originally connected with 6,3!), as well as by the extensive preceding context (4-6). The interpolator has forgotten that the context of the letter concerned the Judaizers and has gone on to apply it to those who contest the bishop's authority. For him union can only be achieved "*materially and spiritually*", that is, by submission to the bishop and to God (see Mg. 13,2).

Ignatius always employs ἕνωσις without the article. He asks that the communities may realize the same union that there is between the Body and Spirit of Jesus the Messiah, between faith and love and especially between Jesus and the Father (Mg. 1,2). God himself proclaims this union, which binds together Head and members, that is, Jesus (Tr. 11,2), and arises from the Eucharistic celebration (Phld. 4ab).

104. "*Shun divisions* (τοὺς μερισμούς)" (4). This is the logical consequence of the preceding invitation. In Sm. 7,2f the

forger uses exactly the same expression, followed by the invitation
to obey the bishop and presbytery (8,1). The two other instances
he uses this term occur in the present context. Here also, for both
expressions he was inspired by the preceding Ignatian context
(φεύγετε οὖν τὰς κακοτεχνίας κτλ.: Phld. 6,2) and the posterior one
(οὗ δὲ μερισμός ἐστιν κτλ.: 8,1). Nevertheless, unlike him, the
forger does not understand this term in the sense of legal observances that could divide (μερίσαι: Mg. 6,2e) the community, which
was the objective of the Judaizers' propaganda (σχίζοντι: Phld.
3,3), but as an internal division occasioned by lack of submission
to the hierarchy. It is to be noted here that, in spite of having
left in Mg. the clause where Ignatius specified that he had no news
of Judaizing deviations in that community (Mg. 11), it was not
possible to do the same with reference to Phld. 3,1 (οὐχ ὅτι παρ' ὑμῖν
μερισμὸν εὗρον, ἀλλ' ἀποδιϋλισμόν), which was in contradiction with
the phrase that he places in the mouth of Ignatius (ὡς προειδότα
τὸν μερισμόν τινων: 7,2a). The correction introduced in 3,2b (see
nr. 96) is an endeavour to avoid this.

Ignatius repeats twice in the letter to the Magnesians (Mg.
11 and Phld. = Mg* 3,1) that there is no division among them but
only a " filtering " (meaning that the Christians at Magnesia hat
' filtered out ' from their church the impurity of the noxius weeds
of schism). He only speaks of division (μερισμός) in this anti-
Judaizing letter (Phld. = Mg* 2,1; 3,1 and 8,1; μερίσαι, Mg. 6,2;
σχίζων, Phld. 3,3). Of the Gnostics he employs the much more
incisive term αἵρεσις. The remaining passages (Phld. 7,2a.g and
Sm. 7,2f) are the interpolator's own.

105. " *Be imitators* (μιμηταὶ) *of Jesus Christ, as he himself
also* (ὡς καὶ) *was of his Father* " (5). It is the only instance the
interpolator uses the term μιμητής. Reciprocity shown by the
conjunctive particle ὡς is a distinguishing feature of the interpolator's style (Eph. 2,1h [330]; 3,2e; 4,1c; 5,1 [2x]; 6,1 [2x]; 21,1 [2x];
Mg. 2 [2x: see nr. 84, and n. 282]; 13,2; Tr. 2,1a.2b.3c; 3,1 [4x];
13,2b; Phld. 1,2; 4c; 7,2; 10,2; 11,1; Sm. 8,1 [3x]; Pol. 1,2; 2,2
[2x]. 3 [2x]; 3,1; 5,1: total 35 times). In this way the interpolator

---

[330] ὡς καὶ αὐτὸν ὁ πατὴρ Ἰησοῦ Χριστοῦ ἀναψύξαι: the subject in the nominative, requires that the ambivalent form of ἀναψύξαι be understood as optative and
not infinitive aorist.

endorses his " prophecy " with the example of Jesus Christ in all things submitted to his Father (see Eph. 5,1; Mg. 7,1; 13,2; Sm. 8,1).

Ignatius always refers the term μιμητής to Jesus the Messiah, as model for imitation (see n. 307, and the statement in nr. 89), only once does he use the particle ὡς with a conjunctive function (Pol. = Eph* 6,2h) [331] and he never proposes Jesus as model of submission to his Father.

106. As confirmation, we hold that, once removed the interpolated clause (Phld. 7), the nexus that originally existed between Phld. 6,3 and 8,1 is restored:

" But I thank my God, for I have a good conscience towards you, and that no one can boast either privately or publicly that I was a burden to anyone in matters great or small. And to all those before whom I spoke, I pray that they may not turn it into a testimony against themselves " [332] (Phld. 6,3). " On my part, I tried to do my best as a man made ready to (create) union. But where there is division and passion God does not dwell ... " (8,1).

In the first phrase there is a clear distinction between the community as such (ἐν ὑμῖν) and the delegates sent to Smyrna from the several communities, with special reference to the delegates from Magnesia (καὶ πᾶσι δέ [333], ἐν οἷς ἐλάλησα). Ignatius take pleasure in recalling to the Magnesian community that he has not been a burden to them: neither himself nor those who came after him from Syria stayed in Magnesia. All the data of the original letter to the Magnesians are unanimous on this point: (a) Ignatius knew the community only through its delegates (Mg. 2a and 6,1a); (b) He is perfectly well aware that up to the present Judaizing propaganda has had no effect on them (Mg. 11); (c) On the contrary, there has been an inward clarification as regards the sowers

---

[331] The only doubtful passage is Phld. 5,1h: προσφυγὼν τῷ εὐαγγελίῳ ὡς σαρκὶ Ἰησοῦ καὶ τοῖς ἀποστόλοις ὡς πρεσβυτερίῳ ἐκκλησίας. The fact that neither σαρκὶ nor πρεσβυτερίῳ have the article inclines us to consider the two sentences preceded by ὡς as simple qualifications. In the quarrel with the Judaizers, who shielded themselves behind the Old Testament Archives as the only criteria of canonicity (Phld. 8,2), Ign. took refuge in the Gospel, Body of Jesus, and in the Apostles, Senate of the Church. See Phld. 9,1e and 9,2a-c. Ign. uses ὡς to introduce qualifying sentences in 19 instances; the interpolator 9 times.

[332] See the parallel of Tr. 12,3.

[333] + δέ GL: > ACg.

of discord (Phld. 3,1) [334]; (d) But he hastens to tell the delegates that they should not take on as a testimony against themselves the fact (αὐτὸ) of having spoken with him and having been charged with this mission (Phld. 6,3). [335]

The primitive letter to the Magnesians was a reiterated exhortation to do all (positive) in agreement with God Jesus the Messiah (Mg. 6,1b +e: see nr. 86) and to do nothing (negative) with a sectarian spirit (Phld. 8,2), the only way to be forewarned against the imminent assault of the Judaizers. For this reason he has left evidence of this preoccupation in the farewell formula of the primitive conclusion of Mg* (Ἔρρωσθε ἐν ὁμονοίᾳ θεοῦ κτλ., Mg. 15f). In the paraenesis of the letter Ignatius refers to a discussion with conservative elements — which happened probably in Syria — who accepted as canonical and inspired Scripture only the Old Testament (Phld. 8,2). By including Phld. 7, the interpolator has succeeded in giving the reader the impression that this dispute took place in Philadelphia and that it was basically due to discrepancies of a disciplinary nature occasioned by schismatic elements.

107. We have repeatedly questioned ourselves on the unconfessed motives that could have induced the forger to risk such a big undertaking. Gradually the investigation centred on Philadelphia. Indeed, if his only aim was to put into Ignatius' mouth the ecclesiology of his time, focused on the authority of the bishop and presbytery, and to back up the new compilation with the unquestionable authority of Polycarp, he would have limited himself to displacing Ignatius' itinerary to Troas — to link up in Philippi with Polycarp's letter to the Philippians — and to write only two new letters (Sm. and Pol.) with materials taken from

---

[334] ZAHN, *I. v. A.* 262, forced by the interpolated passages of Phld. 7 and 11,1 affirms: " Nur in Philadelphia selbst kann also Ignatius den dortigen Bischof kennen gelernt haben, und dass er die ganze Gemeinde persönlich kennen gelernt, folgt aus c. 3: οὐχ ὅτι παρ' ὑμῖν μερισμὸν εὖρον, ἀλλ' ἀποδιϋλισμόν." LIGHTFOOT, *AA. FF.* II: II/1, 256, is of the same opinion: " ' *I found* '. This implies that Ignatius had himself visited Philadelphia." In Tr. 1,2, where he had certainly not been, he says: εὑρὼν ὑμᾶς, ὡς ἔγνων κτλ. Here also he knew it through the delegates from Magnesia!

[335] BAUER, *W. z. N. T.*, s. v. κτάομαι interprets αὐτὸ of his message (nämlich meine Rede). Likewise LIGHTFOOT, *AA. FF.* II: II/1, 265f. (my words). ἐν οἷς ἐλάλησα is a parenthetical sentence that limits the extention of πᾶσι in contrast with ἐν ὑμῖν; αὐτὸ refers to the matter treated of in the previous phrase.

the authentic ones.   What led to the Phld. redaction and the forced passage of Ignatius by way of Philadelphia?   Were there hidden intentions behind the verification of insistent quarrels within that community?   Was the bishop of Philadelphia himself responsible for the falsifying of this compilation?   Did he project into Ignatius' letters his contemporary problematic?   As new elements arose we tried to answer these questions.   Now, after analyzing Phld. 7 we can already provide an approximate solution.   The forger is an Asian.   That is why he knows nothing of Ignatius' letter to the Romans and of the situation in Syria at this time.   He is much later than Polycarp.   If this were not so he could not have feigned personal relations between Ignatius and Polycarp.   It presupposes a much more evolved ecclesiology, including that of Irenaeus' times.   Bishops already reside in each one of the chief cities.   From the tone of the interpolation and its problematic it can be implied that he is a bishop and, concretely, of Philadelphia.   The fact that he corrects almost all expressions in which Ignatius makes appeal to the true experience of the Lord in the Eucharistic celebration as the efficacious means of defence against heresy or schism, replacing these with formulas of respect for authority, supposes that the communities he claims to address lack that experience and need, therefore, a visible authority to give them cohesion. Finally, the juxtaposition of a new problematic — without modifying the specific Ignatian one — provides sufficient data to outline what was the object of contestation.

108.   *Phld.* 8,1e. — There is still a very short interpolated sentence in the letter to the Phld., in which it is stressed that there is no unity with God without the " *bishop's senate* ":

" 8,1 ^cTo all men, then, who repent (μετανοοῦσιν) the Lord forgives, ^dif their repentance (μετανοήσωσιν) [336] leads to the unity of God ^e*and the senate of the bishop* (καὶ συνέδριον τοῦ ἐπισκόπου) " (Phld. 8,1c-e).

" *Senate* " already occurred in Mg. 6,1c (*the presbyters representing the senate of the Apostles*) and Tr. 3,1c (*let them respect ... the presbyters as the senate of God and the college of the Apostles*). Since the bishop takes the place of God, the presbyters went on to occupy the place of God's senate, in that they are the bishop's senate.

---

[336] See Phld. 3,2c; Sm. 4,1; 5,3; 9,1b.   Only in authentic passages.

109. *Sm.* 7,2f-8,2. — Like Phld. 7, the whole paragraph is spurious. Except for LIGHTFOOT [337], the commentators divide this pericope badly. Indeed, from Sm. 7,2f there is a sudden change of style: (a) Four sentences constructed on the particle ὡς with a conjunctive function (7,2f; 8,1a.b.c); (b) Five in imperative form (7,2f; 8,1a.c.d.e); (c) Clear contrast between Ignatius' remark on the advisability of keeping at a distance (ἀπέχεσθαι, in the present tense) from the Docetic Gnostics (7,2a) and the imperious order given by the interpolator to avoid (φεύγετε, imperative) internal divisions (7,2f); [338] (d) The coincidence of 7,2f with the interpolated sentence of Phld. 7,2g — the two single instances where he uses the plural μερισμούς.

The interpolated paragraph falls into three parts: (I.) The first, based on five imperatives, converges on the validity of the Eucharistic celebration (7,2f-8,1); (II.) The second is an invitation to respond massively to the celebrations presided over by the bishop, built up on the correlation: the bishop is to the community what Jesus Christ is to the church (8,2ab): (III.) The third treats of questions of liceity (8,2c-end). To make this clear, we give a structured translation:

I.   " [7,2f]*Shun divisions*
          as the beginning of every evil.
      [8,1]*ᵃDo you all follow the bishop,*
            as Jesus Christ (followed) the Father,
        ᵇ*and the presbytery*
           as the Apostles.
       ᶜ*Respect the deacons*
           as (you would respect) a precept of God.[339]
       ᵈ*Let no one do anything without the bishop*
           in what concerns the church.
       ᵉ*Let that only be considered a valid Eucharist*
           which is held under the control of the bishop
           or anyone to whom he has committed it.

---

[337] *AA. FF.* II: II/1, 308.

[338] As we already pointed out (nr. 17) Ign. does not speak of μερισμός in connection with the Gnostics, but of αἵρεσις. The confusion introduced by the interpolator with the sentence of Sm. 7,2f has created problems between commentators (see for example LIGHTFOOT, *AA. FF.* II: II/1, 308f.).

[339] In the active sense: see nr. 84, and n. 282. LIGHTFOOT, *AA. FF.* II: II/1, 309: " *As the voice of God enjoining you.* The deacons speak with the authority of God; they command in God's place." But Pearson interprets it in a passive sense: " Tamquam Dei praecepto institutos."

II.   8,2 *ªWherever the bishop appears in public,*
        let the community (τὸ πλῆθος) be present;
    ᵇjust as wherever Jesus Christ is,
        there (is) the Catholic church (ἡ καθολικὴ ἐκκλησία).

III.   *ᶜIt is not licit without the bishop*
        to baptize,
        or to hold an agape.
    ᵈBut whatever he approves
        this is also pleasing to God,
    ᵉthus everything you do will be firm and valid "
    (Sm. 7,2h-8,2).

There are numerous coincidences with Phld. 7 in the present passage:

" *Shun divisions* " (7,2f): see Phld. 7,2g. " *Follow the bishop, presbytery, deacons* " (8,1a.b.c): see Phld. 7,1g. " *As Jesus Christ to the Father* " (8,1a): see Phld. 7,2h. " *Do nothing without the bishop* " (8,1d): see Phld. 7,2d. The gathering of imperatives in an asyndetic form: five in Sm. 7,2f-8,1, another five in Phld. 7,2.

The present development, nevertheless, is not a simple repetition of Phld. 7. There we are surprised to find a prophecy from the Spirit placed in Ignatius' mouth. Before the turn of events in Philadelphia, the interpolator thinks it insufficient to support his thesis by Ignatius' chains (Phld. 7,2b). For this reason, he cites as witness Jesus Christ (ἐν ᾧ δέδεμαι) and uses textual words of the Spirit (7,2c) to confirm his pretensions for verticality. Here, though, he surprises us by his juridical technical language, when he treats questions of validity regarding the Eucharist, and of liceity with regard to the agape and baptism.

110. *Sm. 9,1c-e.* — We have come to the transition from the body of the letter (exhortation) to the paraenesis of Eph*. Once removed the whole interpolated paragraph we have just identified, the Ignatian sequence left in 7,2 (πρέπον οὖν ἐστὶν up to τετελείωται) continued in 9,1 (εὐλογόν ἐστιν λοιπὸν up to μετανοεῖν). But in 9,2 (πάντα οὖν κτλ.) the long Eph* ending began. Note the passage from the exhortation in the first person plural (9,1ab) to the congratulations addressed to the community in the second person plural (9,2).

The identification of these brief interpolated sentences is relatively easy. (a) The analogy God/bishop underlies 9,1c; (b) The same in 9,1d, where besides this the interpolator twice employs

— in the active and passive voice to express reciprocity — the verb τιμάω (together with Phld. 11,2 also interpolated are the only instances where this verb is used); (c) In 9,1e we meet with an equivalent expression (with the particle λάθρα used prepositionally) of the well-known phrase: " *Without the bishop do nothing* ", but explaining that whoever does so " *worships the devil* ".

Let us see it (in brackets and italics) in the context of Ignatius' letter:

" ⁹,¹ *ᵃFinally, it is reasonable that we wake up,* ᵇwhile we still have time to repent and turn to God. { ᶜ*It is advantageous to recognize God and the bishop.* ᵈ*Whoever honours a bishop has been honoured by God.* ᵉ*Whoever does anything hidden from the bishop worships the devil.*}
⁹,² ᵃMay all things therefore abound to you in grace ᵇfor you deserve it. ᶜYou have relieved me in every way, ᵈmay Jesus the Messiah also (relieve) you. ᵉAbsent or present you have shown me your affection, ᶠGod reward you! ᵍIf you endure all things for his sake, you shall attain to him " (Sm. 9).

Here also Ignatius' sentences are easily recognizable.

(a) Thus in 9,1a he uses λοιπὸν adverbially, as in Eph. 11,1; (b) In 9,1b he forms a temporal clause with ὡς ἔτι, as in Rom. 2,2 (not to be confused with Phld. 5,1, simple apposition); μετανοέω is used only by Ignatius: the same construction (εἰς + acc.) in Phld. 8,1 and Sm. 5,3; (c) The impersonal form of the imperative, in 9,2a, πάντα οὖν ὑμῖν — περισσευέτω, equals an optative; this makes Jacobson's conjecture very plausible, he reads ἀμείβοι instead of ἀμοίβει G; this is followed by the greater number of editors up to the discovery of P (ἀμοιβή); (d) The sentence κατὰ πάντα με ἀνεπαύσατε is typically Ignatian (Eph. 2,1g; Mg. 15d; Tr. 12,1; Rom. 10,2; Sm. 10,1; the interpolator imitates it in Sm. 12,1); (e) Note in 9,2cd how Ignatius marks reciprocity without the conjunctive particle ὡς; other forms, through repetition of the verb, in 10,2; Eph. 2,2, etc.; (f) In 9,2e, ἀπόντα με καὶ παρόντα, refer to Ignatius' stay in Ephesus (Sm. = Eph*!); (g) Finally note the parallel of 9,2g with Mg. 1,2e.

111. The phenomenon we have observed in the last interpolations of progressive accumulation of arguments from authority and of gradual explicitation of the interpolator's ideology, reaches its climax in the first part of the letter to Polycarp (Pol. 1-5[6,1c]) and in the consequent interpolation of Polycarp's letter

to the Philippians (Pol. Phil. 13). Is this conclusion simply accidental? It is well-known that the order modern editors give to the Ignatian letters arises from internal rather than external criteria. Indeed, that supported by the mixed compilations of Ussher and Voss, as well as by the archtype from which the oriental versions derive (SAB and C) and by the series of quotations of the Sacra Parallela Rupefucaldina (Dam.) and Severus of Antioch, corresponds with the order attributed by the interpolator to the Polycarpian compilation: (1) Letters addressed to Polycarp and his community (Sm. and Pol.); (2) Letters pretendedly collected by Polycarp from the nearby communities (Eph., Mg., Tr. and Phld.). The letter to the Romans was added much later to this compilation. Hence, either it is not included among the other letters or else it is placed last. The editors follow in general, however, the order supported by Eusebius: (1) Letters from Smyrna (Eph., Mg., Tr. and Rom.); (2) Letters from Troas (Phld., Sm. and Pol.). The best of it is that the *crescendo* we verified fits in with the topological order testified to by Eusebius and followed (not merely for its internal logic but also for its archaism) by the greater number of editors. From this we conclude: (a) that this was precisely the order the forger followed in creating the Polycarpian compilation and in the interpolation of the letters; (b) that the better to conceal it he set out the letters in the order testified to by Polycarp, Ussher, Voss, Damascenus, Severus of Antioch and the oriental versions; (c) that Eusebius, without knowing it, fitted in with the original order of the compilation, by inverting for topological motives the order testified to by the manuscript tradition and incorporating Rom. at the end of the letters from Smyrna; (d) that the forger's stratagems to hide his compilation had the desired effect until the modern editors preferred the order given by Eusebius, namely: (aa) to prepare the reader, by placing Sm. and Pol. at the head of the compilation, who was faced with the logical bewilderment that the interruption of Eph. and the promising of a second letter could cause (Pol. 8,1, in fact, distracts attention from Eph. 20,1); (bb) to give a semblance of truth to his compilation by spelling out in advance in Pol. Phil. 13,2 the order the reader would find in the letters; (cc) to avoid possible suspicion by placing Phld. last, which at the same time had the advantage of making it occupy the first place in the reader's memory.

112. The vicissitudes the text of the Ignatian letters underwent can be summed up in the following outline:

I.   Ignatius: (1)   Rom.
                             (2)   Mg*; (3)   Tr. and (4)   Eph*.

II.   Forger/Interpolator/Compiler:
                             (a)   Personal letters: (1)   Sm. and (2)   Pol.
                             (b)   Recompiled letters: (3)   Eph.; (4)   Mg.;
                                   (5)   Tr. and (6)   Phld.

III.   Eusebius: (a)   Written from Smyrna: (1)   Eph.; (2)   Mg.;
                                   (3)   Tr. and (4)   Rom.
                             (b)   Written from Troas: (5)   Phld.; (6)   Sm. and
                                   (7)   Pol.

IV.   Archtype of the mixed compilation of Ussher (Voss): The same order and number of letters as in II. [340]

V.   Archtype X (SAB and C): The same order as in II. and IV. plus (7) Rom.

VI.   Sacra Parallela Rupefucaldina: The same order and number of letters as in II., but with a quotation of Rom. (see n. 161), coming probably from the so-called Martyrium Colbertinum.

Annotations:

(1) The probable order followed by Ignatius in the writing of the letters was the above-mentioned: first, Rom.; last, Eph* (see nrs. 54f.).

(2) The order of the Polycarpian compilation made up by the forger can be inferred from the manuscript tradition, the archtype of the versions and the Sacra Parallela (IV., V., VI.).

(3) Eusebius — or one of his predecessors — has added Rom. in the so-called Polycarpian compilation. As an historian he preferred to set the letters in order according to the place of writing that is recorded at the end of them all. As far as possible he has respected the sequence of the Polycarpian compilation: First those situated in 3., 4. and 5. place, having been written in Smyrna; then Rom., written also there (the fact of occupying the last place

---

[340] In the mixed Ussherian compilation, the positions of Tr. and Phld. are reversed.

among the letters from Smyrna betrays its posterior incorporation); there follows Phld. which comes immediately afterwards (6.) and, finally, the two first (1. and 2.) all of them ascribed to Troas.

(4) The archtype of the mixed collection or ussherian did not contain Rom. In that compilation Rom. comes after the letters belonging to the Long recension (gl) together with the Martyrium Colbertinum (see pp. 16-17 and 22).

(5) In the archtype of the oriental versions we still observe the fresh incorporation of Rom. by its coming last after the six letters of the Polycarpian compilation, and before the six spurious ones of the Long recension.

* * *

At the end of this meticulous search, whose only objective was to fix exactly the extent of the interpolation, a question has remained that — if resolved — may close our investigations. This is the problem raised by the presence in Ignatius and the Didascalia of the same symbolism. Scholars who have perceived this dependence (see below the nn. 342, 343 and 382), carried away by the priority of Ignatius, have no choice but to decide in his favour against the Didascalia. Since, however, all this symbolism appears exclusively in the interpolated passages, the problem needs to be restated.

III.   THE INTERPOLATOR'S SYMBOLISM AND ITS SOURCE

We have repeatedly verified that the interpolator held a very precise idea of the church's organization. On the one hand, the three hierarchical grades — bishop, presbytery and deacons — perfectly ordered from greater to least; on the other, the community. The main objective of the interpolation was to achieve the submission and obedience of the community to the bishop and the presbytery. The arguments he displayed can be reduced to: (a) The example of the presbyters who obey the bishop in every thing, even a young bishop; (b) The exemplary behaviour of the deacons who were in all things submitted to the bishop, at the service of the community; (c) The concrete model of Ignatius, fellow-servant of the deacons and martyr; (d) The authority of

Polycarp, of the Lord and the Holy Spirit who were all on the side of the bishop.

Not satisfied with this, the forger has recourse to symbolism, to confirm his perfect verticalism: (a) The bishop in God's place; (b) The presbyters or the presbytery are a figure of the Apostles or the Apostolic college; (c) The deacons are like Jesus Christ; (d) The community, like the church. The models of submission are the church submitted to Jesus Christ and Jesus Christ submitted to the Father.

Besides, in the Didascalia there are similar correspondences: (a) Bishop/God; (b) Deacon/Jesus Christ; (c) Deaconess/Holy Spirit; (d) Presbyters-presbytery/Apostles-Apostolic college; (e) Widows-orphans/Altar; (f) Community/Church.

The presence of a similar symbolism in both writings is well-known. Before giving an opinion on the priority of either, thus to avoid any partisanship, we shall make a separate study of the interpolator's symbolism and its consistency (§ a: nrs. 113f.); of the symbolism of the Didascalia and its consistency (§ b: nrs. 115-121); only in the third place shall we offer a solution to the question (§ c: nrs. 122-125).

a) *Interpolator's symbolism and its consistency*

113. The interpolator's symbolism relative to the three hierarchical grades can be summed up as follows:

(a) The *bishop* presides over the local church in God's place (εἰς τόπον θεοῦ: Mg. 6,1c: nrs. 86f.); he is a type of the Father (ὄντα τύπον τοῦ πατρός: Tr. 3,1b: nrs. 90f.); the visible bishop, vicar of the universal and invisible Bishop (Mg. 3: nrs. 84f.); we should give the bishop refreshment in honour of the Father of Jesus Christ (Tr. 12,2d: nr. 95); he should be recognized as God himself (Sm. 9,1cd: nr. 110); be received as the One who has sent him (Eph. 6,1: nrs. 81f.). The community should be submitted to the bishop as to a gift of God (Mg. 2c: nrs. 84f.); as to the commandment that comes from God (Tr. 13,2b: nrs. 94f., and n. 282); the community should be as closely united to him as the church is to Jesus Christ and Jesus Christ to the Father (Eph. 5,1: nrs. 81f.); it should submit to the bishop as Jesus Christ to his Father (Mg. 13,2: nr. 57); follow the bishop as Jesus Christ the Father (Sm. 8,1a: nr. 109); be an imitator of Jesus Christ as he also was of his

Father (Phld. 7,2hi: nr. 105); do nothing without the bishop, just as the Lord did nothing without the Father (Mg. 7,1ab: nrs. 86f.). The interpolator sums up in a concise phrase the relations of community-bishop: " *Without the bishop do nothing* " (see nrs. 90, 101) and warns possible transgressors severely: " *Whoever does anything hidden from the bishop worships the devil* " (see nr. 110).

Nevertheless, the interpolator is not always coherent in his use of the correlation God/bishop. The underlying text of Ignatius prevents it. Thus in Eph. 3,2e-4,1 he modifies the invitation Ignatius gives to run in agreement with the Plan of the Father, that is, with Jesus the Messiah, inserting the sentence: " *Just as the bishops ... are included in the plan of Jesus Christ* ", to end up by saying that " *they should run in agreement with the plan of the bishop* " (nrs. 81f.). Logically, he should have suppressed the sentence relative to Jesus the Messiah, as the Plan of the Father, and insert in his place the bishop. But the interpolator always respects the literality of the text (he never suppresses anything) and prefers to adulterate it with a sentence that falsifies the original meaning. In the same way, in Tr. 1,2-2,2 he has been obliged to establish the correlation Jesus Christ/bishop for fear of leaving any loose ends. Ignatius realized that the Trallians were " imitators of God Jesus the Messiah, our hope, in whose company if we persevere we shall be found not living like the people but like Jesus the Messiah, etc. " (nrs. 89, 91). For the interpolator, no one can reach such assimilation with Jesus Christ unless he submits to the bishop as to Jesus Christ (nrs. 90f.). Inadvertently, his usual correlation Jesus Christ/deacons has become Jesus Christ/ bishop. Logically he should have said: " *When you are submitted to the bishop, like Jesus Christ to the Father...* ". But the Ignatian sentences that he had to use immediately afterwards (2,1bc and 2,2bc), prevented this.

(b) The *presbyters* (the presbytery) represent (εἰς τόπον) or figure (εἰς τύπον) the senate of the Apostles (Mg. 6,1c: nr. 87); the community should respect them as the senate of God and the college of the Apostles (Tr. 3,1c: nrs. 90f. and n. 308); submit to the presbytery as to the Apostles (Tr. 2,2b: nr. 91) or to the commandment that comes from God (Tr. 13,2b: nrs. 94f., and n. 282); follow the presbytery as the Apostles (Sm. 8,1b: nr. 109). The interpolator always employs ἀπόστολος in a corporate sense, that is, as definite plural substantive (οἱ ἀπόστολοι: Mg. 6,1c; 13,1.2; Tr. 2,2b; 3,1c; 7,1d; 12,2d; Sm. 8,1b) and in absolute form (only in Tr. 2,2b he determines them as " the Apostles of Jesus the Messiah "; this determination, however, belongs to the Ignatian text! See nr. 89).

Neither here is the interpolator coherent. Firstly, carried away by the trilogy of his time, bishop-presbyters-deacons, he has placed among the correlatives the Apostles before Jesus Christ: God-Apostles-Jesus Christ. This might suggest that at one time the scheme of relationship was: God/bishop, Jesus Christ/deacon and Apostolic college/senate or college of the elders of the community, and that much later the elders became ordained presbyters and rose above the deacons in hierarchical rank. Secondly, as the presbytery were the spiritual crown of the bishop (Mg. 13,2: nr. 57), to express the perfect juncture between the presbyters and the bishop, he could not have taken as model the submission of the Apostles to Jesus Christ, because the bishop occupies the place of God and not of Jesus Christ (following the model: community submitted to the bishop/Jesus Christ submitted to the Father). He uses, on the other hand, the image of the strings harmonized with the zither (Eph. 4,1c: nrs. 81f.). The submission of the Apostles to Christ, to the Father and the Spirit is adduced to arrive at the union of the community (Mg. 13,2: nr. 57). What is more, by putting the phrase in negative form: " *Without the bishop and the presbyters do nothing* ", the logical term of comparison would be: " *Just as the Lord did nothing without the Father or the Apostles*", a phrase from every point of view totally illogical. The interpolator had to modify the term of comparison as follows: " *Just as the Lord did nothing without the Father, neither for himself nor for the Apostles, so neither should you do anything without the bishop or the presbyters* " (Mg. 7,1ab: nr. 87).

If we compare the meaning Ignatius gives to " apostle " with the one given by the interpolator, we find one more anomaly. Ignatius still retains the functional meaning of " founder of communities ": " I do not give you directives like Peter and Paul: they were apostles, I am a condemned man; they were free, I am at present a slave ... " (Rom. 4,3); " It is not my intention to give you directives like an apostle, since I am a condemned man " (Tr. 3,3). Peter and Paul are mentioned in the letter to the

Rom. as founders and educators of the communities in the faith; Ignatius is deeply interested in making clear in three of the four authentic letters that ' he does not give them directives as if he were someone ' (Eph. 3,1), that is, according to the above-mentioned parallels, as if he were an " apostle ". The fact that Ignatius himself, who a short while before introduced himself as " the bishop of Syria " (Rom. 2,2), advises them now that he does not want to give them directives like an apostle, suggests that he considers himself an " apostle " but he does not address them in this capacity, because it is not his church and also because of his situation, above all taking into account that there have been factions from his own communities that provoked his condemnation to death.

So, besides the technical meaning, " the Apostles " (Eph. 11,2; Phld. = Mg* 5,1 and 9,1), Ignatius retains the one deriving from the " charism of apostolate ", belonging specifically to the Apostles and transmitted to the ἐπίσκοποι — Ignatius for Syria and Polycarp later on for Asia as many others — in his capacity of founder of new communities and of educators and inspectors of these (see nr. 89). — The interpolator, on the contrary, understands it exclusively in a stereotyped sense of the Apostles as senate or college (Mg. 6,1c; Tr. 3,1c) or as source of dogmas and prescriptions (Mg. 13,1; Tr. 7,1d: see nrs. 57 and 92). For him, the " successors " of the Apostles would be the presbyters (sic! see above).

(c) The *deacons* do not preside like the bishop or the presbyters (Mg. 6,1cd: see nr. 86): to them had been entrusted the diaconia of Jesus Christ. They are ministers (ὑπηρέται) of the church of God. Hence they have to submit to the bishop and the presbytery (Mg. 2c), just as Jesus Christ was humanly submitted to the Father (13,2). All must respect the deacons as Jesus Christ (Tr. 3,1a), as a precept from God (Sm. 8,1c: nr. 109; see nr. 84 and n. 282). For the interpolator Jesus Christ is the " *deacon* " par excellence. Hence, carried away by Ignatius' Christocentrism and his attitude of service, he has given him the title of " *deacon* ".

The incongruity of relating the deacons (the interpolator always uses the plural, except in the case of some named in particular) to Jesus Christ springs to the eye. It would make sense, on the other hand, if there were only one deacon who stood at

the head of the presbyters. Observe that for the presbyters he
has thought out a collectivity and for the bishop an individuality,
respectively the Apostles and God. Besides this, carried away by
his eagerness to centralize all in the person of the bishop, he has
forgotten to apply the model of submission Jesus Christ/Father
consistently to the deacons in their relations with the bishop; he
proposes this model instead for submission of the community to
the bishop. In Pol. 6,1c he seems to invite the community to
submit to the deacons, as to the bishop and the presbyters. Probably, as in Tr. 7,2c, it is a question of inaccuracies due to his scholasticism. In this last case it could be the slip of an amanuensis
(A omits, against GL, who read " deacon ", and gC " deacons ").

114. In a diagram, the symbolism of the interpolator can be
reduced to:

bishop/God
presbyters-presbytery/Apostles-Apostolic college or senate
deacons/Jesus Christ

The relation between each of these binary systems is expressed
either through the particle ὡς with a conjunctive function or else
with idioms such as " *in honour of* " (εἰς τιμὴν), " *in the place of* "
(εἰς τόπον), " *in the type of* " (εἰς τύπον). The passages which
contain the complete trilogy are Tr. 3,1 and Mg. 6,1cd. In this
last passage the two latter expressions are interchangeable according to the several manuscript traditions. Scholars do not agree
which of the variants is most primitive. Zahn and Lightfoot opt
for the second relying on the Syriac (S) and Armenian (A) versions — to which should be added the newly published Arab (B)
one — and on the parallel of Tr. 3,1 (ὄντα τύπον τοῦ πατρός). Funk,
Hilgenfeld, Bauer, Lelong, Fisher, Camelot prefer the first (εἰς
τόπον), attested to by the Middle (GL) and the Long recension
(gl) and, in Syriac, for Severus of Antioch. ZAHN appeals to the
contradiction that would follow from the first reading. [341] LIGHT-
FOOT adduces several passages of the Apostolic Constitutions that
abound, according to him, in reminiscences of this Ignatian pas-

---

[341] *I. v. A.* 571: " Nicht an der Stelle Gottes ..., der ja nicht abgesetzt ist, sondern als irdisches Abbild Gottes führt der Bischof den Vorsitz in der Gemeinde..."

sage. [342]   As we shall see, these appear first in the Didascalia Apostolorum and not in the Apostolic Constitutions as some have
supposed. [343]

The greater inconsistency in this symbolism is the position
occupied by Jesus Christ below the Apostles and the comparison
of one state, the deacons, with a person in the singular, Jesus Christ.
Has the interpolator made use of elements of a symbolism that
corresponded with a more archaic situation, difficult to adapt to
the ecclesiastical situation of his time?

b) *Symbolism of the Didascalia Apostolorum and its consistency*

115.   The central passage of the Didascalia where this symbolism occurs is in the second book, at the end of the ample development that starts in II. 1,1: " Pastor, qui constituitur in visita-
tione(m) presbyterii et in ecclesiis omnibus et parochiis, oportet... "
and ends in II. 25 (in II. 26 already goes on to address the " laymen ", " the church chosen by God "), that is in *Did.* II. 26.
In this passage we have found the same terminology and the same
correspondences we have just observed in Mg. 6,1 and even a
similar fluctuation as concerns the variants εἰς τόπον/εἰς τύπον. [344]

Far from constituting an isolated affirmation, as was the
case with Mg. 6,1 (Tr. 3,1), this passage of the Didascalia is placed
within the themes developped in chapters 25-36 [345] and announced
in advance incidentally (as was usual in the Didascalia) in 24,4 (7). [346]
The central theme of all this development is the *administration of
goods* contributed by the community, on the part of the bishops
with the deacons.   In 36,9 a new theme is already announced:
The *judiciary power* conferred on the bishops. [347]

---

[342] *AA. FF.* II: II/1, 119f.

[343] ZAHN, *PP. AA.* II 336f.; FUNK, *AA. KK.* 70; H. ACHELIS – J. FLEMMING,
Die syrische Didascalia übersetzt und erklärt (= *Syr. Did.*), Leipzig 1904, T. U.
25,2, Abhandlung II 272 (Achelis): " Das alles nach dem Beispiel des IGNATIUS,
aber doch nicht minder im sinne unseres Autors."

[344] Frequent in sacred and profane authors: ZAHN, *PP. AA.* II 33.

[345] Chaps. VIII-IX of the Syriac Didascalia.

[346] After enumerating ten qualities that a bishop should possess and ten defects
he should avoid, the Didascalist goes on: " Non ut alienis, sed sicut propriis his
quae a Deo dantur utentes, moderatores sicut bonos dispensatores Dei, qui incipiet
rationem ab ea quae in nobis est dispensatione exigere."

[347] " Episcopis vero potestas data est iudicandi, quoniam eis dictum est: ' Estote

116. The first part of this development (Chap. 25) is directed, like the former chapters, to the bishops; the second is already addressed to the " laymen " (26-36,8). The change of addressees is due to the requirements of the theme itself.

The chapter addressed to the bishops is dominated by the analogy of the Tabernacle of the Meeting (ἡ σκηνὴ τοῦ μαρτυρίου), model of the (Christian) Assembly in all its details (ἥτις ἦν τύπος τῆς ἐκκλησίας κατὰ πάντα):

" To this should be added that because of the word 'testimony' the Tabernacle of the (Christian) Assembly was foreshowed " (προσέτι δὲ καὶ ἐκ τοῦ ὀνόματος ' μ α ρ τ ύ ρ ι ο ν ' τῆς ἐκκλησίας ἡ σκηνὴ προωρίζετο) [348] (Did. II. 25,5).

In the Tabernacle of the Christian Assembly the bishops become the " levitical priests " (ἱερεῖς λευῖται), appointed to the liturgical service of the Tabernacle of God, the holy universal Assembly (οἱ λειτουργοῦντες τῇ σκηνῇ τοῦ θεοῦ, [349] τῇ ἁγίᾳ καθολικῇ ἐκκλησίᾳ). [350] All the functions of the People of God are monopolized in their person:

" Thus, you (the bishops) are for your people priests and prophets, princes and guides and kings, the mediators (οἱ μεσῖται) between God and his faithful, the receptacles of the message and the messengers that announce it, the knowers of the Scriptures and speakers of God and witnesses to his plan, those who bear the sins of all and give account of all " (25,7).

Like the Messiah, whom they take as watchman (σκοπὸς), the bishops have to be watchmen (σκοποί) of the laity whom they keep below them (τῶν ὑφ' ὑμᾶς λαικῶν). [351] Underneath this para-

---

prudentes trapezitae '." Developed in II. 37-44 (power of the keys) and 45-57,1 (ecclesiastical tribunal).

[348] S and A. C. differ a little. FUNK, Did. et CC. AA. 94, guesses that the Constitutions " textum Didascaliae hic fidelius vel accuratius tradere videntur quam illa (= S) ". The structural parallel of Did. II. 60,3 agrees with Funk's view: προσέτι δὴ καὶ οὗ ὀνόματος (κενωθέντες) ἑαυτοὺς καλοῦσιν Ἰούδα. Ἰούδας γὰρ ἐξομολόγησις ἑρμηνεύεται κτλ.

[349] Tabernaculo Dei S: τῇ ἱερᾷ σκηνῇ A. C. The A. C. continually tend to sacralize the Did. text.

[350] Did. II. 25,7.

[351] Did. II. 25,12: Reconstruction from S + A. C. The same image and correspondence in II. 6,6 (7).11; 17,6; 24,4 (7).

phrase it is not difficult to recognize the etymology of " episko-
pos ": the " watchman " who is placed " above " his people
(" below " and " above " are correlatives) or, which comes to the
same, " over-seer/super-visor " of the community activities. Just
as they bear the weight of the whole community — it insists that
the mission of watchman (ἡ ἐπισκοπὴ) is a heavy office not easy to
fill —, above all bearing the sins of all, they have also the right
to be the first to feed on the gifts offered by the community and
to distribute them to the needy, in their capacity of " levitical
priests, ministers in the service of God ". [352]

117.   After that he addresses the " laity ", the People of God,
the sacrosanct universal Assembly (II. 26-36). On this subject
he details the correspondences between the Tabernacle of the
Meeting then, and today's Assembly, either in reference to offerings
or persons. In outline they are as follows:

	Then (τότε)		*Now* (νῦν)
(1) *Offerings*: (a)	Sacrifices	(a')	Prayers, intercessions and thanksgivings
(b)	First-fruits, tithes, ransoms and offerings	(b')	Liturgical offerings (prosphorae)
(2) *Persons*: (a)	Levites (comprehensively: the tribe of Levi):	(a')	All those who are at the service of, or who live at the expense of the community :
(aa)	Priests (Aaron and his sons)	(aa')	Bishops (Levitical [High] priests) [353]
(bb)	Levites [354] (Brothers of Aaron and their sons)	(bb')	Deacons, presbyters, widows and orphans

---

[352] Did. II. 25,13-14.   Reconstruction from S + A. C. (S has added the copulas,
as is usual).

[353] The Did. reserves the title " high priest " (II. 26,3.4) as well as " priest "
(II. 25,7.14; 27,3.4; 28,2; 35,3 S) to the bishop. Only once does he refer to the
" High Priest Christ " (II. 26,1). The Constitutor has a special predilection for
these titles as applied to the bishops.

[354] The Did. clearly distinguishes as applied to the universal church, between
the levites (οἱ λευῖται) and levites (λευῖται predicate). This is attested by L (26,

(b) People of Israel   (b') Assembly chosen by God, " laymen "

In this passage appear many of the correspondences between persons we saw in the textus receptus of Ignatius, but together with others not mentioned by the interpolator.

118. Given the present state of the Didascalia text — original Greek (G) lost; preserved in Latin (L) and Syriac (S) versions; recast in Greek by the author of the Apostolic Constitutions (A.C.) — a reconstruction as close as possible is called for.

As for the variant εἰς τόπον/εἰς τύπον (L: 5x *in typum*; S: 3x [2x] *b-duktâ* / 2x [3x] *ba-dmû-tâ*; A.C.: 2x paraphrase [ὡς conj.] / 3x εἰς τύπον), the one which better preserved the original is the *Syriac* (S) version. Indeed, the Didascalist placed the bishop, deacon and deaconess (individuals) " in the place of " (εἰς τόπον) God, the Messiah and the Holy Spirit respectively, for each one, in his own way, reflects in the assembly the action of one person of the Trinity, [355] that is: presidence (God/bishop), masculine deaconship (Messiah/deacon) and feminine deaconship (Holy Spirit/ deaconess); while he proposed the presbyters, widows and orphans (representing collectivities) as " types/figures of " (εἰς τύπον) the Apostles (the presbytery) and the Altar (the needy):

" This (the bishop) is your powerful king who governs you in the place (εἰς τόπον LS: A.C. paraphrase) of the Almighty: let him be honoured by you as God. The bishop, in fact, presides over you (προκάθηται!) in the place (*b-duktâ* S: in *typum* L, A.C. paraphrase) of God Almighty (> L); the (ὁ δὲ) deacon assists in the place (*b-duktâ* S: *in typum* L, A.C. paraphrase) of the Messiah: let him be loved,

---

3.4) and the A. C. when speaking of bishops (25,7: ἱερεῖς λευῖται; 25,14: ἱερεῖς λευίτας, προέδρους, λειτουργούς). S slightly modifies the original of 26,3 (*priests and* levites) inverting the order (*presbyters, deacons*, widows and orphans), thus tacitly establishing the correspondences priests/presbyters, levites/deacons, etc. The A. C. make it definitively explicit, adding orders of more recent creation.

[355] See ACHELIS–FLEMMING, *Syr. Did.*, Abhl. II 272 (Achelis): " Da der Bischof dort den Gottesdienst regelmässig leitet, hatten die Presbyter keine selbstständige Rolle als Prediger und Liturgen. Sie traten nur gemeinsam als Kollegium auf, und kamen daher der Gemeinde wenig ins Bewusstsein. Sie bilden einen Ehrenrat, der nur bei besonderen Gelegenheiten in Funktion tritt. Wenn daher der Verfasser die Hierarchie der Gemeinde mit der des Himmels vergleicht, hat die göttliche Trinität ihr Abbild nicht in Bischof, Presbyter und Diakonen, sondern in Bischof, Diakon und Diakonisse."

then, by all of you; the (ἡ δὲ) deaconess should be honoured by you
in the place (b-duktâ Sp: ba-dmûtâ Smc, in typum L, εἰς τύπον A. C.)
of the Holy Spirit. The (οἴ τε) presbyters should be (ἔστωσαν S A.C.:
sperentur L) for you a type (εἰς τύπον SL A. C.) of the Apostles; the
(αἴ τε) widows and orphans, considered by you as a type (εἰς τύπον
SL A. C.) of the Altar '' (II. 26,4-8).[356]

The first three members — bishop, deacon and deaconess —
are in the singular; the other two — presbyters and widows-orphans — are in the plural denoting a collectivity (οἴ, αἴ). The first
three are connected by one form (δὲ); the two remaining ones,
by another (τε). The first three take the *place* respectively of God,
the Messiah and the Holy Spirit; the two others are *types/images*
of the Apostles and the Altar respectively.

119. The sharp distinction between these groups reflects
perfectly the theological conception of the Didascalist on the ministries. Frequent mention is made of the bishop with his dea-
con(s). [357] On rare occasions the presbyters are also enumerated. [358]
In the Eucharistic celebration the main role is exercised by the
bishop, assisted by his deacon(s). [359] The presbyters occupy only
an honorific place, at each side of the bishop's throne separated
from the laity. [360] In the agapes or paraliturgical celebrations
the bishop, whether or not he presides, has the right, in God's
honour, to a fourfold share of the offerings; [361] each deacon has
the right to a twofold share, in honour of the Messiah; [362] each of
the most needy elderly women who have been convoked, receive
one share. [363] As for the presbyters, this is left to the donors to
decide:

[356] See ZAHN, *PP. AA.* II 337.

[357] Did. II. 10,3; 17,2.3; 30; 31,3; 32,2.3; 37,6; 42,1; 44; III. 8,1.4; 10 (14),
8; 13 (19),1.7; IV. 5,1.

[358] Did. II. 46,6 (episcopum cum presbyteris); 47,1 (presbyteri ac diaconi cum
episcopis); III. 11 (15),5 (neque episcopus nec presbyter nec diaconus nec vidua);
12 (16),3; VI. 12,3.

[359] Did. II. 57,6.

[360] Did. II. 57,3-5.

[361] Pastor (S A. C.) or priest (L) of Did. II. 28,2 is '' the one who presides ''
in 28,3, according as inferred from the twofold motivation: '' in honorem omnipotentis Dei '' (28,2) — '' tamquam in omnipotentis gloriam '' (28,3) and from the
context.

[362] Did. II. 28,3.

[363] '' Sicut ergo unicuique presbyterarum datur, duplum dabitur singulis diaconis

" If anyone wishes to honour the presbyters also, let him give them a twofold share, as to the deacons: for they should also be honoured as the Apostles, and as the counsellors (σύμβουλοι) of the bishop, and as the crown (στέφανος) of the assembly, since they make up the senate and council (συνέδριον καὶ βουλὴ) of the assembly " (II. 28,4).[364]

Office, honour and right to the offerings are correlatives. [365] The *bishop*'s privileged position, in the place of God, gives him the right to dispose freely of the liturgical offerings for his own support and that of his auxiliaries (deacons), assistants or counsellors (presbyters) and protégés (widows and orphans). A lower rank and less rights correspond with the deacons, *deacon* and *deaconess*, because they occupy the place of the Messiah and the Holy Spirit respectively, they being also at the service of the community under the bishop's charge. [366] As far as can be inferred, the author still holds a functional view of the Trinity: God is the administrator, the Messiah and the Spirit are his assistants, through whom he carries out his plan. The same occurs in the assembly: the bishop is the administrator; the deacon and the deaconess, his auxiliaries. But the *presbyters*, apart from the honoured place they occupy in the assemblies, are not said to intervene directly in the liturgical celebration. They are the community elders, in the image of the Apostles. Then come the *widows* (including the presbyters or elderly women) and the *orphans*, who because they habitually live on the communitarian offerings typify the Altar of God or of the Messiah. [367]

The bishop is the centre of the community: mediator between God and the faithful; [368] depositary of the divine power of judging, retaining or forgiving sins " like God " (ὡς θεός); [369]

---

in honorem Christi; quadruplum autem ei, qui praeest, tamquam in omnipotentis gloriam."

[364] ZAHN, *PP. AA.* II 337, has been influenced by the parallels of Ign. and the Ps.-Ign. to reconstruct this passage. The L version does not agree with him.

[365] " Omni ergo dignitati (ἀξιώματι) unusquisque ex laicis venerationem debitam impertiant muneribus et honoribus et verecundia saeculo consentanea " (Did. II. 28,5 S = A. C.).

[366] Did. II. 24,4 (7); 25,2.8.13-14; 35,4; III. 4 (3),2.

[367] Did. II. 26,8; III. 6,3; 7,2; 10,7 (14,1); IV. 3,3; 5,1.2; 7,1.3. ACHELIS-FLEMMING, *Syr. Did.*, Abhl. II 274 (Achelis).

[368] Did. II. 25,7; 26,4; 29; 35,3.

[369] Did. II. 11,1-2; 12,1; 18,2_3; 33,3; 34,4.

object of love, fear, reverence and honour, inasmuch as he is father, king, lord, god after God. [370]

120.   The Didascalist distinguishes closely between παροικία, territory over which the bishop exercises his vigilance, equivalent to our " diocese ", and the ἐκκλησίαι or communities set up within the territory.   Each community has its own presbyters or elders who make up the presbytery.   The bishop with his deacons is the only one responsible for the communities arising in his territory. Hence in the beginning of the second book it is said:

" The pastor who is going to be appointed as supervisor of the presbytery for the communities of each diocese should be blameless, irreproachable, etc." [371]   (Did. II. 1,1).

At the time of the Didascalist, the operative ambit of the bishop was less extended that in Ignatius' or Polycarp's times. Instead of a " province ", he exercised his oversight within a " parish ", a lesser unity, even a very small one, [372] that is, over the communities set up within the limits of this boundary, each one being presided over by a college of elders.

If a brother or sister of another community of the same diocese (ἀπὸ παροικίας) happens to come, the deacon will enquire if they are believers, if they belong to the community or the heretics, etc.   If a presbyter from a community of the diocese (de ecclesia parochiae) comes, he will be received by the presbyters and seated with them in the presbytery.   Should it be a bishop, he will sit beside the local bishop, since he should be object of the same honour.   The local bishop will invite him to speak, because he is a foreigner, for " no one is prophet in his own country ". [373]   Note

---

[370] Did. II. 12,1 (ὡς θεός); 18,2-3 (quasi locum Dei omnipotentis); 20,1 (ὡς... θεὸς μετὰ θεόν S); 26,4; 29-30 (ὡς θεός); 31,3 (deos = praepositos vestros); 34,5 (ut deum); III. 8,1 (sicut deum).

[371] L, S and A. C. differ from each other.   When two coincide, it is a sign they reflect the original: τὸν ποιμένα τὸν καθιστάμενον (A. C. LS) εἰς ἐπισκοπὴν τοῦ πρεσβυτερίου (in visitatione[m] presbyterii L: S translates with an hendiadys: episcopum et principem in presbyterii, ἐπίσκοπον A. C.) εἰς τὰς ἐκκλησίας (A. C., in ecclesiis L: in ecclesia S) ἐν πάσῃ παροικίᾳ (A. C. S: omnibus et parochiis L). In S there is no copula between the three prepositional sentences (unlike the usual construction in S) neither in the A. C.

[372] Did. II. 1,3.

[373] Did. II. 58,1-3.

that in the first instance it is said he comes from the diocese; in the second, from a community in the diocese; in the third there is no precision. This is normal. The foreign bishop is necessarily from another diocese. When speaking of the arrival of authorities or poor people, it is always stated if they are " diocesans or foreigners " (ἢ ἐγχώριος ἢ ξένος). [374]

121. If we now examine the central passage of Did. II. 26 in view of the *consistency* of the symbolism there expressed that is presupposed all through the work, the perfect internal logic and its congruity with the plan of the Didascalia springs to the eye. We shall enlarge on each of these points.

The symbolism of the Didascalist is perfectly *logical* as much in reference to (a) the paradigm taken from the Old Testament, as in what concerns (b) the model probably inspired by the heavenly liturgy.

(a) The paradigm of the *Tabernacle of the Meeting* foretells, throughout, the Tabernacle of the Christian Assembly, the church as gathered in community. The ancient offerings are raised to a spiritual key. The ancient personages, to an ecclesial one. The distinction between Levites and the People of Israel continues to be maintained at any cost. Two groups were separated: on the one hand, bishop, deacons, presbyters, widows and orphans, namely, all those who in any way had access to the Altar; on the other, the Assembly of the elect men, the laity. Between the ancient Levites, in a global sense, were included the priests (Aaronites: Num. 18,1.7-20) and the levites in a strict sense (Num. 18,2-4.6.21.23-24): the bishops now represent the priests/high priests; the deacons, presbyters, widows and orphans, the levites.

(b) The model of the *heavenly Liturgy* included God as supreme Administrator, the Messiah and the Holy Spirit as his Assistants, the Apostles as God's Senate, and the Altar. The bishop takes the place of God; the deacon, the place of the Messiah; the deaconess, the place of the Holy Spirit. The presbyters represent the Apostles; the widows and orphans, the Altar. Here everything fits. Correspondences can be verified along the line of represented and representatives, symbolized and symbolizers. There are two perfect sequences: God-Messiah-Spirit-Apostles-Altar, on

---

[374] Did. II. 58,4-6.

the one hand, and bishop-deacon-deaconess-presbyters-widows and orphans, on the other.

Did. II. 26 *connects up perfectly* with the general plan of the work. The *first* book is dedicated to the church-community, underlying and supporting all the various functions it will treat of directly after. The *second* book deals firstly with the bishops. The first part (II. 1-25) is immediately concerned with the bishops; the second (26-36,8), with the community; the third (36,9-44) is addressed once again to the bishops with the deacons and it develops the power of the keys with regard to the members of the community; the fourth (45-57,1) deals with the ecclesiastical tribunal to resolve cases and litigation among the faithful; the fifth (57,2-63) explains themes relating to order and discipline in the assembly, and relations with other communities, frequency of meetings, frequentation of pagan spectacles, daily work. The *third* book treats of the order of widows, and in passing, of women in general (III. 1-11); of the election of deacons and deaconesses (12-13). The *fourth* treats of orphans and widows in so far as they participate in the offerings of the Altar (IV. 1-10), of children (11). The *fifth* and *sixth* books contain themes relating to the life and behaviour of the community (martyrs, converts, etc.).

The bishop with his deacons (deacon and deaconess) always appears in the foreground. Hardly anything is said of the presbyters. The widows and orphans are the object of special attention on the part of the bishop with the deacons as well as the community.

The only anomaly to be observed in the text of the Didascalia occurs in *Did.* II. 34, the single instance where mention is made of the election of presbyters, deacons and subdeacons in this order. But in III. 12 (16),1 the bishop is invited to choose deacons and deaconesses from among the people. There is evident parallelism between the one and the other. A first anomaly observed in II. 34 collated with III. 12 (16),1 is the twofold election of deacons, very well motivated in the second passage; with no reason given in the first. Another anomaly is the allusion to the subdeacons, singular in the Didascalia. A third is the placing of the presbyters above the deacons, unique of its kind. A fourth, the silence of the Constitutions which are so interested in everything referring to ordinations and hierarchical enumerations. In

the Apostolic Constitutions the presbyters already occupy a leading position, above the deacons.   In them, besides the subdeacons,
lectors, exorcists, etc. are already mentioned.

But the most notable matter is the difficult insertion of
said thematic material in the context of the Didascalia immediately
preceding and following.   It speaks of the honour due to the
bishops and of the tribute to be given them as if to kings, so that
they can feed themselves and their familiars (II. 34,1).   To support this it quotes 1Sam. 8,10-17 (34,2: summed up by the A.C.).
From whence it infers that the bishop also — like the king who
took what he needed from the people in men, animals and in
kind to govern such a multitude — should take from the community what God assigns him (allusion to Num. 18,1-32, developed
in II. 25; likewise summed up by the A.C.) to nourish himself
and his familiars (see II. 25,2-8.13-14).   Thus reads Did. II. 34,1-3,
reconstructed from S + L + A.C. the first part (34,1); from S +
L (+ A.C.), the second (34,2); and from A.C. (and in part from
S + L), the third (34,3).   The present text of 34,3 in S and L
represents a later correction inserted in the Didascalia, which
nevertheless does not affect the copy the Constitutor had before
his eyes.   The intentions of this manipulation of the text are clear:
to sanction with the testimony of the Didascalia the election of
the presbyters, and their superior rank to the deacons and subdeacons.   To work it out the writer used as model III. 12 (16),1 and
the quotation of Os. 1,10.   FUNK [375] as well as ACHELLIS [376] as-
cribe the presence of the subdeacons in the text to a defect in the
manuscript transmission.   The interpolation is deeper.   The immediate posterior context of 34,4-6 corroborates the thematic materials retained by the Apostolic Constitutions.

c) *Priority of the Didascalia, source of the interpolator's symbolism*

There can be no doubt about the interdependence of the interpolator of Ignatius and the Didascalia, in what concerns the symbolism of the hierarchical grades and the terminology used for
the one or the other.   Nevertheless, as we already saw, scholars

---

[375] *AA. KK.* 50f.

[376] *Syr. Did.*, Abhl. II 265, 268 : " so sind wir genötigt, einen Fehler der Ueberlieferung anzunehmen ".

have settled the question in favour of Ignatius. But the detailed
analysis of both writings gives clear evidence that the Didascalia
has priority and that the interpolator of Ignatius was not
only inspired by it in adopting its symbolism (nr. 122), but also
by making his own certain stereotyped formulas (nrs. 123 f.). And
what is more, as far as we can see, he has not even hesitated to
quote it as an Apostolic writing (nr. 125). This is what we are
about to develop.

122.   Independently from the use one or the other made of
the same symbolism and the greater or lesser consistency in its
employment, there are two details that suffice in themselves to
prove the absolute originality of the Didascalia. In fact, unlike
the interpolator of Ignatius who writes and thinks in Greek (we
have already suggested that he is an Asiatic and, so it seems,
from Philadelphia) the author of the Didascalia writes in Greek
but thinks as a *Semitic*. A *first* proof comes to us in the correspondence deaconess/Holy Spirit, based on the Spirit being feminine (*rûhâ*) in Syriac. Only a writer of Semitic origin could relate
a female personage with the third person of the Trinity, the Holy
Spirit, whose equivalent in Greek is neuter (τὸ πνεῦμα τὸ ἅγιον).

The *second* detail is still more convincing. In the first there
is the remote possibility that he was inspired by the Valentinian
gnosis, although there is no trace whatever of gnosticism in the
Didascalia. The second could only occur in a writer familiar with
a Semitic language and, in the concrete, with the Syriac one. In
his attempt to establish a parallelism between the Tabernacle of
the Old Alliance, and the Church as place of assembly or reunion
of the New, the Didascalist did not hesite to correct the mistake
coming from the defective version of the LXX. They had, in
fact, erroneously taken the same Greek word, μαρτύριον, to translate both *mo'ed* (participle derived from *yâ'ad*: " give place and
time for an appointment ") [377] to ἡ σκηνὴ τοῦ μαρτυρίου, as if to
translate '*edut* (derived from '*ud*: " iterate ", from whence " affirm
vigorously ", " testify ") [378] to ἡ κιβωτὸς τοῦ μαρτυρίου, by mistak-
enly making them derive from the same root, because certain
root forms are graphically indistinguishable. But the Didascalist

[377] F. ZORELL, *Lexicon Hebraicum et Aramaicum Veteris Testamenti*, Rome 1968
(reprint), cc. 418f.
[378] ZORELL, *Lexicon* 573f.

underneath the given Greek term recognizes the close etymological relationship that prevails between *mo'ed* (μαρτύριον LXX = " meeting ") and *'edtâ* (ἐκκλησία = " assembly "), both deriving from the same root. In a brief note NESTLE already hints at this solution. [379] Hence the Didascalist can affirm:

" To this should be added that because of the word ' t e s t i m o n y ' (προσέτι δὲ καὶ ἐκ τοῦ ὀνόματος ' μαρτύριον ', according to the LXX!, but instead of ' m e e t i n g ', according to the Semitic original meaning) the Tabernacle of the (Christian) a s s e m b l y was foreshowed (τῆς ἐκκλησίας ἡ σκηνὴ προωρίζετο) " (Did. II. 25,5).

The whole symbolism of the Didascalist is dominated and given unity by the correspondence between the Old Tabernacle of the M e e t i n g and the New Tabernacle of the C h u r c h.

123. If we now compare the interpolated passages in Ignatius' text with parallels from the Didascalia, we shall see that: (1) The interpolator limits himself to support the threefold hierarchical ministry with its corresponding types, while the Didascalist frames them within a perfect harmonic union, the concept of the Tabernacle of the Meeting as complete type of the Christian Assembly; (2) The interpolator is interested only in the threefold ministry (bishop/God; presbyters/Apostles; deacons/Jesus Christ); while the Didascalist clearly distinguishes those who take the place of each person of the Trinity (bishop/God; deacon/Jesus the Messiah; deaconess/Holy Spirit) from those who are types of

---

[379] E. NESTLE, *Miscellen: Apostolische Constitutionen* II, 25, in: *Z. N. W.* 2 (1901) 263f.: " Der Verfasser dieser Literatur scheint aus Kreisen zu stammen, in denen das Hebräische nicht ganz unbekannt war." See also CONNOLLY, *Did. Ap.* LXXXVIIf. As to the region from which the Didascalia comes, he considers " certain points which are suggestive merely of a Semitic environment ". He mentions: (a) Acquaintance with the apocryphal additions to the story of Manasseh; (b) Familiarity with Jewish Sabbath observances; (c) Translation of *raca* ' empty ', deriving it from *rîk*; (d) Interpretation of ' Jew ' as ' confession ', connecting it with a verb which in Hebrew and Aramaic (including Syriac) means ' to confess '; (e) Possible connection of ' tabernacle of *witness* ' (or ' *testimony* ') with the ordinary Syriac word for ' church '; (f) Likeness of the deaconess with the Holy Spirit, doubtless because in Semitic languages ' spirit ' is femenine; (g) Two otherwise unknown O. T. quotations, which he attributes to Isaiah. — Already the Syrian translator (S) had not recognized the underlying connection of μαρτύριον with ' meeting ' and he limited himself to saying that " The Tabernacle of the Testimony (*sâhdûtâ*) foreshowed the Assembly (or Church) ".

the Apostles (presbyters) and the Altar (widows-orphans), thus enlarging the typology to the offerings; (3) The interpolator is inconsistent when he attributes to the presbyters a superior rank to the deacons, since this places the Apostles above Jesus Christ; [380] the Didascalist, on the contrary, is consistent in the order in which he places the types and anti-types, since he holds the service given by the deacons to be more important than the advice given by the presbyters or elders of the community; (4) The interpolator agrees with the Constitutor (tendency already verifiable in the Syriac Didascalia and that probably explains the anomaly of Did. II. 34) by considering the presbyters superior in rank to the deacons; while the Didascalist hints at a still more archaic theology of ministries, in which the service given to the community prevails over the honorary titles; (5) Finally, in the light of the Didascalia text, certain expressions that sound harsh in the text of the interpolator are more easily understood, namely those passages that invite the faithful to fear, reverence, honour and respect the bishop, the presbytery and the deacons; the privileged position of the bishop in the theology of the Didascalia as " lieutenant " of God centres on his person all these and similar expressions. [381]

124. The interpolator does not limit himself to picking out correspondences relative to the three hierarchical grades, but he even imitates formulas, comparisons and images employed by the Didascalist. The formula: " *Without the bishop do nothing* ", so characteristic of the forger (see nrs. 90, 101, and n. 292), is to be found also in the Didascalia:

---

[380] LIGHTFOOT, *AA. FF.* II : II/1, 159, perceived this incongruity : " It will thus appear that both the comparison of the deacons to Jesus Christ and that of the presbyters to the Apostles flow naturally, though in separate channels, from the idea of the bishop as the type of God. But the combined result is incongruous, for the presbyters are made to occupy a lower place in the comparison than the deacons."

[381] Compare *Ignatius*, Eph. 1,3d (ἀγαπᾶν); 6,1b (φοβεῖσθω); Sm. 9,1d (τιμῶν); Eph. 2,1d (εἰς τιμήν); Tr. 12,2d (εἰς τιμήν); Mg. 3,1b (πᾶσαν ἐντροπὴν — ἀπονέμειν); Tr. 3,1a (ἐντρεπέσθωσαν); 3,2e (ἐντρέπεσθαι); Sm. 8,1c (ἐντρέπεσθε) (see nr. 101), with *Didascalia* II. 2,3 (εὐλαβούμενοι καὶ ἐντρεπόμενοι); 18,3 (ἀξίωμα); 20,1 (τιμάτο, ἀγαπάτω, φοβείσθω); 25,16 (εἰς γέρας : Num 18,8); 26,4.6 (τετιμήσθω); 28,2 (εἰς τιμὴν θεοῦ).3 (εἰς γέρας Χριστοῦ).4 (τιμᾶν, τετιμᾶσθαι S).5 (ἑκάστῳ – ἀξιώματι – τὴν προσήκουσαν τιμήν, ἐντροπῇ).9 (τιμᾶν); 29 (ὡς θεοὺς σεβασθήσεσθε); 30,1 (τετιμήσθω); 31,1 (εἰς τιμὴν S); 33,2 (τιμᾶν).3 (εὐλαβούμενοι τιμᾶτε παντοίαις τιμαῖς); 34,1 (δασμοὺς – προσφέρετε).5 (στέργειν, φοβεῖσθαι, τιμᾶν); 58,2.3 (τιμή); III. 8,1 (εὐλαβουμένας, ἐντρεπομένας, φοβουμένας).

" Sicuti ergo non licebat alienigenam, qui non erat levita, offerre aliquid aut accedere ad altare sine sacerdote (ἄνευ τοῦ ἱερέως), ita et vos sine episcopo nolite aliquid facere (οὕτως καὶ ὑμεῖς ἄνευ τοῦ ἐπισκόπου μηδὲν ποιεῖτε.) Si quis autem sine episcopo (ἄνευ τοῦ ἐπισκόπου) facit aliquid, in vano illud facit; non enim illi imputabitur in opus, quia non decet absque sacerdote (ἄνευ τοῦ ἱερέως) aliquid facere " (Did. II. 27,1-2).

The parallel is so evident that Funk goes on to exclaim that the writer of the Didascalia " without doubt borrowed it from Ignatius ". [382] The fact is that, here too, the Didascalist based it on Old Testament discipline, in harmony with the paradigm that sustains all his reasoning.

Even the comparison, " *as Jesus Christ (was submitted, etc.) to the Father* " (see nrs. 56f., 86f., 105, 109 and 113c), appears in the Didascalia in its due context:

" Et omnia diaconus ad episcopum referat, sicut Christus ad Patrem (ὡς ὁ Χριστὸς τῷ πατρί) " (Did. II. 44,3).

The correspondence is perfect: deacon/Messiah as bishop/God the Father (see Did. II. 26,5 and above all the correlation Moses/Aaron, bishop/deacon, god/prophet, of II. 30). The Constitutor will also make use of this comparison. [383] We have already said that the forger of Ignatius' Middle recension employs it inconsistently (see nr. 113).

Let us note to end with that of the three images applied by the forger to the presbytery: στέφανος (Mg. 13,1: see nr. 57), συνέδριον (Mg. 6,1c: nr. 76; Tr. 3,1: nr. 90; and Phld. 8,1e: nr. 108) and σύνδεσμος (Tr. 3,1: nr. 90), two appear in the Didascalia also in connection with the presbyters, but not as " *bishop's crown* " or " *senate of the bishop/God or of the Apostles* ", but as " crown " and " senate " of the Assembly, that is, still keeping its first sense of " elders of the community ", as well as " counsellors of the bishop " (σύμβουλοι τοῦ ἐπισκόπου). [384]

---

[382] FUNK, *Did. et CC. AA.* 106: " Hoc autor haud dubie ex Ignatio mutuavit ...".

[383] A. C. II. 26,5; 44,3, and above all 30,2.

[384] Did. II. 28,4: καὶ γὰρ αὐτοὶ ὡς οἱ ἀπόστολοι καὶ (nam et ipsi tamquam apostoli SL) ὡς σύμβουλοι τοῦ ἐπισκόπου καὶ τῆς ἐκκλησίας στέφανος · εἰσὶν γὰρ συνέδριον καὶ βουλὴ τῆς ἐκκλησίας (SL and A. C.).

125.   The forger's credulity with regard to the Didascalia as an Apostolic writing goes to the extreme of recommending it as a document that validates his ecclesiology, as we saw in connection with Tr. 7,1d (see nr. 92).   The forger of Ignatius' letters to sustain his interpolation, relies on the Didascalia as an Apostolic writing, precisely because he ignores that it was a writing falsely ascribed to the Apostles.   The central position occupied by the bishop as mediator between God and the community (see n. 368) in the Didascalia Apostolorum corresponded perfectly with his plans.

IV.   CONCLUSION

Having uncovered in a first part the primitive structure of the genuine letters of Ignatius, it was appropiate to trace the exact extent of the interpolation which was carried out on the primitive Ignatian compilation.   For this purpose, the specific contents of the interpolation had to be settled accurately from precisely those passages that, in the former analysis, were found to be interpolated.

We set out, then, from a systematical analysis of the contents, style and terminology of the already incriminated passages: (a) the interrupting clauses of Eph. 20 (nr. 56) and Mg. 13 (nr. 57); (b) the beginnings and endings of the newly coined letters, namely Phld. inscr[b].-1 (nrs. 58-61) and 10-11 (nrs. 63-65); Sm. inscr. (nr. 62) and 12 (nr. 65); as also (c) the letter bearing the pretended relationship between Ignatius and Polycarp, Pol. (nrs. 66-72), and (d) the covering note to introduce the new compilation, Pol. Phil. 13 (nr. 73).   In all these we observed the same basic preoccupation: to settle definitely the vertical organization of the church (bishop, presbytery and deacons — community), by availing himself of the authority of the martyr Ignatius, to whom he has assigned the rank of deacon.   Thus he corroborates the basic thesis of his system, namely obedience to the bishop as Jesus Christ to the Father, according to the pattern of the deacon and martyr, Ignatius of Antioch.

Once acquainted with the specific content of the interpolation, we enlarged our analysis to include those passages that, although not key-pieces in the restructuration he imposed on the

Ignatian letters, showed startling anomalies due to the interpolator's ignorance of Ignatius' true identity.

In the first place we examined the passages in which Ignatius is considered to be a simple deacon, "fellow-servant" of certain deacons particularly, Burrhus (Eph. 2,1: nr. 74) and Zotion (Mg. 2: nr. 75), or of the category of deacons in general (Phld. 4c: nr. 77; Sm. 12,2: nr. 78 and Mg. 6,1d: nr. 76); thus contrasting with Rom. 2,2, the letter unknown to the forger, where Ignatius introduces himself as "the bishop of Syria".

In the second place we carefully analyzed the headings of the authentic letters, Eph. 1-6 (nrs. 79-82), Mg. 1-7 (nrs. 83-87) and Tr. 1-3 (nrs. 88-91), because there is mention in them of local bishops, together with their presbyters and deacons, unlike the simpler organization that was current not only in Ignatius' times (one bishop or "overseer" for the whole Roman province of Syria) but also in those of Polycarp and Irenaeus (bishops-overseers of the provinces of Asia and the Gaul). The names ascribed to local bishops, to certain presbyters and deacons, "fellow-servants" of Ignatius, were none other that the names of the delegates of Ephesus, Magnesia and Tralles, sent to Smyrna to represent their respective communities to the bishop of Syria, Ignatius, prisoner of the Romans, so that as far as possible they might alleviate his inhuman captivity. The forger introduced numerous sentences into these headings, to develop his favourite thesis. The identification of these interpolations has been possible thanks to the preceding analysis of the forger's terminology, style and phraseology as well as that of Ignatius himself. Internal parallels and the spontaneous use of specific particles and idioms have contributed decisively towards the identification of authentic or interpolated sentences. The result of this analysis made on a substantial number of interpolated passages agrees with those obtained by the preceding analyses. The forger is obsessed by a type of hierarchical organization of the church, in order to avoid divisions and disunion.

When it became clear that the interpolation was not limited to the structural elements, but that it had now entered fully into the headings of the genuine letters, modifying the Ignatian text or introducing fresh contents, it was easy to foresee that traces would also be found in the body of the letters. The material

16

gathered from previous analyses of the characteristic terminology of the interpolator, the analogies he uses, the way he proceeds to change the original meaning of the phrase and above all his ecclesiological premises have enabled us to detect still more interpolated passages: Tr. 7,1d and 2cd (nrs. 92f.); 12,2d and 13,2b, intercalated in the conclusion of Tr. 12-13 (nrs. 94f.); Phld. 3,2b (nr. 96); Phld. 7, a very biased development, aimed at settling the dissensions that had arisen in Philadelphia by having recourse to prophecy (nrs. 97-107), and Phld. 8,1e (nr. 108); Sm. 7,2f-8,2, a very similar development to Phld. 7 (nr. 109), and Sm. 9,1c-e (nr. 110). The phenomenon observed in Phld. and Sm. of progressive gathering of arguments from authority and gradual explanation of the interpolator's ideology reaches its heights in the first part of the letter presumably addressed to Polycarp (Pol.). The order in which the Ignatian letters appear in the manuscript tradition does not correspond with the order with which the forger has drawn up his own letters, but with the order he attributes — according to Pol. Phil. 13 — to the supposed Polycarpian compilation. Modern editors, however, follow the order testified to by Eusebius (nrs. 111f.).

While progressively identifying and classifying the interpolated sentences many textual and ideological parallels, analogies and terminology very close to the pseudo-Apostolic work of the Didascalia — written at the beginning of the III century — came to the surface. To settle exactly what depends upon whom, we examined separately the interpolator's symbolism and its internal consistency (nrs. 113f.), and in like manner that of the Didascalist (nrs. 115-121). The verdict has been in favour of the primacy of the Didascalia: the interpolator, led astray by the pretended Apostolic character of the latter, has drawn from it a series of analogies and a specific terminology. The Didascalia has turn out to be an original work, written in Greek by an author with a Semitic mentality. An Asiatic author of the middle III century drew inspiration from it to interpolate the Ignatian letters (nrs. 122-125).

The interpolation of the genuine letters of Ignatius (Mg*, Tr* and Eph* [Rom. was unnoticed!], written probably at the end of the first century) was done by a person, very likely the bishop of Philadelphia — as we infer from the existence of the letter to

the Philadelphians and the data derived from it —, who needed
to prop up his authority which was breaking down under grave
internal dissensions, with the authority of the martyr Ignatius,
with the model of Jesus Christ and the strength of prophecy of the
Spirit, thus to vouch for the bishop's authority, which had probably
been compromised by the fact of his youth.

PART THREE

SYSTEMATIC COMPARATIVE STUDY OF THE
INTERPOLATION AND THE GENUINE TEXT OF IGNATIUS

Once the original structure of four genuine Ignatian letters retrieved from the actual textus receptus of seven pretended Ignatian letters (Part One), the exact extent, contents and the most characteristic analogies and terminology of the interpolation identified and the source of its symbolism verified in the Didascalia Apostolorum (Part Two), the moment has come to undertake a systematic study of the genuine letters and the interpolated passages, both separately and comparatively.

By way of Prolegomena (§ I.) we shall, firstly, give in synoptic form the position of the various interpolated passages within the framework of the genuine Ignatian letters (nr. 126); secondly, we shall classify the interpolated clauses and sentences bearing in mind the function the forger gives them and the variety of techniques he used to introduce them. For this purpose in each of their structural (nrs. 127-133) and thematic functions (nrs. 134-145) we shall distinguish between negative (nrs. 127-130 and 134-139) and positive proceedings (nrs. 131-133 and 140-145). Besides the structural and thematic elements we shall consider the specific doctrinal developments of the interpolator (nrs. 146f.). As colophon we shall review the various methods he uses to introduce the interpolations (nr. 148).

After the Prolegomena we shall study systematically (1) the motive/s that induced Ignatius to writte his letters, contrasted with those of the forger (§ II.: nrs. 149-166), and (2) the various literary devices used by each writer (§ III.: nrs. 167-180).

Given the relative shortness of the interpolation and, above all, its fragmentary character and pronounced tendency to imitate Ignatius' style and terminology, an exhaustive study would not be of much use. On the other hand, throughout the whole analysis we point out the outstanding stylistic and terminological features.

I. PROLEGOMENA

a) *Localization in synoptic form of the interpolation*

126. At a halt on the road to his martyrdom, Ignatius wrote four letters, all of them from Smyrna (the four that in their current state still contain this information): one addressed to the community of Rome, and three to the Asian communities of Ephesus, Magnesia and Tralles, which have sent a more or less numerous delegation to Smyrna (as still appears in the headings of Eph., Mg. and Tr., although the greater number of proper names bear a hierarchical title).

The subject of Rom. and that of the three remaining letters is very different, due to their specific mission. Rom. contains a repeated invitation from Ignatius to the Roman community, begging them not to place obstacles in the way of his martyrdom. He asks them to cease trying to exercise influence on higher levels, but to join him in prayer that his immolation may be attained. The Asian letters contain an insistent exhortation to these communities to warn them of the imminent onslaught of Gnostic and Judaizing propaganda which has devastated the church of Syria and caused the condemnation of its bishop.

The four letters were written with the same chiastic [385] structure: (A) Initial greeting; (B) Introduction; (C) Body of the letter: exhortation; (C') Paraenesis; (B') Conclusion; (A') Final greeting.

The *initial greeting* (A) contains the name of the writer, the name and characteristic titles of the community to which the letter was addressed and the ritual greetings.

The *introduction* (B) varies according to the theme: in Rom. it announces in advance the motive of the letter (1,1 + 2,2), after a long digression (1,2-2,1); Eph. (1-2), Mg. (1-5) and Tr. (1,1-2,2) open with a praise of the community and a mention of the delegates, ending with an invitation that fits in with the subject to be developped immediately afterwards.

---

[385] For the chiasm as largely Semitic structure, see N. W. LUND, *Chiasmus in the New Testament*, N. Caroline and London 1942, quoted by J. H. MOULTON – N. TURNER, *A Grammar of New Testament Greek*, vol. III: *Syntax*, Edinburg 1963, p. 345, and F. BLASS – A. DEBRUNNER – R. W. FUNK, *A Greek Grammar of the New Testament and Other Early Christian Literature*, Chicago 1961, nr. 477,2.

The *body of the letter* (C) contains the unfolding of the purpose of each letter in form of exhortation: in the letters dealing with a theological theme there is a separate development of the anti-Docetic (Eph. + Sm., and Tr.) and anti-Judaizing exposition (Mg. + Phld.), using the chiasm or the concentric structure.

The *paraenesis* (C') is a personal exhortation to encourage the community.

In the *conclusion* (B') Ignatius begs prayers for himself and for the church in Syria (in Eph*, once he has become aware of its pacification, he does not ask for prayers but for the sending of a messenger).

Lastly, the *final greeting* (A') contains greetings and the ritual farewell formula.

Except in Rom., which has no specific theological theme, the developments of the three authentic letters addressed to the Asian communities follow a definite pattern, marked by the repetition of certain warnings, admonitions, explanations, etc., with a central axis, around which the exposition or exhortation circles. Hence, as they are schematized a chiastic or concentric structure appears.

The body of the original letter to the Ephesians was thus arranged in a concentric form *a b c d e d' c' b' a'*: *a a'* containing the beginning (Aim) and the end of the exhortation; *b e b'* expressing three warnings (Μηδεὶς πλανάσθω — Μὴ πλανᾶσθε — Μηδεὶς πλανάσθω) at the beginning, centre and end of the exposition; *c d d' c'* constituting the nucleus of the exposition (Constatations that caused the exhortation — Central exposition: first part/Central exposition: second part — Explanation of the meaning of the exhortation).

The body of the original letter to the Magnesians also presents a concentric structure *a b c d c' b' a'*, while a chiastic construction is outlined in the paraenesis *a b c d d' c' b' a'*. The exhortation has numerous points of contact with that of Ephesians: *a a'* containing the aim of the exhortation; *b b'* being warnings (Μὴ πλανᾶσθε); *c c'* constituting the exhortation properly so-called; *d* being the explanation of the meaning of the exhortation; the paraenesis, in Ephesians, depends on the consoling news brought by the envoys from Syria, while in Magnesians it is still influenced by fear of the Judaizers, who — with the Gnostics — caused such grave damage to the church of Syria.

The body of the letter to the Trallians also has its own figure *a b c a' b'*: *a a'* containing the exhortation; *b b'* being an admonition; *c* clarifying the meaning of the exhortation.

In the three letters there appears the same explanation (in Mg* and Tr., in the centre; in Eph*, towards the end): "I say this, my beloved, not because I have learned that any of you behave in this way, but as the last of you I want to warn you beforehand against ... ", Gnostics or Judaizers (Mg. 11; Tr. 8,1; Sm. = Eph* 4,1).

Taken synoptically, the interpolation affects above all the *openings and endings* of the actual letters. Thus, we can distinguish: (a) Fiction of *interrupting clauses* to divide the two long genuine letters, Eph* (Eph. 20) and Mg* (Mg. 13); (b) Creation or arrangement of the *initial greetings* (Mg. inscr. and Phld. inscr[a]. = part of Mg* inscr*; Phld. inscr[b]. = spurious; Sm. inscr. = spurious); (c) Amplification of the genuine *introductions*, after giving hierarchical titles to the delegates from Ephesus (Eph. 1,3-2,2), Magnesia (Mg. 2-5) and Tralles (Tr. 1,2-3,2); creation of a new one for Philadelphia, without mentioning the name of its presumed bishop (Phld. 1); abrupt beginning of Smyrnaeans without any introduction; (d) Creation or arrangement of the *conclusions and final greetings*, cutting up the paraenesis, the original conclusion and the final greeting of Ephesians and spreading them over present *Eph.* (Eph. 21 = arranged summary), present *Sm.* (Sm. 9-13: partly authentic, although arranged [9-11 and 13]; partly spurious [12]), present *Pol.* (Pol. 6-8: partly authentic, although arranged [6-7,1.3; 8,2-3]; partly spurious [7,2 and 8,1]) and present *Phld.* (Phld. 10-11: only the first and the last sentences are authentic [10,1a and 11,2f.]; the rest is spurious); *Mg.* and *Tr.* keep their corresponding conclusions (although in Tr. with substantial disorder and several interpolations).

Generally the interpolator has spared the body of the letters (exhortation) and the paraenesis. He has only introduced those sentences that seem to him unavoidable, either to *modify* the primitive meaning of the text (Eph. 3,3e-4,1a; 5,1.2de.3f-6,1; Mg. 6,1cd.2f.-7,1b; Tr. 7,1d.2cd; Phld. 3,2b; 4c; 8,1e), or to *condense* his ideology (Phld. 7 and Sm. 7,2f-8). The first part of Pol. (1-5) is wholly spurious and belongs to this last model.

b) *Classification of the interpolated clauses and sentences according to their function and the proceedings used by the forger*

The discovery of a massive interpolation of the Ignatian letters has been made possible by placing the problem in a new light. Once discarded the two Long and Short recensions and disavowed one after the other the hypotheses based on historical incongruities, lexical or stylistic questions, problems regarding specific contents, etc., that call in question all or part of the Middle recension, a series of contextual difficulties and internal anomalies went on challenging scholars and compelled them to take up a variety of positions. The posing of the question has changed by taking as a working hypothesis that certain anomalies and irregularities — often solved with benevolent explanations — might be interconnected and form the thread of an analysis that would lead to the discovery of the reasons for their presence in the text.

At the end of this analysis we came to the conclusion that in the actual textus receptus of Ignatius two structures coexist, superimposed one on the other, namely: the primitive Ignatius', made up of four letters written from Smyrna by the bishop of Syria, Ignatius, on his way to martyrdom, and the innovative one, composed of six letters, three written from Smyrna (with the exception of Rom.) and three from Troas by an author closely connected with Philadelphia — probably its bishop. The letter to the Rom. was joined very much later to this compilation, which was supported by Polycarp's authority (Pol. Phil. 13). Indeed, Eusebius already mentions the seven letters, but in the manuscript tradition Rom. continues to be transmitted separately.

In a second moment the characteristic terminology and contents of the clauses forged by the interpolator for his new structure, and contained in certain sentences already suspected as anomalous, allowed us to specify the exact extent of the interpolation.

Thanks to the different function assigned by the interpolator to this or that clause, it has been possible to dissociate structure from content. The structural clauses (§ α) try to create a framework for his restructuration of the Ignatian letters; only incidentally do they deal with questions of content. The thematic ones (§ β) seek deliberately to correct Ignatius' ecclesiology by twisting its contents. This twofold intentionality given to his clauses by the interpolator will be the basis of the present classification. The specific doctrinal developments of the interpolator (§ γ) will complete it.

α) *Structural elements*

1) *Negative proceedings*: *Division of letters, inscriptions and endings*

127. The interpolator possessed three genuine Ignatian letters: Eph*, Mg* and Tr. He was unaware of Rom. The first two were twice as long as the third. And Eph* contained a much longer and more detailed ending than the other two. Thematically, two of them dealt with the Gnostic problem (Eph* and Tr.), while the anti-Judaizing theme was treated only in Mg*. The interpolator had government problems with his community of Philadelphia. To solve them he dug up Ignatius' letters, modified his itinerary, making him pass through Philadelphia to bring him face to face with the contending faction, and created from original materials a new letter for the said community. But the problems he had in his community reflected a much wider issue: the ecclesiastical organization that was gradually imposing itself needed a basis. The authority of the martyr Ignatius could be invoked to legitimize the ecclesiology that already prevailed in Asia.

However, it was not sufficient to cut up his letters in order to insert in them the recent ecclesiastical organization. The new compilation needed to be guaranteed by an irrefutable witness. Polycarp's letter to the Philippians could serve to vouch for a compilation in which there were letters from Ignatius addressed to Polycarp and his community, Smyrna.

We have, thus, three reasons for the recasting of Ignatius' genuine letters: (1) a general motivation, to support the new ecclesiology in process of settlement; (2) a particular one, to silence the contesting faction of Philadelphia; (3) a complementary third motivation, to cover the recasting of the letters with Polycarp's authority.

In order to obtain materials for the new compilation the interpolator has halved the two longest letters leaving the first part in the original ones (Eph. and Mg.) and keeping the second for

the two newly coined ones (Sm. and Phld.). Due to the original
subject matter, the two halves from Eph* contain the same anti-
Gnostic tint, while those from Mg* tend to be anti-Judaizing.
By adding the letter to the Tr., which was also anti-Gnostic and
was too short to be divided, there result three letters against the
Docetists and two against the Judaizers. To compose the letter
addressed to Polycarp, the thematic materials were no use. For
this the forger was obliged to coin a brand-new text (Pol. 1-5),
that is, the part drawn up in the singular. But to disguise this
change of style and contents, and to give an appearance of truth
to the supposed relationship between Ignatius and Polycarp, he
had to use original materials. The paraenesis, the conclusion and
the detailed greetings of Eph* were suitable for this purpose. He
could distribute them skillfully between Sm. and Pol.

The negative proceedings he employed to obtain six letters
from the three genuine ones, were as follows:

128. *Division of the original letters to the Eph* and Mg**. —
The primitive letter addressed to the *Ephesians* was divided in the
central part of the exhortation (between Eph. 19 and Sm. 1).
After stating the four basic articles of his anti-Docetic creed —
virginal conception, birth, baptism, passion and death of Jesus
(Eph. 18,2) — Ignatius explained the ultimate reason for the Gnostics' ignorance of these mysteries: unawareness of the three outstanding mysteries — the virginity of Mary, her child-bearing and
the death of the Lord — for they were hidden from the Chief of
the present order (19,1). There followed a description of the
extraordinary way in which the Star of Jesus showed itself to the
heavenly inhabitants (19,2), thus provoking the overthrow of the
ancient kingdom when God manifested himself as man (19,3).
The exposition went on with Ignatius' own verification of the
Ephesians' perfect knowledge of those four basic articles of faith,
unequivocal sign of their not belonging to the Chief of the present
order (Sm. 1).

The interpolator glimpses the possibility of beginning the fresh
letter to the Smyrnaeans with this last statement. In order that
the division and consequent unfinished character of the letter
could pass unnoticed, he drew up the interrupting clause of Eph.
20, where he alludes to a further explanation of the dispensation just
begun in the second tract he intended to write them (ἐν τῷ δευτέρῳ

βιβλιδίῳ, ὃ μέλλω γράφειν ὑμῖν, προσδηλώσω ὑμῖν, ἧς ἠρξάμην οἰκονο-μίας ...), as long as certain conditions were fulfilled (Ἐάν με κατη-ξιώσῃ Ἰησοῦς Χριστὸς ... καὶ θέλημα ᾖ ... μάλιστα ἐὰν ὁ κύριός μοι ἀποκαλύψῃ ...). The third condition is unusual (see Phld. inscr[b].). The answer to the second is to be found in Pol. 8,1 (οὐκ ἠδυνήθην γράψαι ... ὡς τὸ θέλημα προστάσσει). Thus the interpolator frees himself from writing a second letter since it was not the officer's will. He could not, in fact, write it, since the materials from Eph. II were to be utilized to compose Sm. The themes sketched in Eph. 20 are the same as the beginning in Sm. 1: in the former, a sum-ming up; in the latter, the original development (see nrs. 18-21).

The central exhortation of the primitive letter to the Magne-sians was also split in two parts, after the characteristic Ignatian explanation of the meaning of the exhortation (Mg. 11-12). Since the original was arranged concentrically with said explanation in the middle, and bearing in mind that such an explanation did not fit in with his aim to present the Philadelphian community deeply split into two factions — the one faithful to the bishop and the other contesting him —, the interpolator has made the break at the opportune point leaving this explanation in Mg. But he could not do the same with Phld. 3,1 (οὐχ ὅτι παρ' ὑμῖν μερισμὸν εὗρον, ἀλλ' ἀποδιϋλισμόν). Therefore he tried through the correc-tion of 3,2 to polarize it on the faction obedient to the bishop (see nrs. 96 and 104). Now, if the contestants were for the interpo-lator some schismatics who were not part of the community (ὅσοι γὰρ θεοῦ εἰσὶν καὶ Ἰησοῦ Χριστοῦ, οὗτοι μετὰ τοῦ ἐπισκόπου εἰσίν, 3,2), why then the verification in 7,1, in Ignatius' mouth, that some had tried to deceive him (Εἰ γὰρ κατὰ σάρκα μέ τινες ἠθέλησαν πλανῆσαι κτλ.), the statement in 7,2 which makes Ignatius say that he did not know beforehand that there were divisions among them (οἱ δὲ ὑπο-πτεύσαντές με ὡς προειδότα τὸν μερισμόν τινων λέγειν ταῦτα κτλ.), but it was made known to him by the Spirit himself (τὸ δὲ πνεῦμα ἐκήρυσσεν λέγον τάδε), and the pretended twofold reception for the envoys from Syria in 11,1, one warm, the other indifferent and dishonouring (ὅτι ἐδέξασθε αὐτούς ... οἱ δὲ ἀτιμάσαντες αὐτούς ...)? In spite of all these manipulations, the underlying Ignatian text offers resistance. The Judaizers, against whom Ignatius warned the community (Phld. 6), had not yet harmed it (3,1); the dissidents, with those the interpolator makes Ignatius confront (7,1-2), have already sown divisions in its heart (7,1a.2a and 2g).

On the other hand, the interpolator could not start Phld. suddenly with the second part of the Ignatian exhortation (Mg. II), as he did in Sm., since Smyrna could be supposed to be Polycarp's community, but the Philadelphians had not yet been introduced. To introduce this community, he composed the heading of Phld. inscr.-1 (see nrs. 22-24). Here also, as in Eph. 20, to interrupt the exhortation (Mg. I) he had to write a clause (Σπου-δάζετε οὖν ... ἵνα πάντα, ὅσα ποιεῖτε, κατευοδωθῆτε ..., Mg. 13) where he summed up the ending of the original exhortation (Σπουδάσατε οὖν ..., ἵνα ὃ ἐὰν πράσσητε, κατὰ θεὸν πράσσητε) that he had reserved for Phld. 4 (see nrs. 25-28).

129. *Division and distribution of the Eph* ending between Sm. and Pol. (and Phld.).* — Between the writing of Rom., Mg* and Tr. on the one hand and Eph* on the other, Ignatius found out, through the arrival in Sm. of some envoys from Syria, that the situation in the church there has changed radically (ἀπηγγέλη μοι, εἰρηνεύειν κτλ., Phld. = Eph* 10,1a). Therefore, instead of asking them to remember in their prayers the church which is in Syria (Rom. 9,1; Mg. 14 and Tr. 13,1), he begs the Ephesians to send an embassy with a personal letter from him to congratulate them for the recovery of peace (εἰς τὸ γενόμενον ἕως Συρίας συγχαρῆναι αὐτοῖς, ὅτι εἰρηνεύουσιν κτλ., Sm. 11,2-3). The very detailed final greetings, unlike the ones contained in the other authentic letters (Rom., Mg. and Tr.), were a faithful image of his brief stay in Ephesus and the affection and perfect welcome the Ephesians had given him (Eph. 1,1-2; Sm. 9,2; 10,2; 11,2). The interpolator saw the possibility of making use of this ending to give the impression that Ignatius knew Polycarp and his community well. It sufficed to scatter the sequence between the two spurious letters: Sm. 10-11 and 13, and Pol. 6,1b-7,1.3 and 8,2-3 (see nrs. 42-56, and the reconstructed sequence in nr. 53). In the case of Phld. he has simply plagiarized, if we except the original sentences of Phld. 10,1a and 11,2f. Further on we shall treat of the modifications he found himself obliged to introduce to adapt this ending to the new situation.

130. *Distribution of the inscription of Mg* between Mg. and Phld.* — For his new letters the interpolator had need of the cor-

responding inscriptions. Unlike Sm. and Pol., for which as we shall see, he himself composed the necessary inscriptions, he distributed between Mg. and Phld. the primitive one of Mg*. Keep in mind that this inscription opened a letter of distinctly anti-Judaizing character. By dividing the letter in two he also divided the inscription. In Mg. he left a smaller part; the most representative one he reserved for Phld. Here, though, he made a mistake, led on by his keen desire to set his main theologumenon in the inscription itself. Instead of the ritual opening salutation (πλεῖστα χαίρειν) he conditioned the greetings to the community (ἣν ἀσπάζομαι) on its unity with the bishop, presbyters and deacons (μάλιστα ἐὰν ἐν ἑνὶ ὦσιν κτλ., Phld. inscr[b]: see nrs. 29 and 58). This being a programmatic addition that affects the content, we consider Phld. inscr[b].-1 as a unit belonging not to the structure but to the theme.

2) *Positive proceedings*: *Plagiarism*

131. *The new inscriptions of Sm. and Pol.*; *adaptation of Mg* inscr* to Mg. and Phld.* — The opening salutations (inscriptions) of Ignatius have a peculiar structure:[386] (1) Superscription or sender (Ἰγνάτιος, ὁ καὶ Θεοφόρος), Pagan and Christian name?; (2) Adscription or community addressed (τῇ ... ἐκκλησίᾳ ... τῇ οὔσῃ ἐν ...); (3) Qualifications (εὐλογημένη ...); (4) Salutation: simple ritual greeting (πλεῖστα ... χαίρειν, Eph., Sm.), twofold (ἣν καὶ ἀσπάζομαι ... καὶ εὔχομαι ... πλεῖστα ... χαίρειν, Tr. [Mg. + Phld.]) or complex (ἣν καὶ ἀσπάζομαι ... + dat. + πλεῖστα ... χαίρειν, Rom.).

The interpolator has done no more than imitate them. The only inscription that lacks one of these elements is, as we have seen, Phld., due precisely to the interpolator's eagerness to introduce his own ecclesiology. In the inscription of Mg., the first part of the original one, there is a slight incongruity: the term ἐκκλησία is not found in its usual place (agreeing with εὐλογημένη), as in all the other inscriptions, but in the accusative depending on the singular formula ἐν ᾧ ἀσπάζομαι τὴν ἐκκλησίαν τὴν οὖσαν ἐν ... [387]

---

[386] See H. J. Sieben, *Die Ignatianen als Briefe. Einige formkritische Bemerkungen*, in: *V. Ch.* 32 (1978) 1-18.

[387] Ignatius' usual formula is ἣν καὶ ἀσπάζομαι, Rom., Tr., and Phld. (the interpolator has omitted the καὶ), after naming the community in the dative.

The *Sm.* inscription has been drawn up by the forger follow-ing literally the Ignatian pattern. We noticed slight traces of the interpolator's hand (see nr. 62). That of *Pol.*, on the contrary, is very short and constitutes an adaptation of the Ignatian adscrip-tion (to a community) to a personal letter addressed to Polycarp (see nr. 44). For the inscriptions of *Mg.* and *Phld.* he has had to supply the missing elements, which was relatively easy. Mg. inscr. besides the incongruity noted above, is shorter than the authentic ones (it only mentions a qualification, as in the case of Pol. inscr.), for the simple reason that the forger had to share the material between Mg. and Phld. (see nr. 29).

132. *The new letter endings of Eph., Phld., Sm. and Pol. drawn up from the primitive ending of Eph**. — For the new letters the interpolator needed fresh conclusions. He did not limit him-self, however, by simply plagiarizing the genuine ones. The re-routing of Ignatius' journey forced him to alter the conclusion of Eph. The meeting he made up between Ignatius and Polycarp had to be evidenced in a very detailed ending for Sm. and Pol. The plagiarism is more evident in Phld. ending, while it can be detected — mixed up with the original data — in the other letters.

(1) *First step: The summary of Eph.* — To be able to rely on the Eph* ending for the three new letters written from Troas, the interpolator had first to compose a *summary* for Eph. On the one hand, the re-routing of Ignatius' journey — making him pass through Philadelphia instead of Ephesus — obliged him to refrain from mentioning the change which had come about in the Syrian community, as it appeared in the second half of Eph* now to be found in Sm. On the other hand, there were a few data that did not agree with Sm.: the allusion to the delegates from Ephesus (Eph. 1,3-2,1) and the place of writing, Smyrna (21,1). When he summed up the phrase ἀντίψυχον ὑμῶν κτλ. actually to be found in Sm. 10,2, his lack of understanding of Ignatius' meaning led him to substitute τὸ πνεῦμά μου κτλ. with a simple ἐγώ (Eph. 21,1a) as in Pol. 2,3 and 6,1c. Thus contrasting with the well-testified Ignatian usage in Eph. 18,1; Tr. 13,3; Rom. 9,3. Ignatius devoted his own person (ἀντίψυχον) to the community in his most dynamic and inward dimension ("my spirit"), thus avoiding in passing an excessive personalization of his actions (see Tr. 6,1 and Phld.

5,1). The mention of Smyrna, finally, led the forger to name its presumed bishop, Polycarp, with a twofold participial apposition.

In this brief summary of Eph. 21, the interpolator's characteristic mark of reciprocity (ὡς καὶ with conjunctive function) comes out twice. In none of the three genuine conclusions do we have μνημονεύετέ μου followed by the reciprocal phrase ὡς καὶ ὑμῶν Ἰησοῦς Χριστός that makes Jesus Christ subject of the verb (see Mg. 14; Tr. 13,1; Rom. 9,1, and the other Ignatian usages in Eph. 12,2 and Sm. 5,3). Μνημονεύετέ μου is original. Ignatius at once gives a reason for not asking the Ephesians to remember in their prayer the church which is in Syria: ἡ γὰρ προσευχὴ ὑμῶν ἀπῆλθεν κτλ., which is preserved with its consequent adaptation in Sm. 11,1a. The interpolator could not leave it in Eph. and substitutes it by Προσεύχεσθε ὑπὲρ τῆς ἐκκλησίας τῆς ἐν Συρίᾳ (Eph. 21,2a). Note that Ignatius does not use Προσεύχεσθε in relation to the church which is in Syria, but always Μνημονεύετε κτλ.

The sentence ὅθεν δεδεμένος εἰς Ῥώμην ἀπάγομαι (Eph. 21,1b) is original, but is complemented by its corresponding one in Sm. 11,1b, ὅθεν δεδεμένος θεοπρεπεστάτοις δεσμοῖς [πάντας ἀσπάζομαι], where the plagiarist has let slip an incongruence: Ignatius cannot " greet from " Antioch of Syria (see nr. 30). The two following sentences (Eph. 21,2cd) partly imitate partly complete their corresponding ones in Sm. 11,1c-g.

The interpolator omits everything relating to the sending of an embassy to Syria and concludes with a farewell formula in which he has fused the two original ones. Indeed, both letters to the Smyrnaeans (Sm. 13,1b and 2d) and to Polycarp (Pol. 8,3a and 3d) contain — unlike the other letters — two farewell formulas. To reconstruct the two original ones, we have retained the first of Pol. (8,3a), because of its archaic doxology: ἐρρῶσθαι ὑμᾶς διὰ παντὸς ἐν θεῷ ἡμῶν Ἰησοῦ Χριστῷ κτλ., and the second of Sm. (13,2d) but completed with the one from Eph. (21,2e), because of the already observed tendency of the interpolator to separate θεοῦ from Ἰησοῦ Χριστοῦ, so as to refer the first to God the Father (see nrs. 54,1.4 and 55,4.6).

(2) *Second step*: *The distribution of Eph* ending*. — After drawing up the summary of Eph. 21, the second step consisted in distributing the primitive Eph* ending among the three spurious letters. For this the forger composed three parallel structures

with the same central motive: the sending of an embassy to Syria. Carried away by his craving for triumphalism, he has turned the single embassy to Syria — composed of an envoy from the Ephesian community with a personal congratulatory letter from Ignatius himself — into a cortege of embassies and letters carried by bishops, presbyters and deacons of the neighbouring churches (Phld. 10,2e), by a deacon of Philadelphia (10,1b), by Polycarp or one of his representatives with a letter too from the Philippians (Pol. Phil. 13,1; cf. Pol. 7,2; 8,2), by envoys of the neighbouring churches to Smyrna, carrying letters from the rest of communities (Pol. 8,1). The genuine information about the messengers from Syria that caused the sending of an Ephesian envoy to Syria was left in Sm. 10,1. In Phld. 11,1 the forger has imitated this information, reversing the order of the original sequence: Mention of the messengers → Allusion to the news brought from Syria → Sending of a congratulatory embassy, as can still be inferred from the mutilated but authentic ending that he left in Sm. 10-11 (see nr. 31).

Except for Phld. 10,1a (and 11,2f.), the ending of Phld. is a copy (see nrs. 33f.). And, the parallel of Pol. 7,1a is a copy of Phld. 10,1a with the interpolator's usual touching up (διὰ τὴν προσευχὴν for κατὰ τ. π.; ὡς ἐδηλώθη μοι for ἀπηγγέλη μ., etc.). The continuation of Pol. 7,1b-d, on the contrary, is original: κἀγὼ εὐθυμότερος ἐγενόμην κτλ. Then followed the sequence of Pol. 6,1c-2: καὶ μετ' αὐτῶν μοι κτλ., placed before in the actual textus receptus. With this last sequence Ignatius closed the *paraenesis* (see nrs. 50,1, and 46-49).

(3) The *conclusion* of the primitive letter to the Ephesians began by the petition to be remembered and the inference that the Ephesians' prayers have had effect, as we have just seen. Instead of prayers, Ignatius asks them to complete their good work by appointing an ambassador from the community and sending him to Syria with a personal letter from Ignatius himself to congratulate his Syrian community because it is at peace. Around this information the interpolator has woven two imitations with pertinent touching up, one for Phld. 10,1b-2d and the other for Pol. 7,2. The coincidences are less instructive than the variants, if possible: συμβούλιον ἀγαγεῖν for ἐκκλησία; θεοδρόμος/διάκονον εἰς τὸ πρεσβεῦσαι ἐκεῖ θεοῦ πρεσβείαν for θεοπρεσβευτήν; δοξάσῃ ... εἰς δόξαν θεοῦ/δοξάσαι τὸ ὄνομα for συνδοξάσῃ; θέλουσιν ... θεοῦ for θέλουσιν ... παρέχειν.

The conclusion ended with a reflection, in which Ignatius appealed to the total consecration every Christian has to God (Pol. 7,3). In its place, the interpolator appeals in Phld. 10,2e to the example of the near-by churches of Antioch which sent bishops, presbyters and deacons (ὡς καὶ αἱ ἔγγιστα ἐκκλησίαι κτλ). This statement presuposes that in the most important cities in Syria there were already bishops (see nr. 4). The original information, on the contrary, of Rom. 2,2 ("the bishop of Syria") and 9,1 ("Jesus the Messiah alone will supervise it, with your communion also") excludes them (see nrs. 3-8).

The reconstruction of the original sequence of the paraenesis and the conclusion of Eph* was not easy. Every trace the forger has unknowingly left behind him constitutes a landmark that made it possible to retrace his steps. Here we have concentrated exclusively on the imitations and copies. For the detailed discussion of the reconstruction proposed see above nrs. 30 (first attempt), 46-51 (second attempt) and 52f. (synopsis).

(4) As for the *final greetings*, we have to distinguish those coming from Eph* from those that were composed by the forger. The greeting to Philo (Sm. 13,1c), greetings to Tavia's and Epitropus' families (Sm. 13,2ab and Pol. 8,2a), to Attalus and the messenger that will be appointed to go to Syria, to Alce, Daphnus and Eutecnus (Pol. 8,2b-d and Sm. 13,2c [Pol. 8,3c]) come from Eph*. The interpolator has created the copy of Sm. 13,1a and repeated the greeting to Alce in Pol. 8,3c. He drew up on his own the two parallel clauses of Phld. 11,2 and Sm. 12. Both clauses are inspired by the greetings of the authentic letters. Thus, 'Ασπάζεται ὑμᾶς ἡ ἀγάπη τῶν ἀδελφῶν τῶν ἐν Τρωάδι (Phld. — Sm.) recalls at close the genuine 'Ασπάζεται ὑμᾶς ἡ ἀγάπη Σμυρναίων καὶ 'Εφεσίων (Tr. 13,1: cf. Rom. 9,1.3), with the addition of τῶν ἀδελφῶν, exclusive of the interpolator in the greeting formulas (see also Sm. 12,1c; 13,1a); ὅθεν καὶ γράφω ὑμῖν is a copy from the genuine ones (Eph. 21,1; Mg. 15); διὰ Βούρρου is the new link in Troas between Ignatius and the Smyrnaeans as well as the Ephesians, made up by the forger to take the place of the delegates who went to Smyrna (see nrs. 32, 65). In the genuine letters, the Smyrnaeans are scarcely noticed (see Rom. 10,1; Mg. 15; they are only named in Tr. 13,1 in connection with the Ephesians); in the interpolation they appear in the foreground.

17

The twofold *farewell formula* we have already dealt with above, when speaking of the summary of Eph. 21,2e. For the reconstruction of the greetings and the twofold formula of farewell see above nrs. 54f.

133. *The interrupting clauses of Eph. 20 and Mg. 13; the covering notes of Pol. 8,1 and Pol. Phil. 13.* — The interpolator has also basically made use of plagiarism in drawing up these four clauses. In the first two (Eph. 20 and Mg. 13), according to their suppletive function, he condensed the two respective halves reserved for Sm. and Phld. The equivalents between Eph. 20 and Sm. 1 have already been explained in the first part (see nr. 19). The summarizing aspect of Mg. 13 as compared with Phld. 4 has also been already noted (see nrs. 27f.). The other sentences have no originality whatever: they abound in paratactical enumerations, in sterotyped ternary phrases, in copies of original Ignatian phrases (see nr. 57).

In the last two (Pol. 8,1 and Pol. Phil. 13) he has imitated the theme of the embassy to Syria — as he did in Phld. 10 and Pol. 7,2 — enlarging wearisomely on the original information of Sm. 11,2-3 (and Pol. 8,2c). The two dominant themes are (1) the impossibility for Ignatius to write more letters (οὐκ ἠδυνήθην γράψαι, Pol. 8,1), his request to Polycarp to write them for him (γράψεις, ibid.), the letter written by the Philippians and by Ignatius himself to Polycarp (Ἐγράψατέ μοι καὶ ὑμεῖς καὶ Ἰγνάτιος, Pol. Phil. 13,1), the congratulatory letter written by the Philippians to the church in Syria (τὰ παρ' ὑμῶν ἀποκομίσῃ γράμματα, ibid.), the letters addressed to the same church by the Asian communities which could not send a personal embassy (οἱ δὲ ἐπιστολὰς, Pol. 8,1); (2) the envoy of messengers to Syria on the part of the other Asian churches (οἱ μὲν δυνάμενοι πεζοὺς πέμψαι, ibid.), on the part of Polycarp personally or through his envoy/s (εἴτε ἐγώ, εἴτε ὃν πέμπω πρεσβεύσοντα καὶ περὶ ὑμῶν, Pol. Phil. 13,1 / διὰ τῶν ὑπό σου πεμπομένων, Pol. 8,1 / καὶ τοῦ πέμποντος αὐτὸν Πολυκάρπου, 8,2), the sending to the Philippians of the Ignatian compilation composed by Polycarp (τὰς ἐπιστολὰς Ἰγνατίου ... ἐπέμψαμεν ὑμῖν, καθὼς ἐνετείλασθε, Pol. Phil. 13,2) through Crescens, who, as appears from the context, has been the bearer of Polycarp's authentic letter to the Philippians (αἵτινες ὑποτεταγμέναι εἰσὶν τῇ ἐπιστολῇ ταύτῃ, ibid./Haec vobis scripsi per Crescentem, 14,1). The forger overdoes his plagiarism. He falls into discredit by multiplying letters and envoys unnecessarily, organizing with them an unprecedented affluence of delegates with letters to Syria.

β) *Thematic elements*

Among structural elements the forger has shown sufficiently what his favourite subject matter was, though in general he has limited himself to affirming it. In the case of Eph. 20,2 and Phld. inscr[b]. he goes further: he lays down as ultimate condition (μάλιστα ἐὰν) both in the writing of the second letter to the Ephesians, as well as the initial greeting to the Philadelphians, that the community should remain united to the bishop and the presbyters and obey them.

This subject matter, as we have seen in the second part, is focused on a clear vertical conception of the way to organize the ecclesiastical community: the bishop as peak of the pyramid, the presbytery surrounding him as a crown, the deacons who second his orders, the community at the base. He frequently reinforces this conception with analogies from the Didascalia: the bishop is the vicar and visible representative of God, who is the universal and invisible Bishop; the presbytery represents God's senate and the college of Apostles; the deacons occupy the place of Jesus Christ; the relation of Jesus Christ to the Father is a model of the submission of the community to the bishop, etc.

But when he starts systematically to introduce his thematic elements into Ignatius' letters, he notably distorts the archaic Ignatian ecclesiology centred on Jesus the Messiah and his real presence in the community, making its horizontal dimension vanish in order to polarize it in the bishop's person as God's sole representative. The Christocentric meaning of the Ignatian phrase has been profoundly altered. A new key has prevailed over the primitive one.

In order to insert his themes the forger has used here also negative and positive proceedings. We shall examine them separately.

1) *Negative proceedings*: *Division of periods and sentences with/without alteration of the order, mutilation, abridgement*

Every graft supposes an incision. The forger has in advance to cut Ignatius' text so as to introduce his subject matter. The incision now influences periods or sentences. The choice of places in which the incision is to be made betrays the Ignatian themes he was interested in modifying.

134. On the level of periods in the first place come the *headings* of the three authentic Asian letters. To insert his own themes the forger has chosen the place where the several delegates proceeding from their respective communities were mentioned. Firstly he has cut the period in pieces, either separating the protasis from the apodosis, or dividing the apodosis into fragments and inverting the order. Secondly he has overlain the separated elements with his own theme, so as to compose new periods. In the first two headings, however, the separation of the protasis from its corresponding apodosis has given origin to anacolutha.

Thus, in *Eph.* 1,3-2,2, the primitive protasis ('Επεὶ οὖν τὴν πολυπληθίαν ὑμῶν ἐν ὀνόματι θεοῦ ἀπείληφα κτλ.) has been left in suspense; between the protasis and its respective apodosis the interpolator has inserted a series of sentences in order to introduce two of the delegates respectively as bishop and deacon from Ephesus. In the case of the deacon Burrhus, his " fellow-servant ", he puts in Ignatius' mouth the request that he may be allowed to remain with him (εὔχομαι παραμεῖναι αὐτὸν), thus preparing the future link between the letters written in Troas and the receiving communities (Phld. 11,2 and Sm. 12,1). With the original apodosis (πρέπον ἐστίν, κατὰ πάντα τρόπον δοξάζειν κτλ.) he has constructed an independent clause by merely adding the particle οὖν. Lastly, by means of a participial apposition he has changed the aim of the nuclear sentence of the apodosis, ἐν μιᾷ ὑποταγῇ κατηρτισμένοι, explaining in what way this " one submission " should be understood, that is, ὑποτασσόμενοι τῷ ἐπισκόπῳ καὶ τῷ πρεσβυτερίῳ (see nrs. 79f.).

135. In the heading of *Mg.* 2-5 he has followed the same pattern. Firstly he has detached the initial protasis 'Επεὶ οὖν κτλ. from its corresponding apodosis εἰς τιμὴν ἐκείνου κτλ., leaving the former suspended (see Mg. 2). To each of the proper names in

the protasis he has assigned a corresponding hierarchical rank: Damas has been made bishop; Bassus and Apollonius, presbyters; Zotion, deacon, "fellow-servant" of Ignatius. In place of the apodosis he has introduced very meaningful praise of the deacon Zotion's submission to the bishop and presbytery (2bc: see nr. 84).

The original apodosis (see nr. 83) has been ulteriorly divided into three sentences: 3,2a; 4a and 5. With these he has developed one of the themes with which he is most concerned: the problem of the bishop's youth, his representative position and the obedience due to him as representing God, the universal and invisible Bishop (see nrs. 84f.). The forger has availed himself of the theme of convenience (πρέπον ἐστὶν) of the apodosis, to construct no less than three sentences headed in this way: 3,1a; 3,2a and 4a. He has also been inspired by the contrast of "be called Christians by name" and "be such in fact" to apply it to his own situation (4b). The apodosis ended with a motivation in which Ignatius alluded to the last times (5,1-2). The forger has changed this, by adding one more οὖν, in an independent clause. Thus, he has left two anacolutha in the text (2 and 5,1).

The primitive introduction, reconstructed from the Ignatian sentences — once removed the interpolated ones —, is similar to that of Ephesians: (1) Reference to the situation of the Magnesian community and exposition of Ignatius' purpose in writing to the Asian communities (Mg. 1: see Eph. 1,1-2); (2) Invitation to the community, which he has come to know through its four delegates, not merely to call themselves Christians, but to be such in fact (Mg. 2-5: see Eph. 1,3-2,2).

136. The same proceeding has been used in the heading of *Tr.* 1-3. This time, however, it has not affected the period (division of protasis and apodosis) but only the apodosis, which has been divided into three sentences: 1,2b; 2,2bc and 2,1b-d. As can be seen, the order of the last two sentences has been inverted (see nrs. 88f.). The first cut was made in the formula "imitators of God, Jesus the Messiah, our hope", by separating "God" from "Jesus the Messiah". The second, has been done between the verb εὑρεθησόμεθα and its nominal complement οὐ κατὰ ἀνθρώπους ζῶντες κτλ. Once these cuts were made, the forger could refer "God" to God the Father, thus avoiding, on the one hand, the Christocentrism of the formula and managing, on the other, to

introduce the correlation God/bishop in agreement with his hieratic and vertical theology. The remaining sentences, excepting Tr. 3,3 which begins the exhortation properly so-called, belong to the interpolation (see nrs. 90f.).

137. In *Mg.* 6,1 the cut affects the sentence " strive to do all things in conformity with God, Jesus the Messiah ... ". The forger wants to show that this conformity of mind and unanimity of behaviour can only come about " under the presidency of the bishop in the place of God and the presbyters representing the senate of the Apostles " (6,1c). To attain his purpose, the inter-polator has split up the original sentence, separating " in con-formity with God " from " Jesus the Messiah ", and reversed the order of the phrase. By anticipating the sentence that came at the end, σπουδάζετε πάντα πράσσειν, he was easily able to qualify it with a genitive absolute clause: " presided over by the bishop, etc. ". On the other hand, to link up with the genuine sentence that was left aside: " Jesus the Messiah, who was with the Father before time began and was made manifest at the end of time " (6,1e), inasmuch as they are in the place of Jesus Christ, the forger had to introduce the deacons with a new parenthetical clause: " to the deacons, my beloved, having been entrusted with the dia-conia of *Jesus the Messiah*, who was with the Father, etc. " (6,1de) We have underlined the link point between the two original sen-tences (see nrs. 86f.).

The same tendency to separate " God " from " Jesus the Messiah " is to be seen in the second farewell formula of Eph*, reconstructed from Sm. 13,2c and Eph. 21,2e (see nrs. 54f.).

One more case of division of sentences and inversion of order is found in Pol. 7,1d + 6,1d, according to the proposed recon-struction (see nr. 49).

138. In *Phld.* inscr[b]. we have a case of mutilation of the orig-inal structure. In place of the ritual greeting that ends all the inscriptions (including the spurious ones of Sm. and Pol.), the forger has introduced a condition: " Especially, if they are united with the bishop, etc. ", to whom he has subordinated the saluta-tion Ignatius originally addressed to the Magnesian community (see nrs. 29, 58-61).

Another probable case of mutilation occurs in the farewell formula of Tr. 13,2a with word inversion; the original one is to be found in Phld. 11,2f (see nr. 95).

139. Finally, in *Phld.* 3,2 the forger has markedly compressed the two members of the first correlation: " For as many as are of Jesus the Messiah, these are also of God " into " For as many as are of God and of Jesus the Messiah ", so as to introduce the figure of the bishop: " these are with the bishop ", which can nevertheless be verified by collating it with the second correlation: " and as many as once repentant return to the unity of the church, these will also be of God, so that they may live according to Jesus the Messiah " (see nr. 96).

In all the cases examined up to now the main negative proceeding used by the interpolator has been the division of periods and sentences in order to insert his new theme into them thus changing their primitive meaning. As auxiliary procedures he has inverted sentences or words, mutilated and abridged phrases. However, in the greater number of passages that have been interpolated the scissors had spared the primitive sequence. Only the foreign bodies introduced by the interpolator have modified its original meaning.

2) *Positive proceedings*: *Intercalated sentences to change the original meaning*

Among the sentences merely intercalated that modify the meaning of the phrase without changing Ignatius' underlying text must be numbered the remaining ones that have been inserted into the expositive body or in the paraenesis of the letters.

140. *Eph.* 3,1-6,1. — In the first step (Aim) of the exhortation Ignatius proposed to exhort the Ephesian community to " run in agreement with the Plan of God ", that is, as he specifies subsequently, with Jesus the Messiah, our unwavering life, " for he is the Plan of the Father " (3,2). The interpolator has managed to change the meaning of the phrase by inserting " the bishops " into the " plan of Jesus Christ ", so that the exhortation turns on them: " Hence it is fitting to you to run in agreement with the plan of the bishop ", following the example of the presbytery (3,2e-4,1c).

This first step ended with a recommendation: " It is therefore profitable for you to maintain yourselves in a blameless unity (ἐν ἀμώμῳ ἑνότητι εἶναι), in order that you may always be partakers of God " (4,2gh). The interpolator tried to show, in the form of praise, how quickly Ignatius had gained the confidence of the local bishop in Smyrna, merely as corollary of the perfect attachment of the Ephesian community and its bishop because of their long common life, and ends up by recommending: "that all things may be in symphony with the unity" (ἵνα πάντα ἐν ἑνότητι σύμφωνα ᾖ, 5,1) (see nrs. 81f.).

In the second step (Initial warning) of the exhortation the interpolator has inserted two sentences. The first was introduced in the same way as the one examined before by way of a gradation that reinterprets the preceding Ignatian sentence. It says: "Let no one deceive himself. If any one be not within the precinct of the altar, he lacks the Bread of God" (5,2a-c). For Ignatius the altar is Jesus himself, God's sanctuary in which the Christians meet (Mg. 7,2) to share in his Body and Blood (Phld. 4ab). Only "he that is within the precinct of the altar is clean" (Tr. 7,2a), for he recognizes without hesitation and experiments through the Thanksgiving that Jesus truly died for our sins (Sm. 7,1). The forger guesses that Ignatius is speaking of the Eucharist, and adds a phrase, so as to let it be supposed that this takes place naturally under the presidency of the bishop: "For, if the prayer of one with another has so much strength, how much more that of the bishop together with the whole church!" (Eph. 5,2de). Ignatius went on with a brief admonition: "So then whoever does not come to the common assembly, by that very fact shows pride and has excluded himself. For it is written: 'God resists the proud' (Prov. 3,34)" (5,3a-e). The interpolator in his turn paraphrases the quotation of Proverbs concentrating now on the term "resists", to turn the reader's attention towards the bishop: "Let us strive, therefore, not to 'resist' the bishop, that we may be submitted to God" (5,3fg). There follows a disquisition on one of his favourite themes, the bishop's silence (6,1) (see nrs. 81f.).

141. *Mg.* 6,1-7,2. — A similar interpolation with its subsequent discourse is to be found in the initial invitation (Aim) addressed to the Magnesians to act in conformity with God, Jesus the Messiah. After modifying the first phrase (6,1), as we have just seen (see nr. 137), the forger has divided Ignatius' double, individual and communitarian invitation, turning it into another ternary one (see nrs. 86f.), so as to introduce the bishop and other leaders of the community in accordance with the ecclesiastical

praxis of his times. The interpolation has been inserted in the
right place. The Judaizers divided the members of the community under pretext of particular religious observances (εὔλογόν τι
φαίνεσθαι ἰδίᾳ ὑμῖν). Ignatius invited them insistently to meet in
common (ἐπὶ τὸ αὐτό), sharing in the same prayer, the same way
of thinking, the same hope, to gather all together in the one God's
sanctuary and one altar, Jesus the Messiah. The communitarian
experience of Jesus, immolated (meaning of the " altar ") by the
Jews, defenders of the Mosaic Law and the Temple, was the best
defence against such propagandists of legal observances and practices (6,2a-e. 7,1c-2). The interpolator has other problems. The
adversaries of his ecclesiology are not the Judaizers but the rebels
who refuse to obey the bishop and those presiding at the assemblies on his behalf. For this reason he has to insist imperatively,
both in positive (ἀλλ' ἑνώθητε κτλ., 6,2f) and negative terms (μηδὲ
ὑμεῖς ἄνευ τοῦ ἐπισκόπου καὶ τῶν πρεσβυτέρων μηδὲν πράσσετε, 7,1b),
so that everything be done under the presidency of the bishop and
the presbytery. Moreover he presents this unity as a paradigm
(εἰς τύπον καὶ διδαχὴν ἀφθαρσίας, 6,2f) that he then proceeds to
explain (ὥσπερ οὖν ... οὕτως ..., 7,1ab).

142. *Tr. 7.* — As in Eph. 5,2-6,1, the forger has thought it
necessary to interpolate the second step of the exhortation, the
initial warning, also intercalating two sentences (see nrs. 92f.).
Here too, Ignatius had insisted on the need to be inseparable (οὖσιν
ἀχωρίστοις) from God, Jesus the Messiah (7,1c), to abide within
the precinct of the altar (ἐντὸς θυσιαστηρίου), to remain " clean "
(καθαρός, 7,2ab), that is, not stained by heretical teachings of the
Docetic-Gnostics. The forger reinterprets this term in the sense
of " purity of conscience " (καθαρός — τῇ συνειδήσει, 7,2d ; see Mg.
4c), provided that the community persevere inseparable from the
bishop and the Prescriptions of the Apostles (7,1d: in positive
tone), doing nothing without the bishop, presbytery and deacon
(7,2c: in negative tone), or which comes to the same, " gathering
together in a valid way as it is prescribed " (Mg. 4d). For the
interpolator the only valid form of community meeting for the
Eucharistic celebration is the one that takes place under the bishop
or his delegates (Sm. 8,1) (see nr. 92).

In Ignatius' time this problematic was inexistent. The heretics
abstained from prayer and thanksgiving meetings, so as not to be

obliged to confess the reality of the man Jesus, experienced by
the Christians in the Eucharist (Sm. 7,1). The centre of the community was Jesus, his substantial presence in his Body and Blood.
Ignatius was not worried with who would preside over the Eucharist, but whether this should mean a real commitment to the man
who was born, lived and died in very truth to liberate us from the
slavery in which the Chief of this world kept us, because we had
accepted the coinage, with his inscription (the stamp of this world:
Mg. 5,2); or if, on the contrary, it was a mere charismatic-spiritual
evasion, with no commitment to the social reality of the time (which
was represented by the widows, orphans, the afflicted, prisoners,
the hungry or thirsty, etc.: see Sm. 6,2).

143. *Phld.* 4. — The same interpolation we found in the initial purpose (Aim) of the primitive letter to the Magnesians (Mg.
6,1-7,2: see nr. 141) is repeated in the purpose (Aim) or invitation
that concludes the doctrinal exposition (Phld. = Mg* 4ab.d): the
monarchical bishop with his presbytery and the deacons is a paradigm for the whole gathered community (Phld. 4c). Ignatius invited
them to share in a single thanksgiving act, for one is the Flesh of
our Lord, Jesus the Messiah, one the cup that holds his Blood,
one the altar or precinct within which he is offered (Phld. 4ab).
The interpolator adds a fresh paradigm: "just as the bishop is
one, etc. " (see nr. 77).

In Ignatius' view Jesus is the only mediator between God, to
whom the thanksgiving act is addressed, and the community which
celebrates the Eucharist: there can be only a single Eucharist, because there is only one Flesh, one cup, one altar. In the case of
the interpolator we have a new mediator, the bishop with his presbytery and deacons, as we already saw in the Didascalia (see nr. 119):
there is only one valid Eucharist, because there is only one bishop.
In the first case, the uniqueness of the Body, Blood and altar
— the uniqueness of our Lord, Jesus the Messiah, immolated for
us — brings about that there can be only one Eucharist, since the
substantial presence of Jesus in the midst of the Eucharistic community is constitutive of this thanksgiving; in the second case,
the presence of the bishop or his delegates affects — according to
the canonical categories introduced by the interpolator — the validity of the Eucharist, just as his consent affects the liceity of the
agape or baptism (Sm. 8,1e and 2c: see nr. 109). From one to

the other there has been an evident shift to legal categories, because the language that derived from an authentic experience of the reality of Jesus on the part of the community had been completely lost.

144.   *Phld.* 8,1. — In the paraenesis of the primitive letter to the Magnesians (now to the Philadelphians) Ignatius asserts that the Lord forgives all those who repent, as long as their repentance leads them to unity with God (8,1cd).   There is a question as he said before (3,2cd), of a return to the unity of the community. The interpolator has thought suitable to add " and (to the unity) of the bishop's senate " (8,1e; see nr. 108).   There is no unity with God without unity with the bishop, since the latter is in fact his representative on earth.

145. *Sm.* 9,1. — A similar interpolation appears at the end of the doctrinal section of the primitive letter to the Ephesians (now to the Smyrnaeans).   Ignatius, finally, exhorted the members of the community to wake up while there was still time to repent and turn to God (9,1ab).   The interpolator cannot conceive of an allusion to God that does not include mention of his representative: " It is advantageous to recognize God and the bishop ... " (9,1cd). God is the universal and invisible Bishop; the bishop makes him visible.   Therefore he adds: " Whoever does anything hidden from the bishop worships the devil " (9,1e), since the devil is God's antagonist and the bishop represents and occupies the place of God in the community (see nr. 110).

γ) *Specific doctrinal developments of the interpolator*

In this last paragraph we shall review the passages where the forger expresses himself freely, without being conditioned either by structural reasons, or by questions of content.   They are passages that express synthetically his middle third century ecclesiology, which was inspired — as we have seen — by the Didascalia (see nrs. 113-125).

146.   In the first place we shall consider the ample developments of *Phld.* 7 and *Sm.* 7,2f-8.   Since we have already dealt with their content in the second part, we limit ourselves here to drawing attention to their situation. Phld. 7 was intercalated in the paraenesis of the primitive letter to the Magnesians, taking advantage of the phrase in which Ignatius declares he had written

to them out of fidelity to his conscience and not because he wanted to be a witness for the prosecution against anyone. The expression was useful to evoke the existence of presumed quarrels in the Philadelphian community (see nrs. 97-107). Sm. 7,2f-8, on the other hand, has been inserted in the final exhortation belonging to the body of the primitive letter to the Ephesians. The contrast between Ignatius' exhortative tone (7,2a-e) and the imperative one of the interpolator is evident: the former invited the community to keep away from the Gnostic heretics because they were not committed Christians, and to adhere to the Prophets and especially the Gospel, since they contain the good news of the Passion and Resurrection of Jesus, of his true commitment to men; the interpolator insists to the point of satiety on following the bishop and presbytery, on doing nothing without those who have been appointed in the hierarchy, under pain of performing invalid actions or, at least, illicit ones (see nr. 109).

147. As an independent development we must also consider the first part of the letter to Polycarp: *Pol.* 1-5. This is the section addressed in the singular to Polycarp bishop of Smyrna. Keep in mind that the second part is in the plural and addressed to the community (of Smyrna, as has been held up to now), that is, in reality, to the community of Ephesus, for it was precisely part of the ending of Eph*. The first part, wholly constructed in a prescriptive tone — through juxtaposition of imperatives in asyndetic and paratactic form — differs notably from the exhortative, intentionally non-prescriptive tone of the authentic letters (see nr. 45, and n. 172). As was to be expected, it is full of expressions relative to the bishop's function (see nrs. 66-69).

c) *Methods employed to introduce the interpolations*

148. As colophon of these Prolegomena we thought it opportune to review the various methods used by the forger to intercalate his interpolations in Ignatius' text.

On four occasions the forger limits himself to amplifying Ignatius' development by adding a simple coordinating particle: καὶ τοῦ ἐπισκόπου κτλ. (Tr. 7,1d); καὶ συνέδριον τοῦ ἐπισκόπου (Phld. 8,1e); καὶ τοῦ πέμποντος αὐτὸν Πολυκάρπου (Pol. 8,2d); ἅμα Πολυκάρπου κτλ. (Mg. 15d). On the other hand, in the headings of the three authentic letters, he has enlarged what is relative to the delegates with appositions: ὑμῶν δὲ ἐν σαρκὶ ἐπισκόπῳ ('Ονησίμῳ: Eph. 1,3c); τοῦ κατὰ θεὸν διακόνου ὑμῶν (Βούρρου : 2,1b); τοῦ ἀξιοθέου ὑμῶν ἐπισκόπου (Δαμᾶ: Mg. 2a); πρεσβυτέρων ἀξίων (Βάσσου καὶ 'Απολλωνίου: ibid.); τοῦ συνδούλου μου διακόνου (Ζωτίωνος: ibid.); ὁ ἐπίσκοπος ὑμῶν (Πολύβιος: Tr. 1,1c).

But it is by means of intercalation of short periods (sentences) or whole clauses that he has managed to superimpose his ecclesiology over that of Ignatius. To introduce them he has used:

(1) A simple participial clause in apposition: ὑποτασσόμενοι τῷ ἐπισκόπῳ καὶ τῷ πρεσβυτερίῳ (Eph. 2,2e); εὐχαριστῶν τῷ κυρίῳ, ἀγαπῶν Πολύκαρπον ὡς καὶ ὑμᾶς (21,1cd); προκαθημένου τοῦ ἐπισκόπου up to διακονίαν (Mg. 6,1cd); ὑποτασσόμενοι τῷ ἐπισκόπῳ ὡς τῇ ἐντολῇ, ὁμοίως καὶ τῷ πρεσβυτερίῳ (Tr. 13,2b).

(2) A comparative clause with ὡς: ὡς εἷς ἐπίσκοπος ἅμα τῷ πρεσβυτερίῳ καὶ διακόνοις, τοῖς συνδούλοις μου (Phld. 4c); with ὡς καὶ: ὡς καὶ αὐτὸν ὁ πατὴρ 'Ιησοῦ Χριστοῦ ἀναψῦξαι (Eph. 2,1h); ὡς καὶ οἱ ἐπίσκοποι up to κιθάρᾳ (3,2e-4,1c); ὡς καὶ ὑμῶν 'Ιησοῦς Χριστός (21,1e); with ὥσπερ καὶ: ὥσπερ καί τινες up to συναθροίζεσθαι (Mg. 4b-d); with ὥσπερ ... οὕτως: ὥσπερ οὖν ὁ κύριος ... οὕτως μηδὲ ὑμεῖς up to πράσσετε (7,1ab).

(3) An explanatory clause with τοῦτ' ἔστιν: τοῦτ' ἔστιν, ὁ χωρὶς ἐπισκόπου up to συνειδήσει (Tr. 7,2cd); with γὰρ: ὅταν γὰρ τῷ ἐπισκόπῳ up to φαίνεσθέ μοι (2,1ab); πρέπει γὰρ ὑμῖν up to ἀποστόλων (12,2d).

(4) A conditional clause heightened with πόσῳ μᾶλλον: εἰ γὰρ ἐγὼ ... πόσῳ μᾶλλον ὑμᾶς up to σύμφωνα ἢ (Eph. 5,1); εἰ γὰρ ἑνὸς ... πόσῳ μᾶλλον up to ἐκκλησίας (5,2de); emphasized with μάλιστα ἐὰν: ἐὰν μὲ καταξιώσῃ ... μάλιστα ἐὰν ὁ κύριός μοι ἀποκαλύψῃ up to διὰ παντός (20); μάλιστα ἐὰν ἐν ἑνὶ ὦσιν up to πνεύματι (Phld. inscr[b].); with an adversative meaning: εἰ γὰρ καὶ ... ἀλλὰ up to τοῦ πατρὸς αὐτοῦ (7).

(5) A consecutive sentence with οὖν: σπουδάσωμεν οὖν up to ὑποτασσόμενοι (Eph. 5,3fg); Σπουδάζετε οὖν up to πνευματική (Mg. 13); ἀναγκαῖον οὖν ἐστίν up to πράσσειν ὑμᾶς (Tr. 2,2a); 'Επεὶ οὖν ... γράψεις up to ὡς ἄξιος ὤν (Pol. 8,1). We should mention also those genuine Ignatian periods that, with the addition of a simple οὖν, have been turned into independent periods: πρέπον οὖν ἐστίν ... (Eph. 2,2c); εἰς τιμὴν οὖν ... with the addition of the interpolated

sentence ἐπακούειν up to εἰδότα (Mg. 3,2); πρέπον οὖν εστὶν ... (4a); ἐπεὶ οὖν ... (5,1a).

(6) Various exhortative forms: Περὶ δὲ τοῦ συνδούλου μου Βούρ-ρου ... εὔχομαι up to ἐπισκόπου (Eph. 2,1ab.d); Περὶ δὲ Φίλωνος up to Χριστοῦ (Phld. 11,1); Καὶ ὅσον ... πλειόνως up to προσβλέπειν (Eph. 6,1); Καὶ ὑμῖν δὲ πρέπει up to τῷ πάντων ἐπισκόπῳ (Mg. 3,1) ἀλλ' ἐνώθητε τῷ ἐπισκόπῳ up to ἀφθαρσίας (6,2f); ἀλλ' ὑποτάσσεσθε up to ἀποστόλοις (Tr. 2,2b); δεῖ δὲ καὶ up to ὡς πῦρ (2,3); Ὁμοίως πάντες ἐντρεπέσθωσαν up to ἐντρέπεσθαι (3,1-2); Τοὺς δὲ μερισμοὺς φεύγετε up to πᾶν ὃ πράσσετε (Sm. 7,2f-8); καλῶς ἔχει up to λατρεύει (9,1cd); Τῷ ἐπισκόπῳ προσέχετε up to διακόνοις (Pol. 6,1a-c).

(7) A relative qualifying sentence linked with the mention of a proper noun: ὃν (Onesimus) εὔχομαι up to κεκτῆσθαι (Eph. 1,3de); ὃν (Crocus) ἐξεμπλάριον up to ἀπέλαβον (2,1f); οὗ (Zotion) ἐγὼ ὀναίμην up to Χριστοῦ (Mg. 2bc); Ὃν (anonymous) ἐπίσκοπον up to θεοῦ ζῶντος (Phld. 1).

II. MOTIVES OF THE PRIMITIVE IGNATIAN EPISTOLARY AND OF THE INTERPOLATION

Once the existence of an interpolation in Ignatius' text has been verified (Part One), its content identified, and its exact extent determined (Part Two), the place of the interpolated passages has been fixed, the sentences and clauses classified according to their peculiar specific mission and the proceedings the interpolator used have been described (Prolegomena), the moment has now come to point out the incompatibility of either of the recensions basing ourselves on the motives that induced Ignatius and the interpolator to write their respective epistolaries.

a) *Ignatius' motives for writing his four letters*

In reality, Ignatius wrote five letters. But there has been no evidence as to his congratulatory letter written to the church of Syria (Sm. = Eph* 11,3), after the comforting news brought by the messengers (Sm. = Eph* 10,1; imitated in Phld. 10,1 and Pol. 7,1). We limit ourselves, then, to the four that have turn out to be genuine: Rom. (unknown to the forger and, therefore, not interpolated), Eph* (the body of the primitive letter has been shared out between Eph. and Sm.; its ample conclusion, distributed between Eph., Phld., and above all, Sm. and Pol.), Mg* (divided between Mg. and Phld., as for the body of the exposition, while its primitive ending was left in Mg.) and Tr. (undivided but largely interpolated).

α) *General valid motives for the whole epistolary*

149. Thanks to two explicit allusions, we can verify the *main* motives that led Ignatius to write his letters.

The *first allusion* is to be found in the heading of Magnesians (Mg. 1,2). (Bear in mind that Mg* was in all probability the first of the letters he wrote to the Asian communities). Ignatius' main objective is expressed through a progression of three sentences and a modal conclusive clause:

" For being held worthy to bear such a venerable name, thanks to the chains I carry round me, I sing out to the churches and pray them to realize union in their midst (ἐν αἷς ἕνωσιν εὔχομαι) [388], the union that holds between flesh and spirit of Jesus the Messiah, our life for ever, as also between faith and love, for nothing can be preferred to it, and still more properly, between Jesus and the Father, so that (ἐν ᾧ) [389] after enduring all the machinations of the Chief of this world and having escaped alive, we shall attain to God " (Mg. 1,2).

There is no doubt that Ignatius' main concern was to foment union (ἕνωσιν) among the communities which he was addressing. For this reason he could repeat towards the end of the letter:

---

[388] Commentators usually translate ἐν αἷς (ἕνωσιν εὔχομαι) as if it were a simple dative: " to whom I desire the union of (with) ..." (Lelong, Bauer, Camelot, Quacquarelli, etc.). Lightfoot, Kleist translate well: " I pray that there may be in them union of ...", " I pray for union in their midst ". Ign. uses εὔχομαι with dative in Phld. 6,3 (πᾶσι); Rom. 1,1 (θεῷ); but he employs ἐν + a relative clause in plural (distributively), " before whom " (ἐν οἷς ἐλάλησα), in Phld. 6,3. Commentators also interpret the three pairs of genitives as if it were question of realizing the union of (with) the flesh and the spirit of Jesus, of faith and love, with Jesus and the Father, finding themselves obliged to translate differently (of, into, with). If these three pairs of genitives are taken as models of unity, this difficulty is obviated and Ignatius' purpose becomes clear. Similar elliptical phrases are frequent in Ign.

[389] ἐν ᾧ... θεοῦ τευξόμεθα does not refer to the Father (Camelot?) nor to Jesus (Bauer, Lelong, Lightfoot) but to the three binary pairs, since it equals a modal instrumental clause (the relative is not masculine but neuter). See similar usage in Tr. 13,3 (equivalent to a completive clause) and Pol. 8,3 (equivalent to a consecutive clause).

" On my part, I tried to do my best as a man made ready to create union " (εἰς ἕνωσιν κατηρτισμένος, Phld. = Mg* 8,1).

Nevertheless, the theme of ἕνωσις appears a third time in the same letter (Phld. = Mg* 4), together with the insistent exhortations to " do all things in conformity with God, Jesus the Messiah " (see nr. 86), thus warning the Magnesian community to face the possible tensions that the Judaizers could raise in their midst.

In the letters dealing with the Gnostic problem, ἕνωσις only appears once (Tr. 11,2). The reason is obvious: the Gnostics kept aloof from the communitarian meetings of the church (Sm. 7,1), from which we deduce that they had already set themselves up as a parallel church (αἵρεσις is employed by Ignatius only in an anti-Gnostic context: Eph. 6,2 and Tr. 6,1), while the Judaizers with their legalistic exigencies sowed deep discord and division in the midst of the communities (μερισμός appears only in an anti-Judaizing context, always in the singular: Phld. = Mg* 2,1; 3,1 and 8,1; likewise μερίζω and σχίζω: Mg. 6,2; Phld. = Mg* 3,3).

(1) The *first* of the three models of union proposed is the one that exists between " flesh " and " spirit " (literally), or which comes to the same, between the humanity and the divinity of Jesus the Messiah. The risen Jesus, humanly palpable and visible, while united spiritually to the Father (Sm. 3), is the first paradigm Ignatius presents to the communities for imitation. In the letters with anti-Gnostic subject, he will insist that the reality of the " flesh " of Jesus is inseparable from his " spirit ", his death from the resurrection, because the passion has constituted him " the achieved man " (Sm. 4,2). " Fruit of his divine and blessed passion are we " (1,2), since, as " planting of the Father " (Tr. 11,1), we are " branches of the cross " that give " fruit imperishable " (11,2). In the letters with anti-Judaizing subject, on the contrary, he will stress that " our life ", the definitive life that Jesus gives, " began to shine on the Day of the Lord ", that is, the day when Jesus rose from the dead (Mg. 9,1).

(2) The *second* model he proposes is the close union that holds between " faith " and " love ", between adhesion to Jesus the Messiah and love showed by deeds. The best comment of this paradigm is given by Ignatius himself in Eph. 14,1:

" None of these (heavenly or earthly) things is hidden from you, as long as you maintain to the end this adhesion and this love toward

Jesus the Messiah, for these are the beginning and end of life: faith is the beginning and love the end. When these two come to form a unity, there is God (θεός ἐστιν); all the rest that refers to man's ideal is secondary (ἀκόλουθά ἐστιν)."

To the Gnostic ideal (εἰς καλοκἀγαθίαν, lit. concerning the manners of a perfect gentleman) of knowing every secret relating to the heavenly regions of the angels and archons or principalities (Tr. 5; Sm. = Eph* 6,1) Ignatius opposes the human-divine reality of Jesus. The important thing is to become God; the rest is secondary. Unity of faith and love, of adhesion to Jesus and true commitment, are the main or the whole thing, as he says in a parallel phrase to Sm. 1,2: " For faith and love are the whole: nothing can be preferred to it " (Sm. 6,1).

Faith and love are the two extremities of a totality. They describe the whole process from initial adhesion to definitive union, the divinization of the Christian.

To the human aims of the Judaizers, who judge their neighbour according to appearances and strive to observe certain legal practices that divide the community (Mg. 6,2c.e and 7,1c), he opposes living like Christians according to the Prophets who were disciples of the Messiah through the spirit (8-9), and ends up by saying that " it is absurd to profess Jesus (to be) the Messiah and to practise like a Jew " (10,3).

Faith and law cannot be partners: but faith and love can. Hence he exhorts the Magnesians: " Shun the evil tricks and ambushes of the Chief of this world, lest haply you be oppressed by his ideology, and wax weak in your communion (ἐξασθενήσετε ἐν τῇ ἀγάπῃ): rather, come together, all of you, with undivided heart " (Phld. = Mg* 6,2).

(3)　The *third* model, the model par excellence (τὸ δὲ κυριώτερον), is the union that exists between Jesus and the Father. The union of Jesus with the Father, of the Man-God with God-Father, is the perfect paradigm of personalized unity. For this reason he immediately stresses the urgency of " not only to be called Christians by name but to be such in fact " (Mg. 4a), since " the believers, by love, (have impressed upon them) the stamp of God the Father through Jesus the Messiah " (5,2).

150. The *second explicit allusion* to the motives that led Ignatius to write his four letters, on the way to martyrdom, is to be found in Rom. 4,1:

18

" I am writing to all the churches and insiting to all men that I give my life willingly for God, provided you do not hinder me."

As we have already hinted in the conclusions to the first part (see p. 139ff.), (a) Ignatius' condemnation to be devoured by the wild beasts in Rome (κατάκριτος: Eph. 12,1; Tr. 3,3; Rom. 4,3; θηριωμαχῆσαι: Eph. 1,2; Tr. 10; cf. Rom. 5,1; 4,1-2; 5,2; ὑπὸ κίν-δυνον: Eph. 12,1; Tr. 13,3), (b) his situation — at the time he wrote these letters — of a man " enchained for the sake of the common Name (of Christian) and the common hope " (Eph. 1,2; 3,1; 11,2; 21,2; Mg. 1,2; 12; Tr. 1,1; 5,2; 10; 12,2; Rom. 1,1; 4,3; Phld. 5,1; Sm. 4,2; 10,2; 11,1), (c) his martyrdom really happening in Rome, [390] in a word, his violent death, do not seem to have been due to a more or less generalized persecution.

Not only is there no mention of persecution or invitation to endurance and perseverance, but it is take for granted that it was the sad result of a grave tumult provoked in the heart of the Syrian communities by two opposing factions — Gnostics and Judaizers. Hence he feels the need of writing insistently to the communities and persons he contacts outside Syria, " that I give my life willingly for God " (ὅτι ἐγὼ ἐκὼν ὑπὲρ θεοῦ ἀποθνήσκω, Rom. 4,1); and what is more, he reveals to the Ephesians that " I have delivered myself over to death " (ἑαυτὸν ἔκδοτον δέδωκα τῷ θανάτῳ, Sm. = Eph* 4,2). In times of persecution no one delivered himself up to death — he would have been taken for presumptuous or rash —, nor did any martyr or confessor need to say he died willingly. Ignatius' heroic gesture came from his deep love for his church of Syria: he yields himself up to avoid worse reprisals against his Christian communities. The Roman authorities are satisfied with giving them a lesson by condemning the ringleader of the supposed rebellion.

The letter he writes to the Romans, uniquely to dissuade them from exercising influence in higher spheres to deliver him from death, hardly makes sense in the context of a persecution. If it is a question of a general persecution — as has been held up to now —, how can we explain that the Christians of Rome enjoy

[390] See the evidence of Pol. Phil. 9,1: ἐν τοῖς μακαρίοις Ἰγνατίῳ κτλ. and 9,2: ᾧ καὶ συνέπαθον; and the indirect witness of the interpolator himself, by the mere fact of having invoked the authority of the martyr Ignatius.

such a privileged position that it would allow them to have the sentence annulled? The tight security measures of ten soldiers for a single prisoner, the extreme vigilance, day and night (Rom. 5,1), the possibility Ignatius enjoyed of speaking and writing to Christian communities and individuals (Sm. = Eph* 9,2; 11,3, and passim), the petition for prayers that peace might be restored to the church of Syria (Rom. 9,1; Tr. 13,1 and Mg. 14)[391] and the comforting news brought from Syria by some envoys of that church about restoration of peace, strength and its communitarian body,[392] all this makes no sense if it is understood in the light of a persecution. Otherwise, if the good news brought from Syria should be understood as the end of a persecution, Ignatius' condemnation would be revoked and he himself would have appealed to the responsible authorities.

There is even one statement that makes sense only in the hypothesis of a grave intraecclesiastical conflict that gave rise to intervention of the Roman authorities from outside, just as in the process of Jesus. Owing to a false posing of the question, Ignatius has been labelled as showing an excessive desire for martyrdom with descriptions of the imminence of his being torn to pieces by wild beasts, a desire that would border on the pathological: " Let me be the food of wild beasts ... God's wheat I am, and by the teeth of wild beasts I am to be ground that I may be found God's pure bread. Better still, coax the wild beasts, that they may become my tomb and may leave no part of my body behind ... Entreat the Messiah in my behalf that through these instruments I may be found God's sacrifice ... May I have joy of the beasts that have been prepared for me! And I pray that they may be found to be ready for me. I will even coax them that they may devour me quickly, not as has happened to some people when the beasts refused to touch them through fear. And should they be unwilling while I am willing, I will myself compel them ... " (Rom. 4,1-2; 5,2).

If his letters are interpreted in the light of a persecution, his ardent and passionate desire for martyrdom lacks its main motivation. If, on the contrary, his condemnation is the result of a self-

---

[391] Eph. 21,2 has been tampered with by the forger.

[392] Sm. = Eph* 10,1 (Phld. 11,1 is a copy); Sm. = Eph* 11,2-3; Phld. = Eph* 10,1a; Pol. = Eph* 7,1b-d.

immolation for love of the Christian communities and as an irrefutable witness against Gnostics and Judaizers, we shall understand
how Ignatius takes his martyrdom to be a confirmation of Jesus'
real death and resurrection: " But if ... his suffering was but an
appearance ..., why am I in chains? Why do I even pray that I
may fight wild beasts? So I die in vain! My witness is a lie against
the Lord! " (Tr. 10); " For if these things were done by our
Lord merely in appearance, then I in my chains, too, am in
appearance! And why then have I delivered myself over to death,
to perish by fire or sword or wild beasts? " (Sm. 4,2).

In fact, when he warns the Magnesians against the propaganda
of the Judaizers, he tells them that the Prophets even were persecuted because they lived in conformity with the Messiah, Jesus
(κατὰ Χριστὸν Ἰησοῦν ἔζησαν · διὰ τοῦτο καὶ ἐδιώχθησαν, Mg. 8,2;
cf. 9,2 and Phld. = Mg* 5,2). Likewise, he warns the Ephesians
against the Docetism of the Gnostics telling them that the Apostles
despised death because they believed that Jesus was in the flesh
even after the resurrection (διὰ τοῦτο καὶ θανάτου κατεφρόνησαν,
ηὑρέθησαν δὲ ὑπὲρ θάνατον, Sm. = Eph* 3,2).

Ignatius did not give himself to death carried away by a false
mysticism of martyrdom; if this had been so, he would not have
ceased to invite them all to do so as well. Ignatius wanted to prove
to his adversaries that his beliefs were not mere talk and that in
the silence of his death his true commitment to Jesus' passion and
death could be recognized (cf. Rom. 2,1; Eph. 15,2). When he
writes to the Romans begging them insistently not to interfere in
his journey to martyrdom, he is only trying not to invalidate his
own testimony. Ignatius' adversaries had reproached him for
having put on an act, because he knew beforehand that ultimately
the Roman community would liberate him from the death sentence.

To sum up, Ignatius is the shepherd who gives his life willingly for his sheep (to collate Rom. 4,1 and 9,1 with John 10,17-18);
his ardent desire for martyrdom, supported by the inward prophetic
word that invites him to " Go to the Father " (Δεῦρο πρὸς τὸν πατέρα,
Rom. 7,2), coincides with the desire expressed by Jesus himself
that " his immersion in the waters (of death) be fulfilled " (Lk.
12,50; cf. Mk. 10,38-39; Mtt. 20,22-23). The one who gives him
the strength to endure all things is Jesus himself, " who became
the achieved man " through the passion (αὐτοῦ με ἐνδυναμοῦντος

τοῦ τελείου ἀνθρώπου γενομένου, Sm. 4,2). Ignatius, too, like Jesus was troubled as he faced this supreme moment (John 12,27). He feels an inward struggle and great need of gentleness (Tr. 4). He knows very well that it is not the same thing to be in chains as to be a perfect disciple (Eph. 1,2; 3,1; Phld. 5,1; Tr. 5,2). So he asks the Romans: "Allow me to be an imitator of the passion of my God " (ἐπιτρέψατέ μοι μιμητὴν εἶναι τοῦ πάθους τοῦ θεοῦ μου, Rom. 6,3).

*　*　*

After these two main motives, the Ignatian letters contain — above all in the conclusion — two no less important requests: (1) Petition for prayer for himself so that he might fully reach his objective; (2) Petition for prayers for the church in Syria, in a first moment, that peace might quickly be restablished at its heart; and then, once peace recovered, his congratulations to the people on enjoying such peace.

151. The *first* petition is closely linked with the second motivation that we have just developed. The objective pursued by Ignatius has many different connotations, as are the varied grammatical forms employed to express this desire or petition. Leaving aside the direct connotations with the martyrdom, whether real (to be food for the wild beasts, etc.) or symbolic (to become Bread of God, etc.), and bearing in mind that the next chapter is dedicated to the analysis of literary resources, we shall now simply review the verbs he used to express his request or desire, ending with a detailed analysis of its content.

(a) The *request* is expressed in the following verbal forms: μνημονεύετέ μου (Eph. 21,1; Mg. 14), περὶ ἐμοῦ δὲ προσεύχεσθε (Tr. 12,3), αἰτήσασθε περὶ ἐμοῦ (Rom. 8,3), μόνον μοι δύναμιν αἰτεῖσθε ἔσωθέν τε καὶ ἔξωθεν (3,2), or/and in indirect form with the following expressions: ἡ προσευχὴ ὑμῶν ... με ἀπαρτίσει (Phld. 5,1), τῇ προσευχῇ ὑμῶν κτλ. (Eph. 1,2; 11,2), ἐν τῇ προσευχῇ ὑμῶν κτλ. (Phld. 8,2; Sm. 11,1), ἐν ταῖς προσευχαῖς ὑμῶν κτλ. (Mg. 14), ἐν τῇ αἰτήσει ὑμῶν (Pol. 7,1), when addressed to the Asian communities, or else with εὔχομαι when directed to God (Sm. 11,1).

(b) The *desire* takes preferably the following forms: θέλω, in the positive (Rom. 3,2; 6,1-3; 7,3; Phld. 8,2), οὐκέτι θέλω, in the negative (Rom. 8,1), ζητῶ (6,1), γένοιτό μοι (Eph. 11,2; 12,2; Pol. 6,1), ἐλπίζω (Eph. 1,2), ἠλέημαι (Rom. 9,2).

According to Ignatius, the objective is attained by imitation of the Lord, enduring all kinds of injustice, deprivation, contempt (Eph. 10,3); by imitating the passion of our God, Jesus the Messiah (Rom. 6,3); the apprenticeship is made by following the Christian way of life (Mg. 10,1), by renouncing all desire of power (Rom. 4,3; 6,1; 7,1). Ignatius confesses that in this moment, condemned and surrounded by chains, he is being initiated into discipleship (μαθητεύεσθαι/μαθητὴς εἶναι, Eph. 3,1; Rom. 5,3), enduring injustices on the part of the soldiers (Rom. 5,1). But this, nevertheless, does not mean he has reached his aim (Rom. 5,1; Phld. 8,2; Tr. 5,2). The aim is to become ' a proved complete disciple of Jesus the Messiah ' (Eph. 1,2; Mg. 9,1; 10,1; Tr. 5,2; Rom. 4,2; 5,3; Pol. 7,3), a goal that the Prophets yearned for moved by the Spirit (cf. Mg. 9,2; 8,2).

The goal of this discipleship is expressed in equivalent formulas: θεοῦ ἐπιτυχεῖν/-χω (Eph. 12,2; Mg. 14; Tr. 12,2; 13,3; Rom. 1,2; 2,1; 4,1; 9,2; Sm. 11,1; Pol. 7,1) or merely ἐπιτυχεῖν ἐν ῾Ρώμῃ θηριομαχῆσαι/ἐπιτύχω (Eph. 1,2[2x]; Rom. 8,3), χάριτος ἐπιτύχω (Rom. 1,2), τοῦ κλήρου ἐπιτυχεῖν/-χω (Tr. 12,3; Phld. 5,1), ᾽Ιησοῦ Χριστοῦ ἐπιτύχω (Rom. 5,3: 2x). The favour (cf. Sm. 11,1), share in the inheritance (cf. Eph. 11,2; Rom. 1,2; Pol. 6,1), that Ignatius wants for himself is God Jesus the Messiah, or which is the same, to become God in the way Jesus became God and true Life from within human weakness and death (ἐν σαρκὶ γενόμενος θεός, ἐν θανάτῳ ζωὴ ἀληθινή, Eph. 7,2).

Ignatius' theology on the cross, the source of life, is inspired by the Synoptics. Only the one who resembles Jesus, linking himself to his death and accepting to die like him, has a share in the resurrection to a definitive life (Mg. 5,2; Tr. 2,1; Sm. 5,3; cf. Eph. 11; 17; Mg. 9; Tr. 9,2). The cross is the Tree of life from which Jesus calls his faithful, so that from it may be born the Head with its members (Tr. 11,2). Christians are the branches of the cross that bear incorruptible fruit (Tr. 11,2; Sm. 1,2), since at the instant Jesus exhaled his spirit he breathed it into us: " For this cause the Lord received perfume on his head, that he might breathe incorruption upon the church " (Eph. 17,1). The allusion to Mtt. 26,7, that is, to the perfumes that should prepare the body of Jesus for the sepulture, is interpreted by Ignatius as an advance of the perfumes that Jesus will spill over his Body, the church. For this reason Ignatius could say that " the passion (of Jesus) is our resurrection " (Sm. 5,3; Mg. 5,2; 9,1), because from the cross Jesus has communicated his incorruptible Spirit to us.

152. The content of the *second* petition, generally coupled with the first but destined for the church in Syria, varies according to Ignatius' frame of mind with regard to that community. In the first three letters he wrote, probably in order of urgency, to the Romans, Magnesians and Trallians, he asks them to remember the church of Syria in their prayers (Μνημονεύετε ἐν τῇ/ταῖς προσευχῇ/ -αῖς ὑμῶν τῆς ἐν Συρίᾳ ἐκκλησίας, Rom. 9,1; Mg. 14; Tr. 13,1), because it has been left without a Shepherd (now Jesus will be their only Shepherd and the communion of the churches, Rom. 9,1).

However, in the primitive letter to the Ephesians whose conclusion is now distributed between Eph. (a summary), Phld. (a copy), Sm. and Pol., Ignatius does not ask for prayers, but confirms that their prayers have already attained their goal ('Η ‹γὰρ› προσ- ευχὴ ὑμῶν ἀπῆλθεν ἐπὶ τὴν ἐκκλησίαν τὴν ἐν [...] Συρί‹ᾳ›, Sm. 11,1; 'Επειδὴ κατὰ τὴν προσευχὴν ὑμῶν κτλ., Phld. 10,1a). Indeed, during the short interval that had passed between the writing of the letters, some messengers came from Syria following close upon Ignatius (Sm. 10,1; imitated by the forger in Phld. 11,1) to bring him good and comforting news about the pacification (εἰρηνεύειν, Phld. 10,1a; imitated by the interpolator in Pol. 7,1a; cf. Sm. 11,2) of his church in Syria thanks to the prayers and deep love of the Asian communities. To congratulate the Christians of Syria (συγχαρῆναι, Sm. 11,2; imitated by the forger in Phld. 10,1d) and show his pleasure (συνδοξάσῃ, Sm. 11,3; imitated in Pol. 7,2), Ignatius asks the Ephesians to send an embassy to Syria to represent the community (Sm. 11,2; imitated by the interpolator in Phld. 10,1bc and Pol. 7,2), with a personal letter from him (Sm. 11,3), thus to complete the work begun with the fraternal welcome they gave him (compare Eph. 1,1 with Sm. 11,2 and Pol. 7,3).

The content of the embassy hints at the circumstances that had led to Ignatius' condemnation: Sm. 11,2 alludes to the restoration of peace, strength and the communitarian body (ὅτι εἰρηνεύ- ουσιν καὶ ἀπέλαβον τὸ ἴδιον μέγεθος καὶ ἀπεκατεστάθη αὐτοῖς τὸ ἴδιον σωματεῖον); 11,3 describes the newly regained state as the God-given calm which had come upon them, the safe haven they have reached after the storm (τὴν κατὰ θεὸν αὐτοῖς γενομένην εὐδίαν, καὶ ὅτι λιμένος ἤδη ἔτυχον); in Pol. 7,1b, Ignatius confesses: "I myself also have gathered fresh courage since God has banished my care". This was the worry that tormented him so much. In Mg. 14, in fact, he pointed out to the Magnesians that the church in Syria very much needs the refreshing dew that the other communities can procure it (εἰς τὸ ἀξιωθῆναι τὴν ἐν Συρίᾳ ἐκκλησίαν διὰ τῆς ἐκκλησίας ὑμῶν δροσισθῆναι). Ignatius' condemnation was not due to an external persecution, as we have already said (see pp. 139 ff.), but to internal quarrels brought about by the Gnostic and Judaizing factions among the communities of Syria, that had torn away the members from their corporate body. The uproar forced the Roman authorities to intervene, and Ignatius presented himself as the only responsible man, since he was the bishop of Syria (see Rom. 4,1 and Sm. 4,2).

β) *Specific motives for each letter*

153. If we now examine the explanation of the meaning of the exhortation that he thought necessary to give in each of the three genuine Asian letters, we shall grasp the real problem that troubled him.

We start with the letter to the *Magnesians*, where he deals with the problem of the Judaizers. The explanatory clause is to be found at the end of the present letter to the Magnesians:

" (I say) this, my beloved, not because I have learned that any of you behave in this way, but as the least of you I want to warn you before-hand (προφυλάσσεσθαι ὑμᾶς) so that you do not fall into the lures of these vain opinions, but that you be fully convinced of the birth and the passion and resurrection that happened in the days of Pontius Pilate's government ..." (Mg. 11).

Judaizing propaganda within the church had left aside the obligation of circumcision (Phld. = Mg* 6,1), but it went on insisting on legal observances (Mg. 6,2c.e; 7,1c; 8,1a), the binding character of Jewish Law (8,1b, var. lect.), Sabbath observance (9,1d, indir.), the Jewish way of living (10,3a), supporting Judaizing practices (Phld. = Mg* 6,1a) and preferring the Archives or Canonical Jewish Scriptures to the Gospel (8,2).

Ignatius' basic argument against the Judaizers is the resurrection of Jesus: the Day when life arose as much for the Prophets who lived in conformity with the Messiah, Jesus, as for ourselves (Mg. 8-9). Hence, in the enumeration, birth-passion-resurrection, he places the accent on this last by adding the chronological date: " that happened in the days of ... ". Hence also, he focuses his exhortation on living " in conformity with the Messiah, Jesus " (Mg. 8,2), " no longer observing the Sabbath but living in accord with the Day of the Lord " (9,1), " learning to live in the Christian way " (10,1), to " put away the deteriorated leaven, a leaven stale and sour, exchanging it for the new leaven that is Jesus the Messiah " (10,2), " living in conformity with Jesus the Messiah " (Phld. = Mg* 3,2). For the same reason, too, at the end of this anti-Judaizing letter he declares that his Archives are Jesus the Messiah, his inviolable Archives are the cross, death and resurrection of Jesus, and the faith that comes to us through him (8,2). Jesus is the total newness, " the high Priest to whom is committed the Holy of Holies, for to him alone are committed the hidden designs of God, he himself being the door of the Father " (9,1).

The thematic unity of Mg. + Phld. is absolute. All the argument turns around the explanatory clause of Mg. 11 (see nr. 28). To warn the Magnesian community facing the Judaizers it was not enough, however, to unmask their tactics, nor even to propose Jesus the Messiah to them as a model of life. Ignatius is not a theoretician who defends himself from his adversaries on a doctrinal level. He is a Christian who has experienced the reality of the Lord and his prophetic presence in the midst of the community (Eph. 6,2). Therefore he invites his community to actualize this experience of the Lord in the Eucharist. Thus, the initial exhortation " to do all things in conformity with God, Jesus the Messiah " (ἐν ὁμονοίᾳ θεοῦ [...] Ἰησοῦ Χριστοῦ) (Mg. 6,1b.e) culminates in the repeated call to unity and to " run together as to one sanctuary of God, as to one altar, to one Jesus the Messiah, who came forth from One Father and has returned and is with the One " (Mg. 7,2); likewise, the final exhortation is a fresh invitation " to partake of one Eucharist, for one is the Flesh of our Lord Jesus the Messiah, and one the cup to unite his Blood, and one the altar, in order that whatever you do, you may do it in conformity with God " (Phld. = Mg* 4ab.d).

Summarizing all this we can say that the primitive letter to the Magnesians is full of landmarks which are the insistent invitations to realize the perfect unity of all the members of the community with Jesus the Messiah (see nr. 86). The experience of Jesus in the Eucharist polarizes all the members into a single Body. This experience of unity is the best defence against sowers of division, perverse teachings, noxious weeds, vain doctrines, etc. (cf. Mg. 8,1; 9,1; 11; Phld. 2-3,1.3; 6,2).

154. Of the two letters of an anti-Gnostic character, the one to the *Trallians* constitutes a kind of thematic sketch for Eph*. In spite of its brevity, in regard to Eph*, Tr. too contains the explanatory clause of the exhortation we found in Magnesians:

" Not because I have learned that there is any such thing in your midst, but I warn you beforehand (προφυλάσσω ὑμᾶς) since you are my beloved, for I foresee the snares of the devil ..." (Tr. 8,1).

As we gather from the letter itself, the Gnostics escaped into speculations and lucubrations on the heavenly regions (Tr. 5). Ignatius calls them " heretics " (" separated " from the Christian community, 6,1) who call themselves " Christians " deceitfully, "interweaving their own doctrines with Jesus the Messiah to win credibility " among the faithful (6,2). Concretely, they hold that Jesus " suffered apparently " (10), for they could not admit that the Saviour from above could be contaminated with Matter, as we know from documents of the same sect.

To fight them Ignatius employed a similar strategy to the one we pointed out in Magnesians, though adapted to the particular circumstances of Gnostic propaganda and its contents. He does not limit himself to unmasking them, calling them " foreign weeds " and their fraudulent doctrine " deadly drug mixed with honeyed wine " (Tr. 6), " vile offshoots that engender a deadly fruit " (11,1); neither does he content himself with the formulation of warnings, such as " keep themselves away from them " (6,1c), " beware of such " (7,1a), " turn a deaf ear " (9,1a), " shun those vile offshoots " (11,1a).

Ignatius wields arguments. The chief one, directed against the Gnostic's escapism, is the human reality of Jesus, above all his death:

" Turn a deaf ear, therefore, when anyone speaks to you without mentioning Jesus the Messiah, of David's stock, son of Mary, who was really born, ate and drank, was really persecuted under Pontius Pilate, really crucified and died — in the sight of the inhabitants of heaven, earth and the underworld —, who also really rose from the dead (his own Father having raised him up), who also in like fashion will raise us who believe in him (his Father, I say, through the Messiah, Jesus) apart from whom we have no real life " (Tr. 9).

As secondary argument Ignatius adduces his chains and his free acceptance of martyrdom (Tr. 10: see nr. 150).

Neither does he remain on the theoretical level. Ignatius invites the community to " partake of the Christian food exclusively " (Tr. 6,1b), to " cling inseparably to God, Jesus the Messiah ", " within the precinct of the altar ", that is, the Eucharistic community, without being " puffed up " at possessing esoteric knowledge (7,1bc.2ab). At the centre of his exposition is always the Eucharist, the true experience of the human reality of Jesus:

" Do you therefore arm yourselves with gentleness and recover yourselves through faith, which is the Flesh of the Lord, and through love, which is the Blood of Jesus the Messiah. Let no one of you bear a grudge against his neighbour. Give no pretext to the pagans, lest by reason of a few foolish persons God's own community be outraged, for ' Woe unto him through whose vanity my name is outraged by some ' (cf. Is. 52,5) " (Tr. 8,1d-2).

Faith represents the commitment to the human life of the Lord, love of one's neighbour the commitment to the death of Jesus. The Gnostics reject both Hence Ignatius says " they are not the Father's planting: for if they had been, they would appear as branches of the cross, and their fruit would be incorruptible " (Tr. 11,1c-2b).

Ignatius' exhortation to the Trallians, with respect to the one to the Magnesians, has taken a notable turn. He does not exhort them to " do all things in conformity with God, Jesus the Messiah " (Mg. 6,1), to " live in conformity with the Messiah, Jesus " (8,2), etc., but to remain within the community (Tr. 7,2a), to " abide in mutual concord (ἐν τῇ ὁμονοίᾳ ὑμῶν) and in common prayer " (12,2c), to " love one another with undivided heart " (13,2c). Against the Gnostics who are " separated " (" heretics ") and " unclean " (" without the precinct of the altar ") he invites the community to remain "clinging inseparably to God, Jesus the Messiah", to "be clean" (7,1bc.2ab), so that they may "be found blameless" (13,3d). Against the Judaizers, on the contrary, Ignatius exhorted the Magnesians not to live according to the Law but according to God, that is, Jesus the Messiah, our true life. The reason of this change is clear: facing the Gnostics whose communities were detached from the Christian church because they do not confess the true presence of the Lord in the Eucharistic meetings, Ignatius exhorts the Trallians not to separate themselves from the community which is the meeting place where the human reality of Jesus is experienced.

155.   But it is above all in the letter addressed to the community of *Ephesus*, capital of the province of Asia, that Ignatius develops more in detail his anti-Gnostic exhortation. The body of the letter is constructed in a concentric pattern (see nr. 126): an initial aim and a concluding one, three warnings at the beginning, centre and end of the exposition, two constatations or explanations of the meaning of the exhortation, placed symmetrically before and after the central exposition.

While in the letters to the Magnesians and Trallians the explanatory clause was placed in the centre of the exposition, in the letter to the Ephesians there appear two clauses: one, at the beginning, after the first warning (Eph. 5,2a-c + 3a-e), namely Eph. 6,2-9,3 (Αὐτὸς μὲν οὖν 'Ονήσιμος ὑπερεπαινεῖ ὑμῶν τὴν ἐν θεῷ εὐταξίαν ... ῎Εγνων δὲ παροδεύσαντάς τινας ἐκεῖθεν, ἔχοντας κακὴν διδαχήν ...), and the other towards the end, before the third warning (Sm. = Eph* 6,1), namely Sm. = Eph* 4-5 (Ταῦτα δὲ παραινῶ ὑμῖν, ἀγαπητοί, εἰδώς, ὅτι καὶ ὑμεῖς οὕτως ἔχετε · προφυλάσσω δὲ ὑμᾶς ...). Between both explanations is to be found the long central exposition (I. Part: Eph. 11-15; II. Part: Eph. 18-19 + Sm. 1-3) divided in two by the third warning which is placed in the centre of the body of the letter (Eph. 16-17).

The first explanation has no parallel in the other letters. It starts by verifying the excellent state of the Ephesian community:

"Indeed Onesimus himself praises above mesure your orderly conduct according to God, that is, that you all live according to truth, and no sectarianism (αἵρεσις) has a home among you; nay, you do not even listen to any one else but to Jesus the Messiah who goes on really speaking (to you)" (Eph. 6,2).

Jesus continues to speak, through prophecy, in the midst of the Ephesian community.

Next Ignatius alludes to the Gnostics, who deceitfully try to pass themselves off as Christians, while acting in a manner unworthy of God (Eph. 7,1ab). Repeatedly he insists that the community should avoid them like wild beasts, for they are rabid dogs that bite furtively (7,1cd); they should beware of them, because their bites are hard to cure (7,1e). Then follows a hymn to Jesus, the only Physician (7,2). After this digression, he goes on insisting:

" Let no one, therefore, induce you into error as indeed you have not been induced, for you belong wholly to God. Since there is no rivalry rooted among you, which has power to torment you, it is a sign you live according to God " (Eph. 8,1).

Up to the present he has not revealed the ultimate reason for this persistent warning. Correlatively with the first period, starting by Αὐτὸς μὲν οὖν, he now opens a second period, Ἔγνων δὲ, in which he explains the pressing reason that has moved him to write to them:

" But I have learned that some from there (from Syria) passed through, bringing a perverse teaching, whom you did not allow to sow seed in you; you stopped your ears, so as not to receive the seed sown by them ..." (Eph. 9,1).

On the one hand, in the community of Ephesus there still reigned perfect harmony, for Jesus went on being its only Master; on the other, these same Gnostic propagandists, who had sown deep discord in the community of Syria, had already passed through Ephesus, probably on the way to Rome, but the Ephesians showed themselves to be impervious to their deceitful doctrines. Foreseeing fresh assaults, Ignatius writes them a letter.

Then follows the central exposition. This one concluded, to remove any doubt as to the tone of the exhortation, he composes a new explanatory clause after the pattern of those we have examined in Magnesians and Trallians:

" I am recommending these things to you, beloved, although I know that you maintain the same attitude. But I warn you beforehand (προφυλάσσω δὲ ὑμᾶς) against these wild beasts in human form, whom you should not only not receive, but, if possible, even avoid meeting; only pray for them, if haply they may repent — a difficult thing! " (Sm. = Eph* 4,1).

Unlike the Judaizers who were not completely separated from the community, the Gnostics had already held aloof from the Eucharistic meetings, as they would not confess that the Eucharist is the real Flesh of the Saviour (Sm. 7,1). They totally avoided commitment to the brothers, had no care for the fraternal agape and the needs of the community members (6,2). They were vain about their esoteric knowledge and sure of individual salvation, as a result of a unilateral and distorted experience of the Saviour (6,1; cf. Tr. 5 and Eph. 13,2-14,1; 19,2-3).

Ignatius' strategy against them is very similar to that evidenced in the letter to the Trallians. The defamatory appellatives he gives them are stronger, if possible, that those we found in Tr. He brands them, as we have just seen, as " wild beasts in human form ", camouflaged " Christians ", " rabid dogs ", " heterodox ", " disbelievers ", " contrary to God's plan ", " vain " about their doctrines (Eph. 5,3; 7,1; 8; Sm. = Eph* 2; 6,1-2, etc.); their teaching is " perverse ", " weeds of the devil ", " empowered by Satan ", " malodorous " (Eph. 9,1; 10,3; 13,1; 16,2; 17,1, etc.). Ignatius' warnings are incessant: " you should avoid them like wild beasts ", " beware of them "; " let no one induce you into error ", " do not let yourselves be anointed with the malodorous teaching of the Chief of this world ", " do not be deceived ", " neither should you receive nor meet them ", " it is fitting to keep yourselves away from any such people and not to speak about them either in private or in public " (Eph. 5,2; 7,1; 8,1; 16,1; 17,1; Sm. = Eph* 4,1; 6,1; 7,2).

Here, too, he adduces arguments. He uncovers their origin: their error arises from the unawareness of the Chief of this world about three loudly proclaimed mysteries, the virginity of Mary, the birth of Jesus and his death on the cross (Eph. 19,1). This datum is new with regard to Tr. Later we shall weigh up this mythical language.

He develops his chief argument, the Christological creed of his own Syrian community and the Ephesian one, more fully than in Tr. Both creeds are exact parallels (see nr. 20). The crux of the argument is Jesus' passion and death on the cross:

" For he suffered all these things for our sake, that we might be saved. And he suffered really, just as he really raised himself;[393] not

---

[393] ἀνέστησεν ἑαυτόν (see also Rom. 6,1): Ign. uses ἀνίστημι in the metapho-

as some unbelievers say, that ' he merely suffered in appearance ', being themselves ' mere appearance ';[394] and as they mean so shall it happen to them, since they will be bodiless and ghost-like shapes " (Sm. = Eph* 2).

The Gnostics did not confess that Jesus is " bearer of a mortal body " (σαρκοφόρος), therefore they are " bearers of death " (νεκρο-φόρος). Now, he argues logically, that

" if these things were done by our Lord merely in appearance, then I in my chains, too, am in appearance! And why then have I deliver-ed myself over to death, to perish by fire or sword or wild beasts? (Sm. = Eph* 4,2) ".

Like Jesus, who did not flee from death when faced with the accusation of sedition on the part of the Jewish and Roman author-ities, Ignatius has presented himself willingly to the Roman auth-orities to avoid reprisals falling on his community in Syria. All this would have no sense if Jesus had not really died.

But arguments are not enough. Ignatius passes to the level of experience. He is aware that the Gnostics had reached such a statement because they had avoided — under pretext of spiritual-ism — concrete commitment to the needs of the brothers. They had separated themselves from the community, so as not to be obliged to confess the reality of Jesus and to have to act accordingly. For this reason, in the centre of his exposition, there is also the invitation to be assiduous in frequenting meetings of Thanksgiving and praise, for, when the community meet together frequently, the powers of Satan are destroyed and his attempts to ruin it are neutralized before the concordant adhesion to Jesus of its members (ἐν τῇ ὁμονοίᾳ ὑμῶν τῆς πίστεως, Eph. 13,1). Faith and love, adhe-sion to Jesus and commitment to the brothers until death, if necessary, constitute a man-God (14,1: see nr. 149). In open

---

rical sense of " to rise ": Jesus " raised himself "; but to describe the way in which it has happened he uses the verb ἐγείρω in the metaphorical sense of " to rouse, awaken ", that is, " to rise from the dead " (re-surgere: ἀπὸ/ἐκ νεκρῶν, Mg. 9,2; Tr. 9,2): Tr. 9,2 (ὃς καὶ ἀληθῶς ἠγέρθη ἀπὸ νεκρῶν, ἐγείραντος αὐτὸν τοῦ πατρὸς αὐτοῦ); Sm. 7,1 (ἣν [τὴν σάρκα τοῦ σωτῆρος] τῇ χρηστότητι ὁ πατὴρ ἤγειρεν). Ign. seems to distinguish two moments: (1) The Father has awoken Jesus from his death sleep; (2) Jesus " has raised himself " and " stood up ".

[394] See Tr. 10 and Ir., *A. H.* IV. 33,5.

contrast to the esoteric writings of the Gnostics are the Prophets and, in a special way, the Gospel, since through it his passion has been proved and his resurrection definitely settled (Sm. = Eph* 7,2).

Ignatius' purpose in writing to the Ephesians is, therefore, more explicit than the one manifested in the letter to the Trallians. To counteract efficaciously the individualistic and spiritualistic propaganda of the Gnostics, it was not sufficient to denounce their hypocrisy or to appeal to the human reality of Jesus, which was foretold by the Prophets, contained in the Gospel and expressed in the earlier creeds; he had to encourage the whole experience of the Body of the Lord, who has made himself present in the community gathered together to celebrate the Eucharist, and perceptible through the word by means of prophecy.

156. The letter to the *Romans*, unlike the Asian letters, lacks theological subject matter. Although Ignatius knows the community of Rome at least by hearsay (Rom. inscr.; 3,1; 10,1), he has no definite news that Gnostic or Judaizing propaganda had reached it. The motive of the letter is due to other concerns. Ignatius fears the disorderly affection the Roman Christians have for him, which could be brought to bear on official levels upon the Roman authorities against his will (1,2); he asks them to keep silence, and not let themselves be carried away by their attachment to his person (2,1). The Christians of Rome could hinder his martyrdom. For this reason he exhorts them not to show him unseasonable kindness (4,1). He begs them to be indulgent with him (5,3; 6,2), not to hinder him from living, by wishing for him a life that is death; not to make a gift to the world of one who wishes to be God's, nor to seduce him with material things (6,2; see p. 132).

γ) *Appendix: The Plan of God and the plan of the Chief of this world*

157. The confrontation which originated in Syria between Gnostics, Judaizers and the Christian communities arises in ultimate analysis from the radical opposition between God and the World, between life and death (Mg. 5). Ignatius hopes to avoid its ulterior extension among the Asian communities by warning them of the snares of the Chief of this world.

The world is the materialist system (Rom. 6,2, where κόσμος and ὕλη are equivalents) that incarnates the pleasures of this life (7,3) and the powers that govern the present time (οὐδέν με ὠφελήσει τὰ τερπνὰ [395] τοῦ κόσμου οὐδὲ αἱ βασιλεῖαι τοῦ αἰῶνος τούτου, 6,1.) Christianity is hated by the world (3,3), because the Christians have renounced its values (7,1; cf. also 2,2; 3,2; 4,2). The world is the ancient kingdom that began to be overthrown, when God appeared as man (Eph. 19,3). This " system " of values is personified by the Chief of this world (lit. " the Chief/Prince of this time ": Eph. 17,1; 19,1; Mg. 1,2; Tr. 4,2; Rom. 7,1; Phld. 6,2).

Ignatius twice uses the expression " before the time " (πρὸ αἰώνων) referring to the no-time of God to express the predestination of the church of Ephesus (Eph. inscr.) or of the Messiah (Mg. 6,1). In Sm. 1,2 he seems to refer to the definitive, perpetual time: " he raised an ensign for all time " (εἰς τοὺς αἰῶνας). But on two occasions he certainly means the inhabitants of the higher regions (Eph. 8,1; 19,2: τοῖς αἰῶσιν), the sun, the moon and the other heavenly bodies (Eph. 19,2: cf. 13,2; Tr. 5; Sm. 6,1). Ignatius distinguishes between the invisible Chiefs of the higher regions and the visible ones of our world (Sm. 6,1: οἱ ἄρχοντες ὁρατοί τε καὶ ἀόρατοι; cf. Tr. 5,2 and Rom. 5,3), whose absolute representative is " the Chief of this age ". Under his domination meet all " the kingdoms of this age " established within " the boundaries of the earth " (Rom. 6,1).

God and the Chief of this world each have their own plan or project, which are diametrically opposed to each other. Jesus the Messiah personifies the Plan of God:

" I take the initiative of exhorting you to run in agreement with the Plan of God, for Jesus the Messiah also, our unwavering life, is the Plan of the Father (τοῦ πατρὸς ἡ γνώμη) " (Eph. 3,2).

In the concrete, this project consists in true commitment to man in need. Ignatius describes it indirectly in Sm. 6,2, when he brands the Gnostics as being contrary to God's project: πῶς ἐναντίοι εἰσὶν τῇ γνώμῃ τοῦ θεοῦ · περὶ ἀγάπης οὐ μέλει αὐτοῖς, οὐ περὶ χήρας, οὐ περὶ ὀρφανοῦ, οὐ περὶ θλιβομένου, οὐ περὶ δεδεμένου ἢ λελυμένου, οὐ περὶ πεινῶντος ἢ διψῶντος.

---

[395] See critical apparatus, p. 350, l. 18.

19

We have here a detailed description of the concrete attitudes of the Christian community facing the Gnostic praxis. The Gnosis has succeeded in dissociating the human from the divine by means of the dualism, flesh or matter/spirit. Under pretext of an individual salvation of the spirit they evaded temporal realities, thus leaving " this " world at the mercy of the sovereign Chief who rules it.

The Judaizers are also alien to God's project:

" Do not be deceived, my brethren: whoever follows a schismatic, cannot share in the Kingdom of God; whoever lives according to an alien plan (ἐν ἀλλοτρίᾳ γνώμῃ), does not agree entirely with the passion (of the Lord) " (Phld. 3,3).

Ignatius speaks only twice of the Kingdom of God (βασιλεία θεοῦ): here, in the present, in connection with the Judaizers who were sowing schisms (σχίζοντι), inasmuch as they denied that " our life began to shine on the Day of the Lord through him and his death " (Mg. 9,1: cf. 5,2), and again, in Eph. 16,1 in the future, connected with the Gnostics who have ruined the community-home (οἱ οἰκοφθόροι) and, therefore, " will not share in the Kingdom of God ".

In both letters, the allusion to the Kingdom of God occurs in the context of a warning (Μὴ πλανᾶσθε), key piece in the structure of the letters.

God has already inaugurated his Kingdom through the Messiah, Jesus. From the moment in which God appeared in human form, the ancient kingdom (παλαιὰ βασιλεία) has begun to fall apart (Eph. 19,3).

158. The indiscriminate use Ignatius makes of the symbolic personage, " the Chief of this world ", as much in the two letters with anti-Gnostic subject (Eph*, Tr.) as in the one with anti-Judaizing matter (Mg*), has its reasons (see nrs. 15, 17). In him Ignatius personifies the plan contrary to God's Plan, Jesus the Messiah. The Gnostics, who do not recognize the human reality of the Saviour, as well as the Judaizers, who minimize the newness of his resurrection, both second the plan of the Chief of the present order.

The Chief of this world wants to hinder at all costs that Christianity be propagated, so as not to deprive him of his adepts. His plan is to destroy the Christian community before it succeeds in undermining the foundations of his power over men. He takes advantage of the pluralism of options that unhappily already exist among the Christian communities, and tries by every means to sow disunion and division among them (cf. Mg. 1,2).

On the one hand, he takes sides with the Law: With every kind of evil tricks and ambushes, he tries to distress the Christians with his ideology (τῇ γνώμῃ αὐτοῦ), so that they wax weak in their communion (Phld. 6,2). On the other hand, he sides with the Lawless, the clever and wise men, who are scandalized by the literalness of the cross (Eph. 17-18), because it will lead them to renounce their esoteric teachings which are contrary to God's plan (Sm. = Eph* 6). Being unaware of the three loudly proclaimed mysteries that have moved the universe (Eph. 19,3), both the Chief and his followers hold that Jesus suffered only in appearance and consequently deny that through his passion he became the model of " the achieved man " (Sm. = Eph* 4,2-5,2; cf. 2; Tr. 10).

But he is not content to divide the communities and set them against each other. To prevent Ignatius bearing witness to belief in Jesus the Messiah, he tries to convince him of his heroism and entices him to vanity and impatience (Tr. 4), so as to tear him in pieces before the wild beasts do, and to corrupt his intention of reaching God through martyrdom (τὴν εἰς θεόν μου γνώμην, Rom. 7,1). For this reason Ignatius insists to the Roman Christians that they must not collaborate with him, but rather take his side, that is, God's (ib.). He tells them clearly that his decision to write to them was not inspired by human motives but in agreement with God's plan (κατὰ γνώμην θεοῦ, 8,3).

The Plan of God is, therefore, Jesus the Messiah. Against the Judaizers, whose norm is the Mosaic Law, Ignatius proclaims as norm the *Messiah*, Jesus, our God; against the Gnostics, whose norm is the spirit free from all materiality, he proclaims as norm *Jesus*, true God and true Man. The plan of the Chief of this world consists in fomenting rivalry among the Christian communities, either by means of Judaizing propaganda that will end up by suffocating the Spirit and paralyse the community once more submitted to laws and norms, or else by means of Gnostic propaganda that will leave the community without the Spirit because they tried to separate the Saviour from Jesus, the Spirit from the true Man, and would dissolve it into a thousand speculations and lucubrations. Thus, once the community paralysed and the spiritual men separated from it, the Chief of the present order will have a free hand to govern the world according to his own principles: power, money and pleasure.

b) *The forger's motives for writing his seven letters*

We shall now attempt to find out the motives that induced the forger to carry out his deep recasting of the Ignatian epistolary. We distinguish here between general motives, applicable to the whole compilation, and particular ones, specific of certain letters, which later will enable us to perceive what, in ultimate analysis, led him to achieve his purpose.

α) *General motives applicable to the whole compilation*

The chief motive of the genuine letters was the problem of unity, which was troubled either by the conservative tendencies of the Judaizers, or by the innovative ones of the Gnostics. The forger also has problems about unity. Are they the same as those of Ignatius?

159.   We shall start by examining the active term ἕνωσις that, as we have seen, polarizes around it the triple model of unity proclaimed by Ignatius among the Asian communities. Ignatius used this term preferably (three times) in the letter to the Magnesians, against the Judaizers who could sow divisions among the faithful (Mg. 1,2; Phld. 4b and 8,1); only once in the anti-Gnostic letter to the Trallians (Tr. 11,2) and not at all in Ephesians. The forger employed it four times as well: three times in the sense of active union with the bishop and once with a different meaning, to designate " the matrimonial union " that should be made with the bishop's consent (Pol. 5,2). We leave aside this case that supposes an anachronism in Ignatius' times.

The first mention occurs in the clause forged to interrupt Mg*:

" Submit to the bishop and to one another, as Jesus Christ did humanly to the Father, and as the Apostles did to Christ and the Father and the Spirit, so that there may be both material and spiritual union " (Mg. 13,2: see nr. 57).

The reassumptive function of this interpolated clause has led the forger to summarize in it the theme of union enounced in the genuine introduction of Mg* (Mg. 1,2): To the request of Ignatius, ἐν αἷς ἕνωσιν εὔχομαι σαρκὸς καὶ πνεύματος Ἰησοῦ Χριστοῦ (1,2), the forger responds with a modal clause, ἵνα ἕνωσις ᾖ σαρκική τε καὶ πνευματική (13,2). The parallel is, however, only external. Ignatius invited the Christians to realize in the community the " union that holds between flesh and spirit of Jesus the Messiah ", that is, that the community constitutes an organic body externally recognizable (the united assembly) and inwardly joined (the experience of communion that the Spirit confers on the members of the community: cf. Tr. 11,2; Phld. 4). An individual like Ignatius can " foment union " among the communities (Phld. 8,1), but he cannot substitute the cohesive strength that irradiates from Jesus, truly present in his members (Eph. 6,2). In the interpolator's times, once the inward action of Jesus has lost practically all its cohesive strength, what really mattered was the external union of the community members around the bishop, a union " materially " recognizable, as well the mental union with him as sole representative of God on earth, a " spiritual " or moral union. The bishop has become the visible model of imitation (cf. Eph. 1,3d; Mg. 3,2bc).

In the other two passages in which the forger quotes ἕνωσις, Phld. 7,2f (see nr. 103) and Pol. 1,2 (see nr. 67), he also uses it in this sense: the centre of union of the community has come to be the bishop.

If we now pay attention to the equivalent terms ἐνόω and ἑνότης, we shall reach the same conclusion. The first, ἐνόω, is predicated by Ignatius of the spiritual unity of the risen Jesus with the Father (Sm. 3,3) and above all of the perfect unity of the community with God and his precepts (Eph. inscr.; Mg. 14; Rom. inscr.). The forger, on the contrary, predicates it of the unity to be realized with the bishop (Mg. 6,2f). [396] The second term, ἑνότης, in Ignatius' genuine text means the complete unity of the assembled community (Eph. 4,2: 2x; Phld. 2,2; 3,2), the unity with God (Phld. 8,1; 9,1; Pol. 8,3), Jesus the Messiah (Phld. 5,2). For the interpolator it implies union with the bishop (Eph. 5,1, a copy of 4,2; and Sm. 12,2: ἐν ἑνότητι θεοῦ καὶ ὑμῶν includes unity with the bishop, presbytery, etc.).

---

[396] We leave out Mg. 7,1 (ἡνωμένος ὤν), critically uncertain: see critical apparatus, p. 357, l. 2.

160. The shifting of the community centre from Jesus to the bishop we have just observed is due to the new situation that has arisen in some Asian communities, above all in the Philadelphian one. The adversaries of the forger are no longer the Gnostics nor the Judaizers, but certain groups within the community that still contested the growing all-embracing authority of the bishop. If we except the generic advice the forger gives to Polycarp, οἱ δοκοῦντες ἀξιόπιστοι εἶναι καὶ ἑτεροδιδασκαλοῦντες μή σε καταπλησσέτωσαν (Pol. 3,1), that imitates Phld. 2,2 (λύκοι ἀξιόπιστοι) or else Tr. 6,2 (καταξιοπιστευόμενοι), and draws inspiration from the several passages in which Ignatius speaks of perverse teachings and doctrines (ἑτεροδοξέω: Sm. 6,2; -ία: Mg. 8,1; κακὴ διδαχή: Eph. 9,1; κ. διδασκαλία: 16,2-17,1; κακοδιδασκαλία: Phld. 2,1), the forger does not appear to have doctrinal problems, but only practical ones.

The terms of "ignorance" (ἄγνοια: Eph. 19,3; ἀγνοέω: 17,2; Tr. 6,2; Sm. 5,1), "incredulity" (ἀπιστία: Eph. 8,2 [2x]; ἄπιστος: Mg. 5,2; Tr. 10 [equivalent to ἄθεος]; Sm. 2; 5,3; ἀπιστέω: Eph. 18,1), "blasphemy" (βλασφημέω: Sm. 5,2; in the passive sense cf. Tr. 8,2 [2x]; βλασφημία: Eph. 10,2) with which Ignatius labels both Judaizers and Gnostics, above all the latter who "do not confess" the reality of Jesus in his incarnation or in the Eucharist (μὴ ὁμολογεῖν: Sm. 5,2; 7,1), for both "deny" either the novelty of the resurrection (ὅ τινες ἀρνοῦνται: Mg. 9,1, the Judaizers) or that Jesus has become "the achieved man" through his passion (ὅν τινες ἀγνοοῦντες ἀρνοῦνται: Sm. 4,2-5,1, the Gnostics), all these terms do not occur in the interpolated passages.

Neither are the depreciatory appellatives, "weeds of the devil", "vile offshoots", "wild beasts", "rabid dogs", etc. (cf. Eph. 10,3; Tr. 6,1; Phld. 3,1; Tr. 11,1; Eph. 7,1; 16,1; 17,1; Sm. 4,1), "antiquated fables/practices", "deteriorated, stale and sour leaven" (Mg. 8,1; 10,2), with which he qualifies Gnostics and Judaizers, to be found in the passages proper to the forger.

Every time the interpolator hints at the existence of possible friction or blames some members of the community he relates this either to the person of the bishop: "Let us strive not to resist the bishop" (Eph. 5,3f), respect the "silent" bishop (6,1; Phld. 1,1), "it is fitting not to seek to profit by the bishop's youth" (Mg. 3,1), "to obey without dissimulation" (3,2), "forasmuch as they do not gather together in a valid way as is prescribed " (4d); or else he relates it to Ignatius or his collaborators: " some tried to deceive me humanly " (Phld. 7,1), " treated with dishonour " his companions coming from Cilicia and Syria (11,1). None of these situations appear in the genuine passages.

161. The main preoccupation of the interpolator is the recalcitrant attitude of some members of the community who " do everything without the bishop " (Mg. 4bc; Sm. 9,1e). Hence: (1) His insistent appeal to " do nothing without the bishop and the presbyters " (Mg. 7,1b; Tr. 2,2a; Sm. 8,1-2; Pol. 4,1: with the verb πράσσω; Mg. 13,1; Phld. 7,2; Sm. 8,2; Pol. 5,2: with the verb ποιέω). (2) The repeated use of such locutions as ἄνευ τοῦ ἐπισκόπου κτλ. (Mg. 7,1b; Tr. 2,2a; Pol. 4,1), χωρὶς ἐπισκόπου κτλ. (Mg. 4b; Tr. 3,1; 7,2c; Phld. 7,2; Sm. 8,1-2), λάθρα ἐπισκόπου κτλ. (Sm. 9,1e). (3) The tendency to soften such expressions with a parenthetic sentence referring either to the community (ὅπερ καὶ ποιεῖτε: Eph. 4,1b; ὥσπερ ποιεῖτε: Tr. 2,2a), or to Polycarp (ὥσπερ καὶ ποιεῖς: Pol. 1,2; ὅπερ οὐδὲ πράσσεις: 4,1; cf. Pol. Phil. 13,1: ὅπερ ποιήσω). (4) The consequent explanation that the bishop, in his turn, must do " nothing without God's approval " (μηδὲ σὺ ἄνευ θεοῦ τι πρᾶσσε: Pol. 4,1), since the earthly and visible bishop represents the universal and invisible Bishop (Eph. 1,3c; 5,3fg; 6,1; Mg. 3,1-2; 6,1c; Tr. 3,1; Sm. 8,1; 9,1cd). (5) Finally, the explanation that the model of submission to the bishop for the community is the submission of Jesus Christ to the Father (ὥσπερ οὖν ὁ κύριος ἄνευ τοῦ πατρὸς οὐδὲν ἐποίησεν κτλ., Mg. 7,1), forasmuch as he is entirely submitted to the Father humanly (κατὰ σάρκα, 13,2; cf. Eph. 5,1; Phld. 7,2; Sm. 8,1).

Some members of the Philadelphian community have even tried — according to the interpolator's fiction — to profit by Ignatius' passing there to win him over to their contesting faction. However Ignatius was warned beforehand through the Spirit of these conflicting circumstances and has proclaimed to them in form of prophecy — a fresh forgery — that they should " do nothing without the bishop, etc. " (Phld. 7,1-2). They are the same people that later on affronted the followers of Ignatius from Cilicia and Syria (11,1k).

On the contrary, Ignatius never alludes to internal disorder in the Asian communities, but continues to recognize: (1) The

Ephesians' "orderly conduct according to God" (Eph. 6,2), for they "do everything in conformity with Jesus the Messiah" (ἐν Ἰησοῦ γὰρ Χριστῷ πάντα πράσσετε, 8,2); thus he pledges himself with them to "do everything in the conviction that Jesus dwells in us" (πάντα οὖν ποιῶμεν ὡς αὐτοῦ ἐν ἡμῖν κατοικοῦντος, 15,3) and praises the community for the hospitality they offered to the messengers from Syria as they were "servants of God the Messiah" (καλῶς ἐποιήσατε ὑποδεξάμενοι ὡς διακόνους Χριστοῦ θεοῦ, Sm. = Eph* 10,1); (2) The *Magnesians*' "well-ordered love according to God" (Mg. 1,1) which gave rise to the exhortation "to do everything in conformity with God Jesus the Messiah" (ἐν ὁμονοίᾳ θεοῦ Ἰησοῦ Χριστοῦ ... σπουδάζετε πάντα πράσσειν, Mg. 6,1: see nrs. 86f.); (3) The blameless and undiscriminating disposition of the *Trallians* (Tr. 1,1).

And what is more, in the body of each of the three Asian letters Ignatius takes a special interest in pointing out that the exhortation he addresses them is not due to the existence of any divisions or heresies in their midst, but to the urgent need of warning them against the imminent assault of the Gnostic and Judaizing propagandists who have moved from Syria to Rome and would probably try on the way through Asia to sow dissension among the Christian communities (Sm. = Eph* 4,1: cf. Eph. 9,1; Mg. 11 and Tr. 8,1). The only time Ignatius uses the verb πράσσω to reproach someone for something concerns the Gnostics who deceitfully try to pass themselves off as Christians, but "perform actions that are alien and unworthy of God" (ἄλλα τινὰ πράσσοντες ἀνάξια θεοῦ, Eph. 7,1).

Keeping in mind what we have previously noted with regard to the interpolator and his ways we can state the following oppositions: (1) Ignatius does not use the verbs πράσσω and ποιέω to recriminate against the communities nor to invite them to act in accord with any person in authority, but exclusively to exhort them to do everything in conformity with the unique model who is Jesus the Messiah (Eph. 4,2; 8,2; 14,2; 15; Mg. 6,1; Phld. 4d; 8,2). (2) With the use of the prepositions ἄνευ and χωρίς Ignatius endeavours to manifest the intimate relationship that exists between Jesus, the Head and our life, and the community members (ἄνευ: Tr. 11,2; χωρίς: Eph. 11,2; Mg. 9,2 and Tr. 9,1-2; in 11,2 it functions as adverb); while the interpolator uses them to bind the community to the bishop and the other hierarchical grades. (3) Ignatius makes use of parenthetical sentences to confirm the resistance of the community in face of the deceits of the Gnostics (ὥσπερ οὐδὲ ἐξαπατᾶσθε, Eph. 8,1) or to check their perfect dispositions before God (ὥσπερ καὶ ἀρέσκετε, Rom. 2,1); while the interpolator uses them to corroborate the strict verticality that should exist between God, the bishop and the community. (4) According to Ignatius, the representative of God the Father on earth is none other that Jesus the Messiah, " our God " (Eph. inscr.; 15,3; 18,2; Mg. 6,1 reconstr.; 15; Tr. 1,2b + 2,2b reconstr.; 7,1; 11,2; Rom. inscr. [2x]; 3,3; 6,3; 9,1; Phld. 6,3; Sm. 1,1; 10,1; Pol. 8,3), " God manifested in human form " (θεοῦ ἀνθρωπίνως φανερουμένου, Eph. 19,3), " constituted God from human weakness " (ἐν σαρκὶ γενόμενος θεός, 7,2). (5) Finally, Ignatius never speaks of a submission of Jesus the Messiah to God as model for the community, since it is the very imitation of God Jesus the Messiah which causes us to live not in human fashion, but in the Christian way (Tr. 1,2 + 2,2 + 2,1 reconstr.: see nr. 89). [397]

To express this dependent attitude of the community towards those constituted in hierarchy the forger uses the verb ὑποτάσσω 9 times (Eph. 2,2e; 5,3g; Mg. 2c; 13,2; Tr. 2,1a.2b; 13,2b; Pol. 2,1 and 6,1c) against not once in Ignatius. [398] Other verbs pertaining to the same semantic field used exclusively by the interpolator are ὑπακούω (Eph. 20,2), ἐπακούω (Mg. 3,2), ἐγκεράννυμι (Eph. 5,1), συγχωρέω (Mg. 3,1), συναρμόζω (Eph. 4,1c), συνευριθμίζω (Phld. 1,2), τιμάω (11,2; Sm. 9,1d), προσβλέπω (Eph. 6,1), ἀναψύξω (2,1h; Tr. 12,2d), as also the locutions ἐντροπὴν ἀπονέμειν (Mg. 3,1), ἐν ὁμοιότητι εἶναι (Eph. 1,3d), ἐν ἑνὶ εἶναι (Phld. inscr[b].). In strict dependence of the anterior Ignatian context he employs συντρέχω (Eph. 4,1a: cf. 3,2c; Ign. also uses it in Mg. 7,2 and Pol. 6,1g) and ἀντιτάσσω (Eph. 5,3f: cf. 5,3e, a quotation from Prov. 3,34). Furthermore, in common with Ignatius but with a very different connotation (see nr. 101) he uses ἀκολουθέω (Sm. 8,1: cf. Phld. 2,1 and 3,3), ἐντρέπω (Tr. 3,1.2 and Sm. 8,1: cf. Mg. 6,2), προσέχω (Phld. 7,1 and Pol. 6,1a: cf. Tr. 4,1 and Sm. 7,2), δέχομαι (Eph.

---

[397] See the Ignatian use of μιμητής in Eph. 1,1; 10,3 and Rom. 6,3, plagiarized by the interpolator in Phld. 7,2.

[398] In Eph. 2,2, however, he uses ὑποταγή to stress the perfect union between the community and Jesus.

6,1 and Phld. 11,1: cf. Rom. 9,3), ἐνόω (see nr. 159), φοβέω (Eph. 6,1: cf. 11,1; Tr. 4,1; 5,1; Rom. 1,2 and Phld. 5,1) and ἀγαπάω (Eph. 1,3d and 21,1d), this last directed in both occasions to the person of the bishop; while Ignatius predicates it actively of his or the community's love for God, Jesus, the Prophets, himself and the Christians among themselves (Eph. 9,2; 15,3; Mg. 6,2; Tr. 3,3; 13,2; Phld. 5,1.2; Sm. 9,2, etc.).

162. The interpolator corrects Ignatius' archaic ecclesiology with a much more developed one. To the single bishop, supervisor and coordinator of all the communities of a Roman province (Syria: Ignatius; Asia: Polycarp), he opposes the monarchical bishop, at the head of each of the important communities (Ephesus, Magnesia, Tralles, Philadelphia, Smyrna, Antioch of Syria and adjacent cities, the bishops established to the ends of the earth); with the presbytery or senate of the community elders (even though never mentioned by Ignatius) he contrasts a presbytery depending on the bishop, as his spiritual crown. Even comparing his ecclesiology with that of the Didascalia, from which it takes inspiration (see nrs. 115-125), an ulterior evolution is perceptible: the Didascalia keeps on considering the presbyters as elders of the community, below the bishop with his deacon/s; the interpolator already assigns them the second place after the bishop, above the deacons, as in the Apostolic Constitutions, which also depends on the Didascalia. This detail is very significant, since it excludes the possibility that the interpolator simply tried to transplant the ecclesiology of the Didascalist into the Ignatian letters in order to introduce it into Asia. There existed in Asia, at the time he interpolated the letters of Ignatius, an ecclesiastical organization slightly more developed than the one in the Didascalia. This obliged him to adapt the analogies of this supposedly apostolic writing to his concrete situation.

Will, then, his manipulation of the Ignatian letters correspond to the need of providing a basis to an already existing but slightly wavering ecclesiology? The repeated statements (a) that " the bishops, established in the most distant regions, are included in the plan of Jesus Christ " (ἐν Ἰησοῦ Χριστοῦ γνώμῃ εἰσίν, Eph. 3,2e); (b) that " the bishop with the presbyters and deacons who are with him, were appointed by Jesus Christ's disposition, whom he has established and confirmed according to his own design by his Holy Spirit " (ἀποδεδειγμένοις ἐν γνώμῃ Ἰησοῦ Χριστοῦ, οὓς κατὰ τὸ ἴδιον θέλημα ἐστήριξεν ἐν βεβαιωσύνῃ τῷ ἁγίῳ αὐτοῦ πνεύματι, Phld. inscr[b].); (c) that the pretended bishop of Philadelphia does not possess the ministry for the common weal " by his own initiative nor by any human agency nor yet for vanity, but by the love of God the Father and the Lord Jesus Christ " (1,1), etc.; all this arises from the need the forger feels to prove the apostolic (allusion to the Didascalia) and, what is more, divine origin of the hierarchical trilogy.

163. As for the twofold petition that we verified in the genuine letters — petition for prayers for himself and for the church in Syria — it may be queried if the interpolator amplified and/or altered it to suit his new motivations.

The *first* petition (see nr. 151) addressed to the communities of Asia and Rome, " Remember me in your/s prayer/s " (Μνημονεύετέ μου ἐν τῇ/ταῖς προσευχῇ/-αῖς ὑμῶν, Eph. 21,1; Mg. 14; Tr. 13,1; Rom. 9,1), does not appear in the spurious letters written in Troas with materials taken from the authentic ones redacted in Smyrna. The summary the forger left in Eph. 21, in spite of keeping to the original tenor of the phrase (Μνημονεύετέ μου), empties it by an addition that bears the interpolator's typical mark (ὡς καὶ ὑμῶν Ἰησοῦς Χριστός). On one occasion only does he place in Ignatius' mouth a petition for prayers to the Ephesians that Jesus Christ may consider him worthy to write them a second letter and that this may be allowed by the officer in charge of him. Of course, as was to be expected, it would have no effect, since it was not the officer's will or, which comes to the same thing, it was not the will of the interpolator himself. Compare the well-known condition to which he has subjected the writing of the second tract (or 2Eph.!), Ἐάν με καταξιώσῃ Ἰησοῦς Χριστὸς ἐν τῇ προσευχῇ ὑμῶν καὶ θέλημα ᾖ of Eph. 20,1 with the excuse arising from the impossibility of writing to all the churches, to be found in Pol. 8,1, Ἐπεὶ οὖν πάσαις ταῖς ἐκκλησίαις οὐκ ἠδυνήθην γράψαι διὰ τὸ ἐξαίφνης πλεῖν με ἀπὸ Τρωάδος εἰς Νεάπολιν, ὡς τὸ θέλημα προστάσσει. Similarly, none of the verbs employed by Ignatius to express his *desire* (θέλω: 11x; ζητέω: 1x; γένοιτό μοι: 5x; ἐλπίζω: 2x; πιστεύω: 4x; ἐλεέω: 2x), are used by the interpolator.

As for Ignatius' *martyrdom* (see nr. 150) the forger scarcely notices it. In Phld. 7,2b (cf. 5,1d original), μάρτυς δέ μοι, ἐν ᾧ δέδεμαι, he alludes to his chains, to give greater credence to the witnesses invoked in favour of his cause, namely Jesus and the Spirit. In Pol. 2,3d he does no more that copy Sm. 10,2a, changing — as usual — τὸ πνεῦμά μου for ἐγὼ (see nrs. 47, and 70).

The only allusion of the interpolator to the *imitation* of Jesus (see nr. 151), with his characteristic mark, is to be found in Phld. 7,2h: μιμηταὶ γίνεσθε Ἰησοῦ Χριστοῦ, ὡς καὶ αὐτὸς τοῦ πατρὸς αὐτοῦ. This does not prevent him from presenting in other places the bishop (Eph. 1,3d) or the deacon (Sm. 12,1ef) as the model to be imitated. The theme of discipleship he touches only in Pol. 2,1: καλοὺς μαθητὰς ἐὰν φιλῇς, to minimize it. According to Ignatius, Jesus is the only Master (Eph. 15,1; Mg. 9,1.2); " disciple " can only be predicated of the one who follows in his footsteps so as to give his life if necessary; for the forger, however, Polycarp is a master with his own disciples. In the letter addressed to Polycarp, he will place in Ignatius' mouth a series of imperatives that contrasts with Ignatius' way of exhortation: that Polycarp give himself to unceasing prayer (προσευχαῖς σχόλαζε ἀδιαλείπτοις, Pol. 1,3), that he be given more judgement than he has (αἰτοῦ σύνεσιν πλείονα ἧς ἔχεις, ibid.), that invisible things be revealed to him (τὰ δὲ ἀόρατα αἴτει ἵνα σοι φανερωθῇ, 2,2: cf. on the contrary Tr. 5,2 and Rom. 5,3), etc.

Ignatius' characteristic expression to denote the aim of discipleship, θεοῦ ἐπιτύχω (10x) and equivalents (8x), is applied by the forger only once to Polycarp to designate that his ultimate fight is also imminent:

" As a pilot calls on wind and a storm-tossed mariner on a haven, so the present moment call on you to attain to God " (εἰς τὸ θεοῦ ἐπιτυχεῖν, Pol. 2,3).

The interpolator commits an error of perspective by making Ignatius (who according to the majority of authors had died between 107/115) say that the moment had come for Polycarp to reach God through martyrdom, for his death did not take place until about the years 155/169. Trying to obviate the difficulty, scholars have understood the ship as the church that Polycarp is called on to lead into haven. [399]

---

[399] See LIGHTFOOT, *AA. FF.* II: II/1, 339; LELONG, *PP. AA.* III 99.

The *second* petition (see nr. 152) for prayers was destined for the church of Syria. The forger does not ask prayers for that church, except in the summary of Eph. 21,2. This time however it is not really the interpolator's fault. Indeed, as we saw in treating of this second petition in the authentic letters, between the redaction of Rom., Mg* and Tr., and that of Eph* a circumstance arose that changed Ignatius' attitude: some messengers had arrived from Syria with very comforting news about his community. On his side, the interpolator made use of the primitive conclusion of Ephesians to compose twin conclusions to Sm. and Pol. addressed to the community and the bishop of Smyrna (see nrs. 30-34, 52-55). For the conclusion of Phld. he was also inspired by the same conclusion. Hence, carried away by the basic conclusion of Eph*, instead of asking for prayers, he requested the sending of messengers to congratulate them on the recovered peace. Only it happened that the interpolator having to make such a number of messengers and/or messages (cf. Phld. 10,1.2; Pol. 7,2 and 8,1; Pol. Phil. 13,1) converge on a given address, was forced to change " Syria " into " Antioch of Syria " (Phld. 10,1; Sm. 11,1; Pol. 7,1). In fact, according to him, Ignatius was a deacon of the city of Antioch.

β) *Particular motives, determining the fresh revision*

The general motives already exposed that permeate the whole interpolation prevent us from inferring that the interpolator's design responded to reasons of a dogmatic order, due to the presence of new heresies unknown in Ignatius' times, as will be the case in the long revision of Ps.-Ignatius. The forger does not trouble to add new features to Ignatius' descriptions of his adversaries, be they Gnostics or Judaizers. On the other hand, the hierarchical terminology he slips in frequently, distorting or correcting Ignatius' far more primitive ecclesiology, is already perfectly stereotyped. It is to be found, as we have seen, in the evolutive line that goes from the Didascalia (bishop, deacon/deaconess, presbyters) to the Apostolic Constitutions (bishop, presbyters, deacons, etc.).

While, however, we went on delimiting the extent of the interpolation, there emerged a series of concrete traits whose interpretation allows us to affirm that the forger was an Asian, worried about problems of community obedience to the bishop and presbytery, and concretely, very interested in pointing out divisions among the Philadelphian community members.

164.   There are two facts that incline us to think that the interpolator was himself the bishop of Philadelphia: (1) The existence of a letter for the church of Philadelphia which was at a considerable distance from the coastal route, Smyrna-Troas-Philippi, followed by Ignatius according to the interpolator himself; (2) The denouncement — a very exceptional case — of grave tensions in the heart of that community. He wants to withdraw approval from the contesting faction who refuse to obey him. In order to achieve this he avails himself of the martyr Ignatius' authority, his public debate in Philadelphia with schismatic elements and his presumed letter to the Philadelphians. Thus, he throws in their face that some of their predecessors tried to deceive Ignatius but without success. In fact, the prophetic Spirit himself moved him to say: " Do nothing without the bishop, etc. " (Phld. 7). Polycarp's authority is secondary in this respect. He will use it to authenticate the whole compilation.

If we add the features scattered throughout the strongly interpolated or newly drawn up headings of the actual letters and the freshly composed clauses, we obtain the following portrait of the interpolator and his basic problematic: (a) He is a young bishop: the presbyters or elders have not taken advantage of his youthfulness, thanks to their maturity; but, some immature men have profited by his youth, to act freely without his consent (Mg. 3-4); (b) He is a silent man (Eph. 6,1; Phld. 1,1), prudent, passionless, steadfast, virtuous and observant (Phld. 1,2; Tr. 3,2; Pol. 1,1); (c) As credentials he claims to have been appointed, established and confirmed together with the presbyters and deacons by Jesus Christ himself through his Holy Spirit (Phld. inscr[b].); (d) He presents himself as sent by God (Eph. 6,1); he presides over the community in place of God (Mg. 6,1c; Pol. 1,2); he is the representative of God the Father on earth (Tr. 3,1; Eph. 6,1; Sm. 8), the visible vicar of the universal and invisible Bishop (Mg. 3); (e) He has problems with some dissident elements (Phld. 7; 11,1k) who refuse to obey him (Tr. 2,1a; Eph. 20,2; Mg. 4bc, etc.); (f) To move them to submission, the forger has recourse to the authority arising from the by him previously interpolated letters of the martyr Ignatius (Eph. 5,1; 6,1; 20,2; Phld. 7; Sm. 8; Pol. 6,1a-c, etc.);

(g) He ranks him among the deacons, since he calls him "fellow-servant" of the deacons who are submissive to the bishop and the presbytery (Eph. 2,1a; Mg. 2); (h) He appeals to the authority of the bishop of Smyrna, Polycarp, whom he has previously presented as intimate friend of Ignatius and guarantor of the compilation of his letters (Pol. passim; Pol. Phil. 13); (i) Finally, to witness to the contents of his forgery he calls on God's prophetic Spirit itself (Phld. 7; Eph. 20,2).

In analyzing the motivation of each one of the genuine letters we have seen that Ignatius' aim was no more than to warn the Asian communities of two grave dangers that lay in wait for them, Gnosticism with its false spiritualism and Judaism with its attachment to the Law. At the same time he repeatedly expressed a reserve, i. e. that in none of those communities had there yet been anything similar. We shall now see if in Ignatius there are to be found any of the linguistic fields mentioned above and what form they took. We shall follow point by point the reconstruction we have just presented.

(a) As for the theme of youthfulness (ἡλικία, νεωτερικὴ τάξις, συγχράομαι), there are no traces of it in Ignatian terminology; (b) The theme of silence (σιγάω, the forger; σιγάω, σιγή, σιωπάω, ἡσυχία, Ign.: Eph. 15,1-2; 19,1; Mg. 8,2; Rom. 2,1) is typically Ignatian, due to his own condition of a man forced to silence by his adversaries from Syria (Eph. 15,1-2). He can turn into nothing but a "voice" instead of becoming a "message" through his martyrdom, if the Roman Christians do not keep silence about his identity [400] (Rom. 2,1). The interpolator applies it to the bishop who remains silent before conceited men, thus inviting them to reverential fear (see nr. 60). Likewise the terminology used by the forger to qualify the bishop (ἐνάρετος, τὸ ἀόργητον αὐτοῦ, τὸ ἀκίνητον αὐτοῦ, Phld. 1,2; κατάστημα, μαθητεία, ἐπιείκεια, πραότης, Tr. 3,2; Pol. 1,1) has scarce resonance in the genuine letters; [401] (c) Ignatius needs no credentials: the juridical terminology brandished by the forger (ἀποδείκνυμι, στηρίζω, βεβαιόω, βεβαιωσύνη, βέβαιος/-ίως, ἀσφαλής, ἔξεστιν: Phld. inscr[b].; Mg. 4; 13,1; Sm. 8) is lacking in Igna-

---

[400] i. e. that he is the bishop of Syria or/and a Roman citizen.

[401] ἐπιείκεια appears in Eph. 10,3, and ἀκίνητος in Sm. 1,1, predicated of the community; πραότης, πραΰς, πραϋπάθεια have other connotations: Tr. 4,2; Pol. 6,2; Eph. 10,2; Tr. 8,1.

tius' way of thinking; [402] (d) For Ignatius the unique " God with us " (ὁ θεὸς ἡμῶν/μου) is Jesus the Messiah. He is the only one, who with the communion of the Romans, will shepherd the Syrian community, after the condemnation of its shepherd (Rom. 9,1: cf. Pol. = Eph* 8,3). Ignatius accepts no human mediation, for he is fully convinced that Jesus keeps on really speaking to the community (Eph. 6,2; Rom. 8,2); (e) Ignatius plainly excludes any suspicion of heresy or schism in the Asian communities (see nrs. 153-155). It is significant that while Ignatius always employs πλανάω in a middle-passive sense, the forger uses it preferably in an active one (Mg. 3,2b and Phld. 7,1). Other verbs used exclusively by the interpolator to describe this internal conflictive situation: ἀντιτάσσω (Eph. 5,3f) συγχράομαι (Mg. 3,1), προσλαμβάνω (ibid.), παραλογίζομαι (3,2c), ὑποπτεύω (Phld. 7,2), ἀτιμάζω (11,1), as also their corresponding forms: ὑποτάσσω, ὑπακούω, ἐπακούω, λυτρόω, etc. already identified (see nrs. 159-161); (f) Ignatius never invites to submission and obedience to a human person: the unique centre of the Eucharistic meeting is Jesus; (g) He presents himself as the bishop/supervisor of the whole province of Syria, he is unaware of the ecclesiastical meaning of διάκονος and never uses the term σύνδουλος; (h) He never adduces authorities or models of submission to support his letters or to maintain unity in the community; (i) Notwithstanding the fact that he is fully convinced the only defence against erroneous or restrictive presentation of the message is the experience of the human and divine reality of the Lord in the Eucharist and his presence through prophecy, he does not have recourse to " prophecies " or " revelations " as does the interpolator to reinforce his authority (Eph. 20,2; Phld. 7,2). Compare the simple and natural way Ignatius introduces the inward prophetic word that invites him to go to the Father: " There is living water speaking in me, which says within me: ' Come to the Father ' " (Rom. 7,2), with the solemn and stereotyped prophetic cry the forger places in Ignatius' mouth: " I cried out ... I began to speak ... with God's own voice: ' Give heed to the bishop, etc. ' ... It was the Spirit who praclaimed it saying this: ' Without the bishop do nothing, etc. ' " (Phld. 7).

---

[402] Ign. only uses στηρίζω in Eph. 12,1 of the Ephesians, ἀσφαλίζομαι in Phld. 5,1 of the Magnesians, and βέβαιος, -ίως in Rom. 3,1 and Mg. 11, with very different connotation. See below nr. 176.

165. If we compare the ultimate motives that induced the
forger to draw up the Middle recension with those that appear in
the three authentic letters addressed to the Asian communities, a
remarkably different way of facing the problem becomes manifest.

Ignatius is worried about the imminent danger that the Asian
communities could fall into if they listened to the propagandists
who have come from Syria to sow among them their heretical
doctrines. The most grave one proceeds from the Gnostics. For
that reason he writes two letters, to the Ephesians and the Trallians, to warn them against these esoteric doctrines which tend to
create among Christians a climate of evasion from commitment
to their neighbour by denying the human reality of Jesus. He
warns the Magnesians against the Judaizers, who with their attachment to legal prescriptions could make an end of the absolute
novelty of Christianity.

The forger, on the contrary, is seriously preoccupied by the
presence in his community of a contesting faction that refuses
obedience to the bishop and, consequently, to the other hierarchical ranks.

It is instructive to see the use both make of the term μερισμός.
Ignatius always uses it in the singular, and only in the (primitive)
letter to the Magnesians. Thus he censures the division the Judaizers could introduce into this community by their individualist
practices of a legal nature. Therefore he exhorts them, firstly,
" to do all things in conformity with God, Jesus the Messiah ",
determining in this respect that " there should be nothing among
you that could divide you " (μηδὲν ἔστω ἐν ὑμῖν, ὃ δυνήσεται ὑμᾶς
μερίσαι, Mg. 6,1b.2e). But in continuing the letter along the same
lines as the explanation drawn up in Mg. 11, he wants to make
very clear that he has " found no division among them, but on the
contrary, filtering " (οὐχ ὅτι παρ' ὑμῖν μερισμὸν εὗρον, ἀλλ' ἀποδιϋλισμόν, Phld. 3,1: see nr. 104).

But, although the forger has carefully left the explanatory
clause in Mg. (11), he has not noticed that the Ignatian clause of
Phld. 3,1 contradicts his own falsification in which he alludes to
divisions created in Philadelphia by some who contested the bishop's authority (κατὰ σάρκα μέ τινες ἠθέλησαν πλανῆσαι... οἱ δὲ ὑποπτεύ-
σαντές με ὡς προειδότα τὸν μερισμόν τινων ..., Phld. 7). To dissuade

20

them from " doing everything without the bishop " and " gathering together in an invalid way and not as is prescribed " (Mg. 4), he places twice in Ignatius' mouth the phrase τοὺς μερισμοὺς φεύγετε, with μερισμός in the plural (Phld. 7,2 and Sm. 7,1f).

For Ignatius (see nr. 149) those who provoke division are the Judaizers (σχίζων is that which ἐν ἀλλοτρίᾳ γνώμῃ περιπατεῖ, Phld. 3,3); for the interpolator those who create divisions are the ones who do not respect what is commanded. Thus he makes the commandment equivalent to the bishop's or God's authority (ὑποτασσόμενοι τῷ ἐπισκόπῳ ὡς τῇ ἐντολῇ [403], Tr. 13,2b; cf. also Phld. 1,2 and Sm. 8,1).

γ) *Appendix*: *The bishop's plan*

Having completed the search for the forger's motives, we shall now examine globally, as we did for Ignatius (nrs. 157f.), his use of the term γνώμη, and contrast it with that of Ignatius.

166. The forger employs this term 8 times: [404]

(a) In Eph. 3,2e-4,1c he distorts the Ignatian identification of God's Plan with Jesus the Messiah by introducing the minor, " just as the bishops ... are included in the plan of Jesus Christ ", to conclude inviting the community " to run in agreement with the bishop's plan " (see nr. 81). The same formula, ἐν γνώμῃ Ἰησοῦ Χριστοῦ, to indicate that the bishop and the other hierarchical grades form part of God's plan, appears in Phld. inscr[b]. (cf. also Pol. 1,1 and 8,1).

(b) In Phld. 1,2; Pol. 1,1 and 8,1 it is emphasized that the bishop's plan (in the concrete, Polycarp of Smyrna and the anonymous bishop of Philadelphia) corresponds exactly with God's plan.

(c) In the remaining passages, Pol. 4,1 and 5,2, he points out to the community that " nothing should be done without the bishop's consent ".

On his part, Ignatius used it 7 times: [405]

---

[403] Ign. used ἐντολή to mean the set of precepts of Jesus the Messiah with which the Christian community is adorned (ἐν ταῖς ἐντολαῖς Ἰησοῦ Χριστοῦ, Eph. 9,2; πάσῃ ἐντολῇ αὐτοῦ, Rom. inscr.).

[404] 9 times, if we accept the variant of Pol. 4,1 very well attested to by SAg and the Ps.-Chrysostom, against GL.

[405] By excluding the glosses of Eph. 1,1 (SA) and 2,2 (Gg).

(a) In Eph. 3,2 he identifies the Plan of God with Jesus the Messiah, insofar as he is the true and visible image of the Father's project.

(b) In Phld. 6,2 (" the ideology of the Chief of this world "), 3,3 (the Judaizers' plan, " alien " to God) and Sm. 6,2 (the Gnostics' plan, " contrary to God's plan ") he uses this term to stigmatize his adversaries, Gnostics and Judaizers, and the Chief of both factions which are superficially contrary to one another.

(c) In Rom. 7,1 he denounces the Chief of this world for wanting to corrupt his intention of reaching God through martyrdom, and in 8,3 he specifies to the Romans that he has not written to them for human reasons (κατὰ σάρκα) but according to God's plan (κατὰ γνώμην θεοῦ).

In spite of the fact that both use the same term and even once the same expression (compare Rom. 7,1 Ignatius: τὴν εἰς θεόν μου γνώμην with Phld. 1,2 interpolator: τὴν εἰς θεὸν αὐτοῦ γνώμην), the contents are different. For Ignatius the only Plan of God is Jesus the Messiah, the unique model for the Christian community to imitate. The Gnostics and Judaizers hold a plan " contrary " or " alien " to God's plan, since they deny salvific value to Jesus' flesh and death and/or resurrection, for they consider as an absolute value the Gnosis or the Law. Thus they follow the plan of the Chief of this world. For the interpolator the plan of God consists in submission and respect of the community members to the bishop and the presbytery. Those who disobey and act in anything without the bishop's consent are opposed to God's plan. The circumstances are very different. In Ignatius' time it was a question of contrasting ideologies due to very different conceptions of Christianity, which had grave repercussions on the heart of the Christian communities as well as on their outward image. In the interpolator's time all the problems can be reduced to the basic one of a practical nature: contestation of the hierarchy on the part of certain elements who do not recognize its authority.

III. LITERARY RESOURCES USED BY EACH OF THE REDACTORS

We have just seen that the motives of each of the epistolaries are very different, for they respond to very dissimilar situations. Notwithstanding the fact that the forger tends — so as to pass

unnoticed and reach his aims — to adjust himself to the vocabulary,
style and literary resources employed by Ignatius, it is presumable
that in the use of these latters he does not get close to the lines
laid down by Ignatius. With regard to the style and vocabulary
we have verified it on innumerable occasions. It is undeniable
that the Ignatian letters move deliberately within the exhortatory
genre; the forger unavoidably has to limit himself to this ambit.
As we analyse the gamut of literary resources used by Ignatius and
the interpolator to express it, we shall compare the original and the
adventitious ones, so that fresh motives of differentiation will be
evident between the style of one or other redactor.

a) *Exhortatory, non-prescriptive genre (Ignatius); authoritarian one
   (the forger)*

167.   In three of the four authentic letters we find in an outstanding place the same remark: " I give you no directives as
though I were someone: for although I am in chains for the (Christian) name's sake, I am not yet completed in Jesus the Messiah "
(Eph. 3,1); " It is not my intention to give you directives like an
apostle, since I am a condemned man " (Tr. 3,3); " I do not give
you directives like Peter and Paul: they were apostles, I am a
condemned man; they were free, I am at present a slave " (Rom.
4,3). These are the only three times in which Ignatius uses the
verb διατάσσομαι, allways in the middle voice.

The literary genre choosen by Ignatius to write both to the
communities of Asia and of Rome, is the *exhortatory* one. Ignatius
could have presented himself as " apostle ", [406] in his quality of
bishop/supervisor of the whole province of Syria. But he does
not do it, for in some way he feels himself a condemned man (κατάκριτος: Eph. 12,1; Tr. 3,3; Rom. 4,3), unworthy to be called a
member of the Syrian community, being the last of them (Mg. 14;
Tr. 13,1; Rom. 9,2; Sm. 11,1; Eph. 21,1), an untimely birth
(ἔκτρωμα, Rom. 9,2). When Ignatius considers himself a condemned
man, the least of the Christians of Syria, an abortive fellow, it is
not for the fact of having persecuted the Syrian church before
his conversion, as Zahn and Lightfoot suggest, [407] but for having

---

[406] Note that in Tr. 3,3 and Rom. 4,3 he does not use the article, contrary
to his usage in Eph. 11,2; Phld. 5,1 and 9,1.

[407] ZAHN, *I. v. A.* 402-404, 407; LIGHTFOOT, *AA. FF.* II: II/1, 229f.

been sentenced to death as responsible for the grave riot in that church and for the deplorable state in which he had left it.

Ignatius, "full of faith in Jesus the Messiah, exulting with joy, has proposed to talk with them " (προειλόμην ... προσλαλῆσαι ὑμῖν, Mg. 1,1) "as to his condisciples " (προσλαλῶ ὑμῖν ὡς συνδιδασκαλίταις μου, Eph. 3,1), "for he has been found worthy to converse with them through his letter and to congratulate them " (προσομιλῆσαι ὑμῖν καὶ συγχαρῆναι, 9,2). The decision taken to send them an exhortation "is not personal, but it is the love of Jesus the Messiah " which "will not allow me to keep silence in such circumstances that concern you " (παρακαλῶ οὖν ὑμᾶς, οὐκ ἐγώ, ἀλλ' ἡ ἀγάπη Ἰησοῦ Χριστοῦ, Tr. 6,1; ἀλλ' ἐπεὶ ἡ ἀγάπη οὐκ ἐᾷ με σιωπᾶν περὶ ὑμῶν, διὰ τοῦτο προέλαβον παρακαλεῖν ὑμᾶς, Eph. 3,2). To designate this genre he habitually uses the verb παρακαλέω (8x: Eph. 3,2; Mg. 14; Tr. 6,1; 12,2; Rom. 4,1; 7,2; Phld. 8,2 and Pol. 7,3). On two occasions he employs παραινέω (Mg. 6,1 and Sm. 4,1); once only ἐντέλλομαι (Rom. 4,1) in correlation with the diligence shown by the Romans as teachers of others (3,1); twice he uses the verb προσλαλέω and once προσομιλέω, as we have just seen. To this genre also belongs probably the frequent use of the verb ᾄδω (Eph. 4,1d.2; Mg. 1,2; Rom. 2,2). To be complete, we could list more generic verbs as γράφω, proper to the epistolary genre (Eph. 9,2; 12,1; Tr. 3,3; 5,1; 12,3; Rom. 4,1; 7,2[2x]; 8,3), used especially to indicate the place of writing (Eph. 21,1; Mg. 15; Rom. 10,1), [408] and λαλέω (Phld. 6,3). He employs this last verb also to designate the prophetic word of Jesus or the Spirit (Eph. 6,2; Rom. 8,2 and 7,2), but above all to stigmatize those who talk of Jesus the Messiah but still cling to Judaism (Mg. 10,3; Phld. 6,1), to the values of the world (Rom. 7,1) or to esoteric teachings (Eph. 15,1; Tr. 9,1).

Ignatius feels aversion for the heterodox Gnostics (τοὺς ἑτεροδοξοῦντας, Sm. 6,2) who had formed themselves into a separate sect (αἵρεσις: Eph. 6,2; Tr. 6,1), or for the vain opinions (κενοδοξία, Mg. 11) of the Judaizers with their erroneous teachings and antiquated fables (ἑτεροδοξίαι, μυθεύματα τὰ παλαιά, Mg. 8,1; παλαιὰ πράγματα, 9,1). This aversion is determined by his full conviction that there is only one master, Jesus, who " spoke and it was done "

---

[408] However in Tr. 12,1 he uses ἀσπάζομαι ὑμᾶς ἀπὸ Σμύρνης.

(διδάσκαλος: Eph. 15,1; Mg. 9,1.2). Any teaching or doctrine contrary to his is perverse (κακὴ διδασκαλία, Eph. 16,2; κακοδιδασκα-λία, Phld. 2,1; κακὴ διδαχή, Eph. 9,1), for it emits the ill odour of the teaching of the Chief of this world (δυσωδίαν τῆς διδασκαλίας τοῦ ἄρχοντος τοῦ αἰῶνος τούτου, 17,1). Hence, he prefers " to keep silence and be, than to talk and not to be "; at most he concedes that " it is a good thing to teach, provided the speaker practices (what he preaches) " (15,1). The verb διδάσκω is used by him only here and with respect to the Christians of Rome (Rom. 3,1). It is a eloquent sign.

For Ignatius it is not the moment for esoteric disquisitions on heavenly regions, on superior beings, angels and principalities, on cosmic wars between earthly and heavenly entities, etc., themes much cherished by the Gnostics (Tr. 5; Sm. 6,1; Eph. 13,2-14). Nor is it the moment for private religious practices and observances, as the Judaizers pretend (Mg. 6,2; 7,1c; 8,1; 9,1; 10,1, etc.). " What matters now is not mere profession, but whether one is found with an effective faith to the end ", " whenever Christianity is hated by the world " (Eph. 14,2; Rom. 3,3).

168. The forger does not venture to contradict openly the triple remark Ignatius makes in three of his four letters, although he only knows those of Eph. 3,1 and Tr. 3,3 (he himself does not use διατάσσομαι). But he will try to supply this " lack " by refer-ring the reader to the Prescriptions of the Apostles (τὰ διατάγματα τῶν ἀποστόλων, Tr. 7,1d: cf. Mg. 13,1). In fact, he attributes Apos-tolic value to the Didascalia, from which he drews inspiration, as has been demonstrated (see nrs. 92 and 125). Unaware of the true identity of Ignatius and the equivalence " bishop " — " apostle " in Ignatius' time (the " bishop " of a Roman province was like a " missionary " or " apostle " entrusted by the com-munity to visit and inspect all the communities established there: see Acts 15,36), he does not realize the significance of such pre-cisions.

On the other hand, as can be inferred from every page of the Didascalia from which the forger takes his inspiration, he is con-vinced that the Apostles left everything well and authoritatively settled. It is not strange, then, that he gives his exhortation an authoritarian tone: (a) Placing a monarchical bishop surrounded by his presbytery and assisted by the deacons at the head of each one of the most important communities; (b) Using verbs and expressions that invite to submission and obedience; (c) Adapting to his particular situation the analogies of the Didascalia which justify the separation between clergy and laity and the vertical direction of the community; (d) Employing juridical terms that make certain actions done without the bishop's consent, invalid, illicit or unfitting, etc.

Of those verbs used by Ignatius to give his letters an exhortatory tone, the forger only once uses the verb παρακαλέω, to exhort Polycarp (Pol. 1,2), four times γράφω, twice for the promise of the second tract (Eph. 20,1) and consequently for the excuse for not having been able to write it (Pol. 8,1) and the other two to indicate the new address, Troas (Phld. 11,2 and Sm. 12,1), and once the verb λαλέω (Phld. 7,1).

On his own account he uses προσδηλόω (Eph. 20,1). In the letter to Polycarp he exhorts him to address his faithful using the following verbs and expressions: λάλει (1,3), ὁμιλίαν ποιοῦ, προσλάλει and παράγγελλε (5,1). In Pol. 3,1 he tries to imitate the Ignatian problematic (see nr. 160), but with a verb we do not find in the genuine letters, ἑτεροδιδασκαλέω. Likewise he employs once διδαχή (Mg. 6,2f) and again κενοδοξία (Phld. 1,1) but with a very different connotation. We have also seen that the existence of Polycarp's disciples (Pol. 2,1) presupposes that Polycarp is considered a master, which does not agree with Ignatius' thought.

b) *Warning admonition (Ignatius); recrimination (the forger)*

169. Within the exhortatory genre, Ignatius is especially interested in making it clear that his denouncement of Gnostics or Judaizers is not done in a recriminatory tone: " Not because I have learned, he says, that any of you behave in this way " (Mg. 11; Tr. 8,1); " I am recommending these things to you, beloved, although I know that you maintain the same attitude " (Sm. = Eph* 4,1), that is, Ignatius' own (cf. 3,1). Why then does he write them the letters? The second member of the phrase, built in the same way in the three clauses by means of the verb προφυλάσσω (used only in these clauses), is basic for a correct interpretation of the three Asian letters: Ignatius wants to warn beforehand the Asian communities facing two opposite tendencies, the Gnostics (Tr. 8,1 and Sm. = Eph* 4,1) and the Judaizers (Mg. 11).

Similar explanations are found hinted at in Eph. 6,2-9,1; Mg. 12; Phld. 3,1 (see nrs. 153-155, 161, 165).

These explanatory clauses are nothing else than a condensation of the repeated warnings scattered throughout the letters. Morphologically we can distinguish two classes:

(a) Positive: οὓς δεῖ ὑμᾶς ὡς θηρία ἐκκλίνειν ... φυλάσσεσθαι (Eph. 7,1); φυλάττεσθε (Tr. 7,1); ἀπέχεσθε/-αι (6,1; Phld. 3,1; Sm. 7,2); κωφώθητε (Tr. 9,1); φεύγετε (11,1; Phld. 2,1; 6,2); ὑπέρθεσθε οὖν τὴν κακὴν ζύμην (Mg. 10,2); αἰσχυνθῶμεν, φοβηθῶμεν (Eph. 11,1: cf. Tr. 4,1; 5,1); ὁ χωρῶν χωρείτω (Sm. 6,1); καταμάθετε δὲ τοὺς ἑτεροδοξοῦντας (6,2).

(b) Negative: μηδεὶς πλανάσθω (Eph. 5,2; Sm. 6,1); μὴ πλανᾶσθε (Eph. 16,1; Mg. 8,1; Phld. 3,3); μὴ οὖν τις ὑμᾶς ἐξαπατάτω (Eph. 8,1); μὴ σπουδάζοντες ἀντιμιμήσασθαι αὐτούς (10,2); μὴ ἀλείφεσθε δυσωδίαν τοῦ ἄρχοντος τοῦ αἰῶνος τούτου (17,1); μὴ οὖν ἀναισθητῶμεν τῆς χρηστότητος αὐτοῦ (Mg. 10,1); μὴ ἀκούετε (Phld. 6,1: cf. Eph. 9,1; 6,2; 16,2); μὴ παραδέχεσθαι ... μηδὲ συναντᾶν (Sm. 4,1); μήτε κατ' ἰδίαν περὶ αὐτῶν λαλεῖν μήτε κοινῇ (7,2); μηδὲ γένοιτό μοι αὐτῶν μνημονεύειν (5,3); τόπος μηδένα φυσιούτω (6,1: cf. Mg. 12; Tr. 4,1; 7,1); μηδεὶς κατὰ σάρκα βλεπέτω τὸν πλησίον (Mg. 6,2); μηδεὶς ὑμῶν κατὰ τοῦ πλησίον ἐχέτω, μὴ ἀφορμὰς δίδοτε τοῖς ἔθνεσιν (Tr. 8,2); μηδὲν ἔστω ἐν ὑμῖν, ὃ δυνήσεται ὑμᾶς μερίσαι (Mg. 6,2); μηδὲ πειράσητε εὔλογόν τι φαίνεσθαι ἰδίᾳ ὑμῖν (7,1); μὴ ἐμπεσεῖν εἰς τὰ ἄγκιστρα τῆς κενοδοξίας (11); μηδὲν κατ' ἐρίθειαν πράσσειν, ἀλλὰ κατὰ χριστομαθίαν (Phld. 8,2); πλέον μοι μὴ παράσχησθε τοῦ σπονδισθῆναι θεῷ (Rom. 2,2); μὴ εὔνοια ἄκαιρος γένησθέ μοι (4,1); μηθέν με ζηλῶσαι τῶν ὁρατῶν καὶ ἀοράτων (5,3: cf. 6,1; Tr. 5; Sm. 6,1); μὴ ἐμποδίσητέ μοι ζῆσαι, μὴ θελήσητέ με ἀποθανεῖν, τὸν τοῦ θεοῦ θέλοντα εἶναι κόσμῳ μὴ χαρίσησθε μηδὲ ὕλῃ ἐξαπατήσητε (Rom. 6,2); μηδεὶς οὖν τῶν παρόντων ὑμῶν βοηθείτω αὐτῷ ... μὴ λαλεῖτε Ἰησοῦν Χριστόν, κόσμον δὲ ἐπιθυμεῖτε (7,1); βασκανία ἐν ὑμῖν μὴ κατοικείτω (7,2).

All this ensemble of advice, warnings and admonitions have as scope, in the thematic letters, to block adverse propaganda; in the letter to Romans, their aim is to prevent Ignatius' road to martyrdom being obstructed, still a negative function. There are, however, very perceptible differences of tone: in the thematic letters to the Asian communities he invites them to flee the deceits and fallacies of the adversaries; in the letter to the Romans he begs insistently that they side with him. Even in his warnings against Gnostics and Judaizers he gives a very different stress. Faced with the Gnostics he is categorical: not only they should not receive nor meet them, but it is fitting to keep away from any such people and not to speak about them either in private or in public. For his part, Ignatius prefers not to mention their names nor even to remember them. Faced with the Judaizers he insists rather on not giving any importance to their individualistic religious practices.

170. The interpolator, on the contrary, pays no attention to Ignatius' repeated explanations. Thus in Mg. 4 he states that " there are some persons who call him (Damas) bishop, but in everything act apart from him. Such men do not seem to me to keep a good conscience, forasmuch as they do not gather together in a valid way, as is prescribed ". He reproaches the Philadelphians that " some have tried to deceive me (Ignatius) humanly " (Phld. 7,1) and that " some have suspected me of saying this, because I knew beforehand of the division caused by certain persons " (7,2); and what is more, that " some have treated with dishonour " the companions coming from Syria and Cilicia (11,1).

He never uses the verb προφυλάσσω; on the contrary, he employs πλανάω in an active sense (Mg. 3,2; Phld. 7,1), which Ignatius never does, and he adopts its equivalent παραλογίζομαι (Mg. 3,2), to indicate that the adversaries of his ecclesiology are active and are inside the community itself.

In Phld. 7,2 he tries even to imitate the explanatory clause of the authentic letters, but instead of excluding the existence of divisions among the community members, he makes Ignatius say that he has no human knowledge of such divisions: is it the Spirit who has revealed to him the presence of underhanded enemies in the community of Philadelphia who tried to gain him to their cause, against the recognized rights of those constituted in the hierarchy.

Just as in Ignatius we can distinguish the morphologically positive warnings from the negative ones:

(a) Positive: πλειόνως αὐτὸν φοβείσθω (Eph. 6,1); δέον οὖν αὐτοὺς φυλάσσεσθαι τὰ ἐγκλήματα ὡς πῦρ (Tr. 2,3); τοὺς μερισμοὺς φεύγετε (Phld. 7,2g; Sm. 7,2f); τὰς κακοτεχνίας φεῦγε (Pol. 5,1).

(b) Negative: μὴ ἀντιτάσσεσθαι τῷ ἐπισκόπῳ (Eph. 5,3f); μὴ συγχρᾶσθαι τῇ ἡλικίᾳ τοῦ ἐπισκόπου (Mg. 3,1); μηδὲν πράσσετε (7,1:

cf. 4), μηδὲν πράσσειν (Tr. 2,2: cf. 7,2), μηδεὶς ... τι πρασσέτω (Sm. 8,1: cf. 8,2 and 9,1); μηδὲν ποιεῖτε (Phld. 7,2); μηδὲν ἄνευ γνώμης σου γινέσθω, μηδὲ σὺ ἄνευ θεοῦ τι πρᾶσσε (Pol. 4,1); οἱ δοκοῦντες ... μή σε καταπλησσέτωσαν (3,1); χῆραι μὴ ἀμελείσθωσαν (4,1); δούλους καὶ δούλας μὴ ὑπερηφάνει · ἀλλὰ μηδὲ αὐτοὶ φυσιούσθωσαν ... μὴ ἐρά- τωσαν ἀπὸ τοῦ κοινοῦ ἐλευθεροῦσθαι (4,3).

* * *

If we now compare how each one expresses the warnings, a notable difference springs to the eye. To introduce cautions or warnings, Ignatius very frequently uses the preventive imperative, preceded or not by the negation (Μηδεὶς πλανάσθω, Μὴ πλανᾶσθε, Μὴ ἀλείφεσθε, etc.; Φεύγετε, Φυλάττεσθε, Κωφώθητε, etc.), [409] when he wants to alert the community members against their adversaries, or in its place, the negative subjunctive (μηδὲ πειράσητε, Μὴ οὖν ἀναι- σθητῶμεν, πλέον μοι μὴ παράσχησθε, μὴ ἐμποδίσητε, μὴ θελήσητε, etc.),[410] when he refers to internal community affairs or to deeds that can affect his personal situation. The forger, on the contrary, never uses the negative subjunctive and does not begin any period with the preventive imperative. Thus, Ignatius stresses the verb, while the interpolator emphasizes the object (Τοὺς μερισμοὺς φεύγετε, Χωρὶς τοῦ ἐπισκόπου μηδὲν ποιεῖτε, Χῆραι μὴ ἀμελείσθωσαν, etc.).

Ignatius' admonitions are always addressed to the community and, all things considered, have as only object to warn it against the deceits of Satan or the devil, i.e. the Chief of this world: Eph. 10,3; 13,1; 17,1; 19,1 (letter to the Ephesians); Mg. 1,2; 5; Phld. 6,2 (id. to the Magnesians); Tr. 4,2; 8,1 (id. to the Trallians); Rom. 7,1 (id. to the Romans). The orders imparted by the forger are directed indistinctly to factions or different positions in the community, to the deacons (communitarian letters) or to Polycarp himself (letter to Polycarp, the first part written in the singular), never departing from the intra-ecclesiastical level (submission to the bishop and presbytery, advice to the deacons, problems belonging to the widows, slaves, etc.).

---

[409] Cf. Eph. 5,2; 8,1; 16,1; 17,1c; Mg. 6,2c.e; 8,1; 10,2; Tr. 6,1c; 7,1; 8,2; 9,1; 11,1; Rom. 7,1b.d.2a; Phld. 2,1b; 3,1.3; 6,1.2; Sm. 6,1a.d.2.
[410] Cf. Eph. 11,1; Mg. 7,1c; 10,1; Rom. 2,2; 4,1e; 6,2b.c.d.e.

c) *Invitation to union with Jesus, mutual concord, respect for his decision (Ignatius); to submission to the bishop (the forger)*

171. In his exhortations Ignatius does not limit himself to issuing warnings. His letters are sown with positive invitations, tending to achieve the objectives proposed, introduced by means of the imperative or of the subjunctive, when the first is missing.

When we examine the positive forms employed by Ignatius, three groups of invitations appear according to whether the purpose of the invitation falls on Jesus, the members of the community or Ignatius himself.

Union with Jesus. — Ignatius' main objective for the Asian communities, besides warning them against their adversaries, was the imitation of Jesus the Messiah as the unique model that reproduces the whole project of the Father, and real union with him experienced by the community in the Eucharist. Jesus is our God, he is the achieved and mature Man, placed by the Father as Head of the church thanks to his commitment to men (his Flesh) and his death freely accepted to deliver humanity from the slavery it is bound to by the Chief of this world (his Blood).

This invitation to the community does not appear in the letter to the *Romans*, due to the special tone of this writing. The allusions to the Eucharist, contained in Rom. 4,1-2 and above all 7,3, serve as analogies for its application in the concrete case of Ignatius, who as disciple of Jesus follows his footsteps till he gives his life and blood for love of his brothers.

In the genuine letter to the *Ephesians* (Eph*) he uses either the imperative in the second person plural: οἱ κατ' ἄνδρα δὲ χορὸς γίνεσθε (Eph. 4,2); σπουδάζετε οὖν πυκνότερον συνέρχεσθαι εἰς εὐχαριστίαν θεοῦ καὶ εἰς δόξαν (13,1); or the subjunctive in the first person plural: ἀδελφοὶ αὐτῶν εὑρηθῶμεν τῇ ἐπιεικείᾳ · μιμηταὶ δὲ τοῦ κυρίου σπουδάζωμεν εἶναι κτλ. (10,3); λοιπὸν αἰσχυνθῶμεν, φοβηθῶμεν ... ἢ γάρ ... φοβηθῶμεν, ἢ τὴν ἐνεστῶσαν χάριν ἀγαπήσωμεν κτλ. (11,1); πάντα οὖν ποιῶμεν κτλ. (15,3). Indirectly he invites to Eucharistic meetings when he realizes that the Gnostics keep away from them so as not to have to accept the reality of the Lord's Flesh, i. e. the real commitment to their neighbour (Sm. 7,1: cf. 6,2).

In the letter to the *Trallians* he also invites them imperatively to partake of the unique Christian food of the Eucharist (μόνη τῇ χριστιανῇ τροφῇ χρῆσθε, Tr. 6,1) as defence against the Gnostics.

He draws attention to the correspondence existing between the Flesh of the Lord and the faith that binds the members of the community to him, as well as between the Blood of Jesus the Messiah and the love that they themselves express (ἀνακτήσασθε ἑαυτοὺς ἐν πίστει, ὅ ἐστιν σὰρξ τοῦ κυρίου, καὶ ἐν ἀγάπῃ, ὅ ἐστιν αἷμα Ἰησοῦ Χριστοῦ, 8,1: cf. Mg. 1,2).

The letter to the *Magnesians* (Mg*) also invites them with the imperative to "do all things in conformity with God, Jesus the Messiah" (ἐν ὁμονοίᾳ θεοῦ Ἰησοῦ Χριστοῦ ... σπουδάζετε πάντα πράσσειν, Mg. 6,1 reconstr.), to "run all together as to one sanctuary of God, as to one altar to one Jesus the Messiah" (ὡς εἰς ἕνα ναὸν συντρέχετε θεοῦ κτλ., 7,2), experienced by the community united together in the Eucharist (ἐπὶ τὸ αὐτό, 7,1).

Ignatius exhorts them repeatedly to overcome the ancient sour leaven of Judaizing practices, exchanging it for the new leaven that is Jesus the Messiah (μεταβάλεσθε εἰς νέαν ζύμην, ὅ ἐστιν Ἰησοῦς Χριστός, Mg. 10,2), and to let themselves be seasoned by him (ἁλίσθητε ἐν αὐτῷ, ibid.), so as to escape the corruption and the evil-smelling teachings of the adversaries. As sheep they should follow the footsteps of the only Shepherd (ὅπου δὲ ὁ ποιμήν ἐστιν, ἐκεῖ ὡς πρόβατα ἀκολουθεῖτε, Phld. 2,1: cf. Rom. 9,1).

This conformity of life with Jesus the Messiah can be reached only by participation in the one Eucharist, since one is the Flesh of the Lord and one the cup to unite his Blood, as one is the altar on which he was immolated (σπουδάσατε οὖν μιᾷ εὐχαριστίᾳ χρῆσθαι κτλ., Phld. 4). For this reason he recommends them earnestly to meet all together with undivided heart (πάντες ἐπὶ τὸ αὐτὸ γίνεσθε ἐν ἀμερίστῳ καρδίᾳ, 6,2).

In the same way he employs the subjunctive in the first person plural, to corroborate his invitation to live in the Christian fashion (μάθωμεν κατὰ Χριστιανισμὸν ζῆν, Mg. 10,1: cf. Phld. 8,2: κατὰ χριστομαθίαν) and to profess attachment to the Prophets, because moved by the Spirit, they pointed to the Gospel in their preaching, and they hoped in him and waited for him as their Master, being his disciples through the Spirit; hence, when he came he raised them from the dead (καὶ τοὺς προφήτας δὲ ἀγαπῶμεν κτλ., Phld. 5,2: cf. Mg. 8,2 and 9,2).

The Eucharist for Ignatius is the place where the Christian community experiences the real presence of the Lord, his concrete commitment and his total love until death for mankind. With his death he proclaims the Kingdom as a society of equals, based on a new scale of values, and thus inaugurates the effective reign of God among men. The Eucharist is the actualization of Jesus' life and death in the present moment. To keep away from it signifies evading this real commitment to the needs of one's neighbour. To feed on individual practices, imbued by Judaizing propaganda, sows division and causes confrontation between the members of the community.

The Eucharist is the centre of the exhortation Ignatius addresses to the Asian communities. It still keeps its etymological meaning of " thanksgiving " to God, as an equivalent of " praise " (εἰς εὐχαριστίαν θεοῦ καὶ εἰς δόξαν, Eph. 13,1). The Thanksgiving is expressed by the community when they meet together (ἐπὶ τὸ αὐτό: ibid.; 5,3; Mg. 7,1; Phld. 6,2) forming a chorus (Eph. 4,2: cf. Rom. 2,2) in an attitude of grateful prayer (Sm. 7,1; Mg. 7,1d; Eph. 4,2). It is not to be wondered at, then, that the forger, as we shall soon see, has been especially interested in interpolating the greater number of passages in which allusion is made to the Eucharist, and in copying Ignatian phrases for his own aims.

Mutual concord. — The invitation to frequent community meetings (Eph. 13,1) leads its members to intone in unison the praise of the Father through Jesus the Messiah (ἵνα ... ᾄδετε ἐν φωνῇ μιᾷ διὰ 'Ιησοῦ Χριστοῦ τῷ πατρί, 4,2: cf. Rom. 2,2), so that whatever they do, they may do it in conformity with God (ἵνα, ὃ ἐὰν πράσσητε, κατὰ θεὸν πράσσητε, Phld. 4) and that they may be recognized by their good deeds as members of God's Son (ἵνα ὑμῶν καὶ ἀκούσῃ καὶ ἐπιγινώσκῃ δι' ὧν εὖ πράσσετε, μέλη ὄντας τοῦ υἱοῦ αὐτοῦ, Eph. 4,2). From this Ignatius goes on to exhort them, again with the imperative, generally in the second person plural, to stimulate mutual concord, to collaborate with one another at every moment, to love one another as consecrated men: ἔστε οὖν καὶ σύνοδοι πάντες, θεοφόροι κτλ. (Eph. 9,2); πάντα οὖν ὑμῖν ἐν χάριτι περισσευέτω (Sm. = Eph* 9,2); συγκοπιᾶτε ἀλλήλοις, συναθλεῖτε, συντρέχετε, συμπάσχετε, συγκοιμᾶσθε, συνεγείρεσθε κτλ. (Pol. = Eph* 6,1); ἀρέσκετε ᾧ στρατεύεσθε ... τὸ βάπτισμα ὑμῶν μενέτω ὡς ὅπλα ... μακροθυμήσατε οὖν μετ' ἀλλήλων κτλ. (6,2); ἐντρέπεσθε ἀλλήλους ... ἀλλήλους διὰ παντὸς ἀγαπᾶτε (Mg. 6,2); διαμένετε ἐν τῇ ὁμονοίᾳ ὑμῶν καὶ τῇ μετ' ἀλλήλων προσευχῇ (Tr. 12,2); καὶ οἱ κατ' ἄνδρα ἀλλήλους ἀγαπᾶτε ἐν ἀμερίστῳ καρδίᾳ (13,2).

The exhortation is not limited, however, to the community members, but extends to all men: καὶ ὑπὲρ τῶν ἄλλων δὲ ἀνθρώπων ἀδιαλείπτως προσεύχεσθε ... ἐπιτρέψατε οὖν αὐτοῖς κτλ. (Eph. 10,1), including the Gnostics who have separated themselves from the community: μόνον δὲ προσεύχεσθε ὑπὲρ αὐτῶν κτλ. (Sm. = Eph* 4,1).

Respect for Ignatius' decision. — The third group includes all the passages in which Ignatius insistently begs the community to respect his free decision to give his life for the brothers. Apart from the letter to the Romans, he uses the imperative form only in relation to his personal decision in Tr. 5,1. The Trallians should be indulgent with him, for not having written to them of esoteric knowledge, like the Gnostics, since for lack of capacity to assimilate it they might be stifled: καὶ συγγνωμονεῖτέ μοι, μήποτε οὐ δυνηθέντες χωρῆσαι στραγγαλωθῆτε.

The letter to the *Romans* is one long insistent supplication to the Roman community not to exercise their influence in official quarters to have him liberated from martyrdom. Limiting ourselves to the imperatives in positive form, there is no doubt that these lead us to infer the ardent desire Ignatius had to reach his objective, i. e. to be " an achieved disciple " of Jesus, as long as that was God's will, and he might obtain the divine favour of taking due possession of such an inheritance without hindrance above all from the Romans themselves (ἐάνπερ θέλημα ᾖ τοῦ ἀξιωθῆναί με εἰς τέλος εἶναι, Rom. 1,1; ἐάνπερ χάριτος ἐπιτύχω εἰς τὸ τὸν κλῆρόν μου ἀνεμποδίστως ἀπολαβεῖν, 1,2; ἐάνπερ ὑμεῖς μὴ κωλύσητε, 4,1). Imperatives follow each other, generally in the second person plural: μόνον μοι δύναμιν αἰτεῖσθε ἔσωθέν τε καὶ ἔξωθεν, ἵνα κτλ. (3,2); ἄφετέ με θηρίων εἶναι βοράν κτλ. (4,1); μᾶλλον κολακεύσατε τὰ θηρία, ἵνα κτλ. (4,2); λιτανεύσατε τὸν Χριστὸν ὑπὲρ ἐμοῦ, ἵνα κτλ. (ibid.); συγγνώμην μοι ἔχετε (5,3); κακαὶ κολάσεις τοῦ διαβόλου ἐπ' ἐμὲ ἐρχέσθωσαν, μόνον ἵνα κτλ. (ibid.); σύγγνωτέ μοι, ἀδελφοί (6,2); ἄφετέ με καθαρὸς φῶς λαβεῖν (ibid.); ἐπιτρέψατέ μοι μιμητὴν εἶναι τοῦ πάθους τοῦ θεοῦ μου (6,3); εἴ τις αὐτὸν ἐν ἑαυτῷ ἔχει, νοησάτω, ὃ θέλω, καὶ συμπαθείτω μοι κτλ. (ibid.); μᾶλλον ἐμοῦ γίνεσθε, τουτέστιν τοῦ θεοῦ (7,1); πείσθητέ μοι · τούτοις δὲ μᾶλλον πείσθητε κτλ. (7,2); θελήσατε, ἵνα καὶ ὑμεῖς θεληθῆτε (8,1); πιστεύσατέ μοι (8,2); αἰτήσασθε περὶ ἐμοῦ, ἵνα ἐπιτύχω (8,3).

Before such an ardent and repeated petition the Roman Christians very probably abstained from intervening. Indeed, Polycarp in his letter to the Philippians written half a century later, thinks of him as " blessed ", together with Zosimus and Rufus, other martyrs of the Philippian community, as well as Paul himself and the rest of the Apostles, for their endurance to the end in suffering with the Lord (Pol. Phil. 9).

* * *

The Ignatian positive use of the imperative, generally in the second person plural (when he does not address anybody in particular, he employs the third singular; when he is speaking not to persons, the third plural), and, in its place, the use of the subjunctive first person plural (including himself in the exhortation) is always within the canons of the pressing and supplicating exhortatory genre At no time does it reflect authoritarian tones nor does Ignatius try to impose himself on the community members or make them submit to human leaders.

172. On the contrary, the positive use of the imperative by the forger (he only uses the subjunctive first person plural in Eph. 5,3f to include Ignatius in the community as distinct from the bishop) aims solely at obtaining the total submission of the community members to the appointed authority, the bishop and the presbytery. The interpolator proceeds differently in the use he makes of it, as he is conditioned or not by Ignatius' underlying text.

While he moves within Ignatius' authentic text, his invitation to submission and obedience relies on Ignatian expressions, imitates them or adopts his own forms; in every case he wants to attain his objective by inserting determinate sentences that give the impression it is Ignatius himself who is speaking in favour of the bishop and the presbytery: σπουδάσωμεν οὖν μὴ ἀντιτάσσεσθαι τῷ ἐπισκόπῳ κτλ. (Eph. 5,3f); ἀλλ᾽ ἑνώθητε τῷ ἐπισκόπῳ καὶ τοῖς προκαθημένοις κτλ. (Mg. 6,2f); σπουδάζετε οὖν βεβαιωθῆναι ἐν τοῖς δόγμασιν κτλ. (13,1); ὑποτάγητε τῷ ἐπισκόπῳ καὶ ἀλλήλοις κτλ. (13,2); ἀλλ᾽ ὑποτάσσεσθε καὶ τῷ πρεσβυτερίῳ κτλ. (Tr. 2,2b); τῷ ἐπισκόπῳ προσέχετε κτλ. (Phld. 7,1); πάντες τῷ ἐπισκόπῳ ἀκολουθεῖτε κτλ. (Sm. 8,1a); τοὺς δὲ διακόνους ἐντρέπεσθε κτλ. (8,1c); ἐκείνη βεβαία εὐχαριστία ἡγείσθω, ἡ ὑπὸ τὸν ἐπίσκοπον οὖσα κτλ. (8,1e); ὅπου ἂν φανῇ ὁ ἐπίσκοπος, ἐκεῖ τὸ πλῆθος ἔστω κτλ. (8,2a). Only once (Phld. 7,2) he recommends the members of the community to respect their own bodies as temples of God: τὴν σάρκα ὑμῶν ὡς ναὸν θεοῦ τηρεῖτε; ; to cherish union: τὴν ἔνωσιν ἀγαπᾶτε; and to imitate Jesus Christ: μιμηταὶ γίνεσθε Ἰησοῦ Χριστοῦ κτλ. The first theme frequently recurs in 2Cl. 8,4.6; 9,3; the second with its corresponding one (" Shun divisions ": Phld. 7,2 and Sm. 7,2f) is inspired by Ignatius (Mg. 1,2; Tr. 11,2; Phld. 2; 8,1, etc.); the last also (Eph. 1,1; 10,3; Tr. 1,2b + 2,2b; Rom. 6,3).

In the first part of the letter to *Polycarp* (Pol. 1-5[6,1c]), however, the imperatives follow one another in a dizzy rhythm and crowd on each other without any coordination, in order to give an imperious warning to Polycarp about the right way to guide and to the community about the way to reach cohesion through total submission to the hierarchy: ἐκδίκει σου τὸν τόπον ... τῆς ἑνώσεως φρόντιζε ... πάντας βάσταζε ... πάντων ἀνέχου ἐν ἀγάπῃ ... προσευχαῖς σχόλαζε ἀδιαλείπτοις· αἰτοῦ σύνεσιν πλείονα ἧς ἔχεις· γρηγόρει ... τοῖς κατ' ἄνδρα κατὰ ὁμοήθειαν θεοῦ λάλει (1,2-3d); πάντων τὰς νόσους βάσταζε ... μᾶλλον τοὺς λοιμοτέρους ἐν πραότητι ὑπότασσε ... τοὺς παροξυσμοὺς ἐμβροχαῖς παῦε (1,3e-2,1); φρόνιμος γίνου ὡς <ὁ> ὄφις ... τὰ δὲ ἀόρατα αἴτει ... νῆφε, ὡς θεοῦ ἀθλητής (2,2-3); οἱ ... ἑτεροδιδασκαλοῦντες μή σε καταπλησσέτωσαν· στῆθι ἑδραῖος ... πλέον σπουδαῖος γίνου οὗ εἶ. τοὺς καιροὺς καταμάνθανε. τὸν ὑπὲρ καιρὸν προσδόκα κτλ. (3,1-2); χῆραι μὴ ἀμελείσθωσαν ... αὐτῶν φροντιστὴς ἔσο. μηδὲν ἄνευ γνώμης σου γινέσθω, μηδὲ σὺ ἄνευ θεοῦ τι πρᾶσσε ... εὐστάθει. πυκνότερον συναγωγαὶ γινέσθωσαν. ἐξ ὀνόματος πάντας ζήτει. δούλους καὶ δούλας μὴ ὑπερηφάνει· ἀλλὰ μηδὲ αὐτοῖ φυσιούσθωσαν, ἀλλ' εἰς δόξαν θεοῦ πλέον δουλευέτωσαν ... μὴ ἐράτωσαν ἀπὸ τοῦ κοινοῦ ἐλευθεροῦσθαι ... (4,1-3); τὰς κακοτεχνίας φεῦγε· μᾶλλον δὲ περὶ τούτων ὁμιλίαν ποιοῦ· ταῖς ἀδελφαῖς μου προσλάλει ... ὁμοίως καὶ τοῖς ἀδελφοῖς μου παράγγελλε ... (5,1); εἴ τις δύναται ἐν ἁγνείᾳ μένειν ... ἐν ἀκαυχησίᾳ μενέτω ... πάντα εἰς τιμὴν θεοῦ γινέσθω. τῷ ἐπισκόπῳ προσέχετε κτλ. (5,2-6,1a).

We have retained this time, together with the positive exhortative forms, the negative warning ones so that the reader can give his own opinion on the forger's paratactical and asyndetic style this being the only time when he feels at home and free from Ignatius' underlying text.

Except for the last imperative, in the second person plural

(Pol. 6,1a), needed to link up with Ignatius' primitive paraenesis of Eph*, the rest of the imperatives have been built up on the second person singular (those addressed to Polycarp) or the third singular or plural (those addressed to Polycarp's adversaries or to his community), mixed one with the other.

* * *

If we now compare the usage Ignatius and the interpolator make of both the imperative and the vicarious subjunctive, preceded or not by the negation, we shall observe:

(1) Ignatius' marked tendency to use the subjunctive in the first person plural (10x), [411] contrasted with once in the interpolation. [412]

(2) The exclusive use Ignatius also makes of the subjunctive in the second person plural (7x) [413] and the third singular (2x) [414].

(3) The exclusive use by the interpolator of the imperative in the second person singular (27x: always and only in the first part of Pol.). [415]

(4) As for the use of the imperative in the third person singular, the proportion with regard to the length of the respective texts is almost the same (14x: Ignatius; [416] 7x: the forger [417]).

(5) For the second person plural, Ignatius exceeds the average of 5/7 (71x); [418] while the interpolator is below his average of 2/7 (17x). [419]

---

[411] Eph. 10,3 (2x); 11,1 (4x); 15,3; Mg. 10,1 (2x); Phld. 5,2.

[412] Eph. 5,3.

[413] Mg. 7,1; Rom. 2,2; 4,1; 6,2 (4x).

[414] Sm. 9,2; Pol. 6,2.

[415] Pol. 1,2-6,1c.

[416] Eph. 5,2; 8,1; 11,2; Mg. 6,2 (2x); Tr. 8,2; Rom. 6,3 (2x); 7,1.2; Sm. 6,1 (3x); Pol. 6,2.

[417] Eph. 6,1; Sm. 8,1 (2x).2; Pol. 4,1; 5,2 (2x).

[418] Eph. 4,2; 9,2; 10,1 (2x); 13,1; 16,1; 17,1; 21,1.2 (2x); Mg. 6,1.2 (2x); 7,2; 8,1; 10,2 (3x); 14; 15; Tr. 5,1; 6,1 (2x); 7,1; 8,1.2; 9,1; 11,1; 12,2.3; 13,1.2 (2x); Rom. 3,2; 4,1.2 (2x); 5,3; 6,2 (2x).3; 7,1 (2x).2 (2x); 8,1.2.3; 9,1; 10,2.3; Phld. 2,1 (2x); 3,1.3; 4; 6,1.2 (2x); 11,2; Sm. 4,1; 6,2; 13,2; Pol. 6,1 (6x).2 (2x).

[419] Mg. 6,2; 7,1; 13,1.2; Tr. 2,2; Phld. 7,1.2 (5x); Sm. 7,2; 8,1 (2x); 13,1; Pol. 6,1; 8,3.

21

(6) For the third person plural, finally, the interpolator (7x) [420] outstrips Ignatius (1x). [421]

If we add up separately the number of cases in which one or the other uses the subjunctive, the result is overwhelmingly in favour of Ignatius (19x) compared with the interpolator (1x). Totaling the use of the imperative, the result is favourable to the interpolator (58x) as compared with Ignatius (86x), taking into account that the authentic text consists of little more than 5/7 of the whole.

If, finally, we observe the series of imperatives in each writer, the series of 35 imperatives of the first part of Pol. is in itself striking. This uncommon fact has no parallel in the authentic letters.

Certainly, statistical data are of little value on their own, but they still provide evidence regarding the tendency of each writer. The forger's exclusive preference for the imperative confirms his tendency to authoritarian tones, unlike Ignatius who combines the subjunctive with the imperative so as to tone down the exhortation. Ignatius refuses to exhort the communities in a prescriptive tone, like an apostle, although he is bishop of the whole province of Syria; the forger preaches through Ignatius' mouth submission and obedience to the bishop and his presbytery while he presents Ignatius as a model of a deacon.

d) *Tendency to arguments of convenience (Ignatius); of necessity (the forger)*

The exhortatory genre, proper to the Ignatian letters, shows up not only through verbs of exhortation and petition, in the use of imperative forms or their subjunctive equivalents. Both Ignatius and the interpolator make use of several impersonal forms that denote convenience, necessity, excellence, validity or liceity of the actions prescribed to the community. To complete our analyses, it will be useful to examine them one by one and to look for the tendencies that can be inferred from the usage they make of them. To be able to set up a collation we have placed them in four categories, according to wether they present arguments of conven-

---

[420] Tr. 3,1; Pol. 3,1; 4,1.2.3 (3x).
[421] Rom. 5,3.

ience or valuation that respect the free decision of the communities, or else arguments of necessity or merely juridical ones that hardly leave room for choice.

We shall first deal with the statements that contain reasons of convenience or necessity. Secondly we shall examine those that determine subsequently the objective value or juridical connotation of the actions prescribed. After determining statistically the usage one or the other makes of such expressions, we shall examine their contents. In the final synthesis we shall draw up the pertinent inferences.

173. πρέπω, πρέπον ἐστίν, πρέπει. — *Statistics*: Ignatius uses this verb six times: once in the imperative, μηδὲν ὑμῖν πρεπέτω (Eph. 11,2), in the sense of " let nothing glitter in your eyes/fascinate you [apart from him] "; four times in the periphrastic form, πρέπον ἐστίν (Eph. 2,2; Mg. 3,2; Rom. 10,2 and Sm. 7,2), in the sense of " it is fitting "; and once in the impersonal form, πρέπει (Sm. 11,2) with the accusative of person and the infinitive, signifying also " it is proper that ... ". — The interpolator uses it seven times: twice πρέπον ἐστίν (Mg. 4a, depending on 3,2a and forming an inclusion with it, so as to link up again with Ignatius' text; and Phld. 10,1, a copy of Sm. 11,2) and five times πρέπει (Eph. 4,1a; Mg. 3,1a, depending also of 3,2a; Tr. 12,2d; Pol. 5,2 and 7,2, this last being a copy of Sm. 11,2 as well).

The marked preference of the forger for this paraenetic form becomes obvious, as also his frequent dependence on the underlying Ignatian text.

Content: This mostly impersonal form manifests the reasons of convenience that should move the reader to realize/avoid what is expressed by the subsequent infinitive. If we look at the addressees of the exhortation, qualified as " fitting ", we conclude that for Ignatius these are exclusively the communities of Asia and Rome to whom he writes the four letters, without distinction of persons, while for the forger these are either the communities of Asia as distinct from the bishop (Eph. 4,1; Mg. 3,1.2; Tr. 12,2), or else people about to be married (Pol. 5,2). In all these cases the bishop is the ultimate beneficiary of the exhortation. The two remaining instances (Phld. 10,1 and Pol. 7,2) depend on the underlying Ignatian theme (Sm. = Eph* 11,2). This tendency to centre the exhortation on community relations with the bishop (and the presbytery) becomes evident in the corrections introduced in Eph. 2,2 (ὑποτασσόμενοι κτλ.) and Mg. 3,2-4 (ὥσπερ καί τινες ἐπίσκοπον κτλ.).

If we now turn to the purpose of the exhortation, expressed by the infinitive, we shall see that, according to Ignatius, it is very varied: "to glorify Jesus the Messiah, who has glorified you" (δοξάζειν ... τὸν δοξάσαντα, Eph. 2,2: cf. Sm. 1,1); "not only to be called Christians by name, but also to be such in fact" (καλεῖσθαι ... εἶναι, Mg. 4: cf. Rom. 3,2; Eph. 14,2-15,2); "to give them relief in every way" (ἀναπαῦσαι, with respect to the Syrians who went before Ignatius to Rome, Rom. 10,2); "to keep yourselves away from such people (the Gnostic heretics) ... but to give heed to the Prophets and, especially, to the Gospel" (ἀπέχεσθαι ... προσέχειν ... ἐξαιρέτως δὲ, Sm. 7,2); "that your community appoint God's ambassador" (χειροτονῆσαι, 11,2, copied by the forger in Phld. 10,1 and Pol. 7,2, the only three uses of this verb).

The forger, on the contrary, except for the two paraphrases of Sm. 11,2: "that you, as a church of God, appoint a deacon to carry out God's embassy there" (χειροτονῆσαι, Phld. 10,1) and "to convoke a most venerable plenary meeting and appoint someone ... who can be called God's courier" (συμβούλιον [422] ἀγαγεῖν ... χειροτονῆσαι, Pol. 7,2), polarizes this exhortatory genre into relations with the bishop: "to run in agreement with the plan of the bishop" (συντρέχειν, Eph. 4,1a, a copy of 3,2c: cf. as for the Ignatian use of this verb, Mg. 7,2 and Pol. 6,1); "that men and women who marry contract their union with the bishop's consent" (τὴν ἕνωσιν ποιεῖσθαι, Pol. 5,2); "that you severally ... give the bishop refreshment" (ἀναψύχειν, Tr. 12,2d: cf. Eph. 2,1h, the only two occurrences of this verb, always by the interpolator); "to obey without dissimulation" (ἐπακούειν, Mg. 3,2); "not to seek to profit by the bishop's youth" (μὴ συγχρᾶσθαι, Mg. 3,1). The forger hints at a reason for this change of direction in the exhortation when he explains in Mg. 3,1-2 that the visible bishop is the representative of the invisible and universal Bishop, God (cf. 6,1c).

To complete the foregoing analysis we could adduce the impersonal use Ignatius makes of the verb συμφέρω referring to himself (τί μοι συμφέρει κτλ., Rom. 5,3) or to Gnostic adversaries (συνέ-

---

[422] Note that Ign. uses exclusively the term ἐκκλησία, while the interpolator adds συμβούλιον, συνέδριον, συναγωγή.

φερεν δὲ αὐτοῖς κτλ., Sm. 7,1). This verb is missing in the interpolation.

174. δεῖ, δέον (ἐστίν), ἔδει. — *Statistics*: Ignatius employs this impersonal verb five times: four times δεῖ (of which 3x referred to the community [ὑμᾶς]: Eph. 7,1 [2x] and Sm. 4,1; and 1x referring to himself [με]: Tr. 4,1) and once ἔδει (referring to himself: Eph. 3,1). The forger uses it also five times: in four instances he has δεῖ (2x associating Ignatius with the community as distinct from the bishop [ἡμᾶς]: Eph. 6,1; 1x associating Polycarp with Ignatius [ἡμᾶς]: Pol. 3,1; 1x referring to the deacons: Tr. 2,3) and once δέον (Tr. 2,3, related also to the deacons). In relative terms, the respective frequencies diverge rather notably.

Content: This impersonal form stresses the need to realize/ avoid what is expressed by the infinitive that follows. For Ignatius the addressees are either he himself or the Ephesian community. In this last case, he only uses it to express a negative exigency: "whom (the Gnostic heretics) you should avoid (ἐκκλίνειν) like the wild beasts: for they are rabid dogs that bite furtively; you should beware (φυλάσσεσθαι) of them, because their bites are hard to cure" (Eph. 7,1); "but I warn you beforehand against these wild beasts in human form, whom you should not only not receive (μὴ παραδέχεσθαι), but, if possible, even avoid meeting (μηδὲ συναντᾶν); only pray (προσεύχεσθε) [423] for them, if haply they may repent — a difficult thing!" (Sm. = Eph* 4,1).

But on the two occasions on which he applies this form to himself he gives a glimpse of his difficult personal situation, on the one hand flattered by some as if he were someone important, on the other, full of fear as the decisive moment draws near: "for now I must fear (φοβεῖσθαι) the more, instead of giving heed (μὴ προσέχειν) to those who flatter me" (Tr. 4,1); "for I ought rather to have been anointed for the contest (ἔδει ... ὑπαλειφθῆναι) with your faith, advice, endurance, magnanimity" (Eph. 3,1).

On the contrary, the interpolator uses δεῖ to express a positive exigency, equivalent to an order or command: "for every one whom the owner sends to take charge of his household, we ought so to receive (δέχεσθαι) as him who has sent him. Plainly then,

---

[423] See critical apparatus, p. 379, l. 9. If we retain the infinitive, it would depend from δεῖ.

we ought to regard (προσβλέπειν) the bishop as the Lord himself "
(Eph. 6,1); " it is further needful that those who are deacons of
the mysteries of Jesus Christ please (ἀρέσκειν) all men in every way ...
Consequently, they must shun blame (δέον ... φυλάσσεσθαι) as fire "
(Tr. 2,3); " but above all we should endure (ὑπομένειν) everything
for God's sake " (Pol. 3,1).

Ignatius is mild in formulating exigencies to the Asian communities. He will not give them directives as an apostle, limiting
himself to the (at least morphologically) negative form (" you
should not "), to warn them against the heretics from Syria. But,
since he is not interested in the real motives that moved Ignatius
to write his letters, the interpolator throws out exigency after exigency, putting into Ignatius' mouth orders and categorical directives (" we/you ought to/must "). His lack of critical sense leads
him to recommend the Prescriptions of the Apostles (τὰ διατάγματα
τῶν ἀποστόλων, Tr. 7,1d) contained in the Didascalia, without per-
ceiving that he thus contradicts Ignatius' repeated purpose (οὐ διατάσσομαι ὑμῖν: Eph. 3,1; Tr. 3,3; Rom. 4,3).

To express need (δεῖ) or fittingness (πρέπει) to do something,
Ignatius and the forger use many other locutions. These can be
classified into two series, according to whether they bring positive
reasons that interest the intelligence or merely juridical ones that
move the will.

175. ἄμεινον, ἄτοπον, εὔλογον, καλόν, κρεῖσσον, ὄφελον, χρήσιμόν
ἐστιν. — All the locutions of this first series, excepting ἄτοπον that
is limited to qualifying the contrary conduct as absurd, try to
convince the intelligence, with positive reasons of convenience, so
as to move the will to perform a concrete action. All of them
belong to the exhortatory genre, in the style of πρέπον ἐστίν, since
they do not bind the reader, as is the case with δεῖ and the locutions that we shall examine in the second series, but they suggest
reasons or objective valuations for a free decision.

(1) ἄμεινόν ἐστιν. — Statistics: Ignatius does not use the positive ἀγαθός, but four times the comparative (Eph. 13,2; 15,1; Mg.
7,1 and Phld. 6,1). The interpolator uses once the comparative
(Pol. 1,2). Ignatius employs it twice followed by the infinitive and
twice by a genitive; the forger follows it by a genitive.

Content: Followed by the infinitive it has only comparative
value. Thus Ignatius stresses that a thing is " better " than an-

other: "it is better to keep silence and be (Christian), than to talk and not to be (so)" (Eph. 15,1); "for it is better to listen to a circumcised man speaking about Christianity than to an uncircumcised man about Judaism" (Phld. 6,1). In both cases a relative value is given to the first term, with respect to the second that has no value at all. The best is the third term that in both cases is understood: "to talk and to be Christian", "to listen to an uncircumcised man speaking about Christianity". To express this "best" Ignatius employs the locution οὐδέν ἐστιν ἄμεινον with the genitive: "there is nothing better than peace (= peace is the best thing)" (Eph. 13,2); "with this flawless joy, that is Jesus the Messiah, than whom there is nothing better (= the best that exists)" (Mg. 7,1).

The forger copies this locution in Pol. 1,2: "Take care of (the community) union, for there is nothing better (= the best that exists)" (φροντίζω, here, and φροντιστής of 4,1 are only used by the interpolator).

(2) ἄτοπόν ἐστιν. — Ignatius alone uses it only once: "It is absurd to profess Jesus the Messiah, and to practise like a Jew" (Mg. 10,3). This corresponds with the locution of Phld. 6,1, that we have just examined, belonging to the same letter (Mg*).

(3) εὔλογόν ἐστιν. — This locution is also exclusively Ignatian. As a simple attribute it is to be found in Mg. 7,1. With predicate value it appears in Sm. 9,1: "it is reasonable, finally, that we wake up, while we still have time to repent and turn to God".

(4) καλόν, καλά ἐστιν. — With predicate value (the forger uses 1x the adjective with attributive value in Pol. 2,1) it is used only by Ignatius and even repeatedly: "it is a good thing to teach, provided the speaker practices (what he preaches)" (Eph. 15,1); "it is good to set from the world towards God, that I may rise to him" (Rom. 2,2); "nothing that is apparent is good" (3,3); "it is 'good for me to die' (1Cor. 9,15) binding myself to Jesus the Messiah, rather than to reign over the confines of the earth" (καλόν μοι ... ἤ ..., 6,1); "good, too, are the (Levitic) priests, but better is the High Priest (Jesus)" (καλοὶ ... κρεῖσσον ..., Phld. 9,1); "all these together (the Prophets and the Gospel) are good, provided your faith is rooted in love" (καλά ἐστιν, 9,2).

It seems that Ignatius employs καλός in place of ἀγαθός, as we infer from the absence of this last term in the preceding quotations, above all in Phld. 9,1, where he contrasts κρεῖσσον, one of the comparatives of ἀγαθός, to καλοί.

(5) κρεῖσσον. — With predicate value only Ignatius uses it in Phld. 9,1, as we have just seen. As attribute Ignatius employs it in Rom. 2,1 and the forger in Pol. 4,3.

(6) ὄφελον. — As particle ("utinam") it occurs only once in an interpolated context: "and would that all might imitate him (the deacon Burrhus), for he is an example of God's ministry" (Sm. 12,1).

(7) χρήσιμόν ἐστιν. — Only Ignatius uses this locution in Eph. 4,2: "it is therefore profitable for you to maintain yourselves in a blameless unity".

To sum up: Of the seven locutions with predicate value found in the Ignatian letters belonging to the exhortatory genre, five (2.3.4.5. and 7.) are exclusively Ignatius', one (1.) he shares with the interpolator and one (6.) belongs exclusively to the latter. Adding up the frequencies we obtain the proportion of 14/2 clearly favourable to Ignatius.

176. ἀναγκαῖον, ἀσφαλές, βέβαιον, οὐκ ἐξόν ἐστιν. — The four locutions belonging to this second series have in common that they try to captivate the will, without more reasoning. The juridical content is patent: necessary, firm, valid, licit.

(1) ἀναγκαῖόν ἐστιν. — This locution occurs only once in an interpolated passage: "it is necessary, then, even as you do, that you realize nothing without the bishop" (Tr. 2,2). It is a variant of the forger's insistent appeal to do nothing without the bishop (Mg. 7,1; Pol. 4,1; Phld. 7,2; Sm. 8,1.2), expressed in very varied forms, as we shall see next.

(2) ἀσφαλές. — A variant to the positive of the previous appeal: "thus everything you do will be firm and valid" (ἀσφαλές ... καὶ βέβαιον, Sm. 8,2). Used only by the forger.

(3) βέβαιον. — In the same context as in the former passage, the forger uses again this term to qualify "only as a valid Eucharist that which is held under the control of the bishop or anyone to whom he has committed it" (ἐκείνη βεβαία ... ἥ ..., Sm. 8,1: cf. Mg. 4d).

Ignatius employs this term in Rom. 3,1 to exhort the Romans to be consistent with their own teaching: "but all I want is that what you teach and recommend (to others) will be consistent (in my case) " (βέβαια ἦ). Ignatius refers to recommendations given in writing by the Roman community to other communities (ἄλλους ἐδιδάξατε), about which he is well informed. Scholars have seen here an allusion to the letter of the Roman community to the Corinthians (the so-called first letter of Clement).

(4) οὐκ ἐξόν. — Only the forger uses this locution in Sm. 8,2: " it is not licit without the bishop to baptize, or to hold an agape ". Here it is a question of liceity (in 8,1 it was a question of validity; in Pol. 5,2, of convenience).

To sum up: The four locutions of this second series are characteristic of the forger. Even in the case of βέβαιος used by Ignatius in Rom. 3,1 there is a notable shift from the meaning given by this (" be consistent/really ") to the one given by the interpolator (" be held as valid "). Adding up the frequencies we have a proportion of 1/5, favourable to the forger in absolute and relative terms. The juridical terminology of the latter is in open contradiction with Ignatius' more pastoral tone.

*　　*　　*

Synthesizing the four classes of locutions examined, we can group them into two types of arguments: (a) of *convenience*: " it is fitting " (nr. 173), " it is better ", " there is nothing better than " (nr. 175,1), " it is absurd " (nr. 175,2), " it is reasonable " (nr. 175,3), " good (beautiful, noble) is ... " (nr. 175,4), " better (more excellent) is ... " (nr. 175,5), " would that ... " (nr. 175,6), " it is profitable " (nr. 175,7); (b) of *necessity*: " you should/ought/must ", " you should not " (nr. 174), " it is necessary " (nr. 176,1), " will be firm and valid " (nr. 176,2.3), " it is not licit " (nr. 176,4).

Ignatius' preference for arguments of convenience is evident and fits in with his purpose, clearly expressed on three occasions, not to give " directives ", but to limit himself to exhort. Even in the two instances in which he uses the verb δεῖ, he does so in negative form, to " warn beforehand " the Ephesian community against the onslaught of the heretics coming over from Syria, of whom many had already passed by Ephesus. Likewise, when he employs the term βέβαιος, in the letter to the Romans, he does not give it a juridical nuance.

The forger, on the contrary, prefers arguments of necessity

and although he also makes use of arguments of convenience, in regard to the usage of such locutions there is a notable poverty as compared with the manifold forms that appeared in the first series.

e) *Other forms closely connected with the exhortation*

α) *Use of the optative*

177.   To give greater force to the exhortation or the concomitant petitions, both Ignatius and the interpolator use the optative sporadically.   In general they are not real optatives, but already stereotyped formulas.

Real optatives appear three times in the authentic letters and twice in the interpolation.

Ignatius employs the form εὑρεθείητε in Tr. 13,3 to explain the contents of the petition: πληρῶσαί μου τὴν αἴτησιν καὶ ὑμῶν, ἐν ᾧ εὑρεθείητε ἄμωμοι. The relative ἐν ᾧ has rather the value of a completive clause: "but the Father is faithful to fulfil both your and my prayer through Jesus the Messiah, so that you may be found blameless". In Pol. = Eph* 8,3 we have a similar construction, using the verb of desire, εὔχομαι, as an optative: "I wish that you be always strengthened by our God, Jesus the Messiah, so that you abide in the unity of God and under his oversight" (ἐν ᾧ διαμείνητε ἐν ἑνότητι θεοῦ καὶ ἐπισκοπῇ). A second optative occurs in Rom. 5,3.   Through the form ζηλώσαι[424] he expresses his supreme desire, "that nothing visible or invisible may through envy hinder me from reaching Jesus the Messiah". Finally, in Sm. 9,2 he uses, it seems, ἀμείβοι [425] to express the desire that God reward the Ephesian community for what it has done for him: "God reward you!".

On his part, the forger uses the form ἀναψύξαι in Eph. 2,1h, depending on the ὡς καί with a conjunctive function, one of his most typical marks (see nr. 105, and n. 330).   The conjunction here expresses a consequence: "that the Father of Jesus Christ may refresh him in turn". In Phld. 11,1 he employs the form λυτρωθείησαν to express his desire that "those who treated them (the com-

---

[424] See LIGHTFOOT, *AA. FF.* II: II/1, 215: "The optative is wanted rather than the infinitive."

[425] See critical apparatus, p. 380, l. 24.

panions come from Syria following Ignatius) with dishonour may
be redeemed by the grace of Jesus Christ ''.

Among the stereotyped optative formulas we find ὀναίμην ...
and γένοιτο ... The first is used four times by Ignatius and twice
by the interpolator, but with a notable difference in the use of the
complement. Ignatius employs this formula always as the colophon of a sentence, in a independent clause, and with a plural
object referring it either to the community (ὀναίμην ὑμῶν κτλ.:
Eph. 2,2; Mg. 12; Pol. = Eph* 6,2), or to the wild beasts by which
he has to be devoured (ὀναίμην τῶν θηρίων κτλ.: Rom. 5,2). The
interpolator, on the contrary, always uses it in a relative clause
with singular object referring it either to the deacon Zotion (οὖ
ἐγὼ ὀναίμην, followed by a completive ὅτι: Mg. 2), or to Polycarp
(οὖ ὀναίμην ἐν θεῷ: Pol. 1,1). There is no doubt that the forger
intended to copy this formula which he took for one most characteristic of Ignatius. The Ps.-Ignatius will use the same technique
(see nr. 75).

The second formula is used exclusively by Ignatius on six
occasions. Only once does it refer to the community (ἧς ἐκτραπῆναι μηδενὶ ὑμῶν γένοιτο, Mg. 11. In all the other instances he
refers it to himself (γένοιτό μοι: Eph. 11,2 [2x]; 12,2; Sm. 5,3;
Pol. 6,1).

Statistically, little can be gathered from the frequency of the
optative in Ignatius (13x) and the interpolator (4x). More meaningful, however, is the fact that Ignatius tends to apply it to the community (7x), while the interpolator always applies it to individuals
or a faction. Likewise, the usage Ignatius makes of ὀναίμην is
more correct than the interpolator's one. Ignatius employs it
always as an independent clause, while the forger inserts it in a
relative one. Finally, it is also very significant that γένοιτο does
not appear once in the interpolated passages.

β) *Use of the adverbs* μόνον *and* λοιπόν *as intensive particles*

178. The interpolator uses neither form. Ignatius employs
μόνον with a certain frequency either absolutely or combined with
other particles. It occurs in absolute form in Eph. 11,1 as reply
to an alternative: ἢ γὰρ τὴν μέλλουσαν ὀργὴν φοβηθῶμεν, ἢ τὴν ἐνεστῶσαν χάριν ἀγαπήσωμεν, ἐν τῶν δύο · μόνον ἐν Χριστῷ Ἰησοῦ εὑρεθῆναι
κτλ.; in Rom. 5,3 it appears as expression of his utmost desire,

after enumerating the possible tortures that could fall to him: κακαὶ κολάσεις τοῦ διαβόλου ἐπ᾽ ἐμέ ἐρχέσθωσαν, μόνον ἵνα Ἰησοῦ Χριστοῦ ἐπιτύχω; as well as in the parallel of Sm. 4,2: μόνον ἐν τῷ ὀνόματι Ἰησοῦ Χριστοῦ — εἰς τὸ συμπαθεῖν αὐτῷ — πάντα ὑπομένω. In all these instances Ignatius uses this particle to express his exclusive aim, desire or motive.

Combined with ἀλλά it appears in Mg. 4: πρέπον ἐστὶν μὴ μόνον καλεῖσθαι Χριστιανούς, ἀλλὰ καὶ εἶναι; and in Tr. 13,3: ἁγνίζεται ὑμῶν τὸ ἐμὸν πνεῦμα οὐ μόνον νῦν, ἀλλὰ καὶ ὅταν θεοῦ ἐπιτύχω. Thus he stresses two aspects of the exhortation or encouragement he addresses to the communities.

In double combination it occurs in Sm. 4,1: οὓς οὐ μόνον δεῖ ὑμᾶς μὴ παραδέχεσθαι, ἀλλ᾽ εἰ δυνατὸν μηδὲ συναντᾶν · μόνον δὲ προσεύχεσθε ὑπὲρ αὐτῶν κτλ. Ignatius earnestly warns the Ephesian community against the Gnostic heretics. It must avoid every contact with them. The only efficacious means that can obtain their repentance is prayer.

Finally, he uses it in a triple combination in Rom. 3,2: μόνον μοι δύναμιν αἰτεῖσθε ἔσωθέν τε καὶ ἔξωθεν, ἵνα μὴ μόνον λέγω, ἀλλὰ καὶ θέλω, μὴ ἵνα μόνον λέγωμαι Χριστιανός, ἀλλὰ καὶ εὑρεθῶ κτλ. In Rom. 2,2, the apodosis of 1,1a, after a long digression (1,1b-2,1), we meet with an equivalent expression constructed with πλέον: πλέον [426] μοι μὴ παράσχησθε τοῦ σπονδισθῆναι θεῷ, ὡς ἔτι θυσιαστήριον ἕτοιμόν ἐστιν. By means of these two adverbs Ignatius tries to exclude any human interference of the Roman Christians in regard to his own situation. Their only positive contribution should be prayer and encouragement.

The adverb λοιπόν is used only twice, namely in the preceding context of the phrase quoted above of Eph. 11,1: Ἔσχατοι καιροί · λοιπὸν αἰσχυνθῶμεν, φοβηθῶμεν κτλ., and in Sm. 9,1: Εὔλογόν ἐστιν λοιπὸν ἀνανῆψαι ἡμᾶς, ὡς ἔτι καιρὸν ἔχομεν εἰς θεὸν μετανοεῖν. In both instances he alludes to the time that remains until the end of the world which is imminent (cf. also Mg. 5). Again he emphasizes by means of this particle the only aim of his exhortation.

---

[426] See critical apparatus, p. 349, l. 1.

γ) *Use of the formulas of encouragement* ἀντίψυχον, περίψημα, ἁγνίζομαι, ἀσφαλίζομαι.

179. Ignatius wants to stimulate the communities to whom he writes his letters by making use of certain very characteristic formulas of encouragement. The interpolator will only make use of the first, but substituting the typical Ignatian construction by a personal pronoun. Indeed, in the paraenesis of the primitive letter to the Ephesians (actually to be found in Sm. 10,2, to complete with Eph. 21,1: see nrs. 30f., and n. 116, as well as nr. 132) ἀντίψυχον agreed with τὸ πνεῦμά μου καὶ τὰ δεσμά μου κτλ. The forger has copied this locution no less than three times, doubtless to give an appearance of authenticity to his interpolation, but he has replaced the personal pronoun, ἀντίψυχον ὑμῶν ἐγώ (Eph. 21,1; Pol. 2,3 and 6,1), instead of the genuine Ignatian impersonal subject.

The form περίψημα is exclusively Ignatian. In Eph. 18,1 it is constructed with the same impersonal subject as ἀντίψυχον: περίψημα τὸ ἐμὸν πνεῦμα κτλ.; in 8,1, without subject (or pronoun!): περίψημα ὑμῶν καὶ ἁγνίζομαι ὑμῶν κτλ.

The construction with ἁγνίζομαι is also exclusively Ignatian. In Tr. 13,3 it appears with the same subject as the last two: ἁγνίζεται ὑμῶν τὸ ἐμὸν πνεῦμα κτλ. The other instance where it occurs, Eph. 8,1, has already been mentioned.

In the final greeting Ignatius will use a similar construction: ἀσπάζεται ὑμᾶς τὸ ἐμὸν πνεῦμα καὶ ἡ ἀγάπη τῶν ἐκκλησιῶν κτλ. (Rom. 9,3); ἀσπάζεται ὑμᾶς ἡ ἀγάπη Σμυρναίων καὶ Ἐφεσίων (Tr. 13,1). The forger will copy this last formula in Phld. 11,2 and Sm. 12,1, but adding τῶν ἀδελφῶν.

Ignatius is extremely careful to avoid being a protagonist. Thus, in the use of ἀσφαλίζομαι he states precisely that it is not he who fortifies their faith but the affection Jesus the Messiah professes for them: ἀσφαλίζομαι ὑμᾶς, οὐκ ἐγὼ δέ, ἀλλ᾽ Ἰησοῦς Χριστός (Phld. 5,1). A similar construction with παρακαλῶ in Tr. 6,1.

Ignatius' tendency to substitute the first person pronoun (in the nominative) in formulas of encouragement (twice expressly) agrees with the several passages where he uses this pronoun in formulas of self-abasement (Eph. 12,1; Tr. 5,2; Rom. 4,3; 9,2) and contrasts with the repeated use the forger makes of this pronoun by imitating the genuine Ignatian ἀντίψυχον.

δ) *Use of various particles to introduce complementary clauses*

180. To close the comparative study of the literary devices employed by Ignatius and the interpolator to express their diverse motivations, we have thought well to analyze the particles with complementary function that each one uses.

The conjunction ἵνα, if we except the five instances in which there is allusion to past actions in the life of the Lord (Eph. 17,1; 18,2; Sm. 1,1.2; 2), completes in all other cases the exhortation or petition formulated by the main sentence. In the positive it is used by Ignatius thirteen times with reference to his personal situation (Eph. 1,2; 11,2; Mg. 14; Tr. 3,3; Rom. 2,2f; 4,1.2 [2x]; 5,3 [2x]; 8,3; Phld. 5,1; Sm. 11,1), sixteen times referring to the community as distinct from himself (Eph. 2,2; 4,2 [3x]; 10,1; 15,2 [2x]; Rom. 2,2c; 3,1; 8,1; Phld. 3,2; 4; Sm. 7,1; 11,2.3; Pol. 6,2) and three times to the community including himself (Eph. 15,3; Mg. 9,1; Tr. 2,1 reconstr.). In the negative (ἵνα μή) it is used by Ignatius five times referring to his own situation (Tr. 4,1; 12,3g; Rom. 3,2 [2x]; 4,2), another five times applied simply to the community (Eph. 10,3; Mg. 10,2; Tr. 8,2; 12,3b; Phld. 6,3) and twice including himself in the community (Eph. 11,1; Tr. 5,2).

The interpolator does not use it with a final connotation with regard to the life of the Lord. Neither does he employ it in the exhortation or petition to refer to the personal situation of Ignatius. In the positive he applies it nine times to the community excluding Ignatius: in six of these to invite it to do all things in submission to the bishop and the other hierarchical grades (Eph. 5,1; Mg. 13,1.2; Sm. 8,2; Pol. 5,2; 6,1b), once to instruct it on the problem of the slaves within the community (Pol. 4,3) and twice to imitate situations inspired by the original (7,2; 8,1). On one instance he includes Ignatius in the community as distinct from the bishop (Eph. 5,3). Finally, on three occasions he applies it to Polycarp (Pol. 2,2 [2x]; 3,1). In the negative he uses it only once, with reference to the situation of the slaves within the community (4,3).

The conjunction ὅπως is used by Ignatius in only one instance (Eph. 3,2) and by the forger in another (Pol. 2,2) [427].

As for the construction εἰς τό with infinitive, Ignatius uses it

---

[427] According to G: but g Antioch. and Dam. read ἵνα.

eight times, the forger four. In the negative, Ignatius alone uses
it only once (Eph. 9,1). In the positive, Ignatius applies it once
to the Old Testament Prophets (Mg. 8,2), four times to his own
situation (Tr. 12,3; Rom. 1,2; Sm. 4,2; Pol. 7,1) and twice to the
community (Mg. 14; Sm. 11,2). The interpolator refers it once
to the particular situation of Polycarp (Pol. 2,3), copying Ignatius,
and three times to the community (Eph. 20,2; Phld. 10,1, copy
of Sm. 11,2; Pol. 8,1, idem).

On his side, Ignatius employs in four instances a relative clause
with completive function, constructed either with the optative or
the subjunctive in second person plural: ἐν ᾧ εὑρεθείητε ἄμωμοι
(Tr. 13,3); ἐν ᾧ διαμείνητε ἐν ἑνότητι θεοῦ καὶ ἐπισκοπῇ (Pol. 8,3), or
with the future in first person plural: ἐν ᾧ ὑπομένοντες ... θεοῦ τευξόμεθα (Mg. 1,2); ἐν ᾧ διάγοντες εὑρεθησόμεθα οὐ κατὰ ἀνθρώπους
ζῶντες κτλ. (Tr. 2,2c + 1b reconstr.).

Taking these various usages synoptically we have:

Complementary clauses	in historical context	in exhortatory context			
Terms	Jesus Prophets	Ign.	Comm.	Comm. + Ign.	Pol.
A) Ignatius					
ἵνα	5/—	13	16	3	—
ἵνα μή	—	5	5	2	—
ὅπως	—	—	1	—	—
εἰς τό	—/1	4	2	—	—
εἰς τὸ μή	—	—	1	—	—
ἐν ᾧ	—	—	2	2	—
B) Interpolator					
ἵνα	—	—	9	1	3
ἵνα μή	—	—	1	—	—
ὅπως	—	—	(1)	—	—
εἰς τό	—	—	3	—	1
εἰς τὸ μή	—	—	—	—	—
ἐν ᾧ	—	—	—	—	—

Although the respective frequencies maintain a close proportion to the length of their respective texts (62x Ign./19 Int.), preferences diverge rather sharply: (1) The interpolator never uses these

particles with a final function in past situations; (2) Instead of applying it to the personal situation of Ignatius (22x Ign), the forger refers it to the particular one of Polycarp (4x); (3) Ignatius includes himself very often in his exhortation to the community (7x), according to the interpolator only in one instance; (4) Ignatius alone uses the relative clause with completive function (4x); (5) Referring simply to the community, the forger's usage goes beyond the Ignatian one in relative terms (27x Ign./14x Int.).

If we look at content, the Ignatian exhortation aims exclusively at achieving the unity of the community with Jesus the Messiah (27x) [428] or to avoid its withdrawal from Jesus through adverse propaganda (6x), as also to reach his personal objective (17x) eluding all kinds of obstacles (5x). The interpolator polarizes it above all into submission of the community to the bishop (9x) and in the question of the slaves (2x); on several instances he depends on the Ignatian original (5x).

IV. CONCLUSION

By way of Prolegomena we have, firstly, given in synoptic form the position of the several interpolated passages within the framework of the genuine Ignatian letters.

Taken synoptically, the interpolation affects above all the openings and endings of the letters. We have distinguished: (a) Fictitious interrupting clauses to divide two of the genuine letters into four; (b) Creation or arrangement of initial greetings (inscriptions); (c) Amplification of the genuine introductions, after giving hierarchical titles to the delegates from the respective communities; creation of a new introduction for Philadelphians; abrupt beginning of Smyrnaeans without any introduction; (d) Creation or arrangement of the conclusions and final greetings.

Generally the interpolation has spared the body of the letters (exhortation) and the paraenesis. The interpolator has only introduced those sentences that seem to him unavoidable, either to modify the primitive meaning of the text, or to condense his ideology. The first part of Pol. is wholly spurious and belongs to this last model (nr. 126).

---

[428] Once, in Eph. 10,1, he refers it to the rest of men.

Secondly, we have classified the interpolated clauses and sentences according to the function the forger gave them and the variety of techniques he used to introduce them. Thanks to the different function assigned by the interpolator to this or that clause, it has been possible to dissociate structure from content.

The structural clauses try to create a framework for his restructuration of the Ignatian letters; only incidentally do they deal with questions of content. We have distinguished between negative and positive proceedings.

The negative proceedings employed by the interpolator to obtain six letters from the three genuine ones (Eph*, Mg* and Tr.; the forger was unaware of Rom.) were: (a) Division of the original letters to the Eph* and Mg* into four (Eph. and Sm.; Mg. and Phld.); (b) Division and distribution of the Eph* ending between Sm. and Pol. (and Phld.); (c) Distribution of the inscription of Mg* between Mg. and Phld. (nrs. 127-130).

The plagiarism is the positive proceeding he used (a) to coin the new inscriptions of Sm. and Pol., and to adapt the original inscription of Mg* to Mg. and Phld.; (b) to draw up the new letter endings of Eph., Phld., Sm. and Pol. out of the primitive ending of Eph*; (c) to write the interrupting clauses of Eph. 20 and Mg. 13, the covering notes of Pol. 8,1 and Pol. Phil. 13 (nrs. 131-133).

Thematic elements are used deliberately to correct Ignatius' ecclesiology by twisting its contents. When the interpolator starts systematically introducing his thematic elements into Ignatius' letters, he notably distorts the archaic Ignatian ecclesiology centred on Jesus the Messiah, his real presence through the Eucharist and prophecy in the community, making its horizontal dimension vanish in order to polarize it in the bishop's person as God's sole representative. The Christocentric meaning of the Ignatian phrase has thus been profoundly altered. A new key has prevailed over the primitive one. In order to insert his themes the forger has used here also negative and positive proceedings.

The main negative proceeding has been the division of periods and sentences in order to insert his new theme into them. As auxiliary procedures he has inverted sentences or words, mutilated and abridged phrases. However, in the greater number of passages that have been interpolated the scissors had spared the primi-

22

tive sequence. Only the foreign bodies introduced by the interpolator have modified its original meaning (nrs. 134-139).

As positive proceedings he has intercalated sentences to change
the original Ignatian meaning. Among those merely intercalated
to modify the meaning of the phrase without changing Ignatius'
underlying text must be numbered the remaining ones that have
been inserted into the expositive body or in the paraenesis of the
letters (nrs. 140-145).

Specific doctrinal developments where the forger expresses
himself freely, without being conditioned either by structural reasons, or by questions of content, correspond to a middle third century ecclesiology, which was inspired by the Didascalia Apostolorum (nrs. 146-147).

As colophon of the Prolegomena we have reviewed the various
methods used by the forger to intercalate his interpolations in
Ignatius' text (nr. 148).

After the Prolegomena we have pointed out the incompatibility
of either of the two recensions, the Middle of seven letters or textus
receptus and the authentic Ignatian one of four letters, considering
the motives that induced Ignatius and the forger to write their respective epistolaries.

The two main objectives that led Ignatius to write his letters
and are valid for the whole epistolary are: (1) to foment union
among the communities which he was addressing, and (2) to write
to all the churches and insist to all men that he gives his life willingly
for God.

Faced with the Gnostics, who kept aloof from the communitarian meetings of the church, and the Judaizers, who with their
legalistic exigencies sowed discord and division in the midst of the
communities, Ignatius proposes three models of union: (a) the
one that exists between " flesh " and " spirit ", between the humanity and the divinity of Jesus the Messiah; (b) the close union that
holds between " faith " and " love ", between adhesion to Jesus
the Messiah and love showed by deeds; (c) the model par excellence which is the union that exists between Jesus and the Father
(nr. 149).

The insistence of Ignatius that he dies willingly for God and
his letter to the Roman Christians to dissuade them from exercising influences in higher spheres to deliver him from death, the

tight security measures of ten soldiers for a single prisoner, the possibility Ignatius enjoyed of speaking and writing to Christian communities and individuals, the petition for prayers that peace might be restored to the church of Syria and the comforting news brought from Syria by some envoys of that church about restoration of peace, strength and its communitarian body, all this makes no sense if it is understood in the light of a persecution. If his letters are interpreted so, his ardent and passionate desire for martyrdom lacks its main motivation. If, on the contrary, his condemnation is the result of a self-immolation for love of the Christian communities and an irrefutable witness against Gnostics and Judaizers, we shall understand how Ignatius takes his martyrdom to be a confirmation of Jesus' real death and resurrection (nr. 150).

After these two main motives, the Ignatian letters contain — above all in the conclusion — two no less important requests: (1) Petition for prayers for himself so that he might fully reach his objective; (2) Petition for prayers for the church in Syria, in a first moment, that peace might quickly be restablished at its heart; and then, once peace recovered, his congratulations to the people on enjoying such peace (nrs. 151f.).

Each letter has its specific motive. The three Asian letters deal with the problem of the Judaizers (Magnesians: actually Mg. and Phld.) or the Gnostics (Trallians: Tr.; and Ephesians: actually Eph. and Sm.). In each of these three authentic letters there was an explanatory clause in which we can grasp the real problem that troubled Ignatius. In the letter to the Magnesians he deals with the problem of the Judaizers. The letter to the Trallians constitutes a kind of thematic sketch for Ephesians. But it is in the letter addressed to the community of Ephesus that he develops his anti-Gnostic exhortation. The letter to the Romans, unlike the Asian ones, lacks theological subject. The Roman Christians could hinder his martyrdom. For this reason he exhorts them not to show him unseasonable kindness (nrs. 153-156).

After the generic and specific motives, in an Appendix we have compared the Plan of God that Jesus the Messiah personifies and the plan of the Chief of this world that both Gnostics and Judaizers support. The Gnostics do not recognize the human reality of the saviour and therefore deny true commitment to man in need, and the Judaizers minimize the newness of the resurrection of the Messiah, thus denying that our life has begun to shine on the Lord's Day. Against the Judaizers, whose norm is the Mosaic Law, Ignatius proclaims as norm the Messiah, our God; against the Gnostics, whose norm is the spirit free from all materiality, he proclaims as norm Jesus, true God and true Man (nrs. 157f.).

Once we are acquainted with Ignatius' general and specific motives for writing his four letters, we have attempted to find out the motives that induced the forger to carry out his deep recasting of the Ignatian epistolary. We have also distinguished between general and particular motives.

The forger is no longer worried with Ignatius' martyrdom and its concomitant circumstances. But he is highly preoccupied about unity. In the interpolator's times, once the inward action of Jesus has lost practically all its cohesive strength, what really mattered was the external union of the community members around the bishop, a union " materially " recognizable, as well the mental union with him as sole representative of God on earth, a " spiritual " or moral union. The adversaries of the forger were certain groups within the community that still contested the growing all-embracing authority of the bishop. Ignatius, on the contrary, never alludes to internal disorder in the Asian communities. He points out that the exhortation he addresses them is not due to the existence of any divisions or heresies in their midst, but to the urgent need of warning them against the imminent assault of Gnostic and Judaizing propagandists coming from Syria. The interpolator corrects Ignatius' archaic ecclesiology with a much more developed one. To the single bishop, supervisor and coordinator of all the communities of a Roman province, he opposes the monarchical bishop, at the head of each of the important communities (nrs. 159-162).

As for the twofold petition that we verified in the genuine letters, the first one (prayers for himself) does not appear in the spurious letters written in Troas; the second petition (first, prayers for the church in Syria/then, envoy of an embassy to congratulate them for peace recovered) is only present in the spurious letters in its second modality, as it was to be expected taking into account that the forger has availed himself of the genuine ending of Eph* to compose the three spurious ones of Phld., Sm. and Pol. (nr. 163).

Particular motives, determining the writing of the three spurious letters from Troas, are no longer of dogmatic order. The two letters addressed to Polycarp and his community, Smyrna, fulfill merely a secondary function: to authenticate the whole compilation with Polycarp's authority. But the letter to the Philadelphians reveals the ultimate motive that induced the forger to undertake such a fresh revision. A series of concrete traits that emerged from the interpolated passages allows us to affirm that the interpolator was an Asian, worried about problems of community obedience to the bishop and presbytery, and concretely very interested in pointing out divisions among the Philadelphian community members. He was probably the bishop of Philadelphia. Some immature men have profited by his youth. To move the dissidents to submission, he has recourse to the authority arising from the by him previously interpolated letters of the martyr Ignatius. The deacon Ignatius has already had similar difficulties with schismatic elements on his passing through Philadelphia. Although he was unaware of the existence of divisions, the prophetic Spirit itself would have brought him up-to-date on the presence of such swindlers in the midst of the community. It would be the Spirit of God which has cried out: " Do nothing without the bishop, etc. " (nrs. 164f.).

In an Appendix we have examined the use by both Ignatius and the interpolator of the term γνώμη. In spite of the fact that both use the same term, the contents are different. For Ignatius the only Plan of God is Jesus the Messiah, the unique model for the Christian community to imitate. For the interpolator the plan of God consists in submission and respect of the community members to the bishop and the presbytery. Those who disobey and act in anything without the bishop's consent are opposed to God's plan (nr. 166).

In a third section we have examined the literary resources used by each of the redactors. While Ignatius avails himself of an exhortatory, consciously non-prescriptive genre, the forger makes use of an authoritarian one (nrs. 167f.).

Within the exhortatory genre, Ignatius is especially interested in making it clear that his denouncement of Gnostics or Judaizers is not done in a recriminatory tone. He wants to warn beforehand the Asian communities facing these two opposite tendencies. All the ensemble of advice, warnings and admonitions have as scope to block adverse propaganda. In the letter to the Romans, their aim is to prevent Ignatius' road to martyrdom being obstructed. The interpolator, on the contrary, pays no attention to Ignatius' repeated explanations. He imparts orders indistinctly to factions or states in the community, to the deacons or to Polycarp himself, never departing from the intra-ecclesiastical level (nrs. 169f.).

Ignatius invites to union with Jesus, mutual concord, respect for his decision. The forger invites to submission to the bishop. The forger's exclusive preference for the imperative confirms his tendency to authoritarian tones, unlike Ignatius who combines the subjunctive with the imperative so as to tone down the exhortation. Ignatius refuses to exhort the communities in a prescriptive tone, like an apostle, although he is bishop of the whole province of Syria. The forger preaches through Ignatius' mouth submission and obedience to the bishop and his presbytery while he presents Ignatius as a model of a deacon (nrs. 171f.).

The exhortatory genre, proper to the Ignatian letters, shows up not only through verbs of exhortation and petition, in the use of the imperative forms or their subjunctive equivalents. Both Ignatius and the interpolator make use of several impersonal forms that denote convenience, necessity, excellence, validity or liceity of the actions prescribed to the community. Ignatius' preference for arguments of convenience is evident and fits in with his purpose. The forger, on the contrary, prefers arguments of necessity. The juridical terminology of the latter is in open contradiction with Ignatius' more pastoral tone (nrs. 173-176).

To complete our analysis we have, lastly, examined other forms closely connected with the exhortation. To give greater force to the exhortation or the concomitant petitions, both Ignatius and the forger use the optative sporadically. In general they are not real optatives, but already stereotyped formulas. Statistically, little can be gathered from their frequency. More meaningful, however, is the fact that Ignatius tends to apply the optative to the community, while the interpolator always applies it to individuals or a faction. The usage Ignatius makes of it is more proper and in the case of γένοιτο he uses it exclusively (nr. 177).

Ignatius also uses exclusively the adverbs μόνον and λοιπόν as intensive particles (nr. 178).

In the use of the formulas of encouragement, the interpolator will only make use of ἀντίψυχον by imitating the genuine Ignatian construction, but replacing the personal pronoun instead of the genuine Ignatian impersonal subject. In his turn, Ignatius uses exclusively the equivalent form περίψημα and the constructions with ἁγνίζομαι (ἀσπάζομαι) and ἀσφαλίζομαι (παρακαλῶ). His tendency to substitute the first person pronoun in formulas of encouragement agrees with the several passages where he uses this pronoun in formulas of self-abasement and contrasts with the repeated use the forger makes of it by imitating his own expressions (nr. 179).

To close the comparative study of the literary devices employed by Ignatius and the interpolator to express their diverse motivations, we have analyzed the particles with complementary function that each one uses. Although the respective frequencies maintain a close proportion to the length of their respective texts, preferences diverge rather sharply. If we look at content, the Ignatian exhortation aims exclusively at achieving the unity of the community with Jesus the Messiah or to avoid its withdrawal from Jesus through adverse propaganda, as also to reach his personal objective eluding all kinds of obstacles. The interpolator polarizes it above all into submission of the community to the bishop (nr. 180).

THE FOUR ORIGINAL IGNATIAN LETTERS
(ORIGINAL RECENSION)
RECONSTRUCTED FROM THE SEVEN ONES OF THE MIDDLE RECENSION

As an appendix we are offering the princeps edition of the four authentic Ignatian letters from Smyrna. In our reconstruction from the seven letters of the Middle Recension we have aimed, as far as possible, to give the integral text of the commonly held textus receptus (omitting the first part — written in the singular — of the totally spurious letter to Polycarp); but set out in the new structure of four letters. In the present edition we wished to respect the order given by Ignatius. At the beginning of each letter we give the reasons guiding our choice and other details that can be inferred from the Ignatian text itself.

To facilitate the reading, the text has been printed so as to bring out the chiastic structure proper to the Ignatian epistolary genre. Titles and subdivisions (we have set aside the division into chapters, the only one followed up to now) are to make the theme of each letter clear to the reader. To draw attention to the presence of interpolations we have edited these in smaller print with the use of square brackets. In cases where a reconstruction has been necessary, we have reserved the left-hand column for the original text, printing in bold type to the right one(s) the authentic Ignatian text together with the interpolations, making it correspond exactly with the proposed reconstruction in the left-hand column. When the original order has been changed we have kept to the present order in the right-hand column, reconstructing the primitive order to the left.

To avoid unnecessary repetitions, we have placed outside the normal sequence those clauses or paragraphs that correspond with another places, indicating their new position.

The present edition is accompanied by two apparatus. In the critical apparatus we have taken into account the most important critical variants, above all those placed in a new light because of the reconstruction of the Ignatian text. Besides the manuscripts, versions and doxographers, we have annotated the preferences of editors we have consulted. In the second apparatus there are references to the numbers in our work that justify the reconstruction, changes of order, or indicate the presence of interpolations.

LETTER TO THE ROMANS
(Rom.)

The first of the four letters (the only authentic ones) written from Smyrna by Ignatius, the Godbearer. Reasons: (a) Urgency of the problem; (b) No allusion to the re-establishment of peace in the communities of Syria; (c) Date (see below).

Sender: Ignatius, the bishop-supervisor of the whole province of Syria, on his way from the Orient (Life) to the Occident (Death), to " set " from the world towards God.

Addressees: The Christian community that has the presidency in the country of the region of the Romans.

Theme: Insistent request to the Romans to keep silence, in order to dissuade them from influencing the Imperial authorities to deliver him from martyrdom.

Date: The 24th. August (the only dated letter).

Bearers: Some of the Ephesian delegates sent to Smyrna. Crocus, one of those delegates, well-known to the Romans, remains in Smyrna.

Mention of the envoys from Syria to Rome, who went before him to Rome: Their recommendation to the community.

This letter was not interpolated, since the interpolator who worked in Asia Minor was unaware that Ignatius had written it. Notice its singular manuscript transmission.

A. INITIAL GREETING

Rom. inscr. Ἰγνάτιος, ὁ καὶ Θεοφόρος,
τῇ ἠλεημένῃ ἐν μεγαλειότητι πατρὸς ὑψίστου καὶ Ἰησοῦ
Χριστοῦ τοῦ μόνου υἱοῦ αὐτοῦ ἐκκλησίᾳ,
ἠγαπημένῃ καὶ πεφωτισμένῃ ἐν θελήματι τοῦ θελήσαντος
5 τὰ πάντα, ἅ ἐστιν, κατὰ πίστιν καὶ ἀγάπην Ἰησοῦ Χριστοῦ, τοῦ θεοῦ ἡμῶν,
ἥτις καὶ προκάθηται ἐν τόπῳ χωρίου Ῥωμαίων, ἀξιόθεος,
ἀξιοπρεπής, ἀξιομακάριστος, ἀξιέπαινος, ἀξιοεπίτευκτος, ἀξιόαγνος —
καὶ προκαθημένη τῆς ἀγάπης —, χριστόνομος, πατρώνυμος,
ἣν καὶ ἀσπάζομαι ἐν ὀνόματι Ἰησοῦ Χριστοῦ, υἱοῦ πατρός ·
10 κατὰ σάρκα καὶ πνεῦμα ἡνωμένοις πάσῃ ἐντολῇ αὐτοῦ, πε-
πληρωμένοις χάριτος θεοῦ ἀδιακρίτως καὶ ἀποδιϋλισμένοις ἀπὸ παντὸς
ἀλλοτρίου χρώματος ·
πλεῖστα ἐν Ἰησοῦ Χριστῷ, τῷ θεῷ ἡμῶν, ἀμώμως χαίρειν.

B. INTRODUCTION

**Motive of the letter: You should not procure me anything else but
to be immolated to god**

I, 1. Ἐπεὶ εὐξάμενος θεῷ ἐπέτυχον ἰδεῖν ὑμῶν τὰ ἀξιόθεα πρόσωπα —
15 ὡς καὶ πλέον ⟨ἢ⟩ ἠτούμην λαβεῖν (δεδεμένος γὰρ ἐν Χριστῷ Ἰησοῦ ἐλπίζω ὑμᾶς ἀσπάσασθαι, ἐάνπερ θέλημα ᾖ τοῦ ἀξιωθῆναί με εἰς τέλος
εἶναι. 2. ἡ μὲν γὰρ ἀρχὴ εὐοικονόμητός ἐστιν, ἐάνπερ χάριτος ἐπιτύχω
εἰς τὸ τὸν κλῆρόν μου ἀνεμποδίστως ἀπολαβεῖν · φοβοῦμαι γὰρ τὴν ὑμῶν
ἀγάπην, μὴ αὐτή με ἀδικήσῃ · ὑμῖν γὰρ εὐχερές ἐστιν, ὃ θέλετε ποιῆσαι,
20 ἐμοὶ δὲ δύσκολόν ἐστιν τὸ θεοῦ ἐπιτυχεῖν, ἐάνπερ ὑμεῖς μὴ φείσησθέ
μου · II, 1. οὐ γὰρ θέλω ὑμᾶς ἀνθρωπαρεσκῆσαι, ἀλλὰ θεῷ ἀρέσαι,
ὥσπερ καὶ ἀρέσκετε · οὔτε γὰρ ἐγώ ποτε ἕξω καιρὸν τοιοῦτον θεοῦ ἐπιτυχεῖν, οὔτε ὑμεῖς, ἐὰν σιωπήσητε, κρείττονι ἔργῳ ἔχετε ἐπιγραφῆναι ·
ἐὰν γὰρ σιωπήσητε ἀπ' ἐμοῦ, ἐγὼ λόγος θεοῦ, ἐὰν δὲ ἐρασθῆτε τῆς σαρκός

---

5 πίστιν καὶ TAAmCg Light. Bihl. Perler: > GHKLSmBmM Zahn Funk Hilg.
‖ **14** Ἐπεὶ εὐξάμενος zAAm(C)gM: ἐπευξάμενος (deprecans) Ll (SSm) Hilg.; " but
they seem to be attempts to mend the anacoluthon of ἐπεὶ εὐξάμενος κ.τ.λ." (Light.
II/1, 194). The sentence is not at all an anacoluthon. The corresponding apodosis
comes first after a long digression (1,1c-2,1) in 2,2a: πλέον μοι κτλ., caused by the
specification of 1,1b: ὡς καὶ — λαβεῖν ‖ **15** πλέον ἤ (ἠτούμην) con. Light., cf.
Am (quantum petii, plus etiam accepi): πλέον zL(Sm)ACg editors. For ὡς with
infinitive expressing consequence, see Light. II/1, 195 ‖ **24** ἐγὼ λόγος θεοῦ L(Am)
Light. Funk Hilg. Krüger Bauer Bihl. Fischer: λόγος γενήσομαι θεοῦ SSmC Ioann-
Mon. Zahn, ἐγὼ γενήσομαι θεοῦ z(A)BmgM Camelot.

μου, πάλιν ἔσομαι φωνή) — 2. πλέον μοι μὴ παράσχησθε τοῦ σπονδισθῆναι θεῷ, ὡς ἔτι θυσιαστήριον ἕτοιμόν ἐστιν, ἵνα ἐν ἀγάπῃ χορὸς γενόμενοι ᾄσητε τῷ πατρὶ ἐν Ἰησοῦ Χριστῷ, ὅτι τὸν ἐπίσκοπον Συρίας κατη-
ξίωσεν ὁ θεὸς εὑρεθῆναι εἰς δύσιν ἀπὸ ἀνατολῆς μεταπεμψάμενος. καλὸν
τὸ δῦναι ἀπὸ κόσμου πρὸς θεόν, ἵνα εἰς αὐτὸν ἀνατείλω.   5

C. BODY OF THE LETTER

a. Aim: Be consistent with what you teach, for it is not enough to be called but to be found a Christian

III, 1. Οὐδέποτε ἐβασκάνατε οὐδενί, ἄλλους ἐδιδάξατε. ἐγὼ δὲ θέλω,
ἵνα κἀκεῖνα βέβαια ᾖ, ἃ μαθητεύοντες ἐντέλλεσθε. 2. μόνον μοι δύναμιν
αἰτεῖσθε ἔσωθέν τε καὶ ἔξωθεν, ἵνα μὴ μόνον λέγω, ἀλλὰ καὶ θέλω.
μὴ ἵνα μόνον λέγωμαι Χριστιανός, ἀλλὰ καὶ εὑρεθῶ · ἐὰν γὰρ εὑρεθῶ,
καὶ λέγεσθαι δύναμαι καὶ τότε πιστὸς εἶναι, ὅταν κόσμῳ μὴ φαίνωμαι.   10
3. οὐδὲν φαινόμενον καλόν · ὁ γὰρ θεὸς ἡμῶν Ἰησοῦς Χριστὸς ἐν πατρὶ
ὢν μᾶλλον φαίνεται. οὐ πεισμονῆς τὸ ἔργον, ἀλλὰ μεγέθους ἐστὶν ὁ Χρι-
στιανισμός, ὅταν μισῆται ὑπὸ κόσμου.

b. Exhortation: Do not set obstacles in the way of the decision I freely took to die for God

IV, 1. Ἐγὼ γράφω πάσαις ταῖς ἐκκλησίαις καὶ ἐντέλλομαι πᾶσιν, ὅτι
ἐγὼ ἑκὼν ὑπὲρ θεοῦ ἀποθνήσκω, ἐάνπερ ὑμεῖς μὴ κωλύσητε. παρακαλῶ   15
ὑμᾶς, μὴ εὔνοια ἄκαιρος γένησθέ μοι. ἄφετέ με θηρίων εἶναι βοράν, δι’
ὧν ἔνεστιν θεοῦ ἐπιτυχεῖν. σῖτός εἰμι θεοῦ καὶ δι’ ὀδόντων θηρίων ἀλήθομαι, ἵνα καθαρὸς θεοῦ ἄρτος εὑρεθῶ. 2. μᾶλλον κολακεύσατε τὰ θηρία,
ἵνα μοι τάφος γένωνται καὶ μηθὲν καταλίπωσι τῶν τοῦ σώματός μου,
ἵνα μὴ κοιμηθεὶς βαρύς τινι γένωμαι. τότε ἔσομαι μαθητὴς ἀληθῶς τοῦ   20
Χριστοῦ, ὅτε οὐδὲ τὸ σῶμά μου ὁ κόσμος ὄψεται. λιτανεύσατε τὸν κύριον ὑπὲρ ἐμοῦ, ἵνα διὰ τῶν ὀργάνων τούτων θεοῦ θυσία εὑρεθῶ.

---

1 φωνή LSSm(Am)C Ioann-Mon. Light. Funk Hilg. Krüger Bauer Bihl. Fischer:
τρέχων zABmgM (cf. 1Cor. 9,24) Camelot, ἠχώ con. (Cureton) Bunsen Zahn. " Es
kommt dem Ign. sichtlich auf dem Gegensatz von λόγος und φωνή an " (Bauer II
245) | πλέον GHKSA(C) Zahn (Light.) Funk Lelong Camelot: + δὲ TL(SmAm)gM
Bihl. Fischer. The addition of δὲ turns the apodosis of 1,1a into an independent
period | παράσχησθε GK editors: -εσθαι (sic) H, - ητε T, tribuetis L, -εσθε M,
παρέσχεσθε g || 18 θεοῦ (after εὑρεθῶ SAAm)SSfAAmCg Orig. = Iren. (Schol. 38
in Apoc.) Iren. (panis dei inveniar, A.H. V. 28,4): > Eus. (E.H. III. 36,12) Hieron.
(De viris ill. 16, depending on Eus.) Light., τοῦ Χριστοῦ GHTLSmM Zahn Bihl.
Fischer Camelot || 20 τοῦ Χριστοῦ GHKSmACM Zahn: Χριστοῦ τοῦ θεοῦ T, Ἰησοῦ
Χριστοῦ LSAmg Light. Bihl. Fischer Camelot || 21 κύριον TSSfAAmCg Light.:
Χριστὸν GHKLSm(M) Zahn Bihl. Fischer Camelot.

c. Explanation: I do not give you directives like Peter and Paul

IV, 3a. Οὐχ ὡς Πέτρος καὶ Παῦλος διατάσσομαι ὑμῖν · ἐκεῖνοι ἀπόστολοι, ἐγὼ κατάκριτος · ἐκεῖνοι ἐλεύθεροι, ἐγὼ δὲ μέχρι νῦν δοῦλος. ἀλλ᾽ ἐὰν πάθω, ἀπελεύθερος γενήσομαι Ἰησοῦ Χριστοῦ καὶ ἀναστήσομαι ἐν αὐτῷ ἐλεύθερος.

d. Exposition: Now, in chains, I am learning to desire nothing

5 IV, 3e. Νῦν μανθάνω δεδεμένος μηδὲν ἐπιθυμεῖν · V, 1. ἀπὸ Συρίας μέχρι Ῥώμης θηριομαχῶ, διὰ γῆς καὶ θαλάσσης, νυκτὸς καὶ ἡμέρας, ἐνδεδεμένος δέκα λεοπάρδοις, ὅ ἐστιν στρατιωτικὸν τάγμα, οἳ καὶ εὐεργετούμενοι χείρους γίνονται. ἐν δὲ τοῖς ἀδικήμασιν αὐτῶν μᾶλλον μαθητεύομαι, " ἀλλ᾽ οὐ παρὰ τοῦτο δεδικαίωμαι ". 2. ὀναίμην τῶν θηρίων
10 τῶν ἐμοὶ ἡτοιμασμένων καὶ εὔχομαι σύντομά μοι εὑρεθῆναι · ἃ καὶ κολακεύσω, συντόμως με καταφαγεῖν, οὐχ ὥσπερ τινῶν δειλαινόμενα οὐχ ἥψαντο. κἂν αὐτὰ δὲ ἄκοντα μὴ θελήσῃ, ἐγὼ προσβιάσομαι.

Now I begin to be a disciple

V, 3. Συγγνώμην μοι ἔχετε · τί μοι συμφέρει, ἐγὼ γινώσκω. νῦν ἄρχομαι μαθητὴς εἶναι. μηδέν με ζηλώσαι τῶν ὁρατῶν καὶ ἀοράτων, ἵνα
15 Ἰησοῦ Χριστοῦ ἐπιτύχω. πῦρ καὶ σταυρὸς θηρίων τε συστάσεις, σκορπισμοὶ ὀστέων, συγκοπαὶ μελῶν, ἀλεσμοὶ ὅλου τοῦ σώματος, κακαὶ κολάσεις τοῦ διαβόλου ἐπ᾽ ἐμὲ ἐρχέσθωσαν, μόνον ἵνα Ἰησοῦ Χριστοῦ ἐπιτύχω. VI, 1. οὐδέν με ὠφελήσει τὰ τερπνὰ τοῦ κόσμου οὐδὲ αἱ βασιλεῖαι τοῦ αἰῶνος τούτου. " καλόν μοι ἀποθανεῖν " εἰς Χριστὸν Ἰησοῦν,
20 ἢ βασιλεύειν τῶν περάτων τῆς γῆς. ἐκεῖνον ζητῶ, τὸν ὑπὲρ ἡμῶν ἀποθανόντα · ἐκεῖνον θέλω, τὸν δι᾽ ἡμᾶς ἀναστάντα. ὁ δὲ τοκετός μοι ἐπίκειται.

---

5 νῦν zAmCgM Zahn Light. Funk Camelot: καὶ νῦν LS(Sm)A Bihl. Fischer ‖ **10** σύντομα Smg Eus. editors: promptas L, συντόμως SAAm, ἕτοιμα zBmM ‖ **12** ἄκοντα zBmM Eus. Funk Hilg. Lelong Camelot: ἑκόντα L (volentem) g Zahn Light. Krüger Bauer Bihl. Fischer. ἄ. means that the beasts could *be constrained* (see Liddell-Scott-Jones, s.v.) by God's power to refuse to devour Ign. | θελήσῃ z(M) Zahn Funk Lelong Camelot: velint L, θέλῃ g Eus. Light. Hilg. Fischer ‖ **18** τερπνὰ GHTM(A) Zahn Camelot: πέρατα LSfSmAmg Light. Funk Hilg. Krüger Lelong Bihl. Fischer. τὰ τερπνὰ, *delights, pleasures*, is preferable, since κόσμος is always used by Ign. in a metaphorical sense, as an impersonation of the values system opposed to God (Mg. 5,2[2x]; Rom. 2,2; 3,2.3; 4,2; 6,1.2; 7,1). τὰ πέρατα could " freilich aus dem folgenden eingedrungen sein " (Bauer II 250), see 6,1b ‖ **19** Χριστὸν Ἰησοῦν GHTSmAmM(l): ~ LSfAg Tim.

V,1. The quotation is taken from 1Cor. 4,4.
VI,1. A free quotation from 1Cor. 9,15.

Be indulgent with me: do not prevent me from living

VI, 2. Σύγγνωτέ μοι, ἀδελφοί· μὴ ἐμποδίσητέ μοι ζῆσαι, μὴ θελήσητέ
με ἀποθανεῖν· τὸν τοῦ θεοῦ θέλοντα εἶναι κόσμῳ μὴ χαρίσησθε μηδὲ
ὕλῃ ἐξαπατήσητε. ἄφετέ με καθαρὸν φῶς λαβεῖν· ἐκεῖ παραγενόμενος
ἄνθρωπος ἔσομαι. 3. ἐπιτρέψατέ μοι μιμητὴν εἶναι τοῦ πάθους τοῦ θεοῦ
μου. εἴ τις αὐτὸν ἐν ἑαυτῷ ἔχει, νοησάτω, ὃ θέλω, καὶ συμπαθείτω μοι, 5
εἰδὼς τὰ συνέχοντά με.

C'. PARAENESIS

Place yourselves on my side and not that of the Chief of this world

VII, 1. Ὁ ἄρχων τοῦ αἰῶνος τούτου διαρπάσαι με βούλεται καὶ τὴν εἰς
θεόν μου γνώμην διαφθεῖραι. μηδεὶς οὖν τῶν παρόντων ὑμῶν βοηθείτω
αὐτῷ· μᾶλλον ἐμοῦ γίνεσθε, τουτέστιν τοῦ θεοῦ. μὴ λαλεῖτε Ἰησοῦν
Χριστόν, κόσμον δὲ ἐπιθυμεῖτε. 2. βασκανία ἐν ὑμῖν μὴ κατοικείτω. 10
μηδ' ἂν ἐγὼ παρὼν παρακαλῶ ὑμᾶς, πείσθητέ μοι· τούτοις δὲ μᾶλλον
πείσθητε, οἷς γράφω ὑμῖν. ζῶν γὰρ γράφω ὑμῖν, ἐρῶν τοῦ ἀποθανεῖν.
ὁ ἐμὸς ἔρως ἐσταύρωται, καὶ οὐκ ἔστιν ἐν ἐμοὶ πῦρ φιλόϋλον· ὕδωρ δὲ
ζῶν καὶ λαλοῦν ἐν ἐμοί, ἔσωθέν μοι λέγον· Δεῦρο πρὸς τὸν πατέρα.
3. οὐχ ἥδομαι τροφῇ φθορᾶς οὐδὲ ἡδοναῖς τοῦ βίου τούτου. ἄρτον θεοῦ 15
θέλω, ὅ ἐστιν σὰρξ Ἰησοῦ Χριστοῦ, τοῦ ἐκ σπέρματος Δαυίδ, καὶ πόμα
θέλω τὸ αἷμα αὐτοῦ, ὅ ἐστιν ἀγάπη ἄφθαρτος. VIII, 1. οὐκέτι θέλω κατὰ
ἀνθρώπους ζῆν. τοῦτο δὲ ἔσται, ἐὰν ὑμεῖς θελήσητε. θελήσατε, ἵνα καὶ
ὑμεῖς θεληθῆτε.

Epilogue: Jesus the Messiah will show you my truthfulness

VIII, 2. Δι' ὀλίγων γραμμάτων αἰτοῦμαι ὑμᾶς· πιστεύσατέ μοι. Ἰησοῦς 20
δὲ Χριστὸς ὑμῖν ταῦτα φανερώσει, ὅτι ἀληθῶς λέγω· τὸ ἀψευδὲς στόμα,
ἐν ᾧ ὁ πατὴρ ἀληθῶς ἐλάλησεν.

B'. CONCLUSION

Petition for prayers for himself

VIII, 3. Αἰτήσασθε περὶ ἐμοῦ, ἵνα ἐπιτύχω. οὐ κατὰ σάρκα ὑμῖν ἔγραψα,
ἀλλὰ κατὰ γνώμην θεοῦ. ἐὰν πάθω, ἠθελήσατε· ἐὰν ἀποδοκιμασθῶ,
ἐμισήσατε.   25

Petition for prayers for the church of Syria

IX, 1. Μνημονεύετε ἐν τῇ προσευχῇ ὑμῶν τῆς ἐν Συρίᾳ ἐκκλησίας, ἥτις
ἀντὶ ἐμοῦ ποιμένι τῷ θεῷ χρῆται· μόνος αὐτὴν Ἰησοῦς Χριστὸς ἐπισκοπήσει καὶ ἡ ὑμῶν ἀγάπη. 2. ἐγὼ δὲ αἰσχύνομαι ἐξ αὐτῶν λέγεσθαι·
οὐδὲ γὰρ ἄξιός εἰμι, ὢν ἔσχατος αὐτῶν καὶ ἔκτρωμα· ἀλλ' ἠλέημαί τις
εἶναι, ἐὰν θεοῦ ἐπιτύχω.   30

A'. FINAL GREETING

Personal greetings and greetings from the Asian communities present in Smyrna

IX, 3. Ἀσπάζεται ὑμᾶς τὸ ἐμὸν πνεῦμα καὶ ἡ ἀγάπη τῶν ἐκκλησιῶν τῶν δεξαμένων με εἰς ὄνομα Ἰησοῦ Χριστοῦ, οὐχ ὡς παροδεύοντα · καὶ γὰρ αἱ μὴ προσήκουσαί μοι τῇ ὁδῷ, τῇ κατὰ σάρκα, κατὰ πόλιν με προήγαγον.

Place of writing of the letter and bearers of the same to Rome

5 X, 1. Γράφω δὲ ὑμῖν ταῦτα ἀπὸ Σμύρνης δι᾽ Ἐφεσίων τῶν ἀξιομακαρίστων. ἔστιν δὲ καὶ ἅμα ἐμοὶ σὺν ἄλλοις πολλοῖς καὶ Κρόκος, τὸ ποθητόν μοι ὄνομα.

Recommendations for those who went before him from Syria to Rome

X, 2. Περὶ τῶν προελθόντων με ἀπὸ Συρίας εἰς Ῥώμην εἰς δόξαν θεοῦ πιστεύω ὑμᾶς ἐπεγνωκέναι, οἷς καὶ δηλώσατε ἐγγύς με ὄντα · πάντες γάρ
10 εἰσιν ἄξιοι θεοῦ καὶ ὑμῶν · οὓς πρέπον ὑμῖν ἐστὶν κατὰ πάντα ἀναπαῦσαι.

Date

X, 3a. Ἔγραψα δὲ ὑμῖν ταῦτα τῇ πρὸ ἐννέα καλανδῶν Σεπτεμβρίων.

Farewell formula

X, 3b. Ἔρρωσθε εἰς τέλος ἐν ὑπομονῇ Ἰησοῦ Χριστοῦ.

---

3 προήγαγον g (translated by an aorist or perfect in:) LAAmSm: προῆγον zM (translated by an imperfect in:) S, editors. See Light. II/1, 231, and our n. 234.

PRIMITIVE LETTER TO THE MAGNESIANS
(Mg* = Mg. + Phld.)

Written in second place: (a) Mention of Ignatius' objective in addressing the communities who had sent him delegates; (b) Allusion to the critical situation of the church of Syria; (c) Greetings from the Ephesians present in Smyrna, and from the other delegations.

Sender: Ignatius, the Godbearer, a man ready to create union among the communities.

Addressees: The community which is in Magnesia on the Maeander.

Theme: To warn the community beforehand against the Judaizers. Ignatius is perfectly well aware that up to the present Judaizing propaganda has had no effect on them; on the contrary, there has been an inward clarification as regards the sowers of discord.

Bearers: The four delegates of Magnesia sent to Smyrna.

The original letter (Mg*) has been divided into two (Mg. and Phld.) by cutting the Body of the letter between the explanation of the exhortation (Mg. 11-12) and the exhortation itself (Phld. 2,1-3,2). The original inscr. has again been distributed between Mg. and Phld. The ending has been left in Mg. (14-15). The ending of Phld. is for the most part a copy of that of Sm. Both the newly-composed letters have been heavily interpolated.

A. INITIAL GREETING

Mg* inscr.*

Ἰγνάτιος, ὁ καὶ Θεοφόρος,
τῇ εὐλογημένῃ ἐν χάριτι
θεοῦ πατρὸς ἐν Χριστῷ Ἰησοῦ τῷ σωτῆρι
ἡμῶν οὔσῃ ἐν Μαγνησίᾳ τῇ πρὸς Μαιάνδρῳ,
ἐκκλησίᾳ, τῇ

ἠλεημένῃ καὶ ἡδρασμένῃ ἐν
ὁμονοίᾳ θεοῦ καὶ ἀγαλλιωμένῃ ἐν τῷ πάθει τοῦ κυρίου ἡμῶν ἀδιακρίτως καὶ ἐν
τῇ ἀναστάσει αὐτοῦ,
πεπληροφορημένῃ ἐν παντὶ

ἐλέει·
ἣν <καὶ> ἀσπάζομαι ἐν αἵ-
ματι Ἰησοῦ Χριστοῦ, ἥτις ἐστὶν χαρὰ
αἰώνιος καὶ παράμονος,

καὶ εὔχομαι ἐν θεῷ πατρὶ
καὶ ἐν Ἰησοῦ Χριστῷ πλεῖστα χαίρειν.

Mg. inscr.

Ἰγνάτιος, ὁ καὶ Θεοφόρος,
τῇ εὐλογημένῃ ἐν χάριτι
θεοῦ πατρὸς ἐν Χριστῷ Ἰησοῦ τῷ σωτῆρι
ἡμῶν, ἐν ᾧ ἀσπάζομαι τὴν ἐκκλησίαν τὴν
οὖσαν ἐν Μαγνησίᾳ τῇ πρὸς Μαιάνδρῳ

καὶ εὔχομαι ἐν θεῷ πατρὶ
καὶ ἐν Ἰησοῦ Χριστῷ πλεῖστα χαίρειν.

Phld. inscr.

Ἰγνάτιος, ὁ καὶ Θεοφόρος,
ἐκκλησίᾳ θεοῦ πατρὸς καὶ
κυρίου Ἰησοῦ Χριστοῦ τῇ
οὔσῃ ἐν {Φιλαδελφίᾳ τῆς Ἀσίας,}

ἠλεημένῃ καὶ ἡδρασμένῃ ἐν
ὁμονοίᾳ θεοῦ καὶ ἀγαλλιωμένῃ ἐν τῷ πάθει τοῦ κυρίου ἡμῶν ἀδιακρίτως καὶ ἐν
τῇ ἀναστάσει αὐτοῦ,
πεπληροφορημένῃ ἐν παντὶ
ἐλέει,
ἣν ἀσπάζομαι ἐν αἵ-
ματι Ἰησοῦ Χριστοῦ, ἥτις ἐστὶν χαρὰ
αἰώνιος καὶ παράμονος,

{μάλιστα ἐὰν ἐν ἑνὶ ὦσιν
σὺν τῷ ἐπισκόπῳ καὶ τοῖς σὺν αὐτῷ πρεσβυτέροις καὶ διακόνοις ἀποδεδειγμένοις ἐν
γνώμῃ Ἰησοῦ Χριστοῦ, οὓς κατὰ τὸ ἴδιον
θέλημα ἐστήριξεν ἐν βεβαιωσύνῃ τῷ ἁγίῳ
αὐτοῦ πνεύματι.}

---

3 Χριστῷ Ἰησοῦ LAg editors: ~ G || 12 καὶ add., cf. Tr. inscr.; Rom. inscr.

Mg* inscr*. Reconstructed from Mg. inscr. + Phld. inscr^a.: see nrs. 29, 130.
{Φιλαδελφίᾳ κτλ. Correction introduced by the interp.
{μάλιστα ἐὰν κτλ. For the anomalies in the Phld. inscr., see nrs. 22, 138; for the content of the interpolation, nr. 58.

B. INTRODUCTION

Objective of Ignatius in addressing the communities: perfect union

Mg. I, 1. Γνοὺς ὑμῶν τὸ πολυεύτακτον τῆς κατὰ θεὸν ἀγάπης, ἀγαλλιώμενος προειλόμην ἐν πίστει Ἰησοῦ Χριστοῦ προσλαλῆσαι ὑμῖν · 2. καταξιωθεὶς γὰρ ὀνόματος θεοπρεπεστάτου ἐν οἷς περιφέρω δεσμοῖς ᾄδω τὰς ἐκκλησίας, ἐν αἷς ἕνωσιν εὔχομαι σαρκὸς καὶ πνεύματος Ἰησοῦ Χριστοῦ, τοῦ διὰ παντὸς ἡμῶν ζῆν, πίστεώς τε καὶ ἀγάπης, ἧς οὐδὲν προκέκριται, 5
τὸ δὲ κυριώτερον, Ἰησοῦ καὶ πατρός · ἐν ᾧ ὑπομένοντες τὴν πᾶσαν ἐπήρειαν τοῦ ἄρχοντος τοῦ αἰῶνος τούτου καὶ διαφυγόντες θεοῦ τευξόμεθα.

Mention of delegates: Invitation to be true Christians

II. Ἐπεὶ οὖν ἠξιώθην ἰδεῖν ὑμᾶς διὰ Δαμᾶ
        καὶ
Βάσσου καὶ Ἀπολλωνίου καὶ
        Ζωτίωνος,

II. **Ἐπεὶ οὖν ἠξιώθην ἰδεῖν ὑμᾶς διὰ Δαμᾶ** {τοῦ ἀξιοθέου ὑμῶν ἐπισκόπου} **καὶ** {πρεσβυτέρων ἀξίων} 10 **Βάσσου καὶ Ἀπολλωνίου καὶ** {τοῦ συνδούλου μου διακόνου} **Ζωτίωνος,** {οὗ ἐγὼ ὀναίμην, ὅτι ὑποτάσσεται τῷ ἐπισκόπῳ ὡς χάριτι θεοῦ καὶ τῷ πρεσβυτερίῳ ὡς νόμῳ Ἰησοῦ Χρι- 15 στοῦ. III, 1. καὶ ὑμῖν δὲ πρέπει μὴ συγχρᾶσθαι τῇ ἡλικίᾳ τοῦ ἐπισκόπου, ἀλλὰ κατὰ δύναμιν θεοῦ πατρὸς πᾶσαν ἐντροπὴν αὐτῷ ἀπονέμειν, καθὼς ἔγνων καὶ τοὺς ἁγίους πρεσβυτέ- 20 ρους οὐ προσειληφότας τὴν φαινομένην νεωτερικὴν τάξιν, ἀλλ᾽ ὡς φρονίμους ἐν θεῷ συγχωροῦντας αὐτῷ, οὐκ αὐτῷ δέ, ἀλλὰ τῷ πατρὶ Ἰησοῦ Χρι-

III, 2. εἰς
τιμὴν   ἐκείνου   τοῦ   θελήσαντος
ἡμᾶς πρέπον ἐστὶν

στοῦ, τῷ πάντων ἐπισκόπῳ.} 2. **εἰς** 25 **τιμὴν** {οὖν} **ἐκείνου τοῦ θελήσαντος ἡμᾶς πρέπον ἐστὶν** {ἐπακούειν κατὰ μηδεμίαν ὑπόκρισιν· ἐπεὶ οὐχ ὅτι τὸν ἐπίσκοπον τοῦτον τὸν βλεπόμενον πλανᾷ τις, ἀλλὰ τὸν ἀόρατον παρα- 30

---

27 ἡμᾶς GL Dam.: ὑμᾶς AB(g) Light.

II-V. For the interpolations and the reconstruction of the original sequence, see nrs. 83 f. (85), 135. The first anacoluthon of 2a (᾽Επεὶ οὖν κτλ.), caused by the long digression introduced by the interp., has its corresponding apodosis in 3,2a (εἰς τιμὴν κτλ.). The second anacoluthon of 5,1 (᾽Επεὶ οὖν τέλος κτλ.) is obviated by leaving out the particle οὖν. Thus the sentence of 5,1 recovers its original function: to motivate (ἐπεὶ τέλος κτλ.) the former invitation. As for the explanatory sentence of 5,2a (ὥσπερ γὰρ κτλ.) and its quasi-apodosis of 5,2e (δι᾽ οὗ [sc. διὰ τούτου τοῦ χαρακτῆρος] ἐὰν μὴ κτλ.), see n. 298. (For the indicative with ἐὰν see Bauer II 223.)

λογίζεται. τὸ δὲ τοιοῦτον οὐ πρὸς σάρκα ὁ λόγος, ἀλλὰ πρὸς θεὸν τὸν τὰ κρύφια εἰδότα. IV. πρέπον οὖν

IV.

μὴ μόνον καλεῖσθαι Χριστια-
5 νούς, ἀλλὰ καὶ εἶναι ·

ἐστὶν} **μὴ μόνον καλεῖσθαι Χριστια-νούς, ἀλλὰ καὶ εἶναι** · {ὥσπερ καί τινες ἐπίσκοπον μὲν καλοῦσιν, χωρὶς δὲ αὐτοῦ πάντα πράσσουσιν. οἱ τοι-οῦτοι δὲ οὐκ εὐσυνείδητοί μοι εἶναι φαίνονται διὰ τὸ μὴ βεβαίως κατ' ἐντολὴν συναθροίζεσθαι.}

10 V, 1. ἐπεὶ
τέλος τὰ πράγματα ἔχει καὶ

V, 1. ἐπεὶ {οὖν} **τέλος τὰ πράγματα ἔχει** ...

πρόκειται τὰ δύο ὁμοῦ, ὅ τε θάνατος καὶ ἡ ζωή, καὶ ἕκαστος εἰς τὸν ἴδιον τόπον μέλλει χωρεῖν. 2. ὥσπερ γάρ ἐστιν νομίσματα δύο — ὁ μὲν θεοῦ, ὁ δὲ κόσμου — καὶ ἕκαστον αὐτῶν ἴδιον χαρακτῆρα ἐπικείμενον
15 ἔχει — οἱ ἄπιστοι τοῦ κόσμου τούτου, οἱ δὲ πιστοὶ ἐν ἀγάπῃ χαρακτῆρα θεοῦ πατρὸς διὰ Ἰησοῦ Χριστοῦ —, δι' οὗ ἐὰν μὴ αὐθαιρέτως ἔχομεν τὸ ἀποθανεῖν εἰς τὸ αὐτοῦ πάθος, τὸ ζῆν αὐτοῦ οὐκ ἔστιν ἐν ἡμῖν.

C. BODY OF THE LETTER

a. Aim: Invitation to act in accord with God, Jesus the Messiah

VI, 1. Ἐπεὶ οὖν ἐν τοῖς προγεγραμ-μένοις προσώποις τὸ πᾶν πλῆθος ἐθε-
20 ώρησα ἐν πίστει καὶ ἀγάπῃ, παραινῶ, ἐν ὁμονοίᾳ θεοῦ

VI, 1. **Ἐπεὶ οὖν ἐν τοῖς προγεγραμ-μένοις προσώποις τὸ πᾶν πλῆθος ἐθε-ώρησα ἐν πίστει καὶ ἀγάπῃ, παραινῶ, ἐν ὁμονοίᾳ θεοῦ σπουδάζετε πάντα πράσσειν** {, προκαθημένου τοῦ ἐπι-σκόπου εἰς τόπον θεοῦ καὶ τῶν πρεσ-βυτέρων εἰς τόπον συνεδρίου τῶν ἀποστόλων, καὶ τῶν διακόνων τῶν
25 ἐμοὶ γλυκυτάτων πεπιστευμένων δια-κονίαν} **Ἰησοῦ Χριστοῦ, ὃς πρὸ αἰώ-νων παρὰ πατρὶ ἦν καὶ ἐν τέλει ἐφά-νη** {.}

Ἰησοῦ Χριστοῦ, ὃς πρὸ αἰώ-νων παρὰ πατρὶ ἦν καὶ ἐν τέλει ἐφά-νη, σπουδάζετε πάντα πράσσειν.

30 2. πάντες οὖν ὁμοήθειαν θεοῦ λαβόντες ἐντρέπεσθε ἀλλήλους καὶ μηδεὶς κατὰ σάρκα βλεπέτω τὸν πλησίον, ἀλλ' ἐν Ἰησοῦ Χριστῷ ἀλλήλους διὰ παντὸς ἀγαπᾶτε. μηδὲν ἔστω ἐν ὑμῖν, ὃ δυνήσεται ὑμᾶς μερίσαι, {ἀλλ'

---

16 δι' οὗ GLg editors: propter quod (= δι' ὅ)l, propter eum Sf. See n. 298 ‖ **20** ἀγά-πῃ LSfAl: ἠγάπησα Gg editors ‖ **23** τόπον ... τόπον GLgl Sever. Funk Hilg. Krüger Bihl. Fischer: τύπον ... τύπον SAB (tamquam) Zahn Light. See nrs. 114-115.118.

VI,1. For the reconstruction of the original sequence, see nrs. 86 (87), 137, 141. {προκαθημένου κτλ. Interpolation: see nr. 86.1 (87).
VI,2-VII,1. {ἀλλ' ἑνώθητε κτλ. Interpolation: see nrs. 86.2 (87), 141.

ἐνώθητε τῷ ἐπισκόπῳ καὶ τοῖς προκαθημένοις εἰς τύπον καὶ διδαχὴν ἀφθαρσίας. VII, 1.
ὥσπερ οὖν ὁ κύριος ἄνευ τοῦ πατρὸς οὐδὲν ἐποίησεν οὔτε δι' ἑαυτοῦ οὔτε διὰ τῶν ἀποστόλων · οὕτως μηδὲ ὑμεῖς ἄνευ τοῦ ἐπισκόπου καὶ τῶν πρεσβυτέρων μηδὲν πράσσετε.}
μηδὲ πειράσητε εὔλογόν τι φαίνεσθαι ἰδίᾳ ὑμῖν, ἀλλ' ἐπὶ τὸ αὐτὸ μία
προσευχή, μία δέησις, εἷς νοῦς, μία ἐλπὶς ἐν ἀγάπῃ, ἐν τῇ χαρᾷ τῇ 5
ἀμώμῳ, ὅ ἐστιν Ἰησοῦς Χριστός, οὗ ἄμεινον οὐθέν ἐστιν · 2. πάντες
ὡς εἰς ἕνα ναὸν συντρέχετε θεοῦ, ὡς ἐπὶ ἓν θυσιαστήριον, ἐπὶ ἕνα Ἰησοῦν
Χριστόν, τὸν ἀφ' ἑνὸς πατρὸς προελθόντα καὶ εἰς ἕνα ὄντα καὶ χωρήσαντα.

b.   Warning: Snares of the Judaizers; example of the Prophets

VIII, 1. Μὴ πλανᾶσθε ταῖς ἑτεροδοξίαις μηδὲ μυθεύμασιν τοῖς παλαιοῖς
ἀνωφελέσιν οὖσιν. εἰ γὰρ μέχρι νῦν κατὰ νόμον ἰουδαϊκὸν ζῶμεν, ὁμολο- 10
γοῦμεν χάριν μὴ εἰληφέναι. 2. οἱ γὰρ θειότατοι προφῆται κατὰ Χριστὸν
Ἰησοῦν ἔζησαν · διὰ τοῦτο καὶ ἐδιώχθησαν, ἐμπνεόμενοι ὑπὸ τῆς χάριτος
αὐτοῦ, εἰς τὸ πληροφορηθῆναι τοὺς ἀπειθοῦντας, ὅτι εἷς θεός ἐστιν, ὁ
φανερώσας ἑαυτὸν διὰ Ἰησοῦ Χριστοῦ τοῦ υἱοῦ αὐτοῦ, ὅς ἐστιν αὐτοῦ
λόγος ἀπὸ σιγῆς προελθών, ὃς κατὰ πάντα εὐηρέστησεν τῷ πέμψαντι 15
αὐτόν. IX, 1. εἰ οὖν οἱ ἐν παλαιοῖς πράγμασιν ἀναστραφέντες εἰς καινότητα ἐλπίδος ἦλθον, μηκέτι σαββατίζοντες, ἀλλὰ κατὰ κυριακὴν ζῶντες
— ἐν ᾗ καὶ ἡ ζωὴ ἡμῶν ἀνέτειλεν δι' αὐτοῦ καὶ τοῦ θανάτου αὐτοῦ
(ὅ τινες ἀρνοῦνται, δι' οὗ μυστηρίου ἐλάβομεν τὸ πιστεύειν, καὶ διὰ τοῦτο
ὑπομένομεν, ἵνα εὑρεθῶμεν μαθηταὶ Ἰησοῦ Χριστοῦ τοῦ μόνου διδα- 20
σκάλου ἡμῶν) —, 2. πῶς ἡμεῖς δυνησόμεθα ζῆσαι χωρὶς αὐτοῦ, οὗ καὶ οἱ
προφῆται, μαθηταὶ ὄντες τῷ πνεύματι, ὡς διδάσκαλον αὐτὸν προσεδό-
κων; καὶ διὰ τοῦτο, ὃν δικαίως ἀνέμενον, παρὼν ἤγειρεν αὐτοὺς ἐκ νεκρῶν.

c.   Exhortation: Christianity has held back Judaism

Χ, 1. Μὴ οὖν ἀναισθητῶμεν τῆς χρηστότητος αὐτοῦ · ἐὰν γὰρ ἡμᾶς μιμήσεται καθὰ πράσσομεν, οὐκέτι ἐσμέν. διὰ τοῦτο, μαθηταὶ αὐτοῦ γενό- 25
μενοι, μάθωμεν κατὰ Χριστιανισμὸν ζῆν. ὃς γὰρ ἄλλῳ ὀνόματι καλεῖται
πλέον τούτου, οὐκ ἔστιν τοῦ θεοῦ. 2. ὑπέρθεσθε οὖν τὴν κακὴν ζύμην,
τὴν παλαιωθεῖσαν καὶ ἐνοξίσασαν, καὶ μεταβάλεσθε εἰς νέαν ζύμην, ὅ
ἐστιν Ἰησοῦς Χριστός. ἁλίσθητε ἐν αὐτῷ, ἵνα μὴ διαφθαρῇ τις ἐν ὑμῖν,

---

2 ἐποίησεν SfAB(g) Dam. (Light.): + ἠνωμένος ὤν GL editors. It seems to be a
late theological correction ‖ 6 πάντες LABg: + οὖν G Antioch. See nr. 87 and
n. 301. The οὖν could be authentic ‖ 10 νόμον ἰουδαϊκὸν gAB Petermann: νόμον
ἰουδαϊσμὸν G Zahn, νόμον Camelot, Ἰουδαϊσμὸν L Light. Hilg. Funk Bauer Bihl.
Fischer. See n. 68. Ign. here opposes χάρις to νόμος ‖ 15 λόγος A Sever. Light.
(II/1, 126 f.) modern editors: + ἀΐδιος οὐκ GL Tim. Hilg. The reading of GL seems
to be a late anti-Gnostic correction (Bauer II 225 f.) ‖ 19 ὅ τινες L(A?) recent
editors: οἵτινες G, ὅν τινες (A?) Light. See our n. 70.

VII,1. ἀλλ' ἐπὶ τὸ αὐτὸ [sc. ἔστω] κτλ. constitutes the positive member of the
second Ignatian antithesis: see nr. 87.
IX,1. " The apodosis to εἰ οὖν οἱ ἐν παλαιοῖς κ.τ.λ. at the opening of the section begins with πῶς ἡμεῖς κ.τ.λ. " (Light. II/1, 130). ἐν ᾗ κτλ. (7,1c) is an explanatory sentence of κυριακὴν that again gave rise to the parenthesis ὅ τινες κτλ.
(7,1d-g). See nr. 15.3.

ἐπεὶ ἀπὸ τῆς ὀσμῆς ἐλεγχθήσεσθε. 3. ἄτοπόν ἐστιν, Χριστὸν Ἰησοῦν
λαλεῖν καὶ ἰουδαΐζειν · ὁ γὰρ Χριστιανισμὸς οὐκ εἰς Ἰουδαϊσμὸν ἐπί-
στευσεν, ἀλλ' Ἰουδαϊσμὸς εἰς Χριστιανισμόν, εἰς ὃν " πᾶσα γλῶσσα "
πιστεύσασα εἰς θεὸν " συνήχθη ".

d. Explanation: Meaning of the exhortation

5 XI. Ταῦτα δέ, ἀγαπητοί μου, οὐκ ἐπεὶ ἔγνων τινὰς ἐξ ὑμῶν οὕτως ἔχοντας, ἀλλ' ὡς μικρότερος ὑμῶν θέλω προφυλάσσεσθαι ὑμᾶς, μὴ ἐμπεσεῖν εἰς τὰ ἄγκιστρα τῆς κενοδοξίας, ἀλλὰ πεπληροφορῆσθαι ἐν τῇ γεν-
νήσει καὶ τῷ πάθει καὶ τῇ ἀναστάσει τῇ γενομένῃ ἐν καιρῷ τῆς ἡγεμονίας Ποντίου Πιλάτου · πραχθέντα ἀληθῶς καὶ βεβαίως ὑπὸ Ἰησοῦ
10 Χριστοῦ, τῆς ἐλπίδος ἡμῶν, ἧς ἐκτραπῆναι μηδενὶ ὑμῶν γένοιτο. XII. ὀναίμην ὑμῶν κατὰ πάντα, ἐάνπερ ἄξιος ὦ · εἰ γὰρ καὶ δέδεμαι, πρὸς ἕνα
τῶν λελυμένων ὑμῶν οὐκ εἰμί. οἶδα, ὅτι οὐ φυσιοῦσθε · Ἰησοῦν γὰρ
Χριστὸν ἔχετε ἐν ἑαυτοῖς. καὶ μᾶλλον, ὅταν ἐπαινῶ ὑμᾶς, οἶδα, ὅτι
ἐντρέπεσθε, ὡς γέγραπται, ὅτι " ὁ δίκαιος ἑαυτοῦ κατήγορος ".

{Clause interrupting the primitive sequence of Mg*:

15 XIII, 1. Σπουδάζετε οὖν βεβαιωθῆναι ἐν τοῖς δόγμασιν τοῦ κυρίου καὶ τῶν ἀποστόλων, ἵνα " πάντα, ὅσα ποιεῖτε, κατευοδωθῆτε " σαρκὶ καὶ πνεύματι, πίστει καὶ
ἀγάπῃ, ἐν υἱῷ καὶ πατρὶ καὶ ἐν πνεύματι, ἐν ἀρχῇ καὶ ἐν τέλει, μετὰ τοῦ ἀξιο-
πρεπεστάτου ἐπισκόπου ὑμῶν καὶ ἀξιοπλόκου πνευματικοῦ στεφάνου τοῦ πρεσβυτερίου ὑμῶν καὶ τῶν κατὰ θεὸν διακόνων. 2. ὑποτάγητε τῷ ἐπισκόπῳ καὶ ἀλλή-
20 λοις, ὡς Ἰησοῦς Χριστὸς τῷ πατρὶ κατὰ σάρκα καὶ οἱ ἀπόστολοι τῷ Χριστῷ καὶ
τῷ πατρὶ καὶ τῷ πνεύματι, ἵνα ἕνωσις ᾖ σαρκική τε καὶ πνευματική.}

(Ending of Mg. 14-15: see end of the letter, pp. 361f.).

{Spurious initial greeting of Phld. (inscr.): see beginning of the letter, p. 354}
{Spurious introduction of Phld.:

Phld. I, 1. Ὃν ἐπίσκοπον ἔγνων οὐκ ἀφ' ἑαυτοῦ οὐδὲ δι' ἀνθρώπων κεκτῆσθαι τὴν
διακονίαν τὴν εἰς τὸ κοινὸν ἀνήκουσαν οὐδὲ κατὰ κενοδοξίαν, ἀλλ' ἐν ἀγάπῃ θεοῦ
πατρὸς καὶ κυρίου Ἰησοῦ Χριστοῦ · οὗ καταπέπληγμαι τὴν ἐπιείκειαν, ὃς σιγῶν
25 πλείονα δύναται τῶν μάταια λαλούντων. 2. συνευρύθμισται γὰρ ταῖς ἐντολαῖς ὡς
χορδαῖς κιθάρα. διὸ μακαρίζει μου ἡ ψυχὴ τὴν εἰς θεὸν αὐτοῦ γνώμην, ἐπιγνοὺς
ἐνάρετον καὶ τέλειον οὖσαν, τὸ ἀκίνητον αὐτοῦ καὶ τὸ ἀόργητον αὐτοῦ ἐν πάσῃ ἐπιεικείᾳ θεοῦ ζῶντος.}

---

1 Χριστὸν Ἰησοῦν G Zahn (cf. Mg. inscr. [v. lect.]; 8,2; 10,1.3): ∼ LAg. The
reading of G emphasizes the main theme of this anti-Judaizing letter ‖ 3 εἰς ὃν
gSf (in quo) A (in eum) modern editors: ὡς G(L?), ᾧ Light.

X,3. The fulfillment of the prophecy of Is. 66,18.
XII. Prov. 18,17 LXX.
{Clause interrupting etc. of Mg. 13: see nrs. 25-28, 57.
XIII,1. Adapted quotation from Ps. 1,3.
(Ending of Mg. 14-15: see nr. 35.
{Spurious initial greeting etc.: see nrs. 22, 29, 58, 138.
{Spurious introduction etc. of Phld. 1: see nrs. 23, 59-61.

c'. Exhortation: Jesus the Messiah, unique Shepherd and Gardener

Phld. II,1. Τέκνα οὖν φωτὸς ἀληθείας, φεύγετε τὸν μερισμὸν καὶ τὰς κακοδιδασκαλίας. ὅπου δὲ ὁ ποιμήν ἐστιν, ἐκεῖ ὡς πρόβατα ἀκολουθεῖτε · 2. πολλοὶ γὰρ λύκοι ἀξιόπιστοι ἡδονῇ κακῇ αἰχμαλωτίζουσιν τοὺς θεο-δρόμους. ἀλλ' ἐν τῇ ἑνότητι ὑμῶν οὐχ ἕξουσιν τόπον. III, 1. ἀπέχεσθε τῶν κακῶν βοτανῶν, ἅστινας οὐ γεωργεῖ Ἰησοῦς Χριστός, διὰ τὸ μὴ   5 εἶναι αὐτοὺς φυτείαν πατρός. οὐχ ὅτι παρ' ὑμῖν μερισμὸν εὗρον, ἀλλ' ἀπο-διϋλισμόν ·

2. ὅσοι γὰρ Ἰησοῦ Χριστοῦ εἰσίν,   2. ὅσοι γὰρ θεοῦ εἰσιν καὶ Ἰησοῦ Χριστοῦ, οὗτοι καὶ θεοῦ εἰσίν ·   οὗτοι {μετὰ τοῦ ἐπισκόπου} εἰσίν · καὶ ὅσοι ἂν μετανοήσαντες ἔλθωσιν ἐπὶ τὴν ἑνότητα τῆς ἐκκλησίας, καὶ 10 οὗτοι θεοῦ ἔσονται, ἵνα ὦσιν κατὰ Ἰησοῦν Χριστὸν ζῶντες.

b'. Warning: Whoever follows a schismatic will not inherit the Kingdom

III, 3. " Μὴ πλανᾶσθε, " ἀδελφοί μου · εἴ τις σχίζοντι ἀκολουθεῖ, " βασι-λείαν θεοῦ οὐ κληρονομεῖ " · εἴ τις ἐν ἀλλοτρίᾳ γνώμῃ περιπατεῖ, οὗτος τῷ πάθει οὐ συγκατατίθεται.

a'. Aim: To participate in the same Eucharist leads to acting in harmony with God, Jesus the Messiah

IV. Σπουδάσατε οὖν μιᾷ εὐχαριστίᾳ χρῆσθαι · μία γὰρ σὰρξ τοῦ κυρίου 15 ἡμῶν Ἰησοῦ Χριστοῦ καὶ ἓν ποτήριον εἰς ἕνωσιν τοῦ αἵματος αὐτοῦ, ἓν θυσιαστήριον, {ὡς εἷς ἐπίσκοπος ἅμα τῷ πρεσβυτερίῳ καὶ διακόνοις, τοῖς συνδούλοις μου } ἵνα, ὃ ἐὰν πράσσητε, κατὰ θεὸν πράσσητε.

C'. PARAENESIS

a. Fidelity to the Gospel and the Apostles; recognition of the Prophets

V, 1. Ἀδελφοί μου, λίαν ἐκκέχυμαι ἀγαπῶν ὑμᾶς καὶ ὑπεραγαλλόμενος ἀσφαλίζομαι ὑμᾶς — οὐκ ἐγὼ δέ, ἀλλ' Ἰησοῦς Χριστός, ἐν ᾧ δεδεμένος 20 φοβοῦμαι μᾶλλον, ὡς ἔτι ὢν ἀναπάρτιστος · ἀλλ' ἡ προσευχὴ ὑμῶν εἰς θεόν με ἀπαρτίσει, ἵνα ἐν ᾧ κλήρῳ ἠλεήθην ἐπιτύχω —, προσφυγὼν τῷ εὐαγγελίῳ ὡς σαρκὶ Ἰησοῦ καὶ τοῖς ἀποστόλοις ὡς πρεσβυτερίῳ ἐκκλησίας. 2. καὶ τοὺς προφήτας δὲ ἀγαπῶμεν, διὰ τὸ καὶ αὐτοὺς εἰς τὸ εὐαγγέλιον κατηγγελκέναι καὶ εἰς αὐτὸν ἐλπίζειν καὶ αὐτὸν ἀναμένειν, 25

---

4 οὐχ ἕξουσιν G(C)g Light. Funk-Bihl. Fischer, etc.: οὐκ ἔχουσιν L(A) Zahn Hilg. Krüger Bauer.

III,2. For the reconstruction of the original Ignatian phrase and its smallest inter-polation, see nrs. 96, 139.
III,3. 1Cor. 6,9-10.
IV. {ὡς εἷς ἐπίσκοπος κτλ. Interpolation: see nrs. 77, 143.

ἐν ᾧ καὶ πιστεύσαντες ἐσώθησαν, ἐν ἑνότητι Ἰησοῦ Χριστοῦ ὄντες, ἀξια-
γάπητοι καὶ ἀξιοθαύμαστοι ἅγιοι, ὑπὸ Ἰησοῦ Χριστοῦ μεμαρτυρημένοι
καὶ συνηριθμημένοι ἐν τῷ εὐαγγελίῳ τῆς κοινῆς ἐλπίδος.

b. Beware of the Judaizers!

VI, 1. Ἐὰν δέ τις Ἰουδαϊσμὸν ἑρμηνεύῃ ὑμῖν, μὴ ἀκούετε αὐτοῦ · ἄμει-
5 νον γάρ ἐστιν παρὰ ἀνδρὸς περιτομὴν ἔχοντος Χριστιανισμὸν ἀκούειν,
ἢ παρὰ ἀκροβύστου Ἰουδαϊσμόν. ἐὰν δὲ ἀμφότεροι περὶ Ἰησοῦ Χριστοῦ
μὴ λαλῶσιν, οὗτοι ἐμοὶ στῆλαί εἰσιν καὶ τάφοι νεκρῶν, ἐφ' οἷς γέγραπται
μόνον ὀνόματα ἀνθρώπων.

c. Beware of the Chief of this world!

VI, 2. Φεύγετε οὖν τὰς κακοτεχνίας καὶ ἐνέδρας τοῦ ἄρχοντος τοῦ αἰῶ-
10 νος τούτου, μήποτε θλιβέντες τῇ γνώμῃ αὐτοῦ ἐξασθενήσετε ἐν τῇ ἀγάπῃ ·
ἀλλὰ πάντες ἐπὶ τὸ αὐτὸ γίνεσθε ἐν ἀμερίστῳ καρδίᾳ.

d. In writing to you I am faithful to my conscience

VI, 3. Εὐχαριστῶ δὲ τῷ θεῷ μου, ὅτι εὐσυνείδητός εἰμι ἐν ὑμῖν καὶ
οὐκ ἔχει τις καυχήσασθαι οὔτε λάθρα οὔτε φανερῶς, ὅτι ἐβάρησά τινα
ἐν μικρῷ ἢ ἐν μεγάλῳ · καὶ πᾶσι δέ, ἐν οἷς ἐλάλησα, εὔχομαι, ἵνα μὴ εἰς
15 μαρτύριον αὐτὸ κτήσωνται.

{Explanation of the interpolator:

VII, 1. Εἰ γὰρ καὶ κατὰ σάρκα μέ τινες ἠθέλησαν πλανῆσαι, ἀλλὰ τὸ πνεῦμα οὐ
πλανᾶται ἀπὸ θεοῦ ὄν · " οἶδεν " γάρ, " πόθεν ἔρχεται καὶ ποῦ ὑπάγει ", καὶ τὰ
κρυπτὰ ἐλέγχει. ἐκραύγασα μεταξὺ ὤν, ἐλάλουν μεγάλῃ φωνῇ, θεοῦ φωνῇ · Τῷ
ἐπισκόπῳ προσέχετε καὶ τῷ πρεσβυτερίῳ καὶ διακόνοις. 2. οἱ δὲ ὑποπτεύσαντες
20 με ὡς προειδότα τὸν μερισμόν τινων λέγειν ταῦτα · μάρτυς δέ μοι, ἐν ᾧ δέδεμαι,
ὅτι ἀπὸ σαρκὸς ἀνθρωπίνης οὐκ ἔγνων. τὸ δὲ πνεῦμα ἐκήρυσσεν λέγον τάδε · Χωρὶς
τοῦ ἐπισκόπου μηδὲν ποιεῖτε, τὴν σάρκα ὑμῶν ὡς ναὸν θεοῦ τηρεῖτε, τὴν ἕνωσιν
ἀγαπᾶτε, τοὺς μερισμοὺς φεύγετε, μιμηταὶ γίνεσθε Ἰησοῦ Χριστοῦ, ὡς καὶ αὐτὸς
τοῦ πατρὸς αὐτοῦ.}

d'. I have carried out my mission in favour of union

25 VIII, 1. Ἐγὼ μὲν οὖν τὸ ἴδιον ἐποίουν ὡς ἄνθρωπος εἰς ἕνωσιν κατηρτισμένος. οὗ δὲ μερισμός ἐστιν καὶ ὀργή, θεὸς οὐ κατοικεῖ. πᾶσιν οὖν

---

12 δὲ GL: > AC ‖ 14 δέ GL: > ACg ‖ 20 ὡς προειδότα GL(g) modern editors:
ὡς εἰδότα C, ὥσπερ εἰδότα SfA(?) Zahn Bauer ‖ 21 λέγον g Antioch. editors: λέγων
Gg*.

{Explanation of the interpolator: see nrs. 97-106.
VII,1. John 3,8. (Cf. 1Cor. 2,10; 14,25; Eph. 5,12f.).
VII,2. οἱ δὲ ὑποπτεύσαντες κτλ. A fresh anacoluthon of the interp. (Light. II/1,
267f.; Bauer II 260; Fischer 199, n. 30).

μετανοοῦσιν ἀφίει ὁ κύριος, ἐὰν μετανοήσωσιν εἰς ἑνότητα θεοῦ {καὶ συνέδριον τοῦ ἐπισκόπου}. πιστεύω τῇ χάριτι Ἰησοῦ Χριστοῦ, ὃς λύσει ἀφ' ὑμῶν πάντα δεσμόν.

c'. Do everything with a Christian spirit

VIII, 2. Παρακαλῶ δὲ ὑμᾶς μηδὲν κατ' ἐρίθειαν πράσσειν, ἀλλὰ κατὰ χριστομαθίαν · ἐπεὶ ἤκουσά τινων λεγόντων, ὅτι, Ἐὰν μὴ ἐν τοῖς ἀρ- 5
χείοις εὕρω, ἐν τῷ εὐαγγελίῳ οὐ πιστεύω · καὶ λέγοντός μου αὐτοῖς, ὅτι Γέγραπται, ἀπεκρίθησάν μοι, ὅτι Πρόκειται. ἐμοὶ δὲ ἀρχεῖά ἐστιν Ἰησοῦς Χριστός, τὰ ἄθικτα ἀρχεῖα ὁ σταυρὸς αὐτοῦ καὶ ὁ θάνατος καὶ ἡ ἀνάστασις αὐτοῦ καὶ ἡ πίστις ἡ δι' αὐτοῦ, ἐν οἷς θέλω ἐν τῇ προσευχῇ ὑμῶν δικαιωθῆναι. 10

b'. The High Priest, Jesus, is superior to the Jewish priesthood

IX, 1. Καλοὶ καὶ οἱ ἱερεῖς, κρεῖσσον δὲ ὁ ἀρχιερεὺς ὁ πεπιστευμένος τὰ ἅγια τῶν ἁγίων, ὃς μόνος πεπίστευται τὰ κρυπτὰ τοῦ θεοῦ · αὐτὸς ὢν θύρα τοῦ πατρός, δι' ἧς εἰσέρχονται Ἀβραὰμ καὶ Ἰσαὰκ καὶ Ἰακὼβ καὶ οἱ προφῆται καὶ οἱ ἀπόστολοι καὶ ἡ ἐκκλησία. πάντα ταῦτα εἰς ἑνότητα θεοῦ. 15

a'. The Gospel, fulfillment of the statements of the Prophets

IX, 2. Ἐξαίρετον δέ τι ἔχει τὸ εὐαγγέλιον, τὴν παρουσίαν τοῦ σωτῆρος, κυρίου ἡμῶν Ἰησοῦ Χριστοῦ, τὸ πάθος αὐτοῦ καὶ τὴν ἀνάστασιν. οἱ γὰρ ἀγαπητοὶ προφῆται κατήγγειλαν εἰς αὐτόν · τὸ δὲ εὐαγγέλιον ἀπάρτισμά ἐστιν ἀφθαρσίας. πάντα ὁμοῦ καλά ἐστιν, ἐὰν ἐν ἀγάπῃ πιστεύητε.

{Spurious conclusion of Phld. 10-11,1: see conclusion of Eph*, pp. 381. 383f.}

{Spurious final greeting of Phld. 11,2: see final greeting of Eph*, p. 384}

Epilogue

Mg. XIV, a. Εἰδώς, ὅτι θεοῦ γέμετε, συντόμως παρεκάλεσα ὑμᾶς. 20

---

5 ἀρχείοις g Light. (II/1, 270 f.) editors: ἀρχαίοις GL, scripturis antiquis (prioribus) A. For the punctuation, supported by almost all modern editors, see Light. II/1, 271 f., and our n. 76. We have discussed the whole passage in nr. 16. For πιστεύειν ἐν + dat., see Phld. 5,2: identical rare construction in Mk. 1,15 and John 3,15 (v. lect.) ‖ **7** ἀρχεῖα GCg editors: principium L, scriptura prior A ‖ **8** ἀρχεῖα GL (principia) editors: ἀρχεῖον g ‖ **20** παρεκάλεσα g Light. (cf. Rom. 8,2; Pol. = Eph* 7,3): παρεκάλευσα G, παρεκέλευσα Zahn Funk-Bihl. Fischer etc., deprecatus sum L, peto A, rogavi l. "On the other hand παρακελεύειν does not occur elsewhere in this writer or in the N.T." (Light. II/1, 139).

VIII,1. {καὶ συνέδριον τοῦ ἐπισκόπου. For this very short interpolated sentence, see nrs. 108, 144.
VIII,2. Ἐὰν μὴ κτλ., Γέγραπται (see n. 77 f.), Πρόκειται (see n. 78): Ign. alludes to his discussion in Syria with the Judaizers.
{Spurious conclusion of Phld. 10-11,1: see nrs. 33 f., 53 (synopsis), 63 f.
{Spurious final greeting of Phld. 11,2: see nrs. 54.2, 65.
Mg. XIV-XV, original ending of Mg*: see nr. 35.

B'. CONCLUSION

Petition for prayers for himself and for the church of Syria

XIV, b. Μνημονεύετέ μου ἐν ταῖς προσευχαῖς ὑμῶν, ἵνα θεοῦ ἐπιτύχω, καὶ τῆς ἐν Συρίᾳ ἐκκλησίας, ὅθεν οὐκ ἄξιός εἰμι καλεῖσθαι · ἐπι-
δέομαι γὰρ τῆς ἡνωμένης ὑμῶν ἐν θεῷ προσευχῆς καὶ ἀγάπης, εἰς τὸ
ἀξιωθῆναι τὴν ἐν Συρίᾳ ἐκκλησίαν διὰ τῆς ἐκκλησίας ὑμῶν δροσισθῆναι.

A'. FINAL GREETING

Greetings from the Ephesian delegates from Smyrna

5 XV, a. Ἀσπάζονται ὑμᾶς Ἐφέσιοι ἀπὸ Σμύρνης, ὅθεν καὶ φράφω ὑμῖν,
παρόντες εἰς δόξαν θεοῦ ὥσπερ καὶ ὑμεῖς, οἳ κατὰ πάντα με ἀνέπαυσαν
{ἅμα Πολυκάρπῳ, ἐπισκόπῳ Σμυρναίων}.

Greetings of the other communities present in Smyrna

XV, e. Καὶ αἱ λοιπαὶ δὲ ἐκκλησίαι ἐν τιμῇ Ἰησοῦ Χριστοῦ ἀσπάζονται
ὑμᾶς.

Farewell formula

10 XV, f. Ἔρρωσθε ἐν ὁμονοίᾳ θεοῦ κεκτημένοι ἀδιάκριτον πνεῦμα, ὅς
ἐστιν Ἰησοῦς Χριστός.

XV,a. {ἅμα Πολυκάρπῳ, ἐπισκόπῳ Σμυρναίων}. Adjunction of the interp.: see nr. 43.

LETTER TO THE TRALLIANS
(Tr.)

Written in the third place: (a) Epitomatic character (a kind of thematic sketch of Eph*); (b) Greetings from the Ephesians and Smyrnaeans present in Smyrna.

Sender: Ignatius, the Godbearer, a man who could give them directives as an apostle, but will not, since he considers himself a condemned man.

Addressees: The community which is in Tralles of Asia.

Theme: To warn the community beforehand against the Docetists. Ignatius foresees the snares of the devil, although he knows that such Gnostic speculations are not yet in their midst.

Bearer: The delegate sent by the community to Smyrna.

The original letter has not been divided (it was too short and epitomatic) but heavily interpolated. The original order of the ending has also been altered to give place to the interpolations.

A. INITIAL GREETING

Tr. inscr.   Ἰγνάτιος, ὁ καὶ Θεοφόρος,
           ἠγαπημένη θεῷ πατρὶ Ἰησοῦ Χριστοῦ ἐκκλησίᾳ ἁγίᾳ, τῇ
       οὔσῃ ἐν Τράλλεσιν τῆς Ἀσίας, ἐκλεκτῇ καὶ ἀξιοθέῳ,
           εἰρηνευούσῃ ἐν σαρκὶ καὶ αἵματι Ἰησοῦ Χριστοῦ, τῆς ἐλπί-
5 δος ἡμῶν, ἐν τῇ εἰς αὐτὸν ἀναστάσει·
           ἣν καὶ ἀσπάζομαι ἐν τῷ πληρώματι ἐν ἀποστολικῷ χαρακτῆρι,
       καὶ εὔχομαι πλεῖστα χαίρειν.

B. INTRODUCTION

The Trallians' good nature. Mention of delegate

I, 1. Ἄμωμον διάνοιαν καὶ ἀδιάκριτον ἐν ὑπομονῇ ἔγνων ὑμᾶς ἔχοντας
οὐ κατὰ χρῆσιν, ἀλλὰ κατὰ φύσιν, καθὼς ἐδήλωσέν μοι Πολύβιος, {ὁ ἐπί-
10 σκοπος ὑμῶν,} ὃς παρεγένετο θελήματι θεοῦ καὶ Ἰησοῦ Χριστοῦ ἐν Σμύρνῃ
καὶ οὕτως μοι συνεχάρη δεδεμένῳ ἐν Χριστῷ Ἰησοῦ, ὥστε με τὸ πᾶν
πλῆθος ὑμῶν ἐν αὐτῷ θεωρεῖσθαι.

Invitation to follow close to God, Jesus the Messiah

I, 2. Ἀποδεξάμενος οὖν τὴν κατὰ θεὸν εὔνοιαν δι' αὐτοῦ, ἐδόξασα εὑρὼν
ὑμᾶς — ὡς ἔγνων — μιμητὰς ὄντας θεοῦ{.

---

4 αἵματι (+ τῷ πάθει G, + et passione L) GLABC: πνεύματι (+ ἐν πάθει τῷ κτλ.
after ἡμῶν) g. There is a reference to the Eucharist (cf. Tr. 8,1; Rom. 7,3; Phld. 4).
All modern editors after Zahn propose a conflation of Gg (πνεύματι τῷ πάθει). τῷ
πάθει could be a gloss (see Light. II/1,152: "The alternative would be to omit
τῷ πάθει, as a gloss... The sentence would then be directed against Docetic error".
cf. Sm. 3,2), since it is missing in two independent MSS families: AB (and there-
fore S!) and C || **11** Χριστῷ Ἰησοῦ LAg editors: ~ G Zahn || **12** θεωρεῖσθαι em.
Salv. from G (θεωρῆσθε) Zahn Funk-Bihl. etc.: θεωρῆσαι gC Light. || **13** ἐδόξασα
LA (+ Dominum meum Iesum Christum) C editors: ἔδοξα Gg*.

I,1. {ὁ ἐπίσκοπος ὑμῶν}. Intercalated by the interp.: see nr. 88.
I,2-II,2. The interp. has divided the apodosis of 1,2 (εὑρὼν ὑμᾶς κτλ.) into three
       sentences and inverted the order of the last two: 1,2b; 2,2dc and 2,1b-d.
       See nrs. 136 and 88-91.

II, 1. "Οταν γὰρ τῷ ἐπισκόπῳ ὑποτάσ-
σησθε ὡς Ἰησοῦ Χριστῷ, φαίνεσθέ
μοι} οὐ κατὰ ἀνθρώπους ζῶντες, ἀλλὰ
κατὰ Ἰησοῦν Χριστὸν τὸν δι' ἡμᾶς
ἀποθανόντα, ἵνα πιστεύσαντες εἰς τὸν   5
θάνατον αὐτοῦ τὸ ἀποθανεῖν ἐκφύγητε. 2. {ἀναγκαῖον οὖν ἐστίν, ὥσπερ
ποιεῖτε, ἄνευ τοῦ ἐπισκόπου μηδὲν
πράσσειν ὑμᾶς, ἀλλ' ὑποτάσσεσθε καὶ
τῷ πρεσβυτερίῳ ὡς τοῖς ἀποστόλοις} 10

II, 2b. Ἰησοῦ Χριστοῦ, τῆς ἐλπίδος   Ἰησοῦ Χριστοῦ, τῆς ἐλπίδος
ἡμῶν, ἐν ᾧ διάγοντες εὑρεθησόμεθα   ἡμῶν, ἐν ᾧ διάγοντες εὑρεθησόμεθα {.}
II, 1b. οὐ κατὰ ἀνθρώπους ζῶντες
ἀλλὰ κατὰ Ἰησοῦν Χριστὸν τὸν δι'
ἡμᾶς ἀποθανόντα, ἵνα πιστεύσαντες   15
εἰς τὸν θάνατον αὐτοῦ τὸ ἀποθανεῖν
ἐκφύγ<ωμεν>.
{3. δεῖ δὲ καὶ τοὺς διακόνους ὄντας μυστηρίων Ἰησοῦ Χριστοῦ κατὰ πάντα τρόπον
πᾶσιν ἀρέσκειν · οὐ γὰρ βρωμάτων καὶ ποτῶν εἰσιν διάκονοι, ἀλλ' ἐκκλησίας θεοῦ
ὑπηρέται. δέον οὖν αὐτοὺς φυλάσσεσθαι τὰ ἐγκλήματα ὡς πῦρ. III, 1. ὁμοίως πάντες 20
ἐντρεπέσθωσαν τοὺς διακόνους ὡς Ἰησοῦν Χριστόν, ὡς καὶ τὸν ἐπίσκοπον ὄντα
τύπον τοῦ πατρός, τοὺς δὲ πρεσβυτέρους ὡς συνέδριον θεοῦ καὶ ὡς σύνδεσμον ἀποστόλων. χωρὶς τούτων ἐκκλησία οὐ καλεῖται. 2. περὶ ὧν πέπεισμαι ὑμᾶς οὕτως ἔχειν ·
τὸ γὰρ ἐξεμπλάριον τῆς ἀγάπης ὑμῶν ἔλαβον καὶ ἔχω μεθ' ἑαυτοῦ ἐν τῷ ἐπισκόπῳ
ὑμῶν, οὗ αὐτὸ τὸ κατάστημα μεγάλη μαθητεία, ἡ δὲ πραότης αὐτοῦ δύναμις · ὃν   25
λογίζομαι καὶ τοὺς ἀθέους ἐντρέπεσθαι.}

C. BODY OF THE LETTER

a. Exhortation:

Esoteric doctrines would be self-defeating (a)

III, 3. Ἀγαπῶν ὑμᾶς φείδομαι, συντομώτερον δυνάμενος γράφειν ὑπὲρ
τούτου. οὐκ εἰς τοῦτο ᾠήθην, ἵνα ὢν κατάκριτος ὡς ἀπόστολος ὑμῖν

---

13 κατὰ ἀνθρώπους LC Sever. Zahn Light. (cf. Rom. 8,1): κατὰ ἄνθρωπον Gg Dam.
Funk-Bihlmeyer Fischer Camelot, in corpore SfA ‖ 17 ἐκφύγ<ωμεν> con. (see nr.
89,4): ἐκφύγητε text ‖ 21 ὡς καὶ Gg: καὶ (> ὡς) LSfAC Antioch. ‖ 22 τύπον
SfBClg (A) (Antioch.): υἱὸν GL | καὶ ὡς GC Antioch.: καὶ (> ὡς) LSfA ‖ 27 ἀγα-
πῶν ὑμᾶς φείδομαι gAC Zahn and modern editors: ἀγαπῶντας ὡς οὐ φ. GL | ὑμᾶς:
+ οὕτως Light. | συντομώτερον C (cf. Mg. 14; Rom. 8,2: δι' ὀλίγων γραμμάτων;
Pol. = Eph* 7,3: id.): συντονώτερον gAB editors, ἑαυτὸν πότερον G, ipsum aliqualem
L. Both terms are constantly being confused. Ign.'s aim is not to write *sternly*
to the Tr. (see 8,1) but *briefly*, since he intends to write *more in detail* in the letter
to the Eph* on the subject here only sketched (ὑπὲρ τούτου) ‖ 28 οὐκ AC(g) Zahn
and modern editors: > GL.

II,3-III,2. {δεῖ δὲ καὶ κτλ. Drawn up by the interp.: see nr. 90.

διατάσσομαι. IV, 1. πολλά φρονῶ ἐν θεῷ, ἀλλ' ἐμαυτὸν μετρῶ, ἵνα μὴ
ἐν καυχήσει ἀπόλωμαι · νῦν γάρ με δεῖ πλέον φοβεῖσθαι καὶ μὴ προσέχειν τοῖς φυσιοῦσίν με · οἱ γὰρ λέγοντές μοι μαστιγοῦσίν με. (2. ἀγαπῶ
μὲν γὰρ τὸ παθεῖν, ἀλλ' οὐκ οἶδα, εἰ ἄξιός εἰμι · τὸ γὰρ ζῆλος πολλοῖς μὲν
5 οὐ φαίνεται, ἐμὲ δὲ πλέον πολεμεῖ.) χρήζω οὖν πραότητος, ἐν ᾗ κατα-
λύεται ὁ ἄρχων τοῦ αἰῶνος τούτου. V, 1. μὴ οὐ δύναμαι ὑμῖν τὰ ἐπουράνια γράψαι; ἀλλὰ φοβοῦμαι, μὴ νηπίοις οὖσιν ὑμῖν βλάβην παραθῶ.
καὶ συγγνωμονεῖτέ μοι, μήποτε οὐ δυνηθέντες χωρῆσαι στραγγαλωθῆτε. 2. καὶ γὰρ ἐγώ, οὐ καθότι δέδεμαι καὶ δύναμαι νοεῖν τὰ ἐπουράνια
10 καὶ τὰς τοποθεσίας τὰς ἀγγελικὰς καὶ τὰς συστάσεις τὰς ἀρχοντικάς,
ὁρατά τε καὶ ἀόρατα, παρὰ τοῦτο ἤδη καὶ μαθητής εἰμι · πολλὰ γὰρ ἡμῖν
λείπει, ἵνα θεοῦ μὴ λειπώμεθα.

Take only the Christian Food; keep away from heresy (b)

VI, 1. Παρακαλῶ οὖν ὑμᾶς — οὐκ ἐγώ, ἀλλ' ἡ ἀγάπη Ἰησοῦ Χριστοῦ — ·
μόνῃ τῇ χριστιανῇ τροφῇ χρῆσθε, ἀλλοτρίας δὲ βοτάνης ἀπέχεσθε, ἥτις
15 ἐστὶν αἵρεσις · 2. οἱ ἑαυτοῖς παρεμπλέκουσιν Ἰησοῦν Χριστὸν καταξιοπιστευόμενοι, ὥσπερ θανάσιμον φάρμακον διδόντες μετὰ οἰνομέλιτος,
ὅπερ ὁ ἀγνοῶν ἡδέως λαμβάνει ἐν ἡδονῇ κακῇ τὸ ἀποθανεῖν.

b.   Admonition: Beware of heretics! Do not be separated from the Altar

VII, 1. Φυλάττεσθε οὖν τοὺς τοιούτους. τοῦτο δὲ ἔσται ὑμῖν μὴ φυσιου-
μένοις καὶ οὖσιν ἀχωρίστοις θεοῦ Ἰησοῦ Χριστοῦ {καὶ τοῦ ἐπισκόπου καὶ
20 τῶν διαταγμάτων τῶν ἀποστόλων} · 2. ὁ ἐντὸς θυσιαστηρίου ὢν καθαρός ἐστιν,
ὁ δὲ ἐκτὸς θυσιαστηρίου ὢν οὐ καθαρός ἐστιν {· τοῦτ' ἔστιν, ὁ χωρὶς ἐπισκόπου καὶ πρεσβυτερίου καὶ διακόνου πράσσων τι, οὗτος οὐ καθαρός ἐστιν τῇ
συνειδήσει}.

c.   Explanation of the meaning of the exhortation

VIII, 1a. Οὐκ ἐπεὶ ἔγνων τοιοῦτόν τι ἐν ὑμῖν, ἀλλὰ προφυλάσσω ὑμᾶς
25 ὄντας μου ἀγαπητούς, προορῶν τὰς ἐνέδρας τοῦ διαβόλου.

---

15 οἱ ἑαυτοῖς SfA(C) Zahn Funk-Bihl. Fischer: οἱ καιροὶ G, καὶ Dam., alii alia | κα-
ταξιοπιστευόμενοι Dam. (SfAC): καταξίαν πιστευόμενοι G, > Lg ‖ 21 ὁ δὲ ἐκτὸς
— καθαρός ἐστιν L Light. Funk Hilg. Krüger Bihl. recent editors: ὁ δὲ ἐκτὸς ὢν
gC, > GA (homoeoteleuton) Zahn Bauer. The interp. has undoubtedly read like
L ‖ 22 πρεσβυτερίου GL: τῶν πρεσβυτέρων gAC | διακόνου GL Zahn Bauer Bihl.
Fischer (lectio difficilior): διακόνων gC Light. Funk Lelong Camelot, > A.

VII,1. {καὶ τοῦ ἐπισκόπου κτλ. Addition of the interp.: see nrs. 92, 142.
VII,2. {τοῦτ' ἔστιν κτλ.   Explanation of the interp.: see nrs. 92, 142.

a'. Exhortation:

Fortify yourselves by adhering to Jesus and the love of your neighbour (b')

VIII, 1d. Ὑμεῖς οὖν τὴν πραϋπάθειαν ἀναλαβόντες ἀνακτήσασθε ἑαυτοὺς ἐν πίστει, ὅ ἐστιν σὰρξ τοῦ κυρίου, καὶ ἐν ἀγάπῃ, ὅ ἐστιν αἷμα Ἰησοῦ Χριστοῦ. 2. μηδεὶς ὑμῶν κατὰ τοῦ πλησίον ἐχέτω · μὴ ἀφορμὰς δίδοτε τοῖς ἔθνεσιν, ἵνα μὴ δι' ὀλίγους ἄφρονας τὸ ἐν θεῷ πλῆθος βλασφημῆται · " Οὐαὶ " γάρ, " δι' οὗ ἐπὶ ματαιότητι τὸ ὄνομά μου ἐπί τινων βλασφη- 5 μεῖται ".

Christian doctrine: Anti-Docetic Christological creed (a')

IX, 1. Κωφώθητε οὖν, ὅταν ὑμῖν χωρὶς Ἰησοῦ Χριστοῦ λαλῇ τις,
τοῦ ἐκ γένους Δαυίδ, τοῦ ἐκ Μαρίας,
ὃς ἀληθῶς ἐγεννήθη, ἔφαγέν τε καὶ ἔπιεν,
ἀληθῶς ἐδιώχθη ἐπὶ Ποντίου Πιλάτου,   10
ἀληθῶς ἐσταυρώθη καὶ ἀπέθανεν,
— βλεπόντων τῶν ἐπουρανίων καὶ ἐπιγείων καὶ ὑποχθονίων —,
2. ὃς καὶ ἀληθῶς ἠγέρθη ἀπὸ νεκρῶν
(ἐγείραντος αὐτὸν τοῦ πατρὸς αὐτοῦ) ·
ὃς καὶ ἡμᾶς τοὺς πιστεύοντας αὐτῷ οὕτως ἐγερεῖ   15
(ὁ πατὴρ αὐτοῦ ἐν Χριστῷ Ἰησοῦ),
οὗ χωρὶς τὸ ἀληθινὸν ζῆν οὐκ ἔχομεν. X. εἰ δέ, ὥσπερ τινὲς ἄθεοι ὄντες
— τουτέστιν ἄπιστοι — λέγουσιν · Τὸ δοκεῖν πεπονθέναι αὐτὸν (αὐτοὶ
ὄντες ' τὸ δοκεῖν '), ἐγὼ τί δέδεμαι; τί δὲ καὶ εὔχομαι θηριομαχῆσαι;
δωρεὰν οὖν ἀποθνήσκω. ἄρα οὖν καταψεύδομαι τοῦ κυρίου.   20

b'. Admonition: Beware of the parasite shoots! The cross is the Father's planting

XI, 1. Φεύγετε οὖν τὰς κακὰς παραφυάδας τὰς γεννώσας καρπὸν θανα-
τηφόρον, οὗ ἐὰν γεύσηταί τις, παρ' αὐτὰ ἀποθνήσκει. οὗτοι γὰρ οὔκ εἰσιν

---

1 ἀνακτήσασθε con. Cotelier Light.: ἀνακτίσασθε GL Zahn Funk-Bihl. Fischer Ca melot. The itacisms of G are very frequent. ἀνακτήσασθε ἑαυτοὺς = *recover yourselves* ‖ **13** ὃς καὶ con.: ὡς καὶ CSfA, κατὰ τὸ ὁμοίωμα ὃς καὶ G Light., qui et secundum similitudinem L, οὗ κατὰ τ. ὁ. con. Zahn Krüger Bauer. After Funk, the most recent editors follow the reading of L (ὃς καὶ κ.τ.ὁ.). But κ.τ.ὁ. (> CSfA) seems to be a gloss of ὡς (cf. Paul Rom. 6,5), this being in its turn a scribe's error for ὃς. Note that κατὰ τ. ὁ. (or ὡς!) ... οὕτως is a tautology (Light. II/1, 174) ‖ **20** οὖν C editors: οὐ GL, > g Sever.

VIII,2. A loose quotation from Is. 52,5.
X. Τὸ δοκεῖν κτλ. (see also Sm. 2) seems to be a literal quotation from the Gnostics, who called themselves " Docetists " (see HIPP. Haer. VIII.11: δοκητὰς ἑαυ-τοὺς προσηγόρευσαν ὧν οὐ ' τὸ δοκεῖν ' εἶναι τινὰς κατανοοῦμεν ματαΐζον-τας ...), ' τὸ δοκεῖν ' being the quintessence of their theological terminology (TERT. De Carne Christi 1: " et partus virginis et ipsius exinde infantis τὸ δοκεῖν haberentur "; ORIG., CC. II.16: ἡμεῖς ' τὸ δοκεῖν ' ἐπὶ τοῦ παθεῖν οὐ τάσσομεν ...).

φυτεία πατρός. 2. εἰ γὰρ ἦσαν, ἐφαίνοντο ἂν κλάδοι τοῦ σταυροῦ, καὶ ἦν ἂν ὁ καρπὸς αὐτῶν ἄφθαρτος· δι' οὗ ἐν τῷ πάθει αὐτοῦ προσκαλεῖται ὑμᾶς ὄντας μέλη αὐτοῦ. οὐ δύναται οὖν κεφαλὴ χωρὶς γεννηθῆναι ἄνευ μελῶν, τοῦ θεοῦ ἕνωσιν ἐπαγγελλομένου, ὅ ἐστιν αὐτός.

C'. PARAENESIS

I greet you from Smyrna with the communities here present

5 XII, 1. Ἀσπάζομαι ὑμᾶς ἀπὸ Σμύρνης ἅμα ταῖς συμπαρούσαις μοι ἐκκλησίαις τοῦ θεοῦ, οἳ κατὰ πάντα με ἀνέπαυσαν σαρκί τε καὶ πνεύματι.

My chains exhort you to community prayer and mutual love

XII, 2. Παρακαλεῖ ὑμᾶς τὰ δεσμά μου, ἃ ἕνεκεν Ἰησοῦ Χριστοῦ περιφέρω αἰτούμενος θεοῦ ἐπιτυχεῖν. δια-
10 μένετε ἐν τῇ ὁμονοίᾳ ὑμῶν καὶ τῇ μετ' ἀλλήλων προσευχῇ

XII, 2. Παρακαλεῖ ὑμᾶς τὰ δεσμά μου, ἃ ἕνεκεν Ἰησοῦ Χριστοῦ περιφέρω αἰτούμενος θεοῦ ἐπιτυχεῖν. διαμένετε ἐν τῇ ὁμονοίᾳ ὑμῶν καὶ τῇ μετ' ἀλλήλων προσευχῇ{. πρέπει γὰρ ὑμῖν τοῖς καθ' ἕνα, ἐξαιρέτως καὶ τοῖς πρεσβυτέροις, ἀναψύχειν τὸν ἐπίσκοπον εἰς τιμὴν πατρὸς Ἰησοῦ Χριστοῦ καὶ τῶν ἀποστόλων}. 3. εὔχομαι ὑμᾶς ἐν ἀγάπῃ ἀκοῦσαί μου, ἵνα μὴ εἰς μαρτύριον ὦ ἐν ὑμῖν γράψας. καὶ περὶ ἐμοῦ δὲ προσεύχεσθε, τῆς ἀφ' ὑμῶν ἀγάπης χρῄζοντος ἐν τῷ ἐλέει τοῦ θεοῦ, εἰς τὸ καταξιωθῆναί με τοῦ κλήρου, οὗ περίκειμαι ἐπιτυχεῖν, ἵνα μὴ ἀδόκιμος εὑρεθῶ. XIII, 1. ἀσπάζεται ὑμᾶς ἡ ἀγάπη Σμυρναίων καὶ Ἐφεσίων. μνημονεύετε ἐν ταῖς προσευχαῖς ὑμῶν τῆς ἐν Συρίᾳ ἐκκλησίας, ὅθεν οὐκ ἄξιός εἰμι λέγεσθαι, ὢν ἔσχατος ἐκείνων. 2. ἔρρωσθε ἐν Ἰησοῦ Χριστῷ{, ὑποτασσόμενοι τῷ ἐπισκόπῳ ὡς τῇ ἐντολῇ, ὁμοίως καὶ

30 καὶ οἱ κατ' ἄνδρα ἀλλήλους ἀγαπᾶτε ἐν ἀμερίστῳ καρδίᾳ.

τῷ πρεσβυτερίῳ.} καὶ οἱ κατ' ἄνδρα ἀλλήλους ἀγαπᾶτε ἐν ἀμερίστῳ καρδίᾳ.

---

4 ὅ L recent editors: ὅς G Zahn Light. ‖ **5** μοι LCg editors: μου G ‖ **14** πατρὸς GL Zahn Funk Hilg. Lelong Camelot: + καὶ (+ εἰς τιμὴν g Light.) ACg Bihl. Fischer.

XII–XIII. The ending of Tr. contains two interpolations. The first of them has substituted the original text of Ign. (now placed at the end of the letter, after the shortened and interpolated farewell formula); the second is an explanation of the farewell formula itself. See nrs. 94 f. The whole present ending of Tr. is muddled. We have tried to find out the essential order. Perhaps the greetings of 12,1 should come before 13,1a, as in Mg. 15.

I consecrate my person to you

XIII, 3. ʿΑγνίζεται ὑμῶν τὸ ἐμὸν
πνεῦμα οὐ μόνον νῦν, ἀλλὰ καὶ ὅταν
θεοῦ ἐπιτύχω. ἔτι γὰρ ὑπὸ κίνδυνόν
εἰμι· ἀλλὰ πιστὸς ὁ πατὴρ ἐν ʾΙησοῦ
Χριστῷ πληρῶσαί μου τὴν αἴτησιν
καὶ ὑμῶν, ἐν ᾧ εὑρεθείητε ἄμωμοι.

XIII, 3. ʿΑγνίζεται ὑμῶν τὸ ἐμὸν
πνεῦμα οὐ μόνον νῦν, ἀλλὰ καὶ ὅταν
θεοῦ ἐπιτύχω. ἔτι γὰρ ὑπὸ κίνδυνόν
εἰμι· ἀλλὰ πιστὸς ὁ πατὴρ ἐν ʾΙησοῦ
Χριστῷ πληρῶσαί μου τὴν αἴτησιν 5
καὶ ὑμῶν, ἐν ᾧ εὑρεθείητε ἄμωμοι.

I beg you to listen to me with love

XII, 3a. Εὔχομαι ὑμᾶς ἐν ἀγάπη ἀκοῦσαί
μου, ἵνα μὴ εἰς μαρτύριον ὦ ἐν ὑμῖν
γράψας.

B'. CONCLUSION

I need your prayers

XII, 3c. Καὶ περὶ ἐμοῦ δὲ προσεύχεσθε,   10
τῆς ἀφ᾽ ὑμῶν ἀγάπης χρῄζοντος ἐν τῷ
ἐλέει τοῦ θεοῦ, εἰς τὸ καταξιωθῆναί
με τοῦ κλήρου οὗ περίκειμαι ἐπιτυχεῖν,
ἵνα μὴ ἀδόκιμος εὑρεθῶ.

Remember the church of Syria in your prayers

XIII, 1b. Μνημονεύετε ἐν ταῖς προσευχαῖς   15
ὑμῶν τῆς ἐν Συρίᾳ ἐκκλησίας, ὅθεν οὐκ
ἄξιός εἰμι λέγεσθαι, ὢν ἔσχατος ἐκείνων.

A'. FINAL GREETING

The communities of Smyrna and Ephesus greet you

XIII, 1a. ʾΑσπάζεται ὑμας ἡ ἀγάπη Σμυρναίων καὶ ʾΕφεσίων.

Farewell formula

XIII, 2a. ῎Ερρωσθε ἐν Χριστῷ ʾΙησοῦ <τῇ   20
κοινῇ ἐλπίδι ἡμῶν >.

---

1 ὑμῶν GL: ὑπὲρ ὑμῶν C Zahn. Cf. Eph. 8,1 ‖ 6 εὑρεθείητε GLC (cf. Pol. 8,3)
editors: -ίημεν Ag Light. ‖ 13 οὗ περίκειμαι Gg(A) Zahn Bauer recent editors:
qua conor L, dans lequel je suis impliqué C, οὗπερ ἔγκειμαι Bunsen Light. It
seems to be a parenthetical sentence: see n. 320 ‖ 20 ἔρρωσθε — ἐλπίδι ἡμῶν from
Phld. 11,2f (see nrs. 54,2 and 95): ἔρρωσθε ἐν ʾΙησοῦ Χριστῷ, ὑποτασσόμενοι κτλ. text.

PRIMITIVE LETTER TO THE EPHESIANS
(Eph* = Eph. + Sm. [+ Pol.])

Written last: (a) Allusion to the arrival of envoys coming from Syria; (b) No petition for prayers for the church in Syria, unlike the other three letters; (c) Allusion to the peace restored between the communities of Syria and to the consoling news brought by the messengers; (d) Petition to the church of Ephesus to send a messenger to Syria with an embassy from the community and a personal letter of congratulation from him for having attained peace thanks to the prayers of the communities; (e) Mention of greetings from Philo, one of the envoys from the Syrian church, met by the Ephesians when he passed through Ephesus.

Sender: Ignatius, the Godbearer, a man who could give them directives like an apostle but will not, since although he is in chains for the name of Christian, he is not yet an achieved man in Jesus the Messiah.

Addressees: The community which is in Ephesus of Asia.

Theme: To warn the community beforehand against the Docetists. Ignatius has learned that some Gnostic propagandists from Syria passed through Ephesus, but the Ephesians have stopped their ears. Ignatius invites the community to meet together often for the Eucharist in order to experience the true presence of the Lord in their midst.

Bearers: Some of the delegates sent by the community to Smyrna, others having been sent in turn to Italy to take the letter to the Romans.

Ignatius' brief stay in Ephesus has left traces in the personalized greetings to families and individuals.

The original letter to the Eph* has been divided into two (Eph. and Sm.) by means of a clause interrupting the primitive sequence of the central exposition (Eph. 20). The original inscr. has been left in Eph. Using the original ending the forger has composed new ones for Sm. and Pol. (and a copy for Phld.). Both the newly-constructed letters have been heavily interpolated. The letter to Polycarp is spurious. The second part however (Pol. 6-end), in the plural, retains several passages from the original ending of Eph*.

A. INITIAL GREETING

Eph. inscr. 'Ιγνάτιος, ὁ καὶ Θεοφόρος,
τῇ εὐλογημένῃ ἐν μεγέθει θεοῦ πατρὸς πληρώματι,
τῇ προωρισμένῃ πρὸ αἰώνων εἶναι διὰ παντὸς — εἰς δόξαν
παράμονον — ἄτρεπτον ἡνωμένην καὶ ἐκλελεγμένην ἐν πάθει ἀληθινῷ,
ἐν θελήματι τοῦ πατρὸς καὶ 'Ιησοῦ Χριστοῦ, τοῦ θεοῦ ἡμῶν,　　5
τῇ ἐκκλησίᾳ τῇ ἀξιομακαρίστῳ, τῇ οὔσῃ ἐν 'Εφέσῳ τῆς
'Ασίας ·
πλεῖστα ἐν 'Ιησοῦ Χριστῷ καὶ ἐν ἀμώμῳ χαρᾷ χαίρειν.

B. INTRODUCTION

Solicitude of the Ephesian community

Ι, 1. 'Αποδεξάμενος ἐν θεῷ τὸ πολυαγάπητόν σου ὄνομα, ὃ κέκτησθε
φύσει δικαίᾳ κατὰ πίστιν καὶ ἀγάπην ἐν Χριστῷ 'Ιησοῦ, τῷ σωτῆρι ἡμῶν ·　10
μιμηταὶ ὄντες θεοῦ, ἀναζωπυρήσαντες ἐν αἵματι θεοῦ τὸ συγγενικὸν ἔργον
τελείως ἀπηρτίσατε · 2. ἀκούσαντες γὰρ δεδεμένον ἀπὸ Συρίας ὑπὲρ τοῦ
κοινοῦ ὀνόματος καὶ ἐλπίδος, ἐλπίζοντα τῇ προσευχῇ ὑμῶν ἐπιτυχεῖν
ἐν 'Ρώμῃ θηριομαχῆσαι, ἵνα διὰ τοῦ ἐπιτυχεῖν δυνηθῶ μαθητὴς εἶναι,
ἰδεῖν με ἐσπουδάσατε.　　15

Mention of delegates: Invitation to the community to keep close to the person of Jesus the Messiah

Ι, 3. 'Επεὶ οὖν τὴν πολυπληθίαν ὑμῶν
ἐν ὀνόματι θεοῦ ἀπείληφα ἐν 'Ονησίμῳ,
τῷ ἐν ἀγάπῃ ἀδιηγήτῳ,

Ι, 3. 'Επεὶ οὖν τὴν πολυπληθίαν ὑμῶν
ἐν ὀνόματι θεοῦ ἀπείληφα ἐν 'Ονησίμῳ,
τῷ ἐν ἀγάπῃ ἀδιηγήτῳ, {ὑμῶν δὲ ἐν

---

2 πληρώματι Gg editors, perfectione A: et plenitudine L, et perfectae S. " The μέγεθος describes the moral and spiritual stature of the Ephesian Church itself " (Light. II/1, 23; see Bauer II 191 f.), θεοῦ πατρὸς being related to πλ. ‖ 8 χαρᾷ SAg (cf. Mg. 7,1) editors: χάριτι GL ‖ 10 Χριστῷ 'Ιησοῦ Lg editors: ∼ GSA ‖ 15 ἰδεῖν με (> L editors) ἐσπουδάσατε LSAB: > Gg.

I,1. " Die Worte, mit denen der eigentliche Brief beginnt, werden in der Regel als unvollendetes Satzgefüge betrachtet und auf verschiedene Art vervollständigt. Zuzutrauen ist eine solche Schreibweise dem Ign. sehr wohl ... Nötig ist eine Ergänzung in unserem Fall jedoch nicht. Schon in vorchristlicher Zeit nämlich hat die Volkssprache das Partizipium ganz frei als Verbum finitum verwendet ... " (Bauer II 195; several examples are quoted there).
I,3-II,2. For the identification of the few sentences interpolated in the introduction of Eph*, see nrs. 79 (80), 134. The corresponding apodosis to 'Επεὶ οὖν of 1,3ab is πρέπον ἐστίν of 2,2c: see nr. 79 f.

σαρκὶ ἐπισκόπῳ, ὃν εὔχομαι κατὰ
Ἰησοῦν Χριστὸν ὑμᾶς ἀγαπᾶν καὶ πάντας ὑμᾶς αὐτῷ ἐν ὁμοιότητι εἶναι. εὐ-
λογητὸς γὰρ ὁ χαρισάμενος ὑμῖν ἀξίοις
οὖσι τοιοῦτον ἐπίσκοπον κεκτῆσθαι.

5 II, 1.   <καὶ>
Βούρρ<ῳ>, τ<ῷ>
    ἐν πᾶσιν εὐλογημέν<ῳ>,

II, 1. Περὶ δὲ τοῦ συνδούλου μου}
Βούρρου, τοῦ {κατὰ θεὸν διακόνου
ὑμῶν,} ἐν πᾶσιν εὐλογημένου, {εὔχομαι
παραμεῖναι αὐτὸν εἰς τιμὴν ὑμῶν καὶ

10   καὶ Κρόκ<ῳ> δέ,
<τῷ> θεοῦ ἀξί<ῳ> καὶ ὑμῶν, ὁ<ς>

τοῦ ἐπισκόπου ·} καὶ Κρόκος δέ,
ὁ θεοῦ ἄξιος καὶ ὑμῶν, ὃν {ἐξεμ-
πλάριον τῆς ἀφ' ὑμῶν ἀγάπης ἀπέ-

    κατὰ πάντα με ἀνέπαυσεν

λαβον,} κατὰ πάντα με ἀνέπαυσεν{, ὡς
καὶ αὐτὸν ὁ πατὴρ Ἰησοῦ Χριστοῦ

15   ἄμα Ὀνησίμῳ καὶ Βούρρῳ
καὶ Εὔπλῳ καὶ Φρόντωνι, δι' ὧν πάντας ὑμᾶς κατὰ ἀγάπην εἶδον — 2.
ὀναίμην ὑμῶν διὰ παντός, ἐάνπερ
ἄξιος ὦ —, πρέπον   ἐστίν, κατὰ
20 πάντα τρόπον δοξάζειν Ἰησοῦν Χριστὸν τὸν δοξάσαντα ὑμᾶς, ἵνα ἐν
μιᾷ ὑποταγῇ κατηρτισμένοι

    κατὰ πάντα ἦτε ἡγιασμένοι.

ἀναψύξαι} ἄμα Ὀνησίμῳ καὶ Βούρρῳ
καὶ Εὔπλῳ καὶ Φρόντωνι, δι' ὧν πάντας ὑμᾶς κατὰ ἀγάπην εἶδον — 2.
ὀναίμην ὑμῶν διὰ παντός, ἐάνπερ
ἄξιος ὦ —. πρέπον {οὖν} ἐστίν, κατὰ
πάντα τρόπον δοξάζειν Ἰησοῦν Χριστὸν τὸν δοξάσαντα ὑμᾶς, ἵνα ἐν
μιᾷ ὑποταγῇ κατηρτισμένοι{, ὑποτασσόμενοι τῷ ἐπισκόπῳ καὶ τῷ πρεσβυτερίῳ,} κατὰ πάντα ἦτε ἡγιασμένοι.

C. BODY OF THE LETTER

a. Aim: Not to give directives but to exhort

25 III, 1. Οὐ διατάσσομαι ὑμῖν ὡς ὤν τις · εἰ γὰρ καὶ δέδεμαι ἐν τῷ ὀνόματι, οὔπω ἀπήρτισμαι ἐν Ἰησοῦ Χριστῷ. νῦν γὰρ ἀρχὴν ἔχω τοῦ μαθη-
τεύεσθαι καὶ προσλαλῶ ὑμῖν ὡς συνδιδασκαλίταις μου · ἐμὲ γὰρ ἔδει
ὑφ' ὑμῶν ὑπαλειφθῆναι πίστει, νουθεσίᾳ, ὑπομονῇ, μακροθυμίᾳ. 2. ἀλλ'
ἐπεὶ ἡ ἀγάπη οὐκ ἐᾷ με σιωπᾶν περὶ ὑμῶν, διὰ τοῦτο προέλαβον παρα-
30 καλεῖν ὑμᾶς, ὅπως συντρέχετε τῇ γνώμῃ τοῦ θεοῦ · καὶ γὰρ Ἰησοῦς Χριστός, τὸ ἀδιάκριτον ἡμῶν ζῆν, τοῦ πατρὸς ἡ γνώμη{, ὡς καὶ οἱ ἐπίσκοποι,
οἱ κατὰ τὰ πέρατα ὁρισθέντες, ἐν Ἰησοῦ Χριστοῦ γνώμῃ εἰσίν. IV, 1. ὅθεν πρέπει
ὑμῖν συντρέχειν τῇ τοῦ ἐπισκόπου γνώμῃ, ὅπερ καὶ ποιεῖτε · τὸ γὰρ ἀξιονόμαστον
ὑμῶν πρεσβυτέριον, τοῦ θεοῦ ἄξιον, οὕτως συνήρμοσται τῷ ἐπισκόπῳ, ὡς χορδαὶ κιθάρᾳ}.
35 διὰ τοῦτο ἐν τῇ ὁμονοίᾳ ὑμῶν καὶ συμφώνῳ ἀγάπῃ Ἰησοῦς Χριστὸς
ᾄδεται. 2. καὶ οἱ κατ' ἄνδρα δὲ χορὸς γίνεσθε, ἵνα σύμφωνοι ὄντες ἐν
ὁμονοίᾳ, χρῶμα θεοῦ λαβόντες ἐν ἑνότητι, ᾄδετε ἐν φωνῇ μιᾷ διὰ Ἰησοῦ
Χριστοῦ τῷ πατρί, ἵνα ὑμῶν καὶ ἀκούσῃ καὶ ἐπιγινώσκῃ, δι' ὧν εὖ

31 ἡμῶν LA: ὑμῶν G.

III,2-IV,1. {ὡς καὶ οἱ ἐπίσκοποι κτλ. Paraphrasing interpolation of the preceding
    Ignatian sentence: see nrs. 81.1 (82), 140.

πράσσετε, μέλη ὄντας τοῦ υἱοῦ αὐτοῦ. χρήσιμον οὖν ἐστίν, ὑμᾶς ἐν ἀμώμῳ
ἑνότητι εἶναι, ἵνα καὶ θεοῦ πάντοτε μετέχετε. {V, 1. εἰ γὰρ ἐγὼ ἐν μικρῷ
χρόνῳ τοιαύτην συνήθειαν ἔσχον πρὸς τὸν ἐπίσκοπον ὑμῶν, οὐκ ἀνθρωπίνην οὖσαν,
ἀλλὰ πνευματικήν, πόσῳ μᾶλλον ὑμᾶς μακαρίζω τοὺς ἐνκεκραμένους αὐτῷ, ὡς ἡ
ἐκκλησία Ἰησοῦ Χριστῷ καὶ ὡς Ἰησοῦς Χριστὸς τῷ πατρί, ἵνα πάντα ἐν ἑνότητι 5
σύμφωνα ᾖ;}

b. Initial warning

V, 2. Μηδεὶς πλανάσθω· ἐὰν μή τις ᾖ ἐντὸς τοῦ θυσιαστηρίου, ὑστε-
ρεῖται τοῦ ἄρτου τοῦ θεοῦ. {εἰ γὰρ ἑνὸς καὶ δευτέρου προσευχὴ τοσαύτην ἰσχὺν
ἔχει, πόσῳ μᾶλλον ἥ τε τοῦ ἐπισκόπου καὶ πάσης τῆς ἐκκλησίας;} 3. ὁ οὖν μὴ
ἐρχόμενος ἐπὶ τὸ αὐτό, οὗτος ἤδη ὑπερηφανεῖ καὶ ἑαυτὸν διέκρινεν. γέ- 10
γραπται γάρ· " Ὑπερηφάνοις ὁ θεὸς ἀντιτάσσεται. " {σπουδάσωμεν οὖν
μὴ ἀντιτάσσεσθαι τῷ ἐπισκόπῳ, ἵνα ὦμεν θεῷ ὑποτασσόμενοι. VI, 1. καὶ ὅσον
βλέπει τις σιγῶντα ἐπίσκοπον, πλειόνως αὐτὸν φοβείσθω· πάντα γάρ, ὃν πέμπει
ὁ οἰκοδεσπότης εἰς ἰδίαν οἰκονομίαν, οὕτως δεῖ ἡμᾶς αὐτὸν δέχεσθαι, ὡς αὐτὸν τὸν
πέμψαντα. τὸν οὖν ἐπίσκοπον δῆλον ὅτι ὡς αὐτὸν τὸν κύριον δεῖ προσβλέπειν.} 15

c. Explanation:
The Ephesian community is unsympathetic to the Gnostic heresy

VI, 2. Αὐτὸς μὲν οὖν Ὀνήσιμος ὑπερεπαινεῖ ὑμῶν τὴν ἐν θεῷ εὐταξίαν,
ὅτι πάντες κατὰ ἀλήθειαν ζῆτε καὶ ὅτι ἐν ὑμῖν οὐδεμία αἵρεσις κατοι-
κεῖ· ἀλλ' οὐδὲ ἀκούετέ τινος πλέον, ἥπερ Ἰησοῦ Χριστοῦ λαλοῦντος ἐν
ἀληθείᾳ. VII, 1. εἰώθασιν γάρ τινες δόλῳ πονηρῷ τὸ ὄνομα περιφέ-
ρειν, ἄλλα τινὰ πράσσοντες ἀνάξια θεοῦ. οὓς δεῖ ὑμᾶς ὡς θηρία ἐκκλί- 20
νειν· εἰσὶν γὰρ κύνες λυσσῶντες, λαθροδῆκται, οὓς δεῖ ὑμᾶς   φυλάσσεσθαι ὄντας δυσθεραπεύτους.

         2. εἷς ἰατρός ἐστιν·
         σαρκικός τε καὶ πνευματικός,
         γεννητὸς καὶ ἀγέννητος,   25
         ἐν σαρκὶ γενόμενος θεός,

---

4 ἐνκεκραμένους G, coniunctos L, mixtos A editors: ἀνακεκραμένους g Light. | αὐτῷ
Agl Zahn Camelot: οὕτως GL Light. Funk-Bihl. Lelong Fischer ‖ **18** ἥπερ L (quam),
εἴπερ G Zahn Funk Bauer Bihl. Fischer: εἰ μὴ περὶ A, ἢ περὶ Light. Hilg. (Lelong)
Camelot. To remind the frequent itacisms of G! ‖ **26** ἐν σαρκὶ γενόμενος GL: ἐν
ἀνθρώπῳ Sf B (A deus et filius hominis) Athan. Theodt. Gelas. Sever. (twice) (Light.
II/1, 49) Sf Light. The Athanasian reading seems to be an after-Nicaean theological
correction.

V,1. {εἰ γὰρ ἐγὼ κτλ. The exhortation to unity is tampered with by the interp. in
     order to stress the link of the church with the bishop: see nrs. 81.2 (82), 140.
V,2. {εἰ γὰρ ἑνὸς κτλ. The interp. reinterprets the common prayer by stressing the
     official prayer under the bishop: see nrs. 81.2 (82), 140.
V,3. Prov. 3,34. Cf. 1Pet. 5,5; James 4,6; 1Clem. 30.
V,3-VI,1. {σπουδάσωμεν οὖν κτλ. The interp. again paraphrases Prov. 3,34, since
     for him the bishop personifies God: see nrs. 81.3 (82), 140.

ἐν θανάτῳ ζωὴ ἀληθινή,
καὶ ἐκ Μαρίας καὶ ἐκ θεοῦ,
πρῶτον παθητὸς καὶ τότε ἀπαθής,
Ἰησοῦς Χριστὸς ὁ κύριος ἡμῶν.

5 VIII, 1. μὴ οὖν τις ὑμᾶς ἐξαπατάτω, ὥσπερ οὐδὲ ἐξαπατᾶσθε, ὅλοι ὄντες
θεοῦ · ὅταν γὰρ μηδεμία ἔρις ἐνήρεισται ἐν ὑμῖν, ἡ δυναμένη ὑμᾶς βασα-
νίσαι, ἄρα κατὰ θεὸν ζῆτε. περίψημα ὑμῶν καὶ ἁγνίζομαι ὑμῶν Ἐφεσίων, ἐκκλησίας τῆς διαβοήτου τοῖς αἰῶσιν · 2. οἱ σαρκικοὶ τὰ πνευ-
ματικὰ πράσσειν οὐ δύνανται οὐδὲ οἱ πνευματικοὶ τὰ σαρκικά, ὥσπερ
10 οὐδὲ ἡ πίστις τὰ τῆς ἀπιστίας οὐδὲ ἡ ἀπιστία τὰ τῆς πίστεως. ἃ δὲ καὶ
κατὰ σάρκα πράσσετε, ταῦτα πνευματικά ἐστιν · ἐν Ἰησοῦ γὰρ Χριστῷ
πάντα πράσσετε.

Syrian Gnostics on their way through Ephesus

IX, 1. Ἔγνων δὲ παροδεύσαντάς τινας ἐκεῖθεν, ἔχοντας κακὴν διδαχήν,
οὓς οὐκ εἰάσατε σπεῖραι εἰς ὑμᾶς, βύσαντες τὰ ὦτα, εἰς τὸ μὴ παραδέ-
15 ξασθαι τὰ σπειρόμενα ὑπ᾽ αὐτῶν, ὡς ὄντες λίθοι ναοῦ πατρός, ἡτοι-
μασμένοι εἰς οἰκοδομὴν θεοῦ πατρός, ἀναφερόμενοι εἰς τὰ ὕψη διὰ τῆς
μηχανῆς Ἰησοῦ Χριστοῦ, ὅς ἐστιν σταυρός, σχοινίῳ χρώμενοι τῷ πνεύματι τῷ ἁγίῳ · ἡ δὲ πίστις ὑμῶν ἀναγωγεὺς ὑμῶν, ἡ δὲ ἀγάπη ὁδὸς
ἡ ἀναφέρουσα εἰς θεόν.

Invitation to communitarian assembly and to imitation of the Lord

20 IX, 2. Ἔστε οὖν καὶ σύνοδοι πάντες, θεοφόροι καὶ ναοφόροι, χριστοφόροι,
ἁγιοφόροι, κατὰ πάντα κεκοσμημένοι ἐν ταῖς ἐντολαῖς Ἰησοῦ Χριστοῦ ·
οἷς καὶ ἀγαλλιῶμαι, ὅτι ἠξιώθην δι᾽ ὧν γράφω προσομιλῆσαι ὑμῖν καὶ
συγχαρῆναι, ὅτι κατ᾽ ἄλλον βίον οὐδὲν ἀγαπᾶτε εἰ μὴ μόνον τὸν θεόν.
Χ, 1. καὶ ὑπὲρ τῶν ἄλλων δὲ ἀνθρώπων ἀδιαλείπτως προσεύχεσθε ·
25 ἔστιν γὰρ ἐν αὐτοῖς ἐλπὶς μετανοίας, ἵνα θεοῦ τύχωσιν. ἐπιτρέψατε οὖν
αὐτοῖς κἂν ἐκ τῶν ἔργων ὑμῖν μαθητευθῆναι · 2. πρὸς τὰς ὀργὰς αὐτῶν
ὑμεῖς πραεῖς, πρὸς τὰς μεγαλορημοσύνας αὐτῶν ὑμεῖς ταπεινόφρονες,
πρὸς τὰς βλασφημίας αὐτῶν ὑμεῖς τὰς προσευχάς, πρὸς τὴν πλάνην αὐτῶν
ὑμεῖς ἑδραῖοι τῇ πίστει, πρὸς τὸ ἄγριον αὐτῶν ὑμεῖς ἥμεροι — μὴ σπου-
30 δάζοντες ἀντιμιμήσασθαι αὐτούς, 3. ἀδελφοὶ αὐτῶν εὑρεθῶμεν τῇ ἐπιει-

---

1 ἐν θανάτῳ SfB(A vera vita et in morte vivus) Athan. Theodt. Sever. (twice) Gelas.
editors: ἐν ἀθανάτῳ GL ‖ 4 Ἰησοῦς — ἡμῶν SfAB, Dominus Christus noster L,
Theodt. Sever. (twice) Gelas.: dominus Christus noster L, > G ‖ 6 ἐνήρεισται em.
Zahn modern editors, ἐνείρισται G (itacism!), complexa est L, plantata est SA ‖ 7
ὑμῶν G Light. Funk-Bihl. Fischer (cf. Tr. 13,3): ὑπὲρ ὑμῶν SA Zahn Camelot, a
vestra L ‖ 20 Ἔστε con.: Ἐστὲ editors ‖ 21 ἐν ταῖς gL(in) Antioch. modern editors: (in) omnibus A, ἐν Light., > G.

κεία· μιμηταὶ δὲ τοῦ κυρίου σπουδάζωμεν εἶναι, τίς πλέον ἀδικηθῇ, τίς ἀποστερηθῇ, τίς ἀθετηθῇ — ἵνα μὴ τοῦ διαβόλου βοτάνη τις εὑρεθῇ ἐν ὑμῖν, ἀλλ᾽ ἐν πάσῃ ἁγνείᾳ καὶ σωφροσύνῃ μένητε ἐν Ἰησοῦ Χριστῷ σαρκικῶς καὶ πνευματικῶς.

d. Central exposition (first part):
The end of the world is imminent: only Jesus, the Messiah, matters

XI, 1. Ἔσχατοι καιροί· λοιπὸν αἰσχυνθῶμεν, φοβηθῶμεν τὴν μακρο- 5
θυμίαν τοῦ θεοῦ, ἵνα μὴ ἡμῖν εἰς κρίμα γένηται· ἢ γὰρ τὴν μέλλουσαν
ὀργὴν φοβηθῶμεν, ἢ τὴν ἐνεστῶσαν χάριν ἀγαπήσωμεν, ἐν τῶν δύο·
μόνον ἐν Χριστῷ Ἰησοῦ εὑρεθῆναι εἰς τὸ ἀληθινὸν ζῆν. 2. χωρὶς τούτου
μηδὲν ὑμῖν πρεπέτω, ἐν ᾧ τὰ δεσμὰ περιφέρω, τοὺς πνευματικοὺς μαρ-
γαρίτας, ἐν οἷς γένοιτό μοι ἀναστῆναι τῇ προσευχῇ ὑμῶν, ἧς γένοιτό 10
μοι ἀεὶ μέτοχον εἶναι, ἵνα ἐν κλήρῳ Ἐφεσίων εὑρεθῶ τῶν Χριστιανῶν,
οἳ καὶ τοῖς ἀποστόλοις πάντοτε συνήνεσαν ἐν δυνάμει Ἰησοῦ Χριστοῦ.

Ignatius, a condemned man, exhorts the Ephesians who are gratified and secure

XII, 1. Οἶδα, τίς εἰμι καὶ τίσιν γράφω. ἐγὼ κατάκριτος, ὑμεῖς ἠλεη-
μένοι· ἐγὼ ὑπὸ κίνδυνον, ὑμεῖς ἐστηριγμένοι. 2. πάροδός ἐστε τῶν εἰς
θεὸν ἀναιρουμένων, Παύλου συμμύσται, τοῦ ἡγιασμένου, τοῦ μεμαρτυ- 15
ρημένου, ἀξιομακαρίστου, οὗ γένοιτό μοι ὑπὸ τὰ ἴχνη εὑρεθῆναι, ὅταν
θεοῦ ἐπιτύχω, ὃς ἐν πάσῃ ἐπιστολῇ μνημονεύει ὑμῶν ἐν Χριστῷ Ἰησοῦ.

The best defence is assiduous community meeting

XIII, 1. Σπουδάζετε οὖν πυκνότερον συνέρχεσθαι εἰς εὐχαριστίαν θεοῦ
καὶ εἰς δόξαν· ὅταν γὰρ πυκνῶς ἐπὶ τὸ αὐτὸ γίνεσθε, καθαιροῦνται αἱ
δυνάμεις τοῦ Σατανᾶ, καὶ λύεται ὁ ὄλεθρος αὐτοῦ ἐν τῇ ὁμονοίᾳ ὑμῶν 20
τῆς πίστεως.

Your experience of peace dispels dualism

XIII, 2. Οὐδέν ἐστιν ἄμεινον εἰρήνης, ἐν ᾗ πᾶς πόλεμος καταργεῖται ἐπουρανίων καὶ ἐπιγείων, XIV, 1. ὧν οὐδὲν λανθάνει ὑμᾶς, ἐὰν τελείως εἰς
Ἰησοῦν Χριστὸν ἔχητε τὴν πίστιν καὶ τὴν ἀγάπην, ἥτις ἐστὶν ἀρχὴ ζωῆς
καὶ τέλος· ἀρχὴ μὲν πίστις, τέλος δὲ ἀγάπη. τὰ δὲ δύο ἐν ἑνότητι γενό- 25
μενα θεός ἐστιν, τὰ δὲ ἄλλα πάντα εἰς καλοκἀγαθίαν ἀκόλουθά ἐστιν.

1 ἀδικηθῇ κτλ. G (-θεῖ, itacism!) LS Light. Funk Hilg. Krüger Bauer Fischer: ἀδικηθείς κτλ. em. Hefele Zahn Camelot ‖ 3 μένητε L(A) modern editors: μένετε G Zahn (Light.) ‖ 11 ἐν Lg editors: ἐνὶ G, ἐνὶ Zahn. See Eph. 20,2 for a similar confusion ‖ 12 συνήνεσαν GL editors: συνῆσαν Ag Zahn ‖ 26 θεός ἐστιν LSfA Dam. editors: θεοῦ ἐστιν G, θεοῦ ἄνθρωπον ἀποτελεῖ g. See nr. 149,2.

" You will know them by the kind of fruit they bear "

XIV, 2. Οὐδεὶς πίστιν ἐπαγγελλόμενος ἁμαρτάνει, οὐδὲ ἀγάπην κεκτημένος μισεῖ. " φανερὸν τὸ δένδρον ἀπὸ τοῦ καρποῦ αὐτοῦ " · οὕτως οἱ
ἐπαγγελλόμενοι Χριστοῦ εἶναι, δι᾽ ὧν πράσσουσιν ὀφθήσονται · οὐ γὰρ
νῦν ἐπαγγελίας τὸ ἔργον, ἀλλ᾽ ἐν δυνάμει πίστεως ἐάν τις εὑρεθῇ εἰς
5 τέλος.

My silence is worth more than their vain chatter

XV, 1. Ἄμεινόν ἐστιν σιωπᾶν καὶ εἶναι, ἢ λαλοῦντα μὴ εἶναι. καλὸν
τὸ διδάσκειν, ἐὰν ὁ λέγων ποιῇ. εἷς οὖν διδάσκαλος, ὃς " εἶπεν " καὶ
" ἐγένετο " · καὶ ἃ σιγῶν δὲ πεποίηκεν, ἄξια τοῦ πατρός ἐστιν. 2. ὁ
λόγον Ἰησοῦ κεκτημένος ἀληθῶς δύναται καὶ τῆς ἡσυχίας αὐτοῦ ἀκούειν,
10 ἵνα τέλειος ᾖ, ἵνα δι᾽ ὧν λαλεῖ πράσσῃ καὶ δι᾽ ὧν σιγᾷ γινώσκηται. 3. οὐδὲν λανθάνει τὸν κύριον, ἀλλὰ καὶ τὰ κρυπτὰ ἡμῶν ἐγγὺς αὐτῷ ἐστιν.
πάντα οὖν ποιῶμεν ὡς αὐτοῦ ἐν ἡμῖν κατοικοῦντος, ἵνα ὦμεν αὐτοῦ ναοὶ
καὶ αὐτὸς ᾖ ἐν ἡμῖν θεὸς ἡμῶν, ὅπερ καὶ ἔστιν καὶ φανήσεται πρὸ
προσώπου ἡμῶν, ἐξ ὧν δικαίως ἀγαπῶμεν αὐτόν.

e. Central warning

15 XVI, 1. " Μὴ πλανᾶσθε, " ἀδελφοί μου · οἱ οἰκοφθόροι " βασιλείαν θεοῦ
οὐ κληρονομήσουσιν ". 2. εἰ οὖν οἱ κατὰ σάρκα ταῦτα πράσσοντες ἀπέ-
θανον, πόσῳ μᾶλλον, ἐὰν πίστιν θεοῦ ἐν κακῇ διδασκαλίᾳ φθείρῃ, ὑπὲρ
ἧς Ἰησοῦς Χριστὸς ἐσταυρώθη; ὁ τοιοῦτος, ῥυπαρὸς γενόμενος, εἰς τὸ
πῦρ τὸ ἄσβεστον χωρήσει, ὁμοίως καὶ ὁ ἀκούων αὐτοῦ. XVII, 1. διὰ
20 τοῦτο μύρον ἔλαβεν ἐπὶ τῆς κεφαλῆς αὐτοῦ ὁ κύριος, ἵνα πνέῃ τῇ ἐκκλησίᾳ ἀφθαρσίαν. μὴ ἀλείφεσθε δυσωδίαν τῆς διδασκαλίας τοῦ ἄρχοντος
τοῦ αἰῶνος τούτου, μὴ αἰχμαλωτίσῃ ὑμᾶς ἐκ τοῦ προκειμένου ζῆν. 2. διὰ
τί δὲ οὐ πάντες φρόνιμοι γινόμεθα λαβόντες θεοῦ γνῶσιν, ὅ ἐστιν Ἰησοῦς
Χριστός; τί μωρῶς ἀπολλύμεθα, ἀγνοοῦντες τὸ χάρισμα, ὃ πέπομφεν
25 ἀληθῶς ὁ κύριος;

d'. Central exposition (second part):
a.   The cross, scandal for the heretics, is our liberation and life

XVIII, 1a. Περίψημα τὸ ἐμὸν πνεῦμα τοῦ σταυροῦ, ὅ ἐστιν σκάνδαλον
τοῖς ἀπιστοῦσιν, ἡμῖν δὲ σωτηρία καὶ ζωὴ αἰώνιος.

---

3 Χριστοῦ Ag Dam. Antioch.: Χριστιανοί (sic) GL ‖ 13 ᾖ G(SfA) Zahn: > Lg
Light. modern editors.

XIV,2.   See Mtt. 12,33; Lk. 6,44.
XV,1.   Gen. 1,3.6.9.11, etc. LXX; cf. Ps. 32,9; 148,5 LXX.
XVI,1.   1Cor. 6,9-10.

β. Christological creed of Ignatius' community

XVIII, 1d. " Ποῦ σοφός; ποῦ συζητητής;" ποῦ καύχησις τῶν λεγομένων
συνετῶν; 2. ὁ γὰρ θεὸς ἡμῶν Ἰησοῦς ὁ Χριστὸς
    ἐκυοφορήθη ὑπὸ Μαρίας κατ' οἰκονομίαν θεοῦ
    — ἐκ σπέρματος μὲν Δαυίδ, πνεύματος δὲ ἁγίου —
    ὃς ἐγεννήθη   5
    καὶ ἐβαπτίσθη,
    ἵνα τῷ πάθει τὸ ὕδωρ καθαρίσῃ.

γ. Hiding of these secrets from the Chief of this world

XIX, 1. Καὶ ἔλαθεν τὸν ἄρχοντα τοῦ αἰῶνος τούτου ἡ παρθενία Μαρίας
καὶ ὁ τοκετὸς αὐτῆς, ὁμοίως καὶ ὁ θάνατος τοῦ κυρίου · τρία μυστήρια
κραυγῆς, ἅτινα ἐν ἡσυχίᾳ θεοῦ ἐπράχθη.   10

γ'. Manifestation of the Messiah's star to the other heavenly Chiefs

XIX, 2. Πῶς οὖν ἐφανερώθη τοῖς αἰῶσιν; ἀστὴρ ἐν οὐρανῷ ἔλαμψεν
ὑπὲρ πάντας τοὺς ἀστέρας, καὶ τὸ φῶς αὐτοῦ ἀνεκλάλητον ἦν, καὶ ξε-
νισμὸν παρεῖχεν ἡ καινότης αὐτοῦ, τὰ δὲ λοιπὰ πάντα ἄστρα ἅμα ἡλίῳ
καὶ σελήνῃ χορὸς ἐγένετο τῷ ἀστέρι, αὐτὸς δὲ ἦν ὑπερβάλλων τὸ φῶς
αὐτοῦ ὑπὲρ πάντα · ταραχή τε ἦν, πόθεν ἡ καινότης ἡ ἀνόμοιος αὐτοῖς. 15
3. ὅθεν ἐλύετο πᾶσα μαγεία καὶ πᾶς δεσμὸς ἠφανίζετο κακίας · ἄγνοια
καθῃρεῖτο, παλαιὰ βασιλεία διεφθείρετο θεοῦ ἀνθρωπίνως φανερουμένου
εἰς καινότητα ἀϊδίου ζωῆς · ἀρχὴν δὲ ἐλάμβανεν τὸ παρὰ θεῷ ἀπηρτισ-
μένον. ἔνθεν τὰ πάντα συνεκινεῖτο διὰ τὸ μελετᾶσθαι θανάτου κατά-
λυσιν.   20

{Interrupting clause of the primitive sequence of Eph*:

XX, 1. Ἐάν με καταξιώσῃ Ἰησοῦς Χριστὸς ἐν τῇ προσευχῇ ὑμῶν καὶ θέλημα ᾖ,
ἐν τῷ δευτέρῳ βιβλιδίῳ, ὃ μέλλω γράφειν ὑμῖν, προσδηλώσω ὑμῖν, ἧς ἠρξάμην οἰκονομίας εἰς τὸν καινὸν ἄνθρωπον Ἰησοῦν Χριστόν, ἐν τῇ αὐτοῦ πίστει καὶ ἐν τῇ αὐτοῦ
ἀγάπῃ, ἐν πάθει αὐτοῦ καὶ ἀναστάσει · 2. μάλιστα ἐὰν ὁ κύριός μοι ἀποκαλύψῃ,
ὅτι οἱ κατ' ἄνδρα κοινῇ πάντες ἐν χάριτι ἐξ ὀνόματος συνέρχεσθε ἐν μιᾷ πίστει καὶ 25
ἐν Ἰησοῦ Χριστῷ, τῷ κατὰ σάρκα ἐκ γένους Δαυίδ, τῷ υἱῷ ἀνθρώπου καὶ υἱῷ
θεοῦ, εἰς τὸ ὑπακούειν ὑμᾶς τῷ ἐπισκόπῳ καὶ τῷ πρεσβυτερίῳ ἀπερισπάστῳ δια-
νοίᾳ, ἕνα ἄρτον κλῶντες, ὅς ἐστιν φάρμακον ἀθανασίας, ἀντίδοτος τοῦ μὴ ἀποθανεῖν, ἀλλὰ ζῆν ἐν Ἰησοῦ Χριστῷ διὰ παντός.}

---

25 ὅτι GL(A): εἴ τι Theodt., τι Zahn Krüger, † ὅτι † Light. See nr. 56 ‖ 26 ἐν
GLSf modern editors: ἑνὶ Theodt. Light., in uno Gelas.

XVIII,1d. 1Cor. 1,20(19); cf. Paul Rom. 3,27.
{Interrupting clause etc. of Eph*. Drawn up by the forger to soften the abrupt interruption of the exposition: see nrs. 10 f., 18-21 (with a detailed comparison
with Sm. 1), 56.

(Summary of the conclusion of Eph*: see Paraenesis, p. 381, Conclusion, pp. 382 f., and Final greeting of the letter, p. 385).

{Spurious initial greeting of Sm. (inscr.):

Sm. inscr. Ἰγνάτιος, ὁ καὶ Θεοφόρος, ἐκκλησίᾳ θεοῦ πατρὸς καὶ τοῦ ἠγαπημένου Ἰησοῦ Χριστοῦ, ἠλεημένη ἐν παντὶ χαρίσματι, πεπληρωμένη ἐν πίστει καὶ ἀγάπῃ, ἀνυστερήτῳ οὔσῃ παντὸς χαρίσματος, θεοπρεπεστάτῃ καὶ ἁγιοφόρῳ, τῇ οὔσῃ ἐν Σμύρνῃ τῆς Ἀσίας, ἐν ἀμώμῳ πνεύματι καὶ λόγῳ θεοῦ πλεῖστα χαίρειν.}

β΄. Anti-Docetic Christological creed of the Ephesian community, supported by Ignatius

5 *Sm.* I, 1. Δοξάζω Ἰησοῦν Χριστὸν τὸν θεὸν τὸν οὕτως ὑμᾶς σοφίσαντα · ἐνόησα γὰρ ὑμᾶς κατηρτισμένους ἐν ἀκινήτῳ πίστει — ὥσπερ καθηλωμένους ἐν τῷ σταυρῷ τοῦ κυρίου Ἰησοῦ Χριστοῦ σαρκί τε καὶ πνεύματι — καὶ ἡδρασμένους ἐν ἀγάπῃ ἐν τῷ αἵματι Χριστοῦ, πεπληροφορημένους εἰς τὸν κύριον ἡμῶν,

10 ἀληθῶς ὄντα ἐκ γένους Δαυὶδ κατὰ σάρκα, υἱὸν θεοῦ κατὰ θέλημα καὶ δύναμιν θεοῦ,
γεγεννημένον ἀληθῶς ἐκ παρθένου,
βεβαπτισμένον ἐπὶ Ἰωάννου, ἵνα " πληρωθῇ πᾶσα δικαιοσύνη ὑπ' αὐτοῦ ",

15 2a. ἀληθῶς ὑπὸ Ποντίου Πιλάτου καὶ Ἡρώδου τετράρχου καθηλωμένον ὑπὲρ ἡμῶν ἐν σαρκί.

α΄. Against the Docetic heretics, the resurrection gives evidence that Jesus really suffered

I, 2b. Ἀφ' οὗ καρποῦ ἡμεῖς — ἀπὸ τοῦ θεομακαρίτου αὐτοῦ πάθους —, ἵνα ἄρῃ σύσσημον εἰς τοὺς αἰῶνας διὰ τῆς ἀναστάσεως εἰς τοὺς ἁγίους καὶ πιστοὺς αὐτοῦ — εἴτε ἐν Ἰουδαίοις εἴτε ἐν ἔθνεσιν — ἐν ἑνὶ σώματι
20 τῆς ἐκκλησίας αὐτοῦ · II. ταῦτα γὰρ πάντα ἔπαθεν δι' ἡμᾶς, ἵνα σωθῶμεν. Καὶ ἀληθῶς ἔπαθεν, ὡς καὶ ἀληθῶς ἀνέστησεν ἑαυτόν, οὐχ ὥσπερ ἄπιστοί τινες λέγουσιν · Τὸ δοκεῖν αὐτὸν πεπονθέναι (αὐτοὶ ' τὸ δοκεῖν ' ὄντες · καὶ καθὼς φρονοῦσιν καὶ συμβήσεται αὐτοῖς, οὖσιν ἀσωμάτοις καὶ δαιμονικοῖς) · III, 1. ἐγὼ γὰρ καὶ μετὰ τὴν ἀνάστασιν ἐν σαρκὶ
25 αὐτὸν οἶδα καὶ πιστεύω ὄντα. 2. καὶ ὅτε πρὸς τοὺς περὶ Πέτρον ἦλθεν,

---

5 Δοξάζω LACg Sever. Light. Funk-Bihl.: Δοξάζων G Zahn Bauer Fischer. The participle in G is probably an attempt to tone down the abrupt beginning of Sm. See nr. 18. Perhaps the original reading was Δοξάζω οὖν κτλ.: see n. 95 ‖ **17** ἀφ' οὗ καρποῦ κτλ. See n. 97 | θεομακαρίτου G Zahn: -ίστου Lg Light. modern editors.

(*Summary of the conclusion of Eph*:* see nr. 30.
{*Spurious initial greeting of Sm. (inscr.):* see nr. 62.
Sm. I, 1. According to Mtt. 3,15.
II. See the note on Tr. 10, where similar language is used.

ἔφη αὐτοῖς · " Λάβετε, ψηλαφήσατέ με καὶ ἴδετε, ὅτι οὐκ εἰμὶ δαιμόνιον
ἀσώματον. " καὶ εὐθὺς αὐτοῦ ἥψαντο καὶ ἐπίστευσαν, κραθέντες τῇ
σαρκὶ αὐτοῦ καὶ τῷ πνεύματι · διὰ τοῦτο καὶ θανάτου κατεφρόνησαν,
ηὑρέθησαν δὲ ὑπὲρ θάνατον. 3. μετὰ δὲ τὴν ἀνάστασιν συνέφαγεν αὐτοῖς
καὶ συνέπιεν ὡς σαρκικός, καίπερ πνευματικῶς ἡνωμένος τῷ πατρί.   5

c'. Explanation: Meaning of the exposition

IV, 1. Ταῦτα δὲ παραινῶ ὑμῖν, ἀγαπητοί, εἰδώς, ὅτι καὶ ὑμεῖς οὕτως
ἔχετε · προφυλάσσω δὲ ὑμᾶς ἀπὸ τῶν θηρίων τῶν ἀνθρωπομόρφων, οὓς
οὐ μόνον δεῖ ὑμᾶς μὴ παραδέχεσθαι, ἀλλ' εἰ δυνατὸν μηδὲ συναντᾶν ·
μόνον δὲ προσεύχεσθε ὑπὲρ αὐτῶν, ἐάν πως μετανοήσωσιν, ὅπερ δύσκο-
λον. τούτου δὲ ἔχει ἐξουσίαν Ἰησοῦς Χριστός, τὸ ἀληθινὸν ἡμῶν ζῆν.   10
2. εἰ γὰρ ' τὸ δοκεῖν ' ταῦτα ἐπράχθη ὑπὸ τοῦ κυρίου ἡμῶν, κἀγὼ ' τὸ
δοκεῖν ' δέδεμαι. τί δὲ καὶ ἑαυτὸν ἔκδοτον δέδωκα τῷ θανάτῳ, πρὸς πῦρ,
πρὸς μάχαιραν, πρὸς θηρία; ἀλλ' ἐγγὺς μαχαίρας ἐγγὺς θεοῦ, μεταξὺ
θηρίων μεταξὺ θεοῦ · μόνον ἐν τῷ ὀνόματι Ἰησοῦ Χριστοῦ — εἰς τὸ συμπαθεῖν αὐτῷ — πάντα ὑπομένω, αὐτοῦ με ἐνδυναμοῦντος τοῦ τελείου ἀν- 15
θρώπου γενομένου · V, 1. ὅν τινες ἀγνοοῦντες ἀρνοῦνται, μᾶλλον δὲ
ἠρνήθησαν ὑπ' αὐτοῦ, ὄντες συνήγοροι τοῦ θανάτου μᾶλλον ἢ τῆς ἀληθείας · οὓς οὐκ ἔπεισαν αἱ προφητεῖαι οὐδὲ ὁ νόμος Μωϋσέως, ἀλλ' οὐδὲ
μέχρι νῦν τὸ εὐαγγέλιον οὐδὲ τὰ ἡμέτερα τῶν κατ' ἄνδρα παθήματα ·
2. καὶ γὰρ περὶ ἡμῶν τὸ αὐτὸ φρονοῦσιν. τί γάρ με ὠφελεῖ τις, εἰ ἐμὲ 20
ἐπαινεῖ, τὸν δὲ κύριόν μου βλασφημεῖ, μὴ ὁμολογῶν αὐτὸν σαρκοφόρον;
ὁ δὲ τοῦτο μὴ λέγων τελείως αὐτὸν ἀπήρνηται, ὢν νεκροφόρος. 3. τὰ δὲ
ὀνόματα αὐτῶν, ὄντα ἄπιστα, οὐκ ἔδοξέν μοι ἐγγράψαι. ἀλλὰ μηδὲ
γένοιτό μοι αὐτῶν μνημονεύειν, μέχρις οὗ μετανοήσωσιν εἰς τὸ πάθος,
ὅ ἐστιν ἡμῶν ἀνάστασις.   25

b'. Final warning

VI, 1a. Μηδεὶς πλανάσθω · καὶ τὰ ἐπουράνια καὶ ἡ δόξα τῶν ἀγγέλων
καὶ οἱ ἄρχοντες ὁρατοί τε καὶ ἀόρατοι, ἐὰν μὴ πιστεύσωσιν εἰς τὸ αἷμα
Χριστοῦ, κἀκείνοις κρίσις ἐστίν. " ὁ χωρῶν χωρείτω. "

a'. Final exhortation

VI, 1d. Τόπος μηδένα φυσιούτω · τὸ γὰρ ὅλον ἐστὶν πίστις καὶ ἀγάπη,
ὧν οὐδὲν προκέκριται. 2. καταμάθετε δὲ τοὺς ἑτεροδοξοῦντας εἰς τὴν   30
χάριν Ἰησοῦ Χριστοῦ τὴν εἰς ἡμᾶς ἐλθοῦσαν, πῶς ἐναντίοι εἰσὶν τῇ γνώμῃ

---

5 σαρκικός, καίπερ πνευματικῶς GL: σαρκικ.. καὶ πνευματικως P, σαρκικῶς καὶ
πνευματικῶς Theodt. cf. A, σαρκικὸς καὶ πνευματικὸς C which is perhaps correct ||
9 προσεύχεσθε PSfCg (Cod. c) 1 (Dam.) Light.: -σθαι GLAg (Codd. m n v) Zahn
Funk-Bihl. Fischer. The authority of G is in this occasion of no greater value
because of its frequent itacisms || 16 γενομένου GL editors: > PC Theodt. Light.
See nr. 149,1.

III,2. Preaching of Peter, according to ORIG., PA. praef. 8.   Cf. Lk. 24,38 f.
VI,1a. Taken from Mtt. 19,12.

τοῦ θεοῦ · περὶ ἀγάπης οὐ μέλει αὐτοῖς, οὐ περὶ χήρας, οὐ περὶ ὀρφανοῦ,
οὐ περὶ θλιβομένου, οὐ περὶ δεδεμένου ἢ λελυμένου, οὐ περὶ πεινῶντος
ἢ διψῶντος. VII, 1. εὐχαριστίας καὶ προσευχῆς ἀπέχονται, διὰ τὸ μὴ
ὁμολογεῖν τὴν εὐχαριστίαν σάρκα εἶναι τοῦ σωτῆρος ἡμῶν Ἰησοῦ Χριστοῦ,
5 τὴν ὑπὲρ τῶν ἁμαρτιῶν ἡμῶν παθοῦσαν, ἢν τῇ χρηστότητι ὁ πατὴρ
ἤγειρεν. οἱ οὖν ἀντιλέγοντες τῇ δωρεᾷ τοῦ θεοῦ συζητοῦντες ἀποθνήσκου-
σιν. συνέφερεν δὲ αὐτοῖς ἀγαπᾶν, ἵνα καὶ ἀναστῶσιν. 2. πρέπον οὖν
ἐστὶν ἀπέχεσθαι τῶν τοιούτων καὶ μήτε κατ᾽ ἰδίαν περὶ αὐτῶν λαλεῖν
μήτε κοινῇ, προσέχειν δὲ τοῖς προφήταις, ἐξαιρέτως δὲ τῷ εὐαγγελίῳ,
10 ἐν ᾧ τὸ πάθος ἡμῖν δεδήλωται καὶ ἡ ἀνάστασις τετελείωται. {τοὺς δὲ
μερισμοὺς φεύγετε ὡς ἀρχὴν κακῶν. VIII, 1. πάντες τῷ ἐπισκόπῳ ἀκολουθεῖτε,
ὡς Ἰησοῦς Χριστὸς τῷ πατρί, καὶ τῷ πρεσβυτερίῳ ὡς τοῖς ἀποστόλοις · τοὺς δὲ
διακόνους ἐντρέπεσθε ὡς θεοῦ ἐντολήν. μηδεὶς χωρὶς ἐπισκόπου τι πρασσέτω τῶν
ἀνηκόντων εἰς τὴν ἐκκλησίαν. ἐκείνη βεβαία εὐχαριστία ἡγείσθω, ἡ ὑπὸ τὸν ἐπίσκο-
15 πον οὖσα ἢ ᾧ ἂν αὐτὸς ἐπιτρέψῃ. 2. ὅπου ἂν φανῇ ὁ ἐπίσκοπος, ἐκεῖ τὸ πλῆθος ἔστω,
ὥσπερ ὅπου ἂν ᾖ Ἰησοῦς Χριστός, ἐκεῖ ἡ καθολικὴ ἐκκλησία. οὐκ ἐξόν ἐστιν χωρὶς
ἐπισκόπου οὔτε βαπτίζειν οὔτε ἀγάπην ποιεῖν · ἀλλ᾽ ὃ ἂν ἐκεῖνος δοκιμάσῃ, τοῦτο
καὶ τῷ θεῷ εὐάρεστον, ἵνα ἀσφαλὲς ᾖ καὶ βέβαιον πᾶν ὃ πράσσετε.} IX, 1. Εὐλογόν ἐστιν λοιπὸν ἀνανῆψαι ἡμᾶς, ὡς ἔτι καιρὸν ἔχομεν εἰς θεὸν μετα-
20 νοεῖν. {καλῶς ἔχει, θεὸν καὶ ἐπίσκοπον εἰδέναι. ὁ τιμῶν ἐπίσκοπον ὑπὸ θεοῦ
τετίμηται · ὁ λάθρα ἐπισκόπου τι πράσσων τῷ διαβόλῳ λατρεύει.}

C'. PARAENESIS

Personal thanks

IX, 2. Πάντα οὖν ὑμῖν ἐν χάριτι περισσευέτω · ἄξιοι γάρ ἐστε. κατὰ
πάντα με ἀνεπαύσατε · καὶ ὑμᾶς Ἰησοῦς Χριστός. ἀπόντα με καὶ παρόντα ἠγαπήσατε · ἀμείβοι ὑμῖν ὁ θεός, δι᾽ ὃν πάντα ὑπομένοντες αὐτοῦ
25 τεύξεσθε.

---

7 οὖν GCg: > PLA ‖ **13** χωρὶς Pg Dam. (cf. Sm. 8,2; 9,1; Tr. 7,2) Light. Bihl.
Fischer: + τοῦ G (cf. Phld. 7,2) Zahn Funk Hilg. ‖ **15** ἔστω Gg: ἤτω P Dam.
(Vat.) Antioch., > Dam. (Rup.) ‖ **16** Ἰησοῦς Χριστὸς PA Dam. (Rup.) Bihl.: ~
GL Antioch. Light. and the majority of editors, ὁ Χριστὸς Cg Dam. (Vat.) | χωρὶς
P Dam. (Rup.) recent editors: + τοῦ Gg Dam. (Vat.) Light. Funk ‖ **19** ἡμᾶς PSf
(A)Cg Dam. Bihl. Fischer: καὶ GL Zahn Funk Hilg. ‖ **24** ἀμείβοι con. Jacobson
Zahn Light. Funk Hilg. Camelot: ἀμοιβὴ P Bauer Bihl. Fischer, ἀμοίβει G (the
three forms are phonetically identical, because of the itacism) retribuat L. See nrs.
110 and 177.

VII,2 f-VIII. {τοὺς δὲ μερισμοὺς κτλ. A special doctrinal development of the forger's:
    see nrs. 109, 146.
IX,1. {καλῶς ἔχει κτλ. Interpolation: see nrs. 110, 145.

Thanks to the envoys from Syria (see Synopsis, nr. 53. A)

Χ, 1. Φίλωνα καὶ Γάϊον καὶ Ἀγαθόπουν, οἳ ἐπηκολούθησάν μοι εἰς λόγον
θεοῦ, καλῶς ἐποιήσατε ὑποδεξάμενοι ὡς διακόνους Χριστοῦ θεοῦ · οἳ
καὶ εὐχαριστοῦσιν τῷ κυρίῳ ὑπὲρ ὑμῶν, ὅτι αὐτοὺς ἀνεπαύσατε κατὰ
πάντα τρόπον · οὐδὲν ὑμῖν οὐ μὴ ἀπολεῖται.

{*Phld.* XI, 1. Περὶ δὲ Φίλωνος τοῦ διακόνου ἀπὸ Κιλικίας, ἀνδρὸς μεμαρτυρημένου, 5
ὃς καὶ νῦν ἐν λόγῳ θεοῦ ὑπηρετεῖ μοι ἅμα Γαΐῳ καὶ Ἀγαθόποδι, ἀνδρὶ ἐκλεκτῷ,
ὃς ἀπὸ Συρίας μοι ἀκολουθεῖ ἀποταξάμενος τῷ βίῳ, οἳ καὶ μαρτυροῦσιν ὑμῖν, κἀγὼ
τῷ θεῷ εὐχαριστῶ ὑπὲρ ὑμῶν, ὅτι ἐδέξασθε αὐτούς, ὡς καὶ ὑμᾶς ὁ κύριος. οἱ δὲ
ἀτιμάσαντες αὐτοὺς λυτρωθείησαν ἐν τῇ χάριτι τοῦ Ἰησοῦ Χριστοῦ.}

Personal consecration to the Ephesian community and its delegates
(see Synopsis, nr. 53. B)

Eph*. Ἀντίψυχον ὑμῶν καὶ ὧν ἐπέμψατε εἰς θεοῦ τιμὴν εἰς Σμύρναν, ὅθεν καὶ γράφω ὑμῖν,	*Sm.* Χ, 2. Ἀντίψυχον ὑμῶν	*Eph.* ΧΧΙ, 1a. Ἀντίψυχον 10 ὑμῶν {ἐγὼ} καὶ ὧν ἐπέμψατε εἰς θεοῦ τιμὴν εἰς Σμύρναν, ὅθεν καὶ γράφω ὑμῖν, {εὐχαριστῶν τῷ κυρίῳ, ἀγαπῶν Πολύκαρ- 15 πον ὡς καὶ ὑμᾶς.}
τὸ πνεῦμά μου καὶ τὰ δεσμά μου, ἃ οὐχ ὑπερηφανήσατε οὐδὲ ἐπῃσχύνθητε · οὐδὲ ὑμᾶς ἐπαισχυνθήσεται ἡ τελεία ἐλπίς, Ἰησοῦς Χριστός.	τὸ πνεῦμά μου καὶ τὰ δεσμά μου, ἃ οὐχ ὑπερηφανήσατε οὐδὲ ἐπῃσχύνθητε · οὐδὲ ὑμᾶς ἐπαισχυνθήσεται ἡ τελεία ἐλπίς, Ἰησοῦς Χριστός.	20

Consoling news from Syria (see Synopsis, nr. 53. C)

Eph*. Ἐπειδὴ κατὰ τὴν προσευχὴν ὑμῶν καὶ κατὰ τὰ σπλάγχνα, ἃ ἔχετε ἐν Χριστῷ Ἰησοῦ, ἀπηγγέλη μοι, εἰρηνεύειν τὴν ἐκκλησίαν τὴν ἐν Συρί<ᾳ>,	*Pol.* VII, 1. Ἐπειδὴ {ἡ ἐκκλησία ἡ ἐν Ἀντιοχείᾳ τῆς Συρίας εἰρηνεύει, ὡς ἐδηλώθη μοι, διὰ τὴν προσευχὴν ὑμῶν,}	*Phld.* Χ, 1a. Ἐπειδὴ κατὰ τὴν προσευχὴν ὑμῶν καὶ κατὰ τὰ σπλάγχνα, 25 ἃ ἔχετε ἐν Χριστῷ Ἰησοῦ, ἀπηγγέλη μοι, εἰρηνεύειν τὴν ἐκκλησίαν τὴν ἐν {Ἀντιοχείᾳ τῆς} Συρίας, 30

---

1 Γάϊον PCgl: 'Ρέων G, Reum L, Agrium A. See n. 111 | καὶ LABgl: > GP. See
n. 111 ‖ **2** Χριστοῦ GL editors: > PAB (Light.) See n. 114 ‖ **6** Γαΐῳ Cgl: 'Ρέω
GLAB | καὶ CA (+ ἀδελφῷ) Bgl: > GL. See n. 111 ‖ **11** ὧν g and all the
editors: ὃν GLABl. See n. 109 ‖ **21** ἐλπὶς PACg Bihl. (cf. Eph. 21,2; Mg. 11; Tr.
inscr.; 2,2; Phld. 5,2; 11,2): πίστις GL Zahn Light. Funk Fischer Camelot.

κἀγὼ εὐθυμότερος ἐγε-
νόμην ἐν ἀμεριμνίᾳ θεοῦ,
ἐάνπερ διὰ τοῦ παθεῖν
θεοῦ ἐπιτύχω, εἰς τὸ εὑ-
5 ρεθῆναί με ἐν τῇ αἰτήσει
ὑμῶν μαθητήν,
          καὶ μετ' αὐτῶν
μοι τὸ μέρος γένοιτο
σχεῖν ἐν θεῷ.

κἀγὼ εὐθυμότερος ἐγε-
νόμην ἐν ἀμεριμνίᾳ θεοῦ,
ἐάνπερ διὰ τοῦ παθεῖν
θεοῦ ἐπιτύχω, εἰς τὸ εὑ-
ρεθῆναί με ἐν τῇ αἰτήσει
ὑμῶν μαθητήν.
VI, 1d. καὶ μετ' αὐτῶν
μοι τὸ μέρος γένοιτο
σχεῖν ἐν θεῷ.

Invitation to share everything (see Synopsis, nr. 53. D)

10 *Pol.* VI, 1e. Συγκοπιᾶτε ἀλλήλοις, συναθλεῖτε, συντρέχετε, συμπάσχετε,
συγκοιμᾶσθε, συνεγείρεσθε ὡς θεοῦ οἰκονόμοι καὶ πάρεδροι καὶ ὑπηρέται. 2. ἀρέσκετε ᾧ στρατεύεσθε, ἀφ' οὗ καὶ τὰ ὀψώνια κομίζεσθε ·
μή τις ὑμῶν δεσέρτωρ εὑρεθῇ · τὸ βάπτισμα ὑμῶν μενέτω ὡς ὅπλα, ἡ
πίστις ὡς περικεφαλαία, ἡ ἀγάπη ὡς δόρυ, ἡ ὑπομονὴ ὡς πανοπλία ·
15 τὰ δεπόσιτα ὑμῶν τὰ ἔργα ὑμῶν, ἵνα τὰ ἄκκεπτα ὑμῶν ἄξια κομίσησθε.
μακροθυμήσατε οὖν μετ' ἀλλήλων ἐν πραότητι, ὡς ὁ θεὸς ὑμῶν. ὀναίμην
ὑμῶν διὰ παντός.

Β'. CONCLUSION

Petition for a remembrance of him. Their prayers had already reached the church in Syria (see Synopsis, nr. 53. E)

Eph*.   Μνημο-
νεύετέ μου ·
20

          ἡ <γὰρ> προσευχὴ
ὑμῶν ἀπῆλθεν ἐπὶ τὴν
ἐκκλησίαν τὴν ἐν
          Συρίᾳ, ὅθεν
25 δεδεμένος θεοπρεπεστά-
τοις δεσμοῖς εἰς 'Ρώμην
ἀπάγομαι, οὐκ ὢν ἄξι-
ος ἐκεῖθεν εἶναι ἔσχατος
αὐτῶν ὤν,
30 κατὰ θέλημα δὲ κατηξι-
ώθην

Sm. XI, 1. ῾Η προσευχὴ
ὑμῶν ἀπῆλθεν ἐπὶ τὴν
ἐκκλησίαν τὴν ἐν {'Αντι-
οχείᾳ τῆς} Συρίας, ὅθεν
δεδεμένος θεοπρεπεστά-
τοις δεσμοῖς {πάντας
ἀσπάζ}ομαι, οὐκ ὢν ἄξι-
ος ἐκεῖθεν εἶναι, ἔσχατος
αὐτῶν ὤν,
κατὰ θέλημα δὲ κατηξι-
ώθην,

Eph. XXI, 1e. Μνημο-
νεύετέ μου {, ὡς καὶ
ὑμῶν 'Ιησοῦς Χριστός}.
2. προσεύχ{εσθε ὑπὲρ}
          τῆς
ἐκκλησίας τῆς ἐν
          Συρίᾳ, ὅθεν
δεδεμένος

          εἰς 'Ρώμην
ἀπάγομαι,

          ἔσχατος
ὢν {τῶν ἐκεῖ πιστῶν,
ὥσπερ}   ἠξι-
ώθην

---

5 αἰτήσει gA (cf. Tr. 13,3) Light. Bauer: ἀναστάσει GL Zahn Funk Hilg. Krüger
Bihl. Fischer. See n. 180 ‖ **7** καὶ GL editors: > SSfAg Antioch. Dam. ‖ **9** ἐν GL
Antioch. Dam. editors: παρὰ SSfABg Light. ‖ **16** ὑμῶν G: μεθ' ὑμῶν g Antioch.
Dam. editors ‖ **21** Probably suppressed by the interp. by separating Sm. 11,1 from
its primitive context.

εἰς τιμὴν θεοῦ εὑρεθῆναι,
οὐκ ἐκ συνειδότος, ἀλλ'
ἐκ χάριτος θεοῦ, ἣν εὔ-
χομαι τελείαν μοι δοθῆ-
ναι, ἵνα ἐν τῇ προσευχῇ
ὑμῶν θεοῦ ἐπιτύχω.

οὐκ ἐκ συνειδότος, ἀλλ'
ἐκ χάριτος θεοῦ, ἣν εὔ-
χομαι τελείαν μοι δοθῆ-
ναι, ἵνα ἐν τῇ προσευχῇ
ὑμῶν θεοῦ ἐπιτύχω.

εἰς τιμὴν θεοῦ εὑρεθῆναι.   5

Sending of a messenger (see Synopsis, nr. 53. F)

Sm. XI, 2. Ἵνα οὖν τέλειον
ὑμῶν γένηται τὸ ἔργον καὶ
ἐπὶ γῆς καὶ ἐν οὐρανῷ, πρέπει εἰς τιμὴν θεοῦ χειροτονῆσαι τὴν ἐκκλησίαν ὑμῶν
θεοπρεσβευτήν, εἰς τὸ γε-
νόμενον ἕως Συρίας συγχα-
ρῆναι αὐτοῖς, ὅτι εἰρηνεύουσιν καὶ ἀπέλαβον τὸ
ἴδιον μέγεθος καὶ ἀπεκατεστάθη αὐτοῖς τὸ ἴδιον σω-
ματεῖον.

{*Pol.* VII, 2. πρέπει,
Πολύκαρπε θεομακαρι-
στότατε, συμβούλιον ἀγ-
αγεῖν θεοπρεπέστατον
καὶ χειροτονῆσαί τινα,
ὃν ἀγαπητὸν λίαν ἔχετε
καὶ ἄοκνον, ὃς δυνήσεται
θεοδρόμος καλεῖσθαι ·
τοῦτον καταξιῶσαι, ἵνα
πορευθεὶς εἰς Συρίαν

{*Phld.* X, 1b.. πρέπον
ἐστὶν ὑμῖν ὡς ἐκκλησίᾳ   10
θεοῦ, χειροτονῆσαι διά-
κονον εἰς τὸ πρεσβεῦ-
σαι ἐκεῖ θεοῦ πρεσβείαν,
εἰς τὸ συγχαρῆναι αὐτοῖς
ἐπὶ τὸ αὐτὸ γενομέ-   15
νοις

Sending of a messenger to Syria with a personal letter from him (see Synopsis, nr. 53. G)

Sm. XI, 3a. Ἐφάνη μοι
οὖν θεοῦ ἄξιον πρᾶγμα,
πέμψαι τινὰ τῶν ὑμετέρων
μετ' ἐπιστολῆς, ἵνα συνδοξάσῃ τὴν κατὰ θεὸν αὐτοῖς
γενομένην εὐδίαν, καὶ ὅτι
λιμένος ἤδη ἔτυχον ἐν τῇ
προσευχῇ ὑμῶν.

20

δο-
ξάσῃ ὑμῶν τὴν ἄοκνον
ἀγάπην εἰς δόξαν θεοῦ.}

καὶ δο-
ξάσαι τὸ ὄνομα. 2. μα-
κάριος ἐν Ἰησοῦ Χριστῷ
ὃς καταξιωθήσεται τῆς   25
τοιαύτης διακονίας, καὶ
ὑμεῖς δοξασθήσεσθε.}

Invitation to the Ephesian community to carry out the charge (see Synopsis, nr. 53. H)

Sm. XI, 3d.. Τέλειοι οὖν ὄντες τέλεια
καὶ φρονεῖτε · θέλουσιν γὰρ ὑμῖν εὐ-

{*Phld.* X, 2d. θέλουσιν δὲ ὑμῖν οὐκ ἔστιν

---

12 θεοπρεσβευτήν P Ussher Zahn Hilg. modern editors: θεοπρεσβύτην Gg Light. Funk, deovenerabilem L, praecursorem A ‖ **13** ἕως Συρίας GL editors: ἐν Συρίᾳ Pg Lake, in Syriam A ‖ **25** ἔτυχον ἐν P(A) Bauer Bihl. Fischer: ἐτύγχανεν GL Zahn Funk Hilg., τετύχηκα g, ἐτύγχανον Light. ‖ **28** οὖν P: > MSS, versions, editors.

πράσσειν θεὸς ἕτοιμος εἰς τὸ παρέχειν ·
Pol. VII, 3a. Χριστιανὸς <γὰρ> ἑαυτοῦ ἐξουσίαν οὐκ ἔχει, ἀλλὰ θεῷ
σχολάζει. τοῦτο τὸ ἔργον θεοῦ ἐστὶν
5 καὶ ὑμῶν, ὅταν αὐτὸ ἀπαρτίσητε · πιστεύω γὰρ τῇ χάριτι, ὅτι ἕτοιμοί ἐστε
εἰς εὐποιΐαν θεῷ ἀνήκουσαν.

ἀδύνατον ὑπὲρ ὀνόματος θεοῦ, ὡς
καὶ αἱ ἔγγιστα ἐκκλησίαι ἔπεμψαν
ἐπισκόπους, αἱ δὲ πρεσβυτέρους
καὶ διακόνους.}

Epilogue (see Synopsis, nr. 53. I)

Pol. VII, 3g. Εἰδὼς ὑμῶν τὸ σύντονον τῆς ἀληθείας, δι᾽ ὀλίγων ὑμᾶς
γραμμάτων παρεκάλεσα.

A'. FINAL GREETING

{Spurious final greetings:

10 *Phld.* XI, 2. Ἀσπάζεται ὑμᾶς ἡ ἀγάπη τῶν ἀδελφῶν τῶν ἐν Τρωάδι, ὅθεν καὶ γράφω
ὑμῖν διὰ Βούρρου πεμφθέντος ἅμα ἐμοὶ ἀπὸ Ἐφεσίων καὶ Σμυρναίων εἰς λόγον τιμῆς ·
τιμήσει αὐτοὺς ὁ κύριος Ἰησοῦς Χριστός, εἰς ὃν ἐλπίζουσιν σαρκί, ψυχῇ, πνεύματι,
πίστει, ἀγάπῃ, ὁμονοίᾳ. ἔρρωσθε ἐν Χριστῷ Ἰησοῦ, τῇ κοινῇ ἐλπίδι ἡμῶν.
Sm. XII, 1. Ἀσπάζεται ὑμᾶς ἡ ἀγάπη τῶν ἀδελφῶν τῶν ἐν Τρωάδι, ὅθεν καὶ γράφω
15 ὑμῖν διὰ Βούρρου, ὃν ἀπεστείλατε μετ᾽ ἐμοῦ ἅμα Ἐφεσίοις, τοῖς ἀδελφοῖς ὑμῶν, ὃς
κατὰ πάντα με ἀνέπαυσεν. καὶ ὄφελον πάντες αὐτὸν ἐμιμοῦντο, ὄντα ἐξεμπλάριον
θεοῦ διακονίας, ἀμείψεται αὐτὸν ἡ χάρις κατὰ πάντα. 2. ἀσπάζομαι τὸν ἀξιόθεον
ἐπίσκοπον καὶ θεοπρεπέστατον πρεσβυτέριον, τοὺς συνδούλους μου διακόνους καὶ
τοὺς κατ᾽ ἄνδρα καὶ κοινῇ πάντας ἐν ὀνόματι Ἰησοῦ Χριστοῦ καὶ τῇ σαρκὶ αὐτοῦ
20 καὶ τῷ αἵματι, πάθει τε καὶ ἀναστάσει σαρκικῇ τε καὶ πνευματικῇ, ἐν ἑνότητι θεοῦ
καὶ ὑμῶν. χάρις ὑμῖν, ἔλεος, εἰρήνη, ὑπομονὴ διὰ παντός. XIII, 1a. ἀσπάζομαι
τοὺς οἴκους τῶν ἀδελφῶν μου σὺν γυναιξὶ καὶ τέκνοις καὶ τὰς παρθένους τὰς λεγο-
μένας χήρας. ἔρρωσθέ μοι ἐν δυνάμει πνεύματος.}

Greetings from Philo

Sm. XIII, 1c. Ἀσπάζεται ὑμᾶς Φίλων σὺν ἐμοὶ ὤν.

---

1 παρέχειν P Max. Dam.: παρασχεῖν Gg editors. The reading of P hints at a quasi-
gnomic sentence (see the correspondence θέλουσιν — ἕτοιμοι and εὐπράσσειν — παρέχειν, and the following gnomic sentence Χριστιανὸς κτλ.) ‖ **2** Probably suppressed
by the interp. by separating Pol. 7,3 from its primitive context ‖ **8** Εἰδὼς LCg: +
οὖν GB, nam et A ‖ **18** θεοπρεπέστατον G: θεοπρεπὲς gL(A?) editors | πρεσβυτέριον
G: + καὶ LAg ‖ **23** πνεύματος Gg Zahn Funk (cf. the spurious inscr. of Sm.:
see nr. 62): πατρός LAl Light. Hilg. Bihl. Fischer.

A' FINAL GREETING. For the reconstruction of the original sequence of the final
    greetings of Eph*, see nrs. 54 f.
{*Spurious final greetings* of Phld. 11,2 and Sm. 12: see nrs. 54, 65, 78.

Greetings to the families

Sm. XIII, 2a. 'Ασπάζομαι τὸν οἶκον Ταουίας, ἣν εὔχομαι ἑδρᾶσθαι πίστει καὶ ἀγάπῃ σαρκικῇ τε καὶ πνευματικῇ {.} *Pol.* VIII, 2a. {'Ασπάζομαι πάντας ἐξ ὀνόματος} καὶ τὴν τοῦ 'Επιτρόπου σὺν ὅλῳ τῷ οἴκῳ αὐτῆς καὶ τῶν τέκνων.

Greetings to individuals (first series)

Pol. VIII, 2b. 'Ασπάζομαι "Ατταλον τὸν ἀγαπητόν μου. ἀσπάζομαι τὸν 5 μέλλοντα καταξιοῦσθαι τοῦ εἰς Συρίαν πορεύεσθαι · ἔσται ἡ χάρις μετ' αὐτοῦ διὰ παντός {καὶ τοῦ πέμποντος αὐτὸν Πολυκάρπου}.

First farewell formula

Pol. VIII, 3a. 'Ερρῶσθαι ὑμᾶς διὰ παντὸς ἐν θεῷ ἡμῶν 'Ιησοῦ Χριστῷ εὔχομαι, ἐν ᾧ διαμείνητε ἐν ἑνότητι θεοῦ καὶ ἐπισκοπῇ.

Greetings to individuals (second series)

{*Pol.* VIII, 3c. **'Ασπάζομαι "Αλκην, τὸ ποθητόν μοι ὄνομα. ἔρρωσθε ἐν κυρίῳ.**} 10
Sm. XIII, 2c. 'Ασπάζομαι "Αλκην, τὸ ποθητόν μοι ὄνομα καὶ Δάφνον τὸν ἀσύγκριτον καὶ Εὔτεκνον καὶ πάντας κατ' ὄνομα.

Second farewell formula

Eph*. "Ερρωσθε	*Eph.* XXI, 2e. "Ερρωσθε	*Sm.* XIII, 2d. "Ερρωσθε
ἐν χάριτι θεοῦ	ἐν θεῷ {πατρὶ καὶ ἐν}	ἐν χάριτι θεοῦ.
'Ιησοῦ Χριστοῦ, τῆς κοινῆς	'Ιησοῦ Χριστῷ, τῇ κοινῇ	15
ἐλπίδος ἡμῶν.	ἐλπίδι ἡμῶν.	

---

10 μοι Lg (cf. Rom. 10,1) editors: μου G ‖ **11** μοι Lg (cf. Rom. 10,1) editors: μου G ‖ **13** "Ερρωσθε — ἡμῶν. The second farewell formula of Eph* is reconstructed from Eph. 21,2e + Sm. 13,2d: see nr. 54,3-4.

BIBLIOGRAPHY

(* Fontes ** Subsidia)

*ACHELIS, H. - FLEMMING, J., *Die syrische Didascalia übersetzt und erklärt*, Leipzig 1904, T.U. 25,2 (= *Syr. Did.*).

**ALTANER, B. - STUIBER, A. (IRENEO, D.), *Patrologia*, Turin 1968.

**ARNDT, W. F. - GINGRICH, F. W., *A Greek English Lexicon of the New Testament and Other Early Christian Literature*, Chicago 1957/1971 (an adaptation of W. Bauer, *W.z.N.T.*).

*BARDY, G., *Eusèbe de Césarée, Histoire Ecclésiastique*, t. I-II, Introduction, texte critique, traduction et notes par ..., Paris 1952/1955 (reprinted in 1965), S. Ch. 31 and 41.

BARNARD, L. W., *Studies in the Apostolic Fathers and their Background*, Oxford 1966 (= *Background*).

BARTSCH, H. W., *Gnostisches Gut und Gemeindetradition bei Ignatius von Antiochien*, Gütersloh 1940.

*BASILE, B., *Un ancien témoin arabe des Lettres d'Ignace d'Antioche, Melto* 4 (1968) 107-191.

 Une autre version arabe de la Lettre aux Romains de St. Ignace d'Antioche, Melto 5 (1969) 269-287.

*BAUER, W., *Die Apostolischen Väter*, II. Die Briefe des Ignatius von Antiochia und der Polykarpbrief, Tübingen 1920 (= *AA.VV.* II).

 **Griechisch - Deutsches Wörterbuch zu den Schriften des Neuen Testaments und der übrigen urchristlichen Literatur*, Berlin ⁵1963 (= *W.z.N.T.*).

 Rechtgläubigkeit und Ketzerei im ältesten Christentum, Tübingen ²1964.

**BLAS, F. - DEBRUNNER, A. - FUNK, R. W., *A Greek Grammar of the New Testament and Other Early Christian Literature*, Chicago 1961.

BROWN, M. P., *The authentic Writings of Ignatius. A Study of linguistic Criteria*, Durham, N.C. 1963.

BRUSTON, E., *Ignace d'Antioche, ses épîtres, sa vie, sa théologie*, Paris 1897.

*CAMELOT, Th., *Ignace d'Antioche. Polycarpe de Smyrne. Lettres. Martyre de Polycarpe*, Text grec, introduction, traduction et notes de ..., Paris ⁴1969, S.Ch10A (= *I. d'A.*).

*CONNOLLY, H., *Didascalia Apostolorum. The Syriac Version Translated and Accompanied by the Verona Latin Fragments*, Oxford 1929 (= *Did.Ap.*).

CORWIN, V., *St. Ignatius and Christianity in Antioch*, New Haven 1960.

COTELIER, J. B., *SS. Patrum, qui temporibus Apostolicis floruerunt, Barnabae, Clementis...*, vol. II, Amsterdam 1724.

CURETON, W., *The ancient Syriac version of the Epistles of St. Ignatius to St. Polycarp, the Ephesians, and the Romans ...*, London 1845.

Vindiciae Ignatianae or the genuine writings of St. Ignatius as exhibited in the ancient Syriac version vindicated of the charge of heresy, London 1846.
Corpus Ignatianum: a complete collection of the Ignatian Epistles ... in Syriac, Greek and Latin ..., London 1849.

DAVIES, S. L., *The Predicament of Ignatius of Antioch*, V. Ch. 30 (1976) 175-180.

DIETZE, P., *Die Briefe des Ignatius von Antiochien und das Johannesevangelium*, in Th. Studien und Kritiken, Gotha, 4 (1905) 563-603.

*DIOBOUNIOTIS, C. - HARNACK, A., *Der Scholien-Kommentar des Origenes zur Apokalypse Johannis nebst einem Stück aus Irenaeus*, Lib. V, Graece, Leipzig 1911, T.U. 38,3.

DONAHUE, P. J., *Jewish Cristianity in the Letters of Ignatius of Antioch*, V. Ch. 32 (1978) 81-93.

*FISCHER, J. A., *Die Apostolischen Väter*. Eingeleitet, herausgegeben, übertragen und erläutert von..., Schriften des Urchristentums I, Darmstadt ³1959 (= *AA.VV.*).

FUNK, F. X., *Die Echtheit der Ignatianischen Briefe aufs neue vertheidigt*, Tübingen 1883.
Die Apostolischen Konstitutionen, Eine literar-historische Untersuchung, Rottenburg 1891 (= *AA.KK.*).
Patres Apostolici, vol. I, Tübingen 1901 (= *PP.AA.* I).
Didascalia et Constitutiones Apostolorum, Paderbon 1905 (= *Did. et CC.AA.*).

*FUNK, F. X. - BIHLMEYER, K., *Die Apostolischen Väter*, Tübingen ³1970 (reprinting made on the second edition, Tübingen 1956) (= *AA.VV.*).

*FUNK, F. X. - DIEKAMP, F., *Patres Apostolici*, vol. II, Tübingen 1913 (= *PP.AA.* II).

HAGEDORN, D., *Der Hiobkommentar des Arianers Julian*, Berlin 1973.

HARNACK, A., *Bishop Lightfoot's " Ignatius and Polycarp "*, The Expositor 22 (1885) 401-414; 23 (1886) 9-22; 175-192.
Geschichte der altchristlichen Literatur bis Eusebius, II Chronologie, vol. I, Leipzig 1897.
Miscellen zu den Apostolischen Vätern... II. Zu Ignatius ad Polycarp. 6; III. Zu Polycarp ad Philipp. 11, Leipzig 1900, T.U. 20,3.

HARRISON, P. N., *Polycarp's Two Epistles to the Philippians*, Cambridge 1936.

*HARVEY, W., *Sancti Irenaei episcopi Lugdunensis... libros quinque Adversus Haereses...*, Cambridge 1857 (republished in 1965).

HILGENFELD, A., *Der Brief des Polycarpus an die Philipper*, Z.W.Th. 29 (1886) 180-206.

HOLL, K., *Fragmente vornicänischer Kirchenväter aus den Sacra Parallela herausgegeben*, Leipzig 1899, T.U. 20,2.

JUNGMANN, J. A., *Die Stellung Christi im liturgischen Gebet*, Münster i.W. 1925.

*KLEIST, J. A., *The Epistles of St. Clement of Rome and St. Ignatius of Antioch*, newly translated and annotated by..., London ⁴1961, A.Ch.W. 1 (= *I. of A.*).

KLEVINGHAUS, J., *Die theologische Stellung der Apostolischen Väter zur alttestamentlichen Offenbarung*, Gütersloh 1948.

KOESTER, H., *Synoptische Ueberlieferung bei den apostolischen Vätern*, Berlin 1957, T.U. 65.

**KRAFT, H., *Clavis Patrum Apostolicorum. Konkordanz zu den Schriften der Apostolischen Väter*, München 1963.

*LAKE, K., *The Apostolic Fathers* I, I Clement. II Clement. Ignatius. Polycarp. Didache. Barnabas. Translated by..., London 1975 (= *AA.FF.* I).

*LELONG, A., *Les Pères Apostoliques*. III. Ignace d'Antioche et Polycarpe de Smyrne. Épîtres. Martyre de Polycarpe, Paris ²1927 (= *PP.AA.* III).

LIETZMANN, H., *Ein liturgischer Papyrus des Berliner Museums, Festgabe für A. Jülicher*, Tübingen 1927, pp. 213-228.

    Messe und Herrenmahl. Eine Studie zur Geschichte der Liturgie, Bonn 1926.

*LIGHTFOOT, J. B., *The Apostolic Fathers*, Part II: S. Ignatius. S. Polycarp, vols. I, II/1, II/2, London 1885 (= *AA.FF.* II).

    The Apostolic Fathers..., Revised Texts with Introductions, Notes, Dissertations and Traslations, London 1889. Reprinting (Hildesheim 1973) made on the second edition.

LIPSIUS, R. A., *Ueber die Echtheit der syrischen Recension der Ignatianischen Briefe*, *Z.H.Th.* 26 (1886) 3-160.

LUND, N. W., *Chiasmus in the New Testament*, N. Caroline and London 1942.

McARTHUR, A. A., *The Office of Bishop in the Ignatian Epistles and in the Didascalia Apostolorum compared*, St. Pat. IV, Berlin 1961, T.U. 79, pp. 298-304.

MATEOS, J., *El Aspecto Verbal en el Nuevo Testamento, Estudios de Nuevo Testamento, I.*, Madrid 1977.

MATEOS, J. - ALEPUZ, M., *El imperfecto sucesivo en el NT*, in *Estudios de Nuevo Testamento, II. Cuestiones de gramática y léxico*, Madrid 1977.

MAURER, Ch., *Ignatius von Antiochien und das Johannesevangelium*, Zürich 1949.

MOFFAT, J., *An Approach to Ignatius*, *H.Th.R.* 29 (1936) 1-38.

MOLLAND, E., *The Heretics Combatted by Ignatius of Antioch*, in *Opuscula Patristica*, Oslo 1970, pp. 17-23 (= *J.E.H.* 5, 1954, pp. 1-6).

**MOULTON, J. H. - TURNER, N., *Grammar of the New Testament Greek, vol. III: Syntax*, Edinburg 1963.

MURRAY, R., *Symbols of Church and Kingdom. A Study in Early Syriac Tradition*, Cambridge 1975.

NESTLE, E., *Miscellen: Apostolische Constitutionen II, 25*, in *Z.N.W.* 2 (1901) 263f.

ORBE, A., *La unción del Verbo*, Rome 1961, E.V. III.

    La teología del Espíritu Santo, Rome 1966, E.V. IV.

PAULSEN, H., *Studien zur Theologie des Ignatius von Antiochien*, Göttingen 1978.

PERLER, O., *Pseudo-Ignatius und Eusebius von Emessa*, Hist. Jb. 77 (1958) 73-82.

    Die Briefe des Ignatius von Antiochien. Frage der Echtheit: neue arabische Uebersetzung, Freib. Z. Phil. Theol. 18 (1971) 381-396.

*PETERMANN, J. B., *S. Ignatii Patris Apostolici quae feruntur Epistolae una cum eiusdem Martyrio*, Leipzig 1849.

PRIGENT, P., *L'hérésie asiate et l'église confessante de l'Apocalypse à Ignace*, V. Ch. 31 (1977) 1-22.

*QUACQUARELLI, A., *I Padri Apostolici*, Rome 1976.

RACKL, M., *Die Christologie des heiligen Ignatius von Antiochien*, Freiburg i. Br. 1914.

RATHKE, H., *Ignatius von Antiochien und die Paulusbriefe*, Berlin 1967, T.U. 99.

RIUS-CAMPS, J., *Las Pseudoclementinas. Bases filológicas para una nueva interpretación*, Rev. Cat. Teol. 1 (1976) 79-158.

    Las Cartas auténticas de Ignacio, el obispo de Siria, Rev. Cat. Teol. 2 (1977)

31-149; *La interpolación en las Cartas de Ignacio. Contenido, alcance, simbología y su relación con la Didascalía*, ib. pp. 285-371.

**ROBERTSON, A. T., *A Grammar of the Greek New Testament in the Light of Historical Research*, London ³1919.

SCHERMANN, Th., *Zur Erklärung der Stelle epist. ad Ephes.* 20,2 *des Ignatius von Antiocheia:* φάρμακον ἀθανασίας κ.τ.λ., in *Th. Q.* 92 (1910) 6-19.

*SCHMIDT, C. - SCHUBART, W., *Berliner Klassikertexten, VI. Altchristliche Texte*, Berlin 1910, pp. 3-12.

*SCHWARTZ, E., *Eusebius Kirchengeschichte* herausgegeben von..., Leipzig ⁴1932.

SIEBEN, H. J., *Die Ignatianen als Briefe. Einige formkritische Bemerkungen*, in *V. Ch.* 32 (1978) 1-18.

SNYDER, G. F., *The Text and Syntax of Ignatius* ΠΡΟΣ 'ΕΦΕΣΙΟΥΣ 20:2c, in *V. Ch.* 22 (1968) 8-13.

SOMAL, Pl. S., *Quadro delle opere di vari autori anticamente tradotto in Armeno*, Venice 1885.

SPICQ, C., *Le vocabulaire de l'esclavage dans le Nouveau Testament*, R.Bi. 85 (1978) 208f.

**STEPHANOS, *Thesaurus Graecae Linguae*, Paris 1848-1854.

UHLHORN, G., *Das Verhältnis der kürzeren griechischen Recension der Ignatianischen Briefe zur syrischen Uebersetzung, und die Authentie der Briefe überhaupt*, in *Z.H.Th.* 21 (1851) 3-65; 247-341.

URBÁN, A., *El doble aspecto estático-dinámico de la preposición* ἐν *en el NT*, in *Estudios de Nuevo Testamento, II. Cuestiones de gramática y léxico*, Madrid 1977, pp. 17-60.

USSHER, J., *Polycarpi et Ignatii epistolae. Dissertationes de Ignatii martyris epistolis, indeque occasione data, de Polycarpo quoque scriptis...*, Oxoniae 1644, re-edited by J. B. Cotelier, *SS. Patrum...*, vol. II, Amsterdam 1724, App. pp. 199-250.

VON DER GOLTZ, E. F., *Ignatius von Antiochien als Christ und Theologe. Eine dogmengeschichtliche Untersuchung*, Leipzig 1894, T.U. XII,3.

VON LOEWENICH, W., *Das Johannes-Verständnis in zweiten Jahrhundert*, Giessen 1932.

WAGNER, G., *Zur Herkunft der Apostolischen Konstitutionen*, *Mélanges Liturgiques* offered to B. Botte, Louvain 1972, pp. 525-537.

WEIJENBORG, R., *Les Lettres d'Ignace d'Antioche. Étude de critique littéraire et de théologie*, Leiden 1969.

*WESELY, C., *Neue Materialien zur Textkritik der Ignatius-Briefe*, Vienna 1913.
    Griechische und Koptische Texte theologisches Inhalts, Studien zur Paleographie und Papyruskunde XVIII, Leipzig 1917, pp. 94-96.

ZAHN, Th., *Ignatius von Antiochien*, Gotha 1873 (= *I. v. A.*).
    Patrum Apostolicorum opera II: Ignatii et Polycarpi Epistulae, Martyria, Fragmenta, Leipzig 1876 (= *PP.AA.* II).

**ZORELL, F., *Lexicon Hebraicum et Aramaicum Veteris Testamenti*, Rome 1968.

INDEX OF REFERENCES AND CITATIONS

I. BIBLICAL

II. PATRISTIC

IGNATIUS

26

3 . . . . 125, 126,
127, 128, 129, 186, 209,
255, 257, 293, 297, 304,
330, 335; n. 49, 389, 419

ACTA ROMANA

Ignatius' Martyrdom

10 87

APOSTOLIC CONSTITUTIONS

II. 20 . . . . n. 311
26 . . . . n. 300
26,5 . . . . n. 383
30,2 . . . . n. 292, 383
31,1 . . . . n. 292
34,2 . . . . n. 311, 314
34,5 . . . . n. 311
44,3 . . . . n. 383
61,2 . . . . n. 297

III. 18,1 . . . . n. 297

VI. 5,7 . . . . n. 297

VII. 25,2 . . . . n. 262
26,2 . . . . n. 262
27,2 . . . . n. 262
28,3 . . . . n. 262

VIII. 1,20 . . . . n. 297
5,5 . . . . n. 262
5,7 . . . . n. 262
13,10 . . . . n. 262
15,2 . . . . n. 262
15,9 . . . . n. 262
15,6-9 152
34,10 . . . . n. 297
35,2 . . . . n. 297
39,4 . . . . n. 262
40,2 . . . . n. 262
41,8 . . . . n. 262
47,39 . . . . n. 292
48,3 . . . . n. 262

APOSTOLIC TRADITION

Can. 69 . . . . n. 262

70 . . . . n. 262
72 . . . . n. 262
76 . . . . n. 262

BARNABAS

4 . . . . n. 85
4,3ff. . . . . n. 77
4,9 . . . . n. 90
4,14 . . . . n. 77
5,2 . . . . n. 77
6,5 . . . . n. 90

I CLEMENT

30 373
59,4 . . . . n. 265

II CLEMENT

8,4.6 320
9,3 320

CLEMENT OF ALEXANDRIA

Eclogae Propheticae

5,3 . . . . n. 92
7 . . . . n. 92

DIDACHE

9,2.3 . . . . n. 262
10,2.3 . . . . n. 262

DIDASCALIA APOSTOLORUM

Inscr. . . . . n. 262

II. 1,1 . . . . 226, *232*
1,1-3 185
1,3 . . . . n. 372
1-25 234
2,3 . . . . n. 381
6,6(7) . . . . n. 351
6,11 . . . . n. 351
10,3 . . . . n. 357
11,1-2 . . . . n. 369
12,1 . . . . n. 369, 370

INDEX OF SUBJECT MATTER *

---

* Further references to the subjects in this index may be found by means of the crossreferences provided in the body of the work.

σύμβουλος 239; n. 384.
συναθροίζω n. 297.
σύνδεσμος 195, 239; n. 308, 384.
σύνδουλος 34ff., 37, 130, 163, 169, 171ff., 176, 182f., 220; n. 53, 54.
συνέδριον 172, 195, 214, 231, 239; n. 384.
συνείδησις 200; n. 317.
συντόμως 79, 110 (equiv.); 361,20, 365,27.
σχίζω 51, 211, 272, 290, 306.
σῶμα 210.
σωματεῖον 140, 210, 279; n. 243.

Trajan 85, 143f.
Trinity 63, 155, 229f., 233, 237; n. 355.
Troas 28ff., 74, 88, 95, 104, 111, 124, 133, 136, 167, 174.

τάξις 183ff.
τερπνά, τὰ 289; 350,18.
τιμάω, -ή 209, 217, 225, 230, 297; n. 381.
τόπον, εἰς 186, 221f., 225f., 229f.; n. 341, 344.
τύπον, εἰς 186, 221f., 225f., 227, 229f.; n. 344.

θάνατος 192.
θέλημα 38f., 112, 168, 299; n. 58.
θέλω 182, 277f., 299; n.280.

θεός ἡμῶν, μου, ᾿Ιησοῦς Χριστός 32, 52, 55, 126ff., 161, 189, 193f., 199, 200, 213, 261f., 277, 278, 281, 283, 291, 296, 297, 304; n. 44, 49, 96, 230bis, 307.
θυσία n. 116.
θυσιαστήριον 65, 200, 229f., 233f., 238; n. 116, 316.

Union, unity (see ἑνόω, etc.) 64f., 79, 142, 154f., 157, 164, 173.

ὑποκούω (ἐπ-) 39, 151, 153f., 209, 297, 304, 324.
ὑπομονή 126.
ὑποταγή, -άσσω 155, 178f., 183, 194, 209, 221f., 239, 292, 304, 319; n. 278, 282, 398; ὑποτεταγμέναι 93, 94f.

Valens 96.
Version, Arab (B) 21; Armenian (A) 18f.; Coptic (C) 21; Latin (L 1) 14,16; Syriac (Σ S Sfg.) 18f.; n. 20.
Virgins 125; n. 223.

Warning 65, 312, 313, 314.
Widow(s) 125, 228ff., 233f.; n. 224.